More Than Just a Textbook

Stay Connected
at Glencoe.com

Internet Resources

Step 1   Connect to **History ONLINE** at <u>glencoe.com</u>.

Step 2   Connect to online resources by using *QuickPass* codes.
You can connect directly to the chapter you want.

TAJMT7189c1

Enter this code with the appropriate chapter number.

For Students

Connect to <u>glencoe.com</u> to find all of these resources:

- Online Student Edition
- Test Practice
- Multi-language Glossary
- Interactive Maps
- Workbooks

- Section Spotlight Videos
- Study Central™ and Study-to-Go™
- . . . and more

For Teachers

Connect to standards correlations and professional development content at <u>glencoe.com</u>.

The *American Journey*

Modern Times

Joyce Appleby, Ph.D.

Alan Brinkley, Ph.D.

Albert S. Broussard, Ph.D.

James M. McPherson, Ph.D.

Donald A. Ritchie, Ph.D.

NATIONAL GEOGRAPHIC

McGraw Hill Glencoe

Authors

Joyce Appleby, Ph.D., is Professor of History at UCLA. Dr. Appleby's published works include *Inheriting the Revolution: The First Generation of Americans; Capitalism and a New Social Order: The Jeffersonian Vision of the 1790s;* and *Economic Thought and Ideology in Seventeenth-Century England,* which won the Berkshire Prize. She served as president of both the Organization of American Historians and the American Historical Association, and chaired the Council of the Institute of Early American History and Culture at Williamsburg. Dr. Appleby has been elected to the American Philosophical Society and the American Academy of Arts and Sciences, and is a Corresponding Fellow of the British Academy.

Alan Brinkley, Ph.D., is Allan Nevins Professor of American History at Columbia University. His published works include *Voices of Protest: Huey Long, Father Coughlin, and the Great Depression,* which won the 1983 National Book Award; *The End of Reform: New Deal Liberalism in Recession and War; The Unfinished Nation: A Concise History of the American People;* and *Liberalism and Its Discontents.* He received the Levenson Memorial Teaching Prize at Harvard University.

Albert S. Broussard, Ph.D., is Professor of History and Graduate Coordinator at Texas A&M University. Before joining the Texas A&M faculty, Dr. Broussard was Assistant Professor of History and Director of the African American Studies Program at Southern Methodist University. Among his publications are the books *Black San Francisco: The Struggle for Racial Equality in the West, 1900–1954* and *African American Odyssey: The Stewarts, 1853–1963.* Dr. Broussard has also served as president of the Oral History Association.

Donald A. Ritchie, Ph.D., is Associate Historian of the United States Senate Historical Office. Dr. Ritchie received his doctorate in American history from the University of Maryland after service in the U.S. Marine Corps. He has taught American history at various levels, from high school to university. He edits the Historical Series of the Senate Foreign Relations Committee and is the author of several books, including *Doing Oral History, The Oxford Guide to the United States Government,* and *Press Gallery: Congress and the Washington Correspondents,* which received the Organization of American Historians Richard W. Leopold Prize. Dr. Ritchie has served as president of the Oral History Association and as a council member of the American Historical Association.

James M. McPherson, Ph.D., is George Henry Davis Professor of American History at Princeton University. Dr. McPherson is the author of 11 books about the Civil War era. These include *Battle Cry of Freedom: The Civil War Era,* for which he won the Pulitzer Prize in 1989, and *For Cause and Comrades: Why Men Fought in the Civil War,* for which he won the 1998 Lincoln Prize. He is a member of many professional historical associations, including the Civil War Preservation Trust.

The National Geographic Society, founded in 1888 for the increase and diffusion of geographic knowledge, is the world's largest nonprofit scientific and educational organization. Since its earliest days, the Society has used sophisticated communication technologies, from color photography to holography, to convey knowledge to a worldwide membership. The School Publishing Division supports the Society's mission by developing innovative educational programs—ranging from traditional print materials to multimedia programs including CD-ROMs, videodiscs, and software. "National Geographic Geography & History," featured in each unit of this textbook, was designed and developed by the National Geographic Society's School Publishing Division.

Contributing Author

Dinah Zike, M.Ed., is an award-winning author, educator, and inventor known for designing three-dimensional hands-on manipulatives and graphic organizers known as Foldables®. Foldables are used nationally and internationally by teachers, parents, and educational publishing companies. Dinah has developed over 150 supplemental educational books and materials. She is the author of *The Big Book of Books and Activities,* which was awarded Learning Magazine's Teachers' Choice Award. In 2004 Dinah was honored with the CESI Science Advocacy Award. Dinah received her M.Ed. from Texas A&M, College Station, Texas.

RFB&D learning through listening — Students with print disabilities may be eligible to obtain an accessible, audio version of the pupil edition of this textbook. Please call Recording for the Blind & Dyslexic at 1-800-221-4792 for complete information.

The McGraw-Hill Companies

Glencoe

Send all inquiries to:
Glencoe/McGraw-Hill
8787 Orion Place
Columbus, OH 43240-4027

ISBN: 978-0-07-877718-9
MHID: 0-07-877718-6

Printed in the United States of America.

4 5 6 7 8 9 10 RJE/LEH 12 11 10

Consultants & Reviewers

Academic Consultants

Laura Belmonte, Ph.D.
Associate Professor of
    History
Oklahoma State University
Stillwater, Oklahoma

David Berger, Ph.D.
Broeklundian Professor of
    History
Yeshiva University
New York, New York

**Keith S. Bohannon,
    Ph.D.**
Professor of History
University of West Georgia
Carrollton, Georgia

David Canton, Ph.D.
Jacob & Hilda Blaustein
    Assistant Professor of
    History
Connecticut College
New London, Connecticut

**Jaime Cardenas, Jr.,
    Ph.D.**
Associate Professor of
    History
Seattle Central Community
    College
Seattle, Washington

Jeffrey A. Davis, Ph.D.
Associate Professor of
    History
Bloomsburg University of
    Pennsylvania
Bloomsburg, Pennsylvania

Allison Gough, Ph.D.
Assistant Professor of History
Hawaii Pacific University
Honolulu, Hawaii

Melissa Klapper, Ph.D.
Associate Professor of
    History
Rowan University
Glassboro, New Jersey

Daniel Lewis, Ph.D.
Professor of History
California State Polytechnic
    University
Pomona, California

Teacher Reviewers

Lysa Augustin
Davis Hills Middle School
Huntsville, Alabama

John Brandt
Cumberland County Middle
    School
Cumberland, Virginia

Joanne Cogan
Fairgrounds Middle School
Nashua, New Hampshire

Stephanie Doyle
Breckinridge Middle School
Roanoke, Virginia

Teresa Gallup
York Suburban Middle
    School
York, Pennsylvania

Tina Gersdorf
Jefferson Middle School
Champaign, Illinois

Michael Gordon
Barrington Middle School
Barrington, Illinois

Dawn Grindley
Westlake Middle School
Thornwood, New York

Chris Hartlieb
Highland Middle School
Highland, Illinois

Susan Hawes
Elm Middle School
Elmwood Park, Illinois

Thomas Joice
Clark Middle School
Vincennes, Indiana

Tom Kish
Zimmerman Middle School
Zimmerman, Minnesota

Steven Miller
Blue Ridge Middle School
Purcellville, Virginia

Lisa Ray
Chapin Middle School
Chapin, South Carolina

Terry Robinson
Alden Middle School
Alden, New York

Kathleen Shaeper
Allegany-Limestone Middle
    School
Allegany, New York

Karan Stubbs
Bixby Middle School
Bixby, Oklahoma

Stephanie Sumick
Thompson Middle School
Middletown, New Jersey

Laura Tabachnick
Academy School
Brattleboro, Vermont

Lynn Voorhees
Creekside Middle School
Carmel, Indiana

Marjorie White
Brentwood Middle School
North Charleston, South
    Carolina

Susan Yurkovic
Brownsburg West Middle
    School
Brownsburg, Indiana

Contents

Contents

Features

People IN HISTORY

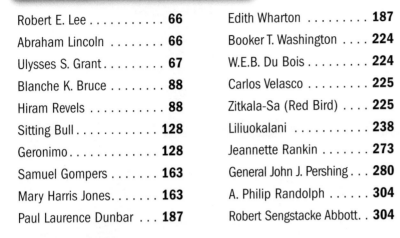

Primary Sources
INTERPRETING
POLITICAL CARTOONS

TIME NOTEBOOK

Features

Chance & Error in History

Skills Handbook

Critical Thinking Skills

Social Studies Skills

1 Learn It!

2 Practice It!

3 Apply It!

Documents of American History

Primary Source Quotes

Primary Source Quotes

◀ Geronimo

Primary Source Quotes

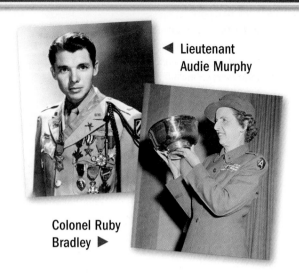

◄ Lieutenant Audie Murphy

Colonel Ruby Bradley ►

Maps, Charts, Graphs, & Diagrams

Maps

Maps In Motion Maps, charts, and graphs with this logo have been enhanced by InMotion graphics in the StudentWorks™ Plus CD-ROM and the Presentation Plus! CD-ROM. These InMotion graphics allow students to interact with layers of data and listen to audio components.

Charts, Graphs, & Diagrams

Scavenger Hunt

The American Journey contains a wealth of information. The trick is to know where to look to access all the information in the book. If you complete this scavenger hunt exercise with your teachers or parents, you will see how the textbook is organized and how to get the most out of your reading and study time. Let's get started!

1. How many units and how many chapters are in this book?

2. Where would you look to quickly find facts about each state, including the capital and the year it was admitted into the Union?

3. You want to read the Declaration of Independence. How will you find it?

4. What time period does Chapter 9 cover?

5. In Chapter 4, what information will the *Foldables* activity help you organize?

6. What Reading History skill will you practice in Unit 3?

7. Where can you find the Essential Questions for each chapter?

8. What is the History Online Web Activity for Chapter 12?

9. Where in the back of the book can you quickly find the meaning of important vocabulary words such as *sodbuster*?

10. Where can you learn about and practice critical thinking and social studies skills?

REFERENCE ATLAS

NATIONAL GEOGRAPHIC

ATLAS KEY

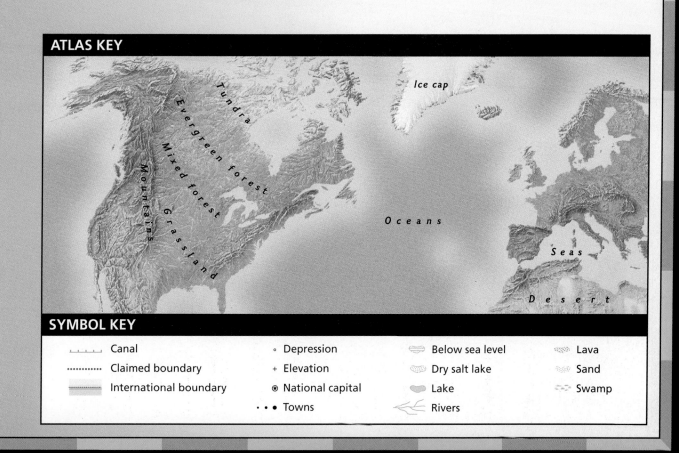

SYMBOL KEY

└┴┴┘ Canal	○ Depression	〰 Below sea level	🌫 Lava
·········· Claimed boundary	+ Elevation	🌫 Dry salt lake	🌫 Sand
▓▓▓ International boundary	⊛ National capital	🌫 Lake	🌫 Swamp
• • • Towns		⟨ Rivers	

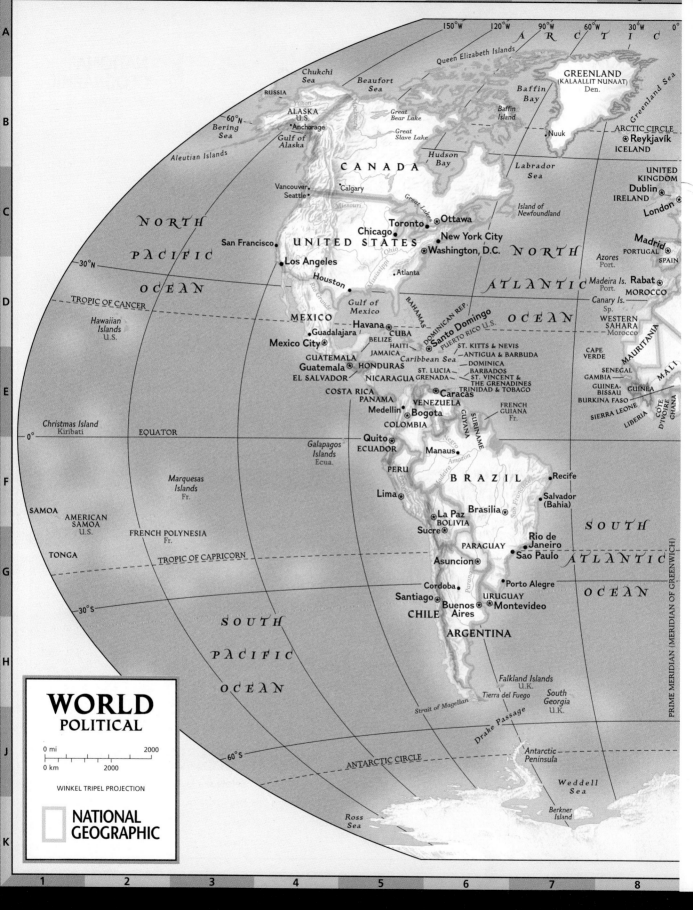

WORLD
POLITICAL

0 mi   2000

0 km   2000

WINKEL TRIPEL PROJECTION

NATIONAL GEOGRAPHIC

NORTH AMERICA
POLITICAL

0 mi   1000
0 km   1000

AZIMUTHAL EQUIDISTANT PROJECTION

NATIONAL GEOGRAPHIC

1. BAJA CALIFORNIA
2. BAJA CALIFORNIA SUR
3. SONORA
4. CHIHUAHUA
5. SINALOA
6. DURANGO
7. COAHUILA
8. NUEVO LEON
9. ZACATECAS
10. TAMAULIPAS
11. NAYARIT
12. AGUASCALIENTES
13. SAN LUIS POTOSI
14. JALISCO
15. GUANAJUATO
16. QUERETARO
17. HIDALGO
18. COLIMA
19. MICHOACAN
20. MEXICO
21. DISTRITO FEDERAL
22. TLAXCALA
23. MORELOS
24. PUEBLA
25. VERACRUZ
26. GUERRERO
27. OAXACA
28. TABASCO
29. CHIAPAS
30. CAMPECHE
31. QUINTANA ROO
32. YUCATAN

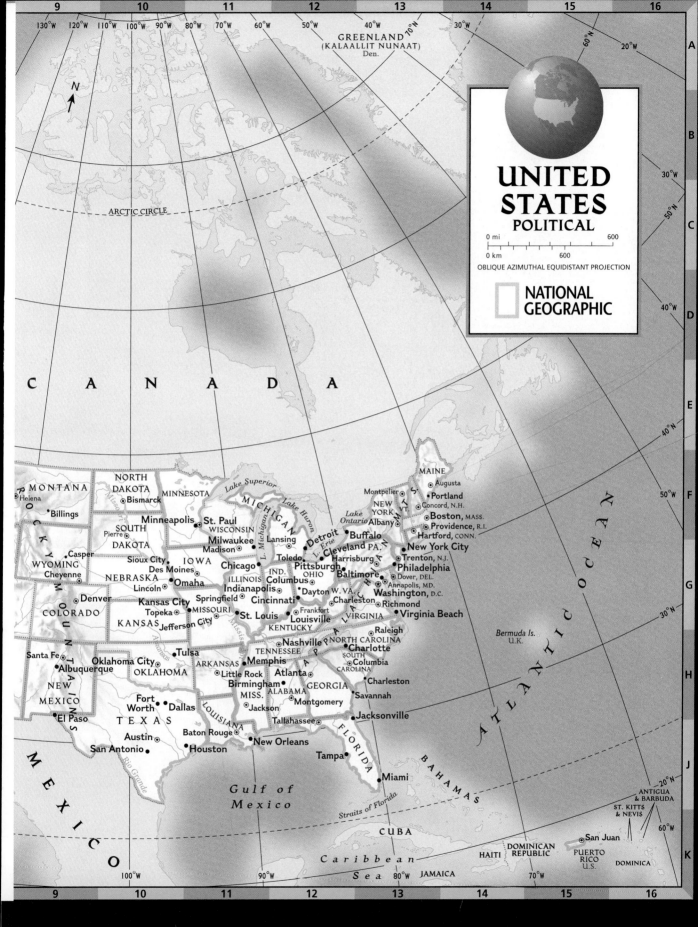

UNITED STATES
POLITICAL

0 mi   600
0 km   600

OBLIQUE AZIMUTHAL EQUIDISTANT PROJECTION

NATIONAL GEOGRAPHIC

GREENLAND (KALAALLIT NUNAAT) Den.

ARCTIC CIRCLE

C A N A D A

MONTANA
Helena
Billings

NORTH DAKOTA
Bismarck

MINNESOTA

Lake Superior

Lake Huron

MICHIGAN

MAINE
Augusta
Portland

Montpelier
Concord, N.H.
NEW YORK
VT.
Boston, MASS.
Albany
Providence, R.I.
Hartford, CONN.

SOUTH DAKOTA
Pierre

Minneapolis
St. Paul
WISCONSIN
Milwaukee
Madison
Lansing

L. Michigan

Lake Ontario

Detroit
L. Erie
Cleveland PA.
Buffalo

New York City

WYOMING
Casper
Cheyenne

IOWA
Sioux City
Des Moines

Chicago
ILLINOIS
IND.

Toledo
Harrisburg
Pittsburgh
OHIO
Columbus
Dayton W. VA.

Trenton, N.J.
Philadelphia
Dover, DEL.
Baltimore
Annapolis, MD.
Washington, D.C.

NEBRASKA
Lincoln
Omaha

Indianapolis
Cincinnati

Charleston

Richmond
Virginia Beach

ROCKY MOUNTAINS

Denver
COLORADO

Kansas City
Topeka
Springfield
MISSOURI
St. Louis
Frankfort

KANSAS
Jefferson City
KENTUCKY
Louisville
VIRGINIA

Raleigh

Santa Fe

Tulsa

Nashville
TENNESSEE

NORTH CAROLINA
Charlotte
SOUTH CAROLINA
Columbia

Albuquerque
Oklahoma City
OKLAHOMA
ARKANSAS
Little Rock
Memphis
Atlanta

Charleston

NEW MEXICO
El Paso

Birmingham
MISS.
ALABAMA
GEORGIA
Montgomery
Jackson

Savannah

Jacksonville

Fort Worth
Dallas
LOUISIANA
Tallahassee
FLORIDA

T E X A S
Baton Rouge
New Orleans

Austin
San Antonio
Houston

Tampa

Miami

Rio Grande

M E X I C O

Gulf of Mexico

Straits of Florida

BAHAMAS

CUBA

Caribbean Sea

JAMAICA

HAITI
DOMINICAN REPUBLIC

San Juan
PUERTO RICO U.S.

Bermuda Is. U.K.

A T L A N T I C   O C E A N

ANTIGUA & BARBUDA
ST. KITTS & NEVIS
DOMINICA

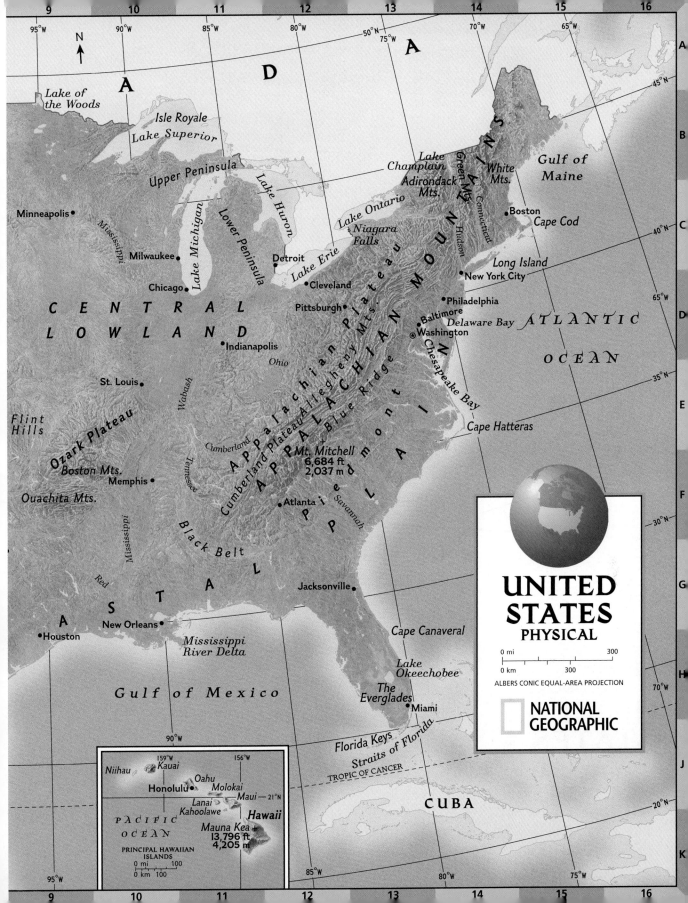

UNITED STATES
PHYSICAL

0 mi ———————— 300
0 km ———————— 300

ALBERS CONIC EQUAL-AREA PROJECTION

NATIONAL GEOGRAPHIC

---

9   10   11   12   13   14   15   16

95°W   90°W   85°W   80°W   75°W   70°W   65°W

N

A   A   D   A

Lake of the Woods

Isle Royale
Lake Superior

Upper Peninsula

Lake Champlain
Adirondack Mts.
Green Mts.
White Mts.
Gulf of Maine

Minneapolis

Mississippi

Lower Peninsula

Lake Huron

Lake Michigan

Lake Ontario
Niagara Falls
Hudson
Connecticut
Boston
Cape Cod

Milwaukee

Detroit

Lake Erie

Cleveland

Chicago

Long Island
New York City

Pittsburgh

Philadelphia

C E N T R A L
L O W L A N D

Indianapolis

Ohio

Appalachian Plateau
Allegheny Mts.

Baltimore
Delaware Bay
Washington

Chesapeake Bay

ATLANTIC
OCEAN

St. Louis

Wabash

Flint Hills

Ozark Plateau

Cumberland Plateau

Cumberland

APPALACHIAN MOUNTAINS

Blue Ridge

Piedmont

Cape Hatteras

Boston Mts.

Memphis

Tennessee

Mt. Mitchell
6,684 ft
2,037 m

Ouachita Mts.

Mississippi

Atlanta

Savannah

C O A S T A L   P L A I N

Black Belt

Red

Jacksonville

New Orleans

Cape Canaveral

Houston

Mississippi
River Delta

Lake Okeechobee

Gulf   of   Mexico

The Everglades

Miami

Florida Keys

Straits of Florida

TROPIC OF CANCER

CUBA

50°N   75°N

45°N

40°N

35°N

30°N

70°W

20°N

Hawaii inset

90°W

159°W   156°W

Niihau

Kauai

Oahu
Honolulu
Molokai
Lanai   Maui — 21°N
Kahoolawe

Hawaii

PACIFIC
OCEAN

Mauna Kea +
13,796 ft
4,205 m

PRINCIPAL HAWAIIAN
ISLANDS

0 mi ———— 100
0 km ———— 100

85°W   80°W   75°W

9   10   11   12   13   14   15   16

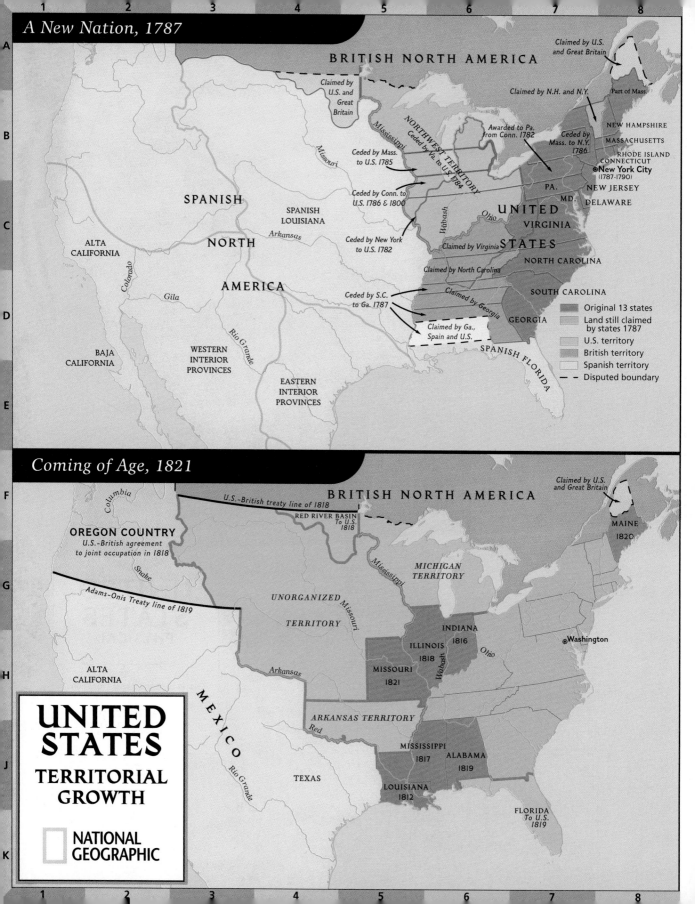

A New Nation, 1787

BRITISH NORTH AMERICA

Claimed by U.S. and Great Britain

Claimed by U.S. and Great Britain

Claimed by N.H. and N.Y.

Part of Mass.

NORTHWEST TERRITORY
Ceded by Va. to U.S. 1784

Awarded to Pa. from Conn. 1782

Ceded by Mass. to N.Y. 1786

Ceded by Mass. to U.S. 1785

NEW HAMPSHIRE

MASSACHUSETTS

RHODE ISLAND

CONNECTICUT

New York City
(1787-1790)

Ceded by Conn. to U.S. 1786 & 1800

PA.

NEW JERSEY

MD.

DELAWARE

Ceded by New York to U.S. 1782

UNITED

VIRGINIA

STATES

Claimed by Virginia

NORTH CAROLINA

Claimed by North Carolina

Claimed by Georgia

SOUTH CAROLINA

Ceded by S.C. to Ga. 1787

GEORGIA

Claimed by Ga., Spain and U.S.

SPANISH FLORIDA

SPANISH

NORTH

AMERICA

SPANISH LOUISIANA

ALTA CALIFORNIA

BAJA CALIFORNIA

WESTERN INTERIOR PROVINCES

EASTERN INTERIOR PROVINCES

Mississippi

Missouri

Arkansas

Colorado

Gila

Rio Grande

Ohio

Wabash

- Original 13 states
- Land still claimed by states 1787
- U.S. territory
- British territory
- Spanish territory
- – – Disputed boundary

Coming of Age, 1821

Claimed by U.S. and Great Britain

BRITISH NORTH AMERICA

U.S.-British treaty line of 1818

RED RIVER BASIN To U.S. 1818

MAINE 1820

OREGON COUNTRY
U.S.-British agreement to joint occupation in 1818

Columbia

Snake

Adams-Onis Treaty line of 1819

ALTA CALIFORNIA

M E X I C O

Rio Grande

TEXAS

UNORGANIZED

TERRITORY

MICHIGAN TERRITORY

Mississippi

Missouri

Arkansas

Red

INDIANA 1816

ILLINOIS 1818

MISSOURI 1821

Wabash

Ohio

Washington

ARKANSAS TERRITORY

MISSISSIPPI 1817

ALABAMA 1819

LOUISIANA 1812

FLORIDA To U.S. 1819

UNITED STATES
TERRITORIAL GROWTH

NATIONAL GEOGRAPHIC

Expanding West of the Mississippi, 1803

BRITISH NORTH AMERICA

Claimed by U.S. and Great Britain

OREGON COUNTRY
Claimed by Great Britain, Russia, Spain, and United States

Claimed by U.S. and Great Britain

VERMONT 1791

Mississippi

Missouri

INDIANA

TERRITORY

OHIO 1803

Philadelphia (1790-1800)

Washington (new capital 1800)

NEW SPAIN
(SPANISH MEXICO)

LOUISIANA PURCHASE
Purchased by U.S. in 1803 from France

Arkansas

Ohio

KENTUCKY 1792

TENNESSEE 1796

Wabash

Red

Rio Grande

Claimed by U.S. and Spain

Ceded by Georgia to U.S. 1802

MISSISSIPPI TERR.

States previously in the Union

States newly admitted

BAJA CALIFORNIA

SPANISH FLORIDA

Claimed by U.S. and Spain

Coast to Coast, 1850 and beyond

BRITISH NORTH AMERICA

Treaty line of 1846

Treaty line of 1842

Treaty line of 1842

WASHINGTON 1889

MONTANA 1889

NORTH DAKOTA 1889

MINNESOTA 1858

OREGON TERRITORY
Added to U.S. in 1846

MINNESOTA TERRITORY

MICHIGAN 1837

OREGON 1859

IDAHO 1890

Snake

SOUTH DAKOTA 1889

WISCONSIN 1848

WYOMING 1890

Missouri

NEVADA 1864

UNORGANIZED

IOWA 1846

UTAH TERRITORY

NEBRASKA 1867

Wabash

Ohio

W. VA. 1863

Washington

TERRITORY

CALIFORNIA 1850

UTAH 1896

COLORADO 1876

KANSAS 1861

Arkansas

Colorado

ARIZONA 1912

Gila

NEW MEXICO TERRITORY

OKLAHOMA 1907

ARKANSAS 1836

Red

Mississippi

GADSDEN PURCHASE
To U.S. 1853

NEW MEXICO 1912

Rio Grande

TEXAS 1845

States admitted after 1850

FLORIDA 1845

RUSSIA

ALASKA 1959
Purchased by U.S. 1867

MEXICO

HAWAII 1959
Annexed by U.S. 1898

9 50°E **10** 60°E **11** 70°E **16** 40°N **A**

Aral Sea

UZBEKISTAN

Tashkent

TAJIKISTAN

Caucasus Mountains

GEORGIA
Tbilisi

Caspian Sea

TURKMENISTAN

Dushanbe

B

Baku

Yerevan
ARMENIA

A S I A

Ashkhabad

Kabul

▲ Mt. Ararat
(16,854 ft.
5,137 m)

AZERBAIJAN

Mashhad

AFGHANISTAN

C

Elburz Mountains

Tigris R.

Tehran

Plateau
of Iran

30°N **D**

Zagros Mountains

IRAQ

IRAN

Baghdad

Euphrates R.

PAKISTAN

E

Al Basrah

KUWAIT

Kuwait

Persian Gulf
(Arabian Gulf)

F

Manama
BAHRAIN

Gulf of Oman

TROPIC OF CANCER

Arabian
Sea

QATAR
Doha

Abu
Dhabi

**SAUDI
ARABIA**

Riyadh

**UNITED
ARAB
EMIRATES**

Masqat

OMAN

20°N **G**

**ARABIAN
PENINSULA**

MIDDLE EAST

PHYSICAL / POLITICAL

H

Makkah
(Mecca)

Rub al Khali
(Empty Quarter)

0 mi   500

0 km   500

AZIMUTHAL EQUIDISTANT PROJECTION

Asir

J

**NATIONAL
GEOGRAPHIC**

N
↑

YEMEN

Sanaa

K

Aden

Gulf of Aden

40°E **9** 50°E **10** **11** **12** **13** **14** **15** **16**

United States Facts

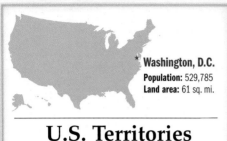

Washington, D.C.
Population: 529,785
Land area: 61 sq. mi.

U.S. Territories

Puerto Rico
Population: 3,987,837
Land area: 3,425 sq. mi.

Guam
Population: 180,692
Land area: 209 sq. mi.

U.S. Virgin Islands
Population: 107,560
Land area: 134 sq. mi.

American Samoa
Population: 57,066
Land area: 77 sq. mi.

The states are listed in the order they were admitted to the Union.

Population figures are based on the U.S. Bureau of the Census projections for July 2010. House of Representatives figures from the 2000 census are from the Clerk of the House of Representatives. States are not drawn to scale.

1 Delaware
Year Admitted: 1787
Population: 884,342
Land area: 1,955 sq. mi.
Representatives: 1
Dover

2 Pennsylvania
Year Admitted: 1787
Population: 12,584,487
Land area: 44,820 sq. mi.
Representatives: 19
Harrisburg

3 New Jersey
Year Admitted: 1787
Population: 9,018,231
Land area: 7,419 sq. mi.
Representatives: 13
Trenton

9 New Hampshire
Year Admitted: 1788
Population: 1,385,560
Land area: 8,969 sq. mi.
Representatives: 2
Concord

10 Virginia
Year Admitted: 1788
Population: 8,010,245
Land area: 39,598 sq. mi.
Representatives: 11
Richmond

11 New York
Year Admitted: 1788
Population: 19,443,672
Land area: 47,224 sq. mi.
Representatives: 29
Albany

17 Ohio
Year Admitted: 1803
Population: 11,576,181
Land area: 40,953 sq. mi.
Representatives: 18
Columbus

18 Louisiana
Year Admitted: 1812
Population: 4,612,679
Land area: 43,566 sq. mi.
Representatives: 7
Baton Rouge

19 Indiana
Year Admitted: 1816
Population: 6,392,139
Land area: 35,870 sq. mi.
Representatives: 9
Indianapolis

24 Missouri
Year Admitted: 1821
Population: 5,922,078
Land area: 68,898 sq. mi.
Representatives: 9
Jefferson City

25 Arkansas
Year Admitted: 1836
Population: 2,875,039
Land area: 52,075 sq. mi.
Representatives: 4
Little Rock

26 Michigan
Year Admitted: 1837
Population: 10,428,683
Land area: 56,809 sq. mi.
Representatives: 15
Lansing

27 Florida
Year Admitted: 1845
Population: 19,251,691
Land area: 53,997 sq. mi.
Representatives: 25
Tallahassee

28 Texas
Year Admitted: 1845
Population: 24,648,888
Land area: 261,914 sq. mi.
Representatives: 32
Austin

33 Oregon
Year Admitted: 1859
Population: 3,790,996
Land area: 96,003 sq. mi.
Representatives: 5
Salem

34 Kansas
Year Admitted: 1861
Population: 2,805,470
Land area: 81,823 sq. mi.
Representatives: 4
Topeka

35 West Virginia
Year Admitted: 1863
Population: 1,829,141
Land area: 24,087 sq. mi.
Representatives: 3
Charleston

36 Nevada
Year Admitted: 1864
Population: 2,690,531
Land area: 109,806 sq. mi.
Representatives: 3
Carson City

37 Nebraska
Year Admitted: 1867
Population: 1,768,997
Land area: 76,878 sq. mi.
Representatives: 3
Lincoln

42 Washington
Year Admitted: 1889
Population: 6,541,963
Land area: 66,582 sq. mi.
Representatives: 9
Olympia

43 Idaho
Year Admitted: 1890
Population: 1,517,291
Land area: 82,751 sq. mi.
Representatives: 2
Boise

44 Wyoming
Year Admitted: 1890
Population: 519,886
Land area: 97,105 sq. mi.
Representatives: 1
Cheyenne

45 Utah
Year Admitted: 1896
Population: 2,595,013
Land area: 82,168 sq. mi.
Representatives: 3
Salt Lake City

46 Oklahoma
Year Admitted: 1907
Population: 3,591,516
Land area: 68,679 sq. mi.
Representatives: 5
Oklahoma City

4 Georgia
Year Admitted: 1788
Population: 9,589,080
Land area: 57,919 sq. mi.
Representatives: 13

★ Atlanta

5 Connecticut
Year Admitted: 1788
Population: 3,577,490
Land area: 4,845 sq. mi.
Representatives: 5

★ Hartford

6 Massachusetts
Year Admitted: 1788
Population: 6,649,441
Land area: 7,838 sq. mi.
Representatives: 10

Boston ★

7 Maryland
Year Admitted: 1788
Population: 5,904,970
Land area: 9,775 sq. mi.
Representatives: 8

Annapolis ★

8 South Carolina
Year Admitted: 1788
Population: 4,446,704
Land area: 30,111 sq. mi.
Representatives: 6

Columbia ★

12 North Carolina
Year Admitted: 1789
Population: 9,345,823
Land area: 48,718 sq. mi.
Representatives: 13

★ Raleigh

13 Rhode Island
Year Admitted: 1790
Population: 1,116,652
Land area: 1,045 sq. mi.
Representatives: 2

★ Providence

14 Vermont
Year Admitted: 1791
Population: 652,512
Land area: 9,249 sq. mi.
Representatives: 1

★ Montpelier

15 Kentucky
Year Admitted: 1792
Population: 4,265,117
Land area: 39,732 sq. mi.
Representatives: 6

Frankfort ★

16 Tennessee
Year Admitted: 1796
Population: 6,230,852
Land area: 41,220 sq. mi.
Representatives: 9

★ Nashville

20 Mississippi
Year Admitted: 1817
Population: 2,971,412
Land area: 46,914 sq. mi.
Representatives: 4

★ Jackson

21 Illinois
Year Admitted: 1818
Population: 12,916,894
Land area: 55,593 sq. mi.
Representatives: 19

★ Springfield

22 Alabama
Year Admitted: 1819
Population: 4,596,330
Land area: 50,750 sq. mi.
Representatives: 7

Montgomery ★

23 Maine
Year Admitted: 1820
Population: 1,357,134
Land area: 30,865 sq. mi.
Representatives: 2

★ Augusta

29 Iowa
Year Admitted: 1846
Population: 3,009,907
Land area: 55,875 sq. mi.
Representatives: 5

Des Moines ★

30 Wisconsin
Year Admitted: 1848
Population: 5,727,426
Land area: 54,314 sq. mi.
Representatives: 8

Madison ★

31 California
Year Admitted: 1850
Population: 38,067,134
Land area: 155,973 sq. mi.
Representatives: 53

Sacramento ★

32 Minnesota
Year Admitted: 1858
Population: 5,420,636
Land area: 79,617 sq. mi.
Representatives: 8

Saint Paul ★

38 Colorado
Year Admitted: 1876
Population: 4,831,554
Land area: 103,730 sq. mi.
Representatives: 7

Denver ★

39 North Dakota
Year Admitted: 1889
Population: 636,623
Land area: 68,994 sq. mi.
Representatives: 1

Bismarck ★

40 South Dakota
Year Admitted: 1889
Population: 786,399
Land area: 75,898 sq. mi.
Representatives: 1

Pierre ★

41 Montana
Year Admitted: 1889
Population: 968,598
Land area: 145,556 sq. mi.
Representatives: 1

★ Helena

47 New Mexico
Year Admitted: 1912
Population: 1,980,225
Land area: 121,365 sq. mi.
Representatives: 3

★ Santa Fe

48 Arizona
Year Admitted: 1912
Population: 6,637,381
Land area: 113,642 sq. mi.
Representatives: 8

Phoenix ★

49 Alaska
Year Admitted: 1959
Population: 694,109
Land area: 570,374 sq. mi.
Representatives: 1

Juneau ★

50 Hawaii
Year Admitted: 1959
Population: 1,340,674
Land area: 6,432 sq. mi.
Representatives: 2

Honolulu ★

Geography Skills Handbook

How Do I Study Geography?

Geographers have created these broad categories and standards as tools to help you understand the relationships among people, places, and environments.

🌐 5 Themes of Geography
🌐 6 Essential Elements
🌐 18 Geography Standards

5
Themes of Geography

1 Location

Location describes where something is. Absolute location describes a place's exact position on the Earth's surface. Relative location expresses where a place is in relation to another place.

2 Place

Place describes the physical and human characteristics that make a location unique.

3 Regions

Regions are areas that share common characteristics.

4 Movement

Movement explains how and why people and things move and are connected.

5 Human-Environment Interaction

Human-Environment Interaction describes the relationship between people and their environment.

6
Essential Elements

18
Geography Standards

I. The World in Spatial Terms
Geographers look to see where a place is located. Location acts as a starting point to answer "Where Is It?" The location of a place helps you orient yourself as to where you are.

1 How to use maps and other tools

2 How to use mental maps to organize information

3 How to analyze the spatial organization of people, places, and environments

II. Places and Regions
Place describes physical characteristics such as landforms, climate, and plant or animal life. It might also describe human characteristics, including language and way of life. Places can also be organized into regions. **Regions** are places united by one or more characteristics.

4 The physical and human characteristics of places

5 How people create regions to interpret Earth's complexity

6 How culture and experience influence people's perceptions of places and regions

III. Physical Systems
Geographers study how physical systems, such as hurricanes, volcanoes, and glaciers, shape the surface of the Earth. They also look at how plants and animals depend upon one another and their surroundings for their survival.

7 The physical processes that shape Earth's surface

8 The distribution of ecosystems on Earth's surface

9 The characteristics, distribution, and migration of human populations

IV. Human Systems
People shape the world in which they live. They settle in certain places but not in others. An ongoing theme in geography is the movement of people, ideas, and goods.

10 The complexity of Earth's cultural mosaics

11 The patterns and networks of economic interdependence

12 The patterns of human settlement

13 The forces of cooperation and conflict

V. Environment and Society
How does the relationship between people and their natural surroundings influence the way people live? Geographers study how people use the environment and how their actions affect the environment.

14 How human actions modify the physical environment

15 How physical systems affect human systems

16 The meaning, use, and distribution of resources

VI. The Uses of Geography
Knowledge of geography helps us understand the relationships among people, places, and environments over time. Applying geographic skills helps you understand the past and prepare for the future.

17 How to apply geography to interpret the past

18 How to apply geography to interpret the present and plan for the future

Globes and Maps

What Is a Globe? ▶

A **globe** is a round model of the Earth that shows its shape, lands, and directions as they truly relate to one another.

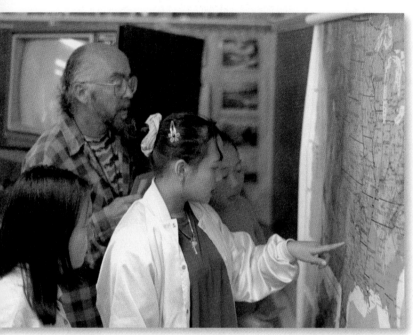

◀ What Is a Map?

A **map** is a flat drawing of all or part of the Earth's surface. Cartographers, or mapmakers, use mathematical formulas to transfer information from the round globe to a flat map.

Globes and Maps ▶

Globes and maps serve different purposes, and each has advantages and disadvantages.

	Advantages	Disadvantages
Globes	• Represent true land shape, distances, and directions	• Cannot show detailed information • Difficult to carry
Maps	• Show small areas in great detail • Display different types of information, such as population densities or natural resources • Transport easily	• Distort, or change, the accuracy of shapes and distances

Map Projections

When the Earth's surface is flattened on a map, big gaps open up. Mapmakers stretch parts of the Earth to show either the correct shapes of places or their correct sizes. Mapmakers have developed different projections, or ways of showing the Earth on a flat piece of paper. Below are different map projections.

Goode's Interrupted Equal-Area Projection ▼

A map with this projection shows continents close to their true shapes and sizes. This projection is helpful to compare land area among continents.

Mercator Projection ▼

The Mercator projection shows land shapes fairly accurately but not size or distance. Areas that are located far from the Equator are quite distorted. The Mercator projection shows true directions, however, making it useful for sea travel.

Robinson Projection ▼

The Robinson projection has minor distortions. Continents and oceans are close to their sizes and shapes, but the North and South Poles appear flattened.

Winkel Tripel Projection ▼

This projection gives a good overall view of the continents' shapes and sizes. Land areas are not as distorted near the poles as they are in the Robinson projection.

Skills Practice

1 **Comparing and Contrasting** Explain the similarities and differences between globes and maps.

2 **Describing** Why do map projections distort some parts of the Earth?

Location

To locate places on Earth, geographers use a system of imaginary lines that crisscross the globe. These lines are called *latitude* and *longitude*.

Latitude ▶

- Lines of **latitude** are imaginary circles that run east to west around the globe. They are known as *parallels*. These parallels divide the globe into units called degrees.

- The **Equator** circles the middle of the Earth like a belt. It is located halfway between the North and South Poles. The Equator is 0° latitude.

- The letter *N* or *S* that follows the degree symbol tells you if the location is north or south of the Equator. The North Pole, for example, is 90°N (north) latitude, and the South Pole is 90°S (south) latitude.

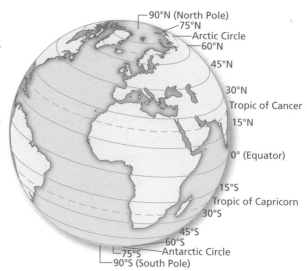

◀ Longitude

- Lines of **longitude,** also known as *meridians*, run from the North Pole to the South Pole. The **Prime Meridian** (also called the Meridian of Greenwich) is 0° longitude and runs through Greenwich, England.

- The letter *E* or *W* that follows the degree symbol tells you if the location is east or west of the Prime Meridian.

- On the opposite side of the Earth is the 180° meridian, also known as the International Date Line.

Absolute Location ▶

A place's exact location can be identified when you use both latitude and longitude. For example, Tokyo, Japan, is 36°N latitude and 140°E longitude.

Hemispheres

The Equator divides the Earth into Northern and Southern Hemispheres. Everything north of the Equator is in the Northern Hemisphere. Everything south of the Equator is in the Southern Hemisphere.

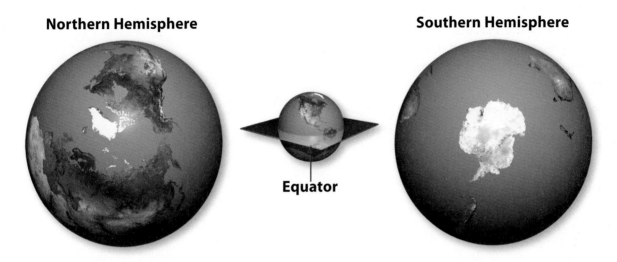

Northern Hemisphere

Southern Hemisphere

Equator

The Prime Meridian divides the Earth into Eastern and Western Hemispheres. Everything east of the Prime Meridian for 180 degrees is in the Eastern Hemisphere. Everything west of the Prime Meridian for 180 degrees is in the Western Hemisphere.

Western Hemisphere

Eastern Hemisphere

Prime Meridian

Skills Practice

1 **Identifying** What country is located at 30°S and 120°E?

2 **Analyzing Visuals** In which hemispheres is Europe located?

Parts of a Map

In addition to latitude and longitude, maps feature other important tools to help you interpret the information they contain.

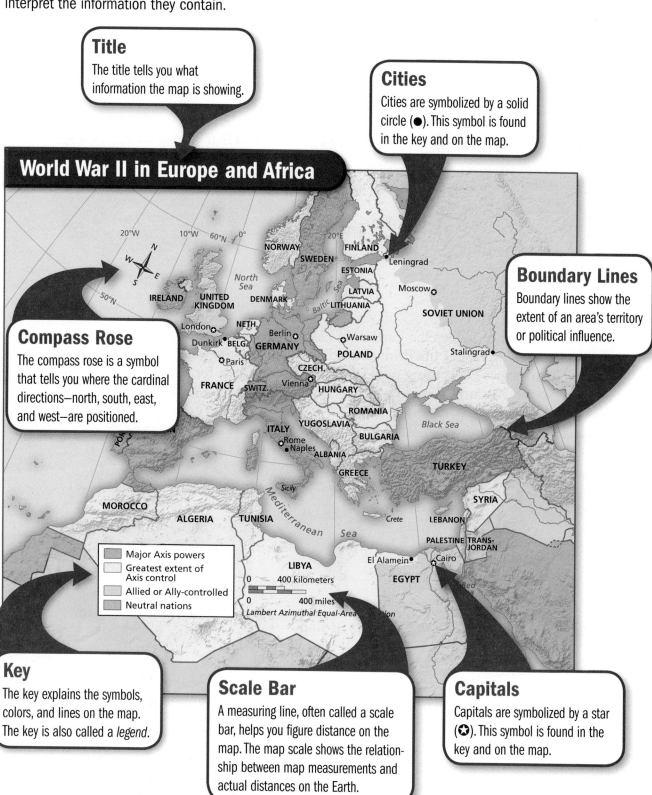

Title
The title tells you what information the map is showing.

Cities
Cities are symbolized by a solid circle (●). This symbol is found in the key and on the map.

World War II in Europe and Africa

Boundary Lines
Boundary lines show the extent of an area's territory or political influence.

Compass Rose
The compass rose is a symbol that tells you where the cardinal directions—north, south, east, and west—are positioned.

Key (map legend):
- Major Axis powers
- Greatest extent of Axis control
- Allied or Ally-controlled
- Neutral nations

0   400 kilometers
0   400 miles
Lambert Azimuthal Equal-Area

Key
The key explains the symbols, colors, and lines on the map. The key is also called a *legend*.

Scale Bar
A measuring line, often called a scale bar, helps you figure distance on the map. The map scale shows the relationship between map measurements and actual distances on the Earth.

Capitals
Capitals are symbolized by a star (✪). This symbol is found in the key and on the map.

Using Scale

All maps are drawn to a certain scale. The scale of a map is the size of the map compared to the size of the actual land surface. Thus, the scale of a map varies with the size of the area shown.

Small-Scale Maps ▼

A small-scale map like this shows a large land area but little detail.

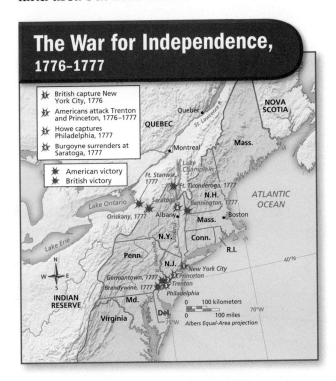

Large-Scale Maps ▼

A large-scale map like this shows a small land area with a great amount of detail.

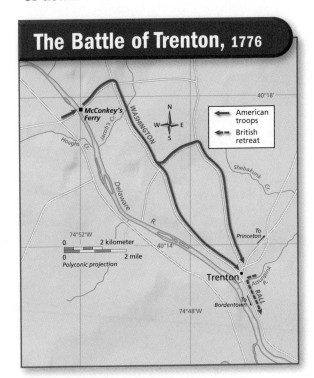

How Do I Use a Scale Bar?

A scale bar helps you determine actual distances that are represented on a map. First, measure the distance between two points on a map with a ruler. Then, check your measurement against the scale bar to find out how many kilometers or miles are represented by that length.

On the scale bar above, about ½ of an inch equals 300 miles. A little more than ½ of a centimeter is equal to 300 kilometers.

Skills Practice

1 **Defining** What is scale?

2 **Contrasting** What is the difference between a small-scale map and a large-scale map?

3 **Identifying** What are the four cardinal directions?

4 **Describing** Would you use a small-scale or a large-scale map to plan a car trip across the United States? Why?

Types of Maps

General Purpose Maps

Maps are amazingly useful tools. You can use them to show information and to make connections between seemingly unrelated topics. Geographers use many different types of maps. Maps that show a wide range of information about an area are called **general purpose maps.** Two of the most common general purpose maps are physical maps and political maps.

Physical Maps ▼

Physical maps call out landforms and water features. The map key explains what each color and symbol stands for.

South Asia: Physical

Physical maps use color and shadings to show **relief,** or how flat or rugged the land surface is.

Colors are used to show **elevation,** the height of an area above sea level.

Elevations
13,100 ft. (4,000 m)
6,500 ft. (2,000 m)
1,600 ft. (500 m)
650 ft. (200 m)
0 ft. (0 m)
Below sea level
▲ Mountain peak

Political Maps ▼

Political maps show the names and political boundaries of states and countries, along with human-made features such as cities or transportation routes.

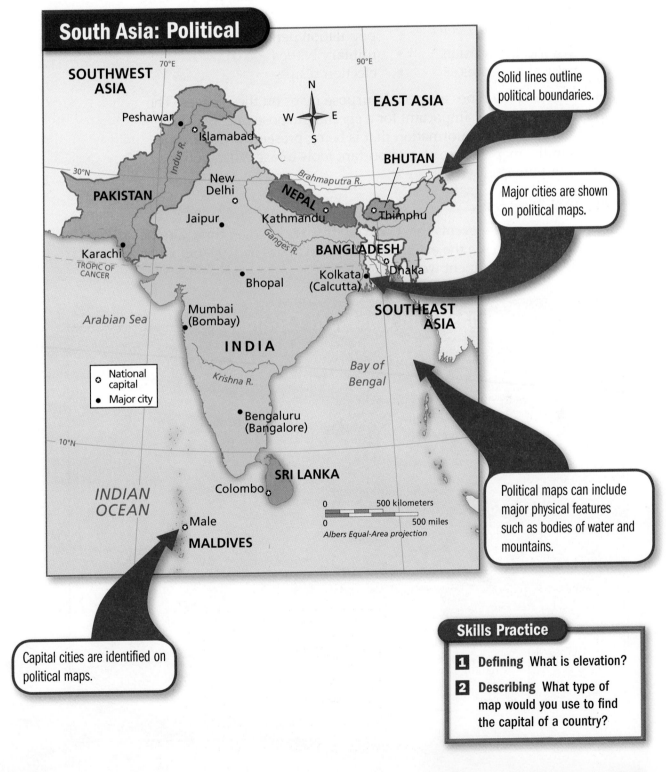

Solid lines outline political boundaries.

Major cities are shown on political maps.

Political maps can include major physical features such as bodies of water and mountains.

Capital cities are identified on political maps.

Types of Maps
Special Purpose Maps

Some maps are made to present specific types of information. These are called **thematic** or **special purpose maps.** These maps usually show specific topics in detail. Special purpose maps may include information about:

- climate
- historical expansion
- natural resources
- population density
- military battles
- election results

Look at some of the types of special purpose maps on these pages. The map's title is especially important for a special purpose map because it tells you the type of information that is being presented. Colors and symbols in the map key are also important tools to use when you read these types of maps.

Historical Maps ▼

Historical maps show events that occurred in a region over time. On the map below, you can see the extent of the United States in 1803 and what other parts of the continent were being explored.

Louisiana Purchase and Westward Expansion

Population Density Maps ▶

Population is not evenly spread across the usable land. Population density is the average number of people that live in a square mile or square kilometer. Population density maps use colors that are explained in a key to indicate how many people live in a given area.

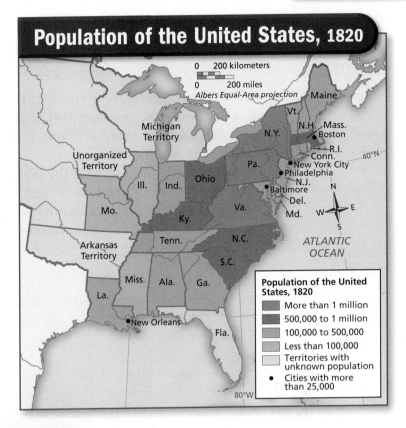

Population of the United States, 1820

0 200 kilometers
0 200 miles
Albers Equal-Area projection

Maine
Vt.
Michigan Territory
N.H. Mass.
N.Y. Boston
R.I.
Unorganized Territory
Conn.
Pa. 40°N
New York City
Ill. Ind. Ohio
Philadelphia
N.J.
Mo.
Baltimore
Va. Del.
Ky. Md.
Arkansas Territory
Tenn.
N.C.
ATLANTIC OCEAN
S.C.
Miss. Ala. Ga.
La.
New Orleans
Fla.
80°W

Population of the United States, 1820
- More than 1 million
- 500,000 to 1 million
- 100,000 to 500,000
- Less than 100,000
- Territories with unknown population
- • Cities with more than 25,000

The Battle of Gettysburg, Day 3

Gettysburg
General Lee
Willoughby Run
Seminary Ridge
Cemetery Hill
Culp's Hill
Rock
Pickett's Charge
Cemetery Ridge
Pitzer's Run
Plum Run
General Meade
Creek
Little Round Top
Big Round Top

- ▬ Confederate troops
- ▬ Union troops
- ◀ Confederate troop movements

0 1 kilometer
0 1 mile
Albers Equal-Area projection

◀ Military Maps

Military maps show the areas where battles occurred, troop movements, who controlled various sites, and who won the battles. Color-coded arrows and symbols shown in the key help you determine the sequence of events. It is also important to notice the geographical features near the battle site and how they could affect military strategy. On larger military maps, battle sites are often symbolized by a burst shell or a star.

Skills Practice

1 Identifying What type of special purpose map might show battles during World War II?

2 Contrasting What is the difference between a general purpose map and a special purpose map?

Graphs, Charts, and Diagrams

Graphs

Graphs present and summarize information visually. The types of graphs you will find in this textbook are described below. Each part of a graph provides useful information. To read a graph, follow these steps:

- Read the graph's title to find out its subject.
- To understand bar and line graphs, read the labels along the **axes**—the horizontal line along the bottom and the vertical line along the left side of the graph. The horizontal axis tells you what is being measured. The vertical axis tells you the unit of measurement being used.

Bar Graphs ▼

Bar graphs use bars or wide lines to compare data visually.

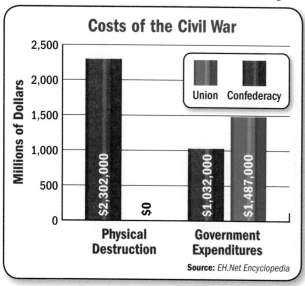

Costs of the Civil War

Source: EH.Net Encyclopedia

Line Graphs ▼

Line graphs help show changes over a period of time. The amounts being measured are plotted on the grid above each year and then are connected by a line.

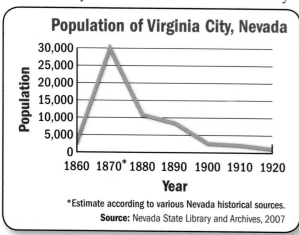

Population of Virginia City, Nevada

*Estimate according to various Nevada historical sources.

Source: Nevada State Library and Archives, 2007

Circle Graphs ▼

You can use circle graphs when you want to show how the whole of something is divided into its parts. Because of their shape, circle graphs are often called *pie graphs*. Each slice represents a part or percentage of the whole pie. The complete circle represents a whole group—or 100 percent.

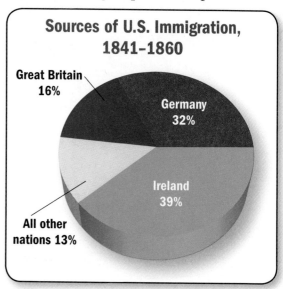

Sources of U.S. Immigration, 1841–1860

Charts

Charts present related facts and numbers in an organized way. One type of chart is a table. A table arranges data, especially numbers, in rows and columns for easy reference. Charts can also be used to summarize ideas or main points of broader topics. This allows you to review material and compare main ideas easily.

Army Salaries (monthly)

Rank	Civil War	World War II 1942	Vietnam War 1965	Iraq War 2007
Private	*$13	$50	$85	$1203 – 1543.20
Corporal	$14	$66	$210	$1699.50
Sergeant	$17	$78	$261	$1854 – 2339.10
Sergeant Major	$21	$138	$486	$4110

*Until 1864, African Americans in the Civil War were paid only $7.00 per month.

Source: *Bureau of Economic Analysis*; Princeton Review; www.militaryfactory.com

Diagrams

Diagrams are drawings that show steps in a process, point out the parts of an object, or explain how something works.

The USS *Maine*

1 **Torpedo tubes** are devices to launch torpedoes.

2 **Steam boilers** power the engines.

3 Munitions were stored in the **magazine**.

4 **Cowls** provided fresh air below deck.

Skills Practice

1 **Identifying** What percentage does the whole circle in a circle graph represent?

2 **Analyzing Information** What type of graph would best show the number of Republicans and Democrats in the U.S. House of Representatives?

Geographic Dictionary

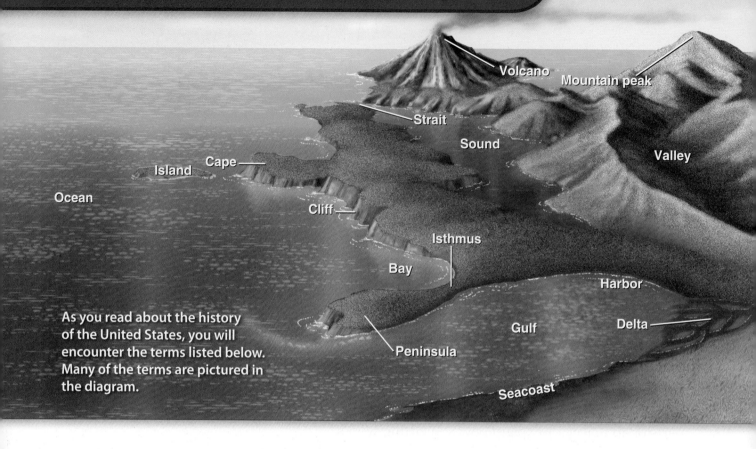

Ocean
Island
Cape
Cliff
Strait
Volcano
Mountain peak
Sound
Valley
Isthmus
Bay
Harbor
Peninsula
Gulf
Delta
Seacoast

As you read about the history of the United States, you will encounter the terms listed below. Many of the terms are pictured in the diagram.

absolute location exact location of a place on the Earth described by global coordinates

basin area of land drained by a given river and its branches; area of land surrounded by lands of higher elevations

bay part of a large body of water that extends into a shoreline, generally smaller than a gulf

canyon deep and narrow valley with steep walls

cape point of land that extends into a river, lake, or ocean

channel wide strait or waterway between two landmasses that lie close to each other; deep part of a river or other waterway

cliff steep, high wall of rock, earth, or ice

continent one of the seven large landmasses on the Earth

cultural feature characteristic that humans have created in a place, such as language, religion, housing, and settlement pattern

delta flat, low-lying land built up from soil carried downstream by a river and deposited at its mouth

divide stretch of high land that separates river systems

downstream direction in which a river or stream flows from its source to its mouth

elevation height of land above sea level

Equator imaginary line that runs around the Earth halfway between the North and South Poles; used as the starting point to measure degrees of north and south latitude

glacier large, thick body of slowly moving ice

gulf part of a large body of water that extends into a shoreline, generally larger and more deeply indented than a bay

harbor a sheltered place along a shoreline where ships can anchor safely

highland elevated land area such as a hill, mountain, or plateau

hill elevated land with sloping sides and rounded summit; generally smaller than a mountain

island land area, smaller than a continent, completely surrounded by water

isthmus narrow stretch of land connecting two larger land areas

lake a large inland body of water

latitude distance north or south of the Equator, measured in degrees

longitude distance east or west of the Prime Meridian, measured in degrees

lowland land, usually level, at a low elevation

map drawing of the Earth shown on a flat surface

meridian one of many lines on the global grid running from the North Pole to the South Pole; used to measure degrees of longitude

Mountain range
Source of river
Channel
Glacier
Highland
Plateau
Lake
Hills
Canyon
Mouth of river
Desert
River
Upstream
Downstream
Plain
Lowland
Basin
Tributary

mesa broad, flat-topped landform with steep sides; smaller than a plateau

mountain land with steep sides that rises sharply (1,000 feet or more) from surrounding land; generally larger and more rugged than a hill

mountain peak pointed top of a mountain

mountain range a series of connected mountains

mouth (of a river) place where a stream or river flows into a larger body of water

ocean one of the four major bodies of salt water that surround the continents

ocean current stream of either cold or warm water that moves in a definite direction through an ocean

parallel one of many lines on the global grid that circle the Earth north and south of the Equator; used to measure degrees of latitude

peninsula body of land jutting into a lake or ocean, surrounded on three sides by water

physical feature characteristic of a place occurring naturally, such as a landform, body of water, climate pattern, or resource

plain area of level land, usually at a low elevation and often covered with grasses

plateau large area of flat or rolling land at a high elevation, about 300 to 3,000 feet (90 to 900 m) high

Prime Meridian line of the global grid running from the North Pole to the South Pole at Greenwich, England; starting point for measuring degrees of east and west longitude

relief changes in elevation over a given area of land

river large natural stream of water that runs through land

sea large body of water completely surrounded by land

seacoast land lying next to a sea or ocean

sea level position on land level with surface of nearby ocean or sea

sound body of water between a coastline and one or more islands off the coast

source (of a river) place where a river or stream begins, often in highlands

strait narrow stretch of water joining two larger bodies of water

tributary small river or stream that flows into a larger river or stream; a branch of the river

upstream direction opposite the flow of a river; toward the source of a river or stream

valley area of low land between hills or mountains

volcano mountain created as ash or liquid rock erupts from inside the Earth

Overview

A prologue is an introduction that sets the stage for what you will be reading and learning later in the text. As you study the prologue, you will learn about the people, events, and movements that shaped the history of the United States from earliest times to the middle of the 1800s. During this period, the first immigrants came to settle the land and develop its resources. Their descendants became Americans, laying the foundation of a democratic nation that eventually spread across the middle of North America.

Looking Back:
Beginnings to 1850

Long before there was a United States, native peoples lived in the Americas. By the A.D. 1500s, Europeans had arrived and established colonies. In the late 1700s, the thirteen British colonies in North America rebelled against Britain and set up a new nation. During the early 1800s, the young republic grew in size and economic strength. In time, however, the country's northern and southern regions divided over slavery and other issues. Unable to settle these differences, the nation moved toward civil war.

▲ The Liberty Bell

Huron and Algonquin taught their customs and traditions to Jean Nicollet and other French fur traders.

The First Americans

Main Idea Native Americans developed different societies and cultures in the Americas during the centuries before 1500.

History and You Have you ever tried to organize a large number of people? It is not easy to get everyone to work together. Read how early Americans organized their societies.

. . . .

For thousands of years, people have been living in what is now the United States. They have come from many different parts of the world to settle a vast territory that stretches across North America. When Europeans first arrived in North America about A.D. 1500, they found Native Americans with advanced cultures already living there. The meeting of Native American and European cultures that occurred in the Western Hemisphere shaped the history of the United States.

Pathway to the Americas

Scientists believe the first Americans were hunters from Asia who crossed over a broad strip of land between Asia and North America that was exposed during the last Ice Age. These early peoples reached the Americas between 15,000 and 30,000 years ago.

Eventually, groups of people spread across the entire landmass, going as far east as the Atlantic Ocean and as far south as the tip of South America. These early people eventually began farming the land. With dependable food supplies, early Americans developed permanent communities. Their descendants today are called Native Americans. Over many centuries, Native American groups developed different ways of life using local resources.

Mesoamerican Civilizations

In what is today Mexico and Central and South America, an area known as Mesoamerica, three large, advanced Native American civilizations developed—the Maya, the Aztec, and the Inca. Each thrived for centuries. They built large cities, developed arts and sciences, and established trading routes.

The Maya The Maya civilization arose in the rain forests of what is now southern Mexico and Central America. By A.D. 300 the Maya had built many cities. Each city was dominated by a stone pyramid that served as a religious and political center. The Maya civilization was a theocracy, a society ruled by religious leaders. Priests performed religious ceremonies and studied the night sky from temples on top of the pyramids. They developed an understanding of astronomy, creating a 365-day calendar to schedule plantings, harvests, and ceremonies. The Maya also traded along Mexico's eastern coast. No one knows why, but around A.D. 800, the Maya civilization began to decline.

The Aztec Centuries after the fall of the Maya, a warlike group of hunters called the Aztec arrived in central Mexico. They settled and farmed on an island in Lake Texcoco, today part of Mexico City. On this island the Aztec built one of the greatest trading cities in the Americas—Tenochtitlán (tay·nawch·teet·LAHN). By A.D. 1500, nearly 200,000 people lived there. The Aztec king, or emperor, ruled over a population divided into four groups: nobles, commoners (farmers, artisans, and merchants), unskilled laborers, and enslaved people.

The Inca A third civilization, the Inca, arose in western South America. The Inca founded their capital city of Cuzco around A.D. 1200. Through military conquest, Inca warriors built an empire that stretched for more than 3,000 miles (4,828 km). It reached from what is today Colombia to northern Argentina. At its height, the Inca Empire had more than 6 million people. To control this vast realm, more than 10,000 miles (16,093 km) of stone-paved roads were built through rain forests and over mountains.

North American Peoples

Meanwhile, many other Native American cultures developed on the North American continent. The Hohokam and the Anasazi lived in the desert Southwest between A.D. 200 and A.D. 1300. The Hohokam developed irrigation canals to carry water from nearby rivers to their settlements. The Anasazi built dwellings in the region's canyons and cliffs. They collected water that ran off the cliffs during heavy rains and channeled it to their fields.

A group of many different peoples called Mound Builders lived in what is today the Midwest. They received this name because they built huge ceremonial mounds made of earth, some in the shape of animals. One of these mound-building groups, the Mississippians, lived in the Mississippi River valley. They grew crops in the rich floodplains along the river. This farming led to the rise of cities.

Ways of Life

Differing Cultures Native American groups across North America developed their own unique ways of life. Styles of lodging and crafts varied from people to people.

Some contained 10,000 or more people. The largest city, Cahokia, may have had 30,000 people. The remains of this city can still be seen in southwestern Illinois.

After the Hohokam, the Anasazi, and the Mound Builders faded away, other Native American civilizations arose to take their place. The Inuit lived in the northern lands along the Arctic Ocean. They learned to build homes made of blocks of snow and ice and to craft clothing from sealskin and thick fur. They fished the coastal waters and hunted for seals, whales, and walruses.

Along the coast of the Pacific Ocean, groups like the Tlingit (TLIHNG·kuht) and Chinook depended on forests for timber and the sea for fish. In the Southwest, groups such as the Hopi, the Acoma, and the Zuni were descended from the Anasazi. They relied on irrigation and built dwellings from sun-dried mud brick called adobe. The people of the Southwest grew corn, squash, and beans.

Southwest Pottery The peoples of the Southwest created beautiful pottery from the same clay with which they built their homes. Pots were used to store water and food. ▶

Buffalo Skin Bag ▶ The Native Americans of the Plains used the skins of the buffalo they hunted to make a number of everyday items. This buffalo skin bag shows a horse and rider.

◀ **Longhouses** People of the East lived in bark-covered longhouses. Each building could shelter several families.

Northwest Artifact This ladle in the form of a bird was used by Native Americans in the Northwest at large parties called potlatches. Potlatches celebrated events such as births, deaths, and weddings. ▼

Critical Thinking

Analyzing Choose one of the items above. What can you infer about the group that made it?

Adapting to the Environment Peoples on the Great Plains were nomads, or people who moved from place to place. They followed the herds of buffalo, deer, and antelope. Some groups, like the Pawnee and Iowa, farmed as well as hunted. The eastern woodlands were home to the Iroquois and Cherokee. They formed federations, or governments that linked different groups. The many Algonquian groups of the East were linked by similar languages.

Wherever they lived in North America, these early Americans developed ways of life that were well suited to their environments, which included deserts, grassy plains, and forests. In the late 1400s, however, they would meet Europeans whose cultures, beliefs, and ways of life were different from anything they had ever known or seen.

Reading Check **Describing** How did the Anasazi adapt to their environment?

Settling North America

Main Idea European colonies in North America developed differently from each other and from Europe.

History and You What would make you want to move to a new place? Read to learn why Europeans settled in North America from the 1500s to the 1700s.

. . . .

Europeans were not aware of the Americas until 1492. That year, explorer Christopher Columbus, financed by the Spanish government, traveled west from Europe in hope of reaching Asia. Instead, he reached islands in the Caribbean Sea. His tales of these new lands excited many Europeans.

In the late 1400s and early 1500s, Spanish explorers arrived in the Americas. They were greatly impressed by the magnificent cities and great riches of the Native Americans.

Conquistadors In the early 1520s, a Spanish army led by Hernán Cortés conquered the Aztecs. About 10 years later, another Spanish explorer, Francisco Pizarro, took over the Inca Empire. The men who led these expeditions were known as conquistadors, or "conquerors." The Spanish soldiers used cannons and swords that the Native Americans did not have. At the same time, the Inca and Aztec were weakened by smallpox and other European diseases.

The Spanish in North America

Throughout the middle and southern parts of the Americas, Spain and its neighbor Portugal built colonies, or overseas settlements. Then, in the 1500s, the Spanish explored what is today the southern United States. They had hoped to find wealthy empires like those of the Aztec and Inca. Instead, they found only small villages of Native Americans. As a result, Spain remained much more interested in its colonies in Mexico, the Caribbean, and South America because these areas had large amounts of silver and gold.

The Spanish, however, did not ignore the lands farther north. They built settlements and forts in what is today the southern United States. These settlements, such as St. Augustine in Florida and Santa Fe in New Mexico, were intended to keep other Europeans out of Spanish territory.

Spanish priests also arrived in North America. They set up missions, or religious communities, to teach Christianity and European ways to the Native Americans. Missions were set up in California, New Mexico, Florida, and other areas of North America.

France Explores America

The French came to North America to make money from fur trading. By the 1600s, beaver fur had become very popular in Europe. In 1608 French merchants hired Samuel de Champlain, a sailor and mapmaker, to help them. Champlain set up a trading post

Spanish Explorers, 1513–1598

NATIONAL GEOGRAPHIC

Ponce de León 1513
Cabeza de Vaca 1528–1536
De Soto 1539–1542
Coronado 1540–1542
Oñate 1598–1605
Present-day boundaries

By the Numbers

American Wealth Sent to Spain

Value of Gold and Silver in Millions of Pesos

1503–05	1536–40	1576–80	1616–20
1	7	17.5	23

Source: *American Treasure and the Price of Revolution in Spain*

Map Skills

Movement Which conquistador explored areas along the southern half of the Mississippi River?

Settling America Most of the early English settlements were founded by private investors who asked the English monarch for charters, or documents, that granted the right to establish colonies in America. Later, England's government placed direct controls on the American colonies.

★ **1590** Settlers at Roanoke vanish

★ **1583** Sir Humphrey Gilbert claims New-foundland for Queen Elizabeth

★ **1607** Colonists settle at Jamestown

Critical Thinking

Theorizing Why do you think people in England invested in the founding of colonies in America?

named Quebec in what is now Canada. Quebec later became the capital of the colony of New France.

From Quebec, fur trappers, explorers, and missionaries moved into other parts of North America. In 1673 the explorers Louis Joliet and Jacques Marquette found the Mississippi River. Then, in 1682 a French explorer named René-Robert Cavelier, Sieur de La Salle followed the Mississippi all the way to the Gulf of Mexico. He named the region Louisiana in honor of King Louis XIV. The French settlers in Louisiana began bringing in enslaved Africans to grow sugarcane, rice, and tobacco.

The English Settle in America

As early as 1585, the English tried to set up a colony on Roanoke Island off the coast of what is today North Carolina. The attempt failed, but it did not stop the English from settling in North America. English settlers came to North America for many reasons. While merchants set up some English colonies to make money, others were set up by people who wanted religious freedom.

England's colonies grew rapidly because of economic problems in England. Many people in England wanted to move to America because their landlords had evicted them from their farms. In America, they had a chance to own land for themselves. Still others came because they were unemployed and needed work.

Why England Colonized By 1600, England's rulers had accepted an economic idea called mercantilism. This idea stated that a country gains power by building up its supply of gold and silver. To get more of this wealth, a country had to sell more goods to other countries than it bought from them. One way to sell more and buy less was to own colonies. Colonies would produce goods the parent country did not have at home. That way, the parent country would not have to import those goods from other countries. During the 1500s and 1600s, colonies and trading posts in Asia and America were making Europe's kingdoms wealthy. The English government believed colonies were needed to keep England strong.

Jamestown Is Founded In 1606 a group of English merchants organized the Virginia Company. It was a joint-stock company, which provided investors in the company partial ownership and a share in its future profits. The colonists sent overseas by the company founded the first permanent English settlement in North America. The settlers named it Jamestown after King James I. Jamestown was the first town in a new colony called Virginia.

Virginia Life in Virginia was very hard. The colonists could barely find enough to eat. Many settlers died from starvation and the cold winters, and others were killed in clashes with Native Americans.

During those first years, the colony made no money for the merchants who had invested in it. It might have collapsed had the settlers not discovered that tobacco could grow in Virginia's soil.

Tobacco was popular in Europe in the 1600s. Soon the colonists in Virginia were growing it in large amounts and selling it for a lot of money. Tobacco became the first cash crop of the English colonies. A cash crop is grown in large quantities to sell for profit.

Eventually tobacco was grown on large farms called plantations. Because plantations needed many workers, the English began bringing in enslaved Africans to work the land. The success of Virginia encouraged the English government to set up more colonies in America to grow cash crops. The colony of South Carolina, for example, began growing rice and indigo. The English also began setting up colonies in the Caribbean to grow sugarcane.

Massachusetts Not all English settlers came to North America in search of wealth. Some came to find religious freedom. Many Protestants in England were Puritans. Puritans

The *Mayflower*

The *Mayflower*
In September 1620, 102 passengers set off on the *Mayflower* on the journey across the Atlantic. The 2,750-mile (4,426 km) trip took more than two months. In early November, the *Mayflower* reached the shores of America.

wanted to rid England's official Anglican Church of Catholic rituals and allow each congregation to choose its own leaders. King James I and his son King Charles I both believed Puritans were a threat to their authority and persecuted them.

In 1620 a group of Puritans known as the Pilgrims decided to go to America so that they could worship freely. They boarded a ship called the *Mayflower* and set out for North America. They landed just north of Cape Cod in what is today the state of Massachusetts. They named their settlement Plymouth.

Seeking Religious Freedom The success of the Pilgrims encouraged other Puritans to begin leaving England for America. Led by John Winthrop, a group of Puritans landed in America and founded the colony of Massachusetts. Others soon followed. By 1643, more than 20,000 Puritans had moved to America. They founded Rhode Island, Connecticut, and New Hampshire.

Fleeing Puritan controls, Roger Williams purchased land from the Narragansett and founded the colony of Rhode Island in 1644. A haven for religious minorities, Rhode Island was the first place in America where people of all faiths—including Jews—could worship freely.

Other people seeking religious freedom set up colonies as well. English Catholics founded Maryland in 1634. The Quakers, another religious group that had been persecuted in England, founded Pennsylvania in 1680. The southernmost part of Pennsylvania later became the separate colony of Delaware.

Expanding Trade Trade and commerce were motives in the founding or taking of other colonies. In 1664 the English seized the valuable trading colony of New Amsterdam from the Dutch. King Charles II gave most of the colony to his brother, the Duke of York, who renamed it New York. The southern part of the Dutch colony became New Jersey. At first, New Jersey was run by landowners who charged settlers rent for farmland. Later, it came under direct royal control.

The Carolinas and Georgia In the South, King Charles II created a large colony south of Virginia named Carolina. Small farmers settled the northern part of Carolina, while large landowners and merchants controlled the more prosperous southern area. Tension between the people of the two areas eventually led to the creation of two separate colonies—North Carolina and South Carolina. Georgia, the last of the English colonies to be established, was founded as a haven where debtors and poor people could make a fresh start.

✔ **Reading Check** Contrasting How was the founding of Jamestown different from the founding of Plymouth?

Mayflower Key

❶ Most of the crew slept in the tiny cabins in the **forecastle,** which also served as the ship's kitchen.

❷ The *Mayflower* was a supply ship. It was not built to carry passengers. **'Tween decks** was where the passengers of the *Mayflower* slept and kept their belongings.

❸ The **main hold** was the main cargo area. It held most of the ship's stores of food, supplies, and tools.

❹ The **helmsman** moved a lever called the **whipstaff,** which moved the rudder and steered the ship.

❺ The **great cabin** was the quarters for the commander of the ship.

Critical Thinking

Drawing Conclusions How comfortable were the passengers on board the *Mayflower*? Explain.

The Thirteen Colonies

Main Idea Britain faced problems in North America because the American colonists objected to new British laws.

History and You Do you like to make your own decisions, without someone else telling you what to do? Read to find out why the American colonies wanted to make decisions without British interference.

. . . .

By the early 1700s, the English had created 13 prosperous colonies along the coast of North America. These colonies had different economies and societies, although farming was the main economic activity in all of them.

In the northern colonies, the poor soil and long winters made farming difficult. The region, however, profited greatly from shipbuilding and fishing. People in the middle colonies grew wheat, raised livestock, ran small businesses and workshops, and relied on trade. In the colonies of the South, the rich soil and warm climate encouraged the growth of large plantations that raised tobacco and rice. Enslaved Africans produced much of this wealth for plantation owners, who controlled the economic and political life of the South.

During the 1700s, the population of the American colonies greatly increased due to immigration and natural increase. The number of people living in the colonies rose from 250,000 in 1700 to 2.5 million in 1775. The colonial population consisted mostly of Europeans (mainly English, Scots, Irish, and Germans), Africans, and Native Americans.

Self-Government in America

Despite their differences, the colonies wanted to govern themselves. The tradition of self-government began early in the English colonies. To attract more settlers, the head of the Virginia Company gave the colonists in Virginia the right to elect burgesses, or representatives, from among men who owned land. The first House of Burgesses met in 1619. It voted on laws for the Virginia colony.

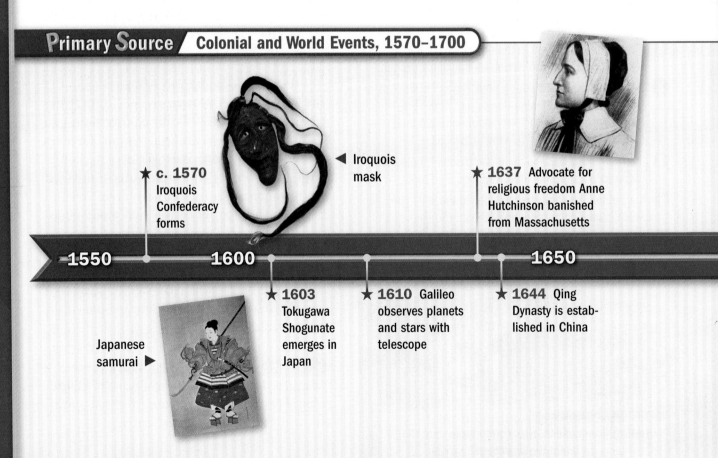

Primary Source / Colonial and World Events, 1570–1700

★ **c. 1570** Iroquois Confederacy forms

◀ Iroquois mask

★ **1637** Advocate for religious freedom Anne Hutchinson banished from Massachusetts

1550 — 1600 — 1650

Japanese samurai ▶

★ **1603** Tokugawa Shogunate emerges in Japan

★ **1610** Galileo observes planets and stars with telescope

★ **1644** Qing Dynasty is established in China

The House of Burgesses set an example for representative government, or a government in which people elect representatives to make laws and conduct government. It was not long before other colonies set up their own legislatures as well.

The Mayflower Compact A year after the Virginia House of Burgesses met, the Pilgrims arrived in North America and began their own tradition of self-government. Before going ashore, the Pilgrims signed an agreement called the Mayflower Compact. They agreed to rule themselves by choosing their own leaders and making their own laws.

Colonial Legislatures Over the years, most of the English colonies began drawing up constitutions, or written plans of government. These documents let the colonists elect legislatures and protected their rights. Colonial legislatures, however, gave only white men who owned property the right to vote. Women, servants, landless and poor people, and enslaved Africans could not vote. In 1619

Dutch traders had sold 20 Africans to work in Virginia tobacco fields. They were the first of many Africans forced to come to America. Until about 1640 some African laborers in Jamestown were free and even owned property. In the years to follow, however, many more shiploads of Africans would arrive in North America, and those unwilling passengers would be sold as enslaved persons.

Colonial Affairs

For many years, Britain allowed the American colonies to run their local affairs. Colonial legislatures passed laws and could tax the people. However, the governor of a colony could veto laws passed by the legislature. The king appointed the governor in most colonies.

Britain controlled the colonies' trade. The American colonies produced raw materials, such as tobacco, rice, indigo, wheat, lumber, and fur. These were then shipped to Britain and traded for manufactured goods and goods from Asia, such as tea and spices.

To control this trade, Britain passed a series of laws called the Navigation Acts in the 1600s. Under these laws, the colonists had to sell their raw materials to Britain even if they could get a better price elsewhere. Any goods bought by the colonies from other countries had to go to England first and be taxed before they could be sent to the Americas. The trade laws also said that all trade goods had to be carried on ships built in Britain or the colonies and that the crews had to be British as well.

The colonists at first accepted the trade laws because the laws guaranteed them a place to sell their raw materials. Later, the colonists came to resent British restrictions. With population in the colonies growing, the colonists wanted to make their own manufactured goods. They also wanted to sell their products elsewhere if they could get higher prices. Many colonial merchants began smuggling, or shipping goods in and out of the country without paying taxes or getting government permission.

★ **c. 1700s**
System of American slavery is fully established

1700

★ **1689**
English Bill of Rights signed

◄ **English rulers William and Mary**

Critical Thinking

Illustrating Create a time line that incorporates events in the British colonies during the 1700s.

A Crisis Over Tea

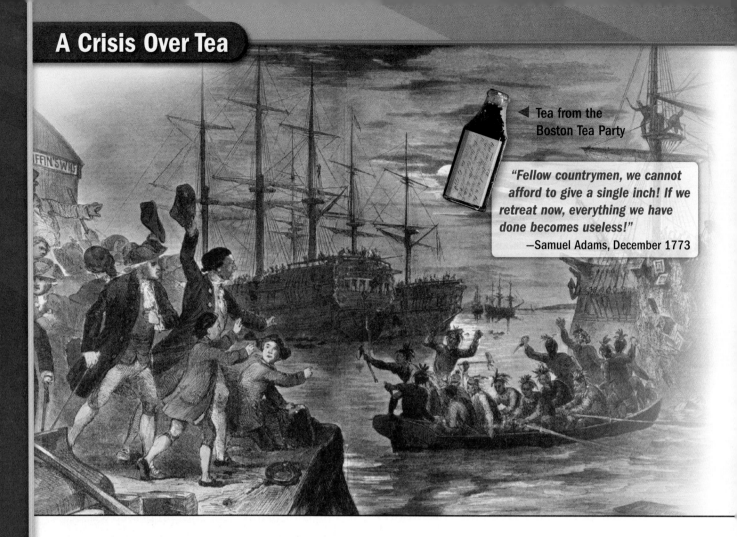

◀ Tea from the Boston Tea Party

"Fellow countrymen, we cannot afford to give a single inch! If we retreat now, everything we have done becomes useless!"
—Samuel Adams, December 1773

Struggle for North America

By the mid-1700s, many changes had taken place in England and its overseas colonies. In 1707 England united with Scotland and became the United Kingdom of Great Britain, or Britain. The term *British* came to mean both the English and the Scots.

The French and Indian War During the 1700s, control of North America shifted dramatically in favor of the British. In 1755 Britain declared war on France, and a global conflict known as the Seven Years' War began. In North America, the war was known as the French and Indian War.

The first years of this struggle were disastrous for the British and their American colonies. Britain's fortunes improved, however. The British government appointed better commanders and exercised tighter control of the war effort. Although Britain ran up an enormous debt fighting the war, British armies finally defeated the French after capturing Quebec in the heart of New France in 1759.

The Treaty of Paris (1763), which finally halted the war, marked the end of France as a power in North America. Britain now controlled all the land east of the Mississippi River. Spain controlled large areas of the continent west of the Mississippi.

Trouble in the Colonies

By 1750 Britain had become the world's most powerful trading empire. In addition to the thirteen American colonies, it had others in India and the Caribbean. For years, Britain and the American colonies seemed to get along well. This relationship changed, however, when the British tried to control trade and impose taxes on the colonies. These efforts angered the colonies.

A Crisis Over Tea The Boston Tea Party is one of the significant events leading to American independence.

- In November 1773, the citizens of Boston refuse to allow three British ships to unload chests of tea.

- On December 16, Boston citizens disguised as Native Americans board the ships and empty the tea into Boston Harbor.

- King George III and Parliament close the port of Boston.

Critical Thinking

Speculating Why do you think the colonists disguised themselves as Native Americans to carry out the Boston Tea Party?

The Stamp Act After the French and Indian War, the British were desperate for money to pay off their war debt. In 1756 the British Parliament passed the Stamp Act, which taxed newspapers and other printed material. The colonists were opposed to the tax. They responded by boycotting, or refusing to buy, British goods.

Finally, delegates from nine colonies met in New York to discuss the Stamp Act. They sent a letter to the British government stating that the colonies could not be taxed except by their own legislatures. The British backed down for a while, but they still needed money. In 1767 Parliament placed taxes on glass, lead, paper, paint, and tea.

From Protests to Revolt

The American colonists grumbled about the new taxes. They bullied the tax collectors, and journalists drew ugly cartoons of King George III. Worried, the British sent more troops to Boston, Massachusetts, where the largest protests had taken place.

Trouble in Boston In March 1770, violence broke out. A crowd of colonists began insulting British soldiers and throwing snowballs at them. The soldiers fired into the crowd. Five people were killed. This event came to be called the Boston Massacre. Shortly thereafter, all of the taxes were repealed, or canceled, except the one on tea.

In 1773 Parliament passed the Tea Act. It allowed a British trading company to ship tea to the colonies without paying taxes. This allowed the company to sell its tea very cheaply and threatened to drive the colonial tea merchants out of business.

In Massachusetts, angry colonists decided to take action. A group of protestors dressed as Native Americans boarded several British ships in Boston Harbor and dumped their cargoes of tea into the water. The event became known as the Boston Tea Party.

To punish the colonists, Parliament in 1774 passed laws that closed down Boston Harbor and put Massachusetts under military rule. It also said that British troops should be quartered, or given a place to live, in colonists' homes. The colonists called these laws the Intolerable Acts, or laws they could not bear.

The First Continental Congress The Intolerable Acts made the colonists more determined to fight for their liberties. In September 1774, delegates from 12 colonies met in Philadelphia. They called themselves the First Continental Congress. The Congress spoke out against the Intolerable Acts and called for their repeal.

Colonial leaders were divided about what to do. Some, like George Washington of Virginia, hoped to settle the differences with Britain. Others, like Samuel Adams of Massachusetts and Patrick Henry of Virginia, demanded independence.

Reading Check **Explaining** Why did the Stamp Act anger the colonists?

Creating a Nation

Main Idea The American colonists formed a new nation, the United States of America.

History and You Why do you think governments are formed? How does the government help you, and what could you do if the government stopped helping you? Read to find out how the Declaration of Independence addressed these questions.

B efore the colonists could decide what to do, fighting broke out in Massachusetts. British troops set out to destroy a store of weapons at Concord. On April 19, 1775, they met colonial militia at Lexington and fought the first battle of the American Revolution.

In May 1775, the Second Continental Congress met in Philadelphia. George Washington was named head of a new colonial army. The Congress then tried again to settle its differences with Britain. They appealed to King George III, who refused to listen.

More and more Americans began to think that independence was the answer to their dissatisfaction. In January 1776, a writer named Thomas Paine convinced many people when he wrote a pamphlet called *Common Sense*. Paine used strong words to condemn the king and urge colonists to separate from Britain.

The Declaration of Independence

On July 4, 1776, the Second Continental Congress issued the document known as the Declaration of Independence. Written by Thomas Jefferson of Virginia, the Declaration stated that the colonies were separating from Great Britain and forming a new nation, the United States of America.

In the Declaration, Jefferson explained why the colonists were founding a new nation. To do so, Jefferson borrowed the ideas of English thinker John Locke. Locke believed that people have a right to overthrow governments that violate their rights. The Declaration stated

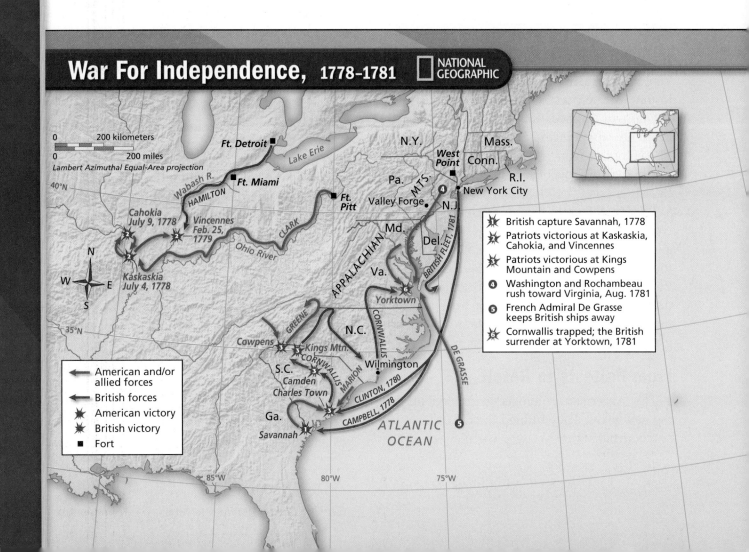

War For Independence, 1778–1781 NATIONAL GEOGRAPHIC

0 ___ 200 kilometers
0 ___ 200 miles
Lambert Azimuthal Equal-Area projection

40°N

Ft. Detroit
Lake Erie
Wabash R.
HAMILTON
Ft. Miami
Cahokia July 9, 1778
Vincennes Feb. 25, 1779
CLARK
Ohio River
Ft. Pitt
Valley Forge
Pa.
MTS.
West Point
Conn.
New York City
N.Y.
Mass.
R.I.
N.J.
Md.
Del.
BRITISH FLEET, 1781
Kaskaskia July 4, 1778
35°N
APPALACHIAN
Va.
Yorktown
GREENE
Cowpens
Kings Mtn.
N.C.
CORNWALLIS
CORNWALLIS
S.C.
Camden
Charles Town
MARION
Wilmington
CLINTON, 1780
DE GRASSE
Ga.
CAMPBELL, 1778
Savannah
ATLANTIC OCEAN

Legend:
- ← American and/or allied forces
- ← British forces
- ✳ American victory
- ✳ British victory
- ■ Fort

✳ British capture Savannah, 1778
✳ Patriots victorious at Kaskaskia, Cahokia, and Vincennes
✳ Patriots victorious at Kings Mountain and Cowpens
4 Washington and Rochambeau rush toward Virginia, Aug. 1781
5 French Admiral De Grasse keeps British ships away
✳ Cornwallis trapped; the British surrender at Yorktown, 1781

85°W   80°W   75°W

that "all men are created equal" and have certain God-given rights. It said that King George III had violated colonists' rights, and so they had the right to rebel.

The Declaration also drew from earlier English documents, such as the Magna Carta and the English Bill of Rights. Both documents established the idea that governments are not all-powerful and that rulers had to obey the laws and treat citizens fairly.

Copies of the Declaration went out to the newly declared states. Washington had it read aloud to the militiamen he was training.

The American Revolution

After the Declaration was issued, the war between the British and Americans dragged on. The most important American victory came in 1777 at the Battle of Saratoga in New York. This battle marked a turning point in the war. France realized that the United States might actually win. In 1778 France agreed to help the Americans.

The French were very important in the final victory. The American victory came in 1781 at the Battle of Yorktown on the coast of Virginia. The French navy blocked the British from escaping by sea, while American and French forces surrounded and trapped the British inside Yorktown. Realizing they could not win, the British surrendered.

While the victory at Yorktown did not end all the fighting, it convinced the British that the war was too costly to pursue. Peace negotiations began, and two years later, the Treaty of Paris ended the war. In this agreement, the British recognized the United States as an independent nation. The treaty also awarded to the United States land from the Appalachian Mountains to the Mississippi River.

The Articles of Confederation

While Americans were fighting for their independence on the battlefield, they were also creating new governments. After rejecting British rule, they needed to establish their own political institutions at both the state and national levels. Additionally, the new nation needed to demonstrate strength and the ability to command respect from the rest of the world.

Creating a Government The Americans' experience with British rule made them cautious about strong governments. For that reason, the states adopted constitutions that limited governmental power. They also divided government functions between the governor and the legislature.

Establishing separate state governments was a much easier task than creating a single national government. Americans agreed that their nation should be a republic, a government in which citizens ruled through elected representatives.

At first the United States was a confederation, or a loose union of independent states. Its plan of government was a document called the Articles of Confederation. The Articles created a national government, but the states held most of the powers.

The Road to Independence

1763	French and Indian War ends; Proclamation of 1763 issued
1764	Sugar Act passes
1765	Stamp Act passes; colonists protest
1767	Townshend Acts passes
1770	Boston Massacre
1773	Tea Act passes; Boston Tea Party held in protest
1774	First Continental Congress meets
1775	Battles of Lexington and Concord
1776	Declaration of Independence signed
1778	France recognizes the United States
1781	British surrender at Yorktown
1783	In the Treaty of Paris, Britain recognizes independence of United States

Map Skills

Region What can you conclude about the strength of the Patriot army based on the events in the West and the South?

A Weak National Government The national government had the authority to conduct foreign affairs, maintain armed forces, borrow money, and issue currency. Yet it could not regulate trade, force soldiers to join the army, or impose taxes.

If the Confederation Congress needed to raise money or troops, it had to ask the state legislatures—but the states were not required to contribute. In addition, the new national government lacked a chief executive to enforce its laws. The Congress could not pass a law unless nine states voted in favor. Any attempt to change the Articles required the consent of all 13 states.

Unfortunately, the Confederation government had so little power that it could not deal with the nation's large war debt. Lacking the power to tax, the Confederation could not pay its debts to the American citizens and foreign nations that had financed the Revolutionary War effort.

It soon became clear that the Articles of Confederation were too weak to deal with the new nation's problems. In September 1786, James Madison, a Virginia planter, proposed calling a convention in Philadelphia to discuss trade issues. He also suggested that this convention consider amending the Articles.

The United States Constitution

Deciding to close their doors to the public and to keep the proceedings secret to permit an atmosphere of free debate, the delegates began their discussions in May 1787. Madison called for the creation of a strong republic that would balance the need to act quickly and decisively with the need to protect people from misuse of power. His carefully thought-out proposal became known as the Virginia Plan.

Compromise The Virginia Plan called for a two-house legislature, a chief executive, and a court system. The members of the lower house of the legislature would be elected by the people. The members of the upper house would be chosen by the lower house. In

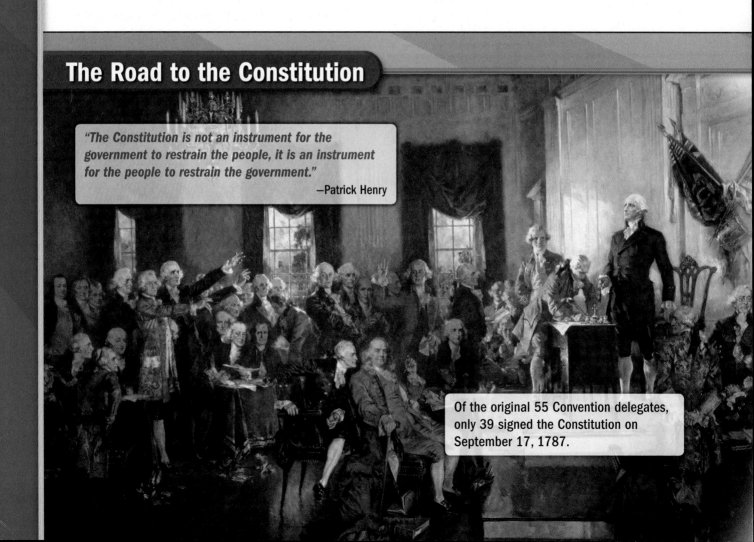

The Road to the Constitution

"The Constitution is not an instrument for the government to restrain the people, it is an instrument for the people to restrain the government."

—Patrick Henry

Of the original 55 Convention delegates, only 39 signed the Constitution on September 17, 1787.

both houses, the number of representatives would correspond in size to the population of each state.

Delegates from small states were unhappy with the Virginia Plan because it centered power in states with large populations. An alternative New Jersey Plan modified the Articles of Confederation. It kept the Confederation's one-house Congress with equal representation and gave the Congress expanded powers to tax and to regulate trade.

Roger Sherman of Connecticut proposed a compromise that aimed at pleasing both large and small states. He suggested a bicameral, or two-house, legislature. In the lower house—the House of Representatives—the number of seats for each state would vary according to the state's population. The upper house—the Senate—would have two members from each state.

Sherman's plan also addressed another disagreement between Northern and Southern states. Enslaved persons were counted as three-fifths of a free person for both taxation and representation. This method prevented over-representing the South's free population, while not increasing the South's tax burden. The delegates also agreed to allow the U.S. slave trade to continue for the time being.

Approving the Constitution Before this new government could go into effect, nine of the 13 states had to approve it. In late 1787, state legislatures set up special committees to debate the document. Those who supported the Constitution were called Federalists. They had enjoyed the support of most of the delegates who approved the document in Philadelphia, including the respected figures of Ben Franklin and George Washington.

The opponents of the new Constitution, called Anti-Federalists by the Federalist group, mainly argued that the new Constitution would take away the liberties fought for in the Revolution. These opponents considered the strong powers of the federal government to be threatening to the states.

Most effectively, the Anti-Federalists criticized the lack of a bill of rights—common in state constitutions—to specifically protect individual freedoms. After vigorous and persuasive arguments by both sides, Delaware became the first state to approve the Constitution on December 7, 1787. Six months later, New Hampshire became the ninth state needed to approve the Constitution.

Though the new government was technically now in force, the nation's two largest states—New York and Virginia—had not yet voted. To move these important states toward approval, the Federalists agreed to add a bill of rights to the Constitution. Finally, in May 1790, Rhode Island became the thirteenth state to approve the new document. The Bill of Rights would be added in 1791, after the new government took office. Now it was time for the nation to elect leaders and begin the work of government.

Reading Check **Explaining** Why did the colonists decide to separate from Britain and create a new nation?

Debating the Constitution During the national debate over ratification of the Constitution, newspapers published articles for and against it. The most famous of these articles appeared as a series of essays published under the pen name "Publius" in New York newspapers. "Publius" was actually three men—John Jay, Alexander Hamilton, and James Madison. Their essays explained the benefits of the new Constitution and became known as the Federalist Papers.

After taking a leading role in shaping the Constitution, James Madison argued for its ratification. ▶

Critical Thinking

Speculating Why do you think that Jay, Hamilton, and Madison signed their essays with a single pen name?

The Young Republic

Main Idea The new American republic faced many challenges but was successful in establishing peace and order.

History and You Think about a time when you disagreed with something that one of your classmates said. Did you voice your opinion? Read to find out what happened when Americans in the new republic began to take opposing sides on issues.

· ·

Under the Constitution, the United States was a republic with an elected president instead of a king. Elections held in 1789 made George Washington the first president of the United States.

Washington and the new Congress made many important decisions about the structure of the government. For example, the Constitution gave Congress the power to establish departments. The precedents, or traditions, they established would shape the future of the United States.

Washington's Administration

During the summer of 1789, Congress set up departments in the executive branch of government to assist the president. Washington chose the leaders of each department. He also requested that the heads of each department meet with him regularly. This group of advisors became known as the cabinet.

The first Congress also created the nation's court system with the Judiciary Act of 1789. In this act, Congress established a federal court system with 13 district courts and three circuit courts. State laws would remain, but the federal courts had the power to reverse state decisions. The nation's Supreme Court served as the final authority on many issues.

Once the basic structures of the new government had been set, Congress considered constitutional amendments for the promised bill of rights. Congress passed 12 amendments and the states agreed on 10 of them. In December 1791, the 10 amendments were added to the Constitution and became known as the Bill of Rights.

Launching the New Government

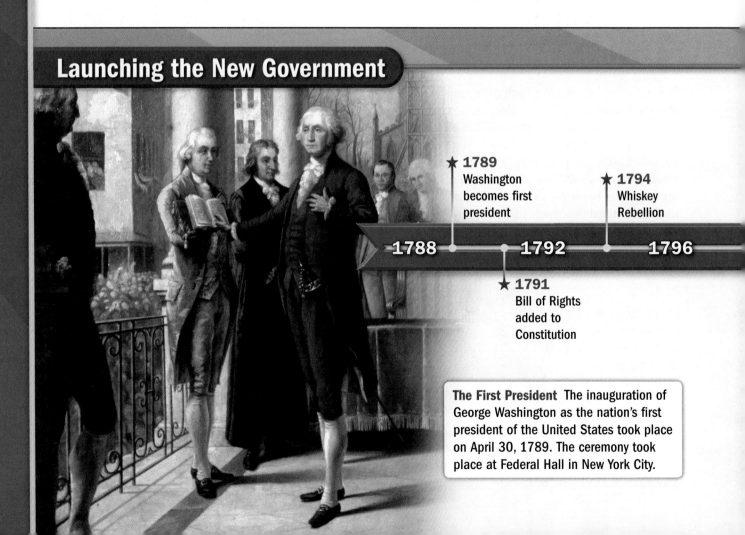

1789 Washington becomes first president

1794 Whiskey Rebellion

1788 — 1792 — 1796

1791 Bill of Rights added to Constitution

The First President The inauguration of George Washington as the nation's first president of the United States took place on April 30, 1789. The ceremony took place at Federal Hall in New York City.

Early Challenges

Meanwhile, the new government faced many financial problems. As a result, Secretary of the Treasury Alexander Hamilton called for new national taxes. The taxes upset many Americans. In western Pennsylvania, farmers rebelled. The armed protest, called the Whiskey Rebellion, alarmed government leaders. President Washington sent 13,000 soldiers to put down the uprising.

The federal government also faced other problems in the West. The Native Americans who lived between the Appalachian Mountains and the Mississippi River resisted United States authority. President Washington used treaties and armed attacks to control the Native Americans and to open most of this area to white settlement.

Washington declined to seek a third term as president in the spring of 1796. In his farewell address, Washington attacked the evils of the developing political parties in the United States and urged the nation to avoid alliances with any other nation.

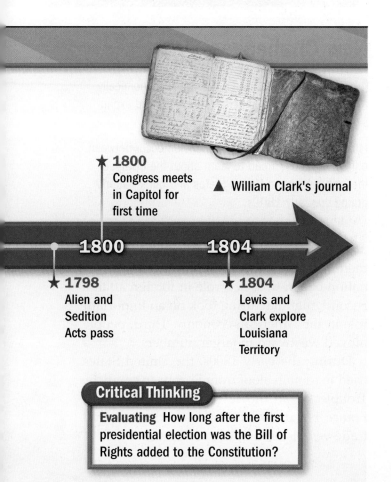

★ **1800**
Congress meets in Capitol for first time

▲ William Clark's journal

1800

1804

★ **1798**
Alien and Sedition Acts pass

★ **1804**
Lewis and Clark explore Louisiana Territory

Critical Thinking

Evaluating How long after the first presidential election was the Bill of Rights added to the Constitution?

Political Parties

During Washington's presidency, the nation's first political parties arose. Each party was centered on a political leader and his supporters. Secretary of the Treasury Alexander Hamilton and his supporters were known as Federalists. They wanted a strong federal government that would create banks and advance trade.

Secretary of State Thomas Jefferson and his backers were known as Democratic-Republicans and they wanted to leave as much power as possible to the state governments rather than giving more power to the national government.

Adams Becomes President In the presidential election of 1796, candidates sought office for the first time as members of a party rather than as individuals. The Federalist candidate, John Adams, won the election and took office as president on March 4, 1797.

As president, Adams faced a growing threat of war with France. During this time of international conflict, many Americans were concerned about the nation's security. Federalists in Congress passed the Alien and Sedition Acts to punish those who spoke out against the government's actions. Opposing these measures, the Democratic-Republicans looked to the states to protect the people's freedoms and to fight what they regarded as Federalist tyranny.

The Jefferson Administration The Federalist and Democratic-Republican parties fought a bitter election campaign in 1800. As a result of the close race, the House of Representatives had to decide the election. Thomas Jefferson, a Democratic-Republican candidate, became president by a single vote.

When Jefferson entered office, he aimed to reduce the size of the federal government, protect individual liberties, and reduce the national debt. The new president hoped that some Federalists would support his policies. However, bitter feelings between the parties continued.

Judicial Review Much ill will resulted from a disagreement between Jefferson and the Supreme Court. The Court's Chief Justice John Marshall, a Federalist, made the Supreme Court an equal partner in government. He did this by declaring that the Supreme Court could review the actions of the executive and legislative branches. This power of judicial review has become a basic part of the system of checks and balances of our government today. Under Marshall, the Court usually upheld the power of the national government over the rights of the states.

The Louisiana Purchase

During the early republic, the United States began to expand beyond the Atlantic Coast. In 1802 France decided to sell the large Louisiana Territory that stretched west of the Mississippi River. President Thomas Jefferson could not resist the opportunity to buy the Louisiana Territory, which would provide cheap and abundant land for American farmers and settlers. The Senate approved the purchase in October 1803, and the size of the United States doubled.

Lewis and Clark Expedition In the spring of 1804, Meriwether Lewis and William Clark led an expedition to explore the Louisiana Territory and to chart its geography. Among the crew was a young Shoshone woman named Sacagawea (SA·kuh·juh·WEE·uh). Married to a guide, she served as an interpreter and helped the explorers survive.

After reaching the Pacific Ocean, the explorers returned east on two separate routes. Both explorers arrived in St. Louis in September 1806. The expedition had collected valuable information on people, plants, animals, and the geography of the West. Perhaps most important, Lewis and Clark's expedition gave hope to a nation of people eager to move westward.

✓ **Reading Check** **Evaluating** How did Chief Justice John Marshall contribute to the strengthening of the Supreme Court in the U.S. government?

Primary Source / **Burning of Washington**

New Challenges

Main Idea The United States grew economically and became more democratic, but westward expansion led to conflict.

History and You Why does tension occur between different groups? Read to learn about the disagreements between the United States and other nations during the early 1800s.

Between 1790 and 1850, three developments changed the United States. First, the nation began to seek a role in foreign affairs. Second, manufacturing took on an important role in the American economy. Third, people moved westward in larger numbers.

During the early 1800s, the United States tried to remain aloof from European conflicts. Trouble began, however, when Britain and France began to stop and search American trade vessels on the Atlantic Ocean.

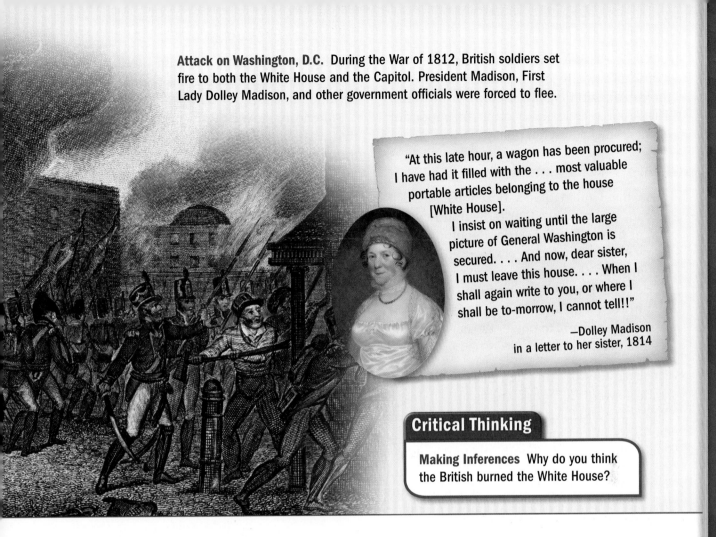

Attack on Washington, D.C. During the War of 1812, British soldiers set fire to both the White House and the Capitol. President Madison, First Lady Dolley Madison, and other government officials were forced to flee.

"At this late hour, a wagon has been procured; I have had it filled with the . . . most valuable portable articles belonging to the house [White House].

I insist on waiting until the large picture of General Washington is secured. . . . And now, dear sister, I must leave this house. . . . When I shall again write to you, or where I shall be to-morrow, I cannot tell!!"

—Dolley Madison
in a letter to her sister, 1814

Critical Thinking

Making Inferences Why do you think the British burned the White House?

Angry at this interference, American officials tried banning trade with Europe, but this policy failed. Meanwhile, the United States faced growing unrest among Native Americans who opposed American settlers in the Ohio Valley. Democratic-Republicans in Congress known as War Hawks blamed the British for stirring up the Native Americans.

The War of 1812 These trade and Native American issues eventually led the United States to declare war on Britain. In what became known as the War of 1812, American forces fought the British mainly in the Northeast, along the Great Lakes, and along the Atlantic Coast and the Gulf of Mexico.

The Treaty of Ghent officially ended the war in December 1814. It did not change any existing borders. Before news of the treaty had reached the United States, an American army led by Major General Andrew Jackson defeated a British invasion of New Orleans.

Jackson became a hero, even though the battle did not affect the war's outcome.

The Monroe Doctrine After the War of 1812, the United States won greater respect in world affairs. During the 1820s, the country began to direct its attention to events in neighboring Latin America. All throughout Spain's American empire—which stretched from the present-day southwestern United States through Mexico, Central America, and most of South America—struggles for independence were breaking out. The possibility that European powers would act against these revolutionary movements led President Monroe to issue a statement known as the Monroe Doctrine.

In this statement, made in 1823, Monroe declared that while the United States would not interfere with any existing European colonies in the Americas, it would oppose any new ones.

North America and South America "are henceforth not to be considered as subjects for colonization by any European powers." The Monroe Doctrine became an important element in U.S. foreign policy.

Growth and Expansion

As the United States flexed its muscles abroad, it experienced an Industrial Revolution at home. The Industrial Revolution was a new system in which workers used machinery instead of hand tools to perform their work. The Industrial Revolution appeared first in New England. This region had many streams and rivers to power the new machinery used in factories.

Economic Growth Although many New Englanders went to work in factories, most Americans still lived and worked on farms. In the 1820s, more than 65 percent of Americans were farmers. In the South, plantation owners used enslaved workers to plant, tend, and pick cotton. Eli Whitney of Connecticut invented the cotton gin, a simple machine that quickly separated cotton seeds from the fiber, in 1793. The cotton gin made it possible to clean cotton much faster and more cheaply than by hand. Cotton production and demand grew steadily with the rise of industrial textile mills in New England and Europe.

Population Growth An increase in population accompanied economic growth. In 1790 the population of the United States was nearly 4 million. Most Americans lived east of the Appalachian Mountains and within a few hundred miles of the Atlantic Coast. By 1820, the population of the country had reached about 10 million, with nearly 2 million living west of the Appalachian Mountains.

The nation needed good inland roads for travel and for the shipment of goods to and from seaports. Private companies built many roads and charged fees to help recover construction costs. When Ohio joined the Union in 1803, it asked the federal government to build a road to connect it with the East. In 1806 Congress approved funds for a National Road to the West.

Americans moved westward in waves. The first wave began before the 1790s and led to the admission of four new states between 1791 and 1803—Vermont, Kentucky, Tennessee, and Ohio. During the next 13 years, however, only one new state, Louisiana, entered the Union.

After the War of 1812, a second wave of westward growth began. Between 1816 and 1821, five new western states were created—Indiana, Illinois, Mississippi, Alabama, and Missouri.

Political Changes

As the nation grew economically and geographically, its political unity became strained. At this time, many Americans sensed a greater loyalty to their region than to the country as a whole. Regional loyalty, or sectionalism, became more intense as differences arose over national policies.

Primary Source / Growth of Industry

Growth of Industry New England was the perfect location for the Industrial Revolution to begin in the United States because its rushing rivers provided power to run the machinery. The industrial growth that began in New England spread to other areas of the country. By 1870, the nation's industrial cities were growing.

Slater Mill in Pawtucket, Rhode Island Because Britain prohibited the export of textile machinery, Slater had to design his factory and build the machines from memory. It was an immediate success. ▼

Slavery and the States Sectional tension reached new heights in 1820 over the issue of slavery and how to admit new states to the Union. The South wanted Missouri, part of the Louisiana Purchase, admitted as a slave state. Northerners wanted Missouri to be free of slavery. Eventually, Speaker of the House Henry Clay helped work out a compromise that preserved the balance between North and South.

The Missouri Compromise, reached in March 1820, provided for the admission of Missouri as a slave state and Maine as a free state. The agreement banned slavery in the remainder of the Louisiana Territory north of the 36°30'N parallel. The question was settled, but only temporarily.

The Supreme Court The Supreme Court also became involved in sectional and states' rights issues at this time. The state of Maryland imposed a tax on the Baltimore branch of the Second Bank of the United States—a federal institution. The Bank refused to pay the state tax, and the case reached the Court in 1819.

In *McCulloch* v. *Maryland*, the Supreme Court ruled that, since the Bank was a creation of the federal government, the state had no right to interfere with it.

The Supreme Court's ruling strengthened the national government. It also contributed to the debate over sectional issues. People who supported states' rights believed the decision was a threat to individual liberties. Strong nationalists welcomed the decision's support for national power.

Building Democracy During the 1820s and 1830s, the United States moved toward greater democracy. As a result, more and more people were able to vote and participate in government.

One of the outstanding political figures of this period was Andrew Jackson of Tennessee, a hero of the War of 1812. Raised in poverty, Jackson claimed to speak for Americans who had been left out of the political process. His supporters included farmers in the South, settlers in the West, and laborers in Eastern cities.

"If thou canst do this thing, I invite thee to come to Rhode Island, and have the credit of introducing cotton-manufacture into America."
—Moses Brown, in a letter to Samuel Slater in 1789

Growth of Industrial Cities   NATIONAL GEOGRAPHIC

Textile Mill The Lowell factory system was designed to bring work and workers together. A typical Lowell textile mill in 1830 housed 4,500 spindles, 120 power looms, and more than 200 employees under one roof.

◄ A water frame was used to spin thread.

Critical Thinking

Determining Cause and Effect Did the increase of factories lead to better technology, or did better technology lead to more factories? Explain.

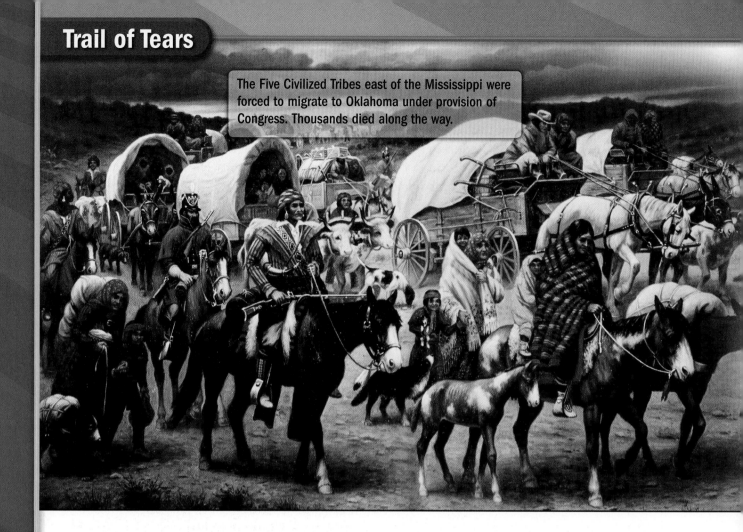

The Five Civilized Tribes east of the Mississippi were forced to migrate to Oklahoma under provision of Congress. Thousands died along the way.

Elected president in 1828, Jackson promised "equal protection and equal benefits" for all Americans—at least for all white American men. During his first term, a spirit of equality and flourishing democracy spread through American politics. Between 1824 and 1828, the percentage of white males voting in presidential elections increased from 36.9 to 57.6 percent. By 1828, 22 of the 24 states had also changed their constitutions to allow the people, rather than the state legislatures, to choose presidential electors.

The Jackson Era

As president, Andrew Jackson faced a number of challenges. First, there was the growing rift over trade policy between the nation's Northern and Southern regions.

The Tariff Debate One of the most divisive issues in American politics was the use of tariffs, fees paid by merchants who imported goods. While Northeastern manufacturers believed tariffs made American-produced goods more affordable, Southerners hated tariffs. The South traded cotton to Europe for manufactured goods, and the new tariff made these items more expensive.

Southern politicians and plantation owners were so outraged by the rise of high tariffs during the 1820s and 1830s that some threatened to secede, or break away, from the United States and form their own country.

President Jackson supported a bill in Congress to lower the tariff, while also persuading Congress to pass another bill that allowed him to use the military to enforce congressional acts. The message was clear: If the South did not obey the law, it would face the army.

For a time, a crisis was avoided. Yet the South would remember this lesson—that the federal government would not allow a state to go its own way without a fight.

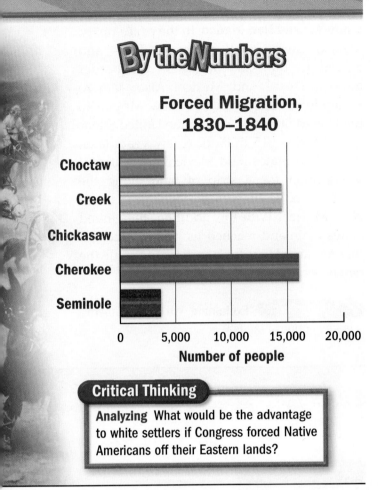

By the Numbers

Forced Migration, 1830–1840

	Number of people
Choctaw	
Creek	
Chickasaw	
Cherokee	
Seminole	

Number of people: 0   5,000   10,000   15,000   20,000

Critical Thinking

Analyzing What would be the advantage to white settlers if Congress forced Native Americans off their Eastern lands?

Jackson and the Bank Another area of conflict during Jackson's time as president was the Second Bank of the United States. For years, Jackson attacked the Bank as an organization of wealthy Easterners. The Bank held the federal government's money and controlled much of the country's money supply.

In 1832 Jackson rejected a congressional bill to renew the Bank's charter for another twenty years. After he started his second term of office in 1833, Jackson decided to "kill" the Bank by ordering the withdrawal of all government deposits from the Bank. The Bank was eventually forced to close.

Conflicts Over Land The United States had expanded westward by the 1830s, but large numbers of Native Americans still held valuable lands in the eastern part of the country. In 1830 Congress passed the Indian Removal Act, which allowed the federal government to pay Native Americans to move west. Most

Native Americans agreed to move, and in 1834, Congress created the Indian Territory in present-day Oklahoma.

Some Native Americans did not agree to move. In 1838 Jackson ordered federal troops to remove the Cherokee from their homes and lead them west. Brutal weather along the way claimed thousands of Cherokee lives. Their forced journey west became known to Cherokee people as the Trail Where They Cried. Historians call it the Trail of Tears.

Manifest Destiny

After the Louisiana Purchase, the United States gained Florida from Spain and the Oregon Territory from Britain. Many Americans came to believe in Manifest Destiny, the idea that the United States was destined—set apart for a special purpose—to expand its territory and spread freedom all the way to the Pacific Ocean.

Texas The territory of Texas, once a part of Spain's empire, was at this time under the rule of Mexico. Wanting to attract settlers to Texas, Mexican leaders offered land at low prices. In return, colonists agreed to obey Mexican law, convert to Catholicism, and learn Spanish. By 1830, Americans in Texas far outnumbered Mexicans. Further, these American settlers had not adopted Mexican ways.

When Mexico tried to assert its authority, American settlers called for independence. The American settlers fought the Mexican army in several battles—the most famous at a Catholic mission called the Alamo. Despite losing at the Alamo, the Americans eventually won independence for Texas in 1836. The Republic of Texas lasted for nine years before becoming part of the United States in 1845.

War With Mexico Relations between Mexico and the United States had been strained for some years. When the United States annexed, or took control of, Texas in 1845, the situation worsened. Mexico, which had never accepted the independence of Texas, charged that the annexation was illegal.

Words turned into blows on April 24, 1846, when Mexican soldiers attacked a small force of American soldiers. Polk's government decided that the attack was grounds for war with Mexico. Although Polk had clearly provoked the Mexicans, most Americans supported a war with Mexico. On May 13, Congress passed a declaration of war against Mexico. American forces won hard-fought victories in New Mexico and California. Then U.S. forces invaded Mexico, capturing Vera Cruz and Mexico City. Mexican forces surrendered on September 14, 1847.

Thousands on both sides lost their lives. Most casualties were due to disease and accident, not to enemy fire. Mexico also lost more than half its territory in the war.

California and New Mexico In the peace treaty, Mexico gave up all claims to Texas and agreed to the Rio Grande as the border between Texas and Mexico. Also, Mexico surrendered California and New Mexico to the United States. In return, the United States gave Mexico $15 million. A few years later, the United States paid Mexico an additional $10 million for a strip of land along the southern edge of present-day Arizona and New Mexico. With this addition, the United States mainland reached its present size. All that remained was for Americans to settle the newly acquired territories.

Reading Check Explaining Why did Southern leaders oppose tariffs?

Westward Expansion

New Mexico

- The territory includes all of present-day New Mexico, Arizona, Nevada, and Utah and parts of Colorado and Wyoming.
- The first American trader arrives in New Mexico in 1821.
- The Santa Fe Trail trade route begins near Independence, Missouri, and ends in New Mexico.

California

- Spanish explorers and Mexican missionaries settle the region.
- In June 1846, American settlers proclaim California's independence from Mexico.
- After the war with Mexico, the United States buys California and New Mexico for $15 million.
- The Gold Rush fuels settlement and economic growth.
- California becomes a state in 1850.

Utah Territory

- The Mormons, founded by Joseph Smith, seek to escape religious persecution.
- In 1846 Brigham Young leads the Mormons west; they settle near the Great Salt Lake.
- The Mormons establish successful farming communities.
- Utah becomes a state in 1896.

Critical Thinking

1. **Explaining** How did the United States acquire New Mexico?
2. **Analyzing** How did the Gold Rush affect California's population?

Immigration in the Mid-1800s

Sources of Immigration Newcomers came to America from many different countries in the mid-1800s, but the overwhelming majority came from Ireland and Germany.

Sources of U.S. Immigration, 1841–1860

- Great Britain 16%
- Germany 32%
- Ireland 39%
- All other nations 13%

Immigration, 1820–1860

Annual Immigration (in thousands) vs Year (1820, 1830, 1840, 1850, 1860)

Critical Thinking

Predicting Why might people leave their homeland for another country?

Regions and Reform

Main Idea As the North and the South developed distinct societies, reformers worked to improve education, free enslaved people, and expand women's rights.

History and You Think of a person or leader whom you admire. Does he or she stand up for others? Read to learn how a number of individuals and groups set out to improve life for other Americans during the early 1800s.

As the United States moved westward, different ways of life developed in the Northern and Southern states.

The North

By 1860, Northern factories were producing two-thirds of the country's manufactured goods. A wave of inventions and new technology spurred new industry. The success of these new industries was linked to the building of roads, canals (artificial waterways), and railroads. These improvements in transportation speeded the flow of goods.

Slavery had largely disappeared from the North by 1820. African Americans, however, suffered the cruel and lasting effects of discrimination. Most communities would not allow free African Americans to attend public schools and forced them to use separate hospitals, theaters, and other public facilities.

The North also received a growing number of immigrants, mainly from Ireland and Germany. American manufacturers welcomed the tide of immigrants, many of whom were willing to work for long hours and low pay.

The South

As industry advanced in the North, agriculture dominated the South. States in the Upper South produced tobacco, hemp, wheat, and vegetables. Those in the Deep South were committed to cotton and, in some areas, to rice and sugarcane.

Industry never caught on in the South in the 1800s, in part because cotton growing was so profitable. Another reason was the lack of investment. Most wealthy Southerners invested their money in land and enslaved Africans, not industry.

Looking Back: Beginnings to 1850   **Prologue 25**

Comparing North and South

The North and the South developed differently during the first half of the 1800s.

	North	South
Economy	• Industrial • New technology fuels growth of industry • Industry develops rapidly Power loom ▶	• Agricultural • Revolutionary cotton gin makes cotton crop highly profitable • Industry develops slowly
People	• Immigrants, including many from Ireland, work factory jobs • Slavery has mostly disappeared by 1830s, but racial prejudice and discrimination remain ◀ Mill workers	• The South had more small farms than large plantations • Most small farmers work land themselves • Slavery on large cotton plantations grows due to increased demand for labor • By 1860 about 4 million African Americans lived under slavery

Critical Thinking

1. **Making Connections** How did immigration have an impact on industries and cities?
2. **Inferring** What was the main reason the South remained largely agricultural?

Most whites in the South were yeomen—farmers who owned land but did not have enslaved workers. Other Southern whites were tenant farmers, who rented land or worked on landlords' estates. A small group of plantation owners—about 12 percent—lived comfortable lives and held more than half of enslaved workers. Life for the enslaved worker on the plantation was one of hardship and misery. They worked hard, earned no money, and had little hope of freedom.

Although the South was primarily agricultural, it had several growing cities, including New Orleans, Baltimore, Charleston, Richmond, and Memphis. The population of these cities included white city dwellers, some enslaved workers, and about 250,000 of the South's free African Americans. Between 1830 and 1860, Southern states passed laws that limited the rights of these free African Americans.

The Age of Reform

During the first half of the 1800s, many Americans were interested in perfecting their society. The result was an age of social reform. Some reformers sought to improve society by forming utopias, communities based on a vision of a perfect society. Others were motivated by religious faith. In the early 1800s, a wave of religious fervor—known as the Second Great Awakening—stirred the nation. The Second Great Awakening increased church membership, especially among Methodists and Baptists. It also inspired people to become involved in missionary work and reform.

In the early 1800s, many reformers began to push for a system of public education—government-funded schools open to all citizens. In 1852 Massachusetts passed the first mandatory school attendance law. New York passed a similar measure the next year.

The Abolitionists Reform in the early 1800s also included the efforts of abolitionists—reformers who worked to end slavery. The religious revival and the reform movements of the time gave new life to the antislavery movement. Many Americans came to believe that slavery was wrong.

The Underground Railroad Some abolitionists risked prison—even death—by secretly helping enslaved Africans escape. The network of escape routes out of the South became known as the Underground Railroad. Harriet Tubman escaped from slavery to become the most famous conductor on the Underground Railroad.

The antislavery movement led to an intense reaction against abolitionism. Southern slaveholders claimed that slavery was essential to economic prosperity in the South. They also argued that they treated enslaved people well, and that for African Americans, slavery was preferable to factory work in the North.

The Women's Movement Women played a major role in all the American reform movements of the 1800s. In July 1848, Elizabeth Cady Stanton, Lucretia Mott, and a few other women organized the first women's rights convention in Seneca Falls, New York. The convention issued a Declaration of Sentiments and Resolutions modeled on the Declaration of Independence.

The women's declaration called for an end to all laws that discriminated against women. It demanded that women be allowed to enter the all-male world of trades, professions, and businesses. The most controversial issue at the Seneca Falls Convention was the demand to allow women the right to vote. The Seneca Falls Convention paved the way for the growth of the women's rights movement.

An Uncertain Future The period of time from the 1820s to the 1860s was an era of conflict, compromise, and reform. The most pressing source of division remained the existence of slavery. Slavery became the focus of numerous arguments and conflicts in the United States. This issue would eventually serve to split the nation in two.

✓ **Reading Check** **Evaluating** Why was the Seneca Falls Convention important?

Prologue Review

Main Ideas

1. **Comparing and Contrasting** How did the lifestyle of the Inuit compare with that of the Hopi?

2. **Analyzing** What ideas are expressed in the Declaration of Independence?

3. **Describing** What effect did Eli Whitney's cotton gin have on the South?

Critical Thinking

4. **Analyzing** Why did Britain's colonies in America grow quickly?

5. **Analyzing** How did the idea of Manifest Destiny help Americans justify their desire to extend the United States to the Pacific Ocean?

6. **Organizing Information** Re-create the chart below. List the issues that Jackson dealt with during his presidency. Then describe how he responded to each issue.

Issues	Jackson's Response

7. **Informative Writing** Research the life of a reformer in mid-1800s America. Write a one-page biography of the important events in his or her life. Make sure your biography is clear and concise.

The Declaration of Independence

In Congress, July 4, 1776. The unanimous Declaration of the thirteen United States of America,

Words spelled as originally written.

What It Means

The Preamble The Declaration of Independence has four parts. The Preamble explains why the Continental Congress drew up the Declaration.

impel: force

What It Means

Natural Rights The second part, the Declaration of Natural Rights, lists the rights of the citizens. It goes on to explain that, in a republic, people form a government to protect their rights.

endowed: provided

usurpations: unjust uses of power

despotism: unlimited power

What It Means

List of Grievances The third part of the Declaration lists the colonists' complaints against the British government. Notice that King George III is singled out for blame.

[Preamble]

When in the Course of human events, it becomes necessary for one people to dissolve the political bands which have connected them with another, and to assume among the powers of the earth, the separate and equal station to which the Laws of Nature and of Nature's God entitle them, a decent respect to the opinions of mankind requires that they should declare the causes which **impel** them to the separation.

[Declaration of Natural Rights]

We hold these truths to be self-evident, that all men are created equal, that they are **endowed** by their Creator with certain unalienable Rights, that among these are Life, Liberty, and the pursuit of Happiness.

That to secure these rights, Governments are instituted among Men, deriving their just powers from the consent of the governed,

That whenever any Form of Government becomes destructive of these ends, it is the Right of the People to alter or to abolish it, and to institute new Government, laying its foundation on such principles and organizing its powers in such form, as to them shall seem most likely to effect their Safety and Happiness. Prudence, indeed, will dictate that Governments long established should not be changed for light and transient causes; and accordingly all experience hath shewn, that mankind are more disposed to suffer, while evils are sufferable, than to right themselves by abolishing the forms to which they are accustomed. But when a long train of abuses and **usurpations,** pursuing invariably the same Object evinces a design to reduce them under absolute **Despotism,** it is their right, it is their duty, to throw off such Government, and to provide new Guards for their future security.

[List of Grievances]

Such has been the patient sufferance of these Colonies; and such is now the necessity which constrains them to alter their former Systems of Government. The history of the present King of Great Britain is a history of repeated injuries and usurpations, all having in direct object the establishment of an absolute Tyranny over these States. To prove this, let Facts be submitted to a candid world.

He has refused his Assent to Laws, the most wholesome and necessary for the public good.

He has forbidden his Governors to pass Laws of immediate and pressing importance, unless suspended in their operation till his Assent should be obtained; and when so suspended, he has utterly neglected to attend to them.

He has refused to pass other Laws for the accommodation of large districts of people, unless those people would **relinquish** the right of Representation in the Legislature, a right **inestimable** to them and formidable to tyrants only.

relinquish: give up
inestimable: priceless

He has called together legislative bodies at places unusual, uncomfortable, and distant from the depository of their public Records, for the sole purpose of fatiguing them into compliance with his measures.

He has dissolved Representative Houses repeatedly, for opposing with manly firmness his invasions on the rights of the people.

He has refused for a long time, after such dissolutions, to cause others to be elected; whereby the Legislative Powers, incapable of **Annihilation,** have returned to the People at large for their exercise; the State remaining in the mean time exposed to all the dangers of invasion from without, and **convulsions** within.

annihilation: destruction

convulsions: violent disturbances

He has endeavoured to prevent the population of these States; for that purpose obstructing the Laws for **Naturalization of Foreigners;** refusing to pass others to encourage their migrations hither, and raising the conditions of new Appropriations of Lands.

Naturalization of Foreigners: process by which foreign-born persons become citizens

He has obstructed the Administration of Justice, by refusing his Assent to Laws for establishing Judiciary powers.

He has made Judges dependent on his Will alone, for the **tenure** of their offices, and the amount and payment of their salaries.

tenure: term

He has erected a multitude of New Offices, and sent hither swarms of Officers to harass our people, and eat out their substance.

He has kept among us, in times of peace, Standing Armies without the Consent of our legislatures.

He has affected to render the Military independent of and superior to the Civil power.

He has combined with others to subject us to a jurisdiction foreign to our constitution, and unacknowledged by our laws; giving his Assent to their Acts of pretended Legislation:

quartering: lodging

For **Quartering** large bodies of armed troops among us:

For protecting them, by a mock Trial, from punishment for any Murders which they should commit on the Inhabitants of these States:

For cutting off our Trade with all parts of the world:

For imposing Taxes on us without our Consent:

For depriving us in many cases, of the benefits of Trial by Jury:

For transporting us beyond Seas to be tried for pretended offences:

For abolishing the free System of English Laws in a neighbouring Province, establishing therein an Arbitrary government, and enlarging its Boundaries so as to **render** it at once an example and fit instrument for introducing the same absolute rule into these Colonies:

render: make

For taking away our Charters, abolishing our most valuable Laws, and altering fundamentally the Forms of our Governments:

For suspending our own Legislatures, and declaring themselves invested with power to legislate for us in all cases whatsoever.

abdicated: given up

He has **abdicated** Government here, by declaring us out of his Protection and waging War against us.

He has plundered our seas, ravaged our Coasts, burnt our towns, and destroyed the lives of our people.

He is at this time transporting large Armies of foreign Mercenaries to compleat the works of death, desolation and tyranny, already begun with circumstances of Cruelty & **perfidy** scarcely paralleled in the most barbarous ages, and totally unworthy the Head of a civilized nation.

perfidy: violation of trust

He has constrained our fellow Citizens taken Captive on the high Seas to bear Arms against their Country, to become the executioners of their friends and Brethren, or to fall themselves by their Hands.

insurrections: rebellions

He has excited domestic **insurrections** amongst us, and has endeavoured to bring on the inhabitants of our frontiers, the merciless Indian Savages, whose known rule of warfare, is an undistinguished destruction of all ages, sexes and conditions.

petitioned for redress: asked formally for a correction of wrongs

In every stage of these Oppressions We have **Petitioned for Redress** in the most humble terms: Our repeated Petitions have been answered only by repeated injury. A Prince whose character is thus marked by every act which may define a Tyrant, is unfit to be the ruler of a free People.

Nor have We been wanting in attentions to our Brittish brethren. We have warned them from time to time of attempts by their legislature to extend an **unwarrantable jurisdiction** over us. We have reminded them of the circumstances of our emigration and settlement here. We have appealed to their native justice and magnanimity, and we have conjured them by the ties of our common kindred to disavow these usurpations, which, would inevitably interrupt our connections and correspondence.

unwarrantable jurisdiction: unjustified authority

They too have been deaf to the voice of justice and of **consanguinity.** We must, therefore, acquiesce in the necessity, which denounces our Separation, and hold them, as we hold the rest of mankind, Enemies in War, in Peace Friends.

[Resolution of Independence by the United States]

We, therefore, the Representatives of the united States of America, in General Congress, Assembled, appealing to the Supreme Judge of the world for the **rectitude** of our intentions, do, in the Name, and by Authority of the good People of these Colonies, solemnly publish and declare, That these United Colonies are, and of Right ought to be Free and Independent States; that they are Absolved from all Allegiance to the British Crown, and that all political connection between them and the State of Great Britain, is and ought to be totally dissolved; and that as Free and Independent States, they have full Power to levy War, conclude Peace, contract Alliances, establish Commerce, and to do all other Acts and Things which Independent States may of right do. And for the support of this Declaration, with a firm reliance on the protection of divine Providence, we mutually pledge to each other our Lives, our Fortunes and our sacred Honor.

John Hancock
    President from
    Massachusetts

Georgia
Button Gwinnett
Lyman Hall
George Walton

North Carolina
William Hooper
Joseph Hewes
John Penn

South Carolina
Edward Rutledge
Thomas Heyward, Jr.
Thomas Lynch, Jr.
Arthur Middleton

Maryland
Samuel Chase
William Paca
Thomas Stone
Charles Carroll
    of Carrollton

Virginia
George Wythe
Richard Henry Lee
Thomas Jefferson
Benjamin Harrison
Thomas Nelson, Jr.
Francis Lightfoot Lee
Carter Braxton

Pennsylvania
Robert Morris
Benjamin Rush
Benjamin Franklin
John Morton
George Clymer
James Smith
George Taylor
James Wilson
George Ross

Delaware
Caesar Rodney
George Read
Thomas McKean

New York
William Floyd
Philip Livingston
Francis Lewis
Lewis Morris

New Jersey
Richard Stockton
John Witherspoon
Francis Hopkinson
John Hart
Abraham Clark

New Hampshire
Josiah Bartlett
William Whipple
Matthew Thornton

Massachusetts
Samuel Adams
John Adams
Robert Treat Paine
Elbridge Gerry

Rhode Island
Stephen Hopkins
William Ellery

Connecticut
Roger Sherman
Samuel Huntington
William Williams
Oliver Wolcott

consanguinity: originating from the same ancestor

What It Means

Resolution of Independence The final section declares that the colonies are "Free and Independent States" with the full power to make war, to form alliances, and to trade with other countries.

rectitude: rightness

What It Means

Signers of the Declaration The signers, as representatives of the American people, declared the colonies independent from Great Britain. Most members signed the document on August 2, 1776.

Constitution Handbook

For more than 200 years, the Constitution has provided the framework for the United States government and has helped preserve the basic rights of American citizens. It is the highest authority in the nation and the basic law of the United States. It is also a symbol of our nation, representing our system of government and our basic ideals, such as liberty and freedom.

Essential Question ◄

Why is citizen participation essential to the preservation of the U.S. political system?

Reading Guide

Content Vocabulary

Preamble *(P33)*	reserved powers *(P34)*
popular sovereignty *(P33)*	concurrent powers *(P34)*
republicanism *(P33)*	amend *(P36)*
federalism *(P34)*	implied powers *(P37)*
enumerated powers *(P34)*	

Academic Vocabulary

involve *(P39)*   diminish *(P41)*

Reading Strategy

Taking Notes As you read, use a diagram like the one below to identify the seven major principles on which the Constitution is based.

Federalism

Major Principles

The Constitution

Main Idea The Constitution sets forth the basic principles of government.

History and You What principles do you live by? Read to learn how the basic principles of the Constitution assure the rights of the people.

• •

The **Preamble,** or introduction, to the Constitution reflects the basic idea of American government—the right of the people to govern themselves. It also lists six goals for the United States government:

PRIMARY SOURCE

"to form a more perfect Union, establish Justice, insure domestic Tranquility [peace], provide for the common defence, promote the general Welfare, and secure the Blessings of Liberty to ourselves and our Posterity [descendents]."

—United States Constitution

Major Principles

The principles outlined in the Constitution were the Framers' solution to the problems of a representative government. The Constitution rests on seven major principles: (1) popular sovereignty, (2) republicanism, (3) limited government, (4) federalism, (5) separation of powers, (6) checks and balances, and (7) individual rights.

Popular Sovereignty The Declaration of Independence states that governments derive their powers from "the consent of the governed." The opening words of the Constitution, "We the People," reinforce this idea of **popular sovereignty**—or "authority of the people."

Republicanism Under **republicanism,** voters hold sovereign power. The people elect representatives and give them the responsibility to make laws and conduct government. For most Americans today, the terms *republic* and *representative democracy* mean the same thing: a system of limited government in which the people are the ultimate source of governmental power.

Limited Government The Framers saw both benefits and risks in creating a powerful national government. They agreed that the nation needed strong central authority but feared misuse of power. They wanted to prevent the government from using its power to give one group special advantages or to deprive another group of its rights. By creating a limited government, they made certain the government would have only those powers granted by the people.

Article I of the Constitution states the powers that the government has and the powers that it does not have. Other limits on government appear in the Bill of Rights, which guarantees certain rights and liberties to the people.

Limited government can be described as the "rule of law." No person or group of people is above the law. Government officials must obey the law.

Federalism When the states banded together under the Constitution, they gave up some independence. States could no longer print their own money or tax items imported from other states. Nevertheless, each state governed itself much as it had in the past.

This system, in which the power to govern is shared between the national government and the states, is called the federal system, or **federalism.** Our federal system allows the people of each state to deal with their needs in their own way. At the same time, it lets the states act together to deal with matters that affect all Americans.

The Constitution defines three types of government powers. **Enumerated powers** belong only to the federal government. These include the power to coin money, regulate interstate and foreign trade, maintain the armed forces, and create federal courts (Article I, Section 8).

The second kind of powers are those retained by the states, known as **reserved powers.** They include such rights as the power to establish schools, pass marriage and divorce laws, and regulate trade within a state. Although reserved powers are not listed specifically in the Constitution, the Tenth Amendment says that all powers not specifically granted to the federal government "are reserved to the States."

The third set of powers defined by the Constitution are **concurrent powers**—powers shared by the state and federal governments. Among these powers are the right to raise taxes, borrow money, provide for public welfare, and administer criminal justice.

When conflicts arise between state law and federal law, the Constitution declares that the Constitution is "the supreme Law of the Land." Conflicts between state law and federal law must be settled in a federal court.

Separation of Powers To prevent any single group or institution in government from gaining too much authority, the Framers divided the federal government into three branches: legislative, executive, and judicial. Each branch has its own functions and powers. The legislative branch, Congress, makes the laws. The executive branch, headed by the president, carries out the laws. The judicial branch, consisting of the Supreme Court and other federal courts, interprets and applies the laws.

Checks and Balances As an additional safeguard, the Framers established a system of checks and balances in which each branch of government can check, or limit, the power of the other branches. This system helps maintain a balance in the power of the three branches. For example, Congress can pass a

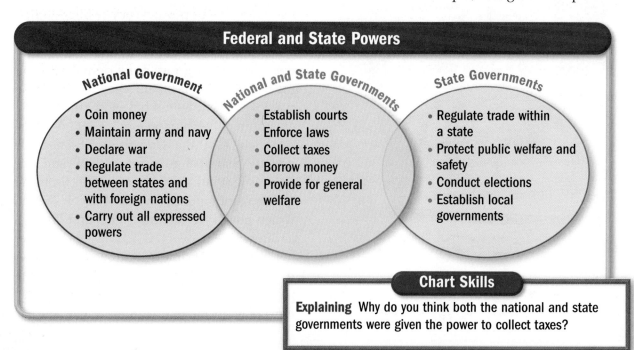

Federal and State Powers

National Government
- Coin money
- Maintain army and navy
- Declare war
- Regulate trade between states and with foreign nations
- Carry out all expressed powers

National and State Governments
- Establish courts
- Enforce laws
- Collect taxes
- Borrow money
- Provide for general welfare

State Governments
- Regulate trade within a state
- Protect public welfare and safety
- Conduct elections
- Establish local governments

Chart Skills

Explaining Why do you think both the national and state governments were given the power to collect taxes?

A System of Checks and Balances

Can impeach president;
Can override veto;
Can reject appointments;
Can refuse to approve treaties

Can impeach judges;
Can reject appointment
of judges

Can veto
legislation

Can declare
acts of legislature
unconstitutional

LEGISLATIVE BRANCH

Can appoint judges

Can declare presidential
actions unconstitutional

EXECUTIVE BRANCH

JUDICIAL BRANCH

Critical Thinking

1. **Describing** How can the judicial branch check the power of the executive branch?
2. **Describing** How can the executive branch check the power of the judicial branch?

law. Then the president can reject the law by vetoing it. However, Congress can override, or reverse, the president's veto if two-thirds of the members of both houses vote again to approve the law.

Over the years, the Supreme Court has acquired the power to determine the meaning of the Constitution and to declare that a law or a government policy goes against the Constitution. In doing so, the Court provides a check on the powers of Congress and the president. Judicial decisions—those made by the courts—can be overruled by amending the Constitution. The president and the Senate provide a check on the judicial branch through their power to appoint and approve federal judges. Congress can also change a law so that it no longer conflicts with the Constitution, or it can amend the Constitution. The Fourteenth Amendment, passed by Congress in 1866, overturned the Supreme Court's rul-

ing in the *Dred Scott* decision, which had ruled that enslaved African Americans were not citizens.

Individual Rights The Bill of Rights became part of the U.S. Constitution in 1791. These first 10 consitutional amendments protect basic liberties and rights that you may have taken for granted—including freedom of speech, freedom of the press, freedom of assembly, freedom of religion, and the right to a trial by jury.

The 17 amendments that follow the Bill of Rights expand the rights of Americans and adjust certain provisions of the Constitution. Included among them are amendments that abolish slavery, define citizenship, guarantee the right to vote to all citizens aged 18 years and older, authorize an income tax, establish the direct election of senators, and set a two-term limit on the presidency.

Many people have come to the United States in search of religious freedom. The principle of religious freedom became rooted in early America as people of different religions learned to live and work together.

In 1777 Thomas Jefferson wrote a resolution on religious freedom that was adopted by the Virginia State legislature in 1786. ▶

The Virginia Statute for Religious Freedom

"No man shall be compelled to frequent or support any religious worship, place, or ministry whatsoever, nor shall be enforced, restrained, molested, or [burdened] in his body or goods, nor shall otherwise suffer on account of his religious opinions or belief; but that all men shall be free to profess, and by argument to maintain, their opinion in matters of religion, and that the same shall in no [way] diminish enlarge, or affect their civil capacities."

—from Thomas Jefferson, "The Virginia Statute for Religious Freedom"

Freedom of religion became one of the principles upon which the United States was founded. In 1791 the First Amendment to the Constitution barred the federal government from establishing a religion or from adopting any law limiting religious freedom.

Critical Thinking

Explaining Why do you think Americans regard religious freedom as an important principle?

A Living Constitution

Two years after the Constitutional Convention, Benjamin Franklin wrote, "Our Constitution is in actual operation; everything appears to promise that it will last; but in this world nothing is certain but death and taxes."

Despite Franklin's uncertainty about the Constitution's future, it is still very much alive today. The Constitution has survived because the Framers wrote a document that the nation could alter and adapt to meet changing needs. The result is a flexible document that can be interpreted in different ways in keeping with the conditions of a particular time. The Constitution's flexibility allows the government to deal with matters the Framers never anticipated—such as regulating nuclear power plants or developing a space program. In addition, the Constitution contains a provision for **amending**—changing or adding to—the document.

Amending the Constitution The Framers intentionally made the amendment process difficult to discourage minor or frequent changes. Although thousands of amendments—changes to the Constitution—have been proposed since 1788, only 27 of them have actually become part of the Constitution.

An amendment can be proposed in two ways: by the vote of two-thirds of both houses of Congress or by two-thirds of the state legislatures asking for a special convention on the amendment. The second method has never been used. Ratification of an amendment requires approval by three-fourths of the states. States ratify amendments by the approval of state legislatures or by special state conventions.

Only the Twenty-first Amendment—which repealed the Eighteenth Amendment, banning the sale of alcoholic beverages—was ratified by state conventions. Voters in each state chose the delegates to the special conventions.

Interpreting the Constitution The Constitution includes two provisions that give Congress the power to act as needed to meet changing conditions. The first of these provisions is what is known as the "elastic clause" (Article I, Section 8). It directs Congress to "make all Laws which shall be necessary and proper" for executing all the powers of government. Congress has interpreted this clause to mean that it has certain

implied powers, powers not specifically defined in the Constitution. Over the years, Congress has drawn on its implied powers to pass laws to deal with the needs of society.

The second provision used to expand congressional authority, the "commerce clause" (Article I, Section 8), gives Congress the power to "regulate Commerce with foreign Nations, and among the several States." Congress has used this clause to expand its powers into a number of areas, such as regulation of the airline industry, radio and television, and nuclear energy.

The process of amending the Constitution and applying its principles in new areas helps keep our government functioning well. In 1974 Barbara Jordan, an African American member of Congress and a constitutional scholar, spoke about her faith in the constitutional process:

PRIMARY SOURCE

"Through the process of amendment, interpretation, and court decision I have finally been included in 'We, the people.' . . . My faith in the Constitution is whole; it is complete; it is total.

—from her speech before the House, July 25, 1974

 Reading Check **Explaining** What are reserved powers?

The Federal Government

Main Idea The U.S. federal government has three branches: the legislative branch, the executive branch, and the judicial branch.

History and You Have you ever written to a representative, senator, president, or chief justice? Read to learn about the duties of officials in the different branches of the federal government.

The Constitution explains how our federal, or national, government is set up and how it works. The federal government is divided among the three branches: legislative, executive, and judicial.

The Legislative Branch

Congress, the legislative branch, makes laws, imposes taxes, and declares war. It has two parts—the House of Representatives and the Senate. The House of Representatives has 435 voting members and 5 nonvoting delegates from the District of Columbia, Puerto Rico, Guam, American Samoa, and the Virgin Islands. The number of representatives from each state is determined by the state's population. Representatives, who must be at least 25 years old, serve two-year terms.

Women in Congress

Firsts Patsy Mink of Hawaii, elected in 1964, became the first Asian American woman and the first woman of color in the U.S. Congress. In 1968 Shirley Chisholm of Brooklyn, New York, was the first African American woman elected to Congress. The first Latino woman elected to Congress was Ileana Ros-Lehtinen of Florida. She was elected in 1988.

Nancy Pelosi
First woman Speaker of
the U.S. House (2007) ▶

◀ **Jeanette Rankin**
First woman in U.S.
Congress (1917)

Critical Thinking

Making Generalizations Does democracy require participation in government by all groups? Explain.

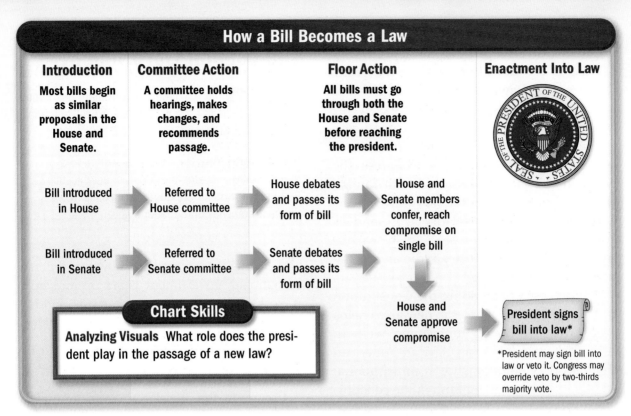

How a Bill Becomes a Law

Introduction	Committee Action	Floor Action	Enactment Into Law
Most bills begin as similar proposals in the House and Senate.	A committee holds hearings, makes changes, and recommends passage.	All bills must go through both the House and Senate before reaching the president.	

Bill introduced in House → Referred to House committee → House debates and passes its form of bill → House and Senate members confer, reach compromise on single bill

Bill introduced in Senate → Referred to Senate committee → Senate debates and passes its form of bill

House and Senate approve compromise → President signs bill into law*

*President may sign bill into law or veto it. Congress may override veto by two-thirds majority vote.

Chart Skills

Analyzing Visuals What role does the president play in the passage of a new law?

The Senate has 100 senators, 2 from each state. Senators, who must be at least 30 years old, serve six-year terms. One-third of Senate seats come up for election every 2 years.

The Role of Congress Congress makes the nation's laws and controls government spending. All tax and spending bills begin in the House of Representatives and are approved in both the House and the Senate before the president signs them into law.

Congress also keeps a check on the actions of the executive branch. The House can impeach, or bring charges against, any federal official suspected of wrongdoing. Officials found guilty may be removed from office. The Senate also holds certain special powers. It can ratify treaties and approve presidential appointments of federal officials.

The Executive Branch

The executive branch carries out the laws passed by Congress. It includes the president, the vice president, and various offices, departments, and agencies.

The President The president carries out the nation's laws with the help of many executive offices, departments, and agencies. As head of the executive branch, the president has the following roles, each with specific powers and duties:

- **Chief Diplomat:** directs foreign policy, appoints ambassadors, and negotiates treaties with other nations.

- **Commander in Chief:** uses the military in crises at home and abroad with congressional approval or declaration of war.

- **Head of State:** representative of all Americans; receives foreign dignitaries; bestows honors on Americans.

- **Legislative Leader:** proposes laws to Congress; sets goals for legislation and working to see that they are passed. In the annual State of the Union address, the president presents goals for legislation. The vice president also serves in the Legislative branch as the President of the Senate.

Cabinet and Vice President The secretaries, or heads, of departments form the cabinet, a group that helps the president set government policy. Members of the cabinet advise the president on issues related to their departments. The Constitution gives the vice president no duties aside from presiding over the Senate. It is the president who determines what the vice president will do, such as working with Congress or making trips abroad.

The Judicial Branch

The Constitution calls for a Supreme Court and the creation of lower courts as Congress wishes. In 1789 Congress passed a Judiciary Act, which added a series of district courts to the federal court system. Appeals, or circuit courts, were added in 1891 to ease the workload of the Supreme Court.

Lower Federal Courts The duties of the lower federal courts are the following:

- **District Courts:** handle civil and criminal cases that come under federal authority; 91 district courts, with at least 1 in every state.

- **Appeals Courts:** review disctrict court decisions; overturn a verdict of the district court or order a retrial; 14 appeals courts in the United States.

The Supreme Court The Supreme Court stands at the top of the American legal system. It is one of the coequal branches of the national government, along with Congress and the president. The Supreme Court is comprised of nine justices: the chief justice of the United States and eight associate justices. Congress has the power to set this number and the power to change it.

The Constitution does not describe the duties of the justices, which have developed from laws and customs in response to national needs. The main duty of the justices is to hear and rule on cases. This duty **involves** them in three tasks: deciding which cases to hear from among thousands of appeals each year; deciding the case itself; and explaining the decision, called the Court's opinion.

The role of the judicial branch has grown as the powers implied in the Constitution have been put into practice. In the 1803 case *Marbury* v. *Madison*, Chief Justice John Marshall expanded Supreme Court powers by striking down an act of Congress. In that decision, the Court defined its right to determine whether a law violates the Constitution. Although not mentioned in the Constitution, this principle, known as judicial review, has become a major power of the judicial branch.

Reading Check **Describing** What is Congress's role in government spending?

The Supreme Court

◀ Seated left to right: Anthony Kennedy, John Paul Stevens, Chief Justice John G. Roberts, Jr., Antonin Scalia, David Souter. Standing left to right: Stephen Breyer, Clarence Thomas, Ruth Bader Ginsburg, Samuel Alito, Jr.

Critical Thinking

Describing Why do you think the number of justices is set at an uneven number?

Rights, Duties, and Responsibilities

Rights	Duties	Responsibilities
Security protection by government **Equality** equal treatment under the law **Liberty** rights guaranteed under the Constitution	• Obey the law • Pay taxes • Defend the nation • Serve in court • Attend school	• Be informed and vote • Participate in your community and government • Respect the rights and property of others • Respect different opinions and ways of life

Chart Skills

Contrasting How do duties differ from responsibilities?

Rights and Citizen Participation

Main Idea U.S. citizenship brings with it certain rights and responsibilities.

History and You Are you a good citizen? What are the rights and responsibilities of citizenship? Read to learn why American citizens have a responsibility to their community, the environment, and the law.

. . . .

All American citizens have certain basic rights, but they also have specific responsibilities. Living in a democracy means that every citizen is partly responsible for how society is governed and for the actions the government takes on each citizen's behalf.

The Rights of American Citizens

The rights of Americans fall into three broad categories: the right to be protected from unfair government actions, to have equal treatment under the law, and to enjoy basic freedoms.

Due Process The Fifth Amendment states that no person shall "be deprived of life, liberty, or property, without due process of law." Due process of law means that the government must follow procedures established by law and guaranteed by the Constitution, treating all people according to these principles.

Equal Protection All Americans, regardless of race, religion, or political beliefs, have the right to be treated the same under the law.

The Fourteenth Amendment requires every state to grant its citizens "equal protection of the laws."

Basic Freedoms The basic freedoms involve the liberties outlined in the First Amendment—freedom of speech, freedom of religion, freedom of the press, freedom of assembly, and the right to petition. In a democratic society, power exists in the hands of the people. Therefore, its citizens must be able to exchange ideas freely.

Limits on Rights Our rights are not unlimited. The government can establish laws or rules to protect the health, safety, security, and moral standards of a community. Moreover, rights may be limited to prevent one person's rights from interfering with the rights of others. The restrictions of rights, however, must be reasonable and must apply to everyone equally.

Citizen Participation

A citizen is a person who owes loyalty to and is entitled to the protection of a state or nation. How do you become an American citizen? Generally, citizenship is granted to anyone born within the borders of the United States. Citizenship is also granted to anyone born outside of the United States if one parent is a U.S. citizen. A person of foreign birth can become a citizen through the process of naturalization. Before being admitted citizenship, applicants must be willing to give up any foreign allegiance and must promise to obey the Constitution and the laws of the United States.

As citizens of the United States, we are expected to carry out certain duties and responsibilities. Duties are things we are required to do by law. Responsibilities are things we should do. Fulfilling both our duties and our responsibilities helps ensure that we have a good government and that we continue to enjoy our rights.

Duties One of the duties of all Americans is to obey the law. Laws help keep order; protect the health, safety, and property of citizens; and make it possible for people to live together peacefully. If you believe a law needs to be changed, you can work through your elected representatives to improve it.

Americans also have a duty to pay taxes. The government uses tax money for purposes, such as defending the nation, providing health insurance for senior citizens, and building roads and bridges.

Another duty of citizens is to defend the nation. All males aged 18 and older must register with the government in case they are needed for military service.

The Constitution guarantees all Americans the right to a trial by a jury of their peers (equals). For this reason, citizens are often called to serve on juries after they become eligible at the age of 18. Having jurors on hand is necessary to guarantee the right to a fair and speedy trial.

Responsibilities Responsibilities are not as clear-cut as duties. Because responsibilities are voluntary, people are not arrested or punished if they do not fulfill these obligations. The quality of our lives **diminishes** if responsibilities are neglected.

Perhaps your most important responsibility as a citizen will be to vote when you reach the age of 18. Voting allows you to participate in government and guide its direction. When you vote for people in government, you will be exercising your right of self-government. If you disapprove of the job your representatives are doing, you can express your views to them or help elect other people in the next election.

Reading Check **Summarizing** What is the difference between a duty and a responsibility?

Constitution Handbook Review

Vocabulary

1. Use each of these terms in a sentence: Preamble, popular sovereignty, republicanism, federalism, enumerated powers, reserved powers, concurrent powers, amend, implied powers, involve, diminish.

Main Ideas

2. Making Connections How are popular sovereignty and voting connected?

3. Explaining Are the rights of American citizens unlimited? Explain.

Critical Thinking

4. Evaluating What is the importance of federalism in the Constitution?

5. Comparing Re-create the chart below, and describe how each branch of government has power over another branch.

Branch	Power
Legislative	
Executive	
Judicial	

6. Expository Writing Write a short essay summarizing the major principles found in the Preamble.

Answer the
7. Essential Question
Why is citizen participation essential to the preservation of the U.S. political system?

The Constitution
of the United States

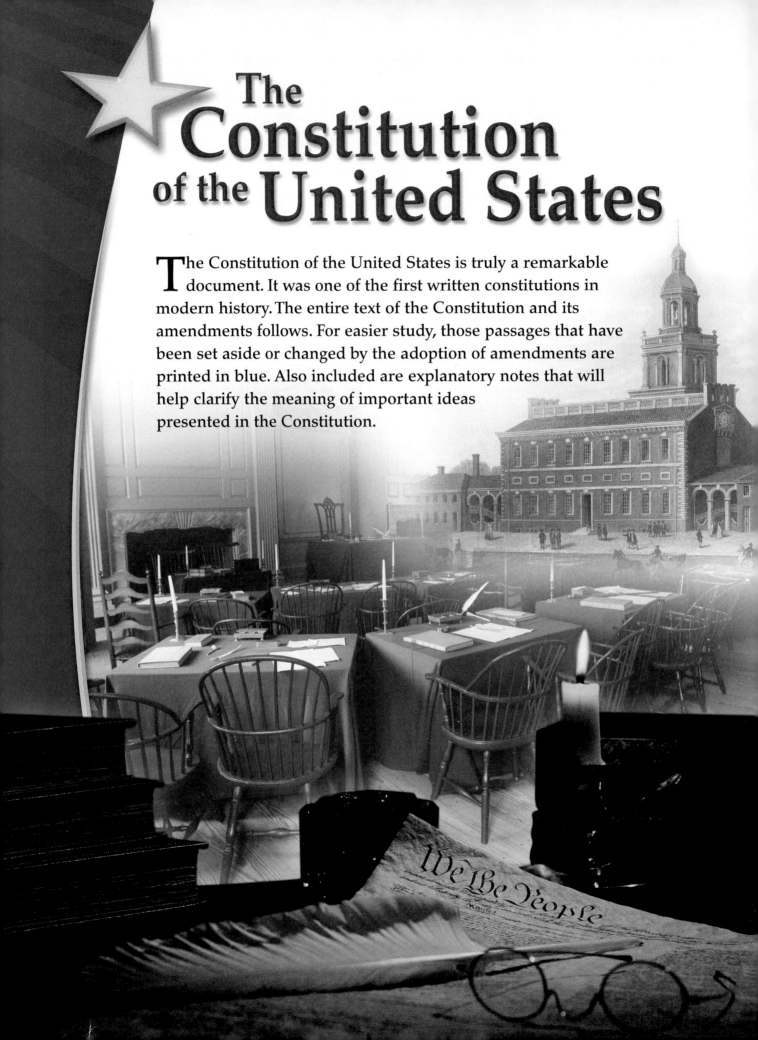

The Constitution of the United States is truly a remarkable document. It was one of the first written constitutions in modern history. The entire text of the Constitution and its amendments follows. For easier study, those passages that have been set aside or changed by the adoption of amendments are printed in blue. Also included are explanatory notes that will help clarify the meaning of important ideas presented in the Constitution.

Preamble

We the People of the United States, in Order to form a more perfect Union, establish Justice, insure domestic Tranquility, provide for the common defence, promote the general Welfare, and secure the Blessings of Liberty to ourselves and our Posterity, do ordain and establish this **Constitution** for the United States of America.

Article I

Section 1

All legislative Powers herein granted shall be vested in a Congress of the United States, which shall consist of a Senate and House of Representatives.

Section 2

[1.] The House of Representatives shall be composed of Members chosen every second Year by the People of the several States, and the Electors in each State shall have the Qualifications requisite for Electors of the most numerous Branch of the State Legislature.

[2.] No Person shall be a Representative who shall not have attained the Age of twenty five Years, and been seven Years a Citizen of the United States, and who shall not, when elected, be an Inhabitant of that State in which he shall be chosen.

[3.] Representatives and direct Taxes shall be apportioned among the several States which may be included within this Union, according to their respective Numbers, which shall be determined by adding to the whole Number of free Persons, including those bound to Service for a Term of Years, and excluding Indians not taxed, three fifths of all other Persons. The actual **Enumeration** shall be made within three Years after the first Meeting of the Congress of the United States, and within every subsequent Term of ten Years, in such Manner as they shall by Law direct. The Number of Representatives shall not exceed one for every thirty Thousand, but each State shall have at Least one Representative; and until such enumeration shall be made, the State of New Hampshire shall be entitled to chuse three, Massachusetts eight, Rhode-Island and Providence Plantations one, Connecticut five, New-York six, New Jersey four, Pennsylvania eight, Delaware one, Maryland six, Virginia ten, North Carolina five, South Carolina five, and Georgia three.

[4.] When vacancies happen in the Representation from any State, the Executive Authority thereof shall issue Writs of Election to fill such Vacancies.

[5.] The House of Representatives shall chuse their Speaker and other Officers; and shall have the sole Power of **Impeachment.**

The **Preamble** introduces the Constitution and sets forth the general purposes for which the government was established. The Preamble also declares that the power of the government comes from the people.

The printed text of the document shows the spelling and punctuation of the parchment original.

What It Means

Article I. The Legislative Branch The Constitution contains seven divisions called articles. Each article covers a general topic. For example, Articles I, II, and III create the three branches of the national government—the legislative, executive, and judicial branches. Most of the articles are divided into sections.

What It Means

Representation The number of representatives from each state is based on the size of the state's population. Each state is entitled to at least one representative. *What are the qualifications for members of the House of Representatives?*

Vocabulary

preamble: introduction

constitution: principles and laws of a nation

enumeration: a census or population count

impeachment: the bringing of charges against an official

Electing Senators Originally, senators were chosen by the state legislators of their own states. The Seventeenth Amendment changed this so that senators are now elected by the people. There are 100 senators, 2 from each state. The vice president serves as president of the Senate.

▲ John Adams, the first vice president

Impeachment One of Congress's powers is the power to impeach—to accuse government officials of wrongdoing, put them on trial, and if necessary remove them from office. *Which body has the power to decide the official's guilt or innocence?*

Vocabulary

president pro tempore: the presiding officer of Senate who serves when the vice president is absent

indictment: the charging of a person with an offense

quorum: the minimum number of members that must be present to conduct sessions

adjourn: to suspend a session

emolument: salary

bill: the draft of a proposed law

revenue: income raised by government

Section 3

[1.] The Senate of the United States shall be composed of two Senators from each State, chosen by the Legislature thereof, for six Years; and each Senator shall have one Vote.

[2.] Immediately after they shall be assembled in Consequence of the first Election, they shall be divided as equally as may be into three Classes. The Seats of the Senators of the first Class shall be vacated at the Expiration of the second Year, of the second Class at the Expiration of the fourth Year, and of the third Class at the Expiration of the sixth Year, so that one third may be chosen every second Year; and if Vacancies happen by Resignation, or otherwise, during the Recess of the Legislature of any State, the Executive thereof may make temporary Appointments until the next Meeting of the Legislature, which shall then fill such Vacancies.

[3.] No Person shall be a Senator who shall not have attained to the Age of thirty Years, and been nine Years a Citizen of the United States, and who shall not, when elected, be an Inhabitant of that State for which he shall be chosen.

[4.] The Vice President of the United States shall be President of the Senate, but shall have no Vote, unless they be equally divided.

[5.] The Senate shall chuse their other Officers, and also a **President pro tempore,** in the Absence of the Vice President, or when he shall exercise the Office of the President of the United States.

[6.] The Senate shall have the sole Power to try all Impeachments. When sitting for that Purpose, they shall be on Oath or Affirmation. When the President of the United States is tried, the Chief Justice shall preside: And no Person shall be convicted without the Concurrence of two thirds of the Members present.

[7.] Judgment in Cases of Impeachment shall not extend further than to removal from Office, and disqualification to hold and enjoy any Office of honor, Trust or Profit under the United States: but the Party convicted shall nevertheless be liable and subject to **Indictment,** Trial, Judgment and Punishment, according to Law.

Section 4

[1.] The Times, Places and Manner of holding Elections for Senators and Representatives, shall be prescribed in each State by the Legislature thereof; but the Congress may at any time by Law make or alter such Regulations, except as to the Places of chusing Senators.

[2.] The Congress shall assemble at least once in every Year, and such Meeting shall be on the first Monday in December, unless they shall by Law appoint a different Day.

Section 5

[1.] Each House shall be the Judge of the Elections, Returns and Qualifications of its own Members, and a Majority of each shall constitute a **Quorum** to do Business; but a smaller Number may **adjourn** from day to day, and may be authorized to compel the Attendance of absent Members, in such Manner, and under such Penalties as each House may provide.

[2.] Each House may determine the Rules of its Proceedings, punish its Members for disorderly Behaviour, and, with the Concurrence of two thirds, expel a Member.

[3.] Each House shall keep a Journal of its Proceedings, and from time to time publish the same, excepting such Parts as may in their Judgment require Secrecy; and the Yeas and Nays of the Members of either House on any question shall, at the Desire of one fifth of those Present, be entered on the Journal.

[4.] Neither House, during the Session of Congress, shall, without the Consent of the other, adjourn for more than three days, nor to any other Place than that in which the two Houses shall be sitting.

Section 6

[1.] The Senators and Representatives shall receive a Compensation for their Services, to be ascertained by Law, and paid out of the Treasury of the United States. They shall in all Cases, except Treason, Felony and Breach of the Peace, be privileged from Arrest during their Attendance at the Session of their respective Houses, and in going to and returning from the same; and for any Speech or Debate in either House, they shall not be questioned in any other Place.

[2.] No Senator or Representative shall, during the Time for which he was elected, be appointed to any civil Office under the Authority of the United States, which shall have been created, or the **Emoluments** whereof shall have been encreased during such time; and no Person holding any Office under the United States, shall be a Member of either House during his Continuance in Office.

Section 7

[1.] All **Bills** for raising **Revenue** shall originate in the House of Representatives; but the Senate may propose or concur with Amendments as on other Bills,

[2.] Every Bill which shall have passed the House of Representatives and the Senate, shall, before it become a Law, be presented to the President of the United States: If he approve he shall sign it, but if not he shall return it, with his Objections to that House in which it shall have originated, who shall enter the Objections at large on their Journal, and proceed to reconsider it. If after such Reconsideration two thirds

▲ Congresswoman Nydia Velázquez represents New York's 12th District.

What It Means

Congressional Salaries To strengthen the federal government, the Founders set congressional salaries to be paid by the United States Treasury rather than by members' respective states. Originally, members were paid $6 per day. In 2006 all members of Congress received a base salary of $165,200.

What It Means

Where Tax Laws Begin All tax laws must originate in the House of Representatives. This ensures that the branch of Congress that is elected by the people every two years has the major role in determining taxes.

What It Means

How Bills Become Laws A bill may become a law only by passing both houses of Congress and by being signed by the president. The president can check Congress by rejecting—vetoing—its legislation. *How can Congress override the president's veto?*

of that House shall agree to pass the Bill, it shall be sent, together with the Objections, to the other House, by which it shall likewise be reconsidered, and if approved by two thirds of that House, it shall become a Law. But in all such Cases the Votes of both Houses shall be determined by yeas and Nays, and the Names of the Persons voting for and against the Bill shall be entered on the Journal of each House respectively. If any Bill shall not be returned by the President within ten Days (Sundays excepted) after it shall have been presented to him, the Same shall be a Law, in like Manner as if he had signed it, unless the Congress by their Adjournment prevent its Return, in which Case it shall not be a Law.

[3.] Every Order, **Resolution,** or Vote to which the Concurrence of the Senate and House of Representatives may be necessary (except on a question of Adjournment) shall be presented to the President of the United States; and before the Same shall take Effect, shall be approved by him, or being disapproved by him, shall be repassed by two thirds of the Senate and House of Representatives, according to the Rules and Limitations prescribed in the Case of a Bill.

Section 8

[1.] The Congress shall have the Power To lay and collect Taxes, Duties, **Imposts** and Excises, to pay the Debts and provide for the common Defence and general Welfare of the United States; but all Duties, Imposts and Excises shall be uniform throughout the United States;

[2.] To borrow Money on the credit of the United States;

[3.] To regulate Commerce with foreign Nations, and among the several States, and with the Indian Tribes;

[4.] To establish an uniform Rule of **Naturalization,** and uniform Laws on the subject of Bankruptcies throughout the United States;

[5.] To coin Money, regulate the Value thereof, and of foreign Coin, and fix the Standard of Weights and Measures;

[6.] To provide for the Punishment of counterfeiting the Securities and current Coin of the United States;

[7.] To establish Post Offices and post Roads;

[8.] To promote the Progress of Science and useful Arts, by securing for limited Times to Authors and Inventors the exclusive Right to their respective Writings and Discoveries;

[9.] To constitute **Tribunals** inferior to the supreme Court;

[10.] To define and punish Piracies and Felonies committed on the high Seas, and Offences against the Law of Nations;

[11.] To declare War, grant **Letters of Marque** and **Reprisal,** and make Rules concerning Captures on Land and Water;

[12.] To raise and support Armies, but no Appropriation of Money to that Use shall be for a longer Term than two Years;

[13.] To provide and maintain a Navy;

What It Means

Powers of Congress Expressed powers are those powers directly stated in the Constitution. Most of the expressed powers of Congress are listed in Article I, Section 8. These powers are also called enumerated powers because they are numbered 1–18. *Which clause gives Congress the power to declare war?*

▲ Civil War money

Vocabulary

resolution: legislature's formal expression of opinion

impost: tax

naturalization: procedure by which a citizen of a foreign nation becomes a citizen of the United States

tribunal: a court

letter of marque: authority given to a citizen to outfit an armed ship and use it to attack enemy ships in time of war

reprisal: taking by force property or territory belonging to another country or to its citizens

[14.] To make Rules for the Government and Regulation of the land and naval Forces;

[15.] To provide for calling forth the Militia to execute the Laws of the Union, suppress **Insurrections** and repel Invasions;

[16.] To provide for organizing, arming, and disciplining, the Militia, and for governing such Part of them as may be employed in the Service of the United States, reserving to the States respectively, the Appointment of the Officers, and the Authority of training the Militia according to the discipline prescribed by Congress;

[17.] To exercise exclusive Legislation in all Cases whatsoever, over such District (not exceeding ten Miles square) as may, by Cession of particular States, and the Acceptance of Congress, become the Seat of Government of the United States, and to exercise like Authority over all Places purchased by the Consent of the Legislature of the State in which the Same shall be, for the Erection of Forts, Magazines, Arsenals, dock-Yards, and other needful Buildings;—And

[18.] To make all Laws which shall be necessary and proper for carrying into Execution the foregoing Powers, and all other Powers vested by this Constitution in the Government of the United States, or in any Department or Officer thereof.

Section 9

[1]. The Migration or Importation of such Persons as any of the States now existing shall think proper to admit, shall not be prohibited by the Congress prior to the Year one thousand eight hundred and eight, but a Tax or **duty** may be imposed on such Importation, not exceeding ten dollars for each Person.

[2.] The Privilege of the Writ of Habeas Corpus shall not be suspended, unless when in Cases of Rebellion or Invasion the public Safety may require it.

[3.] No Bill of Attainder or ex post facto Law shall be passed.

[4.] No Capitation, or other direct, Tax shall be laid, unless in Proportion to the Census or enumeration herein before directed to be taken.

[5.] No Tax or Duty shall be laid on Articles exported from any State.

[6.] No Preference shall be given by any Regulation of Commerce or Revenue to the Ports of one State over those of another; nor shall Vessels bound to, or from, one State, be obliged to enter, clear, or pay Duties in another.

[7.] No Money shall be drawn from the Treasury, but in Consequence of **Appropriations** made by Law; and a regular Statement and Account of the Receipts and Expenditures of all public Money shall be published from time to time.

[8.] No Title of Nobility shall be granted by the United States: And no Person holding any Office of Profit or Trust under them, shall, without the Consent of the Congress, accept of any present, Emolument, Office, or Title, of any kind whatever, from any King, Prince, or foreign State.

What It Means

Elastic Clause The final enumerated power is often called the "elastic clause." This clause gives Congress the right to make all laws "necessary and proper" to carry out the powers expressed in the other clauses of **Article I.** It is called the elastic clause because it lets Congress "stretch" its powers to meet situations the Founders could never have anticipated.

What does the phrase **"necessary and proper"** in the elastic clause mean? Almost from the beginning, this phrase was a subject of dispute. The issue was whether a strict or a broad interpretation of the Constitution should be applied. The dispute was first addressed in 1819, in the case of *McCulloch* v. *Maryland*, when the Supreme Court ruled in favor of a broad interpretation.

What It Means

Habeas Corpus A writ of habeas corpus issued by a judge requires a law official to bring a prisoner to court and show cause for holding the prisoner. A bill of attainder is a bill that punished a person without a jury trial. An "ex post facto" law is one that makes an act a crime after the act has been committed. *What does the Constitution say about bills of attainder?*

Vocabulary

insurrection: rebellion

duty: tax

appropriations: funds set aside for a specific use

What It Means

Limitations on the States Section 10 lists limits on the states. These restrictions were designed, in part, to prevent an overlapping in functions and authority with the federal government.

Section 10

[1.] No State shall enter into any Treaty, Alliance, or Confederation; grant Letters of Marque and Reprisal; coin Money; emit Bills of Credit; make any Thing but gold and silver Coin a Tender in Payment of Debts; pass any Bill of Attainder, ex post facto Law, or Law impairing the Obligation of Contracts, or grant any Title of Nobility.

[2.] No State shall, without the Consent of the Congress, lay any Imposts or Duties on Imports or Exports, except what may be absolutely necessary for executing it's inspection Laws: and the net Produce of all Duties and Imposts, laid by any State on Imports or Exports, shall be for the Use of the Treasury of the United States; and all such Laws shall be subject to the Revision and Controul of the Congress.

[3.] No State shall, without the Consent of Congress, lay any Duty of Tonnage, keep Troops, or Ships of War in time of Peace, enter into any Agreement or Compact with another State, or with a foreign Power, or engage in War, unless actually invaded, or in such imminent Danger as will not admit of delay.

Article II

What It Means

Article II. The Executive Branch Article II creates an executive branch to carry out laws passed by Congress. Article II lists the powers and duties of the presidency, describes qualifications for office and procedures for electing the president, and provides for a vice president.

Section 1

[1.] The executive Power shall be vested in a President of the United States of America. He shall hold his Office during the Term of four Years, and, together with the Vice President, chosen for the same Term, be elected, as follows:

[2.] Each State shall appoint, in such Manner as the Legislature thereof may direct, a Number of Electors, equal to the whole Number of Senators and Representatives to which the State may be entitled in the Congress: but no Senator or Representative, or Person holding an Office of Trust or Profit under the United States, shall be appointed an Elector.

[3.] The Electors shall meet in their respective States, and vote by Ballot for two Persons, of whom one at least shall not be an Inhabitant of the same State with themselves. And they shall make a List of all the Persons voted for, and of the Number of Votes for each; which List they shall sign and certify, and transmit sealed to the Seat of the Government of the United States, directed to the President of the Senate. The President of the Senate shall, in the Presence of the Senate and House of Representatives, open all the Certificates, and the Votes shall then be counted. The Person having the greatest Number of Votes shall be the President, if such Number be a Majority of the whole Number of Electors appointed; and if there be more than one who have such Majority, and have an equal Number of Votes, then the House of Representatives shall immediately chuse by Ballot one of them for President; and if no person have a Majority,

▲ United States coins

then from the five highest on the List the said House shall in like Manner chuse the President. But in chusing the President, the Votes shall be taken by States, the Representation from each State having one Vote; A quorum for this Purpose shall consist of a Member or Members from two thirds of the States, and a Majority of all the States shall be necessary to a Choice. In every Case, after the Choice of the President, the Person having the greatest Number of Votes of the Electors shall be the Vice President. But if there should remain two or more who have equal Votes, the Senate shall chuse from them by Ballot the Vice President.

[4.] The Congress may determine the Time of chusing the Electors, and the Day on which they shall give their Votes; which Day shall be the same throughout the United States.

[5.] No Person except a natural born Citizen, or a Citizen of the United States, at the time of the Adoption of this Constitution, shall be eligible to the Office of President; neither shall any Person be eligible to that Office who shall not have attained to the Age of thirty five Years, and been fourteen Years a Resident within the United States.

[6.] In Case of the Removal of the President from Office, or of his Death, Resignation, or Inability to discharge the Powers and Duties of the said Office, the Same shall devolve on the Vice President, and the Congress may by Law provide for the Case of Removal, Death, Resignation or Inability, both of the President and Vice President, declaring what Officer shall then act as President, and such Officer shall act accordingly, until the Disability be removed, or a President shall be elected.

[7.] The President shall, at stated Times, receive for his Services, a Compensation, which shall neither be increased nor diminished during the Period for which he shall have been elected, and he shall not receive within that Period any other Emolument from the United States, or any of them.

[8.] Before he enter on the Execution of his Office, he shall take the following Oath or Affirmation:—"I do solemnly swear (or affirm) that I will faithfully execute the Office of President of the United States, and will to the best of my Ability, preserve, protect and defend the Constitution of the United States."

Section 2

[1.] The President shall be Commander in Chief of the Army and Navy of the United States, and of the Militia of the several States, when called into the actual Service of the United States; he may require the Opinion, in writing, of the principal Officer in each of the executive Departments, upon any Subject relating to the Duties of their respective Offices, and he shall have Power to grant Reprieves and Pardons for Offences against the United States, except in Cases of Impeachment.

What It Means

Previous Elections The Twelfth Amendment, added in 1804, changed the method of electing the president stated in Article II, Section 3. The Twelfth Amendment requires that the electors cast separate ballots for president and vice president.

What It Means

Qualifications The president must be a citizen of the United States by birth, at least 35 years of age, and a resident of the United States for 14 years.

What It Means

Vacancies If the president dies, resigns, is removed from office by impeachment, or is unable to carry out the duties of the office, the vice president becomes president. The Twenty-fifth Amendment sets procedures for presidential succession.

What It Means

Salary Originally, the president's salary was $25,000 per year. The president's current salary is $400,000 plus a $50,000 nontaxable expense account per year. The president also receives living accommodations in two residences—the White House and Camp David.

What It Means

The Cabinet Mention of "the principal officer in each of the executive departments" is the only suggestion of the president's cabinet to be found in the Constitution. The cabinet is an advisory body, and its power depends on the president. Section 2, Clause 1, also makes the president—a civilian—the head of the armed services. This established the principle of civilian control of the military.

Presidential Powers An executive order is a command issued by a president to exercise a power which he or she has been given by the U.S. Constitution or by a federal statute. In times of emergency, presidents sometimes have used the executive order to override the Constitution of the United States and the Congress. During the Civil War, President Lincoln suspended many fundamental rights guaranteed in the Constitution and the Bill of Rights. He closed down newspapers that opposed his policies and imprisoned some who disagreed with him. Lincoln said that these actions were justified to preserve the Union.

Article III. The Judicial Branch The term "judicial" refers to courts. The Constitution set up only the Supreme Court but provided for the establishment of other federal courts. The judiciary of the United States has two different systems of courts. One system consists of the federal courts, whose powers derive from the Constitution and federal laws. The other includes the courts of each of the 50 states, whose powers derive from state constitutions and laws.

Statute Law Federal courts deal mostly with "statute law," or laws passed by Congress, treaties, and cases involving the Constitution itself.

[2.] He shall have Power, by and with the Advice and Consent of the Senate, to make Treaties, provided two thirds of the Senators present concur; and he shall nominate, and by and with the Advice and Consent of the Senate, shall appoint Ambassadors, other public Ministers and Consuls, Judges of the supreme Court, and all other Officers of the United States, whose Appointments are not herein otherwise provided for, and which shall be established by Law: but the Congress may by Law vest the Appointment of such inferior Officers, as they think proper, in the President alone, in the Courts of Law, or in the Heads of Departments.

[3.] The President shall have Power to fill up all Vacancies that may happen during the Recess of the Senate, by granting Commissions which shall expire at the End of their next Session.

Section 3

He shall from time to time give to the Congress Information of the State of the Union, and recommend to their Consideration such Measures as he shall judge necessary and expedient; he may, on extraordinary Occasions, convene both Houses, or either of them, and in Case of Disagreement between them, with Respect to the Time of Adjournment, he may adjourn them to such Time as he shall think proper; he shall receive Ambassadors and other public Ministers; he shall take Care that the Laws be faithfully executed, and shall Commission all the Officers of the United States.

Section 4

The President, Vice President and all civil Officers of the United States, shall be removed from Office on Impeachment for, and Conviction of, Treason, Bribery, or other high Crimes and Misdemeanors.

Article III

Section 1

The judicial Power of the United States shall be vested in one supreme Court, and in such inferior Courts as the Congress may from time to time ordain and establish. The Judges, both of the supreme and inferior Courts, shall hold their Offices during good Behaviour, and shall, at stated Times, receive for their Services a Compensation, which shall not be diminished during their Continuance in Office.

Section 2

[1.] The judicial Power shall extend to all Cases, in Law and Equity, arising under this Constitution, the Laws of the United States, and Treaties made, or which shall be made, under their Authority;—to all Cases affecting Ambassadors, other public Ministers and Consuls;—to all Cases of admiralty and maritime Jurisdiction;—to Controversies to which the United States shall be a Party;—to Controversies between two or more States;—between a State and Citizens of another State;—between Citizens of different States;—between Citizens of the same State claiming Lands under Grants of different States, and between a State, or the Citizens thereof, and foreign States, Citizens or Subjects.

[2.] In all Cases affecting Ambassadors, other public Ministers and Consuls, and those in which a State shall be Party, the supreme Court shall have **original Jurisdiction.** In all the other Cases before mentioned, the supreme Court shall have **appellate Jurisdiction,** both as to Law and Fact, with such Exceptions, and under such Regulations as the Congress shall make.

[3.] The Trial of all Crimes, except in Cases of Impeachment, shall be by Jury; and such Trial shall be held in the State where the said Crimes shall have been committed; but when not committed within any State, the Trial shall be at such Place or Places as the Congress may by Law have directed.

Section 3

[1.] **Treason** against the United States, shall consist only in levying War against them, or in adhering to their Enemies, giving them Aid and Comfort. No Person shall be convicted of Treason unless on the Testimony of two Witnesses to the same overt Act, or on Confession in open Court.

[2.] The Congress shall have Power to declare the Punishment of Treason, but no Attainder of Treason shall work Corruption of Blood, or Forfeiture except during the Life of the Person attainted.

Article IV

Section 1

Full Faith and Credit shall be given in each State to the public Acts, Records, and judicial Proceedings of every other State. And the Congress may by general Laws prescribe the Manner in which such Acts, Records and Proceedings shall be proved, and the Effect thereof.

Section 2

[1.] The Citizens of each State shall be entitled to all Privileges and Immunities of Citizens in the several States.

[2.] A Person charged in any State with Treason, Felony, or other Crime, who shall flee from Justice, and be found in another State, shall on Demand of the executive Authority of the State from which he fled, be delivered up, to be removed to the State having Jurisdiction of the Crime.

[3.] No Person held to Service of Labour in one State, under the Laws thereof, escaping into another, shall, in Consequence of any Law or Regulation therein, be discharged from such Service or Labour, but shall be delivered up on Claim of the Party to whom such Service or Labour may be due.

What It Means

The Supreme Court A court with "original jurisdiction" has the authority to be the first court to hear a case. The Supreme Court has "appellate jurisdiction" and mostly hears cases appealed from lower courts.

What It Means

Article IV. Relations Among the States Article IV explains the relationship of the states to one another and to the national government. This article requires each state to give citizens of other states the same rights as its own citizens, addresses admitting new states, and guarantees that the national government will protect the states.

Vocabulary

original jurisdiction: authority to be the first court to hear a case

appellate jurisdiction: authority to hear cases that have been appealed from lower courts

treason: violation of the allegiance owed by a person to his or her own country, for example, by aiding an enemy

Section 3

[1.] New States may be admitted by the Congress into this Union; but no new State shall be formed or erected within the Jurisdiction of any other State; nor any State be formed by the Junction of two or more States, or Parts of States, without the Consent of the Legislatures of the States concerned as well as of the Congress.

[2.] The Congress shall have Power to dispose of and make all needful Rules and Regulations respecting the Territory or other Property belonging to the United States; and nothing in this Constitution shall be so construed as to Prejudice any Claims of the United States, or of any particular State.

Section 4

The United States shall guarantee to every State in this Union a Republican Form of Government, and shall protect each of them against Invasion; and on Application of the Legislature, or of the Executive (when the Legislature cannot be convened), against domestic Violence.

Article V

The Congress, whenever two thirds of both Houses shall deem it necessary, shall propose **Amendments** to this Constitution, or, on the Application of the Legislatures of two thirds of the several States, shall call a Convention for proposing Amendments, which, in either Case, shall be valid to all Intents and Purposes, as Part of this Constitution, when ratified by the Legislatures of three fourths of the several States, or by Conventions in three fourths thereof, as the one or the other Mode of **Ratification** may be proposed by the Congress; Provided that no Amendment which may be made prior to the Year One thousand eight hundred and eight shall in any Manner affect the first and fourth Clauses in the Ninth Section of the first Article; and that no State, without its Consent, shall be deprived of its equal Suffrage in the Senate.

Article VI

[1.] All Debts contracted and Engagements entered into, before the Adoption of this Constitution, shall be as valid against the United States under this Constitution, as under the Confederation.

[2.] This Constitution, and the Laws of the United States which shall be made in Pursuance thereof; and all Treaties made, or which shall be made, under the Authority of the United States, shall be the supreme Law of the Land; and the Judges in every State shall be bound thereby, any Thing in the Constitution or Laws of any State to the Contrary notwithstanding.

[3.] The Senators and Representatives before mentioned, and the Members of the several State Legislatures, and all executive

---

What It Means

Republic Government can be classified in many different ways. The ancient Greek philosopher Aristotle classified government based on the question: Who governs? According to Aristotle, all governments belong to one of three major groups: (1) autocracy—rule by one person; (2) oligarchy—rule by a few persons; or (3) democracy—rule by many persons. A republic is a form of democracy in which the people elect representatives to make the laws and conduct government.

What It Means

Article VI. National Supremacy
Article VI contains the "supremacy clause." This clause establishes that the Constitution, laws passed by Congress, and treaties of the United States "shall be the supreme Law of the Land." The "supremacy clause" recognized the Constitution and federal laws as supreme when in conflict with those of the states.

Vocabulary

amendment: a change to the Constitution
ratification: the process by which an amendment is approved

and judicial Officers, both of the United States and of the several States, shall be bound by Oath or Affirmation, to support this Constitution; but no religious Test shall ever be required as a Qualification to any Office or public Trust under the United States.

Article VII

The Ratification of the Conventions of nine States, shall be sufficient for the Establishment of this Constitution between the States so ratifying the Same.

Done in Convention by the Unanimous Consent of the States present the Seventeenth Day of September in the Year of our Lord one thousand seven hundred and Eighty seven and of the Independence of the United States of America the Twelfth. In witness whereof We have hereunto subscribed our Names,

What It Means

Article VII. Ratification Article VII addresses ratification and declares that the Constitution would take effect after it was ratified by nine states.

Signers

**George Washington,
President and Deputy
from Virginia**

New Hampshire
John Langdon
Nicholas Gilman

Massachusetts
Nathaniel Gorham
Rufus King

Connecticut
William Samuel Johnson
Roger Sherman

New York
Alexander Hamilton

New Jersey
William Livingston
David Brearley
William Paterson
Jonathan Dayton

Pennsylvania
Benjamin Franklin
Thomas Mifflin
Robert Morris
George Clymer
Thomas FitzSimons
Jared Ingersoll
James Wilson
Gouverneur Morris

Delaware
George Read
Gunning Bedford, Jr.
John Dickinson
Richard Bassett
Jacob Broom

Maryland
James McHenry
Daniel of
    St. Thomas Jenifer
Daniel Carroll

Virginia
John Blair
James Madison, Jr.

North Carolina
William Blount
Richard Dobbs Spaight
Hugh Williamson

South Carolina
John Rutledge
Charles Cotesworth
    Pinckney
Charles Pinckney
Pierce Butler

Georgia
William Few
Abraham Baldwin

Attest:
William Jackson, Secretary

Amendment I

Congress shall make no law respecting an establishment of religion, or prohibiting the free exercise thereof; or abridging the freedom of speech, or of the press; or the right of the people peaceably to assemble, and to petition the Government for a redress of grievances.

Amendment II

A well regulated Militia, being necessary to the security of a free State, the right of the people to keep and bear Arms, shall not be infringed.

Amendment III

No Soldier shall, in time of peace be **quartered** in any house, without the consent of the Owner, nor in time of war, but in a manner to be prescribed by law.

Amendment IV

The right of the people to be secure in their persons, houses, papers, and effects, against unreasonable searches and seizures, shall not be violated, and no **Warrants** shall issue, but upon **probable cause,** supported by Oath or affirmation, and particularly describing the place to be searched, and the persons or things to be seized.

Amendment V

No person shall be held to answer for a capital, or otherwise infamous crime, unless on a presentment or indictment of a Grand Jury, except in cases arising in the land or naval forces, or in the Militia, when in actual service in time of War or public danger; nor shall any person be subject for the same offence to be twice put in jeopardy of life or limb; nor shall be compelled in any criminal case to be a witness against himself, nor be deprived of life, liberty, or property, without due process of law; nor shall private property be taken for public use, without just compensation.

Amendment VI

In all criminal prosecutions, the accused shall enjoy the right to a speedy and public trial, by an impartial jury of the State and district wherein the crime shall have been committed, which district shall have been previously ascertained by law, and to be informed of the nature and cause of the accusation; to be confronted with the witnesses against him; to have compulsory process for obtaining

Vocabulary

quarter: to provide living accommodations

warrant: a document that gives police particular rights or powers

probable cause: a reasonable basis to believe a person is linked to a crime witnesses in his favor, and to have the Assistance of Counsel for his defence.

Amendment VII

In Suits at **common law,** where the value in controversy shall exceed twenty dollars, the right of trial by jury shall be preserved, and no fact tried by a jury, shall be otherwise re-examined in any Court of the United States, than according to the rules of common law.

Amendment VIII

Excessive **bail** shall not be required, nor excessive fines imposed, nor cruel and unusual punishments inflicted.

Amendment IX

The enumeration in the Constitution, of certain rights, shall not be construed to deny or disparage others retained by the people.

Amendment X

The powers not delegated to the United States by the Constitution, nor prohibited by it to the States, are reserved to the States respectively, or to the people.

Amendment XI

The Judicial power of the United States shall not be construed to extend to any suit in law or equity, commenced or prosecuted against one of the United States by Citizens of another State, or by Citizens or Subjects of any Foreign State.

Amendment XII

The electors shall meet in their respective states and vote by ballot for President and Vice-President, one of whom, at least, shall not be an inhabitant of the same state with themselves; they shall name in their ballots the person voted for as President, and in distinct ballots the person voted for as Vice-President, and they shall make distinct lists of all persons voted for as President, and of all persons voted for as Vice-President, and of the number of votes for each, which lists they shall sign and certify, and transmit sealed to the seat of the government of the United States, directed to the President of the Senate;— The President of the Senate shall, in the presence of the Senate and House of Representatives, open all the certificates and the votes shall then be counted;—The person

What It Means

Powers Reserved to the People This amendment prevents government from claiming that the only rights people have are those listed in the Bill of Rights.

What It Means

Powers Reserved to the States The final amendment of the Bill of Rights protects the states and the people from an all-powerful federal government. It establishes that powers not given to the national government—or denied to the states—by the Constitution belong to the states or to the people.

What It Means

Suits Against States The Eleventh Amendment (1795) limits the jurisdiction of the federal courts. The Supreme Court had ruled that a federal court could try a lawsuit brought by citizens of South Carolina against the state of Georgia. This case, *Chisholm* v. *Georgia*, decided in 1793, raised a storm of protest, leading to passage of the Eleventh Amendment.

Vocabulary

common law: law established by previous court decisions

bail: money that an accused person provides to the court as a guarantee that he or she will be present for a trial

Vocabulary

majority: more than half

devolve: to pass on

abridge: to reduce

having the greatest number of votes for President, shall be the President, if such number be a majority of the whole number of Electors appointed; and if no person have such majority, then from the persons having the highest numbers not exceeding three on the list of those voted for as President, the House of Representatives shall choose immediately, by ballot, the President. But in choosing the President, the votes shall be taken by states, the representation from each state having one vote; a quorum for this purpose shall consist of a member or members from two-thirds of the states, and a **majority** of all the states shall be necessary to a choice. And if the House of Representatives shall not choose a President whenever the right of choice shall **devolve** upon them, before the fourth day of March next following, then the Vice-President shall act as President, as in the case of the death or other constitutional disability of the President. The person having the greatest number of votes as Vice-President, shall be the Vice-President, if such number be a majority of the whole number of Electors appointed, and if no person have a majority, then from the two highest numbers on the list, the Senate shall choose the Vice-President; a quorum for the purpose shall consist of two-thirds of the whole number of Senators, and a majority of the whole number shall be necessary to a choice. But no person constitutionally ineligible to the office of President shall be eligible to that of Vice-President of the United States.

Amendment XIII

Section 1

Neither slavery nor involuntary servitude, except as a punishment for crime whereof the party shall have been duly convicted, shall exist within the United States, or any place subject to their jurisdiction.

Section 2

Congress shall have power to enforce this article by appropriate legislation.

Amendment XIV

Section 1

All persons born or naturalized in the United States, and subject to the jurisdiction thereof, are citizens of the United States and of the State wherein they reside. No State shall make or enforce any law which shall **abridge** the privileges or immunities of citizens of the United States; nor shall any State deprive any person of life, liberty, or property, without due process of law; nor deny to any person within its jurisdiction the equal protection of the laws.

Section 2

Representatives shall be apportioned among the several States according to their respective numbers, counting the whole number of persons in each State, excluding Indians not taxed. But when the right to vote at any election for the choice of electors for President and Vice-President of the United States, Representatives in Congress, the Executive and Judicial officers of a State, or the members of the Legislature thereof, is denied to any of the male inhabitants of such State, being twenty-one years of age, and citizens of the United States, or in any way abridged, except for participation in rebellion, or other crime, the basis of representation therein shall be reduced in the proportion which the number of such male citizens shall bear to the whole number of male citizens twenty-one years of age in such State.

Section 3

No person shall be a Senator or Representative in Congress, or elector of President and Vice-President, or hold any office, civil or military, under the United States, or under any State, who, having previously taken an oath, as a member of Congress, or as an officer of the United States, or as a member of any State legislature, or as an executive or judicial officer of any State, to support the Constitution of the United States, shall have engaged in **insurrection** or rebellion against the same, or given aid or comfort to the enemies thereof. But Congress may by a vote of two-thirds of each House, remove such disability.

Section 4

The validity of the public debt of the United States, authorized by law, including debts incurred for payment of pensions and bounties for service in suppressing insurrection or rebellion, shall not be questioned. But neither the United States nor any State shall assume or pay any debt or obligation incurred in aid of insurrection or rebellion against the United States, or any claim for the loss or **emancipation** of any slave; but all such debts, obligations and claims shall be held illegal and void.

Section 5

The Congress shall have power to enforce, by appropriate legislation, the provisions of this article.

What It Means

Representation in Congress This section reduced the number of members a state had in the House of Representatives if it denied its citizens the right to vote. Later civil rights laws and the Twenty-fourth Amendment guaranteed the vote to African Americans.

What It Means

Penalty for Engaging in Insurrection The leaders of the Confederacy were barred from state or federal offices unless Congress agreed to remove this ban. By the end of Reconstruction all but a few Confederate leaders were allowed to return to public life.

What It Means

Public Debt The public debt acquired by the federal government during the Civil War was valid and could not be questioned by the South. However, the debts of the Confederacy were declared to be illegal. *Could former slaveholders collect payment for the loss of their slaves?*

Vocabulary

insurrection: rebellion against the government

emancipation: freedom from slavery

What It Means

Right to Vote The Fifteenth Amendment (1870) prohibits the government from denying a person's right to vote on the basis of race. Despite the law, many states denied African Americans the right to vote by such means as poll taxes, literacy tests, and white primaries. During the 1950s and 1960s, Congress passed successively stronger laws to end racial discrimination in voting rights.

What It Means

Direct Election of Senators The Seventeenth Amendment (1913) states that the people, instead of state legislatures, elect United States senators. *How many years are in a Senate term?*

Amendment XV

Section 1

The right of citizens of the United States to vote shall not be denied or abridged by the United States or by any State on account of race, color, or previous condition of servitude.

Section 2

The Congress shall have power to enforce this article by appropriate legislation.

Amendment XVI

The Congress shall have power to lay and collect taxes on incomes, from whatever source derived, without **apportionment** among the several States, and without regard to any census or enumeration.

Amendment XVII

Section 1

The Senate of the United States shall be composed of two Senators from each State, elected by the people thereof, for six years; and each Senator shall have one vote. The electors in each State shall have the qualifications requisite for electors of the most numerous branch of the State legislatures.

Section 2

When vacancies happen in the representation of any State in the Senate, the executive authority of such State shall issue writs of election to fill such vacancies: *Provided,* That the legislature of any State may empower the executive thereof to make temporary appointments until the people fill the vacancies by election as the legislature may direct.

Section 3

This amendment shall not be so construed as to affect the election or term of any Senator chosen before it becomes valid as part of the Constitution.

Amendment XVIII

Section 1

After one year from ratification of this article, the manufacture, sale, or transportation of intoxicating liquors within, the importation thereof into, or the exportation

Vocabulary

apportionment: the distribution of seats in the House based on population thereof from the United States and all territory subject to the jurisdiction thereof for beverage purposes is hereby prohibited.

Section 2

The Congress and the several States shall have concurrent power to enforce this article by appropriate legislation.

Section 3

This article shall be inoperative unless it shall have been ratified as an amendment to the Constitution by the legislatures of the several States, as provided in the Constitution, within seven years from the date of the submission hereof to the States by the Congress.

Amendment XIX

Section 1

The right of citizens of the United States to vote shall not be denied or abridged by the United States or by any State on account of sex.

Section 2

Congress shall have power by appropriate legislation to enforce the provisions of this article.

Amendment XX

Section 1

The terms of the President and Vice President shall end at noon on the 20th day of January, and the terms of the Senators and Representatives at noon on the 3d day of January, of the years in which such terms would have ended if this article had not been ratified; and the terms of their successors shall then begin.

Section 2

The Congress shall assemble at least once in every year, and such meeting shall begin at noon on the 3d day of January, unless they shall by law appoint a different day.

Section 3

If, at the time fixed for the beginning of the term of the President, the **President elect** shall have died, the Vice President elect shall become President. If a President shall not have been chosen before the time fixed for the beginning of his term, or if the President elect shall have failed to qualify, then the Vice President elect shall act as President until a President shall have qualified; and the Congress may by law

What It Means

Woman Suffrage The Nineteenth Amendment (1920) guaranteed women the right to vote. By then women had already won the vote in many state elections, but the amendment made their right to vote in all state and national elections constitutional.

What It Means

"Lame Duck" The Twentieth Amendment (1933) set new dates for Congress to begin its term and for the inauguration of the president and vice president. Under the original Constitution, elected officials who retired or who had been defeated remained in office for several months. For the outgoing president, this period ran from November until March. Such outgoing officials, referred to as "lame ducks," could accomplish little. *What date was fixed as Inauguration Day?*

Vocabulary

president elect: the individual who is elected president but has not yet begun serving his or her term provide for the case wherein neither a President elect nor a Vice President elect shall have qualified, declaring who shall then act as President, or the manner in which one who is to act shall be selected, and such person shall act accordingly until a President or Vice President shall have qualified.

Section 4

The Congress may by law provide for the case of the death of any of the persons from whom the House of Representatives may choose a President whenever the right of choice shall have devolved upon them, and for the case of the death of any of the persons from whom the Senate may choose a Vice President whenever the right of choice shall have devolved upon them.

Section 5

Sections 1 and 2 shall take effect on the 15th day of October following the ratification of this article.

Section 6

This article shall be inoperative unless it shall have been ratified as an amendment to the Constitution by the legislatures of three-fourths of the several States within seven years from the date of its submission.

Amendment XXI

Section 1

The eighteenth article of amendment to the Constitution of the United States is hereby repealed.

Section 2

The transportation or importation into any State, Territory, or Possession of the United States for delivery or use therein of intoxicating liquors, in violation of the laws thereof, is hereby prohibited.

Section 3

This article shall be inoperative unless it shall have been ratified as an amendment to the Constitution by conventions in the several States, as provided in the Constitution, within seven years from the date of the submission hereof to the States by the Congress.

Amendment XXII

Section 1

No person shall be elected to the office of the President more than twice, and no person who has held the office of

What It Means

Repeal of Prohibition Amendment The Twenty-first Amendment (1933) repeals the Eighteenth Amendment. It is the only amendment ever passed to overturn an earlier amendment. It is also the only amendment ratified by special state conventions instead of state legislatures.

What It Means

Limit on Presidential Terms The Twenty-second Amendment (1951) limits presidents to a maximum of two elected terms. It was passed largely as a reaction to Franklin D. Roosevelt's election to four terms between 1933 and 1945.

President, or acted as President, for more than two years of a term to which some other person was elected President shall be elected to the office of the President more than once. But this Article shall not apply to any person holding the office of President when this Article was proposed by the Congress, and shall not prevent any person who may be holding the office of President, or acting as President, during the term within which this Article becomes operative from holding the office of President or acting as President during the remainder of such term.

Section 2

This article shall be inoperative unless it shall have been ratified as an amendment to the Constitution by the legislatures of three-fourths of the several States within seven years from the date of its submission to the States by the Congress.

Amendment XXIII

Section 1

The **District** constituting the seat of Government of the United States shall appoint in such manner as the Congress may direct:

A number of electors of President and Vice President equal to the whole number of Senators and Representatives in Congress to which the District would be entitled if it were a State, but in no event more than the least populous State; they shall be in addition to those appointed by the States, but they shall be considered, for the purposes of the election of President and Vice President, to be electors appointed by a State; and they shall meet in the District and perform such duties as provided by the twelfth article of amendment.

Section 2

The Congress shall have power to enforce this article by appropriate legislation.

Amendment XXIV

Section 1

The right of citizens of the United States to vote in any primary or other election for President or Vice President, for electors for President or Vice President, or for Senator or Representative in Congress, shall not be denied or abridged by the United States or any State by reason of failure to pay any poll tax or other tax.

What It Means

Presidential Electors for the District of Columbia The Twenty-third Amendment (1961) allows citizens living in Washington, D.C., to vote for president and vice president, a right previously denied residents of the nation's capital. The District of Columbia now has three presidential electors, the number to which it would be entitled if it were a state.

What It Means

Abolition of Poll Tax The Twenty-fourth Amendment (1964) prohibits poll taxes in federal elections. Prior to the passage of this amendment, some states had used such taxes to keep low-income African Americans from voting. In 1966 the Supreme Court banned poll taxes in state elections as well.

Vocabulary

District: the site of the nation's capital, occupying an area between Maryland and Virginia

Presidential Disability and Succession The Twenty-fifth Amendment (1967) established a process for the vice president to take over leadership of the nation when a president is disabled. It also set procedures for filling a vacancy in the office of vice president.

This amendment was used in 1973, when Vice President Spiro Agnew resigned from office after being charged with accepting bribes. President Richard Nixon then appointed Gerald R. Ford as vice president in accordance with the provisions of the 25th Amendment. A year later, President Nixon resigned during the Watergate scandal and Ford became president. President Ford then had to fill the vice presidency, which he had left vacant upon assuming the presidency. He named Nelson A. Rockefeller as vice president. Thus, individuals who had not been elected held both the presidency and the vice presidency. *Whom does the president inform if he or she cannot carry out the duties of the office?*

▲ President Gerald Ford

Vocabulary

vacancy: an office or position that is unfilled or unoccupied

Section 2

The Congress shall have power to enforce this article by appropriate legislation.

Amendment XXV

Section 1

In case of the removal of the President from office or of his death or resignation, the Vice President shall become President.

Section 2

Whenever there is a **vacancy** in the office of the Vice President, the President shall nominate a Vice President who shall take the office upon confirmation by a majority vote of both Houses of Congress.

Section 3

Whenever the President transmits to the President pro tempore of the Senate and the Speaker of the House of Representatives his written declaration that he is unable to discharge the powers and duties of his office, and until he transmits to them a written declaration to the contrary, such powers and duties shall be discharged by the Vice President as Acting President.

Section 4

Whenever the Vice President and a majority of either the principal officers of the executive departments or of such other body as Congress may by law provide, transmit to the President pro tempore of the Senate and the Speaker of the House of Representatives their written declaration that the President is unable to discharge the powers and duties of his office, the Vice President shall immediately assume the power and duties of the office of Acting President.

Thereafter, when the President transmits to the President pro tempore of the Senate and the Speaker of the House of Representatives his written declaration that no inability exists, he shall resume the powers and duties of his office unless the Vice President and a majority of either the principal officers of the executive department or of such other body as Congress may by law provide, transmit within four days to the President pro tempore of the Senate and the Speaker of the House of Representatives their written declaration that the President is unable to discharge the powers and duties of his office. Thereupon Congress shall decide the issue, assembling within forty-eight hours for that purpose if not in session. If the Congress, within twenty-one days after receipt of the latter written declaration, or, if Congress is not in session, within twenty-one days after Congress is required to assemble, determines by two-thirds vote of both Houses that the President is unable to discharge the powers and duties of his office, the Vice President shall continue to discharge the same as Acting President; otherwise, the President shall resume the power and duties of his office.

Amendment XXVI

Section 1

The right of citizens of the United States, who are eighteen years of age or older, to vote shall not be denied or abridged by the United States or by any State on account of age.

Section 2

The Congress shall have power to enforce this article by appropriate legislation.

Amendment XXVII

No law, varying the compensation for the services of Senators and Representatives, shall take effect, until an election of representatives shall have intervened.

What It Means

Eighteen-Year-Old Vote The Twenty-sixth Amendment (1971) guarantees the right to vote to all citizens 18 years of age and older.

What It Means

Restraint on Congressional Salaries The Twenty-seventh Amendment (1992) makes congressional pay raises effective during the term following their passage. James Madison offered the amendment in 1789, but it was never adopted. In 1982 Gregory Watson, then a student at the University of Texas, discovered the forgotten amendment while doing research for a school paper. Watson made the amendment's passage his crusade.

▼ Joint meeting of Congress

Civil War and Reconstruction
1840–1896

Spent cannon round from the attack on Fort Sumter, April 1861

FIRED FROM FORT MOULTRIE INTO CHARLESTON, S.C. 1861

"It is well that war is so terrible; we would grow too fond of it."
—Robert E. Lee

Union soldiers with a cannon, June 1862

Reading History

 Identifying Cause and Effect

Learn It!

A *cause* is an action or event that makes something happen. What happens as a result is the *effect*.

> **Cause**
> The slavery issue splits the Democratic Party.

> **Effect**
> Northern Democrats nominate Stephen Douglas.

> **Effect**
> Southern Democrats nominate John C. Breckinridge.

—from Chapter 1, p. 21

The issue of slavery split the Democratic Party. The northern Democrats nominated Stephen Douglas. They supported popular sovereignty. Southern Democrats vowed to uphold slavery. Their candidate was John C. Breckinridge.

Practice It!

Read the paragraph and write down the cause and effect(s) on another sheet of paper.

—from Chapter 3, p. 89

In the 1870s, Reconstruction governments created public schools for both races. Within a few years, about 50 percent of white children and 40 percent of African American children in the South were enrolled.

> **Cause**
> _____

> **Effect**
> _____
> _____

> **Effect**
> _____
> _____

Academic Vocabulary Preview

In addition to content vocabulary, you will also find academic vocabulary in this unit. Knowing academic vocabulary will help you understand content that is taught in all of your classes, not just social studies. Learning these words will also help you perform well on tests. Below are the academic vocabulary terms that appear in Unit 1.

Academic Vocabulary	Definition	Practice It!
Chapter 1 Toward Civil War		
temporary (TEHM · puh · REHR · ee) *p. 7*	brief	**Identify** *the term from Chapter 1 that best completes the sentences.*
regulate (REH · gyuh · LAYT) *p. 8*	to control	1. The Underground Railroad was a secret _____ of people opposed to slavery.
network (NEHT · WUHRK) *p. 11*	an interconnected system	
inevitable (ih · NEH · vuh · tuh · buhl) *p. 13*	unavoidable	2. When Southern states seceded from the Union, it signaled the _____ coming of the Civil War.
rigid (RIH · juhd) *p. 16*	firm and inflexible	
topic (TAH · pihk) *p. 18*	a subject of discussion	3. The _____ of slavery was one that divided families as well as the nation.
reject (rih · JEHKT) *p. 22*	to refuse to accept	
justify (JUHS · tuh · FY) *p. 22*	to find reason(s) to support	
Chapter 2 The Civil War		
contrast (kuhn · TRAST) *p. 34*	completely opposite	**Identify** *the term from Chapter 2 that best matches the underlined term or terms.*
challenge (CHA · luhnj) *p. 37*	a demanding situation	
abandon (uh · BAN · duhn) *p. 39*	to leave behind	4. Many women collected food, clothing, and medicine to <u>give out</u> to the troops.
impact (ihm · PAKT) *p. 45*	to effect or influence	
distribute (dih · STRIH · byuht) *p. 51*	to divide and give out	5. A person could avoid the draft by hiring a <u>replacement</u> to serve in his place.
substitute (SUHB · stuh · TOOT) *p. 54*	a replacement	
nevertheless (NEH · vuhr · thuh · LEHS) *p. 59*	however	6. Under attack, Union soldiers decided to <u>leave</u> the fort.
encounter (ihn · KAUN · tuhr) *p. 60*	to come upon; meet	
series (SIHR · eez) *p. 65*	sequence	
interpret (ihn · TUHR · pruht) *p. 67*	to explain the meaning of something	
Chapter 3 Reconstruction and the New South		
radical (RA · dih · kuhl) *p. 78*	extreme	**Choose** *the synonym that best matches the meaning of each vocabulary word listed below.*
adjust (uh · JUHST) *p. 78*	to adapt	

convince (kuhn · VIHNS) *p. 81*	to persuade (someone) that something is true	7. **radical** 9. **suspend**
		    a. method a. believe
		    b. drastic b. eliminate
		    c. envy c. delay

suspend (suh · SPEHND) *p. 84*	to temporarily prevent	

credit (KREH · diht) *p. 88*	extra time to pay for purchased goods	8. **convince** 10. **outcome**
		    a. bother a. conclusion
		    b. believe b. expense
		    c. persuade c. anew

academy (uh · KA · duh · mee) *p. 89*	a school that provides special training	
outcome (AUT · KUHM) *p. 94*	a result	
commission (kuh · MIH · shuhn) *p. 94*	a special group	

Toward Civil War 1840–1861

Confederate forces bombarded Fort Sumter on April 12, 1861. The attack on the fort, located in Charleston Harbor, South Carolina, marked the beginning of the Civil War.

WILLIAM HENRY HARRISON 1841

JOHN TYLER 1841–1845

JAMES POLK 1845–1849

★ 1846 Congress establishes the Smithsonian Institution

ZACHARY TAYLOR 1849–1850

MILLARD FILLMORE 1850–1853

PRESIDENTS

U.S. Events

World Events

1840 — 1845 — 1850

1843 ★ Charles Dickens: *A Christmas Carol* published

1845 ★ Many Irish emigrate to escape famine

1848 ★ Marx publishes *The Communist Manifesto*

History ONLINE
Chapter Overview Visit glencoe.com and click on **Chapter 1—Chapter Overviews** to preview chapter information.

Section 1: Slavery and the West

Essential Question Did the compromises that Congress made effectively address slavery and sectionalism?

Section 2: A Nation Dividing

Essential Question How did popular sovereignty lead to violence in Kansas?

Section 3: Challenges to Slavery

Essential Question What was the significance of the *Dred Scott* decision?

Section 4: Secession and War

Essential Question What role did the theory of states' rights play in the outbreak of the Civil War?

FOLDABLES
Study Organizer

Organizing Information

Make this Foldable to help organize what you learn about events leading up to the Civil War.

Step 1 Fold an 11" x 17" sheet of paper accordion style.

Step 2 Fold the bottom edge up three inches. Glue the edges to make pockets.

Step 3 Label the panels with the section titles as shown. Use the pockets to hold notes taken on index cards.

Reading and Writing As you read the chapter, take notes on key issues and key events in the years leading up to war.

◄ Edwin Drake drills the first oil well near Titusville, Pennsylvania.

FRANKLIN PIERCE 1853–1857

1854 ★
Kansas-Nebraska Act passes

1857 ★
U.S. Supreme Court makes *Dred Scott* decision

JAMES BUCHANAN 1857–1861

1859 ★
The Drake Well becomes first U.S. oil well

1861 ★
Civil War begins

ABRAHAM LINCOLN 1861–1865

1855

1860

1855 ★
Florence Nightingale improves health care during Crimean War

1856 ★
Henry Bessemer introduces process for making steel inexpensively

1861 ★
Alexander II frees serfs in Russia

Slavery and the West

Essential Question ◄

Did the compromises that Congress made effectively address slavery and sectionalism?

Reading Guide

Content Vocabulary

sectionalism *(p. 7)*   secede *(p. 9)*

fugitive *(p. 9)*   abstain *(p. 9)*

Academic Vocabulary

temporary *(p. 7)*   regulate *(p. 8)*

Key People and Events

Missouri Compromise *(p. 7)*

Stephen A. Douglas *(p. 9)*

Compromise of 1850 *(p. 9)*

Reading Strategy

Taking Notes As you read, use a diagram like the one below to describe how two compromises addressed the issue of slavery in new states.

Slavery in New States
- Missouri Compromise:
- Compromise of 1850:

American Diary

When Missouri applied for statehood in 1819, controversy arose in Congress. Slavery was legal in Missouri, and Missouri's admission would change the balance between free states and slave states. The Missouri debate became so bitter that Thomas Jefferson wrote: "This momentous question, like a fire bell in the night, awakened and filled me with terror. I considered it at once as the knell [funeral bell] of the Union."

—letter to John Holmes

A riverboat traveling on the Mississippi River at St. Louis

The Missouri Compromise

Main Idea The Missouri Compromise temporarily resolved the issue of whether new states would be slave states or free states.

History and You Do you feel loyalty to your school during a contest with another school? Read how differences between the North and the South created feelings of loyalty to a region.

. . . .

Many settlers brought enslaved African Americans into Missouri with them. When Missouri applied for statehood, its constitution allowed slavery. The request sparked an angry debate in Congress. In 1819, 11 states permitted slavery and 11 did not. The Senate—with two members from each state—was, therefore, evenly balanced between slave and free states. The admission of a new state would upset that balance.

In addition, the North and the South, with their different economic systems, were competing for new lands in the western territories. At the same time, a growing number of Northerners wanted to restrict or ban slavery. Southerners, even those who disliked slavery, opposed these antislavery efforts. They resented the interference by outsiders in Southerners' affairs. These differences between the North and the South grew into **sectionalism**—an exaggerated loyalty to a particular region of the country.

The Senate suggested a way to resolve the crisis—allow Missouri to join as a slave state and admit Maine at the same time as a free state. Maine, formerly part of Massachusetts, had also applied for statehood. The Senate wanted to settle the issue of slavery in the territories for good. It proposed banning slavery in the rest of the Louisiana Purchase north of 36°30′ N latitude.

Speaker of the House Henry Clay carefully guided the bill through the House of Representatives, which passed it by a close vote in 1820. Maine joined the union that year. In 1821 Missouri became the twenty-fourth state. The **Missouri Compromise** preserved the balance between slave and free states in the Senate. It also brought about a **temporary,** or brief, lull in the debate over slavery.

✓ Reading Check **Explaining** Why was the admission of a new state controversial in 1819?

By the Numbers / The Missouri Compromise

The Vote The map shows how the House of Representatives voted on provisions in a law restricting slavery.

Legend:
- For extending slavery
- Against extending slavery
- Tie vote

N.H., Me., Vt., N.Y., Mass., R.I., Pa., N.J., Conn., Del., Md., Ill., Ind., Ohio, Va., Ky., Tenn., N.C., S.C., Miss., Ala., Ga., La., Fla. Terr., ATLANTIC OCEAN, Gulf of Mexico

40°N, 30°N, 70°W, 80°W, 90°W

0 200 kilometers
0 200 miles
Albers Equal-Area projection

Critical Thinking

Comparing Which region united in favor of extending slavery? Which region opposed extending slavery?

A New Party Forms The acquisition of New Mexico and California brought the slavery issue into the open. Many Southern senators argued that Congress had no constitutional power to forbid slavery in the new territories. In 1848, a new party—the Free-Soil Party—formed. Free-Soilers supported the Wilmot Proviso, which banned the spread of slavery into the new territories gained from Mexico.

▲ The Van Buren-Adams Free-Soil ticket received nearly 300,000 votes in 1848. Later the Republican Party would adopt many principles from the Free-Soil Party.

"Gen. [Zachary] Taylor and Gen. [Lewis] Cass are proslavery candidates. Mr. Van Buren and Mr. Adams are antislavery candidates. The former are the shameless tools of the slave-power. The latter bravely resist it."

—Gerrit Smith, New York abolitionist, August 1848

Critical Thinking

Finding the Main Idea What led to the formation of the Free-Soil Party?

A New Compromise

Main Idea The Compromise of 1850 addressed several issues, including slavery in the territories.

History and You Do you engage in some give and take in order to settle an argument? Read how Congress settled its differences in 1850.

The debate over slavery in new territories erupted again in the 1840s. The annexation of Texas, where slavery already existed, became the main issue in the presidential election of 1844. Democrat James Polk won the election and pressed forward on acquiring Texas. Texas became a state in 1845. At the same time, support grew in the South for taking New Mexico and California from Mexico. Government actions led to war with Mexico.

Conflicting Views

Soon after the Mexican War began, Representative David Wilmot of Pennsylvania introduced a proposal. Called the Wilmot Proviso, it would ban slavery in any lands that might be acquired from Mexico.

Southerners protested. They believed that any antislavery policy about the territories endangered slavery everywhere. They wanted California and New Mexico to remain open to slavery. Senator John C. Calhoun of South Carolina countered with another proposal. It stated that neither Congress nor any territorial government had the authority to ban slavery from a territory or **regulate,** or control, it.

Neither proposal passed, but both caused bitter debate. By the 1848 presidential election, the United States had gained California and New Mexico from Mexico but took no action on slavery in those areas.

The Free-Soil Party

In 1848 the Whigs selected Zachary Taylor, a Southerner and a hero of the Mexican War, as their candidate. The Democrats chose Senator Lewis Cass of Michigan. Both candidates ignored the slavery issue.

This failure to take a stand angered voters. Many opponents of slavery left their parties and formed the Free-Soil Party. Adopting the slogan "Free Soil, Free Speech, Free Labor, and Free Men," they chose former president Martin Van Buren as their candidate. Taylor won, but the Free-Soil Party gained several seats in Congress.

The Compromise of 1850

With the backing of President Taylor, California applied to become a free state in 1849. Meanwhile, antislavery forces wanted to ban slavery in Washington, D.C. Southerners, however, wanted a strong national law that required states to return **fugitive,** or runaway, enslaved people. The key issue, however, remained the balance of power in the Senate. If California entered as a free state, the slave-holding states would be outvoted in the Senate. Southerners talked about **seceding** from, or leaving, the Union.

In 1850 Senator Henry Clay tried to find a compromise. He proposed that California enter as a free state, while the rest of the new territories would have no limits on slavery. In addition, the slave trade, but not slavery itself, would be banned in Washington, D.C. Finally, Clay pushed for a stronger fugitive slave law.

A heated debate began in Congress. Senator Calhoun opposed Clay's plan. He felt that the Union could be saved only by protecting slavery. Senator Daniel Webster supported the plan. He reasoned that slavery had little chance in the new territories because the land was not suited to plantations.

When President Taylor—an opponent of Clay's plan—died unexpectedly, Vice President Millard Fillmore succeeded him and favored a compromise. To end the crisis, Illinois Senator **Stephen A. Douglas** divided Clay's plan into parts that could be voted on separately. Fillmore had several Whigs **abstain,** or not vote, on the parts they opposed. Congress finally passed five bills in 1850. Taken together, these laws became known as the **Compromise of 1850.**

Reading Check **Explaining** Who formed the Free-Soil Party and why?

Section 1 Review

History ONLINE **Study Central™** To review this section, go to glencoe.com.

Vocabulary

1. Use each of the following terms in a sentence that clearly expresses its meaning: sectionalism, temporary, regulate, fugitive, secede, abstain.

Main Ideas

2. Describing How did the Missouri Compromise preserve the balance of power in the U.S. Senate?

3. Explaining How did Stephen Douglas help win approval of the Compromise of 1850?

Critical Thinking

4. Analyzing What was the Wilmot Proviso? Why was this amendment to a bill so controversial?

5. Comparing Describe what the North and South each gained from the Compromise of 1850. Use a diagram like the one below.

Compromise of 1850

North Gains:

South Gains:

6. Creative Writing Write a dialogue in the form of a conversation in which John Calhoun and Daniel Webster express their views on the Compromise of 1850.

Answer the
7. Essential Question Did the compromises that Congress made effectively address slavery and sectionalism?

A Nation Dividing

Essential Question ◄
How did popular sovereignty lead to violence in Kansas?

Reading Guide

Content Vocabulary
popular sovereignty   civil war
  (p. 12)   (p. 13)
border ruffians (p. 13)

Academic Vocabulary
network (p. 11)   inevitable (p. 13)

Key People and Events
Fugitive Slave Act (p. 11)
Kansas-Nebraska Act (p. 12)
John Brown (p. 13)

Reading Strategy
Taking Notes Use a diagram like the one below to note reactions to the Kansas-Nebraska Act. Also, summarize the reasons for these reactions.

Kansas-Nebraska Act	
Antislavery:	Proslavery:

American Diary

On May 24, 1854, the people of Boston erupted in outrage. Federal officers had seized Anthony Burns, a runaway enslaved African American who lived in Boston, to return him to slavery. Abolitionists tried to rescue Burns from the federal courthouse, and city leaders attempted to buy his freedom. All efforts failed. Federal troops escorted Burns to a ship that would carry him back to Virginia and into slavery. In a gesture of bitter protest, Bostonians draped buildings in black and hung the American flag upside down.

The Underground Railroad by James Michael Newell

The Fugitive Slave Act

Main Idea The Fugitive Slave Act required all citizens to help catch runaways, yet many Northerners refused to cooperate.

History and You Have you ever tried to protect someone from a bully? Read how Northerners tried to thwart the efforts of slave hunters.

. . . .

As part of the Compromise of 1850, Senator Henry Clay of Kentucky convinced Congress to pass the **Fugitive Slave Act** as an attempt to pacify slaveholders. The Fugitive Slave Act of 1850 required all citizens to help catch runaways. Anyone who aided a fugitive could be fined or imprisoned. People in the South believed the law would force Northerners to recognize the rights of Southerners. Instead, enforcement of the law convinced more people in the North of the evils of slavery.

After the passage of the Fugitive Slave Act, slaveholders stepped up their efforts to catch runaway enslaved people. They even tried to capture runaways who had lived in freedom in the North for years. Sometimes they seized African Americans who were not trying to escape and forced them into slavery.

History ONLINE

Student Web Activity Visit glencoe.com and complete the Chapter 1 Web Activity about the Underground Railroad.

In spite of the penalties, some Northerners refused to cooperate with the law. They justified their opposition on moral grounds. In his 1849 essay "Civil Disobedience," Henry David Thoreau wrote that if the law "requires you to be the agent [cause] of injustice to another, then I say, break the law."

The Underground Railroad, a **network,** or interconnected system, of free African Americans and whites, helped runaways make their way to freedom. Antislavery groups tried to rescue African Americans who were being pursued or to free those who were captured. In Boston, members of one such group followed federal agents shouting, "Slave hunters—there go the slave hunters." People contributed funds to buy the freedom of African Americans. Northern juries refused to convict those accused of violating the Fugitive Slave Act.

✔ **Reading Check** **Explaining** What was the purpose of the Underground Railroad?

Primary Source / Reward Poster

A poster advertises a substantial reward for a runaway enslaved man.

$150 REWARD

RANAWAY from the subscriber, on the night of the 2d instant, a negro man, who calls himself *Henry May*, about 22 years old, 5 feet 6 or 8 inches high, ordinary color, rather chunky built, bushy head, and has it divided mostly on one side, and keeps it very nicely combed; has been raised in the house, and is a first rate dining-room servant, and was in a tavern in Louisville for 18 months. I expect he is now in Louisville trying to make his escape to a free state, (in all probability to Cincinnati, Ohio.) Perhaps he may try to get employment on a steamboat. He is a good cook, and in any capacity as a house servant. Had on when he left, a dark dark striped cassinett pantaloons, new—he had other reward if taken in Louisvill; 100 dollars if taken out ... State, and 150 dollars if taken out ... that I can get him ... RKI.

Critical Thinking

Making Inferences Under the Fugitive Slave Act of 1850, any citizen might be required to help capture a runaway slave. Why do you think some people condemned this law?

Slavery and Sectionalism

The Compromise of 1850

Oregon Territory
Minnesota Territory
Unorganized Territory
Utah Territory
Calif. (1850)
New Mexico Territory
PACIFIC OCEAN
ATLANTIC OCEAN
0 600 kilometers
MEXICO
Gulf of Mexico
0 600 miles
Albers Equal-Area projection

Kansas-Nebraska Act, 1854

Washington Territory
Oregon Territory
Nebraska Territory
Minnesota Territory
Utah Territory
Kansas Territory
New Mexico Territory
PACIFIC OCEAN
ATLANTIC OCEAN
MEXICO 0 600 kilometers
0 600 miles
Albers Equal-Area projection

Free states
Slave states
Indian Territory
Territory open to slaveholding
Territory closed to slaveholding

◄ Stephen Douglas sponsored the controversial Kansas-Nebraska Act.

Map Skills

Regions What territories were non-slaveholding in 1854?

Maps In Motion See StudentWorks™ Plus or glencoe.com.

The Kansas-Nebraska Act

Main Idea The Kansas-Nebraska Act resulted from another dispute over slavery in Congress.

History and You Do you recall how the Missouri Compromise limited slavery in the territories? Read how this agreement fell apart in the 1850s.

Franklin Pierce, a New Hampshire Democrat, became president in 1853. Pierce intended to enforce the Fugitive Slave Act.

In 1854 Stephen A. Douglas, the Illinois senator who forged the Compromise of 1850, introduced a bill in Congress. He proposed organizing the region west of Missouri and Iowa as the territories of Kansas and Nebraska. Douglas hoped his plan to expand the nation would be acceptable to both the North and the South.

Because of their location, Kansas and Nebraska seemed likely to become free states. Both lay north of 36°30′N latitude, the line set in the Missouri Compromise as the limit of slavery. Douglas knew Southerners would object to admitting Kansas and Nebraska as free states because it would give free states more votes in the Senate. As a result, Douglas proposed abandoning the Missouri Compromise and letting the settlers in each territory vote on whether to allow slavery. He called this **popular sovereignty**—allowing the people to decide.

Passage of the Act

Many Northerners protested. Douglas's plan to repeal the Missouri Compromise would allow slavery into areas that had been free for more than 30 years. Southerners in Congress, however, supported the bill. They expected Kansas to be settled mostly by slaveholders from Missouri who would vote to keep slavery legal. With some support from Northern Democrats and the backing of President Pierce, Congress passed the **Kansas-Nebraska Act** in 1854.

Conflict in Kansas

Right after the law passed, pro-slavery and antislavery groups rushed into Kansas. When elections took place, a pro-slavery legislature was elected.

Although only about 1,500 voters lived in Kansas at the time, more than 6,000 people cast ballots. Thousands of pro-slavery supporters from Missouri crossed the border just to vote in the election. These Missourians traveled in armed groups and became known as **border ruffians.**

Soon, the new Kansas legislature passed laws supporting slavery. One law even restricted political office to pro-slavery candidates.

The antislavery people refused to accept these laws. Instead they armed themselves, held their own elections, and adopted a constitution that banned slavery. By January 1856, rival governments existed in Kansas—one for and one against slavery.

"Bleeding Kansas"

With both sides arming themselves, an outbreak of violence became **inevitable,** or unavoidable. In May 1856, 800 slavery supporters attacked the town of Lawrence, a stronghold of antislavery settlers. The attackers burned the Free State Hotel and destroyed two newspaper offices and many homes. Soon after, antislavery forces retaliated.

John Brown, a fervent abolitionist, believed God chose him to end slavery. The attack on Lawrence enraged Brown. He vowed to "strike terror in the hearts of the pro-slavery people." One night Brown led a group along Pottawatomie Creek, where they seized and killed five supporters of slavery.

Armed bands soon roamed the territory. Newspapers referred to "Bleeding Kansas" and "the Civil War in Kansas." A **civil war** is a conflict between citizens of the same country. In October 1856 the territorial governor sent federal troops to stop the bloodshed.

Violence also broke out in Congress. Senator Charles Sumner of Massachusetts lashed out against pro-slavery forces in Kansas. He also criticized pro-slavery senators, such as Andrew P. Butler of South Carolina. Two days later, Butler's cousin, Representative Preston Brooks, walked into the Senate chamber and hit Sumner with a cane. Sumner fell to the floor, unconscious and bleeding. This incident and the Kansas feud revealed the rising hostility between North and South.

✔ **Reading Check** **Explaining** What events led to "Bleeding Kansas"?

History ONLINE
Study Central™ To review this section, go to glencoe.com.

Section 2 Review

Vocabulary

1. Use each of these terms in a sentence that will help explain its meaning: network, popular sovereignty, border ruffians, inevitable, civil war.

Main Ideas

2. Listing What were some ways that Northerners defied the Fugitive Slave Act?

3. Explaining How would the issue of slavery in Kansas and Nebraska be decided under the Kansas-Nebraska Act?

Critical Thinking

4. Contrasting How did Southerners expect Northerners to react to the Fugitive Slave Act? How did Northerners actually react?

5. Sequencing Use a diagram like the one below to list the steps leading to bloodshed in Kansas.

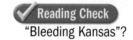

Step → Step → Step → **Bloodshed in Kansas**

6. Persuasive Writing Decide whether you would have been for or against the Kansas-Nebraska Act and the concept of popular sovereignty. Then write a newspaper editorial arguing your position.

Answer the

7. Essential Question
How did popular sovereignty lead to violence in Kansas?

Challenges to Slavery

Reading Guide

Content Vocabulary

arsenal *(p. 19)*   martyr *(p. 19)*

Academic Vocabulary

rigid *(p. 16)*   topic *(p. 18)*

Key People and Events

Republican Party *(p. 15)*

John C. Frémont *(p. 15)*

James Buchanan *(p. 15)*

Dred Scott *(p. 16)*

Abraham Lincoln *(p. 18)*

Reading Strategy

Taking Notes As you read, use a diagram like the one below to note each party's candidate and platform in the 1856 presidential election. Also record the election result.

Republican:	Platform:
Democrat:	Platform:
American Party:	Platform:

Election Result:

American Diary

A few years after the attacks in Kansas, John Brown led a raid in Harpers Ferry, Virginia. Many people considered Brown and his followers to be ruthless murderers. The Fredericksburg Herald declared that, "shooting is a mercy they should be denied." Others viewed Brown as a freedom fighter. When Brown was executed in 1859, writer Henry David Thoreau wrote, "He is not Old Brown any longer, [but] an angel of light."

—quoted in "John Brown at Harpers Ferry" and from Thoreau's "A Plea for Capt. John Brown"

John Brown leaving Charleston jail on his way to his execution

A New Political Party

Main Idea Opponents of slavery from different political parties came together to form the new Republican Party.

History and You Which of today's political issues is most important to your family? Read to learn how the parties stood on key issues of the 1854 and 1856 elections.

· ·

Even before Brown's raid, other events drove the North and South further apart. After the Kansas-Nebraska Act, the Democratic Party began to divide along sectional lines, with Northern Democrats leaving the party. Differing views over the slavery issue destroyed the Whig Party.

The Election of 1854

In 1854 additional antislavery Whigs and Democrats joined forces with Free-Soilers to form the **Republican Party.** The Republicans challenged the pro-slavery Whigs and Democrats, choosing candidates to run in the state and congressional elections of 1854. Their main message was that the government should ban slavery from new territories. The Republican Party quickly showed its strength in the North. In the election, the Republicans won control of the House of Representatives and of several state governments. In the South, the Republican Party had almost no support.

Almost three-fourths of the Democratic candidates from free states lost in 1854. The Democrats were increasingly becoming a Southern party.

The Election of 1856

Democrats and Republicans met again in the presidential election of 1856. The Whig Party, disintegrating over the slavery issue, did not offer a candidate of its own.

The Republicans chose **John C. Frémont** of California as their candidate for president. Frémont gained fame as an explorer in the West. The party platform called for free territories, and its campaign slogan became "Free soil, Free speech, and Frémont."

The Democratic Party nominated **James Buchanan** of Pennsylvania, an experienced diplomat and former member of Congress. Buchanan wanted to appease the South in order to save the Union. As a result, the party endorsed the idea of popular sovereignty.

Primary Source / **Hero or Villain?**

Views of John Brown Some Northerners regarded John Brown as a hero. In a letter to Brown, a free African American in Indiana wrote: "I thank you that you have been brave enough to reach out your hands to the crushed and blighted of my race." A Southern newspaper, however, wrote: "The miserable old traitor and murderer belongs to the gallows, and the gallows will have its own."

Critical Thinking

Evaluating In what ways might a Northerner and a Southerner view John Brown's actions differently?

The Election of 1856

NATIONAL GEOGRAPHIC

Map Legend:
- Buchanan (Democratic)
- Frémont (Republican)
- Fillmore (American/Know Nothing)

Candidate	Popular Vote (%)	Electoral Vote (%)
Buchanan	1,838,169 (45%)	174 (59%)
Frémont	1,341,264 (33%)	114 (38%)
Fillmore	874,534 (22%)	8 (3%)

▲ Third-party candidate Fillmore appealed to voters concerned about immigration and Catholicism.

Democrats stressed that Buchanan was the candidate of conciliation and stability and believed that a Frémont victory would lead to civil war. ▶

Northern States for Buchanan The presidential election of 1856 was decided in the swing states of Pennsylvania, Illinois, and Indiana. Democratic candidate James Buchanan won all three. Only 1,200 of Republican John Frémont's 1.34 million popular votes came from slaveholding states.

The Republican ticket of John C. Frémont and William L. Dayton opposed slavery's expansion into the territories. ▶

JAMES BUCHANAN, DEMOCRATIC CANDIDATE FOR PRESIDENT OF THE UNITED STATES.

Map Skills

Regions In which region was Frémont most successful? Which states in that area did he not win?

Maps In Motion See StudentWorks™ Plus or glencoe.com.

The American Party, or Know Nothings, grew quickly between 1853 and 1856 by attacking immigrants. The Know Nothings nominated former president Millard Fillmore. Most of the Northern delegates, however, walked out of the convention when the party refused to call for the repeal of the Kansas-Nebraska Act.

The presidential vote divided along **rigid**—firm and inflexible—sectional lines. Buchanan won the election. He took all Southern states except Maryland and received 174 electoral votes compared to 114 for Frémont and 8 for Fillmore. Frémont did not receive a single electoral vote south of the Mason-Dixon line, but he carried 11 of the 16 free states.

✓ **Reading Check** **Identifying** Which political party was emerging as the party of the South in the 1854 and 1856 elections?

The *Dred Scott* Case

Main Idea The Supreme Court's decision in the *Dred Scott* case dealt a severe blow to antislavery forces and further divided the country.

History and You How would you feel if the Supreme Court decided that you were "property"? Read to find out how the decision in the *Dred Scott* case shocked the nation.

· ·

Dred **Scott** was an enslaved African American bought by an army doctor in Missouri, a slave state. In the 1830s, the doctor moved his household to Illinois, a free state, and then to the Wisconsin Territory, where slavery was banned by the Northwest Ordinance of 1787. Later the family returned to Missouri, where the doctor died. In 1846, with the help of antislavery lawyers, Scott sued for his freedom.

Scott claimed he should be free because he once lived in areas of the North where slavery was prohibited.

Eleven years later, as anger grew over the slavery issue, the case reached the Supreme Court. The case attracted enormous attention across the country. While the immediate issue was Dred Scott's status, the Court also had the opportunity to rule on the question of slavery in the territories.

The Court's Decision

The Court's decision electrified the nation. Chief Justice Roger B. Taney (TAW•nee) said that Dred Scott was still an enslaved person. As such, Scott was not a citizen and had no right to bring a lawsuit. Taney continued on, addressing broader issues.

Taney wrote that Scott's residence on free soil did not make him free. An enslaved person was property, and the Fifth Amendment prohibits Congress from taking away property without "due process of law."

Finally, Taney wrote that Congress had no power to prohibit slavery in any territory. The Missouri Compromise—which banned slavery north of 36°30′N latitude—was unconstitutional. For that matter, so was popular sovereignty. Not even the voters in a territory could prohibit slavery because that would amount to taking away a person's property. In effect, the decision meant that the Constitution protected slavery.

Reaction to the Decision

Rather than settling the issue, the decision divided the country even more. The Court upheld what many in the South had always maintained: Nothing could legally stop the spread of slavery. The Republicans' main issue—limiting the spread of slavery—was ruled unconstitutional.

Republicans and other antislavery groups were outraged. They called the *Dred Scott* decision "a wicked and false judgment" and "the greatest crime" ever committed in the nation's courts.

✓ **Reading Check** Applying Based on the *Dred Scott* decision, could voters ban slavery? Explain.

Primary Source | The *Dred Scott* Decision

A Controversial Ruling In his ruling in the *Dred Scott* case, Chief Justice Roger B. Taney declared the Missouri Compromise unconstitutional because it deprived slaveholders of their property without due process or compensation. Southerners praised the decision, which opened all U.S. territory to slavery.

Supreme Court Chief Justice Roger B. Taney ▶

◀ Newspaper announcing the *Dred Scott* decision

"They [African Americans] had for more than a century before been regarded as beings of an inferior order and altogether unfit to associate with the white race . . . and so far inferior that they had no rights which the white man was bound to respect. . . . No one . . . should induce the Court to give to the words of the Constitution a more liberal construction in their favor than they were intended to bear when the instrument was framed and adopted."

—Roger Taney, *Dred Scott* v. *Sandford* decision, March 1857

▲ The Old Courthouse in St. Louis where the *Dred Scott* case was heard

Critical Thinking

Assessing How do you think the *Dred Scott* decision affected sectional tensions in the country?

A Raid to Fight Slavery John Brown gained notoriety fighting against pro-slavery forces in Kansas in the mid-1850s. Financed by wealthy abolitionists, Brown led a raid in 1859 to capture the federal arsenal at Harpers Ferry, Virginia. Brown hoped to use the weapons at the arsenal to spark an uprising by enslaved people in Virginia.

John Brown and his men barricaded themselves in this brick engine house to fight off attacks from federal troops. ▼

"Now if . . . I should forfeit my life for the furtherance of the ends of justice and MINGLE MY BLOOD . . . with the blood of millions in this slave country whose rights are disregarded by wicked, cruel, and unjust enactments—I submit; so LET IT BE DONE."

—John Brown's statement to the Virginia Court

▲ Federal troops commanded by Colonel Robert E. Lee crushed Brown's raid. More than half of Brown's force, including two of his sons, died in the fighting. Brown and his surviving men were captured and Brown was later hanged.

Critical Thinking

Drawing Conclusions Was the raid on Harpers Ferry a success for abolitionists? Why or why not?

Lincoln and Douglas

Main Idea The Lincoln-Douglas debates placed the little-known Lincoln into the national spotlight.

History and You Do you like to root for the underdog? Read how Abraham Lincoln skillfully debated against the powerful Stephen Douglas.
· ·

In the congressional election of 1858, the Senate race in Illinois was the center of national attention. The contest pitted the current senator, Democrat Stephen A. Douglas, against Republican challenger **Abraham Lincoln.** People considered Douglas a likely candidate for president in 1860. Lincoln was nearly an unknown.

Douglas, a successful lawyer, joined the Democratic Party and won election to the House in 1842 and to the Senate in 1846. Short, stocky, and powerful, Douglas was called "the Little Giant." He disliked slavery but thought that the controversy over it would interfere with the nation's growth. He believed the issue could be resolved through popular sovereignty.

Born in the poor backcountry of Kentucky, Abraham Lincoln moved to Indiana as a child, and later to Illinois. Like Douglas, Lincoln was intelligent, ambitious, and a successful lawyer. He had little formal education—but excellent political skills. He had served in the Illinois legislature and in the U.S. House of Representatives. Lincoln saw slavery as morally wrong but admitted there was no easy way to end slavery where it existed. He was certain, though, that slavery should not be allowed to spread.

The Lincoln-Douglas Debates

Not as well-known as Douglas, Lincoln challenged the senator to a series of debates. Douglas reluctantly agreed. The two met seven times in August, September, and October of 1858 in cities and villages throughout Illinois. Thousands came to these debates. The main **topic,** or subject of discussion, was slavery.

During the debate at Freeport, Lincoln pressed Douglas about his views on popular sovereignty. Could the people of a territory legally exclude slavery before becoming a state? Douglas replied that the people could exclude slavery by refusing to pass laws protecting slaveholders' rights. Douglas's response, which satisfied antislavery followers but lost him support in the South, became known as the Freeport Doctrine.

Douglas claimed that Lincoln wanted African Americans to be fully equal to whites. Lincoln denied this. Still, Lincoln said, "in the right to eat the bread . . . which his own hand earns, [an African American] is my equal and the equal of [Senator] Douglas, and the equal of every living man." The real issue, Lincoln said, is "between the men who think slavery a wrong and those who do not think it wrong. The Republican Party think it wrong."

Following the debates, Douglas won a narrow victory in the election. Lincoln lost the election but did not come away empty-handed. He gained a national reputation as a man of clear thinking who could argue with force and persuasion.

The Raid on Harpers Ferry

After the 1858 election, Southerners felt threatened by Republicans. In late 1859, an act of violence added to their fears. On October 16 the abolitionist John Brown led a group on a raid on Harpers Ferry, Virginia. His target was an **arsenal,** a storage site for weapons. Brown hoped to arm enslaved African Americans and start a revolt against slaveholders. Abolitionists had paid for the raid.

Brown's raid was defeated by local citizens and federal troops. Convicted of treason and murder, Brown was sentenced to hang. His execution shook the North. Some antislavery Northerners denounced Brown's use of violence. Others saw Brown as a **martyr**—a person who dies for a great cause.

John Brown's death rallied abolitionists. When Southerners learned of Brown's abolitionist ties, their fears of a great Northern conspiracy against them seemed to be confirmed. The nation was on the brink of disaster.

Reading Check **Identifying** Why did John Brown raid the arsenal at Harpers Ferry?

Section 3 Review

History ONLINE
Study Central™ To review this section, go to glencoe.com.

Vocabulary

1. Define each of the following terms, and use each in a sentence: rigid, topic, arsenal, martyr.

Main Ideas

2. Specifying What issue led to the formation of the Republican Party, and what stand did the new party take on that issue?

3. Explaining What reasons did Taney give for Dred Scott's status as an enslaved person?

4. Identifying How did the Lincoln-Douglas debates benefit Lincoln?

Critical Thinking

5. Identifying Points of View Use a diagram like the one below to compare the views of Lincoln and Douglas on the issue of slavery.

6. Making Inferences Why do you think the raid on Harpers Ferry by a mere 18 men seemed so threatening to Southerners?

7. Persuasive Writing Write a rebuttal, or response, to Roger B. Taney on the *Dred Scott* decision. Address the points he made in his remarks on the Court's decision.

Answer the
8. Essential Question

What was the significance of the *Dred Scott* decision?

Essential Question ◄

What role did the theory of states' rights play in the outbreak of the Civil War?

Reading Guide

Content Vocabulary

secession *(p. 21)*   states' rights *(p. 22)*

Academic Vocabulary

reject *(p. 22)*   justify *(p. 22)*

Key People and Events

John Crittenden *(p. 21)*
Confederate States of America *(p. 22)*
Jefferson Davis *(p. 22)*
Fort Sumter *(p. 24)*

Reading Strategy

Taking Notes As you read, list the major events on a time line like the one below.

| Nov. 1860 | Feb. 1861 | April 1861 |

| Dec. 1860 | March 1861 |

American Diary

The events at Harpers Ferry inflamed slaveholders. In 1859 the Charleston Mercury *declared "The day of compromise is passed. . . . There is no peace for the South in the Union." Republicans argued that the South leaving the Union was a tactic to frighten voters from casting their ballots for Abraham Lincoln. To many Southerners, however, Lincoln's election would signal that their position in the Union was hopeless.*

—*from the* **Charleston Mercury**

The Wigwam in Chicago was the site of the 1860 Republican Convention.

Secession

Main Idea Fearing that President Lincoln would not protect Southern rights, first South Carolina and then other states voted to leave the Union.

History and You Have you ever been so angry that you needed to leave a room? Read to learn about the South's decision to secede.

. . . .

Would the Union break up? That was the burning question as the presidential election of November 1860 approached.

The Election of 1860

The issue of slavery split the Democratic Party. The northern Democrats nominated Stephen Douglas. They supported popular sovereignty. Southern Democrats vowed to uphold slavery. Their candidate was John C. Breckinridge. Moderates from the North and the South who formed the Constitutional Union Party chose John Bell. This party took no position on slavery.

The Republicans nominated Abraham Lincoln. Their platform was that slavery should be left undisturbed where it existed, but that it should be excluded from the territories.

Many Southerners feared, however, that a Republican victory would encourage slave revolts.

With the Democrats divided, Lincoln won a clear majority of the electoral votes. The vote was along purely sectional lines. Lincoln's name did not even appear on the ballot in most Southern states, but he won every Northern state. In effect, the more populous North outvoted the South.

Attempt at Compromise

The Republicans promised not to disturb slavery where it already existed. Many Southerners, though, did not trust the Republican Party to protect their rights. On December 20, 1860, South Carolina voted to secede from the Union.

As other Southern states debated the question of **secession,** or withdrawal from the Union, leaders in Congress worked frantically to fashion a compromise. Senator **John Crittenden** of Kentucky proposed a series of amendments to the Constitution. Central to his plan was a provision to protect slavery south of 36°30′N latitude—the line set by the Missouri Compromise—in all territories "now held or hereafter acquired."

Primary Source | **Secession Ribbon**

Supporting Separation *Secession* means "separation from the Union." Some Southerners wore ribbons like this one to show their support for separating from the United States. The words on the ribbon are mottoes, or well-known expressions, from the American Revolution.

PALMETTO

LIBERTY OR DEATH!

DON'T TREAD ON ME

Critical Thinking

Analyzing What did the mottoes mean during the American Revolution? Why do you think secessionists used these mottoes?

This cartoon was created in 1861, just before the outbreak of the Civil War. Secession was breaking up the United States.

1. **Interpreting** What do the men in the cartoon represent?

2. **Analyzing** Look at each person's expression. How would you describe their expressions?

3. **Identifying Points of View** What does the cartoonist think will result from the men's action?

SECESSIONISTS LEAVING THE UNION

Republicans **rejected,** or refused to accept, this provision. They had just won an election on the principle that slavery would not be extended in any territories. "Now we are told . . ." Lincoln wrote, "the government shall be broken up unless we surrender to those we have beaten." Leaders in the South also rejected the plan. "We spit upon every plan to compromise," exclaimed one Southern leader. "No human power can save the Union," wrote another.

The Confederacy

By February 1861, Texas, Louisiana, Mississippi, Alabama, Florida, and Georgia joined South Carolina and also seceded. On February 4, delegates from these states and South Carolina met to form a new nation. Calling themselves the **Confederate States of America,** they chose **Jefferson Davis** as their president.

Southerners **justified,** or found reasons to support, secession with the theory of **states' rights.** The states, they argued, had voluntarily chosen to enter the Union. They defined the Constitution as a contract among the independent states. They believed the national government violated that contract by refusing to enforce the Fugitive Slave Act and by denying the Southern states equal rights in the territories. As a result, they argued, the states had a right to leave the Union.

Reactions to Secession

Many Southerners welcomed secession, ringing church bells and celebrating in the streets. Other Southerners, however, were alarmed. Virginian Robert E. Lee expressed concern about the future. "I only see that a fearful calamity is upon us," he wrote.

In the North, some abolitionists preferred to allow the Southern states to leave. If the Union could be kept together only by compromising on slavery, they declared, then let the Union be destroyed. Most Northerners, however, believed that the Union must be preserved. For Lincoln the issue was "whether in a free government the minority have the right to break up the government whenever they choose."

Lincoln Takes Office

Lincoln had won the election, but he was not yet president. James Buchanan's term ran until March 4, 1861. In December 1860, Buchanan sent a message to Congress saying that the Southern states had no right to secede from the Union. Then he added that he had no power to stop them from doing so.

As Lincoln prepared for his inauguration on March 4, 1861, people throughout the United States wondered what he would say and do. They wondered, too, what would happen in Virginia, North Carolina, Kentucky, Tennessee, Missouri, and Arkansas. These slave states chose to remain in the Union, but the decision was not final. If the United States used force against the Confederate States of America, the remaining slave states also might secede.

In his Inaugural Address, Lincoln spoke to the seceding states directly, mixing tough-ness with words of peace. He said that secession would not be permitted, that "the Union of these States is perpetual [forever]." He vowed to hold federal property in the South, including a number of forts and military installations, and to enforce the laws of the United States. At the same time, Lincoln pleaded with the South:

PRIMARY SOURCE

"In your hands, my dissatisfied fellow countrymen, and not in mine, are the momentous issues of *civil war*. The Government will not assail you. You can have no conflict without being yourselves the aggressors. . . . We are not *enemies*, but *friends*. We must not be enemies. Though passion may have strained, it must not break our bonds of affection."

—Abraham Lincoln, on reconciliation

Reading Check **Explaining** What was John Crittenden's proposal to save the Union?

Seceding States, 1860–1861

NATIONAL GEOGRAPHIC

West Virginia separated from Virginia in 1861 and was admitted to the Union in 1863.

Jefferson Davis ▶

On February 4, 1861, delegates met in Alabama to form a new nation.

South Carolina was the first state to secede from the Union.

Lambert Azimuthal Equal-Area projection

0 — 600 kilometers
0 — 600 miles

Legend:
- Union territories
- Union free state
- Union slave state
- Slave state seceding before siege of Ft. Sumter, April 1861
- Slave state seceding after siege of Ft. Sumter, April 1861
- Boundary between Union & Confederacy

Map Skills

1. **Regions** Which states seceded before the attack on Fort Sumter?

2. **Regions** Which states did not secede until after the attack on Fort Sumter?

Maps In Motion See StudentWorks™ Plus or glencoe.com.

Fort Sumter

Main Idea The Civil War began when Confederate forces attacked Fort Sumter in South Carolina.

History and You Have you ever argued with a family member over an item that you each felt you owned? Read to learn about events at Fort Sumter.

. . . .

Confederate forces had already seized some U.S. forts within their states. Although Lincoln did not want to start a war by trying to take the forts back, allowing the Confederates to keep them would amount to admitting their right to secede.

The day after taking office, Lincoln received a message from the commander of **Fort Sumter,** a U.S. fort on an island guarding Charleston Harbor. The message warned that the fort was low on supplies and the Confederates demanded its surrender.

Lincoln responded by sending a message to Governor Francis Pickens of South Carolina. He informed Pickens that he was sending an unarmed expedition with supplies to Fort Sumter. Lincoln promised that Union forces would not "throw in men, arms, or ammunition" unless they were fired upon. The president thus left the decision to start shooting up to the Confederates.

Jefferson Davis made a fateful choice. He ordered his forces to attack Fort Sumter before the Union supplies could arrive. Confederate guns opened fire early on April 12, 1861. Union captain Abner Doubleday witnessed the attack from inside the fort:

PRIMARY SOURCE

"Showers of balls . . . and shells . . . poured into the fort in one incessant stream, causing great flakes of masonry to fall in all directions."

—quoted in *Fort Sumter*

High seas kept Union relief ships from reaching the fort. Fort Sumter surrendered on April 14. Thousands of shots were fired during the siege, but there was no loss of life.

President Lincoln issued a call for troops, and volunteers quickly signed up. Meanwhile, Virginia, North Carolina, Tennessee, and Arkansas voted to join the Confederacy. The Civil War had begun.

Reading Check **Explaining** Why did Lincoln decide not to send armed troops to Fort Sumter?

Section 4 Review

History ONLINE
Study Central™ To review this section, go to glencoe.com.

Vocabulary

1. Use each of the following vocabulary terms in a sentence that will help explain its meaning: secession, reject, justify, states' rights.

Main Ideas

2. **Specifying** What action did South Carolina take after Lincoln won the election of 1860? Why?

3. **Explaining** What was the significance of the attack on Fort Sumter?

Critical Thinking

4. **Drawing Conclusions** How would you describe President Lincoln's priorities as he took office in March 1861?

5. **Sequencing** In a diagram like the one below, trace the events leading to the surrender of Fort Sumter.

Fort Sumter surrenders

6. **Descriptive Writing** Imagine that you are a Confederate journalist. Write a brief announcement about the attack on Fort Sumter for your newspaper. Then write another brief announcement of the event—this time from a Union journalist's point of view.

Answer the
7. **Essential Question**
What role did the theory of states' rights play in the outbreak of the Civil War?

1848–1854

1848 The Free-Soil Party forms to oppose slavery in territories.

Van Buren-Adams poster, 1848 ▶

1850

- The Compromise of 1850 temporarily eases debate on slavery in Congress.
- The Fugitive Slave Act stirs up antislavery feelings in North.

1854

- The Kansas-Nebraska Act declares popular sovereignty in territories.
- Missouri voters help elect pro-slavery legislature in Kansas.
- The Republican Party forms as antislavery party.

1855–1859

1856

Jan. Kansas antislavery forces set up a rival government.

May Slavery supporters unleash violence in Kansas.

Oct. Federal troops are sent to end violence in "Bleeding Kansas."

1857 The *Dred Scott* decision rules that slavery is protected by the Constitution.

1858 Lincoln-Douglas debates focus on slavery and give Lincoln national recognition.

1859

Oct. John Brown raids Harpers Ferry arsenal uniting abolitionists.

1860–1861

1860

Nov. Lincoln is elected president.

Dec. South Carolina secedes; other Southern states follow.

1861

Feb. Southern states form Confederate States of America.

March Lincoln speaks of preserving the Union and preventing war in his Inaugural Address.

April The Confederate attack on Fort Sumter begins the Civil War.

▲ Confederate attack on Fort Sumter

◀ Fighting at Harpers Ferry

STUDY TO GO Study anywhere, anytime! Download quizzes and flash cards to your PDA from <u>glencoe.com</u>.

Did the South Have the Right to Secede?

Building Background

When Abraham Lincoln was inaugurated to his first term as president, on March 4, 1861, the unfinished Capitol dome seemed to reflect the uncertain future of the United States. Seven Southern states had already voted to secede from the Union and form the Confederate States of America.

The Confederate president, Jefferson Davis, had been inaugurated earlier, on February 18. Each man's inauguration address presented a different view on the basic question of whether a state had the right to secede from the Union.

Abraham Lincoln's first inauguration, March 4, 1861

NO

ABRAHAM LINCOLN

One section of our country believes slavery is right and ought to be extended, while the other believes it is wrong and ought not to be extended. This is the only substantial dispute. . . .

The [President] derives all his authority from the people, and they have referred none upon him to fix terms for the separation of the States. The people themselves can do this if also they choose, but the Executive as such has nothing to do with it. His duty is to administer[1] the present Government as it came to his hands and to transmit it unimpaired[2] by him to his successor. . . .

We are not enemies, but friends. We must not be enemies. Though passion may have strained it must not break our bonds of affection. The mystic chords of memory, stretching from every battlefield and patriot grave to every living heart and hearthstone all over this broad land, will yet swell the chorus of the Union, when again touched, as surely they will be, by the better angels of our nature.

---

[1] **administer** manage
[2] **unimpaired** unharmed

YES

JEFFERSON DAVIS

An agricultural people, whose chief interest is the export of a commodity required in every manufacturing country, our true policy is peace, and the freest trade which our necessities will permit. . . . There can be but little rivalry between ours and any manufacturing or navigating community, such as the Northeastern States of the American Union. It must follow, therefore, that a mutual interest would invite good will and kind offices. If, however, passion or the lust of dominion[3] should cloud the judgment or inflame the ambition of those States, we must prepare to meet the emergency and to maintain, by the final arbitrament[4] of the sword, the position which we have assumed among the nations of the earth. We have entered upon the career of independence, and it must be inflexibly pursued. . . . As a necessity, not a choice, we have resorted to the remedy of separation; and henceforth our energies must be directed to the conduct of our own affairs, and the perpetuity[5] of the Confederacy which we have formed.

---

[3] **dominion** territory

[4] **arbitrament** power to decide

[5] **perpetuity** lasting life

DBQ Document-Based Questions

1. **Identifying** What are Abraham Lincoln's and Jefferson Davis's basic arguments against or in favor of secession?

2. **Making Inferences** What issue seems most important to Lincoln? To Davis?

3. **Analyzing** Did either president refer to the economies of the different regions? If so, how were they described?

4. **Evaluating** In your opinion, which of the two addresses makes the more powerful appeal to emotions? Explain your answer in a short essay.

Jefferson Davis's inauguration in Montgomery, Alabama, February 18, 1861

Chapter 1 Assessment

STANDARDIZED TEST PRACTICE

Reviewing Main Ideas

Directions: Choose the best answer for each of the following questions.

1. Which of the following was a proposal to ban slavery in any lands acquired from Mexico?

   A Compromise of 1850

   B Wilmot Proviso

   C Missouri Compromise

   D Freeport Doctrine

2. What resulted from the Fugitive Slave Act?

   A Passage of the law quieted widespread violence in Kansas and Nebraska.

   B Most Northerners believed Southern slaveholders' rights should be upheld.

   C Abolitionists were jailed in the North.

   D The law angered the North, convincing many of the evils of slavery.

3. The Supreme Court's decision in the *Dred Scott* case stated that

   A enslaved persons could bring lawsuits.

   B Congress had no power to prohibit slavery in any territory.

   C the slave trade should be abolished.

   D the Missouri Compromise was constitutional.

4. Which was included in the Republican Party platform of the election of 1860?

   A The question of slavery should be decided by popular sovereignty.

   B In a free society, the minority has the right to break up the government.

   C Slavery should be left where it existed but be excluded from the territories.

   D Slavery should be protected in all territories south of 36°30′N latitude.

Short-Answer Question

Directions: Base your answer to question 5 on the political cartoon below and on your knowledge of social studies.

SOUTHERN CHIVALRY — ARGUMENT versus CLUB'S.

Source: Bettmann/CORBIS

5. This cartoon shows the attack on Massachusetts Senator Charles Sumner in the Senate chamber. What emotions might the event in this cartoon have stirred up in the North and in the South?

Review the Essential Questions

6. **Essay** Describe the various attempts to find a compromise between the demands of the North and the South.

To help you write your essay, review your answers to the Essential Questions in the section reviews and the chapter Foldables Study Organizer. Your essay should include:

- the compromises Congress made regarding sectionalism and slavery; and
- reactions by antislavery and pro-slavery forces.

GO ON

History ONLINE

For additional test practice, use **Self-Check Quizzes**—Chapter 1 at <u>glencoe.com</u>.

Document-Based Questions

Directions: Analyze the documents and answer the short-answer questions that follow.

Document 1

In this passage, Erastus D. Ladd describes voters from Missouri crossing the border to vote in an 1855 election in Kansas.

> They claimed to have a legal right to vote in the Territory [Kansas], and that they were residents by virtue of their being then in the Territory. They said they were free to confess that they came from Missouri; that they lived in Missouri, and voted as Missourians.

Source: Albert Bushnell Hart, *Source-Book of American History*

7. Were the actions of these voters legal? How did the voters from Missouri justify voting in Kansas?

Document 2

This is an excerpt from a speech by Georgia congressperson Robert Toombs in 1849.

> I do not . . . hesitate to avow [admit] before this House and the country, and in the presence of the living God, that if by your legislation you seek to drive us from the territories of California and New Mexico, purchased by the common blood and treasure of the whole people, and to abolish slavery in this District, thereby attempting to fix a national degradation [shame] upon half the States of this Confederacy, I am for disunion.

Source: Representative Robert Toombs of Georgia, 1849

8. Based on the excerpt, do you think Toombs favored or opposed the legalization of slavery in California and New Mexico? On what did Toombs base his views?

Document 3

In this passage from 1851, Richard Henry Dana, Jr., speaks of the Fugitive Slave Act of 1850.

> If the law were constitutional, which I firmly believe it is not, it would be the duty of a citizen not to resist it by force, unless he was prepared for revolution and civil war; but we rejoice in the escape of a victim of an unjust law as we would in the escape of an ill-treated captive deer or bird.

Source: Charles Francis Adams, *Richard Henry Dana*

9. Suppose Dana was a member of a jury during a trial of someone accused of breaking the Fugitive Slave Act. Based on the passage, do you think he would find the accused guilty or not guilty? Why?

Document 4

This is a campaign ribbon from the 1856 presidential election.

FREMONT AND DAYTON.

Source: David J. & Janice L. Frent Collection/CORBIS

10. Does this ribbon support or oppose John C. Frémont for president? Explain.

11. Expository Writing Using the information from the four documents and your knowledge of social studies, write an essay in which you:

- identify ways Northerners and Southerners appealed to emotion *and* to legal arguments to justify their positions; and

- explain which type of argument you find most persuasive, and why.

Need Extra Help?											
If you missed questions. . .	1	2	3	4	5	6	7	8	9	10	11
Go to page. . .	8	11	16–17	21	13	6–24	12–13	9	11	15–16	6–24

The Civil War
1861–1865

Civil War: First at Vicksburg, 1863 by H. Charles McBarron, Jr.

PRESIDENTS

ABRAHAM LINCOLN

U.S. Events

World Events

1861 ★ **1861**
Conflict at Fort Sumter, South Carolina, begins Civil War

1861
Robert E. Lee named commander of Confederate armies

1861

★ **1861**
• Russia emancipates serfs
• First ironclad warship completed in England

1862

★ **1862**
International Red Cross established; American Red Cross organized 10 years later

Section 1: The Two Sides

Essential Question What were the strengths and weaknesses of the North and the South?

Section 2: Early Stages of the War

Essential Question Why did neither the Union nor the Confederacy gain a strong advantage during the early years of the war?

Section 3: Life During the War

Essential Question What social, political, and economic changes resulted from the war?

Section 4: The Strain of War

Essential Question How did the events at Gettysburg and Vicksburg change the course of the war?

Section 5: The War's Final Stages

Essential Question What events led to the end of the war?

FOLDABLES® Study Organizer

Organizing Information
Make this Foldable to help organize what you learn about the Civil War.

Step 1 Fold a sheet of paper in half from side to side.

Fold it so the left edge lies about $\frac{1}{2}$ inch from the right edge.

Step 2 Turn the paper and fold it into thirds.

This will make three tabs.

Step 3 Unfold and cut the top layer only along both folds.

Step 4 Label your Foldable as shown.

Before the War | During the War | After the War
The Civil War

Reading and Writing As you read the chapter, list events that occurred before, during, and after the Civil War under the appropriate tabs of your Foldable.

1863
- Emancipation Proclamation issued
- Grant named commander of Union armies

1864
Sherman's March to the Sea begins

ANDREW JOHNSON

1865
Civil War ends

1863

1864

1865

1863
London subway opens

1864
First Geneva Convention establishes rules for treatment of prisoners of war

1865
French writer Jules Verne publishes a novel about a trip to the moon

The Two Sides

Essential Question ◄
What were the strengths and weaknesses of the North and the South?

Reading Guide

Content Vocabulary

border state *(p. 33)* export *(p. 35)*
blockade *(p. 35)*

Academic Vocabulary

contrast *(p. 34)* challenge *(p. 37)*

Key People and Events

Abraham Lincoln *(p. 33)*
Anaconda Plan *(p. 35)*

Reading Strategy

Taking Notes As you read, take notes on the differences and similarities between the two sides.

North   South

American Diary

At the Battle of Malvern Hill in 1862, a Union sergeant named Driscoll shot a young Confederate soldier. Hurrying forward, Driscoll turned the soldier's face up to see if the young man was dead. But when he looked at the dying soldier's face, he received a terrible shock. Looking up, the boy murmured, "Father," and then closed his eyes forever. The soldier was his son, who had gone south before the war.

Goals and Strategies

Main Idea The North and the South had many different strengths, strategies, and purposes in the Civil War.

History and You Is it better for an army to have plenty of soldiers or a powerful will to fight? Why? Read to learn how these characteristics affected the Civil War.

. . . .

Like the Driscolls, many families were divided by the war. Neither side imagined, however, that the war would cost such a terrible price in human life. During the four years of fighting, hundreds of thousands of Americans had lost their lives. Many thousands more were wounded in battle.

The Border States

For most states, choosing sides in the Civil War was easy. The **border states** of Delaware, Maryland, Kentucky, and Missouri, however, were bitterly divided. Slavery was legal in all four states, though none had many enslaved people. All four had ties to the North and the South.

These states were vital to the Union because of their strategic locations. Missouri could control parts of the Mississippi River and major routes to the West. Kentucky controlled the Ohio River. Delaware was close to Philadelphia.

Maryland, perhaps the most important of the border states, was close to Richmond, the Confederate capital. Most significantly, Washington, D.C., lay within the state. If Maryland seceded, the North's government would be surrounded.

President **Abraham Lincoln** worked tirelessly to keep the four border states in the Union. In the end, he was successful.

Still, many border state residents supported the Confederacy. The president had his hands full trying to restrain these opponents of the war. In September 1861, Lincoln wrote:

PRIMARY SOURCE

"I think to lose Kentucky is nearly the same as to lose the whole game. . . . We would as well consent to separation at once, including the surrender of this capitol."

—from *Abraham Lincoln: His Speeches and Writings*

More than 400,000 Union and Confederate soldiers were wounded in battle during the Civil War.

By the Numbers / The Fighting Forces

Organization of the Armies The smaller Confederate army and the larger Union army were organized in roughly the same way.

1861–1865

Union soldiers 2,100,000

Confederate soldiers 900,000

50 Soldiers	= 1 Platoon
2 Platoons	= 1 Company
10 Companies	= 1 Regiment
4–6 Regiments	= 1 Brigade
4–5 Brigades	= 1 Division
3 Divisions	= 1 Corps

Critical Thinking

Concluding Why do you think the armed forces were divided into units?

Source: U.S. Census Bureau, *Historical Statistics of the United States*

Graph Skills

Comparing In what areas did the North have the greatest advantage over the South?

Graphs In Motion See StudentWorks™ Plus or glencoe.com.

Comparing North and South

When the war began, both sides had advantages and disadvantages. How they would use those strengths and weaknesses would determine the war's outcome.

The North had a larger population and better resources than the South. The South had other advantages, such as excellent military leaders and a strong fighting spirit. Also, because most of the war was fought in the South, the Confederacy knew the land and had the will to defend it.

War Aims

The North and the South had different aims in fighting the Civil War. The South's goal was to establish itself as an independent nation. To do this, the South did not have to invade the North or destroy the Union army. The Confederacy needed only to fight hard enough and long enough to convince Northerners that the war was not worth its cost.

In **contrast,** the Northern goal was to restore the Union. That meant invading the South and forcing the breakaway states to give up their quest for sovereignty. Although slavery helped drive a wedge between Northerners and Southerners, President Lincoln's original aim was not to defeat slavery. He wrote in 1862:

PRIMARY SOURCE

"If I could save the Union without freeing *any* slave I would do it."
—from *Abraham Lincoln: His Speeches and Writings*

Confederate Strategies

The South expected support from Britain and France, whose supply of Southern cotton was being disrupted by the war. Southerners reasoned that these nations might pressure the North to end the war.

The South's basic strategy, however, was to conduct a defensive war. This meant that the South would hold on to as much territory as possible. Southerners felt that if they showed determination to be independent, Northerners would tire of the war. The only exception to this defensive strategy was a plan to attack Washington, D.C.

Union Strategies

The North's war plan came from General Winfield Scott, hero of the war with Mexico. Knowing that the North would have to subdue the South completely, he proposed three main strategies for winning the war.

First, the Union should **blockade,** or close, Southern ports. This strategy would prevent supplies from reaching the Confederacy. It also would keep the South from **exporting** its cotton crop—or selling it to other countries.

Second, the North intended to gain control of the entire Mississippi River, which would split the Confederacy in two and cut Southern supply lines. Scott's plan was called the **Anaconda Plan,** after the snake that squeezes its prey to death.

Third, the North planned to capture Richmond, Virginia, the Confederate capital.

✔ **Reading Check** **Explaining** Why was it to the South's advantage to fight a defensive war?

Americans Against Americans

Main Idea Soldiers in the Civil War came from every region, and each side expected an early victory.

History and You What motivates men and women to join the armed forces today? Read to find out about the backgrounds of the Civil War soldiers.

. . . .

The Civil War was more than a war between the states. It pitted brother against brother and neighbor against neighbor. Kentucky senator John Crittenden had two sons who became generals. One fought for the Confederacy, the other for the Union. Even President Lincoln's wife, Mary Todd Lincoln, had relatives in the Confederate army.

Many left their homes and families to enlist in the Union or Confederate armies. Soldiers on both sides had many reasons for signing up. Some were motivated by patriotism and loyalty to their causes.

Economics & History

Enlisted men in both the Union and Confederate armies were paid monthly. Compare the pay rates to those in later wars.

Army Salaries (monthly)

Rank	Civil War	World War II 1942	Vietnam War 1965	Iraq War 2007
Private	*$13	$50	$85	$1,203 – 1,543.20
Corporal	$14	$66	$210	$1,699.50
Sergeant	$17	$78	$261	$1,854 – 2,339.10
Sergeant Major	$21	$138	$486	$4,110

*Until 1864, African Americans in the Civil War were paid only $7.00 per month.

Source: *Bureau of Economic Analysis;* Princeton Review; www.militaryfactory.com

$7.20	Overcoat	$1.14	Pair of Shoes
$6.71	Dress Coat	$1.35	Hat
$2.95	Blanket	$0.88	Undershirt
$2.63	Blouse	$0.55	Underwear
$3.03	Trousers	$0.26	Socks

Soldiers had to replace any of the clothing they lost out of their own pay.

Union soldier's cap ▲

$100 BOUNTY
$13 PAY PER MONTH
$6 STATE PAY for MARRIED MEN
$4 STATE PAY for SINGLE MEN
$3.50 PER MONTH FOR CLOTHES & RATIONS FOUND.
THE
N GUARDS!
LEGION, Colonel William Bryan, now encamped at Beverly. A few more
YOUNG MEN WANTED
N AND PROCEED TO CAMP AT ONCE
TING STATION,
AN'S, SECOND ST.
Market and Plum Sts.
N, N. JERSEY.
APT. R. GRAHAM CLARKE.

▲

To get more men to enlist, Union recruiters put up posters offering a sign-up bonus or bounty.

Critical Thinking

Calculating What was a private's weekly salary in the Civil War?

On Average The typical soldier was 5'8", 143 pounds, nearly 26 years of age, and unmarried. He grew up on a farm and practiced the Protestant religion.

Private Edwin Francis Jennison, 2nd Louisiana Cavalry

Private George A. Stryker, New York Regiment

Critical Thinking

Explaining Why do you think many new soldiers had their picture taken in uniform?

Others thought they would be called cowards if they did not serve. Still others yearned for excitement. The sister of William Stone of Louisiana wrote that her brother was:

PRIMARY SOURCE

"wild to be off to Virginia [to join the Confederate army]. He so fears that the fighting will be over before he can get there."

—from *Brokenburn: The Journal of Kate Stone*

The quest for excitement was especially strong among younger soldiers. Many recruits on both sides were hardly adults. Tens of thousands of soldiers were under 18, and some were younger than 14. To get into the army, many teenagers ran away from home or lied about their ages.

Although teenage boys were accepted into military service, one group of men was not permitted to fight during the early days of the war. Unwilling to provide enslaved people with weapons, the Confederacy barred African Americans from the army. The Union also refused to let freed people enlist. Northern leaders worried that white troops would

not accept African American soldiers. Later in the war, though, this policy was changed.

False Hopes

When the war began, each side expected an easy victory. Northerners could not imagine the Confederates holding out for long against the Union's greater resources. They boasted that the war would end in a quick and glorious triumph for the Union.

Confederates found it impossible to believe that the North could ever subdue the fighting spirit of the South. Both sides were wrong. In the end, the war lasted far longer than most Americans could have guessed.

Who Were the Soldiers?

Soldiers came from every region and all walks of life. Most, though, came from farms. Almost half of the North's troops and more than 60 percent of the South's had owned or worked on farms. Lincoln's early terms of enlistment asked governors to supply soldiers for 90 days. When the conflict did not end quickly, soldiers' terms became longer.

By the summer of 1861, the Confederate army had about 112,000 soldiers, who were sometimes called Rebels. The Union had about 187,000 soldiers, or Yankees, as they were also known. By the end of the war, about 900,000 men fought for the Confederacy and about 2.1 million men for the Union. The Union army included just under 200,000 African Americans and about 10,000 Latino soldiers.

The Life of a Soldier

In both the North and the South, civilians and soldiers suffered terrible hardships and faced new **challenges.** In letters to their families and friends at home, soldiers described what they saw and how they felt. Many wrote about their boredom, discomfort, sickness, fear, and horror.

Most of the time the soldiers lived in camps. Camp life had its pleasant moments of songs, stories, letters from home, and baseball games. Often, however, a soldier's life was dull—a seemingly unchanging routine of drills, bad food, marches, and rain.

During lulls between battles, Confederate and Union soldiers sometimes forgot they were enemies. A private described his wartime experiences:

"A part of Co K and some of the enemy came together and stacked arms and talked for a long time. Our men cooked coffee and treated them and [afterward] . . . each one took up his position again and they began to fire at each other again, but not as hard as before."

—from *The Life of Billy Yank*

The Reality of War

In spite of fleeting moments of calm, the reality of war was never far away. Both sides suffered terrible losses. The new rifles used during the Civil War fired with greater accuracy than the muskets of earlier wars.

Medical facilities were overwhelmed by the thousands of casualties. After the Battle of Shiloh, the wounded lay in the rain for more than 24 hours waiting for treatment. A Union soldier recalled, "Many had died there, and others were in the last agonies as we passed. Their groans and cries were heart-rending."

Faced with such horrors, many men deserted. About one of every 11 Union soldiers and one of every 8 Confederates ran away because of fear, hunger, or sickness.

Reading Check **Explaining** Why did both sides think the war would end quickly?

Section 1 Review

History ONLINE
Study Central™ To review this section, go to glencoe.com.

Vocabulary

1. Write a short paragraph in which you use all the following vocabulary terms: border state, contrast, blockade, export, challenge.

Main Ideas

2. **Explaining** Why were the border states important to both the North and South?

3. **Evaluating** What was the purpose of the Anaconda Plan?

Critical Thinking

4. **Predicting** What do you think would be the South's greatest advantage in the war?

5. **Comparing** Create a diagram to compare Northern and Southern aims and strategies.

	North	South
Aims		
Strategies		

6. **Descriptive Writing** You are a Southerner or Northerner in 1861. Write a journal entry that explains your reasons for joining the Confederate or Union army.

Answer the
7. **Essential Question**
What were the strengths and weaknesses of the North and the South?

Essential Question ◄

Why did neither the Union nor the Confederacy gain a strong advantage during the early years of the war?

Reading Guide

Content Vocabulary

tributary *(p. 40)*   casualty *(p. 41)*

ironclad *(p. 41)*

Academic Vocabulary

abandon *(p. 39)*   impact *(p. 45)*

Key People and Events

Stonewall Jackson *(p. 39)*

Ulysses S. Grant *(p. 40)*

Battle of Shiloh *(p. 41)*

Robert E. Lee *(p. 43)*

Battle of Antietam *(p. 44)*

Frederick Douglass *(p. 45)*

Emancipation Proclamation *(p. 45)*

Reading Strategy

Taking Notes As you read, place the early Civil War battles described in the text on a time line and take notes on what happened during each one.

1861   1862   1863

American Diary

Captain Van Brunt, of the U.S. Navy, described the historic first battle between metal-plated ships in 1862: "[The Monitor] laid herself right alongside of the Merrimack, and the contrast was that of a pigmy to a giant. Gun after gun was fired by the Monitor, which was returned with whole broadsides from the rebels with no more effect, apparently, than so many pebblestones thrown by a child."

—*quoted in* Official Records of the Union and Confederate Navies in the War of the Rebellion, *1898*

War on Land and Sea

Main Idea The Confederates decisively won the First Battle of Bull Run.

History and You Would you eat a picnic lunch while a battle was raging all around you? Read to learn what happened in 1861 when many people did exactly that.

. . . .

The Civil War was fought on sea as well as on land. While the Union and Confederacy mobilized their armies, the Union navy began operations against the South. In April 1861, President Lincoln proclaimed a blockade of all Confederate ports.

Southerners hoped to break the Union blockade with a secret weapon—the *Merrimack*, an abandoned Union warship. The Confederates rebuilt and covered the wooden ship in iron. The armored vessel, renamed the *Virginia*, could withstand Union cannon fire.

First Battle of Bull Run

Pressure mounted in the summer of 1861, leading to the first major battle of the Civil War. On July 21, about 30,000 inexperienced Union troops commanded by General Irvin McDowell attacked a smaller, equally inexperienced Confederate force led by General P. G. T. Beauregard. The fighting took place in northern Virginia, about 5 miles (8 km) from the town of Manassas Junction near a small river called Bull Run. Hundreds of Washington, D.C., residents went to the battle site to picnic and watch.

The Yankees drove the Confederates back at first. Then the Rebels rallied, inspired by reinforcements under General Thomas Jackson. Jackson was seen holding out heroically, "like a stone wall," and became known thereafter as **"Stonewall" Jackson.** The Confederates unleashed a savage counterattack that forced Union lines to break. The Union retreat turned into a mad stampede when retreating Union troops collided with the civilians, fleeing in panic back to Washington, D.C.

The outcome shocked Northerners. They began to understand that the war could be a long, difficult, and costly struggle. President Lincoln appointed a new general, George B. McClellan, to head and organize the Union army of the East—called the Army of the Potomac—and to train the troops.

Primary Source / Naval Warfare

The Ironclads The *Monitor* was small for a warship—about 172 feet (52 m) long—and constructed almost entirely of iron. A revolving armored tower called a turret housed the guns.

11-inch (28-cm) cannon housed inside rotating turret

iron turret rotates on a pivot

The Union's *Monitor* (below) battled the ironclad *Merrimack* (left), called the *Virginia* by the Confederates, on March 9, 1862.

layered armor plating

Critical Thinking

Making Inferences What advantages would an iron warship have over a wooden ship? Explain.

The loss at Bull Run discouraged Union supporters. Although dismayed by the results, President Lincoln was also determined. Within days he issued a call for more volunteers for the army. He signed two bills requesting a total of 1 million soldiers to serve for three years. Victories in the West raised Northern spirits and also increased enlistment.

The War in the West

In the West, the major Union goal was to control the Mississippi River and its **tributaries,** the smaller rivers that flow into a larger river. With control of the river, Union ships on the Mississippi could prevent the states of Louisiana, Arkansas, and Texas from supplying the rest of the Confederacy. Control would also let Union gunboats and troops move into the heart of the South.

The battle for the rivers began in February 1862 when Union forces captured Fort Henry on the Tennessee River. The assault was led by naval commander Andrew Foote and army general **Ulysses S. Grant.** Soon afterward, Grant and Foote moved against Fort Donelson on the Cumberland River. The Confederates in Fort Donelson realized that they had no chance of winning the battle, so they asked Grant what terms, or incentives, he would give them to give up the fort. Grant said:

PRIMARY SOURCE

"No terms except an unconditional and immediate surrender can be accepted."
—General Grant to General Buckner, February 1862

"Unconditional Surrender" Grant became the North's new hero.

War of the Ironclads

As conflict was raging on the rivers of the West, ships of the Union and Confederate navies were fighting in the Atlantic Ocean.

War in the West, 1862–1863

NATIONAL GEOGRAPHIC

Shiloh April 7, 1862
At dawn, Union forces launched a counterattack **A** against Confederate forces **B**. By mid-afternoon, the Confederate forces were driven back **C**. Confederate General Beauregard ordered a retreat, forming a rear guard. The remaining Confederate forces moved south toward Corinth **D**.

Union states
Confederate states
Union victory
Confederate victory

0   200 kilometers
0   200 miles
Albers Equal-Area projection

On March 8, 1862, the *Merrimack*, renamed the *Virginia*, attacked a group of Union ships off the coast of Virginia. The North's wooden warships could not damage the Confederate ship—shells simply bounced off its iron sides. Some Northern leaders feared the South would use the **ironclad** warship to destroy the Union navy, steam up the Potomac River, and bombard Washington, D.C.

The North, though, had an ironclad ship of its own, the *Monitor*, and this ship rushed toward Virginia. On March 9, the two ironclads met in battle. Neither ship could sink the other. Although the battle was indecisive, it was also historic because it was the first ever between metal-covered ships.

The Battle of Shiloh

Meanwhile, in the West, General Grant and about 40,000 troops headed south along the Tennessee River toward Corinth, Mississippi, an important railroad junction. In early April 1862, the Union army camped at Pittsburg Landing, 20 miles (32 km) from Corinth. Nearby was a church named Shiloh. Additional Union forces came from Nashville to join Grant.

Confederate leaders decided to strike first, before the reinforcements arrived. Early in the morning of April 6, Confederate forces led by Albert Sidney Johnston and P. G. T. Beauregard launched a surprise attack on the Union troops. The **Battle of Shiloh** lasted two days, with some of the most bitter, bloody fighting of the war. Even though Shiloh was a narrow victory for the Union forces, the losses were enormous. Together the two armies suffered more than 23,000 **casualties**—people killed or wounded.

After Shiloh, Union forces gained control of Corinth on May 30. Memphis, Tennessee, fell to Union armies on June 6. The North seemed well on its way to controlling the Mississippi River.

The Battle of Shiloh

More than 23,000 troops were killed or wounded in the Battle of Shiloh. This was the highest number of casualties of any Civil War battle to date. The Union victory was an important step toward the goal of controlling the Mississippi River.

Day One

A surprise attack by the Confederate army gave it an early advantage. Union general William T. Sherman remarked to General Grant, *"Well, Grant, we've had the devil's own day of it, haven't we?"*

"Yes," Grant replied, *"Lick 'em tomorrow, though."*

◀ William T. Sherman

Day Two

With Union reinforcements, the battle changed direction, resulting in a Union victory. Confederate general P. G. T. Beauregard lamented, *"I thought I had General Grant just where I wanted him and could finish him up in the morning."*

P. G. T. Beauregard ▶

Critical Thinking

Analyzing Did either Beauregard or Sherman accept the fact that his side might lose the Battle of Shiloh? Do you think their statements reflect what most military leaders would say in this situation? Explain.

War in the East, 1862-1863

Battle Dates

Monitor & Virginia
Mar. 9, 1862

Seven Days
June 25–July 1, 1862

Bull Run
(2nd Battle)
Aug. 29–30, 1862

Antietam
Sept. 17, 1862

Fredericksburg
Dec. 13, 1862

Chancellorsville
May 1–4, 1863

Gettysburg
July 1–3, 1863

Union advance
Union retreat
Confederate advance
Confederate retreat
Union victory
Confederate victory
Inconclusive battle

0   40 kilometers
0   40 miles
Albers Equal-Area projection

New Orleans Falls

A few weeks after Shiloh, the North won another important victory. On April 25, 1862, Union naval forces under David Farragut captured New Orleans, Louisiana, the largest city in the South. Farragut, who was of Spanish descent, grew up in the South but remained loyal to the Union. His capture of New Orleans, near the mouth of the Mississippi River, meant that the Confederacy could no longer use the river to carry its goods to sea. Together with Grant's victories to the north, the capture of New Orleans gave the Union control of most of the Mississippi River. Only the city of Vicksburg, Mississippi, blocked Union control of the river and the success of the Union's western strategy.

Reading Check Comparing and Contrasting
How was the Battle of Shiloh like the First Battle of Bull Run? How were the two battles different?

War in the East

Main Idea The South won several important victories in the East during 1862, but the Union responded with a vital triumph of its own.

History and You What is the most valuable thing you have lost? Read to learn what happened when a Confederate officer lost some important papers.

While Union and Confederate forces were struggling for control of Tennessee and the Mississippi River, another major campaign was being waged in the East to capture Richmond, Virginia. Richmond, the capital of the Confederacy, was close to the northern Confederate border and vulnerable to attack. Yet it was a matter of pride to defend it at all costs. Repelling one Union advance after another, Confederate armies prevented the fall of Richmond until the end of the war.

By the Numbers

The Battle of Antietam was the bloodiest one-day battle in the war and in American history. Several battles in the East were costly in terms of total casualties (killed, wounded, missing, and captured).

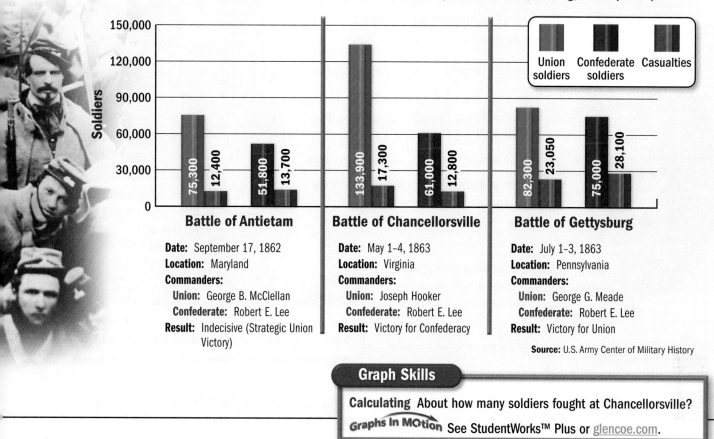

Battle of Antietam
Date: September 17, 1862
Location: Maryland
Commanders:
 Union: George B. McClellan
 Confederate: Robert E. Lee
Result: Indecisive (Strategic Union Victory)

Battle of Chancellorsville
Date: May 1-4, 1863
Location: Virginia
Commanders:
 Union: Joseph Hooker
 Confederate: Robert E. Lee
Result: Victory for Confederacy

Battle of Gettysburg
Date: July 1-3, 1863
Location: Pennsylvania
Commanders:
 Union: George G. Meade
 Confederate: Robert E. Lee
Result: Victory for Union

Source: U.S. Army Center of Military History

Graph Skills

Calculating About how many soldiers fought at Chancellorsville?

Graphs In Motion See StudentWorks™ Plus or glencoe.com.

Victories for the Confederacy

Southern victories in the East were largely the result of the leadership of General **Robert E. Lee** and Stonewall Jackson. Through knowledge of the terrain, speed of movement, and the ability to inspire their troops, Confederate forces managed to defeat Union forces sometimes twice as large as their own.

In 1862 Confederate forces turned back General George B. McClellan at the Seven Days' Battle, General John Pope at the Second Battle of Bull Run, and General Ambrose Burnside at Fredericksburg. In May 1863, at Chancellorsville, Virginia, Lee's army defeated a Union army twice its size. "My God, my God," Lincoln said when he learned of the defeat, "What will the country say!"

Victories in the East did not include victories outside the Confederacy. Lee's two attempts to invade the North failed. In September 1862,

Lee's army was turned back at the Battle of Antietam. Less than a year later, Confederate forces would face the same fate at Gettysburg. You will read about the Battle of Gettysburg in Section 4.

Invasion of the North

Washington, D.C., presented a tempting target for the Confederates, but the city was too well guarded for Lee to consider an attack. On the urging of Confederate president Jefferson Davis, Lee moved his troops instead into western Maryland—Union territory. His goal now was to sweep into Pennsylvania and carry the war into the Northern states. Lee knew that McClellan was pursuing him with a sizable force, so he concentrated on moving forward. Lee's forces crossed into Maryland and began an invasion of the North.

The Civil War **Chapter 2** 43

Lincoln declared in the Emancipation Proclamation that:

"all persons held as slaves within any state . . . in rebellion against the United States, shall be then, thenceforward and forever free."

Results of the Proclamation

✔ It sent a clear message to enslaved people and the Confederacy that slavery would no longer be tolerated.

✔ African American military units were formed.

✔ Europe was strongly opposed to slavery. No European government would defend the South in its war to protect the institution of slavery.

"The white man's happiness cannot be purchased by the black man's misery."
—Frederick Douglass, 1849

"If my name ever goes into history, it will be for this act."
—Abraham Lincoln, 1863

Critical Thinking

Explaining What political reasons did Lincoln have for issuing the Emancipation Proclamation?

The Battle of Antietam

Once in Maryland, Lee split his army in four parts and instructed them to move in different directions. He hoped to confuse McClellan about the size and destination of his army. A Confederate officer, however, lost his copy of Lee's orders describing this plan. The paper was found by two Union soldiers, who brought it to McClellan.

McClellan did not attack immediately. Lee reassembled his troops, and on September 17, 1862, the two sides met in the **Battle of Antietam** near Sharpsburg, Maryland.

About 6,000 soldiers were killed. About 17,000 more were badly wounded. It was the deadliest single day of fighting during the war. Antietam was an important victory for the Union. Because of the great losses, Lee chose to retreat to Virginia after the fighting. At least for the time being, his strategy of invading the North had failed. The Union could breathe a little more easily.

Reading Check **Summarizing** What was the outcome of the Battle of Antietam?

The Emancipation Proclamation

Main Idea Lincoln's Emancipation Proclamation had an enormous effect in America and abroad.

History and You How do you make difficult decisions? Read to learn about the debate over the war's purpose and how Lincoln eventually settled on a course of action.

At first, Abraham Lincoln cast the Civil War as a battle for the Union rather than as a fight against slavery. As the conflict progressed, however, Lincoln changed the way he thought about slavery and its role in the war.

The Debate

Lincoln hated slavery, yet he was reluctant to make the Civil War a battle to end it. He feared that many Union supporters would strongly oppose such a decision. At the beginning of the war, Lincoln hesitated to move against slavery because of the border states.

Even many Northerners who disapproved of slavery were not eager to risk their lives to end it. Other Americans held a different opinion, however.

From the start of the war, abolitionists, including orator **Frederick Douglass** and newspaper editor Horace Greeley, urged Lincoln to make the war a fight to end slavery. These Northerners made several arguments to support their position. First, they argued, slavery was a moral wrong that needed to be abolished. Second, they pointed out that slavery was the root of the divisions between North and South. Therefore, the nation could never be fully restored if slavery continued.

Finally, Douglass and others brought up the issue of foreign policy. Britain and France each sympathized with the South for economic reasons. Southern leaders were trying to persuade Britain and France to recognize the Confederacy's independence.

Public opinion in England and France was strongly antislavery. By casting the war as a fight for freedom, Douglass pointed out, Lincoln would make Britain and France less willing to support the South. That, in turn, would help the Union cause.

Lincoln Decides

Lincoln knew that the Constitution did not give him the power to end slavery. The Constitution did, however, give him the power to take property from an enemy in wartime—and, by law, enslaved people were property. On September 22, 1862, soon after the North's victory at Antietam, Lincoln announced that he would issue the **Emancipation Proclamation**—a decree freeing all enslaved people in rebel territory on January 1, 1863.

Effects of the Proclamation

The Emancipation Proclamation did not actually free a single enslaved person. The proclamation applied only to enslaved people in areas held by the Confederacy. There Lincoln had no power to enforce the new policy.

The proclamation had an important **impact** in America, however. By issuing the Emancipation Proclamation, the government declared slavery to be wrong. If the Union won the war, slavery would be banned forever.

✔ Reading Check **Summarizing** Why did abolitionists believe that Lincoln should make the end of slavery a goal of the war?

History ONLINE
Study Central™ To review this section, go to glencoe.com.

Section 2 Review

Vocabulary

1. Use each of these terms in a sentence that will help explain its meaning: abandon, tributary, ironclad, casualty, impact.

Main Ideas

2. **Analyzing** What factors helped the Confederates win the First Battle of Bull Run?

3. **Summarizing** What was the final outcome of the Battle of Shiloh?

4. **Explaining** What did the Emancipation Proclamation state?

Critical Thinking

5. **Analyzing** Why was controlling the Mississippi River vital to the North and the South? Explain your answer in a diagram like the one shown here.

Control of the Mississippi

6. **Evaluating** Which of Frederick Douglass's arguments for making the abolition of slavery an aim of the war do you find most convincing? Why?

7. **Expository Writing** You read about General Lee's lost battle orders. Write a short paragraph explaining the role of chance and error in this discovery, as well as General McClellan's use of the information.

Answer the
8. **Essential Question**
Why did neither the Union nor the Confederacy gain a strong advantage during the early years of the war?

Meet the Author

Stephen Crane (1871–1900) had never seen a battlefield when he wrote *The Red Badge of Courage,* which he based on accounts of the Confederate victory at Chancellorsville. Even so, he described the experience of war so realistically that even combat veterans admired his work.

Building Background

The American novelist Stephen Crane, who created the most famous depiction of Civil War combat in his 1895 novel *The Red Badge of Courage,* did not describe warfare in traditional, heroic terms. Instead, he tried to present an objective, almost scientific examination of the effect of battle on individuals. As you read this excerpt from *The Red Badge of Courage,* be aware of how Crane creates an effect of realism.

Vocabulary

careering speeding

exasperation extreme irritation

impotency powerlessness

imprecations curses

pummeling beating

exultant very joyful

THE RED BADGE OF COURAGE

Stephen Crane

He was at a task. He was like a carpenter who has made many boxes, making still another box, only there was furious haste in his movements. He, in his thought, was **careering** off in other places, even as the carpenter who as he works whistles and thinks of his friend or his enemy, his home or a saloon. And these jolted dreams were never perfect to him afterward, but remained a mass of blurred shapes.

Presently he began to feel the effects of the war atmosphere—a blistering sweat, a sensation that his eyeballs were about to crack like hot stones. A burning roar filled his ears.

Following this came a red rage. He developed the acute **exasperation** of a pestered animal, a well-meaning cow worried by dogs. He had a mad feeling against his rifle, which could only be used against one life at a time. He wished to rush forward and strangle with his fingers. He craved a power that would enable him to make a world-sweeping gesture and brush all back. His **impotency** appeared to him, and made his rage into that of a driven beast.

A burning roar filled his ears.

Buried in the smoke of many rifles his anger was directed not so much against the men whom he knew were rushing toward him as against the swirling battle phantoms which were choking him, stuffing their smoke robes down his parched throat. He fought frantically for respite for his senses, for air, as a babe being smothered attacks the deadly blankets.

There was a blare of heated rage mingled with a certain expression of intentness on all faces. Many of the men were making low-toned noises with their mouths, and these subdued cheers, snarls, **imprecations,** prayers, made a wild, barbaric song that went as an undercurrent of sound, strange and chantlike with the resounding chords of the war march. The man at the youth's elbow was babbling. In it there was something soft and tender like the monologue of a babe. . . .

The lieutenant of the youth's company had encountered a soldier who had fled screaming at the first volley of his comrades. Behind the lines these two were acting a little isolated scene. The man was blubbering and staring with sheeplike eyes at the lieutenant, who had seized him by the collar and was **pummeling** him. He drove him back into the ranks with many blows. The soldier went mechanically, dully, with his animal-like eyes upon the officer. Perhaps there was to him a divinity expressed in the voice of the other—stern, hard, with no reflection of fear in it. He tried to reload his gun, but his shaking hands prevented. The lieutenant was obliged to assist him.

The men dropped here and there like bundles. The captain of the youth's company had been killed in an early part of the action. His body lay stretched out in the position of a tired man resting, but upon his face there was an astonished and sorrowful look, as if he thought some friend had done him an ill turn. . . .

At last an **exultant** yell went along the quivering line. The firing dwindled from an uproar to a last vindictive popping. As the smoke slowly eddied away, the youth saw that the charge had been repulsed. The enemy were scattered into reluctant groups. He saw a man climb to the top of the fence, straddle the rail, and fire a parting shot. The waves had receded, leaving bits of dark *débris* upon the ground.

Analyzing Literature

1. **Respond** What surprised you most about Stephen Crane's description of combat?

2. **Recall and Interpret**
   (a) What is the "dark *débris*" left on the battlefield?
   (b) What is the effect of using this phrase?

3. **Evaluate and Connect**
   (a) In your opinion, which details in this passage contribute most powerfully to the effect of realism Crane was striving to create?
   (b) What conclusions can you draw from Crane's depiction of battle?

Life During the War

Essential Question ◀

What social, political, and economic changes resulted from the war?

Reading Guide

Content Vocabulary

habeas corpus (p. 53)

greenback (p. 55)

draft (p. 54)

inflation (p. 55)

bounty (p. 54)

Academic Vocabulary

distribute (p. 51)   substitute (p. 54)

Key People and Events

Mary Edwards Walker (p. 50)

Dorothea Dix (p. 50)

Clara Barton (p. 50)

Sally Tompkins (p. 50)

bread riots (p. 52)

Reading Strategy

Taking Notes As you read the section, complete a diagram like the one below by describing three ways that women in the North and the South contributed to the war effort.

Contributions

American Diary

Drummer boy Delavan Miller, who served in a New York Regiment, recalls: "The day after a battle is always a sad one in a regiment. Men search for missing comrades and some are found cold in death who were full of life the day before. No jests are spoken. The terribleness of war has been forcibly impressed on all participants."

—*from* Drum Taps in Dixie

Men with the 36th Pennsylvania Infantry Regiment drill at their winter quarters near Langley, Virginia.

A Different Way of Life

Main Idea The Civil War affected civilians as well as soldiers.

History and You How does war change the everyday life of citizens? Read on to find out how Americans tried to adjust to wartime conditions.

. . . .

Thirteen-year-old Delavan Miller served as a drummer for a New York regiment. He recalls that:

PRIMARY SOURCE

"The great majority of the men really felt that the war would be ended before we had a chance to take a hand in. I may say that the drummer boys, full of young red blood, were as eager for [battle] as the older men, but most of us had got enough of war before we reached Appomattox."

—from *Drum Taps in Dixie*

Life at Home

When the Civil War began, Miller, like many other teenagers, left everything that was familiar to him to serve in the military. This meant leaving family, friends, and school.

Almost everyone who stayed home was touched in some way by the war. Only about one-half of the 12 million school-age children attended school. Many of those who did not worked to help support their families. Schools closed during the war in some areas, especially those near the scenes of battles and skirmishes. Many schools and churches served as hospitals for the wounded.

Shortages in the South

Although the war affected everyone, life in the South changed most dramatically. Both armies spent most of their time on Southern soil, and the South therefore suffered the greatest destruction. Southerners who lived in the paths of marching armies lost crops and homes. Thousands became refugees, and even those who lived outside the war zones suffered. As one observer noted, the South depended on the outside world "for everything from a hairpin to a toothpick, and from a cradle to a coffin." As the war dragged on, shortages of food, supplies, and even household items became commonplace.

Reading Check **Explaining** What problems did the Southern people face during the war?

If You Were There / **Drummer Boys in the Civil War**

Duties and Tasks At 13, you join the army and train as a drummer. Your day begins at 5 A.M. Your drums call the soldiers to meals, roll call, drills, bed, and lights out. You also do chores for officers and surgeons. Your meals, when you can eat, are usually plain biscuits called hardtack and barely cooked bacon.

◀ "Drummer" Jackson served with an African American regiment.

Critical Thinking

Making Inferences What is your daily routine like? How do you think you would have handled the life of a drummer?

New Roles for Women

Main Idea Many Northern and Southern women took on new responsibilities during the war.

History and You Think of ways that your family would be affected by a war in your backyard. Read to learn the many ways families were affected by the Civil War.

Against the advice of family and friends, Kate Cumming, a young woman from Mobile, Alabama, left home to begin a career as a nurse with the Confederate Army of the Mississippi. Cumming was one of the many women whose lives changed greatly because of the Civil War.

In both the North and the South, women kept the farms and factories going. They ran offices, taught school, and kept government records. Women suffered the stress of having husbands away at war and the pain of losing family members. They scrimped and saved to make do without many things they were used to, and they prayed to keep their families together.

Treating the Sick and Wounded

In the Civil War, for the first time, thousands of women served as nurses. At first many doctors did not want women nurses, saying that women were too delicate for the grisly work required on the battlefields. Men thought of nursing as work for males and believed it was improper for women to tend the bodies of unknown men.

Strong-minded women disregarded these objections. **Mary Edwards Walker** became the first woman army surgeon and later received the Congressional Medal of Honor. **Dorothea Dix** convinced officials to let women work as nurses and recruited large numbers of women to serve. Another Northerner, **Clara Barton,** became famous for her work with wounded soldiers. In the South, **Sally Tompkins** established a hospital for soldiers in Richmond, Virginia.

Kate Cumming, who nursed the wounded in Corinth after the Battle of Shiloh, wrote, "Nothing that I had ever heard or read had given me the faintest idea of the horrors witnessed here."

Primary Source / Women in the War

New Roles Women filled many roles during the Civil War. Many offered their services as nurses. A few were spies, and as many as 400 disguised themselves as men to serve as Union or Confederate soldiers. They cut their hair, donned men's clothing, and changed their names to fight alongside men in battle. Many were following brothers or husbands to war, but some wanted to fight because they believed in the cause.

"Francis Clailin" ▶

Nurse in field hospital ▼

Frances Louisa Clayton changed her name to Francis Clailin and enlisted as a Union soldier to be with her husband. Like the woman described below, Clayton's identity was revealed in a hospital.

"Maybe she would have remained undiscovered for a long time if she hadn't fainted. She was given a warm bath which gave the secret away."

Frances Clayton ▶

Spies

Some women were spies. Rose O'Neal Greenhow entertained Union leaders in Washington, D.C. She gathered information about Union plans that she passed to the South. Greenhow eventually was caught, convicted of treason, and exiled. Belle Boyd, of Front Royal, Virginia, informed Confederate generals of Union army movements in the Shenandoah Valley.

Some women disguised themselves as men and became soldiers. Loretta Janeta Velázquez fought for the South at the First Battle of Bull Run and at the Battle of Shiloh. Later she became a Confederate spy.

Harriet Tubman, an important "conductor" on the Underground Railroad, also served as a spy and scout for the Union. In 1863 Tubman led a mission that freed hundreds of enslaved people and disrupted southern supply lines.

Reading Check Making Inferences How do you think women felt about how the war changed their lives?

Elizabeth Van Lew lived in Richmond and secretly sent information about Confederate activities to President Lincoln.

"For my loyalty to my country I have two beautiful names— here I am called 'Traitor,' farther North a 'Spy.'"

Elizabeth Van Lew ▲

Critical Thinking

Analyzing Did the Civil War change the traditional roles of women? How?

Prison Camps and Field Hospitals

Main Idea When Americans went to war, most were not prepared for the horrors of battle.

History and You What goes through the mind of a doctor or nurse in the middle of battle? Read to learn about battlefield medicine.

· ·

After the terror on the battlefield, many men suffered the agony of their wounds. Still others faced the humiliation and suffering of being taken prisoner.

In the Hands of the Enemy

Throughout the war, each side treated its enemy soldiers with a mixture of sympathy and hostility. At first, the two sides exchanged prisoners. However, when each realized that the men simply returned to fight again, they set up prison camps. Prisoners were generally allowed to keep their blanket and a cup or canteen when they were captured. These few provisions were all they had during their imprisonment. Food shortages also added to the suffering. Volunteers **distributed,** or gave out, bread and soup among the wounded, but in the prisons there was little or nothing to eat.

Andersonville prison, in Georgia, was opened in early 1864. It was built to hold 10,000 prisoners, but by August, 33,000 were crammed into it. The men slept in shallow holes dug in the ground and daily received a teaspoon of salt, three tablespoons of beans, and eight ounces of cornmeal. They drank and cooked with water from a stream that also served as a sewer. Almost 13,000 Union prisoners died there, mostly from disease.

The Union prison in Elmira, New York, was no better. Captured soldiers from the sunny South suffered through the winter months without blankets and warm clothes. The hospital was in a flooded basement, and a pond within the compound served as both toilet and garbage dump. Almost one quarter of all prisoners at Elmira died.

Field Hospitals

Surgeons traveled with the troops and set up hospitals near battlefields. There, with bullets and cannonballs flying past their heads, they bandaged wounds and amputated limbs. A nurse recalls:

PRIMARY SOURCE

"We have to walk, and when we give the men anything kneel, in blood and water; but we think nothing of it."
—from *Kate: The Journal of a Confederate Nurse*

The war produced many casualties, and doctors struggled to tend to the wounded. Disease was a constant threat, and some regiments lost half their men to illness before ever going into battle. Crowded together in army camps and drinking from unsanitary water supplies, many soldiers became sick. Smallpox, when it erupted, could be deadly, as could a number of other diseases, including dysentery, typhoid, and pneumonia.

✔ **Reading Check** Comparing and Contrasting
How were the prison camps at Andersonville and Elmira alike, and how were they different?

Political and Economic Change

Main Idea The Civil War led to political change and strained the economies of the North and the South.

History and You Can you think of a time when you disagreed with or opposed something? Did you take action? Read to learn why and how people opposed the Civil War, and how Presidents Lincoln and Davis responded.

. . . .

Throughout the Civil War, numerous smaller "civil wars" raged in the North and the South.

In the South

Many Southerners opposed the war in the first place. After two years, the war had taken huge amounts of food, materials, and money, and shortages were widespread.

Bread riots erupted throughout the South as hungry people took to the streets. In Richmond, a mob, mostly made of women and

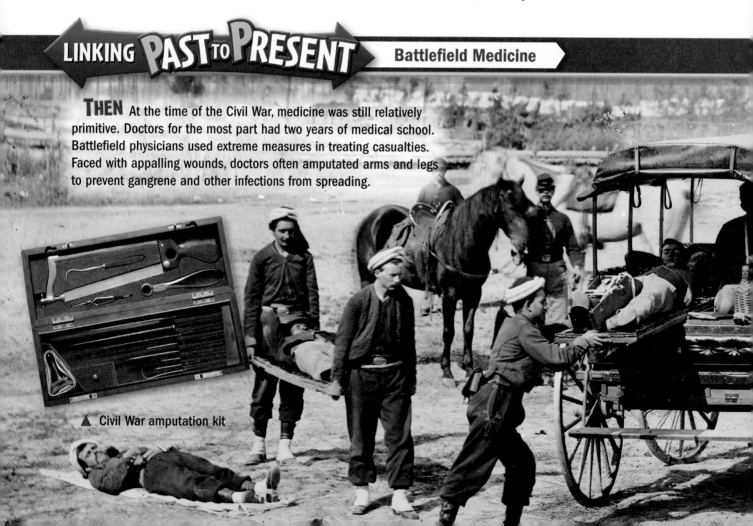

LINKING PAST TO PRESENT   Battlefield Medicine

THEN At the time of the Civil War, medicine was still relatively primitive. Doctors for the most part had two years of medical school. Battlefield physicians used extreme measures in treating casualties. Faced with appalling wounds, doctors often amputated arms and legs to prevent gangrene and other infections from spreading.

▲ Civil War amputation kit

children, gathered peacefully to protest but soon started smashing shop windows and stealing food.

In the North

The Union, too, had its war opponents. The Democratic Party, which always opposed Lincoln, was split down the middle. The War Democrats were sharply critical of how the Republican administration was running the war. The Peace Democrats, in contrast, argued for an immediate end to fighting. They called for reuniting the states through negotiation. Mostly from the Midwestern states of Ohio, Illinois, and Indiana, the Peace Democrats were viewed by some as traitors. This earned them the nickname Copperheads, after the poisonous snake. However, by 1863, they proudly embraced this label and wore copper pennies as badges because the coins had "Lady Liberty" on them.

As in the South, some Northerners who opposed the war discouraged enlistment. Occasionally they went further, helping Confederate prisoners of war escape. Some historians claim that the activities of the Peace Democrats encouraged the South and that the war dragged on because the South believed that the North would abandon the struggle.

Jail Without Trial

As a way of dealing with war opponents in the North, President Lincoln suspended **habeas corpus.** This legal proceeding is a protection against unlawful imprisonment. A prisoner uses it to ask for a court hearing to determine if he or she is being held lawfully. The Constitution provides that habeas corpus can be suspended only "when in cases of rebellion or invasion, the public safety may require it."

As a result of Lincoln's action, thousands of Northerners were jailed without trials. When people—even supporters of the war—spoke out against the suspension, they were labeled treasonous Copperheads. Lincoln's critics were right to be concerned. Although many who were in jail actively helped the enemy, others were simply political leaders who had stated their opinions.

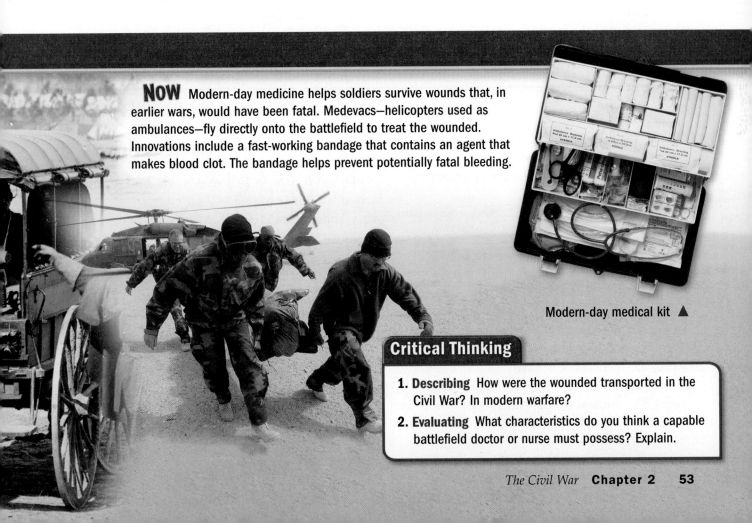

NOW Modern-day medicine helps soldiers survive wounds that, in earlier wars, would have been fatal. Medevacs—helicopters used as ambulances—fly directly onto the battlefield to treat the wounded. Innovations include a fast-working bandage that contains an agent that makes blood clot. The bandage helps prevent potentially fatal bleeding.

Modern-day medical kit ▲

Critical Thinking

1. **Describing** How were the wounded transported in the Civil War? In modern warfare?

2. **Evaluating** What characteristics do you think a capable battlefield doctor or nurse must possess? Explain.

A Northern newspaper ran this cartoon in 1863. It shows Lady Liberty warding off an attack of the Peace Democrats, or Copperheads.

1. **Identify** Who does the woman represent?
2. **Points of View** What is the cartoonist expressing about the Peace Democrats? How can you tell?

A. Lady Liberty   B. Copperheads

THE COPPERHEAD PARTY—IN FAVOR OF A VIGOROUS PROSECUTION OF PEACE!

In the South, President Jefferson Davis also suspended the right of habeas corpus. He, too, believed he needed to deal harshly with opponents of the war. However, by suspending habeas corpus, Davis upset many loyal supporters. In early 1864, North Carolina's Governor Vance wrote him:

PRIMARY SOURCE

"I hear with deep regret that a bill is certainly expected to pass . . . suspending the writ of habeas corpus, throughout the Confederacy, and that certain arrests will immediately be made."
—letter to Confederate President Jefferson Davis

Draft Laws

After the initial excitement of the war had disappeared, both the North and the South had trouble recruiting troops. In 1862 the Confederate Congress passed a **draft** law requiring able-bodied white men between 18 and 35 to serve for three years. Later the range was extended to cover men between 17 and 50. There were several exceptions. If he could afford it, a man could hire a **substitute,** or replacement, to serve for him. Later, if a man had 20 or more enslaved people, he did not have to serve.

The North, at first, offered a **bounty,** or a sum of money paid to encourage volunteers. Then, in March 1863, it too passed a draft law. All men from age 20 to 45 had to register. As in the South, a man could avoid the draft, either by hiring a substitute or by paying $300. Such exceptions met with great protest. In both the North and the South, people complained it was "a rich man's war and a poor man's fight."

Antidraft sentiment led to riots in several Northern cities. The worst disturbance was the New York City draft riots in July 1863. Members of the working class, many of them Irish immigrants, attacked government and military buildings. Then mobs turned their attacks against African Americans. Many white workers had opposed the Emancipation Proclamation, fearing that freed blacks would take their jobs. After four days of terror, more than 100 people were dead. Federal troops had to be rushed in to stop the riots.

Economic Effects

The war strained the economies of the North and the South. However, the North, with its greater resources, was better able to cope with the immense costs of the war.

The two governments had three ways of paying for the war:

1. They borrowed money by selling war bonds that promised high interest.
2. They imposed new taxes, including income taxes.
3. They printed money. Northern money was called **greenbacks** because of its color.

The North Prospers

Northern industry profited from the war effort. It produced guns, ammunition, shoes, and uniforms. Farmers prospered as they sold their crops to provide a steady supply of food for the troops. However, prices rose faster than wages because goods were in high demand. This **inflation,** or general increase in prices, caused a great hardship for working people. Still, the Northern economy boomed during the war years.

Economic Troubles in the South

The war's economic strain was felt more sharply in the South, where warfare destroyed farmland and railroad lines. Also, the blockade prevented the shipping of trade goods. Vital materials could not reach the Confederacy. Salt was so desperately needed that women scraped the floors of smokehouses to recover it. Food shortages led to riots in Atlanta, Richmond, and other cities.

Inflation, too, was much worse in the South. As early as 1862, citizens begged Confederate leaders for help. In North Carolina, citizens wrote desperate letters to the governor:

PRIMARY SOURCE

"If it is Constitutional, and if your position . . . gives you the power to do so, in the name of . . . suffering humanity, of the cries of widows and orphans, *do* put down the Speculation and extortion in this . . . State."

—R. L. Abernethy to Governor Zebulon Vance, 1862

Reading Check **Determining Cause and Effect**
Describe at least three causes of discontent among people in the North and the South.

Section 3 Review

History ONLINE
Study Central™ To review this section, go to glencoe.com.

Vocabulary

1. Use each of these terms in a complete sentence that will help explain its meaning: distribute, habeas corpus, draft, substitute, bounty, greenback, inflation.

Main Ideas

2. **Describing** What role did Sally Tompkins play in the war effort? Which women played a similar role in the North?

3. **Summarizing** Who were the Copperheads? What was their position on fighting the war?

4. **Explaining** Why did the Union and the Confederacy institute drafts?

Critical Thinking

5. **Describing** Explain three ways that the governments raised money for the war effort.

Raising Funds

6. **Persuasive Writing** President Lincoln suspended writs of habeas corpus to prevent interference with the draft. Do you think suspending civil liberties is justified in some situations? Write a short essay explaining your position and defend it.

Answer the
7. **Essential Question**
What social, political, and economic changes resulted from the war?

The Strain of War

Essential Question ◄

How did the events at Gettysburg and Vicksburg change the course of the war?

Reading Guide

Content Vocabulary

entrench *(p. 57)*   siege *(p. 63)*

Academic Vocabulary

nevertheless *(p. 59)*   encounter *(p. 60)*

Key People and Events

54th Massachusetts *(p. 59)*

Pickett's Charge *(p. 61)*

Gettysburg Address *(p. 63)*

Reading Strategy

Taking Notes As you read, use a chart like the one shown below to write at least one important fact about each of these battles.

Battle	Importance
Fredericksburg	
Chancellorsville	
Gettysburg	
Siege of Vicksburg	

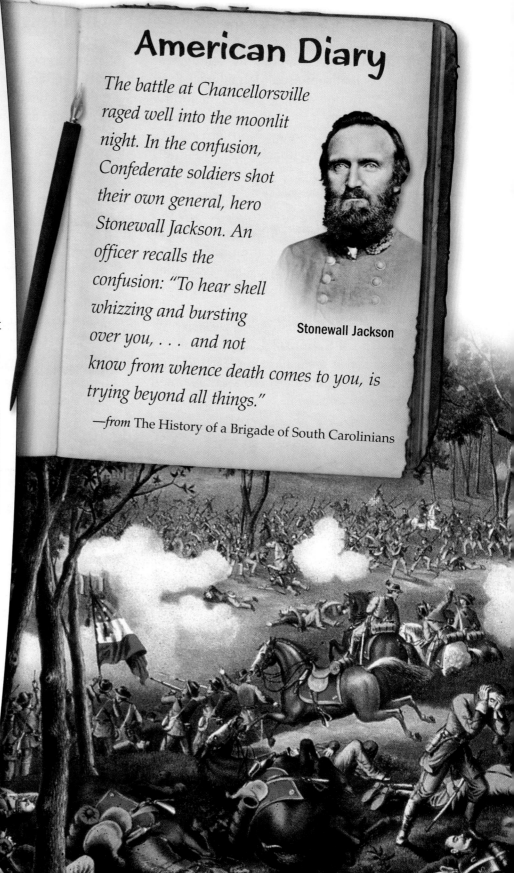

American Diary

The battle at Chancellorsville raged well into the moonlit night. In the confusion, Confederate soldiers shot their own general, hero Stonewall Jackson. An officer recalls the confusion: "To hear shell whizzing and bursting over you, . . . and not know from whence death comes to you, is trying beyond all things."

—from The History of a Brigade of South Carolinians

Stonewall Jackson

Southern Victories

Main Idea In the winter of 1862 and the spring of 1863, the South seemed to be winning the Civil War.

History and You How do leadership qualities make a difference to what happens in life? Read to learn the qualities of some Civil War battle commanders that led to victories and to defeat.

• •

Southern victories in the East were largely the result of the military leadership of generals Robert E. Lee and Stonewall Jackson. Through knowledge of the terrain and the ability to inspire troops, these two managed to defeat larger Union forces. Jackson's death at Chancellorsville not only removed one of the South's great strategists, it affected the morale of its army and its citizens. As Jackson lay dying, Lee said, "He has lost his left arm; I have lost my right."

Battle of Fredericksburg

After Antietam, Robert E. Lee moved his army out of Maryland into Virginia. This encouraged Union leaders to attack. The new Union commander, General Ambrose Burnside, boldly marched his troops toward the Confederate capital at Richmond.

Lee chose to intercept the Union troops near the town of Fredericksburg. He moved his forces to hills south of the town and ordered them to dig trenches so they could fire down on the enemy from a protected position. On December 13, 1862, the Union army attacked. Lee's **entrenched** forces drove the Union troops back soundly. Devastated by his failure, General Burnside resigned and was replaced by General Joseph Hooker.

Battle of Chancellorsville

In May 1863, Lee again used strategy brilliantly. He divided his forces in Virginia in response to General Hooker's having done the same thing—even though Hooker had twice as many men. Some Confederate troops stayed to defend Fredericksburg, and some confronted the main Union force at Chancellorsville. A third group made a daring maneuver that caught the Union army by surprise. Under the leadership of Stonewall Jackson, Confederate troops marched around the side of Hooker's position.

Stonewall Jackson mortally wounded at the battle of Chancellorsville in Virginia

Critical Thinking

Speculating What do you think is the main reason some leaders decided to fight for the Confederacy? For the Union?

Then, suddenly, Jackson's army turned and attacked the Union forces in the rear. At the same time, Lee struck from the front. Sandwiched between the two Confederate forces, Hooker eventually withdrew his men. One of the Confederate companies fired on Stonewall Jackson's company by mistake, wounding the general in the left arm. Jackson's arm had to be amputated, and he died a week later.

Weak Union Generals

In less than a year, three different generals led the Union forces. Lincoln was frustrated by their conduct of the war. Major General George McClellan commanded the Union forces at the Battle of Antietam in March 1862. He prepared well but was reluctant to engage the enemy. Said Lincoln, "If McClellan doesn't want to use the army, I'd like to borrow it for awhile."

The last straw came when, after victory at Antietam, McClellan failed to obey Lincoln's order to follow the retreating Confederate troops and "destroy the rebel army."

Lincoln pushed his next commander, General Ambrose Burnside, to take aggressive action. Burnside quickly lost the president's favor after a crushing loss at Fredericksburg.

Next, Lincoln appointed Major General Joseph Hooker, who had often been critical of other generals. Hooker's attitude matched the president's.

PRIMARY SOURCE

"May God have mercy on General Lee, for I will have none."

—General Joseph Hooker to his staff, April 1863

Words, however, were not enough to defeat Lee, who crushed Hooker's forces at Chancellorsville. Within two months, Hooker resigned.

Lincoln's next commander needed to prove himself quickly. Major General George Meade assumed command three days before one of the most important battles of the war.

Reading Check **Synthesizing** What strategies did General Lee use to defeat Union armies that were much larger than his?

Primary Source / African American Soldiers

Union Recruits Of the more than 2 million soldiers who served in the Union army and navy, nearly 200,000 were African American. As news of the Emancipation Proclamation spread, many African Americans from the North and the South enlisted. More than half were formerly enslaved.

▼ Union soldiers

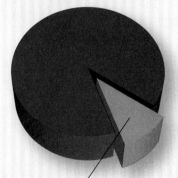

Union Army

Nearly 10% of the soldiers in the Union army were African American.

Union Navy

About 18% of sailors in the Union navy were African American.

African Americans in the War

Main Idea African Americans showed courage and skill as soldiers in the Union army.

History and You What does it mean to act bravely? Read to learn about the 54th Massachusetts regiment and the battle for Fort Wagner.

. . . .

At first, both the North and the South barred African Americans from serving in their armies. As time passed, the North relaxed its rules.

In the South

African Americans made up more than 30 percent of the Southern population, but Confederate leaders never seriously considered allowing them to enlist. Confederate leaders feared that African American soldiers, once armed, would attack their fellow troops or even begin a general revolt. The Confederates felt that the advantage of having more soldiers in their army did not justify this risk.

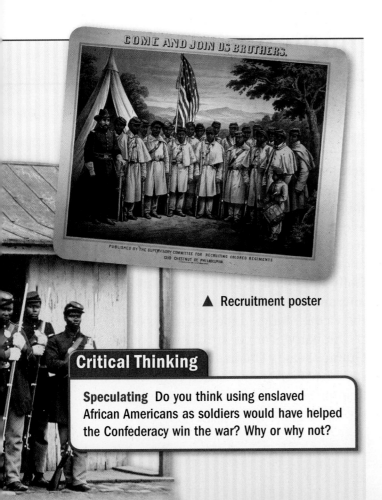

▲ Recruitment poster

Critical Thinking

Speculating Do you think using enslaved African Americans as soldiers would have helped the Confederacy win the war? Why or why not?

History ONLINE
Student Web Activity Visit glencoe.com and complete the Chapter 2 Web Activity about African Americans in the war.

In the North

President Lincoln at first resisted appeals to enlist African Americans in the Union army. He feared that such a policy would be resented in the border states. By 1862, though, it was evident that the North needed more soldiers, and many Union African Americans were eager to fight. As a result, Congress decided to allow the formation of all-African American regiments.

These new soldiers were in a tough position. Many white regiments from the North doubted their fighting ability. Others resented their presence. Many Southern troops hated the African American soldiers and often focused their fiercest gunfire on African American Northern regiments.

Still, African Americans joined. By the end of the war, they comprised about 10 percent of the Union army. Some were freed people from the North; others were runaway enslaved African Americans from the South. These men fought hard and effectively, too. As one white Union officer wrote about an all-African American Kansas regiment:

PRIMARY SOURCE

"They make better soldiers in every respect than any troops I have ever had under my command."
—Union general James G. Blunt

The 54th Massachusetts

The best-known African American regiment was the **54th Massachusetts.** In 1863 this regiment took part in an assault on Fort Wagner in South Carolina. The 54th served in the front lines of this battle. Confederate gunfire battered the men, causing nearly 300 casualties in this regiment alone. **Nevertheless,** the soldiers bravely fought on. Though the Union could not capture the fort, the 54th became famous for the courage and sacrifice of its members.

✔ **Reading Check** **Comparing and Contrasting** How were Union and Confederate policies regarding African American soldiers alike and different?

YOU DECIDE

Should Lee Have Invaded the North?

The war was fought in Southern territory for the most part. Lee's first invasion was turned back at Antietam. In 1863 he tried again.

The Alternatives

Play it safe

Should the South continue its defensive strategy?

Be bold

Should Lee launch a second invasion of the North?

Considering the Consequences

If the invasion fails

- The Confederacy makes no further attempt to invade the North.
- The tide of war turns in favor of the North.

If the invasion succeeds

- The Confederacy likely gains support from Europe.
- Union antiwar feeling grows.

The Decision

Could Lee's forces conquer the army of the Potomac on its own soil? Confident after the brilliant victory at Chancellorsville, Lee decided to invade the North.

The Results

- Lee's army in northern Virginia is defeated.
- The Confederacy makes no further attempt to invade the North.
- The tide of war turns in favor of the North.

DBQ Document-Based Questions

1. **Analyzing** In your opinion, did Lee have valid reasons for invading the North?

2. **Explaining** What do you think was the best reason for not invading the North?

The Tide of War Turns

Main Idea The Battle of Gettysburg marked a turn in the war as the Union forces defeated the Confederates.

History and You Have you ever made a decision that seemed right at the time but turned out to be disastrous? Read to learn what happened when General Lee decided to invade the North.

. . . .

In spring of 1863, the South had the upper hand, but that was soon to change. The Confederate victory at Chancellorsville ruined Union plans for attacking Richmond. Robert E. Lee, emboldened by his victories, decided to take the war into the North. A win there might impress France and Britain.

The South's strategy recalled that of the colonies in the Revolutionary War—though far outnumbered, they were aided by France and had won. Now, France and Britain missed the goods—especially cotton—they were accustomed to buying from Southern planters. If the Confederates appeared to be winning, those nations might help.

The Battle of Gettysburg

In July 1863, a small town in southern Pennsylvania became the site of one of the most decisive battles in the Civil War. Gettysburg was not a capital, a strategic port, or the location of an important fort. That such serious fighting took place there was almost an accident.

The Confederates entered the town for much-needed supplies. General Lee hoped to avoid fighting troops in an unfamiliar area. However, the two sides **encountered** one another. When Lee's armies crawled out of Gettysburg four grueling days later, it was after sustaining 25,000 casualties. The Union—the victor—suffered the loss of 23,000.

The battle started at 5:30 A.M. on July 1. Outnumbered, Union troops retreated to a section of high ground called Cemetery Ridge. Reinforcements for both sides arrived, and on the second day of fighting, Southern generals tried to dislodge Union forces from hills named Round Top and Little Round Top. However, after furious fighting, Union forces under the command of General George Meade held their positions.

That night, Meade made the decision not to retreat. The next day, Lee also made an important decision. He ordered an attack designed to "create a panic and virtually destroy the [Union] army."

The Confederates started by firing nearly 140 cannons at the Union lines. Then, under the leadership of General George Pickett, thousands of Confederate troops attacked the Union's center position at Cemetery Ridge. Putting themselves directly in the way of musket and artillery fire, they advanced across open land.

At first, it seemed that **Pickett's Charge** might work—the Confederates broke the first line of Union defense. In the end, however, three-quarters of those who started the attack lay dead or wounded on the ground. Lee later wrote:

"The army did all it could. I fear I required of it impossibilities."

—from *Memoirs of Robert E. Lee*

Gettysburg put an end to one goal of Confederate foreign policy: gaining help from Britain and France. The South hoped to receive from the British two ironclads that would be used to sweep Union shipping from the Atlantic. However, in October 1863, the British government decided not to release the ships.

The Vicksburg Siege

On July 4, the day that Lee retreated from Gettysburg, the Confederacy suffered another major military blow. The important river city of Vicksburg, Mississippi, fell under the control of Union troops led by Ulysses S. Grant.

The Battle of Gettysburg, Day 3 NATIONAL GEOGRAPHIC

Confederate troops

Union troops

Confederate troop movements

0 1 kilometer
0 1 mile
Albers Equal-Area projection

Pickett's Charge came at the height of the three-day battle. More than 12,000 Confederate troops marched across an open field to attack the Union's center position. The effort ended in disaster.

▲ Today, the Gettysburg battlefield's 1,400 monuments commemorate "the great deeds of valor."

"The sacrifice of life on that blood soaked field . . . was too awful for the heralding of victory, even for our victorious foe."

—George E. Pickett, in a letter to his fiancée

Critical Thinking

Concluding Why did Pickett think that the North did not want to celebrate the victory?

Primary Source

The Gettysburg Address

On November 19, 1863, President Abraham Lincoln gave a short speech at the dedication of a national cemetery on the battlefield of Gettysburg. His simple yet eloquent words expressed his hopes for a nation divided by civil war.

▲ Monument at Gettysburg

Four **score** and seven years ago our fathers brought forth on this continent a new nation, conceived in liberty, and dedicated to the **proposition** that all men are created equal.

> Lincoln is referring to the nation declaring its independence in 1776—87 years before.

Now we are engaged in a great civil war, testing whether that nation, or any nation so conceived and so dedicated, can long **endure.** We are met on a great battlefield of that war. We have come to dedicate a portion of that field as a final resting place for those who here gave their lives that that nation might live. It is altogether fitting and proper that we should do this.

> Union soldiers were fighting to keep the nation (North and South) together.

But, in a larger sense, we can not dedicate—we can not **consecrate**—we can not **hallow**—this ground. The brave men, living and dead, who struggled here, have consecrated it far above our poor power to add or detract. The world will little note nor long remember what we say here, but it can never forget what they did here. It is for us, the living, rather, to be dedicated here to the unfinished work which they who fought here have thus far so nobly advanced. It is rather for us to be here dedicated to the great task remaining before us—that from these honored dead we take increased devotion to that cause for which they gave the last full measure of devotion; that we here highly **resolve** that these dead shall not have died in vain; that this nation, under God, shall have a new birth of freedom; and that government of the people, by the people, for the people, shall not perish from the earth.

> The soldiers who died made the supreme sacrifice. Lincoln believes it is up to those who are still living to carry on their unfinished work.

> The U.S. government was created to serve the people. People are the source of the government's power.

VOCABULARY

score: twenty

proposition (PRAH·puh·ZI·shun): an idea or a belief

endure: to continue or last

consecrate (KAHN·suh·KRAT): to dedicate to a sacred purpose

hallow (HA·LOH): to respect greatly

resolve: to make a firm decision

Critical Thinking

1. **Making Inferences** How is the Civil War going to "test" whether or not the United States can endure?

2. **Interpreting** Why do you think Lincoln thought it was so important to honor those who fought and died at Gettysburg?

3. **Finding the Main Idea** According to Lincoln, why was the war being fought?

Grant first launched his attack in April, surrounding the 30,000 Confederate troops holding Vicksburg. In May, Grant began a **siege** against the town, blockading it to prevent food and supplies from entering. Union gunships on the river supported Grant's 77,000 troops by firing thousands of mortar shells into the city.

During the 47-day siege, both sides suffered heavy casualties. More than 9,000 Confederate and 10,000 Union troops died, many of disease or starvation. Remarkably, fewer than 20 civilians were killed in the siege.

The bad news did not end there for the South, though. A few days later, it lost Port Hudson in Louisiana, its last stronghold on the vital Mississippi River. The Union strategy to split the South in two had succeeded. Arkansas, Louisiana, and Texas were now cut off. In a single month, July 1863, the Civil War reached a major turning point.

Lincoln's Gettysburg Address

On November 19, 1863, Soldiers' National Cemetery was dedicated at Gettysburg. At the ceremony, former governor of Massachusetts Edward Everett delivered a two-hour speech. After him, President Abraham Lincoln spoke for about two minutes. In 272 words, Lincoln was able to honor the soldiers and the cause for which they had fought and died, as well as state his vision for the country.

PRIMARY SOURCE

"These dead shall not have died in vain. . . . Government of the people, by the people, for the people shall not perish from the earth."

—from the Gettysburg Address

Reactions to Lincoln's **Gettysburg Address** in the press were mixed. Everett, along with the *New York Times*, *Chicago Tribune*, and *Springfield* (Mass.) *Republican*, thought the speech was a success. The *Republican* wrote, "His little speech is a perfect gem; deep in feeling, compact in thought and expression, and tasteful . . . in every word and comma."

Reading Check **Explaining** How do the events of this section demonstrate that the "tide" of war turned?

Section 4 Review

Vocabulary

1. Define each of these terms in a sentence that will help explain its meaning: entrench, nevertheless, encounter, siege.

Main Ideas

2. **Explaining** Why was the battle of Chancellorsville important?

3. **Contrasting** How were African American soldiers treated differently than white soldiers?

4. **Explaining** In the Gettysburg Address, what did Lincoln say was the duty of "the living" to accomplish?

Critical Thinking

5. **Making Inferences** Why do you think many leaders called for African Americans to be allowed to fight in the Civil War?

6. **Organizing** Using a graphic organizer similar to the one below, list the results of the Battle of Gettysburg.

7. **Expository Writing** Refer to Lincoln's Gettysburg Address in this section. Write an essay discussing Lincoln's ideas on freedom and the importance of saving the Union.

Answer the
8. **Essential Question**
How did the events at Gettysburg and Vicksburg change the course of the war?

The War's Final Stages

Essential Question

What events led to the end of the war?

Reading Guide

Content Vocabulary

total war *(p. 65)*   resistance *(p. 67)*

Academic Vocabulary

series *(p. 65)*   interpret *(p. 67)*

Key People and Events

David Farragut *(p. 67)*

March to the Sea *(p. 68)*

Appomattox Court House *(p. 70)*

Reading Strategy

Taking Notes As you read, take notes on the significance of battles late in the war.

Battle	Importance

American Diary

After Union forces took control of Atlanta on September 2, 1864, General William Sherman ordered the city burned and the citizens to leave. When the mayor of Atlanta pleaded with Sherman to change his mind, Sherman refused. He responded: "War is cruelty, and you cannot refine it. . . . You might as well appeal against the thunderstorm as against these terrible hardships of war."

—from Memoirs of General William T. Sherman

Atlanta and many other Southern cities, including Richmond as shown here, suffered large-scale destruction as the war continued.

Total War Strikes the South

Main Idea After a long, bloody summer, Union forces captured major Southern strongholds, and as a result, Lincoln won reelection.

History and You Have you ever had a goal that was difficult to reach? Did you have a strategy to reach your goal? Read to learn how Grant and the Union forces executed their plan.

· ·

General William Sherman's destruction of Atlanta and other areas of the South was part of a deliberate strategy to bring the horrors of war—terror, starvation, violence, and homelessness—to the Southern people. This systematic destruction of an entire land—not just its army—is called **total war**.

Union Strategy

By 1864, Union forces surrounded the South. Union ships blocked the Confederate coast, strangling its export economy and cutting off supplies. The Union controlled the Mississippi River, and the western Confederate states were cut off. A bold plan of attack was needed. General Grant would be the one to draw up such a plan.

Grant in Charge

Ulysses S. Grant was only an average student and a failure as a farmer and businessperson. At soldiering, however, he was brilliant. He chalked up victories at Shiloh and Vicksburg and at another important battle in Chattanooga, Tennessee. In March 1864, President Lincoln put General Grant in charge of all the Union armies.

Grant then devised his plan. He would deliver killing blows from all sides. His armies would move on to Richmond, the Confederate capital. At the same time, William Tecumseh Sherman would lead his troops in attacks across the Deep South.

Grant soon put his strategy into effect. In May and June of 1864, Grant's army of 115,000 men smashed into Lee's 64,000 troops in a **series** of three battles near Richmond, Virginia—the battles of the Wilderness, Spotsylvania Courthouse, and Cold Harbor. Each time Confederate lines held, but each time Grant quickly resumed the attack.

"Whatever happens, there will be no turning back," Grant promised Lincoln. He was determined to march southward, attacking Lee's forces relentlessly until the Confederacy surrendered.

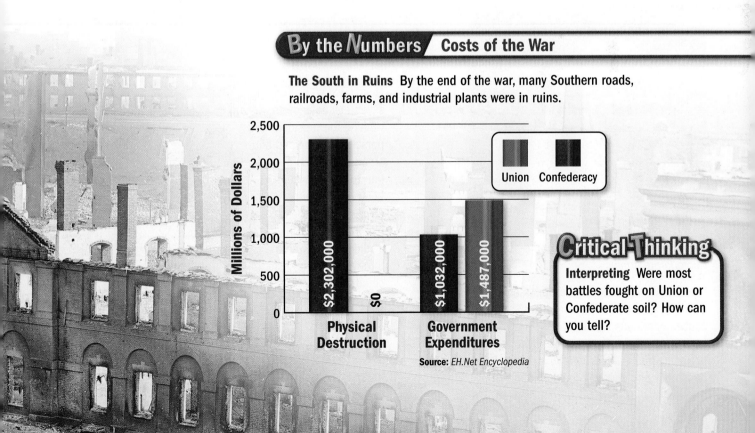

By the Numbers / Costs of the War

The South in Ruins By the end of the war, many Southern roads, railroads, farms, and industrial plants were in ruins.

Millions of Dollars

	Union	Confederacy
Physical Destruction	$0	$2,302,000
Government Expenditures	$1,032,000	$1,487,000

Source: *EH.Net Encyclopedia*

Critical Thinking

Interpreting Were most battles fought on Union or Confederate soil? How can you tell?

The Wilderness Campaign

In the northeast corner of the Confederacy, about halfway between Washington, D.C., and Richmond, Virginia, lay an area of dense woods called the Wilderness. Here, on May 5, 1864, the six bloodiest weeks of the war began. For two days, the forces of Grant and Lee struggled among a tangle of trees through which they could scarcely see. Said a Union private, "It was a blind and bloody hunt to the death."

Lee had only about 60,000 men to Grant's more than 100,000. Both sides suffered huge casualties. Grant, who lost 17,000 men, cried in his tent at the end of the second day. Meanwhile, brushfires raged through the forest, burning alive 200 wounded men. On the morning of the third day, with no clear winner, Grant moved his forces south toward Richmond.

The next battles were fought at nearby Spotsylvania Courthouse and at Cold Harbor. On June 2, the night before this third battle began, a Union general observed that men were "writing their names and home addresses on slips of paper and pinning them to the backs of their coats" to help people identify their bodies. The war seemed hopeless. Grant, however, was determined. He explained to the White House:

PRIMARY SOURCE

"I propose to fight it out on this line, if it takes all summer."

—Dispatch to Washington, May 11, 1864

Grant's critics in the North called him a "butcher" because of the huge loss of life among his own troops—50,000 in 30 days. Lincoln, however, said, "I can't spare this man. He fights."

People IN HISTORY

Robert E. Lee

General, commander in chief of the Confederate armies

Lee, a brilliant scholar and a daring soldier, was willing to take risks. However, when his orders caused enormous loss of lives, he was filled with sadness. When he finally surrendered, he told his troops he had *"unceasing admiration of your constancy and devotion to your country."*

Abraham Lincoln

Sixteenth president of the United States

Lincoln would not give up. He lost seven elections on the way to winning the presidency. His perseverance helped him stand against all opposition to the war. He believed, *"A house divided against itself cannot stand."* He would see the war through until the country was reunited.

The Petersburg Siege

Continuing his movement south, Grant went on to Petersburg, a railroad center that was vital to the Confederate movement of troops and supplies. If Grant could take Petersburg, then Richmond would be cut off from the rest of the Confederacy. Grant laid siege. The Confederates defended the city, but they could not win. Trains brought food and reinforcements to the Union troops. The Confederates could get neither. For nine long months, however, they held out.

Sherman in Georgia

Meanwhile, William Tecumseh Sherman took off for Georgia. In early July, his troops circled Atlanta. There they faced the brilliant Confederate general, John Hood, whose forces put up major **resistance.** Sherman laid siege. Finally, on September 1, Hood abandoned the

Ulysses S. Grant

General of the United States Army and eighteenth president of the United States

Grant was a fearless soldier and an expert horseman at a time when soldiers rode horses in battle. Grant's strategy seemed ruthless at times, but he said, *"I have never advocated [war] except as a means of peace."*

CRITICAL Thinking

1. **Synthesizing** What characteristics do you think these three men shared?

2. **Describing** Select a quote from one of the men described. What does the quote reveal about that person?

city. The mood in the South was desperate. Mary Chesnut, a Georgian who kept a diary throughout the war, wrote, "There is no hope, but we will try to have no fear."

Farragut at Mobile Bay

The highest-ranking officer in the Union navy was **David Farragut,** the son of a Latino military man. Young David Farragut joined the navy when he was only 12 years old. Now, in August 1864, he was leading a fleet of 18 ships through a narrow channel into Mobile Bay in Alabama. The Confederates had two forts on either side of the channel, and they had mined the waters with torpedoes. Guns were firing from both forts. What was Farragut to do? He gave his famous order, "Damn the torpedoes, full speed ahead!"

Farragut, who was suffering from dizziness, had himself tied to the ship's rigging so he could stay in the battle. His invasion was a success, and the last Southern port east of the Mississippi was blocked.

The Election of 1864

Through most of 1864, opposition to the war in the North grew stronger. A presidential election was coming up in November, and it looked unlikely that Lincoln would win reelection. His loss could mean an end to the war and recognition of the Confederate government as an independent country. Southerners clung to this hope.

After Atlanta fell and Mobile Bay was blocked, Northerners began to believe again that they could win. Lincoln won a second term handsomely—with 55 percent of the popular vote, 212 to 21 electoral votes.

Lincoln **interpreted,** or explained, his reelection as a clear sign from the voters to end slavery permanently by amending the Constitution. On January 31, 1865, Congress passed the Thirteenth Amendment, which banned slavery in the United States.

Reading Check **Summarizing** What was the Union strategy in 1864, and what were the results?

Battle Dates

The Wilderness
May 5–6, 1864

Cold Harbor
June 3, 1864

Petersburg siege
June 5, 1864–April 3, 1865

Kennesaw Mountain
June 27, 1864

Atlanta
July 20–Sept. 2, 1864

Franklin
Nov. 30, 1864

Nashville
Dec. 15–16, 1864

Wilmington
Feb. 12–22, 1865

Bentonville
March 19–21, 1865

Appomattox Court House
April 9, 1865

Map Skills

1. **Location** Where did Sherman's March to the Sea begin and end?
2. **Analyzing Information** Which battle was considered "indecisive"? Why?

Maps In MOtion See StudentWorks™ Plus or glencoe.com.

The War's End

Main Idea After four years of fighting against unfavorable odds, the South finally surrendered.

History and You How would you treat an enemy who said, "I give up"?

From the beginning of the war, the Union army wanted to capture the Confederate capital. When Grant finally drove Lee's army out of Petersburg, Virginia, Jefferson Davis knew that Richmond was doomed.

Sherman's March to the Sea

The last months of the war saw the Union determined to break the will of the South. Sherman and his men became destroyers.

Before Sherman's army left Atlanta in November, it burned much of this beautiful city. From Atlanta, Sherman's troops burned cities and farmlands as they marched across Georgia to the Atlantic coast. This trail of destruction is known as Sherman's **March to the Sea.**

Sherman continued his path of destruction through the Carolinas to join Grant's forces near Richmond. Union troops took what food they needed, tore up railroad lines and fields, and killed livestock in an effort to destroy anything that was useful to the South.

White Southerners deplored Sherman's march, but thousands of African Americans left their plantations to follow the protection of his army. For them, this was a march to freedom.

The Union Advances

1861

Early Stages Confederate troops won most of the battles in the first year of the Civil War.

1863

Union Gains Union control of the Mississippi River cut off Texas and Arkansas, the South's leading food producers, from the Confederacy.

1865

Final Stages By 1865, the Union controlled large parts of the Confederacy.

By the Numbers

Lives Lost More lives were lost in the Civil War than in any other major American conflict. Deadly weapons, poor medical practices, infection, and disease all contributed.

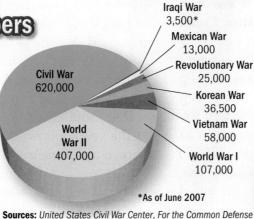

Civil War 620,000

World War II 407,000

Iraqi War 3,500*

Mexican War 13,000

Revolutionary War 25,000

Korean War 36,500

Vietnam War 58,000

World War I 107,000

*As of June 2007

Sources: *United States Civil War Center, For the Common Defense*

Unknown Soldiers A gravestone in Gettysburg Cemetery commemorates the loss of 425 Civil War soldiers who were never identified.

The Fall of Richmond

Meanwhile, Grant continued the siege of Petersburg. Lee and his troops defended the town, but sickness, casualties, and desertion weakened them. Finally, on April 2, 1865, the Confederate lines broke and Lee withdrew.

Word of Lee's retreat came to the Confederate president. As the Union army marched toward Richmond, Davis and his cabinet gathered documents, gave orders that bridges and weapons useful to the enemy be set on fire, and fled the city. An observer wrote:

PRIMARY SOURCE

"The trains came and went, wagons, vehicles, and horsemen rumbled and dashed to and fro. . . . As night came on . . . rioting and robbing took place."

—from *Battles and Leaders of the Civil War*

The armory, with its stores of ammunition, exploded. Boom after boom rang through the city, and fires raged out of control.

Two days later, President Lincoln and his son Tad arrived to tour the fallen capital. Said Lincoln, "Thank God I have lived to see this. It seems to me that I have been dreaming a horrid nightmare for four years, and now the nightmare is over."

Joyful African Americans followed Lincoln everywhere, singing, laughing, and reaching out to touch him. When one man knelt down to thank him, Lincoln replied, "Don't kneel to me. You must kneel to God only, and thank Him for your freedom."

At the Confederate president's house, Lincoln sat in a chair in Davis's office and "looked far off with a dreamy expression."

At Libby Prison, where the Union held Confederate prisoners of war, Lincoln was asked what to do with the prisoners and replied, "If I were in your place, I'd let 'em up easy, let 'em up easy."

Surrender at Appomattox

The formal end of the war came a few days later, on April 9, 1865. Two days earlier, Grant asked Lee to surrender, writing, "The result of last week must convince you of the hopelessness of further resistance."

Yet Lee believed he must fight on. However, when the Union captured the train carrying food to his troops and Lee was completely surrounded, he knew it was over.

In the little town of **Appomattox Court House,** Virginia, Grant met with Lee. They shook hands and talked a little. Then Grant offered his terms. Lee's soldiers could keep their small firearms, the officers could keep their horses, and no one would disturb the soldiers as they made their way home. In an act of generosity, Grant also gave 25,000 rations to feed Lee's troops. Dignity and compassion were the order of the day that ended America's deadliest war.

The Toll of War

More lives were lost in the Civil War than in any other conflict in American history. More than 600,000 soldiers died. The war cost billions of dollars. In the South, cities and farmlands were destroyed, and it would take years and a massive national effort to rebuild.

The war had other consequences as well. The North's victory saved the Union. The federal government was strengthened and was now clearly more powerful than the states. Finally, the war freed millions of African Americans. The end of slavery, however, did not solve the problems that the newly freed African Americans were to face.

Following the war, many questions remained. No one yet knew how to bring the Southern states back into the Union, nor what the status of African Americans would be in Southern society. Americans from the North and the South tried to answer these questions in the years following the Civil War—an era known as Reconstruction.

 Reading Check **Evaluating** What events led to Lee's surrender?

Section 5 Review

 History ONLINE
Study Central™ To review this section, go to glencoe.com.

Vocabulary

1. Define each of the following terms, and use them in a paragraph about the last year of the Civil War: total war, series resistance, interpret.

Main Ideas

2. Explaining How did events on the battlefield affect Lincoln's reelection?

3. Describing Why did Sherman burn and destroy the South's land?

4. Explaining What were Grant's terms of surrender at Appomattox Court House?

Critical Thinking

5. Analyzing Complete a graphic organizer similar to the one below to explain the effects of the Civil War on the nation.

6. Descriptive Writing Take on the role of a reporter living in Georgia during Sherman's March to the Sea. Write a brief article describing the Union's actions and their effects on the people living there.

Answer the
7. Essential Question
What events led to the end of the war?

Visual Summary

1861

Feb. Southern states form the Confederacy

Apr. Union surrenders Fort Sumter

June Four border states stay in the Union

July First major battle fought at Bull Run in Virginia

1862

Mar. The *Monitor* and the *Virginia* fight the first battle between ironclad ships

Virginia

Apr. Farragut's naval forces capture New Orleans

Sept. Antietam is the first major battle on Northern soil

1863

Jan. Lincoln issues Emancipation Proclamation

July Lee's invasion of the North turned back at Gettysburg

July Fall of Vicksburg results in Union control of the Mississippi River

1864

Mar. General Ulysses Grant assumes command of all Union armies

Nov. Lincoln reelected to second term

1865

Feb. Sherman's forces march through the Carolinas

Apr. 2 Lee evacuates Richmond; Union forces capture capital

Apr. 9 Surrender at Appomattox Court House

Apr. 14 Lincoln is assassinated

▲ A Union soldier with his family in a Washington, D.C., camp in 1862

STUDY TO GO Study anywhere, anytime! Download quizzes and flash cards to your PDA from glencoe.com.

TEST-TAKING TIP

Answer the questions you know first and go back to those for which you need more time.

Reviewing Main Ideas

Directions: Choose the best answer for each of the following questions.

1. What was one advantage the Southern states had during the Civil War?

A They received military support from Britain and France.

B Many battles occurred on lands with which Southerners were more familiar.

C The largest weapons factories were located in the South.

D Most people in the country agreed with the position of the Southern states.

2. By gaining control of the Mississippi and Tennessee Rivers, what was the Union able to do?

A capture Fort Sumter

B force the Confederacy to surrender

C split the Confederacy

D defeat the Confederate forces at Gettysburg

3. During the war, the economy of the South

A was severely strained from the blockade instituted by the North and the destruction of Southern land and property.

B remained unchanged because most of the battles took place on Northern soil.

C was strengthened due to inflation.

D was strengthened because bounties were paid to army recruits.

4. Which Union general proved to be most effective?

A General McClellan **C** General Burnside

B General Grant **D** General Hooker

Short-Answer Question

Directions: Base your answer to question 5 on the excerpt below and on your knowledge of social studies.

> With malice toward none, with charity for all, with firmness in the right as God gives us to see the right, let us strive on to finish the work we are in, to bind up the nation's wounds, to care for him who shall have borne the battle and for his widow and his orphan—to do all which may achieve and cherish a just and lasting peace among ourselves and with all nations.
>
> —from Abraham Lincoln's second Inaugural Address

5. In his address, Lincoln did not focus on the Union victory in the Civil War. State *two* reasons why this is so.

Review the Essential Questions

6. Essay How did the Civil War affect the North and the South?

To help you write your essay, review your answers to the Essential Questions in the section reviews and the chapter Foldables Study Organizer. Your essay should include:

- the strengths and weaknesses of the two sides;
- the results of early battles;
- social, political, and economic changes;
- how Vicksburg and Gettysburg changed the course of the war; and
- the aftermath of war.

GO ON

History ONLINE

For additional test practice, use **Self-Check Quizzes**—Chapter 2 at glencoe.com.

Document-Based Questions

Directions: Analyze the documents and answer the short-answer questions that follow.

Document 1

In July 1861 Confederate diplomat John Slidell describes one advantage the South holds.

> We shall have the enormous advantage of fighting on our own territory and for our very existence.

Source: James M. McPherson, *Ordeal By Fire*

7. Why would fighting on familiar territory be an advantage?

Document 2

A Union cavalry man taken prisoner describes the conditions of the Andersonville prison.

> July 6. Boiling hot, camp reeking with filth, and no sanitary privileges; men dying off over 140 per day . . . .Disease is here and mowing down good and true men. . . .Bread today and it is so coarse as to do more hurt than good to a majority of the prisoners.

Source: *Eyewitness to America*

8. What was life like for prisoners during the Civil War?

Document 3

The diaries of Mary Chesnut of South Carolina describe life in the South during the Civil War.

> Since we left Chester nothing but solitude, nothing but tall blackened chimneys, to show that any man has trod here before. This is Sherman's track.

Source: Mary Boykin Chesnut, *A Diary From Dixie*

9. What does this excerpt reveal about Sherman's strategy in fighting the South?

Document 4

This political cartoon appeared in an August 1862 edition of *Punch,* a British magazine.

LINCOLN'S TWO DIFFICULTIES.

Lin. "WHAT? NO MONEY! NO MEN!"

Source: Corbis

10. Based on this cartoon, identify *two* challenges the Union faced in fighting the war.

Document 5

Frederick Douglass led the movement to allow African American men to enlist.

> Once let the black man get upon his person the brass letters U.S. . . . and a musket on his shoulder and bullets in his pocket, and there is no power on earth which can deny that he has earned the right to citizenship [in the United States].

Source: James M. McPherson, *Battle Cry of Freedom*

11. Based on this document, identify *one* reason Douglass wanted African American men to fight in the war.

12. Expository Writing Using the information from the five documents and your knowledge of social studies, write an essay in which you:

- discuss the main goals for the Union and the Confederacy in fighting the Civil War; and

- discuss the effects of the war on soldiers and civilians.

Need Extra Help?												
If you missed questions...	1	2	3	4	5	6	7	8	9	10	11	12
Go to page...	34	40–41	52–53	58	64–65	30–70	33–34	51	64–68	56–63	59	30–70

Chapter 3

Reconstruction and the New South 1865–1896

A teacher and her students in front of the Freedmen's School in North Carolina

ABRAHAM
LINCOLN
1861–1865

ANDREW
JOHNSON
1865–1869

1867
• Alaska purchased
• First Recon-
  struction Act
  passed

1870
Fifteenth
Amendment
ratified

ULYSSES S.
GRANT
1869–1877

1877
Reconstruction
ends

PRESIDENTS

U.S. Events

World Events

1860

1870

1866
First transatlantic
cable connects
North America to
Europe

1868
Meiji era
begins in
Japan

1871
Bismarck
unifies
Germany

1874
First major
exhibit of
impressionist
art in Paris

History ONLINE
Chapter Overview Visit glencoe.com
and click on **Chapter 3—Chapter Overviews**
to preview chapter information.

Section 1: Reconstruction Plans

Essential Question How did plans to unify the nation differ after the Civil War?

Section 2: Radicals in Control

Essential Question What were the results of Radical Reconstruction?

Section 3: The South During Reconstruction

Essential Question In what ways did government in the Southern states change during Reconstruction?

Section 4: Change in the South

Essential Question How did the South change politically, economically, and socially when Reconstruction ended?

FOLDABLES®
Study Organizer

Organizing Information

Make this Foldable to help you summarize what you learn about Reconstruction and the New South.

Step 1 Fold an 11" x 17" piece of paper lengthwise to create a shutterfold.

Step 2 Fold a 3-inch tab along the bottom, and glue or staple the seams to create four pockets.

Step 3 Label the Foldable as shown.

Reading and Writing
As you read the chapter, take notes on notecards about key events and issues covered in each section. Use your Foldable to store the cards, and then answer the Essential Questions for each section.

Jane Addams, founder of Hull House ▶

RUTHERFORD B. HAYES
1877–1881

JAMES GARFIELD
1881

CHESTER ARTHUR
1881–1885

GROVER CLEVELAND
1885–1889

★ **1890**
Hull House opens in Chicago

BENJAMIN HARRISON
1889–1893

GROVER CLEVELAND
1893–1897

1880   **1890**   **1900**

★ **1882**
Beginning of British occupation of Egypt

★ **1886**
First May Day celebration held in Paris

★ **1891**
Famine spreads throughout Russia

★ **1896**
Ethiopia defeats invading Italians

Chapter 3   75

Reconstruction Plans

Essential Question ◄

How did plans to unify the nation differ after the Civil War?

Reading Guide

Content Vocabulary

Reconstruction (p. 77)

amnesty (p. 77)

Academic Vocabulary

radical (p. 78)

adjust (p. 78)

Key People and Events

Ten Percent Plan (p. 77)

Radical Republicans (p. 78)

Thaddeus Stevens (p. 78)

Wade-Davis Bill (p. 78)

Freedmen's Bureau (p. 78)

John Wilkes Booth (p. 79)

Andrew Johnson (p. 79)

Reading Strategy

Taking Notes As you read, use a diagram like the one below to describe each Reconstruction plan.

Ten Percent Plan	→	
Wade-Davis Plan	→	
Restoration	→	

American Diary

Major Henry Rathbone tried to seize John Wilkes Booth after Booth shot President Lincoln at Ford's Theater. As Booth leaped over the railing of the presidential box onto the stage, Rathbone cried, "Stop that man." Rathbone later stated: "I then turned to the President. . . . I saw that he was unconscious, and, supposing him mortally wounded, rushed to the door for the purpose of calling medical aid."

—from **The Assassination of President Lincoln and the Trial of the Conspirators**

The funeral train that carried Lincoln's body traveled more than 1,700 miles (2,736 km) and stopped in 10 major cities before arriving in Springfield, Illinois.

Reconstruction Debate

Main Idea Government leaders disagreed about how Southern states could rejoin the Union.

History and You Have you ever had an argument with a friend? How did you resolve your differences? Read to learn how the North and South tried to work out their problems after the Civil War.

. . . .

Major Henry Rathbone and the rest of the nation were deeply shocked by Abraham Lincoln's assassination. Four years of civil war, followed by the president's death, shook the nation. The Union was saved, but Americans still faced the difficult challenges of reuniting and rebuilding their country.

Southern states, because they had left the Union in 1861, needed to be readmitted. The economy and society of the devastated South also needed to be rebuilt. Americans disagreed bitterly, however, about how to accomplish these tasks. This period of rebuilding is called **Reconstruction.** This term also refers to the various plans for readmitting Southern states to the Union.

Lincoln's Plan

Before his assassination, President Lincoln offered the first plan for accepting the Southern states back into the Union. In December 1863, during the Civil War, the president announced what came to be known as the **Ten Percent Plan.** When 10 percent of the voters of a state took an oath of loyalty to the Union, the state could form a new government and adopt a new constitution that banned slavery.

Lincoln wanted to encourage Southerners who supported the Union to take charge of the state governments. He believed that punishing the South would serve no useful purpose and would only delay healing the torn nation. Lincoln offered **amnesty**—a pardon—to all white Southerners who were willing to swear loyalty to the Union, except Confederate leaders. In 1864 three states under Union occupation—Louisiana, Arkansas, and Tennessee—set up governments under the plan. These states then became caught in controversy when Congress refused to seat the states' representatives.

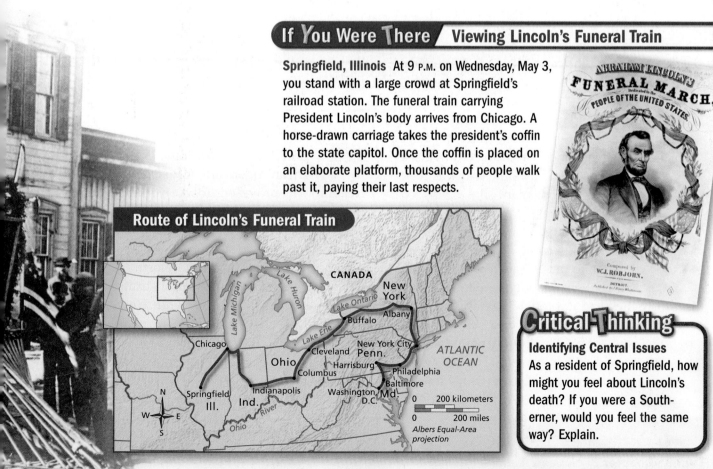

If You Were There / **Viewing Lincoln's Funeral Train**

Springfield, Illinois At 9 P.M. on Wednesday, May 3, you stand with a large crowd at Springfield's railroad station. The funeral train carrying President Lincoln's body arrives from Chicago. A horse-drawn carriage takes the president's coffin to the state capitol. Once the coffin is placed on an elaborate platform, thousands of people walk past it, paying their last respects.

ABRAHAM LINCOLN'S
FUNERAL MARCH,
Dedicated to the
PEOPLE OF THE UNITED STATES

Composed by
W.J. ROBJOHN.

DETROIT.
Published by J. Henry Whittemore

Route of Lincoln's Funeral Train

CANADA
Lake Michigan
Lake Huron
Lake Ontario
New York
Buffalo
Albany
Chicago
Lake Erie
Cleveland
New York City
Penn.
ATLANTIC OCEAN
Ohio
Columbus
Harrisburg
Springfield
Ill.
Indianapolis
Ind.
Philadelphia
Baltimore
Washington
D.C.
Md.
Ohio River

N
W E
S

0   200 kilometers
0   200 miles
Albers Equal-Area projection

Critical Thinking

Identifying Central Issues
As a resident of Springfield, how might you feel about Lincoln's death? If you were a Southerner, would you feel the same way? Explain.

Course of Study African Americans who were enrolled in freedmen's schools learned practical skills such as sewing as well as academic subjects. A popular textbook was Lydia Maria Child's *Freedmen's Book,* a collection of essays and poems used to teach and inspire freed African Americans.

▼ Freedmen's Bureau School, Edisto Island, South Carolina

"Yesterday . . . my sister and I formally opened school. . . . We had more than one thousand (1,000) children, and seventy-five adults; and found time, after disciplining them, to hear the readers, to instruct the writers, and to teach the multitude from the blackboard."
—Lucy Chase, April 1865

"We have glorious schools in full blast—And I am so satisfied with the work here that nothing in the world could make me wish to be in another place, or doing anything else."
—Sarah Chase, February 1866

Critical Thinking

Analyzing Why do you think practical skills and academic subjects were taught at freed people's schools?

The Radicals' Plan

Some Republicans considered Lincoln's plan too forgiving. They favored a more **radical,** or extreme, approach and were called **Radical Republicans.** Radical Republican **Thaddeus Stevens** declared that Southern institutions "must be broken up and relaid, or all our blood and treasure have been spent in vain." Congress was controlled by the Radical Republicans and voted to deny seats to representatives from any state that was readmitted under Lincoln's plan.

In July 1864, Congress passed the **Wade-Davis Bill.** To rejoin the Union, a state had to meet several requirements. First, a majority of the state's white males had to swear loyalty to the Union. Second, only white males who swore they had not fought against the Union could vote for delegates to a state constitutional convention. Finally, any new state constitution had to ban slavery. The bill would also bar former Confederates from holding public office.

Lincoln refused to sign the bill, but he wanted new state governments to form quickly so that order could be restored in the South as soon as possible. Lincoln realized that he would have to compromise with the Radical Republicans.

The Freedmen's Bureau

In March 1865, Lincoln and Congress set up the **Freedmen's Bureau.** The bureau helped African Americans **adjust,** or adapt, to freedom. It provided food, clothing, and medical services. It helped freed people acquire land or find work for fair wages.

The bureau also set up schools, staffed mostly by teachers from the North. It gave aid to new African American institutions of higher learning, such as Atlanta University, Howard University, and Fisk University.

Reading Check **Contrasting** What were the differences between Lincoln's views and the Radical Republicans' views concerning Reconstruction?

Johnson's Plan

Main Idea After Lincoln was assassinated, Andrew Johnson became president and announced his plan of "Restoration."

History and You How do you think Abraham Lincoln's death might affect plans to unify the nation? Read about President Johnson's Reconstruction plan.

Shortly after the Freedmen's Bureau was founded, a tragic event took place that shocked the nation. On April 14, 1865, President Lincoln attended a play at Ford's Theater in Washington, D.C. **John Wilkes Booth,** an actor and Confederate sympathizer, entered the private box and shot Lincoln in the head. Lincoln died several hours later.

News of the president's assassination swept across the nation. African Americans mourned the man who helped them win their freedom. Northern whites grieved for the leader who had saved the Union.

When Lincoln died, Vice President **Andrew Johnson** became president. Johnson was born in the South but supported the Union during the war. Johnson soon revealed his plan for Reconstruction. Called "Restoration," his plan would grant amnesty to most Southerners once they swore loyalty to the Union. High-ranking Confederates could be pardoned only by appealing to the president. This provision revealed Johnson's desire to humiliate the leaders who he believed had tricked the South's people into seceding.

Johnson also allowed only loyal, pardoned whites to vote for delegates to the state constitutional conventions. Stating that "white men alone must manage the South," Johnson opposed equal rights for African Americans.

Before a state could reenter the Union, it had to denounce secession and ban slavery. States also had to ratify the Thirteenth Amendment to the Constitution, passed by Congress in January 1865. This amendment abolished slavery throughout the United States. By the end of 1865, all former Confederate states, except Texas, had new governments and were ready to rejoin the Union.

Reading Check **Specifying** What did the Thirteenth Amendment accomplish?

Section 1 Review

History ONLINE
Study Central™ To review this section, go to glencoe.com.

Vocabulary

1. Write a short paragraph in which you use all of the following vocabulary terms:
   Reconstruction, amnesty, radical, adjust.

Main Ideas

2. **Explaining** Why did Lincoln disagree with the harsh Reconstruction plan of the Radical Republicans?

3. **Specifying** Under Johnson's Restoration plan, how could high-ranking or wealthy Confederates gain a pardon?

Critical Thinking

4. **Contrasting** Using a diagram like the one below, compare the Reconstruction plans of Lincoln and the Radical Republicans.

Reconstruction Plans

Lincoln	Radical Republicans

5. **Drawing Conclusions** Do you think President Johnson's Southern heritage influenced his Reconstruction plan? Explain your answer.

6. **Persuasive Writing** Write a one-paragraph response to the Radical Republicans' plan for Reconstruction from Abraham Lincoln's point of view. Explain why you think the South should be treated less harshly.

Answer the
7. **Essential Question**
   How did plans to unify the nation differ after the Civil War?

Essential Question ◄

What were the results of Radical Reconstruction?

Reading Guide

Content Vocabulary

black codes (p. 81)   impeach (p. 85)
override (p. 82)

Academic Vocabulary

convince (p. 81)   suspend (p. 84)

Key People and Events

Civil Rights Act of 1866 (p. 81)
First Reconstruction Act (p. 83)
Second Reconstruction Act (p. 84)
Tenure of Office Act (p. 84)
Edwin Stanton (p. 84)
Ulysses S. Grant (p. 85)

Reading Strategy

Taking Notes As you read, use a diagram like the one below to answer the questions about impeachment.

- Impeachment
  - What Is It?
  - Who Was Impeached?
  - Outcome of Trial?

American Diary

For three days in May 1866, white mobs in Memphis, Tennessee, burned African American churches, schools, and homes. An army officer investigating the causes of the riot later reported: "Three [African American] churches were burned, also . . . about fifty (50) private dwellings, owned, occupied or inhabited by freedmen as homes, and . . . in many instances containing the hard earnings of months of labor."

—from the report on Memphis riot investigation, by Charles F. Johnson, 1866

Memphis rioters set fire to an African American schoolhouse built by the Freedmen's Bureau.

African Americans' Rights

Main Idea When Northerners realized that African Americans in the South were still being mistreated, they worked to find a way to help them.

History and You Think about the rights American citizens have. Read to find out how Congress made sure that formerly enslaved African Americans became citizens.

· ·

Many Northerners saw the Memphis riot as an attempt by whites to terrorize African Americans and keep them from enjoying and practicing their new freedoms. The Memphis incident and similar riots in other Southern cities helped **convince,** or persuade, Radical Republicans that President Johnson's Reconstruction plan was not strong enough.

During the fall of 1865, Southern states created new governments based on Johnson's plan. They also elected new representatives to Congress. When the Southern representatives arrived in Washington, D.C., however, Congress refused to seat them. Many Republicans refused to readmit the Southern states on such easy terms.

Black Codes

By early 1866, Southern states had passed **black codes,** or laws to control freed men and women. The black codes trampled the rights of African Americans. They allowed plantation owners to exploit African American workers and allowed officials to arrest and fine jobless African Americans. The codes also banned African Americans from owning or renting farms. To freed men and women and many Northerners, the black codes resembled slavery.

In early 1866, Congress passed a bill giving the Freedmen's Bureau new powers. The agency could now set up special courts to try individuals charged with violating the rights of African Americans. African Americans could also serve on juries in these courts.

Congress then passed the **Civil Rights Act of 1866.** This act granted full citizenship to African Americans and gave the federal government the power to intervene in state affairs to protect their rights. The law overturned the black codes. It also contradicted the 1857 *Dred Scott* decision of the Supreme Court, which had ruled that African Americans were not citizens.

Primary Source / Freed People's Schools

Freedom to Learn Throughout the South, African Americans of all ages attended freed men and women's schools to learn basic reading, writing, and mathematical skills. As one freed person declared, education was "the next best thing to liberty." Many white Southerners, however, opposed schooling for African Americans. During the Memphis riots, white mobs burned down freed people's schools and attacked teachers and students. Despite the violence, African Americans continued to enroll in the schools.

—from *Forever Free: The Story of Emancipation and Reconstruction*

▲ Freed people's school, Richmond, Virginia, 1866

Critical Thinking

Hypothesizing Why do you think freed African Americans were eager to receive an education?

Protection of Rights The Fourteenth Amendment gave African American males their citizenship and tried to prevent the Southern states from taking away their rights. Since its ratification in 1868, the Supreme Court has written several landmark decisions related to the Fourteenth Amendment.

During the 2000 presidential election, the Supreme Court ruled in *Bush* v. *Gore* that the Florida recount violated the equal protection clause. The Court argued that since vote counters used different standards to count the votes, the recount did not treat all voters equally.

"All persons born or naturalized in the United States, and subject to the jurisdiction thereof, are citizens of the United States and of the State wherein they reside. No State shall make or enforce any law which shall abridge the privileges or immunities of citizens of the United States; nor shall any State deprive any person of life, liberty, or property, without due process of law; nor deny to any person within its jurisdiction the equal protection of the laws."

—Fourteenth Amendment, Section I

The Supreme Court limited the Fourteenth Amendment in a series of rulings in the late 1800s. These rulings led to segregation and voter restrictions in the South.

Responding to an ▶ appeal by Clarence Gideon, the Supreme Court in 1963 ruled in *Gideon* v. *Wainwright* that all defendants were entitled to legal counsel in cases involving possible jail time, including those who were too poor to hire a lawyer.

In 1954 the Supreme Court ruled in *Brown* v. *Board of Education, Topeka, Kansas* that the equal protection clause forbade segregation. The Court ordered the desegregation of the nation's public schools. ▶

Critical Thinking

Assessing How has the Fourteenth Amendment influenced the rights of individual Americans?

President Johnson vetoed both bills. He argued that the federal government was overstepping its authority. He also argued that the Freedmen's Bureau bill and the Civil Rights Act were unconstitutional because they were approved by a Congress that did not include representatives from all of the states. By raising this issue, Johnson indirectly threatened to veto any law passed by this Congress.

Republicans in Congress had enough votes to **override,** or defeat, both vetoes, and the bills became law. The chances of the president and Congress working together faded. The Radical Republicans abandoned the idea of compromise and drafted a new Reconstruction plan—one created by Congress.

The Fourteenth Amendment

Fearing that the Civil Rights Act might be overturned in court, Congress passed a new amendment to the Constitution in 1866. The Fourteenth Amendment was enacted in 1868. It granted full citizenship to all people born in the United States. Because most African Americans in the United States had been born in the country, they became full citizens.

The amendment also stated that no state could take away a citizen's life, liberty, or property "without due process of law." In addition to this, every citizen was entitled to "equal protection of the laws." If a state prevented any adult male citizen from voting, then it could lose some of its representation in Congress.

The amendment also barred former Confederate leaders from holding national or state office unless pardoned by Congress. The Fourteenth Amendment also excluded Native Americans from citizenship.

Congress declared that Southern states had to ratify the amendment to rejoin the Union. Of the 11 Southern states, only Tennessee ratified it. The refusal of the other Southern states to ratify delayed the amendment's adoption until 1868.

Republican Victory

In the congressional elections of 1866, President Johnson campaigned vigorously against the Radical Republicans. Many Northerners objected to the nasty tone of Johnson's campaign and feared clashes between whites and African Americans. The Republicans won a solid victory, giving Congress the signal to take Reconstruction into its own hands.

✓ **Reading Check** **Explaining** Why did Johnson consider the civil rights bill unconstitutional?

Radical Reconstruction

Main Idea Radical Republicans were able to put their version of Reconstruction into action.

History and You If you were a member of Congress at this time, what changes would you like to see in a Reconstruction plan? Read to find out how the Radical Republicans shaped Reconstruction.

President Johnson could do little to stop Republicans because they could easily override his vetoes in Congress. Thus began a period known as Radical Reconstruction.

Reconstruction Acts of 1867

The **First Reconstruction Act** passed in 1867 called for the creation of new governments in the 10 Southern states that had not ratified the Fourteenth Amendment. Tennessee, which ratified, kept its government and rejoined the Union.

History ONLINE
Student Web Activity Visit glencoe.com and complete the Chapter 3 Web Activity about Reconstruction.

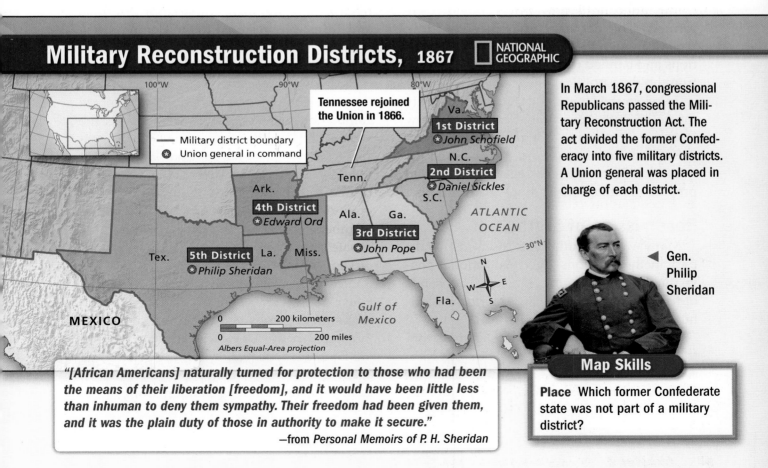

Military Reconstruction Districts, 1867 — NATIONAL GEOGRAPHIC

Tennessee rejoined the Union in 1866.

— Military district boundary
⭐ Union general in command

1st District — Va., John Schofield
2nd District — N.C., S.C., Daniel Sickles
3rd District — Ala., Ga., John Pope
4th District — Ark., Edward Ord
5th District — Tex., La., Miss., Philip Sheridan

Tenn.

ATLANTIC OCEAN
Gulf of Mexico
Fla.
MEXICO

0   200 kilometers
0   200 miles
Albers Equal-Area projection

In March 1867, congressional Republicans passed the Military Reconstruction Act. The act divided the former Confederacy into five military districts. A Union general was placed in charge of each district.

◀ Gen. Philip Sheridan

"[African Americans] naturally turned for protection to those who had been the means of their liberation [freedom], and it would have been little less than inhuman to deny them sympathy. Their freedom had been given them, and it was the plain duty of those in authority to make it secure."
—from *Personal Memoirs of P. H. Sheridan*

Map Skills

Place Which former Confederate state was not part of a military district?

What If Lincoln Had Survived?

Abraham Lincoln wanted the South to be treated compassionately when the war ended. The Radicals expected that the new president, Andrew Johnson, would adopt a firm policy toward the South.

Second Inaugural Address, March 1865

"With malice toward none, with charity for all, with firmness in the right as God gives us to see the right, let us strive on to finish the work we are in, to bind up the nation's wounds, to care for him who shall have borne the battle and for his widow and his orphan."

—Abraham Lincoln

◀ Lincoln's funeral procession, Columbus, Ohio

Critical Thinking

1. **Contrasting** Describe the leadership qualities of Abraham Lincoln and Andrew Johnson.

2. **Speculating** How do you think Reconstruction might have been different if Lincoln had not been assassinated? Explain.

◀ President Johnson and the Radicals had little in common, and Johnson had little popular support. Many people thought Johnson was self-righteous, hot-tempered, stubborn, and crude.

The act divided the 10 Southern states into 5 military districts, each run by a military commander until new governments were formed. The act also guaranteed African American men the right to vote in state elections and banned former Confederate leaders from holding political office.

To rejoin the Union, the states had to ratify the Fourteenth Amendment and submit new state constitutions to Congress for approval. A **Second Reconstruction Act** required the military commanders to register voters and prepare for state constitutional conventions.

Readmission of States

Many white Southerners refused to take part in the elections for constitutional conventions and state governments. Thousands of newly registered African American voters, however, voted.

In the elections, Republicans gained control of Southern state governments. By 1868, seven Southern states—Alabama, Arkansas, Florida, Georgia, Louisiana, North Carolina, and South Carolina—had established new governments and met the requirements for readmission. By 1870, Mississippi, Virginia, and Texas were restored to the Union.

Impeaching the President

Strongly opposed to Radical Reconstruction, President Johnson had the power as commander in chief of the army to direct the actions of the military governors. For this reason, Congress passed a series of laws to limit the president's power, such as the **Tenure of Office Act.** It prohibited the president from removing government officials, including members of his own cabinet, without the Senate's approval.

The conflict between Johnson and the Radicals grew more intense. In August 1867—when Congress was not in session—Johnson **suspended** (removed from office temporarily) Secretary of War **Edwin Stanton** without the Senate's approval. When the Senate met again and refused to approve the suspension, Johnson removed Stanton from office.

This action was a deliberate violation of the Tenure of Office Act. Johnson also appointed people who the Radical Republicans opposed to command some of the Southern military districts.

Outraged by Johnson's actions, the House of Representatives voted to **impeach** the president, or formally charge him, with wrongdoing. In 1868 the case went to the Senate for a trial that lasted almost three months. Johnson's defenders claimed that the president was exercising his right to challenge laws he considered unconstitutional. They argued that Congress impeached the president because of politics, without accusing him of a crime. Johnson's critics disputed that Congress held supreme power to make the laws and that Johnson's use of the veto improperly interfered with this function.

The senators failed to achieve the two-thirds majority required for conviction. Some moderate Republicans supported the president, arguing that Johnson should not be removed from office because of political differences. As a result, Johnson stayed in office until the end of his term in March 1869.

The Fifteenth Amendment

By the presidential election of 1868, most Southern states had rejoined the Union, and many Americans hoped that Reconstruction was over. Abandoning Johnson, the Republicans nominated **Ulysses S. Grant,** the Civil War hero. The Democrats chose Horatio Seymour. Grant received most of the African American votes in the South and won the presidency. The 1868 election showed that voters supported the Republican approach to Reconstruction.

In 1869 Congress passed the Fifteenth Amendment. It prohibited the state and federal governments from denying the right to vote to any male citizen because of "race, color, or previous condition of servitude."

African American men won the right to vote when the amendment was ratified and became law in 1870. Republicans thought the power of the vote would enable African Americans to protect themselves. That belief, however, was too optimistic.

Reading Check **Explaining** How did Republicans organize the South during Reconstruction?

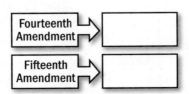

Section 2 Review

Vocabulary

1. Define each of the following terms and use it in a sentence: convince, black codes, override, suspend, impeach.

Main Ideas

2. **Specifying** What requirement was necessary for African Americans to become citizens under the Fourteenth Amendment?

3. **Explaining** Why was President Johnson unable to stop Radical Republicans from putting their Reconstruction plan into action?

Critical Thinking

4. **Comparing** How were black codes similar to slavery?

5. **Determining Cause and Effect** Describe the impact of the Fourteenth and Fifteenth Amendments on African Americans. Use a diagram like the one below.

| Fourteenth Amendment | → | |
| Fifteenth Amendment | → | |

6. **Persuasive Writing** Assume the role of Andrew Johnson. Write a short speech to give at your trial, explaining why the senators should not convict you of wrongdoing.

7. **Answer the Essential Question** What were the results of Radical Reconstruction?

The South During Reconstruction

Essential Question ◄

In what ways did government in the Southern states change during Reconstruction?

Reading Guide

Content Vocabulary

scalawag (p. 87)

integrate (p. 89)

carpetbagger (p. 88)

sharecropping (p. 89)

corruption (p. 88)

Academic Vocabulary

credit (p. 88)

academy (p. 89)

Key People and Events

Hiram Revels (p. 87)

Blanche K. Bruce (p. 87)

Reading Strategy

Taking Notes As you read, use a diagram like the one below to describe improvements in the South in the field of education.

Improvements in Education

American Diary

John Roy Lynch, once enslaved, ran a business in Mississippi. In the 1869 election—the first in which African Americans could vote—Lynch was elected to the Mississippi state legislature. Lynch later recalled that "the campaign was aggressive . . . the election resulted in a sweeping Republican victory. That party not only elected the state ticket . . . but also had a large majority in . . . the state legislature."

—*from* Reminiscences of an Active Life: The Autobiography of John Roy Lynch

Newly freed African Americans from rural areas moved to Southern cities, such as Richmond, where they sought jobs, voted for the first time, and joined local branches of the Republican Party.

Reconstruction Politics

Main Idea As African Americans began to take part in civic life in the South, they faced resistance, including violence, from whites.

History and You Do some people today use mean names to refer to someone they don't like? Read to learn what former Confederates called Republican supporters in the South.

. . . .

During Reconstruction, Republicans dominated Southern politics. Support for the Republican Party came from African Americans, white Southerners who supported Republican policies, and white settlers from the North. These groups were in charge of the state governments.

African Americans in Government

African Americans played an important role in Reconstruction politics, both as voters and as elected officials. In some states they contributed heavily to Republican victories. African Americans did not control any state government, although they briefly held a majority in the lower house of the South Carolina legislature. In other Southern states, they held important positions, but never in proportion to their numbers.

At the national level, 16 African Americans served in the House of Representatives and 2 in the Senate between 1869 and 1880. **Hiram Revels,** one of the African American senators, was an ordained minister who had recruited African Americans for the Union army. He also started a school for freed African Americans in Missouri and served as chaplain of an African American regiment in Mississippi. Revels remained in Mississippi after the war and was elected to the U.S. Senate in 1870.

Blanche K. Bruce, the other African American senator, also came from Mississippi. A former escaped slave, Bruce taught in a school for African Americans in Missouri when the war began. In 1869 he went to Mississippi, entered politics, and was elected to the U.S. Senate in 1874.

Scalawags and Carpetbaggers

Some Southern whites—such as pro-Union business leaders and non-slaveholding farmers—backed the Republicans. Former Confederates called them **scalawags,** a term meaning "scoundrel" or "worthless rascal."

Primary Source / The African American Church

Creating a Community After the Civil War, many African Americans formed their own churches free of white control. In addition to providing a place of worship, churches supported schools, social events, and political meetings. Elias Campbell Morris was a popular African American preacher and a leader of the Republican Party in Arkansas. He encouraged African Americans to participate in politics, saying that improvements in society "will depend in a large measure upon what we prove able to do for ourselves."

—from *This Far by Faith: Stories from the African American Religious Experience*

◀ In many African American homes, the social, political, and economic life of the family centered around religion.

Critical Thinking

Analyzing Information Why do you think churches played such an important political and social role in the African American community?

People IN HISTORY

Blanche K. Bruce

African American senator from Mississippi

In Mississippi, the election of 1876 was controversial. Many people thought that African Americans were pressured to vote for white Democrats. Bruce stated: *"The conduct of the late election in Mississippi . . . put in question and jeopardy the sacred rights of the citizen."*

Hiram Revels

First African American senator

Revels wanted to find common ground between African Americans and white Southerners. He felt that in most places in Mississippi, *"white people . . . accept as a fact that all men are born free and equal, and . . . are ready to guarantee to my people every right and privilege guaranteed to an American citizen."*

CRITICAL Thinking

1. **Analyzing** How do Revels and Bruce differ in their views of Mississippi politics?
2. **Evaluating** Which view of Mississippi politics do you think is more accurate? Explain your answer.

Many Northern whites who moved to the South after the war also supported the Republicans. Critics called these Northerners **carpetbaggers** because they arrived with all their belongings in cheap suitcases made of carpet fabric. Although some carpetbaggers were dishonest, most were not. Many were reformers who wanted to help the South.

Many Southerners accused Reconstruction governments of **corruption**—or dishonest or illegal actions. Although some officials made money illegally, probably less corruption occurred in the South than in the North.

Resistance to Reconstruction

Most Southern whites opposed efforts to expand African Americans' rights. Life soon became difficult for African Americans. Most white landowners refused to rent land to freed people. Store owners refused them **credit**—extra time to pay for goods—and employers would not hire them.

Secret societies, such as the Ku Klux Klan, used fear and violence to deny rights to freed men and women. Wearing white sheets and hoods, Klan members killed thousands of African Americans and their white friends. They beat and wounded many more and burned African American homes, schools, and churches. Many Southerners, especially planters and Democrats, backed the Klan. These people, who had the most to gain from the return of white supremacy, saw violence as a defense against Republican rule.

In 1870 and 1871, Congress passed several laws to try to stop the growing violence of the Klan. These laws met with limited success. Most white Southerners refused to testify against those who attacked African Americans and their white supporters.

Reading Check **Explaining** Who were the scalawags and carpetbaggers? Why did many Southerners resent them?

Education and Farming

Main Idea Education improved for both races in the South, but the sharecropping system limited economic opportunities for African Americans.

History and You If you could not attend school, how would the course of your life change? Read about advances in education in the South.

. . . .

During Reconstruction, African Americans created their own schools. The Freedmen's Bureau also helped spread education. Northern women and African Americans came south to teach in schools. In the 1870s, Reconstruction governments created public schools for both races. Within a few years, about 50 percent of white children and 40 percent of African American children in the South were enrolled. Northern missionary societies set up **academies**—schools for special training. These academies grew into a network of African American colleges and universities, including Fisk University in Tennessee and Morehouse College in Georgia.

Generally, African American and white students attended different schools. Only a very few states required that schools be **integrated**—include both whites and African Americans—but the laws were not enforced.

Along with education, most freed people wanted land. Some African Americans purchased land with the help of the Freedmen's Bank, but most failed to get their own land. The most common form of farmwork for freed people was **sharecropping.** In this system, a landowner rented a plot of land to a sharecropper, or farmer, along with a crude shack, some seeds and tools, and perhaps a mule. In return, sharecroppers shared a percentage of their crops with the landowners.

After paying the landowners, sharecroppers often had little left to sell. Sometimes there was barely enough to feed their families. For many, sharecropping was little better than slavery.

✓ **Reading Check** **Describing** What was the relationship between sharecroppers and landowners?

Section 3 Review

History ONLINE
Study Central™ To review this section, go to glencoe.com.

Vocabulary

1. Use each of these terms in a sentence that will help explain its meaning: scalawag, carpetbagger, corruption, credit, academy, integrate, sharecropping.

Main Ideas

2. Specifying What kinds of resistance did African Americans face as they tried to exercise their rights as citizens in the South?

3. Describing How did Reconstruction governments reform education in the South?

Critical Thinking

4. Organizing Use a diagram like the one below to identify the three main groups that made up the Southern Republican Party.

Southern Republican Party

5. Analyzing How did the sharecropping system work to keep African Americans from improving their lives?

6. Expository Writing Imagine that you are a journalist in 1869. You are preparing to interview an African American senator from Mississippi, a carpetbagger, and a white Southern planter. Write three questions you would ask each about Reconstruction. Suggest how each person would respond.

Answer the
7. Essential Question

In what ways did government in the Southern states change during Reconstruction?

TIME NOTEBOOK

What were people's lives like in the past?

These two pages will give you some clues to everyday life in the United States as you step back in time with TIME Notebook.

PHOTO RESEARCHERS

New Railway Crosses the Country

GETTING THERE

By now, you have probably heard that the tracks of the Union Pacific and Central Pacific railways met up in Utah on May 10, 1869—completing the first transcontinental railroad in the United States. A pioneer named **ALEXANDER TOPONCE** *wrote about the events that day:*

"When they came to drive the last spike, Governor Stanford, president of the Central Pacific, took the sledge, and the first time he struck he missed the spike and hit the rail.

"What a howl went up! Irish, Chinese, Mexicans, and everybody yelled with delight. 'He missed it. Yee.' The engineers blew the whistles and rang their bells. Then Stanford tried it again and tapped the spike and the telegraph operators had fixed their instruments so that the tap was reported in all the offices east and west, and set bells to tapping in hundreds of towns and cities. . . . Then Vice President T. C. Durant of the Union Pacific took up the sledge and he missed the spike the first time. Then everybody slapped everybody else again and yelled, 'He missed it too, yow!'

"It was a great occasion, everyone carried off souvenirs and there are enough splinters of the last tie in museums to make a good bonfire."

NORTH WIND PICTURE ARCHIVES / ALAMY

VIRGINIA STATS
State of the Union

Richmond had been the capital of the Confederacy—and Virginia paid the price after the Civil War. One of the states most ravaged by battles, Virginia's farm values sank from fifth in the country to tenth. The state tried to get new business by lowering taxes. That led to more factories, but they produced less than in the past.

CORBIS

	1860	1870
Number of Farms	86,468	73,849
Value of Farm Land	$371.8 million	$213 million
Number of Factories	5,385	5,933
Value of Manufactured Products	$50.7 million	$38.4 million

MILESTONES
EVENTS AND PEOPLE OF THE TIME

DRAWN. An elephant to represent jittery Republican voters by Thomas Nast before the presidential election in 1874. Looks like his symbol for Republicans might stick—after all, Nast is the artist who drew a mule to represent Democrats.

STRETCHED. Baseball fans in 1882 in what is becoming known as the "seventh inning stretch." The athletic director of New York's Manhattan College baseball team felt sorry for fidgety students in the crowd and told them to stand up and stretch during a game. Word has it that New York Giants fans will copy the practice.

DRIVEN OUT. African American members of the Georgia legislature in 1868, after white members claimed that African Americans might vote but not hold office.

THE REPUBLICAN VOTE

BETTMANN / CORBIS

NUMBERS
UNITED STATES AT THE TIME

2 cents About the price per acre the United States paid for Alaska in 1867—the total price is $7.2 million

600,000 Approximate number of African Americans in the South who had enrolled in school by 1877

$125 Price of a typewriter, invented by Christopher Sholes in 1868

120,000,000,000 Number of locusts in a swarm that reached a mile high, 100 miles wide (161 km), and up to 300 miles long (483 km), wiping out crops in the West in 1874

MARY EVANS PICTURE LIBRARY / ALAMY

10,000 Number of people who went to the first Kentucky Derby horse race in 1875

CRITICAL THINKING

Speculating Based on Susan B. Anthony's reaction to her voting fine, what personal and philosophical qualities do you think she had?

Assessing How might the values of Virginia's farm and manufacturing economies have affected the lives of its citizens after the Civil War? Use the table to help explain your answer.

Change in the South

Essential Question ◄

How did the South change politically, economically, and socially when Reconstruction ended?

Reading Guide

Content Vocabulary

cash crop
(p. 97)

grandfather clause
(p. 97)

poll tax
(p. 97)

segregation
(p. 98)

literacy test
(p. 97)

lynching
(p. 98)

Academic Vocabulary

outcome
(p. 94)

commission
(p. 94)

Key People and Events

Amnesty Act (p. 93)

Rutherford B. Hayes (p. 94)

Compromise of 1877 (p. 94)

Jim Crow laws (p. 98)

Plessy v. Ferguson (p. 98)

Reading Strategy

Taking Notes As you read, use a diagram like the one below to summarize the goals for industry and for agriculture that leaders hoped to achieve in the "New South."

```
        The New South
        /           \
  Goal for        Goal for
  Industry:       Agriculture:
```

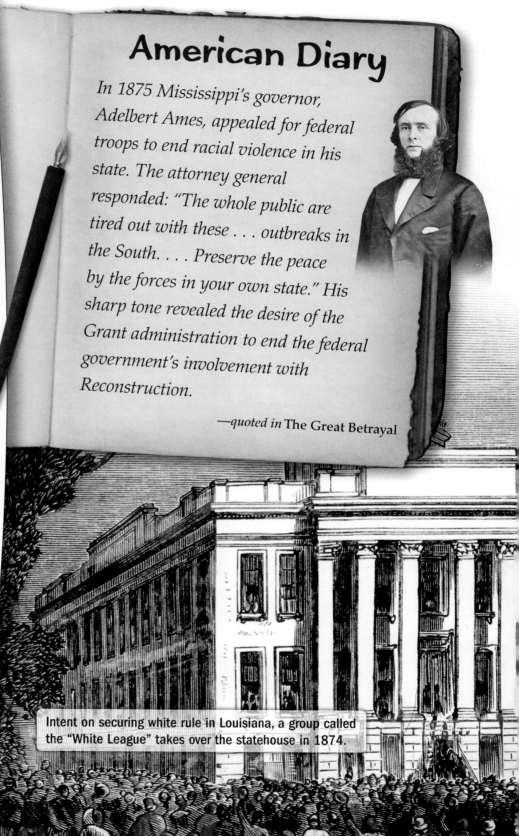

American Diary

In 1875 Mississippi's governor, Adelbert Ames, appealed for federal troops to end racial violence in his state. The attorney general responded: "The whole public are tired out with these . . . outbreaks in the South. . . . Preserve the peace by the forces in your own state." His sharp tone revealed the desire of the Grant administration to end the federal government's involvement with Reconstruction.

—*quoted in* The Great Betrayal

Intent on securing white rule in Louisiana, a group called the "White League" takes over the statehouse in 1874.

The End of Reconstruction

Main Idea Democrats steadily regained control of Southern governments as support for Radical Reconstruction policies decreased.

History and You Would you lose respect for a famous sports star if you learned he or she was cheating? Read how scandals weakened public support for the Radical Republicans.

. . . .

During the Grant administration, Northerners began losing interest in Reconstruction. Many believed it was time for the South to solve its own problems.

Reconstruction declined for other reasons as well. The old Radical leaders began to disappear from politics. Thaddeus Stevens died in 1868. Others retired or lost elections.

Opponents of Reconstruction also exploited racial prejudice in the North. They argued that only Southerners really knew how to deal with African Americans and that the fate of the freed people should be left to the South. Southerners protested what they called "bayonet rule"—the use of federal troops to support Reconstruction governments. Grant tried to avoid any clashes with the South.

Republican Revolt

In the early 1870s, reports of corruption in Grant's administration and in Reconstruction governments spread. Some Republicans split with the party over the issue of corruption. Another group broke with the party over Reconstruction, proposing peaceful reconciliation—coming together again—with Southern whites. Calling themselves Liberal Republicans, these two groups nominated Horace Greeley, a newspaper editor, to run against Grant in 1872. Despite the split among Republicans, Grant was reelected.

Democrats Regain Power

In 1872 Liberal Republicans helped pass the **Amnesty Act,** which pardoned most former Confederates. Nearly all white Southerners could vote and hold office again. The amnesty changed the political balance in the South by restoring full rights to people who supported the Democratic Party.

In Southern states where a majority of voters were white, Democrats soon regained control of state governments. In states where African Americans held a majority, the Ku Klux Klan helped the Democrats take power by terrorizing Republican voters.

By the Numbers / Politics in Mississippi

Mississippi House of Representatives

1870

- 82 Republicans
- 25 Democrats

1875

- 97 Democrats
- 20 Republicans

End of Reconstruction After the Civil War, Republican state governments in Mississippi and other Southern states set up schools, built hospitals, and ended racial discrimination laws. By 1880, these reforms that began under Reconstruction came to an end as the more conservative Democrats returned to power throughout the South.

Mississippi State Budgets	
1870	$1,061,250
1871	$1,729,046
1876	$518,709
1877	$697,019
1880	$803,191

Source: *Cyclopaedia of Political Science,* 1899.

Critical Thinking

Interpreting Why do you think state government spending in Mississippi declined around 1876? How do you think the state's African American population was affected by this and other changes?

The Republicans had other problems as well. In 1873 a series of political scandals came to light. Investigations uncovered top government officials making unfair business deals, scheming to withhold public tax money, and accepting bribes. One scandal involved the vice president and another the secretary of war. These scandals further damaged the Grant administration and the Republicans.

In addition to political scandals, Grant and the nation endured a severe economic depression. The crisis began in 1873 when a series of bad railroad investments forced the powerful banking firm of Jay Cooke and Company to declare bankruptcy. A wave of fear known as the Panic of 1873 quickly spread through the nation's financial community. The panic forced small banks to close and the stock market to plummet. Thousands of businesses shut down, and tens of thousands of Americans were thrown out of work. Blame for the hard times fell on the Republicans.

In the congressional elections of 1874, Democrats gained seats in the Senate and won control of the House. For the first time since the Civil War, the Democratic Party controlled a part of the federal government. This situation further weakened Congress's commitment to Reconstruction and protecting the rights of African Americans.

The Election of 1876

President Grant considered running for a third term in 1876. Most Republican leaders preferred a new candidate—one who could win back the Liberal Republicans and unite the party. The Republicans nominated **Rutherford B. Hayes,** governor of Ohio. A champion of political reform, Hayes had a reputation for honesty, and he held moderate views on Reconstruction. The Democrats nominated New York governor Samuel Tilden. Tilden gained fame for fighting political corruption in New York City.

After the election, Tilden appeared to be the winner, receiving almost 250,000 more votes than Hayes. However, disputed returns from four states—representing 20 electoral

Struggle of Reconstruction

Extending Liberties Laws and amendments were passed during Reconstruction to extend civil liberties to African Americans.

Civil Rights Amendments and Laws

Civil Rights Act of 1866

Granted citizenship and equal rights to all persons born in the United States (except Native Americans)

Fourteenth Amendment (1870)

Granted citizenship and equal protection of the laws to all persons born in the United States (except Native Americans)

Fifteenth Amendment (1870)

Protected the voting rights of African Americans

Civil Rights Act of 1875

Outlawed racial segregation in public services
Ensured the right of African Americans to serve as jurors

votes—kept the **outcome,** or results, in doubt. Tilden had 184 electoral votes, only 1 short of what he needed to win. Yet if Hayes received all 20 of the disputed votes, he would have the 185 electoral votes required for victory.

To review the election results, Congress created a special **commission,** or group, of 15 persons made up equally of members of the House of Representatives, the Senate, and the Supreme Court. The commission had 7 Republicans, 7 Democrats, and 1 independent. But the independent resigned, and a Republican took his place. The commission voted 8 to 7 to award all 20 electoral votes, and the election, to Hayes. The vote followed party lines.

Compromise of 1877

Democrats in Congress threatened to fight the commission's decision. Republican and Southern Democratic leaders reportedly met in secret to work out an agreement. On March 2, 1877, Congress declared Hayes the winner.

The agreement—called the **Compromise of 1877**—included some favors to the South.

Disputed Election of 1876 NATIONAL GEOGRAPHIC

Rutherford B. Hayes ▶

One of Oregon's three electoral votes was in doubt.

Disputed electoral vote

Washington Territory 3

Montana Territory

Dakota Territory 5

Idaho Territory

Wyoming Territory

3

3

Utah Terr.

3

6

Arizona Territory

New Mexico Territory

Unorg. Terr.

10

11

35

7

5 5 13

4

6

29

8 9 3

5

11

10

11

21 15 22

5

15

12

6

12

10

8 10 11 7

8 8

4

People living in territories could not vote in national elections.

Northern troops still occupied three states.

Candidate	Electoral Vote	Popular Vote	Political Party
Hayes	185	4,036,572	Republican
Tilden	184	4,284,020	Democrat

Critical Thinking

Comparing Which laws are most similar to each other?

The new government would give more aid to the South. Republicans agreed to withdraw all remaining troops from Southern states. Without soldiers to support them, the remaining Republican governments in South Carolina and Louisiana quickly collapsed. The Democrats, in turn, promised to maintain African American rights.

A New Policy

In his Inaugural Address, Hayes declared that what the South needed most was the restoration of "wise, honest, and peaceful local self-government." During a goodwill trip to the South, Hayes announced his intention of letting Southerners handle racial issues. Hayes's message was clear. The federal government would no longer attempt to reshape Southern society. Reconstruction had come to an end.

Reading Check **Summarizing** How did the Compromise of 1877 affect Reconstruction?

Change in the South

Main Idea After Reconstruction, the South experienced a political shift and industrial growth.

History and You Do you recall that lack of industry put the South at a disadvantage during the Civil War? Read to learn how Southerners vowed to create a strong industrial "New South."

Many Southern whites hated Republicans for their role in the Civil War and in Reconstruction. When Reconstruction ended, power in the South shifted to the Democrats.

Democrats in Control

In some regions, the ruling Democrats were the large landowners and other groups that held power before the Civil War. In many areas, however, new leaders took charge. Among their ranks were merchants, bankers, and other business leaders who supported economic development.

Change in Politics

These Democrats called themselves "Redeemers" because they had "redeemed," or saved, the South from Republican rule. The Redeemers adopted conservative policies, such as lower taxes and reduced government spending. They drastically cut, or even eliminated, many social services started during Reconstruction, including public education. Their one-party rule and conservative policies dominated Southern politics well into the 1900s.

Rise of the "New South"

By the 1880s, forward-looking Southerners were convinced that their region must develop a strong industrial economy. They argued that the South lost the Civil War because its industry did not match the North's. Henry Grady, editor of the *Atlanta Constitution,* headed a group that urged Southerners to "out-Yankee the Yankees" and build a "New South." This "New South" would have industries based on the region's abundant coal, iron, tobacco, cotton, and lumber. Southerners would create this new economy by embracing a spirit of hard work and regional pride.

Industry in the South made dramatic gains in the 1880s. Textile mills sprang up across the South. The American Tobacco Company, developed largely by James Duke of North Carolina, eventually controlled almost all tobacco manufacturing in the nation. By 1890, Southern mills produced nearly 20 percent of the nation's iron and steel. Much of the industry was in Alabama near deposits of iron ore.

Southern industry grew as a result of a cheap and reliable workforce. Most factory workers put in long hours for low wages. A railroad-building boom also aided industrial development. By 1870, the Southern railroad system, which had been destroyed during the war, was largely rebuilt. The miles of rail track more than doubled between 1880 and 1890. Still, the South did not develop an industrial economy as strong as the North's. Agriculture remained the South's main economic activity.

Primary Source | Sharecropping

Denied Land During the Civil War, formerly enslaved African Americans hoped to acquire abandoned or confiscated Confederate lands. The government under President Johnson, however, returned Southern plantations to their former slaveholders.

Formerly enslaved African Americans often ended up working as sharecroppers on land that belonged to their former owners. ▼

Southern laws forced sharecroppers to work the land until they paid off their debts. A system emerged in the South that closely resembled slavery. ▼

Typical sharecropper contract ▶

To secure payment of said rent and supply bill, the said Dawson [the sharecropper] grants unto said Solid South [the landowner] a special privilege and right of pledge on all the products raised on said land, and on all his stock, farming implements, and personal property, and hereby waives in favor of said Solid South the benefit of any and all homestead laws and exemption laws now in force, or which may be in force, in Louisiana, and agrees that all his property shall be seized and sold to pay said rent and supply bill in default of payment thereof as herein agreed. Any violation of this contract shall render the lease void.

Rural Economy

Supporters of the New South hoped to change Southern agriculture as well as industry. Their goal was small, profitable farms raising a variety of crops rather than large plantations devoted to cotton. A different economy emerged, however. Some plantations were broken up, but many large landowners held on to their land. When estates were divided, much of the land went to sharecropping and tenant farming, neither of which was profitable.

Debt also caused problems. Poor farmers used credit to buy supplies. Merchants who sold on credit charged high prices, and farmers' debts rose. To repay debts, farmers grew **cash crops**—crops that could be sold for money. As in the past, the main cash crop was cotton. Too much cotton forced prices down, however. Farmers then had to grow even more cotton to try to recover their losses. Sharecropping and reliance on one cash crop kept Southern agriculture from advancing.

✓ Reading Check **Describing** Why did industry in the South grow during this period?

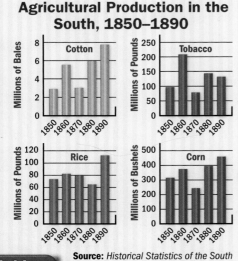

Agricultural Production in the South, 1850–1890

Increased production lowered cotton prices and left much of the rural South in poverty after the Civil War. ▶

Cotton — Millions of Bales
Tobacco — Millions of Pounds
Rice — Millions of Pounds
Corn — Millions of Bushels

Source: *Historical Statistics of the South*

Critical Thinking

Comparing and Contrasting How was the South after the Civil War similar to and different from the South before the Civil War?

Graphs In Motion See StudentWorks™ Plus or glencoe.com.

A Divided Society

Main Idea As Reconstruction ended, true freedom for African Americans became a distant dream.

History and You How would you feel if you had to pass a test on a subject you never studied in order to graduate? Read to learn about a test African Americans in the South had to pass in order to vote.

· ·

As Reconstruction ended, African Americans' dreams for justice faded. In the last 20 years of the 1800s, racism became firmly set in the culture. Individuals took steps to keep African Americans separated from whites and to deny them basic rights.

Voting Restrictions

The Fifteenth Amendment prohibited any state from denying an individual the right to vote because of race. Southern leaders, however, found ways to get around the amendment and prevent African Americans from voting.

Many Southern states required a **poll tax,** a fee people had to pay to vote. Because many African Americans could not afford the tax, they could not vote. The tax also kept many poor whites from voting.

Another approach was to make prospective voters take a **literacy test** in which they had to read and explain difficult parts of state constitutions or the federal Constitution. Because most African Americans had little education, literacy tests prevented many from voting.

Literacy tests could also keep some whites from voting. For this reason some states passed **grandfather clauses.** These laws allowed people who did not pass the literacy test to vote if their fathers or grandfathers voted before Reconstruction. Because African Americans could not vote until 1867, they were excluded. By the end of the 1800s, such laws and the constant threat of violence caused African American voting to decline drastically.

Jim Crow Laws

By the 1890s, **segregation,** or the separation of the races, had become a common feature of the South. Southern states passed so-called **Jim Crow laws** that required African Americans and whites to be separated in almost every public place.

In 1896 the Supreme Court upheld segregation laws in ***Plessy v. Ferguson.*** The case involved a Louisiana law requiring separate sections on trains for African Americans. The Court ruled that segregation was legal as long as African Americans had access to public places equal to those of whites.

One problem, however, was that the facilities were separate but in no way equal. Southern states spent much more money on schools and other facilities for whites than on those for African Americans. This "separate but equal" doctrine gave legal support to Southern segregation for more than 50 years. White violence against African Americans also rose. One form of violence was **lynching,** in which an angry mob killed a person by hanging. African Americans were lynched because they were suspected of crimes—or because they did not behave as whites thought they should behave.

Reconstruction's Impact

Reconstruction was both a success and a failure. It helped the South rebuild its economy. Yet much of the South remained agricultural and poor. African Americans gained greater equality, created their own institutions, and shared in government with whites. Their advances, however, did not last. In the words of African American writer and civil rights leader W.E.B. Du Bois, "The slave went free; stood a brief moment in the sun; then moved back again toward slavery."

✔ **Reading Check** **Describing** How was segregation applied?

Section 4 Review

History ONLINE
Study Central™ To review this section, go to glencoe.com.

Vocabulary

1. Use each of these terms in a sentence that will help explain its meaning: outcome, commission, cash crop, poll tax, literacy test, grandfather clause, segregation, lynching.

Main Ideas

2. **Explaining** How did the Amnesty Act help Democrats regain control of Southern state governments?

3. **Describing** How did forward-thinking Southerners want to change the South's economy?

4. **Explaining** Why did African American voting in the South decline drastically by the late 1800s?

Critical Thinking

5. **Determining Cause and Effect** Use a diagram like the one below to describe the two issues that split the Republican Party for the 1872 election. Then name the group these dissatisfied Republicans came together to form.

Issues That Divided Republicans

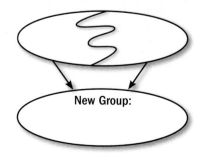

New Group:

6. **Analyzing** Did agriculture in the New South achieve the shift envisioned by its supporters? Why or why not?

7. **Descriptive Writing** You are an African American in 1899. When you took a seat on a train, the white conductor told you to move to a separate section. Write a letter to W.E.B. Du Bois, describing the incident and your feelings about it.

8. **Answer the Essential Question** How did the South change politically, economically, and socially when Reconstruction ended?

Visual Summary

◀ Freedmen's school

Reconstruction Plans

- The South is rebuilt and readmitted to the Union during Reconstruction.
- Lincoln's Ten Percent Plan is designed to heal the Union quickly.
- The Radical Republicans' Wade-Davis Bill has strict requirements for states to be readmitted.
- The Freedmen's Bureau helps African Americans adjust to freedom.
- Abraham Lincoln is assassinated in April 1865.
- President Johnson's "Restoration" plan calls for states to ratify the amendment to abolish slavery.

Lincoln's funeral ▼

Radical Reconstruction

- Radical Republicans believe Johnson's plan is too easy on the South.
- Southern states pass black codes to control freed African Americans, but Congress passes the Civil Rights Act of 1866 to protect their freedoms.
- The Fourteenth Amendment gives African Americans citizenship and equal protection of the laws.
- Radical Republicans win Congress and enact their own Reconstruction plans.
- Congress impeaches Johnson but fails to convict him.
- The Fifteenth Amendment gives African American men the right to vote.

Andrew Johnson ▲

Reconstruction in the South

- African Americans vote and take part in Southern politics.
- Some whites resist the expansion of African Americans' rights and form the Ku Klux Klan.
- Sharecropping limits economic opportunities for African Americans.

Reconstruction Ends

- Republicans lose power as a result of political corruption and economic crisis.
- Democrats regain control of Southern state governments.
- Southern Democrats encourage economic growth but limit the rights of African Americans.

STUDY TO GO Study anywhere, anytime! Download quizzes and flash cards to your PDA from glencoe.com.

Southern Industry After the Civil War

Before the Civil War, the backbone of the Southern economy was agriculture. After Reconstruction, industry in the South made dramatic gains.

How Did Geography Affect Southern Industry?

Many Southern industries after the Civil War centered around regional agricultural products such as tobacco and cotton. In the 1880s textile mills sprang up throughout the South. Additionally, Southern forests provided lumber for new homes, factories, railroad ties, and above all, furniture.

Other Southern industries centered on the region's rich reserves of coal and iron. By 1900, the South led the world in coal production; this same period saw a large growth in iron and steel mills.

🎩 Coal	🌊 Lumber	
🗳 Cotton	🐚 Textiles	
⚡ Iron	🌾 Tobacco	

▲ While the economy of the Old South focused on cotton and tobacco production, distinct industrial regions began to develop after the Civil War.

Manufacturing in the Southern States, 1860–1900*

State	1860	1880	1900
Alabama	1,459	2,070	5,602
Arkansas	518	1,202	4,794
Florida	185	426	2,056
Georgia	1,890	3,593	7,504
Louisiana	1,744	1,553	4,350
Mississippi	976	1,479	4,772
North Carolina	3,689	3,802	7,226
South Carolina	1,230	2,078	3,762
Tennessee	2,572	4,326	8,016
Texas	983	2,996	12,289
TOTAL	15,246	23,525	60,371

*Number of Manufacturing Establishments

Thomas Nast's illustration for an 1882 cover of *Harper's Weekly* compares the Old South's "King Cotton" of 1861 to the New South's "Queen of Industry." ▶

What they were saying . . .

Atlanta *Constitution* editor Henry Grady was one of the leaders calling for a "New South," a South that is industrialized and part of a modern national economy.

"We are going to take a noble revenge . . . by invading every inch of your territory [the North] with iron, as you invaded ours twenty-nine years ago."

After the Civil War, Southerners built a number of iron and steel mills. Many mills were located near the iron ore deposits around Birmingham, Alabama. Founded in 1871, Birmingham became a prime industrial center of the New South. Between 1880 and 1900, the area in and around Birmingham was second only to Pittsburgh, Pennsylvania, in the number of new furnaces for making iron.

Although tobacco was grown in the South before the Civil War, it was rarely processed there. By 1900, tobacco processing had become a major Southern industry. ▶

One of the first industries to gain strength in the "New South" was the textile industry. Textile mills produced cotton cloth.

▲ The lumber industry thrived in many parts of the South.

Analyzing Geography

1. **Location** In which parts of the "New South" did coal mining predominate? Textile manufacturing? Tobacco?

2. **Human-Environment Interaction** In what ways did Southern agriculture influence the types of industries that arose in the New South?

STANDARDIZED TEST PRACTICE

Be sure to pay attention to specific words in a question. Words can act as clues to help you identify the correct answer.

Reviewing Main Ideas

Directions: Choose the best answer for each of the following questions.

1. Which of the following was a provision of the 1864 Wade-Davis bill?

   A African American males in a state had to swear loyalty to the Union.

   B Ex-Confederates could not hold public office.

   C Confederate states could be readmitted to the Union even if they kept slavery.

   D Half of all delegates to a constitutional convention had to be formerly enslaved people.

2. What was Andrew Johnson's reaction to the Civil Rights Act of 1866?

   A He supported the law even though he believed it did not protect African Americans.

   B He said it was unconstitutional because it was passed by a Congress that did not include representatives from all the states.

   C He persuaded Congress to pass the bill.

   D He vetoed it because it gave states too much power.

3. Southern whites who supported the Republicans were called

   A scalawags.   **C** carpetbaggers.

   B sharecroppers.   **D** freed men and women.

4. During the Grant administration,

   A Radical Republicans became more powerful.

   B corruption charges weakened Democrats.

   C many Northerners began to think the South should solve its own problems.

   D most white Southerners supported Republicans.

Short-Answer Question

Directions: Base your answer to question 5 on the excerpt below and on your knowledge of social studies.

I have confidence . . . in the endurance, capacity, and destiny of my people [African Americans]. We will . . . seek our places, sometimes in the field of letters, arts, sciences, and the professions. More frequently mechanical pursuits will attract and elicit our efforts; more still of my people will find employment . . . as the cultivators of the soil. The bulk of this people—by surroundings, habits, adaptation, and choice—will continue to find their homes in the South. . . . Whatever our ultimate position in the . . . Republic . . . we will not forget our instincts for freedom nor our love of country.

   —Senator Blanche K. Bruce, from a speech in 1876

5. According to the document, how did Bruce expect most African Americans to earn a living? How did he view their futures?

Review the Essential Questions

6. Essay What do you think was Reconstruction's greatest success? What was its greatest failure? Explain your answers.

To help you write your essay, review your answers to the Essential Questions in the section reviews and the chapter Foldables Study Organizer. Your essay should include:

   • the various plans for Reconstruction;
   • the actions of the Radical Republicans and their conflicts with Johnson;
   • the changes in the South and white Southern responses; and
   • reasons why Reconstruction ended.

GO ON ▶

History ONLINE

For additional test practice, use **Self-Check Quizzes**—Chapter 3 at glencoe.com.

Document-Based Questions

Directions: Analyze the documents and answer the short-answer questions that follow.

Document 1

New England journalist Sidney Andrews recorded these remarks in 1865 from a man in Charleston, South Carolina.

> You Northern people are making a great mistake in your treatment of the South. We are thoroughly whipped; we give up slavery forever; and now we want you to quit [criticizing] us. Let us back into the Union, and then come down here and help us build up the country.

Source: Sidney Andrews, *The South Since the War*

7. Based on the excerpt, do you think the person Andrews spoke to would most likely support Lincoln's Ten Percent Plan or the Wade-Davis Bill? Explain.

Document 2

President Andrew Johnson made these remarks in his veto of the First Reconstruction Act of 1867.

> The power . . . given to the commanding officer . . . of each district is that of an absolute monarch. His mere will is to take the place of all law. . . .
> It reduces the whole population of the ten States . . . to the most abject and degrading slavery.

Source: Andrew Johnson, "From Revolution to Reconstruction"

8. According to the document, why did Johnson veto the First Reconstruction Act?

Document 3

The illustration at the top right is from the December 28, 1868, *Harper's Weekly* magazine. It shows two members of the Ku Klux Klan.

Source: Corbis

9. Why did Klan members wear disguises?

Document 4

The following are examples of Jim Crow laws passed throughout the South.

> No person or corporation shall require any white female nurse to nurse in wards or rooms in hospitals, either public or private, in which negro men are placed. *Alabama*
>
> The schools for white children and the schools for negro children shall be conducted separately. *Florida*
>
> Books shall not be interchangeable between the white and colored schools, but shall continue to be used by the race first using them. *North Carolina*

Source: Martin Luther King, Jr., National Historic Site

10. How were African American freedoms limited?

11. **Expository Writing** Using the information from the four documents and your knowledge of social studies, write an essay in which you:

- describe the political issues related to Reconstruction, including the effect of Lincoln's death on the process; and

- describe how Reconstruction affected the various groups in the South.

Need Extra Help?											
If you missed questions. . .	1	2	3	4	5	6	7	8	9	10	11
Go to page. . .	78	82	87	93	88	76–98	77–78	83	88	97–98	76–98

Unit
2

Reshaping the Nation
1858–1914

The gramophone was an early player of musical recordings.

"*Once I moved about like the wind. Now I surrender to you and that is all.*"
—Geronimo

Grand Opening of the Brooklyn Bridge, May 24, 1883

Reading History

Comparing and Contrasting

Learn It! When you *compare* people, things, or ideas, you look for similarities among them. When you *contrast*, you look for differences.

Central Pacific
Hired Chinese laborers

Similarities
Both companies were working to build the transcontinental railroad. Workers labored for low wages in harsh conditions.

Union Pacific
Hired Irish and African American workers

—from Chapter 4, p. 114

Two companies accepted the challenge to build the [transcontinental] railroad. . . .The Central Pacific hired about 10,000 Chinese laborers to work on its tracks. The first Chinese were hired in 1865 at about $28 per month. The Union Pacific relied on Irish and African American workers. All workers toiled for low wages in harsh conditions.

Practice It! Read the paragraph. Then on another sheet of paper, draw a Venn diagram and compare and contrast forms of public transportation in the late 1800s.

—from Chapter 6, p. 183

As cities grew, people needed new means of transportation. Streetcars, which horses pulled on tracks, provided public transportation at the time. In 1873 San Francisco began construction of cable-car lines. A large underground cable powered by a motor at one end of the rail line moved passengers along.

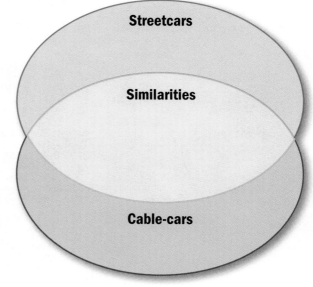

Streetcars

Similarities

Cable-cars

Academic Vocabulary Preview

Listed below are the academic vocabulary words and their definitions that you will come across as you study Unit 2. The activities in the Practice It! column will help you study the words and definitions.

Academic Vocabulary	Definition	Practice It!
Chapter 4 Opening the West		
sum (SUHM) *p. 111*	amount; total	**Identify** *the term from Chapter 4 that best completes each sentence.*
extract (ehk · STRAKT) *p. 111*	to remove, usually by force	**1.** Mining companies use machinery to _____ ore from the land.
locate (LOH · kayt) *p. 119*	to establish; settle	**2.** At one time, the United States had a gold-based _____, instead of metal coins and paper notes.
factor (FAK · tuhr) *p. 121*	contributing circumstance	
ensure (ihn · SHUR) *p. 125*	make certain	**3.** Some prospectors made large _____(s) of money during the California Gold Rush.
widespread (WYD · SPREHD) *p. 127*	far-reaching	
create (kree · AYT) *p. 133*	to form; to make	
currency (KUHR · uhnt · see) *p. 135*	metal coins and paper notes used as money	
Chapter 5 The Industrial Age		
labor (LAY · buhr) *p. 143*	to work	**Identify** *the term from Chapter 5 that best matches the underlined word or phrase.*
individual (IHN · duh · VIHJ · wuhl) *p. 143*	person	**4.** The telegraph was used to <u>send</u> messages in Morse code.
transmit (trants · MIHT) *p. 147*	send from one place to another	
mechanism (MEH · kuh · NIH · zuhm) *p. 150*	mechanical device	**5.** In the early 1900s, labor unions helped create safer <u>working conditions</u> in urban factories.
partner (PAHRT · nuhr) *p. 155*	associate who agrees to operate a business with another	**6.** African American inventors developed much-needed <u>mechanical devices</u> for consumers and industry.
trend (TREHND) *p. 157*	general direction or movement	
identify (eye · DEHN · tuh · FY) *p. 162*	recognize	
environment (ihn · VY · ruhn · muhnt) *p. 163*	the conditions of a location	
Chapter 6 An Urban Society		
attitude (A · tuh · TOOD) *p. 175*	way of thinking and acting	**Choose** *the word that best matches the meaning of each vocabulary term listed below.*
affect (uh · FEHKT) *p. 175*	to have an impact on	

major (MAY · juhr) *p. 179*	greater in size, extent, or importance	**7. major** **9. minor**
		    a. greater **a.** equal
		    b. lower **b.** lesser
		    c. wiser **c.** greater

minor (MY · nuhr) *p. 181*	lesser in size, extent, or importance	

philosophy (fuh · LAH · suh · fee) *p. 185*	a set of ideas and beliefs	**8. philosophy** **10. isolate**
		    a. education **a.** gather
		    b. beliefs **b.** control
		    c. government **c.** separate

isolate (EYE · suh · LAYT) *p. 186*	cut off; separate	

Chapter 4

Opening the West 1858–1896

Railroad companies hired buffalo hunters to provide their workers with fresh meat.

▲ Ruins after Chicago Fire

★ **1871**
Great Chicago Fire destroys most of city

PRESIDENTS

JAMES BUCHANAN 1857–1861

ABRAHAM LINCOLN 1861–1865

ANDREW JOHNSON 1865–1869

ULYSSES S. GRANT 1869–1877

RUTHERFORD B. HAYES 1877–1881

JAMES GARFIELD 1881

U.S. Events

World Events

1860

1870

1880

★ **1861**
Italians establish a united kingdom

★ **1869**
Suez Canal opens

1871 ★
Stanley and Livingstone meet in Africa

★ **1878**
Russo-Turkish War ends

History ONLINE
Chapter Overview Visit glencoe.com
and click on **Chapter 4—Chapter
Overviews** to preview chapter information.

Section 1: The Mining Booms
Essential Question What were the causes and effects of mining booms in the West?

Section 2: Ranchers and Farmers
Essential Question How did cattle ranchers and farmers adapt to life in the West?

Section 3: Native American Struggles
Essential Question How did westward expansion affect Native Americans?

Section 4: Farmers in Protest
Essential Question Why did economic reform movements develop in the late 1800s?

Organizing Information
Make this Foldable to help organize what you learn about the opening of the West in the late 1800s.

Step 1 Fold an 11" x 17" piece of paper lengthwise to create 4 equal sections.

Step 2 Label your Foldable as shown.

The Mining Booms	Ranchers & Farmers	Native American Struggles	Farmers in Protest

Reading and Writing As you read the chapter, use the Foldable to take notes on each section. Be sure to write down important people, dates, and events.

Apache leader
Geronimo ▶

CHESTER ARTHUR 1881–1885

★ **1882**
Congress limits immigration with Chinese Exclusion Act

GROVER CLEVELAND 1885–1889

★ **1886**
• Geronimo surrenders to U.S. military
• U.S. accepts Statue of Liberty from France

BENJAMIN HARRISON 1889–1893

★ **1892**
• Populist Party forms
• Sierra Club organizes in San Francisco

GROVER CLEVELAND 1893–1897

1890 — **1900**

★ **1882**
Triple Alliance forms among Germany, Austria, Italy

★ **1885**
European powers divide Africa

★ **1891**
Construction of Trans-Siberian railroad begins

★ **1896**
First modern Olympics held in Athens

The Mining Booms

Essential Question ◄

What were the causes and effects of mining booms in the West?

Reading Guide

Content Vocabulary

vigilante *(p. 111)*

subsidy *(p. 113)*

transcontinental *(p. 113)*

time zone *(p. 115)*

Academic Vocabulary

sum *(p. 111)*   extract *(p. 111)*

Key People and Events

Comstock Lode *(p. 111)*

Leland Stanford *(p. 114)*

Reading Strategy

Taking Notes As you read, identify the effects of the mining booms.

American Diary

In 1859 a Kansas newspaper article tried to inspire people to travel to Pikes Peak in Colorado where gold had been discovered: "Hurra for Pike's Peak! Hurra for Pike's Peak! / There's gold in the Mount'n, there's gold in the vale, / There's plenty for all who are willing to seek / Believe me; believe me—'tis no idle tale. / Come, hurra for Pike's Peak!" Stories about the discoveries of gold and silver lured thousands of fortune seekers west.

—*from "A Call to the Mines"*

People traveled west to Colorado in search of gold and silver.

Gold, Silver, and Boomtowns

Main Idea Miners found gold in the West, leading to the creation of new states.

History and You What opportunities today might tempt your family to move to a new state? Read to learn how the discovery of gold encouraged people to move West.

. . . .

By the mid-1850s, the California Gold Rush had ended. Disappointed miners, still hoping to strike it rich, began prospecting in other parts of the West.

In 1858 gold was found at Pikes Peak in the Colorado Rockies. Newspapers claimed that miners were making $20 a day panning for gold—a large **sum,** or amount of money, at a time when servants earned less than a dollar a day. By the spring of 1859, about 50,000 prospectors had flocked to the goldfields of Colorado.

Prospectors skimmed gold dust from streams or scratched gold particles from the land. Most of the gold, however, was deep in underground lodes, which are rich streaks of ore running between rock layers. Mining this ore and then **extracting,** or removing, the gold particles required machinery, workers, and an organized business. Companies stood a better chance of getting rich from mining for gold than did individuals.

Boom and Bust

In 1859 several prospectors found one of the world's richest deposits of silver-bearing ore near Nevada's Carson River. The discovery was called the **Comstock Lode** after Henry Comstock, who owned a share of the claim. Thousands of mines opened near the site, but only a few were profitable.

Gold strikes created boomtowns—towns that developed almost overnight around mining sites. The Comstock boomtown was Virginia City, Nevada. Boomtowns were lively, and often lawless, places. Money came quickly—and was often lost just as quickly through spending and gambling. Violence was also part of life in boomtowns, where many people carried guns and a lot of cash. Few boomtowns had police or prisons, so ordinary people known as **vigilantes** sometimes acted to punish criminals.

Men mostly lived in boomtowns, but some women opened businesses or worked as laundresses, cooks, or entertainers. Women often founded schools and churches.

By the Numbers / Life of a Mining Boomtown

A Boomtown's Population Virginia City, Nevada, became one of the largest cities in the West after gold was discovered in the region. Once all of the gold was extracted from the ground, however, Virginia City's population declined.

Population of Virginia City, Nevada

*Estimate according to various Nevada historical sources

Source: Nevada State Library and Archives, 2007.

Critical Thinking

Summarizing Describe the changes in population in Virginia City, Nevada, from 1860 to 1920.

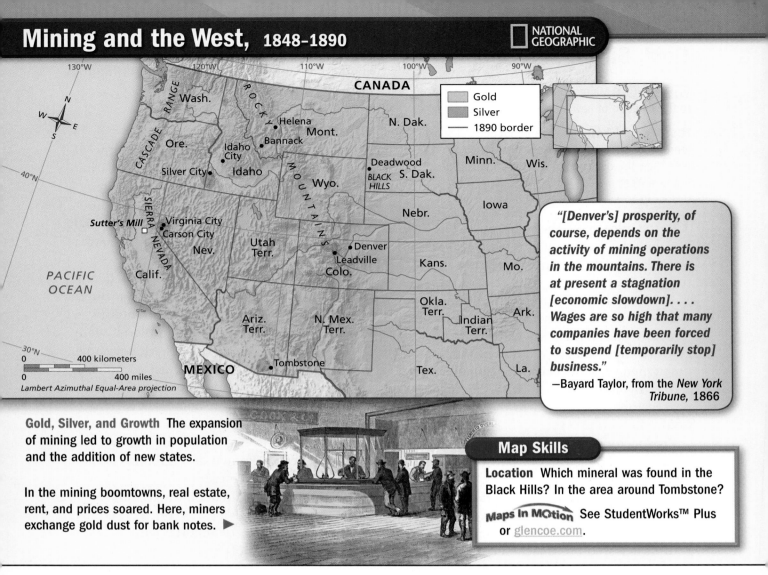

Gold
Silver
— 1890 border

"[Denver's] prosperity, of course, depends on the activity of mining operations in the mountains. There is at present a stagnation [economic slowdown]. . . . Wages are so high that many companies have been forced to suspend [temporarily stop] business."

—Bayard Taylor, from the *New York Tribune*, 1866

Gold, Silver, and Growth The expansion of mining led to growth in population and the addition of new states.

In the mining boomtowns, real estate, rent, and prices soared. Here, miners exchange gold dust for bank notes. ▶

Map Skills

Location Which mineral was found in the Black Hills? In the area around Tombstone?

Maps In Motion See StudentWorks™ Plus or glencoe.com.

Despite the promise of prosperity, many mining "booms" were followed by "busts." When the ore was gone, people left, and the boomtowns became ghost towns.

The United States Expands West

As the gold and silver disappeared, the mining of other metals, including copper, lead, and zinc, increased. As these mining areas developed and became more populated, they eventually became states. Colorado joined the United States in 1876. North Dakota, South Dakota, Washington, and Montana became states in 1889. Wyoming and Idaho were admitted to the Union in 1890.

Reading Check **Explaining** Why did many boomtowns turn into ghost towns?

Railroads Connect East and West

Main Idea Railroads transported gold and silver to market and brought supplies to the miners.

History and You What type of transportation would you take if you had to travel from the East Coast to the West Coast? Read to learn how people and goods were transported in the mid-1800s.

The western mines operated far from the industrial centers of the East and Midwest. For this reason, transportation played a vital role in the survival of mining communities. Gold and silver had little value unless they could reach factories, ports, and markets.

At the same time, people living in the boom-towns needed shipments of food and other supplies.

Wagons and stagecoaches could not move people and goods fast enough to meet these demands, but railroads did. The nation's railroad network expanded rapidly between 1865 and 1890. During that time, the length of track in the United States soared from about 35,000 miles (56,327 km) to more than 150,000 miles (241,402 km).

Government and the Railroads

Railroad construction was often supported by large government subsidies—financial aid and land grants from the government. Railroad executives made the argument that their companies should receive free public land on which to lay track because a rail network connecting East and West would bring important benefits to the entire nation.

The national government and states agreed. In all, the federal government granted more than 130 million acres (52,609,180 ha) of land to the railroad companies. Much of the land was purchased or obtained by treaties from Native Americans. The government grants included the land for the tracks plus strips of land along the railway, 20 to 80 miles (32 to 129 km) wide. Railroad companies sold those strips of land to raise additional money.

States and local communities also helped the railroads. Towns offered cash subsidies to make sure that the railroads were constructed near their communities. For example, Los Angeles gave the Southern Pacific Railroad money and paid for a passenger terminal to ensure that the railroad would be built near the town.

Spanning the Continent

The search for a route for a transcontinental rail line—one that would span the continent and connect the Atlantic and Pacific coasts—began in the 1850s. Southerners wanted the route to run through the South, and Northerners wanted it to pass through the North. During the Civil War, the Union government chose a northerly route. The government offered land grants to railroad companies willing to build the transcontinental line.

The challenge was enormous—laying track for more than 1,700 miles (2,736 km) across hot plains and through rugged mountains.

The Steam Locomotive

The railroads that were so important to the growth of the West were dependent upon the technology of the steam locomotive.

1 The firebox burns coal, wood, or sometimes oil.

2 Water in the boiler, heated by gases from the firebox, creates steam.

3 The smoke box draws hot gases from the firebox and keeps an even fire burning.

4 In the steam header tank, the heated steam expands and creates great pressure.

5 Hot steam is piped to the pistons. The pistons power the drive rods, which in turn push the drive wheels.

Critical Thinking

Making Inferences What advantages did steam locomotives have over other forms of transportation available in the mid-1800s?

Improving Travel When it was completed in May 1869, America's first transcontinental railroad spanned more than 1,700 miles (2,736 km). A rail trip coast to coast took a week. Before the railroad, the same trip would have taken months.

"We witnessed here the fabulous speed with which the Railroad was built. . . . The only limit . . . was the power of the road behind to bring forward the materials."

—Samuel Bowles, *Our New West*, 1869

▲ The "golden spike" ceremony signified the completion of the railroad line.

Critical Thinking

Speculating What was the significance of using a golden spike to link the Central Pacific and Union Pacific railroads?

Two companies accepted the challenge to build the railroad. The Union Pacific Company began laying track westward from Omaha, Nebraska, while the Central Pacific Company worked eastward from the city of Sacramento, California.

The two companies competed furiously. Each wanted to cover a greater distance than the other in order to receive more of the government subsidies.

The Central Pacific hired about 10,000 Chinese laborers to work on its tracks. The first Chinese were hired in 1865 at about $28 per month. The Union Pacific relied on Irish and African American workers. All workers toiled for low wages in harsh conditions. In the choking heat of summer and the icy winds of winter, the workers cleared forests, blasted tunnels through mountains, and laid hundreds of miles of track across the vast center of the country. In the end, the Central Pacific workers, who covered a much harsher terrain, laid 742 miles (1,194 km) of track. The Union Pacific workers laid 1,038 miles (1,670 km) of track.

The Transcontinental Railway

On May 10, 1869, construction was completed. A Chinese crew was chosen to lay the final 10 miles (16 km) of track, which was completed in only 12 hours. The two sets of track met at Promontory Summit in Utah Territory. **Leland Stanford,** governor of California, drove a final golden spike into a tie to join the two railroads. Almost as the event occurred, telegraph lines flashed the news across the country: "The last rail is laid. . . . [T]he last spike driven. . . . The Pacific Railroad is completed."

Effects of the Railroads

By 1883, two more transcontinental lines and dozens of shorter lines connected cities in the West with the rest of the nation. The economic consequences were enormous. The railroads brought thousands of workers west. Trains carried metals and produce east and manufactured goods west. As more tracks were laid, more steel was needed, and the demand boosted the nation's steel industry.

Coal producers, railroad car manufacturers, and construction companies also benefited from the expansion.

Numerous towns sprang up along the rail lines that carried the settlers' agricultural goods to market. Some of these towns eventually grew into large cities such as Denver, Colorado. Railroads also brought the next wave of settlers to the West—ranchers and farmers.

Railroads even changed how people measured time. Before the 1880s, each community kept its own time based on the sun's position at noon. Clocks in Boston, for example, were 11 minutes ahead of clocks in New York City. Having local time zones interfered with train scheduling, however, and at times even threatened passenger safety. When two trains were traveling on the same track, collisions could result from scheduling errors caused by differences in timekeeping.

To make rail service across the country safer and more reliable, the American Railway Association—an organization that included the nation's railroad companies—divided the country into four **time zones** in 1883. All of the communities located within a time zone would share the same time. Each zone was exactly one hour later than the zone to its west. Congress made the time zones official in 1918.

Meanwhile, new locomotive technology and the invention of air brakes enabled railroads to pull longer and heavier trains on their lines. When combined with large, well-organized railroad systems, operations became so efficient that the average cost per mile for a ton of freight dropped from two cents in 1860 to three-quarters of a cent in 1900.

The nationwide rail network also helped unite Americans in different regions. The *Omaha Daily Republican* newspaper in Nebraska observed in 1883 that railroads had "made the people of the country homogenous [alike], breaking the peculiarities and provincialisms [local ways] which marked separate and unmingling regions." This was a bit of an exaggeration, but it recognized that railroads were changing American society.

✔ **Reading Check** **Determining Cause and Effect** How did railroads affect the American economy in the middle to late 1800s?

Section 1 Review

History ONLINE
Study Central™ To review this section, go to glencoe.com.

Vocabulary

1. Use each of these terms in a sentence that will help explain its meaning: sum, extract, vigilante, subsidy, transcontinental, time zone.

Main Ideas

2. **Describing** What was life like in the boomtowns?

3. **Explaining** Why did the government provide subsidies to railroad companies?

Critical Thinking

4. **Evaluating** What are some problems that might be caused by allowing vigilantes to punish people for crimes? Record your ideas in a diagram like this one.

5. **Making Inferences** Why do you think the government chose a northern route for the transcontinental railroad?

6. **Descriptive Writing** From the point of view of a miner in a boomtown, write a letter to your family in Boston describing your new life and your reasons for moving west.

Answer the
7. **Essential Question**
What were the causes and effects of mining booms in the West?

America's LITERATURE

Meet the Author

Mark Twain (1835–1910) was born Samuel Longhorne Clemens in Missouri. He took his pen name from a phrase used by pilots on Mississippi riverboats. A legendary American writer, lecturer, and humorist, Twain published newspaper and magazine articles as well as novels and short stories. *Roughing It,* Twain's second major work, contains the imagery and humor that serve as hallmarks of Twain's writing.

Building Background

Roughing It is the personal account of Mark Twain's travels to the Nevada Territory in 1861, when few Americans had first-hand knowledge about the West. The following excerpt is Twain's description of his arrival in Carson City. As you read the passage, think about Twain's choice of words and note the images that his words bring to mind.

Vocabulary

barren bare

alkali salt mixture

burthen burden

serenity calmness

impertinent bothersome

intermeddling interfering

rebuke scold

rivulets streams

Miner, Nevada Territory, 1867 ▶

ROUGHING IT

Mark Twain

WE were approaching the end of our long journey. It was the morning of the twentieth day. At noon we would reach Carson City, the capital of Nevada Territory. . . .

Visibly our new home was a desert, walled in by **barren,** snow-clad mountains. There was not a tree in sight. There was no vegetation but the endless sage-brush and greasewood. All nature was gray with it. We were plowing through great deeps of powdery **alkali** dust that rose in thick clouds and floated across the plain like smoke from a burning house. . . . Every twenty steps we passed the skeleton of some dead beast of **burthen,** with its dust-coated skin stretched tightly over its empty ribs. Frequently a solemn raven sat upon the skull or the hips and contemplated the passing coach with meditative **serenity**. . . .

We arrived, disembarked, and the stage went on. [Carson City] was a "wooden" town; its population two thousand souls. The main street consisted of four or five blocks of little white frame stores which were too high to sit down on, but not too high for various other purposes; in fact, hardly high enough. They were packed close together, side by side, as if room were scarce in that mighty plain. . . .

We were introduced to several citizens, at the stage-office and on the way up to the Governor's from the hotel—among others, to a Mr. Harris, who was on horseback; he began to say something, but interrupted himself with the remark:

"I'll have to get you to excuse me a minute; yonder is the witness that swore I helped to rob the California coach—a piece of **impertinent intermeddling,** sir, for I am not even acquainted with the man."

Then he rode over and began to **rebuke** the stranger with a six-shooter, and the stranger began to explain with another. When the pistols were emptied, the stranger resumed his work . . . and Mr. Harris rode by with a polite nod, homeward bound, with a bullet through one of his lungs, and several in his hips; and from them issued little **rivulets** of blood that coursed down the horse's sides. . . . This was all we saw that day, for it was two o'clock, now, and according to custom the

daily "Washoe Zephyr" set in; a soaring dust-drift about the size of the United States set up edgewise came with it, and the capital of Nevada Territory disappeared from view.

Every twenty steps we passed the skeleton of some dead beast of burthen, with its dust-coated skin stretched tightly over its empty ribs.

Still, there were sights to be seen which were not wholly uninteresting to new comers; for the vast dust cloud was thickly freckled with things strange to the upper air—things living and dead . . . appearing and disappearing among the rolling billows of dust—hats, chickens and parasols sailing in the remote heavens; blankets, tin signs, sage-brush and shingles a shade lower; door-mats and buffalo robes lower still; shovels and coal scuttles on the next grade; glass doors, cats and little children on the next; disrupted lumber yards, light buggies and wheelbarrows on the next; and down only thirty or forty feet above ground was a scurrying storm of emigrating roofs and vacant lots.

It was something to see that much. I could have seen more, if I could have kept the dust out of my eyes.

Analyzing Literature

1. **Respond** After reading the passage, how would you describe Carson City?

2. **Recall and Interpret** What occurred between Mr. Harris and the stranger? Why?

3. **Evaluate**
   (a) In Twain's description of the dust cloud, how did he create the image of movement?
   (b) In your opinion, is the description of the dust cloud meant to inform, entertain readers, or both? Explain your thinking.

Ranchers and Farmers

Essential Question

How did cattle ranchers and farmers adapt to life in the West?

Reading Guide

Content Vocabulary

Long Drive (p. 119)   sodbuster (p. 123)

vaquero (p. 120)   dry farming (p. 123)

homestead (p. 121)

Academic Vocabulary

locate (p. 119)   factor (p. 121)

Key Event

Homestead Act (p. 121)

Reading Strategy

Taking Notes As you read, use a cause-and-effect diagram like the one below to identify reasons people settled on the Great Plains.

People Settle on the Great Plains

American Diary

Texas cowhand E. C. Abbott recalled the early days of riding the trail: "Here [were] all these cheap long-horned steers overrunning Texas; here was the rest of the country crying for beef—and no railroads to get them out. So they trailed them out, across hundreds of miles of wild country that was thick with Indians. . . . In 1867 the town of Abilene was founded at the end of the Kansas Pacific railroad and that was when the trail really started."

—from We Pointed Them North

In his painting *The Trail Boss*, western painter Charles Russell depicted a cattle drive in the American Southwest.

Cattle on the Plains

Main Idea Ranchers herded their cattle to railroad towns and shipped them to new markets in the North and East.

History and You Have you ever wondered whether the beef in your grocery store was raised in your state or another state? Read to learn how ranchers got their cattle to market.

. . . .

When the Spanish settled Mexico and Texas, they brought a tough breed of cattle with them. Called longhorns because of their prominent horns, these cattle gradually spread across Texas.

Even though very large cattle ranches were found throughout the state, much of Texas was open range—which means it was not fenced or divided into lots. Cattle roamed free on the open range. Ranchers added to their own herds by rounding up wild cattle. The ranchers burned a brand, or symbol, into the animals' hides to show who owned the cattle.

Railroads and Cow Towns

Although Texas ranchers had plenty of cattle, the markets for beef were in the North and the East. By 1865, the Missouri Pacific Railroad reached Kansas City, Missouri, and the value of Texas cattle suddenly increased. Texas cattle could now be herded to Missouri and loaded onto trains for shipment to northern and eastern cities, where new markets for beef were expanding. Some Texans drove their combined herds—sometimes 260,000 head of cattle—north to Sedalia, Missouri, the nearest rail point. Longhorns that were worth $3 each quickly rose in value to $40.

The Long Drive

This increase in the longhorns' value set off what became known as the **Long Drive**—the herding of cattle 1,000 miles (1,609 km) or more to meet the railroads. Cattle drives left Texas in the spring, when there was enough grass along the way to feed the cattle. They traveled to cow towns—towns **located,** or established, near railroads. Some of the largest Long Drives led from central Texas to Abilene, Kansas, on the Chisholm Trail. From the late 1860s to the mid-1880s, more than 5 million cattle moved north on cattle drives.

✔ **Reading Check** Determining Cause and Effect How did railroads increase the value of Texas cattle?

If You Were There / African American Cowboys

A New Life Following the Civil War, a large number of formerly enslaved persons moved to the West to work in the cattle industry. Many became cowhands, working the cattle trails that headed north from Texas. African American cowhands faced some of the same prejudices found in the South and the East. They could not stay in the same hotels or eat in the same restaurants as whites. Despite these differences, however, African American cowhands often received the same pay as white cowhands.

Critical Thinking

Inferring How do you think life was different for formerly enslaved persons who went west to work as cowhands?

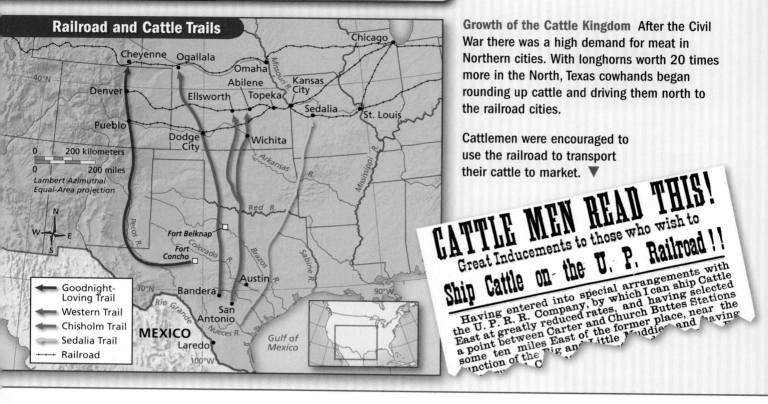

Railroad and Cattle Trails

Chicago
Cheyenne Ogallala
40°N Omaha
Denver Abilene Kansas City
Ellsworth Topeka
Sedalia St. Louis
Pueblo
Dodge City Wichita
Arkansas R.

0   200 kilometers
0   200 miles
Lambert Azimuthal
Equal-Area projection

Red R.
Fort Belknap
Pecos R.
Fort Concho Colorado R.
Brazos R.
Sabine R.
Austin
Bandera 30°N 90°W
Rio Grande
San Antonio
MEXICO Nueces R.
Laredo Gulf of Mexico
100°W

Goodnight-Loving Trail
Western Trail
Chisholm Trail
Sedalia Trail
Railroad

Growth of the Cattle Kingdom After the Civil War there was a high demand for meat in Northern cities. With longhorns worth 20 times more in the North, Texas cowhands began rounding up cattle and driving them north to the railroad cities.

Cattlemen were encouraged to use the railroad to transport their cattle to market. ▼

CATTLE MEN READ THIS!
Great Inducements to those who wish to
Ship Cattle on the U. P. Railroad !!

Having entered into special arrangements with the U. P. R. R. Company, by which I can ship Cattle East at greatly reduced rates, and having selected a point between Carter and Church Buttes Stations some ten miles East of the former place, near the junction of the Big and Little Muddies, and having

Life on the Great Plains

Main Idea Cowhands and ranchers lived difficult lives on the Plains.

History and You Think about Old West movies you have seen. Read to find out what life was really like on the Plains.

. . . .

The cattle drives and the cowhands who worked on them captured the imagination of the nation. Cattle driving was hard work. Cowhands rode in the saddle up to 15 hours every day, in driving rain, dust storms, and blazing sun. Life on the trail was lonely, too. Cowhands saw few outsiders. Cowhands also faced many dangers: violent storms, "rustlers" who tried to steal cattle, and stampedes, when thousands of cattle ran in panic. During a stampede, cowhands had to race on horseback and bring the cattle under control.

Cowhands included veterans of the Civil War and African Americans who moved west in search of a better life. Some cowhands were Hispanics. In fact, cattle herding traditions began in the Spanish Southwest when Hispanic ranch hands, known as **vaqueros,** developed the riding, roping, and branding skills used by cowhands. Much of the language of the rancher today comes from Spanish words used by vaqueros for centuries. Even the word *ranch* comes from the Spanish word *rancho.*

The Cattle Kingdom Ends

Ranching eventually began to replace the cattle drives, because ranchers were able to produce hardier, plumper cattle. The ranchers became rich when cattle prices boomed. Then, as a result of too many cattle for sale on the beef market, cattle prices fell, bringing an end to the "Cattle Kingdom." The cattle industry survived but was changed forever. Another type of economic activity would rise in the Plains—farming.

Reading Check Describing Why were the trails dangerous for cowhands?

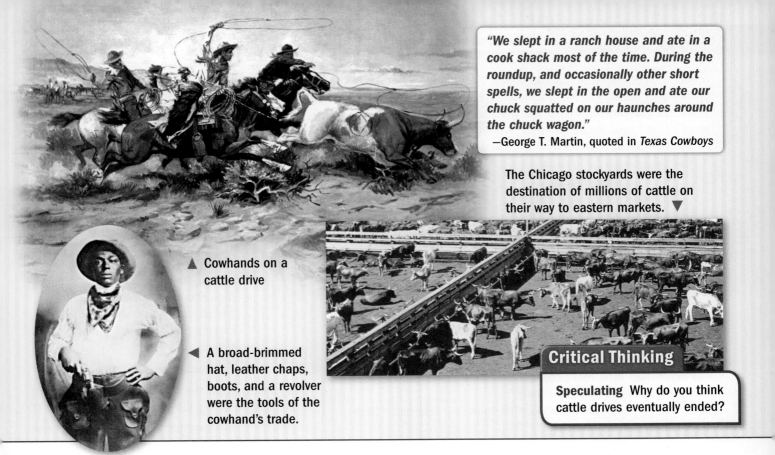

"We slept in a ranch house and ate in a cook shack most of the time. During the roundup, and occasionally other short spells, we slept in the open and ate our chuck squatted on our haunches around the chuck wagon."

—George T. Martin, quoted in *Texas Cowboys*

The Chicago stockyards were the destination of millions of cattle on their way to eastern markets. ▼

▲ Cowhands on a cattle drive

◄ A broad-brimmed hat, leather chaps, boots, and a revolver were the tools of the cowhand's trade.

Critical Thinking

Speculating Why do you think cattle drives eventually ended?

Farmers Settle the Plains

Main Idea Free land and new farming methods brought many settlers to the Great Plains.

History and You Have you ever experienced a drought or flood? Read on to learn about the challenges farmers faced on the Great Plains.

. . . .

The early pioneers who reached the Great Plains did not believe they could farm the dry, treeless area. In the late 1860s, however, farmers began settling there. Much of the Plains soon changed from "wilderness" to farmland. In 1872 a Nebraska farmer wrote, "One year ago this was a vast, houseless, uninhabited prairie. . . . Today I can see more than thirty dwellings from my door."

Several **factors,** or contributing circumstances, brought settlers to the Plains. Railroads made the journey west easier and cheaper. New laws offered free land. Finally, above-average rainfall in the late 1870s made the land better suited to farming.

The Homestead Act

In 1862 the government encouraged settlement on the Plains by passing the **Homestead Act.** This law gave up to 160 free acres (65 ha) of land to a settler who paid a $10 filing fee and lived on the land for five years. Later government acts increased the size of the tracts available. The federal land policy brought farmers to the Plains to **homestead**— earn ownership of land by settling on it.

Homesteading attracted thousands of new settlers to the Plains. With their property rights secured, settlers were more willing to move west. Some of these settlers were immigrants who had begun the process of becoming American citizens and were eligible to file for land. Other homesteaders were women. Although married women could not claim land, single women and widows had the same rights as men—and they used the Homestead Act to acquire property. In Colorado and Wyoming, for example, 12 percent of all those who filed claims were women.

Open for Settlement During the 1880s, pressure increased to open Indian Territory in Oklahoma to white settlement. Early in 1889, the government yielded and purchased nearly 2 million acres of land from Native Americans. The Oklahoma Land Rush officially began at noon on April 22, 1889.

◄ Oklahoma City on the first day of the land rush.

◄ On horseback, in wagons, in buggies, and on foot, thousands raced forward to claim land.

▲ Men line up outside a land office. The chaotic land rush led to many disputed land claims.

"The race was not over when you reached the particular lot. . . . The contest still was who should drive their stakes first, who would erect their little tents soonest, and then, who would quickest build a little wooden shanty."
—Hamilton S. Wicks, "The Opening of Oklahoma," 1889

Critical Thinking

Sequencing What steps were involved in claiming land during the Oklahoma Land Rush?

New Groups of Settlers

Homesteaders settled on the Plains to own land and be independent. Advertising paid for by railroads, steamship companies, land speculators, and western states and territories also lured people to the Plains. Railroad companies sold the strips of land alongside the rail lines to raise cash. Steamship travel companies advertised the Plains in Scandinavia where many people were searching for economic opportunities. Scandinavian influence remains strong in Minnesota and the Dakotas today.

Thousands of African Americans also migrated from the Southern states to Kansas in the late 1870s. They called themselves "Exodusters," from the biblical book of Exodus, which describes the Jews' escape from slavery in Egypt.

The end of Reconstruction in 1877 had meant the end of federal protection for African Americans. Fearing for their safety in former slave regions, freed people sought land farther west. By 1881, more than 40,000 African Americans had migrated to Kansas.

Challenges of Farming the Frontier

The climate of the Plains presented farmers with their greatest challenge. During some years excessive rainfall caused flooding. The region, however, also experienced drought. In times of drought, brushfires swept rapidly through a region, destroying crops, livestock, and homes. Summer might bring plagues of grasshoppers.

Winters presented even greater dangers. Winds howled across the open Plains, and deep snow could bury animals and trap families in their homes. Farm families had to plan ahead and store food for the winter.

Meeting the challenges of farming on the Great Plains was a family affair. Men labored hard in the fields. Women often did the same work, but they also cared for the children, sewed clothing, made candles, and cooked and preserved food. When the men were away, women bore all responsibility for keeping the farm running. When children grew old enough, they helped work on the farm. Farmwork often kept children from attending school.

New Farming Methods

The Plains could not be farmed by the methods of the 1860s. Most of the region had little rainfall and few streams for irrigation. Plains farmers, known as **sodbusters,** needed new methods and tools.

One approach, called **dry farming,** was to plant seeds deep in moist ground. However, wooden plows could not penetrate the tough layer of sod. By the late 1870s, farmers could use the new lightweight steel plow that was better for digging into sod.

The sodbusters had other tools to help them—windmills to pump water from deep in the ground and a new fencing called barbed wire. Farmers did not have wood to build fences, so they substituted these wire fences to protect their land.

Dry farming, however, did not produce large yields, and the 160-acre (65 ha) grants were too small. Most farmers needed at least 300 acres (121 ha) and advanced machinery, to make a profit. Many farmers went into debt. Others lost ownership of their farms and then had to pay rent for the land.

The Oklahoma Land Rush

The last region of the Plains to be settled was the Oklahoma Territory, which Congress designated as "Indian Territory" in the 1830s. In 1889, after years of pressure from land dealers and settlers, the government opened Oklahoma to homesteaders.

On the morning of April 22, 1889—the official opening day—more than 10,000 people lined up on the edge of this land. At the sound of a bugle, the homesteaders charged across the border to stake their claims. The eager boomers, as the homesteaders were called, discovered that some settlers had already slipped into Oklahoma. These "sooners" already claimed most of the best land. Within a few years, all of Oklahoma was opened to settlement.

Not long after the land rush, the 1890 census revealed that the frontier was no more. Settlement had greatly changed the Plains, especially for Native Americans.

✓ Reading Check **Identifying** What new farming methods were used on the Great Plains?

Section 2 Review

History ONLINE
Study Central™ To review this section, go to glencoe.com.

Vocabulary

1. Use each of these terms in a sentence that will help explain its meaning: Long Drive, locate, vaquero, factor, homestead, sodbuster, dry farming.

Main Ideas

2. **Explaining** Why did the Long Drive develop?

3. **Analyzing** Why do you think cowhands captured the imaginations of many Americans?

4. **Predicting** How do you think the Oklahoma Land Rush affected Native Americans?

Critical Thinking

5. **Analyzing** Create a diagram that shows how new farming methods solved some of the problems of farming on the Plains.

Problem   Solution

6. **Explaining** Why did many African Americans move west?

7. **Persuasive Writing** Design a brochure that might have been printed by a steamship company in Scandinavia. Include a few sentences explaining why Scandinavians should move to the American plains.

Answer the Essential Question

8. How did cattle ranchers and farmers adapt to life in the West?

Native American Struggles

Reading Guide

Content Vocabulary

nomadic
(p. 125)

reservation
(p. 126)

Academic Vocabulary

ensure
(p. 125)

widespread
(p. 127)

Key People and Events

Crazy Horse (p. 127)

Sitting Bull (p. 128)

Geronimo (p. 129)

Dawes Act (p. 129)

Wounded Knee (p. 129)

Reading Strategy

Taking Notes As you read, record the actions of the U.S. government toward Native Americans.

Government Actions

American Diary

In 1867 government officials traveled to Fort Laramie, Wyoming, to sign a peace treaty with Red Cloud and other Sioux chiefs. After the U.S. troops were withdrawn, at Red Cloud's request, the treaty was signed. One Crow leader, Bear Tooth, however, sharply criticized the actions of white people. "If I went into your country to kill your animals, what would you say? Would I not be wrong, and would you not make war on me?"

—*from* The Mammoth Book of Native Americans

Signers of the Treaty of Fort Laramie, May 1868

Following the Buffalo

Main Idea Native Americans of the Great Plains depended on buffalo to survive, but railroads threatened this lifestyle.

History and You What is one thing in your life that you could not live without? Read to learn what Native Americans were forced to give up.

. . . .

The government officials who met with Red Cloud wanted to **ensure,** or make certain of, the safety of whites moving into Native American territory. In the mid-1850s, miners, ranchers, and farmers began to settle on the Plains. Conflict between Native Americans and whites grew as Native Americans tried to preserve their civilizations. Red Cloud mourned, "The white children [settlers] have surrounded me and left me nothing but an island."

The Great Plains had been home to many Native American nations for centuries. Some, like the Omaha and the Osage nations, lived in communities as farmers and hunters. Most of the Plains Indians, however, including the Sioux, the Comanche, and the Blackfeet, lived a **nomadic** life. They traveled vast distances following their main source of food—great herds of buffalo.

Despite their differences, the people of the Plains were similar in many ways. Their nations, sometimes numbering several thousand people, were divided into bands consisting of up to 500 people each. A governing council headed each band, but most members participated in decisions.

The women raised the children, cooked, and prepared hides. The men hunted, traded, and performed military tasks. Most Native Americans of the Plains believed in the spiritual power of the natural world.

For most of their history, the Plains Native Americans had millions of buffalo to supply their needs. After the Civil War, however, American hunters hired by the railroads began slaughtering the animals to feed the crews building the railroads. The railroad companies also wanted to prevent the giant herds of buffalo from blocking the trains. Starting in 1872, hunters targeted buffalo to sell the hides back East.

✔ **Reading Check** **Comparing and Contrasting** How were the lifestyles of different Plains people similar? How were they different?

If You Were There / Life on the Plains

Skills of a Warrior Young Native Americans on the Plains learned the skills they would need in battle. Boys ran races, wrestled, rode horses, and learned how to shoot arrows. As they grew older, they learned about battle strategies, including the tactic of sending young men to fight hand-to-hand with the enemy while other warriors surrounded and attacked the opponents. Courage during battle was highly valued by the Native Americans of the Plains. Before a battle, for example, the Lakota would often yell, "It is a good day to die!"

Critical Thinking

Making Connections What types of skills are you learning that will help you as an adult?

Conflict

Main Idea Conflict between Native Americans and whites grew as Native Americans were forced onto reservations.

History and You Think about how you might feel if the government told you where to live. Read to learn how this affected Native Americans.

. . . .

When white people began to settle the Plains, conflict developed with Native American groups. In 1867 the federal government appointed the Indian Peace Commission to develop a policy toward Native Americans. The commission recommended moving the Native Americans to a few large **reservations**—tracts of land set aside for them. The army was given authority to deal with any groups that would not move. Moving Native Americans to reservations was not a new policy, but the government increased its efforts in that direction.

Reservation Life

One large reservation was in Oklahoma, the "Indian Territory" that Congress created in the 1830s for Native Americans who were relocated from the Southeast. A second large reservation was created for the Sioux in the Dakota Territory. The federal Bureau of Indian Affairs would manage the reservations.

Government agents often used trickery to persuade Native American nations to move to the reservations. Many reservations were located on poor land. In addition, the government often failed to deliver promised food and supplies, and the goods that were delivered were of poor quality.

A great many Native Americans accepted the reservation policy at first, and they agreed to move to the lands that had been set aside for them. However, some Native Americans refused to move, while others who tried reservation life eventually abandoned it. The stage was set for conflict.

Primary Source / Conflicts With Native Americans

Cultures Under Pressure Westward migration of white settlers in the mid-1800s caused conflicts with Native Americans on the Great Plains. White settlers fought with many groups, including the Sioux, Cheyenne, Apache, and Navajo. After the Civil War, the U.S. government implemented a reservation policy. Some Native Americans agreed to move to reservations; others resisted.

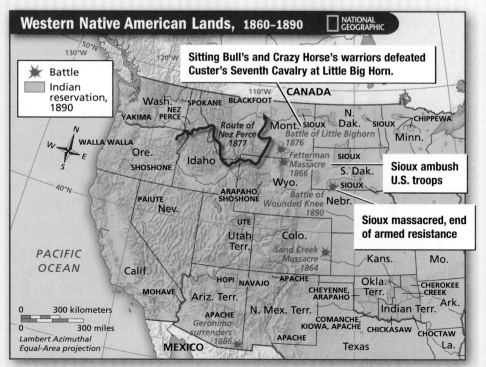

Western Native American Lands, 1860–1890

Sitting Bull's and Crazy Horse's warriors defeated Custer's Seventh Cavalry at Little Big Horn.

Sioux ambush U.S. troops

Sioux massacred, end of armed resistance

Native American Population

"You might as well expect all rivers to run backward as that any man who was born a free man should be contented when penned up and denied liberty to go where he pleases."

—Chief Joseph of the Nez Perce, on a visit to Washington, D.C., 1879

Conflict Begins

During the 1860s, many armed clashes between Native Americans and whites took place. Minnesota Territory was the site of one especially bloody confrontation. Resentful of the settlers, Sioux warriors led by Red Cloud burned and looted white settlers' homes in the summer of 1862. Hundreds died before troops put down the uprising.

The Sioux, along with Cheyenne and Arapaho, staged a series of attacks from 1865 to 1867. The bloodiest occurred on December 21, 1866. Army troops were stationed at a fort on the Bozeman Trail, which was used by prospectors to reach gold mines in Montana. A Sioux military leader, **Crazy Horse,** acting as a decoy, lured the troops into a deadly trap, where hundreds of warriors wiped out the entire detachment. This incident was known as the Fetterman Massacre.

Colorado was another site of conflict between Native Americans and whites. A growing number of miners flocked to Colorado in search of gold and silver. Bands of Cheyenne and Arapaho began raiding wagon trains and stealing cattle and horses from ranches. By the summer of 1864, white people traveling to Denver or the mining camps were no longer safe. Many ranches were burned, and about 200 settlers were killed. The territorial governor of Colorado ordered the Native Americans to surrender at Fort Lyon, where he said they would be given food and protection.

Although several hundred Native Americans surrendered at the fort, many did not. In November 1864, Chief Black Kettle traveled with several hundred Cheyenne to negotiate a peace agreement. They camped at Sand Creek. On their way to the fort, Colonel John Chivington led the Colorado Volunteers on an attack against the unsuspecting Cheyenne. Fourteen volunteers and hundreds of Cheyenne died. Retaliation by the Cheyenne was swift, provoking **widespread,** or far-reaching, uprisings before some of the Cheyenne and Arapaho leaders agreed to stop the fighting in October 1865.

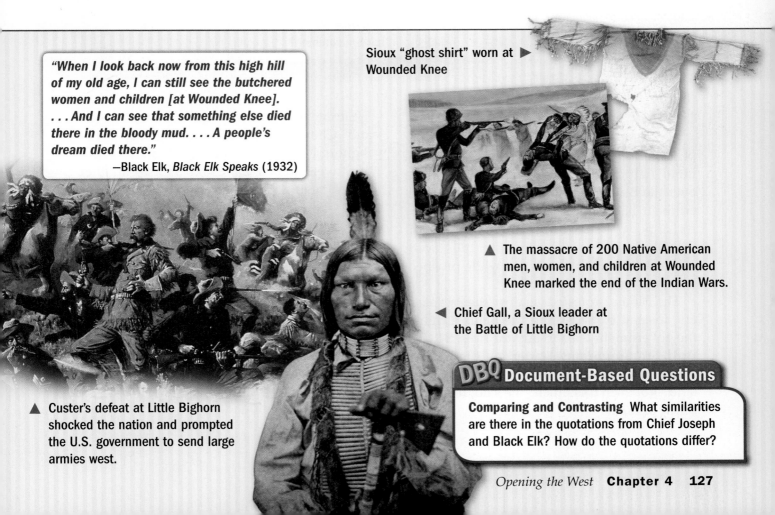

"When I look back now from this high hill of my old age, I can still see the butchered women and children [at Wounded Knee]. . . . And I can see that something else died there in the bloody mud. . . . A people's dream died there."
—Black Elk, *Black Elk Speaks* (1932)

Sioux "ghost shirt" worn at ▶ Wounded Knee

▲ The massacre of 200 Native American men, women, and children at Wounded Knee marked the end of the Indian Wars.

◀ Chief Gall, a Sioux leader at the Battle of Little Bighorn

▲ Custer's defeat at Little Bighorn shocked the nation and prompted the U.S. government to send large armies west.

DBQ Document-Based Questions

Comparing and Contrasting What similarities are there in the quotations from Chief Joseph and Black Elk? How do the quotations differ?

People IN HISTORY

Sitting Bull

Sioux Chief

Sitting Bull distrusted the U.S. government and resisted its attempts to control the Sioux. One journalist reported that Sitting Bull said, *"I never taught my people to trust Americans. I have told them the truth—that the Americans are great liars. I never dealt with the Americans. Why should I? The land belonged to my people."*

Geronimo

Leader of the Apache

Geronimo once said that he might have lived peacefully with white settlers if their promises to his people had been kept. Instead, he wrote, *"We were reckless of our lives, because we felt that every man's hand was against us. If we returned to the reservation we would be put in prison and killed; if we stayed in Mexico they would continue to send soldiers to fight us."*

CRITICAL Thinking

1. **Interpreting** Why did Sitting Bull choose not to negotiate with the U.S. government?
2. **Analyzing** What did Sitting Bull and Geronimo have in common?

Little Bighorn

An 1868 treaty was supposed to bring peace, but tensions remained and erupted in more fighting. This time the conflict arose over the Black Hills of the Dakotas. The government had promised that "No white person or persons shall be permitted" to settle on the Black Hills. However, the hills were rumored to contain gold, and white prospectors swarmed into the area.

The Sioux protested against the trespassers. Instead of protecting the Sioux's rights, the government tried to buy the hills. **Sitting Bull,** an important leader of the Lakota Sioux, refused. "I do not want to sell any land. Not even this much," he said, holding a pinch of dust.

Sitting Bull gathered the combined Sioux and Cheyenne warriors along the Little Bighorn River in present-day Montana. There they were joined by Crazy Horse, another Sioux chief, and his forces. With only about 210 soldiers, Lieutenant Colonel George Custer of the U.S. Army faced thousands of Sioux and Cheyenne warriors. In less than 30 minutes, Custer and almost all of his men lost their lives at Little Bighorn.

News of the army's defeat shocked the nation. Yet the army soon crushed the uprising, sending most of the Native Americans to reservations. Sitting Bull and his followers fled north to Canada. By 1881, exhausted and starving, the Lakota and Cheyenne agreed to live on a reservation.

The Apache Wars

Trouble also broke out in the Southwest. In the 1870s, the Chiracahua Apache were moved to a reservation in Arizona. The Apache leader, **Geronimo,** then fled to Mexico. During the 1880s, he led raids in Arizona. Thousands of troops pursued Geronimo and his warriors. In 1886 Geronimo finally gave up—the last Native American to surrender.

A Changing Culture

Many factors changed Native American life—the movement of whites onto their lands, the slaughter of the buffalo, U.S. army attacks, and the reservation policy. Change also came from reformers who wanted to absorb Native Americans into white culture.

In 1887 Congress passed the **Dawes Act.** It aimed to remove what whites regarded as two weaknesses of Native American life: the lack of private property and the nomadic tradition. The act called for the breakup of reservations and an end to identification with a tribal group. Each Native American would receive a plot of reservation land. Reformers hoped that the native peoples would become farmers and, in time, American citizens. Some Native Americans succeeded as farmers or ranchers, but many had little training or enthusiasm for either pursuit. Like homesteaders, they often found their land too small to be profitable, and so they sold it.

Wounded Knee

A ceremony called the Ghost Dance became popular with many western Native Americans. The ceremony celebrated a hoped-for day when the settlers would disappear and the buffalo would return. As the Ghost Dance spread, white officials became alarmed and banned the ritual. Believing that Sitting Bull led the movement, police tried to arrest him. During a scuffle, they shot and killed him.

After Sitting Bull's death, several hundred Lakota Sioux gathered at a creek called **Wounded Knee** in southwestern South Dakota. In December 1890, the army went there to collect Sioux weapons. When a shot rang out, the army responded with fire. More than 200 Sioux and 25 soldiers were killed. Wounded Knee marked the end of armed conflict beween the U.S. government and Native Americans.

✔ **Reading Check** **Evaluating** How effective was the Dawes Act?

Section 3 Review

History ONLINE
Study Central™ To review this section, go to glencoe.com.

Vocabulary

1. Define each of the following terms: ensure, nomadic, reservation, widespread.

Main Ideas

2. **Specifying** Why did American railroad workers hunt buffalo?

3. **Evaluating** Was the Dawes Act an improvement on previous government policy toward Native Americans? Why or why not?

Critical Thinking

4. **Predicting** What do you think happened to Native Americans after Wounded Knee?

5. **Contrasting** List the similarities and differences between nomadic life and reservation life. Use a Venn diagram like the one below.

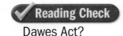

Nomadic Life — Both — Reservation Life

6. **Creative Writing** Write a poem describing the Ghost Dance and its importance to Native Americans.

Answer the
7. **Essential Question**
How did westward expansion affect Native Americans?

GEOGRAPHY & HISTORY

Skin Houses, Sod Houses: Plains Indians and Homesteaders

As many as 100,000 Native Americans lived on the Great Plains in the middle of the 1800s. Many groups, such as the Crow and Sioux, were nomadic hunters who trekked across the plains following game: deer, elk, antelope, and most importantly buffalo. Over time Native Americans had learned to live in the harsh landscape. By contrast white settlers who entered the region in the mid-1800s were accustomed to entirely different surroundings.

How Did Geography Affect Housing on the Great Plains?

Great Plains Native Americans lived in portable shelters that they could carry from place to place. These shelters, called tepees, were made from buffalo skins. Most homesteaders, however, were farmers who wanted more permanent homes. The Great Plains had few trees, so little wood was available for building. Some settlers built shelters called dugouts by tunneling directly into the sides of hills. Others constructed freestanding sod houses—or *soddies*—made of bricks cut from the ground.

The Great Plains Covering most of the central United States is a vast area called the Great Plains. In the early 1800s, the area's relative lack of water and wood made it seem unfit for settlement and farming. The region was labeled the "Great American Desert" on many maps of the day. This inhospitable environment made the Great Plains the last refuge of independent Native Americans.

Native American Lands

Native American Lands
- 1860
- 1890
- Great Plains (Great American Desert)

0   400 kilometers
0   400 miles

Lambert Azimuthal Equal-Area projection

Handbill promoting Plains settlement

◄ "Boomers" race into the Oklahoma Territory to claim land, April 1889

Skin Houses A tepee had a cover made of tanned buffalo skins fastened together and stretched over a cone-like framework of poles. Typically 3 or 4 poles were tied together near the top and raised upright. Up to 12 additional poles were leaned against these, again tied at the top. The cover was then positioned around the frame and tied to an anchor inside the tepee. The bottom was tied down or held down with stones. A door flap was pinned into place. Two women could typically raise a tepee in less than an hour.

A completed tepee was about 15 feet in diameter. Objects inside the tepee were used in specific ways: ceremonial items at the back, beds and pillows along the sides.

Where the sides of the tepee cover met, pins acted as a wooden seam. The door flap was also attached with a pin.

Plains Indians built other structures besides tepees, such as earth lodges, sweat lodges, storage pits, and platforms for drying food.

About 36 tons of sod were needed to make a house.

Only grass that had strong roots could be used so that the soil held together.

The direction of the bricks was reversed every few layers to make the wall strong.

◀ **Sod Houses** Homesteaders built *soddies* by plowing ground into strips 12 inches wide and 4 inches thick; these strips were then cut into about 3-foot lengths. The builder laid two bricks side by side lengthwise to construct a wall, placing every third layer crosswise to bind the walls. Sod was laid with the grass side down. Wooden door and window frames were set in place with wooden pegs as the walls reached proper height. Roofs were thin wooden planks nailed to rafters and topped with a layer of sod.

A sod house needed to be at least 8 x 10 feet to meet the requirements of the Homestead Act of 1862. The sun-hardened sod created a solid structure. The house's thick walls provided good insulation.

Analyzing Geography

1. **Human-Environment Interaction** Do you think living in a *soddie* was comfortable? What kinds of problems do you think homesteaders typically had with their *soddies?* Explain your answer.

2. **Human-Environment Interaction** What materials did Native Americans use to build their tepees?

Farmers in Protest

Essential Question

Why did economic reform movements develop in the late 1800s?

Reading Guide

Content Vocabulary

National Grange *(p. 133)*

cooperative *(p. 133)*

populism *(p. 135)*

Academic Vocabulary

create *(p. 133)*   currency *(p. 135)*

Key People and Events

William Jennings Bryan *(p. 136)*

William McKinley *(p. 136)*

Reading Strategy

Taking Notes As you read, use a chart like the one below to identify the successes and failures of the National Grange, Farmers' Alliances, and the Populist Party.

	Successes	Failures
National Grange		
Farmers' Alliances		
Populist Party		

American Diary

In the late 1800s, farmers experienced great economic hardships, suffering from falling prices and rising costs. They expressed their frustration in the following popular song called "The Farmer Is the Man":

"The farmer is the man,
Lives on credit till the fall—
With the interest rates so high
It's a wonder he don't die,
For the mortgage man's the one
who gets it all."

—from Songs of Work and Protest

Farmworkers on a combine harvester and thresher, 1903

The Farmers Organize

Main Idea The National Grange and the Farmers' Alliances tried to help farmers.

History and You Are you a member of any groups or organizations? Read to find out why farmers united in groups.

. . . .

After the Civil War, farming expanded in the West and South. The supply of crops grew faster than the demand for them, however, and prices fell steadily. In 1866 a bushel of wheat sold for $1.45. By the mid-1880s, the price dropped to 80 cents, and by the mid-1890s, it dropped to 49 cents. At the same time, farmers' expenses—for transporting their goods to market, for seed, and for equipment and other manufactured goods—remained high.

Farmers blamed their troubles on three groups in particular. They resented the railroad companies, which charged farmers more to ship crops than they charged manufacturers to ship goods. They were angry at Eastern manufacturers, who charged high prices for their products. They also resented bankers, who charged high interest rates to farmers when they borrowed money for seed, equipment, and other necessary items. Senator William A. Peffer of Kansas summarized farmers' problems when he noted that the railroad companies "took possession of the land" and the bankers "took possession of the farmer."

The National Grange

Farmers began to organize in an effort to solve their problems. Within a short time, they had **created,** or formed, a mass political movement.

The first farmers' organization was a network of local organizations that eventually was called the **National Grange.** The Grange offered farmers education, fellowship, and support. For inexperienced farmers, the Grange provided a library with books on planting and livestock raising. For lonely farm families, it also organized social gatherings.

Above all, the Grange tried to encourage economic self-sufficiency for farmers. It set up "cash-only" **cooperatives,** stores where farmers bought products from each other.

Critical Thinking
Predicting What might happen to the price of a product if there were not enough of it available to sell?

By the Numbers / **Farmers Face Hard Times**

A Drop in Crop Prices As farming grew, so did the amount of crops grown, such as wheat. The price of wheat dropped because there was too much wheat available to sell.

Wheat Production

Millions of Bushels

500		
400		
300		
200		
1870	1880	1890

Year

Wheat Prices

$ per Bushel

1.50		
1.20		
0.90		
0.60		
1870	1880	1890

Year

Source: U.S. Census Bureau, Historical Statistics of the United States.

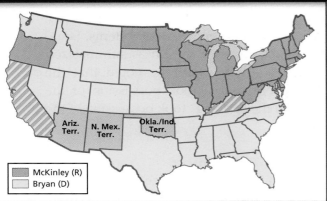

McKinley (R)
Bryan (D)

Campaigns in Contrast In 1896 the Democratic presidential nominee was William Jennings Bryan, who ran on a free-silver platform. The Republicans nominated William McKinley, a pro-business candidate who favored the gold standard and a high tariff.

◀ Democrat William Jennings Bryan campaigned that free silver would help farmers and the working class.

▲ Republican William McKinley said that the gold standard would ensure prosperity for all.

Map Skills

Regions In the 1896 election, which candidate carried most of the industrial states? Which candidate carried most of the agricultural states?

Cooperatives charged lower prices than regular stores while also providing an outlet for farmers' crops. The cash-only policy prevented farmers from buying items on credit, which often led to debt.

In the 1870s, the Grange tried to cut farmers' costs by getting state legislatures to limit railroad shipping rates. Many Midwestern states passed such laws. By 1878, however, the railroads put so much pressure on state legislatures that these states repealed the rate regulations.

The Grange's cooperatives also failed. Farmers were always short of cash and had to borrow money until their next crop was sold. The cash-only cooperatives could not survive if borrowing was necessary. By the late 1870s, the Grange had declined.

The Farmers' Alliances

The Farmers' Alliances were a network of organizations that sprang up in the West and the South in the 1880s. The alliances grew rapidly. By 1890, the Southern Alliance had more than 3 million members, and the Colored Farmers' National Alliance, a separate organization of African American farmers, had 1 million members.

Like the Grange, the Farmers' Alliances sponsored education and cooperative buying and selling. The alliances also proposed a plan in which the federal government would store farmers' crops in warehouses and lend money to the farmers. When the crops were sold, the farmers would pay back the loans. It was hoped that such a plan would reduce the power that railroads, banks, and merchants had over farmers. The plan would also offer farmers some federal protection.

The alliances could have been a powerful force. Regional differences and personality clashes, however, kept the alliances apart.

✓ **Reading Check** **Determining Cause and Effect** Why did farmers create organizations such as the Grange and the Farmers' Alliances?

A Party of the People

Main Idea The Populist Party supported the views of farmers and the common people.

History and You What political parties exist in the United States today? Read to learn about the People's, or Populist, Party that was created in 1890.

· ·

In the 1890 election, the Farmers' Alliances became active in political campaigns. Their candidates won 6 governorships, 3 seats in the U.S. Senate, and 50 seats in the House of Representatives.

As a result of their successes, Alliance leaders worked to turn the movement into a national political party. In February 1890, Alliance members had formed the People's Party of the U.S.A., also known as the Populist Party. The goals of this new party were rooted in **populism,** or appeal to the common people.

The Populist Party

The Populist Party claimed that the government, not private companies, should

History ONLINE
Student Web Activity Visit glencoe.com and complete the **Chapter 4** Web Activity about farming in the late 1800s.

own the railroads and telegraph lines. The Populists also wanted to replace the country's gold-based **currency,** or money, system with a flexible currency system that was based on free silver, or the unlimited production of silver coins. They believed that putting more silver coins into the economy would give farmers more money to pay their debts.

The Populist Party also supported several political and labor reforms. They promoted political reforms such as limiting the president and vice president to a single term, electing senators directly, and introducing the use of secret ballots. They also called for shorter hours for workers and the creation of a national income tax that would tax higher earnings more heavily.

In 1892 the Populists nominated James B. Weaver of Iowa as its presidential candidate. Although Weaver did not win, support for the Populist Party strengthened.

Primary Sources
ANALYZING POLITICAL CARTOONS

In 1896 William Jennings Bryan campaigned for the unlimited production of silver coins to help poor farmers. Opponents viewed free silver as repudiation, or a refusal to pay their debts.

1. **Identifying Points of View** Does the cartoon support or oppose free silver? How do you know?

2. **Interpreting** According to the cartoon, what is happening to the free-silver movement?

Supporters of the free-silver movement:
A. Senator Ben Tillman of South Carolina B. William Jennings Bryan C. Governor John P. Altgeld of Illinois

The Populists did well in the state and local elections of 1894 and had hopes for building even more support in the presidential election of 1896. Despite having energetic candidates, however, the Populists lacked money and organization.

Free Silver

In addition to these problems, hostility between the North and the South following the Civil War caused divisions within the Populist Party. Also, many white Southerners could not bring themselves to join forces with Populists who were African American.

Another problem for populism was that in the 1890s, Democrat-controlled Southern state legislatures placed limits on the rights of African Americans to vote. Many freedmen—who might have supported the Populists—were unable to vote.

Farmers were joined by debtors in supporting free silver. Debtors hoped that free silver would mean their loans could be repaid more cheaply. Silver-mining companies in the West also supported the cause. If the government coined large quantities of silver, the mining companies would have a place to sell their metal.

The Election of 1896

In 1896 the Democrats chose a candidate for president who supported free silver and other Populist goals. He was 36-year-old **William Jennings Bryan,** known as the Great Commoner because of his appeal to average Americans. Bryan passionately believed in farmers' causes. The Populists endorsed Bryan as their candidate. His opponent was Republican **William McKinley** of Ohio, who opposed free silver.

Bryan was a fiery speaker and proved to be an outstanding campaigner. He traveled across the nation giving dynamic speeches, attacking bankers and other money interests. Yet by the time of the election, the economic depression that had slowed business in the early 1890s was nearly over. Bryan's message no longer seemed urgent. McKinley won the election in a landslide.

Despite the loss, Populist ideas made an impact. In the 1900s, the United States abandoned the gold standard and adopted an eight-hour workday, an income tax, the secret ballot, and the direct election of senators.

Reading Check Evaluating Why did people support the Populist Party?

Section 4 Review

Vocabulary

1. Define each of the following terms, and use each of them in a sentence: create, National Grange, cooperative, populism, currency.

Main Ideas

2. **Explaining** How did cooperatives help farmers? Why did the cooperatives fail?

3. **Analyzing** Why did the Populists believe free silver would help farmers and debtors?

Critical Thinking

4. **Evaluating** Was the Populist Party successful? Explain your answer.

5. **Identifying Points of View** Use a chart to describe what each person's opinion might be about the Populist Party.

	Opinion
Factory Worker	
Wealthy Factory Owner	
Southern African American Farmer	

6. **Persuasive Writing** Write a speech that William Jennings Bryan might have given during the election of 1896.

Answer the Essential Question

7. Why did economic reform movements develop in the late 1800s?

Miners

- Pikes Peak in Colorado and the Comstock Lode in Nevada bring many miners west.
- Boomtowns spring up near mining sites and are abandoned when mining ended.
- Population growth leads to statehood for Colorado, North Dakota, South Dakota, Washington, Montana, Wyoming, and Idaho.

Ranchers

- Railroads open up profitable new markets for beef in the North and East.
- Cowhands herd cattle from Texas on long drives.
- Ranching spreads from Texas to the northern Plains.
- The "Cattle Kingdom" ends when a surplus of cattle causes prices to fall.

Farmers

- The Homestead Act attracts thousands of settlers with the promise of free land on the Great Plains.
- New technology helps pioneers overcome the harsh realities of farming on the Plains.
- Organizations such as the Grange and Farmers' Alliances help farmers financially and politically.

Native Americans

- Plains Indians are forced off their lands with the promise of receiving new land.
- White settlers move into land promised to Native Americans.
- The slaughter of the buffalo removes a major part of the Native American way of life.
- The Dawes Act aims to break up reservations and end tribal identification among Native Americans.

STUDY TO GO — Study anywhere, anytime! Download quizzes and flash cards to your PDA from glencoe.com.

STANDARDIZED TEST PRACTICE

TEST-TAKING TIP

Answer the questions you know first and go back to those for which you need more time.

Reviewing Main Ideas

Directions: Choose the best answer for each of the following questions.

1. Discovered in 1859, Nevada's Comstock Lode contained
   A scattered deposits of gold and iron ore.
   B large concentrations of coal.
   C the biggest seam of copper ever found.
   D a rich lode of silver-bearing ore.

2. Who were the "Exodusters"?
   A Hispanic ranch hands in the Southwest
   B African Americans who migrated into Kansas
   C settlers who staked claims in Oklahoma
   D ordinary citizens who punished criminals

3. Which of the following events occurred in 1868 along the Little Bighorn River in present-day Montana?
   A Several hundred Cheyenne negotiated a peace deal with the U.S. government.
   B Sioux and Cheyenne warriors defeated a U.S. army unit led by Lt. Col. George Custer.
   C Apache leader Geronimo was the last Native American to surrender formally to the U.S.
   D Thousands of Lakota Sioux gathered for a Ghost Dance ritual.

4. One of the goals of the Populist Party was
   A returning to the gold currency standard.
   B government ownership of railroads.
   C extending the term of the president.
   D passage of the Fifteenth Amendment.

Short-Answer Question

Directions: Base your answer to question 5 on the excerpt below and on your knowledge of social studies.

> My brothers, I bring to you the promise of a day in which there will be no white man to lay his hand on the bridle of the Indian's horse; when the red men of the prairie will rule the world and not be turned from the hunting-grounds by any man. I bring you word from your fathers the ghosts, that they are now marching to join you, led by the Messiah who came once to live on earth with the white men, but was cast out and killed by them. I have seen the wonders of the spirit-land, and have talked with the ghosts.
>
> —from Kicking Bear's speech to a council of Sioux, 1890

5. According to the document, what changes did Kicking Bear expect to occur in the relationship between Native Americans and whites? Why did he think this?

Review the Essential Questions

6. **Essay** Discuss the contributions of different ethnic groups to the history of the American West in the middle to late 1800s.

To help you write your essay, review your answers to the Essential Questions in the section reviews and the chapter Foldables Study Organizer. Your essay should include:

- western mining booms;
- westward expansion;
- ranchers and homesteaders;
- settlers' relations with Native Americans; and
- Populist Party activities.

History ONLINE

For additional test practice, use **Self-Check Quizzes**—Chapter 4 at glencoe.com.

Document-Based Questions

Directions: Analyze the documents and answer the short-answer questions that follow.

Document 1

This is an excerpt from Grenville M. Dodge's 1869 report on the transcontinental railway.

> Telegraphic wires were so connected that each blow of the descending [sledgehammer] could be reported instantly to all parts of the United States. . . . And with the last blow of the sledge a cannon was fired at Fort Point [in San Francisco].

Source: David Colbert, *Eyewitness to America*

7. Based on the excerpt, was the completion of the railroad considered an important national event? How do you know?

Document 2

J. Ross Browne recorded these impressions of Virginia City, Nevada, in 1865.

> The business part of the town has been built up with astonishing rapidity. In the spring of 1860 there was nothing of it save a few frame shanties and canvas tents, and one or two rough stone cabins. It now presents some of the distinguishing features of a metropolitan city.

Source: *The Mammoth Book of Eyewitness America*

8. According to Browne, how had Virginia City changed?

9. What might be distinguishing features of a metropolitan city in 1865?

Document 3

This 1891 cartoon is about the Populist Party.

A PARTY OF PATCHES.

Source: The Granger Collection, New York

10. The title of the cartoon is "A Party of Patches." What does this say about the organization of the party?

11. Expository Writing Using the information from the three documents and your knowledge of social studies, write an essay in which you:

- explain why railroads are the key to understanding the development of the American West; and

- discuss at least one problem or conflict directly related to the spread of railroads in the West.

Need Extra Help?											
If you missed questions...	1	2	3	4	5	6	7	8	9	10	11
Go to page...	111	122	128	135	126–129	110–136	112–115	115	115	135–136	110–136

The Industrial Age 1865–1914

Working at a factory in Dayton, Ohio, 1902

PRESIDENTS

U.S. Events

World Events

A. JOHNSON
1865–1869

1869 ★
First trans-continental railroad completed

U. S. GRANT
1869–1877

1870
Rockefeller organizes Standard Oil Company

1876 ★
Bell patents the telephone

R. B. HAYES
1877–1881

1879 ★
Edison invents electric light

J. GARFIELD
1881

1860

1870

1880

1867 ★
Diamonds discovered in Cape Colony, a province in South Africa

★ **1880**
Unions win the right to strike in Great Britain

Section 1: Railroads Lead the Way

Essential Question How did railroad expansion affect the United States economy?

Section 2: Inventions

Essential Question How did the inventions of the late 1800s revolutionize society?

Section 3: An Age of Big Business

Essential Question How did Americans build fortunes in the oil and steel industries?

Section 4: Industrial Workers

Essential Question Why did workers form labor unions in the middle to late 1800s?

FOLDABLES Study Organizer

Organizing Information Make this Foldable to help organize what you learn about the growth of industry in the late 1800s.

Step 1 Fold four sheets of paper in half from top to bottom.

Step 2 On each folded paper, make a cut 1 inch from the side on the top flap.

Step 3 Place the folded papers one on top of the other, and staple the sections together. Label the pages with headings appropriate for the sections.

Railroad Industry

Main ideas, dates, events, diagrams, etc.

Reading and Writing As you read, note dates, events, and visuals from the chapter to help you summarize its main ideas.

◄ Model T touring car, 1908

C. ARTHUR 1881–1885

G. CLEVELAND 1885–1889

B. HARRISON 1889–1893

★ **1890** Sherman Antitrust Act passes

★ **1892** Iron- and steel-workers strike in the U.S.

G. CLEVELAND 1893–1897

W. MCKINLEY 1897–1901

T. ROOSEVELT 1901–1909

★ **1903** First powered flight by Wright brothers

★ **1908** Ford introduces Model T

1890

1900

1893 ★ Karl Benz builds four-wheel car

1895 ★ Marconi sends first radio signals

1895 Lumière brothers introduce motion pictures

◄ French inventor Louis Lumière

Railroads Lead the Way

Essential Question

How did railroad expansion affect the United States economy?

Reading Guide

Content Vocabulary

consolidation (p. 143)

rebate (p. 145)

railroad baron (p. 143)

pool (p. 145)

standard gauge (p. 144)

Academic Vocabulary

labor (p. 143)   individual (p. 143)

Key People and Events

George Westinghouse (p. 145)

Eli H. Janney (p. 145)

Gustavus Swift (p. 145)

George M. Pullman (p. 145)

Reading Strategy

Taking Notes As you read, use a diagram like the one below to record the effects of railroad expansion in the United States.

Railroad Expansion

American Diary

In 1869 writer Samuel Bowles described his journey west: "Marked, indeed, was the contrast between the stage [stagecoach] ride . . . and the Railroad ride . . . across the Plains. The then long-drawn, tedious [boring] endurance of six days and nights, running the gauntlet of hostile Indians, was now accomplished in a single twenty-four hours, safe in a swiftly-moving train, and in a car that was an elegant drawing-room by day and a luxurious bedroom at night."

—from **Our New West**

Railroad Expansion

Main Idea The railroad system expanded rapidly in the late 1800s, building large fortunes for some wealthy businesspeople.

History and You In what industries do people make large amounts of money today? Read to learn about the profits generated by railroad expansion.

During the Civil War, trains carried troops and supplies to the front. After the war, the railroad system grew rapidly and drove economic growth in the United States. In 1860 the United States had about 30,000 miles (48,280 km) of railroad track. By 1900, the nation had nearly 193,000 miles (310,603 km) of track. Work songs such as "John Henry" and "I've Been Working on the Railroad" were popular among those who **labored,** or worked, to build these miles of track.

Railroad expansion was accompanied by **consolidation**—the practice of combining separate companies—in the industry. Large railroad companies bought smaller companies or drove them out of business. Consolidation made the large companies more efficient. These companies established standard prices and made industrial processes more uniform.

Railroad Barons

After consolidation, a few powerful **individuals,** or persons, known as **railroad barons** controlled the nation's rail traffic. New Yorker Cornelius Vanderbilt, one of the first railroad barons, made a fortune by consolidating several companies. His railroad empire stretched from New York City to the Great Lakes. Another railroad baron, James J. Hill, built the Great Northern line between Minnesota and Washington State. Other barons, including Collis P. Huntington and Leland Stanford, founded the Central Pacific, which connected California and Utah. The railroad barons were aggressive and competitive. They lived in an age when there were few laws that regulated business.

Reading Check Analyzing What are the advantages and disadvantages of consolidation?

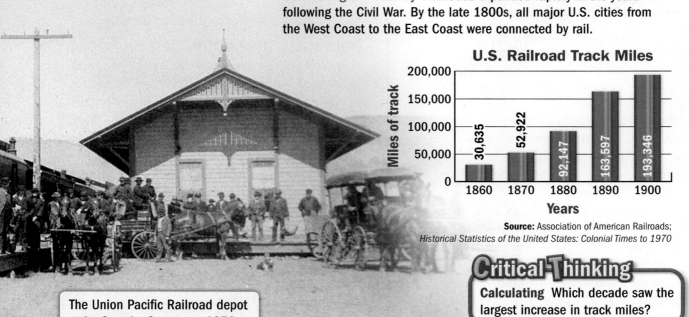

By the Numbers / Railroad Tracks

Connecting the Country Railroads expanded rapidly in the years following the Civil War. By the late 1800s, all major U.S. cities from the West Coast to the East Coast were connected by rail.

U.S. Railroad Track Miles

Years	Miles of track
1860	30,635
1870	52,922
1880	92,147
1890	163,597
1900	193,346

Source: Association of American Railroads; *Historical Statistics of the United States: Colonial Times to 1970*

The Union Pacific Railroad depot at La Grande, Oregon, c. 1870

Critical Thinking
Calculating Which decade saw the largest increase in track miles?

Time Zones Before railroads, each community established its own time. In order to create sensible schedules, the railroad companies divided the country into four time zones. Each zone was one hour apart from the zone on either side of it.

Railroads in 1890

CANADA

0   400 kilometers
0   400 miles
Albers Equal-Area projection

Boston
Chicago
New York City
Washington, D.C.
San Francisco

ATLANTIC OCEAN

PACIFIC OCEAN   MEXICO   Gulf of Mexico

N W E S

Pacific Time Zone
Mountain Time Zone
Central Time Zone
Eastern Time Zone
—— Railroads built by 1870
—— Railroads built by 1890
*Time zones and borders shown as of 1890

This advertisement shows the "Hotel" car introduced by George Pullman in 1867. It had both sleeping and dining facilities and greatly improved the experience of rail travel.

Map Skills

Regions Which time zone regions had the greatest lengths of railroad tracks? Why was that so?

Maps in MOtion See StudentWorks™ Plus or glencoe.com.

Railroads Stimulate the Economy

Main Idea Railroads brought major changes to American industry and American life in general.

History and You Think about how the expansion of one industry leads to the growth of others. Read to learn how railroads influenced other industries.

. . . .

Railroads carried raw materials such as iron ore, coal, and timber to factories. They also carried manufactured goods from factories to markets and transported produce from farming areas to the cities.

At first the demand for iron tracks and locomotives helped the iron mining and processing industries grow. Around 1880, railroad companies began using tracks of steel—a strong metal made by adding carbon and other elements to refined iron. The use of steel in railroad tracks stimulated America's steel industry. Railroads also had an effect on the lumber industry, which supplied wood for railway ties, and the coal industry, which provided fuel. In addition, railroad companies provided work for thousands of people.

Improving the Railroads

Increased use made it necessary for railroads to expand and unify their systems. While railroads were being built across the country, different lines used rails of different gauges, or widths. As a result, trains of one line could not use another line's tracks. The gaps in service made travel extremely slow.

As the railroad companies consolidated, companies adopted a **standard gauge** of 4 feet, 8.5 inches (1 m, 41.6 cm) as the width of the railroad track. A standard gauge allowed faster shipment of goods at a reduced cost. It was no longer necessary to load and unload goods from one train to another.

Railroad Technology

Railway transportation also improved with the introduction of new technology. Four developments were particularly important. Inventor **George Westinghouse** devised air brakes that improved the system for stopping trains, making train travel safer. Janney car couplers, named after inventor **Eli H. Janney,** made it easier for railroad workers to link cars. Refrigerated cars, developed by **Gustavus Swift,** enabled the railroads to ship meat and other perishable goods over long distances. Finally, **George M. Pullman** developed the Pullman sleeping car—a luxury railway car with seats that converted into beds for overnight journeys.

Competing for Customers

Railroad companies competed fiercely with one another to keep old customers and to win new ones. Large railroads offered secret discounts called **rebates** to their biggest customers. Smaller railroads that could not match these rebates were often forced out of business. Giving discounts to big customers, however, raised freight rates for farmers and other customers who shipped small amounts of goods.

The railroad barons also made secret agreements among themselves, known as **pools.** They divided business among their companies and set rates. With no other competition in its region, a railroad could charge higher rates and earn greater profits. There were some laws to regulate the railroads, but they did little to stop the barons.

Railroads Change America

The growing railroad network helped American industry expand into the West. For example, the manufacturing center for agricultural equipment moved from central New York State to Illinois and Wisconsin. Trains also redistributed the American population. They transported homesteaders into the Great Plains and the West and people from rural areas to the cities.

✔ Reading Check **Describing** What were some of the new technologies that improved railroad travel?

Section 1 Review

History ONLINE
Study Central™ To review this section, go to glencoe.com.

Vocabulary

1. Use each of these terms in a sentence that will help explain its meaning: labor, consolidation, individual, railroad baron, standard gauge, rebate, pool.

Main Ideas

2. **Explaining** How did railroad barons build their fortunes?

3. **Evaluating** Do you think Congress should have allowed railroad barons to make agreements about business and rates? Explain your answer.

Critical Thinking

4. **Classifying** What are some industries that benefited from the expansion of the railroad system?

Railroad Industry

5. **Making Inferences** Do you think owners of small farms supported the rebates given by railroad companies?

6. **Expository Writing** Write a paragraph explaining how the adoption of standard-gauge track affected the railroads.

Answer the
7. **Essential Question**
How did railroad expansion affect the United States economy?

Essential Question

How did the inventions of the late 1800s revolutionize society?

Reading Guide

Content Vocabulary

Model T (p. 151)

mass production (p. 151)

assembly line (p. 151)

Academic Vocabulary

transmit (p. 147)

mechanism (p. 150)

Key People and Events

Cyrus Field (p. 147)

Alexander Graham Bell (p. 148)

George Eastman (p. 148)

John Thurman (p. 148)

Lewis Howard Latimer (p. 150)

Granville Woods (p. 150)

Elijah McCoy (p. 150)

Jan E. Matzeliger (p. 150)

Henry Ford (p. 150)

Reading Strategy

Taking Notes As you read, use a chart like the one below to identify the effects of major inventions.

	Effects
Telegraph	
Telephone	
Electric lightbulb	

American Diary

The Cleveland Plain Dealer *described the lighting of a park in 1879:*
"Thousands of people gathered . . . and as the light shot around and through the Park a shout was raised. . . . Soon afterward a section of artillery on the lake shore began firing a salute in honor of the occasion. The Telegraph Supply Company's establishment . . . was thrown open to as many people as could be accommodated . . . [to] inspect the machinery which sends light over the wire."

—*from* Men and Volts

Electricity lights up Luna Park on Coney Island in New York, 1890.

Communications

Main Idea New inventions revolutionized communications, making faraway places seem closer.

History and You Do you talk on a cell phone or e-mail people in other states or countries? Read to learn how long-distance communication changed in the late 1800s.

. . . .

By 1910, Americans in cities drove cars through streets lit with electric lights. They went to department stores where they bought everything from kitchen sinks to shoes. Americans also could do their shopping by mail—or pick up the telephone and order groceries from the local store. The automobile, the electric light, and the telephone were invented after 1870. Within a generation, they became part of everyday life for millions of people. These new inventions helped people communicate more quickly over long distances. Improvements in communication helped unify the country and promoted economic growth.

The Telegraph

Samuel Morse had introduced the telegraph in 1844. By 1860 the United States had thousands of miles of telegraph lines, managed mostly by the Western Union Telegraph Company. At telegraph offices, trained operators **transmitted**, or sent, messages in Morse code.

Telegrams offered almost instant communication and served many purposes. Shopkeepers relied on telegrams to order goods, and reporters used them to transmit stories to their newspapers. Americans also used telegrams to send personal messages.

The telegraph soon linked the United States and Europe. In the 1860s, news from Europe was relayed to the United States by ship and took several weeks. **Cyrus Field** wanted to speed up the process. In 1866, after several unsuccessful attempts, Field managed to lay a telegraph cable across the Atlantic Ocean. The new transatlantic telegraph transmitted messages in a matter of seconds, bringing the United States and Europe closer together.

Primary Source / **Lewis Latimer**

Improving Technology Lewis Latimer was a draftsman and an inventor who received numerous patents for his inventions. In 1876 he was hired to draft the patent drawings for Alexander Graham Bell's telephone. Later, he improved on Edison's version of the lightbulb, creating one that lasted much longer. Latimer directed the installation of electric streetlights in New York City, Philadelphia, Montreal, and London.

Critical Thinking

Making Connections What types of technology today make your life easier?

Primary Source / The Wright Brothers

Taking Flight Inventors experimented with engine-powered aircraft in the 1800s, but attempts were not successful until 1903. Orville and Wilbur Wright made the world's first flight in an engine-powered glider at Kill Devil Hill, near Kitty Hawk, North Carolina.

◀ Orville and his brother Wilbur operated a bicycle shop in Dayton, Ohio, in the 1890s. Both expert mechanics, they became interested in the concept of human flight.

▲ On December 17, 1903, the Wright brothers fitted their glider with a gasoline engine. They made four flights at Kitty Hawk, the longest covering 852 feet (260 m) and lasting 59 seconds.

◀ The Wright brothers designed and tested gliders. From these experiments, they learned how to control an aircraft.

The Telephone Rings In

Alexander Graham Bell invented a device that revolutionized communications even more. Born and educated in Scotland, Bell moved to the United States, where he studied methods for teaching hearing-impaired people to speak. He also experimented with sending voices through electrical wires.

By 1876 Bell developed a device that transmitted speech—the telephone. While preparing to test the device, he accidentally spilled battery acid on his clothes. Panicked, Bell called out to his assistant in another room: "Mr. Watson, come here. I want you!" Watson heard Bell's voice coming through the telephone. The invention was a success.

Bell formed the Bell Telephone Company in 1877. By the 1890s, he had sold hundreds of thousands of phones. Businesses were the first customers to use telephones. Before long, though, telephones were common in homes.

✔ **Reading Check** Comparing Describe the difference between a telegraph and a telephone.

The Genius of Invention

Main Idea Revolutionary new inventions changed business and everyday life in the 1800s.

History and You Have you ever had an idea for an invention that would make life easier? Read about inventions that improved people's lives.

The late 1800s saw a burst of inventiveness in the United States. Between 1860 and 1890, the United States government granted more than 400,000 patents for new inventions.

Many of the inventions were designed to help businesses operate more efficiently. Among these were Christopher Sholes's typewriter (1868) and William Burroughs's adding machine (1888).

Other inventions affected everyday life. In 1888 **George Eastman** invented a small box camera—the Kodak—that made it easier and less costly to take photographs. **John Thurman** developed a vacuum cleaner in 1899 that simplified housework.

In 1908 Wilbur created a sensation in France by controlling his aircraft in different types of wind. He also set new distance and altitude records. ▶

"The airplane became the promise of the future, and pilots were the popular heroes. . . . Even the routine flights of today retain a touch of magic, reminiscent of the Wright brothers' real intent, which was not speed, money, or military might but simply to break the bonds of Earth and see the world in a new way."

—Astronaut Edwin "Buzz" Aldrin, May 1998

◀ As shown by this aerial bomb test in 1911, the Wrights' invention soon attracted the attention of the U.S. military as well as militaries around the world.

Critical Thinking

Analyzing Primary Sources According to Buzz Aldrin, what was the Wright brothers' greatest accomplishment?

The Wizard of Menlo Park

Thomas Edison was called "dull" by his teachers. Because of his poor hearing, he had trouble in school and often did not attend. His mother finally removed him from school and taught him at home. Edison loved anything related to science, and his mother allowed him to set up a chemistry lab in the family's basement.

When he was 12, Edison got a job working for the railroad, where he set up a new lab in an empty freight car. One day, Edison saved the life of a child who had fallen onto the tracks of an oncoming train. The child's father took an interest in Edison and taught him to use the telegraph. Edison's first invention was a gadget that sent automatic telegraph signals—which he invented so he could sleep on the job.

While still in his 20s, Edison decided to go into the "invention business." In 1876 he set up a workshop in Menlo Park, New Jersey. Out of this famous laboratory came the phonograph, the motion picture projector, the telephone transmitter, and the storage battery. Edison's most important invention by far, though, was the electric lightbulb.

Edison developed the first workable lightbulb in 1879. He then designed power plants that could produce electric power and distribute it to lightbulbs. For Christmas in 1880, Edison used 40 bulbs to light up Menlo Park. Visitors flocked to see the "light of the future." Then, in 1882, Edison built the first central electric power plant in New York City—illuminating 85 buildings!

Inventor George Westinghouse took Thomas Edison's work with electricity even further. In 1885 Westinghouse developed and built transformers that could send electric power more cheaply over longer distances. As a result of Westinghouse's work, factories, trolleys, streetlights, and lamps throughout the United States could be powered by electricity. Westinghouse also created a method for transporting natural gas and invented many safety devices.

Lightbulbs and Vacuum Cleaners The late 1800s could be called the age of invention. The inventions helped change the everyday lives of Americans.

▼ Alexander Graham Bell's first phone

In 1888 George Eastman marketed the Kodak camera. After taking 100 pictures, a user could send it back to the company. The developed photos and a reloaded camera were returned to the customer by mail. ▲

★ **1876** Telephone

★ **1879** Lightbulb

★ **1888** Kodak camera

★ **1868** Typewriter

★ **1877** Phonograph

★ **1888** Adding machine

★ **1899** Motorized vacuum cleaner

▼ Alexander Graham Bell patented the telephone in 1876. There were two million in use by 1900.

◄ Thomas Edison's invention of the phonograph in 1877 attracted worldwide attention.

Critical Thinking

Evaluating Which invention do you think affected people's lives the most? Why?

African American Inventors

A number of African Americans contributed to the era of invention. Engineer **Lewis Howard Latimer** developed an improved wire for the lightbulb and joined Thomas Edison's company. **Granville Woods,** an electrical and mechanical engineer from Ohio, patented dozens of inventions. Among them were an electric incubator and railroad improvements such as an electromagnetic brake and an automatic circuit breaker. **Elijah McCoy** invented a mechanism, or mechanical device, for oiling machinery.

Jan E. Matzeliger, another African American inventor, developed a shoe-making machine that performed many steps previously done by hand. His device, which revolutionized the shoe industry, was used in in the United States and overseas.

Reading Check **Evaluating** Which of Edison's inventions do you think is the most valuable to our world today? Explain your reasoning.

A Changing Society

Main Idea Henry Ford's automobile and assembly line changed industry and society forever.

History and You How might your life be different if the automobile had never been invented? Read to learn about the invention of the automobile.
. . . .

In the 1900s, improvements ushered in a new era of transportation. After much experimentation, the automobile became a practical machine for traveling from place to place.

Henry Ford's Automobiles

Henry Ford had a vision. He wanted to build an inexpensive car that would last a lifetime. While working as an engineer in Detroit, Michigan, in the 1890s, Ford experimented with an automobile engine that was powered by gasoline. In 1903 he established his own auto-making company in Detroit and began designing cars.

In 1906 Ford had an idea for a new type of car. He told Charles Sorenson, later Ford's general superintendent, "We're going to get a car now that we can make in great volume and get the prices way down." For the next year, Ford and Sorenson worked on the **Model T,** building the car and testing it on rough roads. In 1908 Ford introduced the Model T to the public. Sorenson described the sturdy black vehicle as "a car which anyone could afford to buy, which anyone could drive anywhere, and which almost anyone could keep in repair." These qualities made the Model T immensely popular. During the next 18 years, Ford's company sold 15 million Model Ts.

Henry Ford also pioneered a new, less expensive way to manufacture cars—the **assembly line.** On the assembly line, each worker performed an assigned production task again and again. The assembly line revolutionized other industries as well. It enabled manufacturers to produce large quantities of goods more quickly. This **mass production** of goods decreased manufacturing costs, so products could be sold more cheaply.

Selling Goods

Merchants looked for more efficient ways to sell their goods. One method was through the mail. Before 1863 people picked up their mail at post offices. After 1863 mail was delivered directly to people's homes.

Merchants could now send goods cross country nearly as easily as across town. Some firms developed mail order businesses—receiving and shipping orders by mail. Companies such as Montgomery Ward and Sears Roebuck published catalogs that offered a wide range of goods from shoes to farm equipment.

Chain stores—stores with identical branches in many places—grew rapidly. F. W. Woolworth's chain of "five-and-ten-cent stores" specialized in the sale of everyday household and personal items at bargain prices. By 1911, more than 1,000 Woolworths were in operation. The Woolworth Building, erected in New York City in 1913, stood 792 feet (241 m) tall—the tallest building in the world at that time.

Reading Check **Identifying** What was Henry Ford's vision?

History ONLINE
Study Central™ To review this section, go to glencoe.com.

Section 2 Review

Vocabulary

1. Use each of these terms in a sentence that will help explain its meaning: transmit, mechanism, Model T, assembly line, mass production.

Main Ideas

2. **Assessing** What was the significance of the transatlantic telegraph cable?

3. **Explaining** How did George Westinghouse build upon Thomas Edison's inventions?

4. **Analyzing** What effect did the assembly line have on the manufacturing industry?

Critical Thinking

5. **Evaluating** In your opinion, what were the five most important inventions of this time? List them in order in a chart, and provide your reasons.

Top 5 Inventions	Reasons

6. **Concluding** How did companies change the way goods were sold to the public in the late 1800s?

7. **Expository Writing** Some people believe that the Internet has been the most revolutionary invention in communications since the telegraph. Write a paragraph in which you compare the two inventions and explain whether you support this view.

Answer the
8. **Essential Question**
How did the inventions of the late 1800s revolutionize society?

An Age of Big Business

Essential Question ◄

How did Americans build fortunes in the oil and steel industries?

Reading Guide

Content Vocabulary

corporation *(p. 154)*   trust *(p. 155)*
stock *(p. 154)*   monopoly *(p. 155)*
shareholders *(p. 154)*   merger *(p. 157)*
dividend *(p. 154)*

Academic Vocabulary

partner *(p. 155)*   trend *(p. 157)*

Key People and Events

John D. Rockefeller *(p. 155)*
Andrew Carnegie *(p. 156)*
Sherman Antitrust Act *(p. 157)*

Reading Strategy

Taking Notes As you read, create a diagram like the one below to organize information about the oil and steel industries.

- Industry
  - Leader
  - Reason for Growth
  - Method Used

American Diary

A man once told author Ida M. Tarbell that, "The only time I ever saw John Rockefeller enthusiastic was when a report came in from the creek that his buyer had secured a cargo of oil at a figure much below the market price. He bounded from his chair with a shout of joy, danced up and down, hugged me, threw up his hat, acted so like a madman that I have never forgotten it."

—*from* The History of the Standard Oil Company

Oil wells in Los Angeles, California, area during the late 1800s

Foundations for Growth

Main Idea New technology and abundant natural resources led to economic growth.

History and You If you wanted to start your own small business, what resources would you need? Read about the resources that were available for the oil and steel industries.

· ·

In western Pennsylvania, a sticky black substance—petroleum—seeped from the ground. For a while, promoters sold the oil as medicine. Then, in the 1850s, researchers found they could burn petroleum to produce heat and smoke-free light. It could also be used to lubricate machinery. Suddenly, oil became valuable.

Edwin L. Drake believed that he could find petroleum by digging a well. Many people thought Drake was wrong. At that time, few people knew that pools of oil did indeed exist underground. They did not imagine that oil wells could lead to great fortune.

In 1859 Drake drilled a well in Titusville, Pennsylvania, and struck oil. This led to the creation of a multimillion-dollar petroleum industry.

Factors of Production

During the late 1800s, new technology, transportation, and business methods allowed the country to tap its rich supply of natural resources and increase production.

The change from an agricultural economy to an industrial one was possible because the United States had the resources needed for a growing economy. Among these resources were what economists call the factors of production: land, labor, and capital.

The first factor of production, land, refers not just to the land itself but all natural resources. The United States held a variety of natural resources that were useful for industrial production.

The second factor of production is labor. Large numbers of workers were needed to turn raw materials into goods. This need was met by rapid population growth. Between 1860 and 1900, the population of the country more than doubled.

The third factor of production is capital, which are the manufactured goods used to make other goods and services. The machines, buildings, and tools used to assemble automobiles, for example, are capital goods.

Primary Source / Big Business

Monopolies Big corporations were often portrayed as "monopoly monsters" that were too powerful to be controlled.

The United States is swallowed by the Giant of Monopoly, ca. 1890. ▶

Critical Thinking

Evaluating Why might laws be passed to control monopolies?

The term *capital* also means "money for investment." One source of money is the sale of stock by corporations. Another is corporate savings, or businesses investing some of their earnings in better equipment.

Raising Capital

With the economy growing after the Civil War, many railroads and other businesses looked for ways to expand. To do so, they had to raise capital. They needed capital to buy raw materials and equipment, to pay workers, and to cover shipping and advertising costs.

One way a company could raise capital was by becoming a **corporation.** A corporation is a company that sells shares, or **stock,** of its business to the public. People who invest in the corporation by buying stock are its **shareholders,** or partial owners.

During periods of strong economic growth, shareholders earn **dividends**—cash payments from the corporation's profits—on the stock they own. If the company fails, however, the shareholders lose their investment. In the late 1800s, hundreds of thousands of people bought and sold stocks in special markets known as stock exchanges.

The growth of corporations helped fuel America's industrial expansion in the years following the Civil War. Railroads were the first businesses to form corporations, followed by manufacturing firms and other businesses. Banks also played a major role in this period of economic growth. They made profits by lending money to new businesses.

✔ **Reading Check** **Explaining** Why is capital important for economic growth?

Primary Source / Factors of Production

"I am a woman who came from the cotton fields of the South. I was promoted from there to the wash-tub. Then I was promoted to the cook kitchen, and from there I promoted myself into the business of manufacturing hair goods and preparations. . . . I have built my own factory on my own ground."
—Madam C. J. Walker, quoted in *On Her Own Ground*

Land
Natural resources

Labor
Human skills and effort

Capital
Buildings, tools, equipment

▲ Madam C. J. Walker, American entrepreneur

Entrepreneurs People bring together the factors of production to create products and services. They accept the risk of running a business to earn a profit.

Products and Services

Critical Thinking

1. **Categorizing** You use a calculator to complete your math homework. Which factor of production is your calculator?

2. **Theorizing** What qualities should a person have to become a successful entrepreneur?

This 1800s cartoon represents John D. Rockefeller's near-total control of the oil industry.

1. **Identifying** What type of character does Rockefeller represent in this cartoon?

2. **Analyzing** Why is Rockefeller shown holding the world in his hand?

A. John D. Rockefeller
B. oil lamp
C. world

The Oil Business

Main Idea John D. Rockefeller's Standard Oil Company controlled the booming oil industry.

History and You Recall how the railroad barons became powerful. Read how similar events occurred in the oil industry.

. . . .

The oil industry grew rapidly in the late 1800s. As word of Edwin Drake's success spread, prospectors and investors hurried to western Pennsylvania. "Oil rush" towns with names such as Oil City and Petroleum Center sprang up overnight. The oil boom expanded as prospectors struck oil in Ohio and West Virginia.

Great fortunes were made from oil. Born in Richford, New York, in 1839, **John D. Rockefeller** was the most famous figure of the oil industry. When Rockefeller was 26 years old, he and four **partners,** or associates who agree to operate a business together, built an oil refinery—a plant to process oil—in Cleveland, Ohio.

In 1870 Rockefeller organized the Standard Oil Company of Ohio and set out to dominate the oil industry. One method he used was horizontal integration—combining competing companies into one corporation. Standard Oil grew powerful and wealthy.

The Standard Oil Trust

Rockefeller lowered his prices to drive his competitors out of business, pressured customers not to deal with rival companies, and persuaded the railroads to give him special rates. In 1882 he formed a **trust,** a group of companies managed by the same board of directors. Rockefeller did this by acquiring stock in many different oil companies. The shareholders of these companies traded their stock for Standard Oil stock, which paid higher dividends. As a result, Standard Oil became part owner of the other companies. Rockefeller had created a **monopoly**—total control of an industry by a single producer.

✓ **Reading Check** **Describing** How did Standard Oil become a monopoly?

Economics & History

During the late 1800s, vertical and horizontal integration helped businesses grow into monopolies.

Vertical Integration
Purchase of companies at all levels of production

Ace Meat Industries

↑ Delivery wagons

Meat packing plants

Cooled warehouse

Refrigerated railroad cars

Slaughterhouse

Cattle

Horizontal Integration
Purchase of competing companies in same industry

U.S. Oil Company

Independent Oil Refineries

Diagram Skills

Contrasting What is the difference between vertical integration and horizontal integration?

The Steel Business

Main Idea New processes for making steel created an important industry.

History and You Have you heard of Carnegie Hall in New York City? Read to learn about the influential man for whom this cultural landmark is named.

- -

Steel also became a huge business in the late 1800s. A strong and long-lasting form of iron treated with carbon, steel was the ideal material for railroad tracks, bridges, and many other products.

Steel Industry Growth

Two new methods of making steel—the Bessemer process, developed by English inventor Henry Bessemer, and the open-hearth process—changed the industry. With these new methods, mills could produce steel at affordable prices and in large quantities. In the 1870s, large steel mills were built near sources of iron ore in western Pennsylvania and eastern Ohio. Pittsburgh, Pennsylvania, became the steel capital of the United States. Cleveland, Chicago, Detroit, and Birmingham, Alabama, also became important hubs for steel production.

Andrew Carnegie

The leading figure in the early years of the American steel industry was **Andrew Carnegie,** the son of a Scottish immigrant. Starting as a messenger and telegraph operator, Carnegie worked his way up to become manager of the Pennsylvania Railroad. In 1865 he invested in the growing iron industry. Carnegie soon realized that there was an enormous market for steel. After learning about the Bessemer process, he built a steel plant near Pittsburgh.

By 1890 Andrew Carnegie dominated the steel industry. His company became powerful through vertical integration—acquiring companies that provided the equipment and services he needed. Carnegie bought iron and coal mines, warehouses, ore ships, and railroads to gain control of all parts of the business of making and selling steel. By 1900 the Carnegie Steel Company was producing one-third of the nation's steel.

Philanthropists

Andrew Carnegie, John D. Rockefeller, and other industrial millionaires of the era grew interested in philanthropy—the use of money to benefit the community. They used their huge fortunes to found schools, universities, and other civic institutions.

Carnegie donated $350 million to various organizations. He built Carnegie Hall—one of the world's most famous concert halls—in New York City and created more than 2,000 libraries worldwide. Rockefeller used his fortune to establish the University of Chicago in 1890 and New York's Rockefeller Institute for Medical Research.

Corporations Grow Larger

In 1889 New Jersey encouraged the **trend**, or general movement, toward business monopolies by allowing holding companies to obtain charters. A holding company would buy the stock of other companies instead of purchasing the companies outright. Rockefeller formed Standard Oil of New Jersey so that the corporation could expand its holdings. Other states also passed laws that made corporate **mergers**—the combining of companies—easier.

Many Americans admired the efficiencies of large businesses, but others argued that a lack of competition hurt consumers. Without competition, corporations had no reason to improve—or keep prices low.

In 1890 Congress passed the **Sherman Antitrust Act,** which prohibited trusts and monopolies. In its early years, however, the Sherman Antitrust Act did little to curb the power of big business.

Reading Check **Making Inferences** What is one advantage of vertical integration?

History ONLINE
Study Central™ To review this section, go to glencoe.com.

Section 3 Review

Vocabulary

1. Use each of these terms in a sentence that will help explain its meaning: corporation, stock, shareholder, dividend, partner, trust, monopoly, trend, merger.

Main Ideas

2. **Describing** What is the relationship between a corporation and its shareholders?

3. **Explaining** What methods did Rockefeller use to build his oil empire?

4. **Defending** Did the Sherman Antitrust Act support competition? Explain.

Critical Thinking

5. **Speculating** Why do you think the industrial millionaires became philanthropists?

6. **Comparing and Contrasting** Create a diagram to list the similarities and differences between Carnegie and Rockefeller.

Carnegie / Rockefeller

7. **Persuasive Writing** As a member of Congress, write a speech supporting the Sherman Antitrust Act.

Answer the
8. **Essential Question** How did Americans build fortunes in the oil and steel industries?

Were Wealthy Industrialists "Robber Barons"?

Building Background

After the Civil War, businesses, especially those in oil, steel, and railroads, formed a few dominating corporations. Some people viewed the industrial millionaires, such as Andrew Carnegie, as ingenious businesspeople who also gave back to the communities through charity.

Other people, mostly laborers, referred to the leaders of the corporations as robber barons, those who robbed the poor to build their fortunes. In May 1886, after Chicago police fired into a crowd of striking workers, killing several, labor leaders criticized business owners and urged workers to continue their protests.

NO

ANDREW CARNEGIE

The surplus wealth of the few will become, in the best sense, the property of the many. . . . This wealth, passing through the hands of the few, can be made a much more potent[1] force for the elevation of our race than if it had been distributed in small sums to the people themselves. Even the poorest can be made to see this, and to agree that great sums gathered by some of their fellow-citizens and spent for public purposes, from which the masses reap the principal benefit, are more valuable to them than if scattered among them through the course of many years in trifling amounts.

This, then, is held to be the duty of the man of Wealth: . . . to consider all surplus revenues which come to him simply as trust funds, which he is called upon to administer, . . . [in order] to produce the most beneficial result for the community—the man of wealth thus [becomes] the sole agent and trustee for his poorer brethren, bringing to their service his superior wisdom [and] experience . . . doing for them better than they would or could do for themselves.

Carnegie Steel Company plant in Homestead, Pennsylvania

---

[1] **potent** powerful

YES

AD FOR LABOR MEETING

Your masters sent out their bloodhounds—the police—; they killed six of your brothers at McCormicks this afternoon. They killed the poor wretches, because they, like you, had the courage to disobey the supreme will of your bosses. They killed them, because they dared ask for the shortening of the hours of toil. They killed them to show you, "Free American Citizens," that you must be satisfied and contented with whatever your bosses . . . allow you, or you will get killed!

You have for years endured the most abject[2] humiliations . . . you have worked yourself to death; you have endured the pangs of want and hunger; . . . in short: You have been miserable and obedient slaves all these years: Why? To satisfy the insatiable[3] greed, to fill the coffers[4] of your lazy thieving master? When you ask them now to lessen your burden, he sends his bloodhounds out to shoot you, kill you!

If you are men . . . then you will . . . destroy the hideous monster that seeks to destroy you. To arms we call you, to arms!

---

[2] **abject** miserable
[3] **insatiable** unquenchable
[4] **coffers** money boxes

Newspaper engraving of Chicago's Haymarket Riot, May 4, 1886

DBQ Document-Based Questions

1. **Summarizing** According to Andrew Carnegie, what responsibility does a man of wealth have to society?

2. **Making Inferences** Why did Carnegie think that giving his wealth to worthy causes would do more to improve the lives of working people than would paying them higher wages?

3. **Explaining** Why did the author of the advertisement for the meeting in Chicago urge working people to rise up and fight?

4. **Evaluating** Why do you think the phrase "robber barons" developed during this period? Explain your answer.

Industrial Workers

Essential Question ◄

Why did workers form labor unions in the middle to late 1800s?

Reading Guide

Content Vocabulary

sweatshop *(p. 161)*   strikebreaker *(p. 164)*

trade union *(p. 162)*   injunction *(p. 164)*

collective bargaining
    (p. 163)

Academic Vocabulary

identify *(p. 162)*   environment *(p. 163)*

Key People and Events

Knights of Labor *(p. 162)*

Terence V. Powderly *(p. 162)*

American Federation of Labor *(p. 162)*

Samuel Gompers *(p. 163)*

Eugene V. Debs *(p. 164)*

Reading Strategy

Taking Notes As you read, use a chart like the one below to record the reasons why the events occurred and what happened as a result.

	Reason	Outcome
Haymarket Riot		
Homestead Strike		
Pullman Strike		

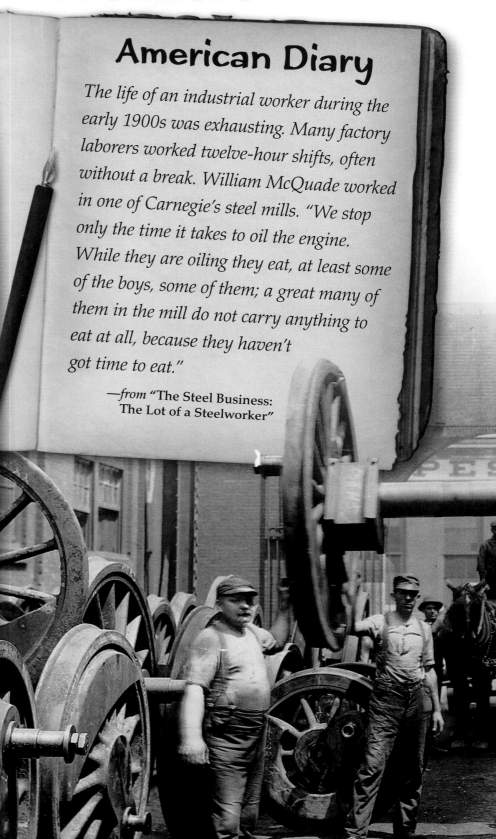

American Diary

The life of an industrial worker during the early 1900s was exhausting. Many factory laborers worked twelve-hour shifts, often without a break. William McQuade worked in one of Carnegie's steel mills. "We stop only the time it takes to oil the engine. While they are oiling they eat, at least some of the boys, some of them; a great many of them in the mill do not carry anything to eat at all, because they haven't got time to eat."

—from "The Steel Business:
The Lot of a Steelworker"

Working Conditions

Main Idea Factory workers toiled under terrible conditions.

History and You When you are working on a project, do you take breaks? Why are breaks necessary? Read to learn what life was like for factory workers.

• •

The industrial growth of the late 1800s created new jobs. Yet factory workers paid a price for economic progress. As mass production increased, factories became larger and less personal.

Industrial laborers worked for 10 or 12 hours a day, six days a week. They could be fired at any time for any reason. Many lost their jobs during business downturns or were replaced by immigrants who were willing to work for lower pay.

People worked in unsafe and unhealthy factory conditions, and accidents were common in factories and mines. Steelworkers suffered burns. Coal miners died in cave-ins and from the effects of gas and coal dust. Garment workers toiled in crowded and dangerous urban factories called **sweatshops.**

Women and Children

By 1900 more than one million women had joined the industrial workforce. Because there were no laws that regulated workers' salaries, women, in general, earned about half of what men did for the same work.

Hundreds of thousands of children under 16 years of age also worked in factories. Many states passed child-labor laws that said children working in factories had to be at least 12 years old and should not work more than 10 hours a day. Employers, however, widely ignored child-labor laws.

✓ **Reading Check** **Calculating** How many hours a week did industrial laborers typically work?

History ONLINE
Student Web Activity Visit glencoe.com and complete the Chapter 5 Web Activity about industrial workers.

By the Numbers / Cost of Living

Working for a Living For industrial workers in the early 1900s, life was difficult. Most family members, including children, worked for long hours and low pay. Employers often hired and paid on a weekly or daily basis. A worker did not get paid if he or she was unable to work because of illness or if an employer closed the factory because business was slow.

Average Hourly Wages*	Average Expenses*
Bricklayers: 50¢	Rent: $4–10 per month
Plasterers: 50¢	Butter: 22¢ per pound
Newspaper compositors: 36¢	Milk: 6¢ per quart
Machine woodworkers: 25¢	Bread: 5¢ per loaf
Construction workers: 17¢	Rib roast: 13¢ per pound
Metalworkers: 16¢	Postage: 2¢ per ounce

(*in Chicago, 1903)   (*in Chicago, 1903)

Critical Thinking

Speculating What do you think is the biggest expense today for workers?

Workers repair train wheels in 1904.

Growth of Labor Unions

Main Idea Workers organized unions in order to acquire better wages, benefits, and working conditions.

History and You Have you ever been a part of a group that was working for a common goal? Did the group achieve its goal? Why or why not? Read to learn about labor unions and their goals.

· ·

Dissatisfied workers organized into groups—labor unions—to demand better pay and working conditions from their employers. Earlier in the 1800s, skilled workers had formed unions to represent workers in certain crafts or trades, such as carpentry. These **trade unions** had little influence because each represented only one trade and were too small to be effective. By the mid-1800s, as working conditions worsened, labor leaders looked to expand their unions.

In 1869 garment cutters in Philadelphia founded a trade union known as the Noble and Holy Order of the **Knights of Labor.** Employers fired workers who joined labor organizations, so the Knights met secretly and used special handshakes to **identify,** or recognize, one another.

Under the leadership of **Terence V. Powderly,** the Knights of Labor became a national labor organization in the 1880s. Unlike most unions, the Knights recruited people who were traditionally kept out of trade unions, including women, African Americans, immigrants, and unskilled laborers.

The Knights of Labor grew to more than 700,000 members by 1886. A wave of strikes, however, turned public opinion against the union, and it lost power in the 1890s.

In 1881 a group of national trade unions formed the **American Federation of Labor** (AFL). The AFL represented skilled workers in various crafts.

The Labor Movement, 1877–1914   NATIONAL GEOGRAPHIC

Unions Struggle After the Civil War, labor leaders sought to organize large national unions. In the late 1800s, however, government opposition, internal divisions, and public disapproval limited the movement's progress.

◀ Unions gained strength in the late 1800s and worked more actively for workers' rights.

▼ Labor unrest during the Pullman Strike, 1894

Critical Thinking

Identifying Which strikes involved miners?

❶ 1877 Great Railway Strike
Workers protest pay cuts

❷ 1886 Haymarket Affair
Labor rally ends in violence

❸ 1892 New Orleans
Workers from 42 unions demand shorter hours and better pay

❹ 1892 Homestead Strike
Steelworkers protest wage cut

❺ 1892 Silver Mine Unrest
State jails hundreds of striking workers

❻ 1894 Pullman Strike
Federal troops end riots

❼ 1902 Anthracite Coal Strike
Miners strike to win union recognition

❽ 1914 Ludlow Massacre
State militia burns striking miners' tent colony

People IN HISTORY

Samuel Gompers

Leader of the American Federation of Labor

Samuel Gompers did not think that unions should always support the same political party. Rather, Gompers argued that unions should support any political party that worked for the unions' goals. He also believed the best way to achieve labor's goals was through collective bargaining. Gompers stressed that *"the*

individual workman is as weak against the combination of wealth as would be a straw in a cyclone." Workers could only *"stand on an equal footing with the employers"* when they were organized into labor unions.

Mary Harris Jones

Labor organizer

Mary Harris Jones, also known as "Mother Jones," traveled across the country organizing workers for the United Mine Workers union. She also supported strikes and tried to sway public opinion in favor of unions. Denounced in the United States Senate, Jones believed that *"there are no limits to which powers of privilege will not go to keep the workers in slavery."*

CRITICAL Thinking

1. **Identifying** According to Gompers, how could labor unions help workers?
2. **Synthesizing** How did Gompers and Jones view employers?

The AFL was led by **Samuel Gompers,** the tough and practical-minded president of the Cigar Makers' Union. The organization pressed for higher wages, shorter hours, better working conditions, and the right to **collective bargaining**—when unions represent workers in labor discussions with management.

Although violent strikes turned public feeling against workers and unions in the late 1880s, the AFL survived and grew. By 1904, the AFL claimed more than 1.6 million members.

Women and the Unions

Many unions would not admit women workers, so some women formed their own unions. Mary Harris Jones, also known as Mother Jones, spent 50 years fighting for workers' rights.

In 1911 a fire broke out at the Triangle Shirtwaist Company factory, a sweatshop in New York City. The workers, mostly young immigrant women, could not escape because the company locked the doors to prevent employees from leaving early. Nearly 150 workers died. The disaster led the International Ladies' Garment Workers Union (ILGWU) to push for a safer working **environment.**

The Unions Act

Economic depressions in the 1870s and the 1890s forced companies to lower wages and, in some cases, fire workers. Unions responded with large strikes that sometimes sparked violence.

After a financial panic in 1873, an economic depression hit the nation. To cut costs, companies forced their workers to take pay cuts.

In July 1877, angry strikers burned rail yards, ripped up track, and destroyed railroad property. The companies hired **strikebreakers** to replace the striking workers, and federal troops restored order.

Antilabor feeling grew stronger after a bloody clash between police and strikers in Chicago's Haymarket Square in May 1886. Striking workers from the McCormick Harvester Company gathered to protest the killings of four strikers the previous day. When police ordered the crowd to break up, an unidentified person threw a bomb that killed a police officer. Several more were killed in a riot that followed. Following the Haymarket Riot, many Americans associated the labor movement with terrorism and disorder.

In 1892 workers went on strike at Andrew Carnegie's steel plant in Homestead, Pennsylvania. In the attempt to weaken the steel-workers' union, plant managers had cut workers' wages. When the union called a strike, Homestead managers hired nonunion workers and brought in 300 armed guards to protect them. A fierce battle left at least 10 people dead.

Pennsylvania's governor sent the state's militia to Homestead to restore order. The plant reopened with nonunion workers, pro-tected by the troops. After the failure of the Homestead Strike, the number of members in the steelworkers' union dwindled.

The employees of George Pullman's railway-car plant near Chicago went on strike in May 1894, when the company cut their wages. Pullman responded by closing the plant. One month later, workers in the American Railway Union supported the strikers by refusing to handle Pullman cars. As a result, rail traffic was paralyzed.

Pullman and the railroad owners fought back with the help of the government. They persuaded U.S. Attorney General Richard Olney to obtain an **injunction,** or court order, to stop the union from "obstructing the railways and holding up the mails." Yet the union and its leader, **Eugene V. Debs,** still refused to end the strike. Debs was sent to jail.

President Grover Cleveland sent federal troops to Chicago, and soon the strike was over. The failure of the Pullman Strike dealt another blow to the union movement. Despite these setbacks, however, workers continued to organize to campaign for better wages and working conditions.

✔ Reading Check **Explaining** Why were there growing antilabor feelings during the late 1800s?

History ONLINE
Study Central™ To review this section, go to glencoe.com.

Section 4 Review

Vocabulary

1. Use each of these terms in a sentence that will help explain its meaning: sweatshop, trade union, identify, collective bargaining, environment, strikebreaker, injunction.

Main Ideas

2. Describing How were women and children treated as members of the industrial workforce?

3. Making Inferences Why did employers fire workers who joined labor organizations?

Critical Thinking

4. Comparing Compare the Pullman Strike and the Homestead Strike. Create a Venn diagram like the one below to identify their similarities.

Pullman Strike   Homestead Strike

5. Evaluating Were the early labor unions successful? Explain.

6. Persuasive Writing As a member of Congress, write a speech supporting federal child-labor laws.

Answer the
7. Essential Question
Why did workers form labor unions in the middle to late 1800s?

Visual Summary

Main Idea	Supporting Details
Expansion of Railroads	• From 1860 to 1900, more than 163,000 miles (262,323 km) of new railroad track is laid in the United States. • The width of railroad track becomes standard, simplifying transport by train. • Improvements are introduced such as air brakes, linking systems, refrigerated cars, and sleeping cars.
New Inventions	• Transatlantic telegraph • Telephone • Camera • Vacuum cleaner • Electric lightbulb • Model-T car
Growth of Big Business	• U.S. has plentiful resources, including those making up the factors of production—land, labor, and capital. • A few giant corporations, especially in oil and steel, hold substantial economic power. • Trusts and monopolies make corporations efficient but create less competiton, hurting consumers.
Philanthropy	• Carnegie builds Carnegie Hall, one of the world's most famous music halls, and more than 2,000 libraries nationwide. • Rockefeller establishes the University of Chicago and New York's Rockefeller Institute for Medical Research.
Workers' Rights	• Factory workers, miners, and other laborers work long hours, often under dangerous conditions. • Trade unions, such as the AFL, expand in order to represent more workers. • Workers strike in several industries, sometimes sparking violence.

◄ Pullman Strike, 1894

Study anywhere, anytime! Download quizzes and flash cards to your PDA from glencoe.com.

STANDARDIZED TEST PRACTICE

TEST-TAKING TIP

Answer the questions you know first. Then go back to answer those for which you need more time.

Reviewing Main Ideas

Directions: Choose the best answer for each of the following questions.

1. Large railroads of the 1800s offered their biggest customers secret discounts called

   A tariffs.

   B tolls.

   C rebates.

   D pools.

2. Which of the following was invented by George Eastman?

   A lightbulb

   B typewriter

   C phonograph

   D Kodak camera

3. Which factor of production refers to buildings, machinery, and tools?

   A land

   B dividends

   C labor

   D capital

4. The 1892 Homestead Strike erupted after

   A railway workers paralyzed rail traffic in protest over job cuts.

   B managers at Andrew Carnegie's steel plant cut workers' wages to weaken the union.

   C workers from the McCormick Harvester Company demanded a 40-hour workweek.

   D a fire killed workers at a garment factory, leading to calls for safer working conditions.

Short-Answer Question

Directions: Base your answer to question 5 on the excerpt below and on your knowledge of social studies.

> We want eight hours [work day] and nothing less. We have been accused of being selfish, and it has been said that we will want more; that last year we got an advance of ten cents and now we want more. We do want more. You will find that a man generally wants more. . . . You ask a workingman, who is getting two dollars a day, and he will say that he wants ten cents more. . . . The man who receives five thousand dollars a year wants six thousand dollars a year, and the man who owns eight or nine hundred thousand dollars will want a hundred thousand dollars more to make it a million.
>
> —Samuel Gompers, labor union leader

5. Restate the main idea of this excerpt in your own words.

Review the Essential Questions

6. **Essay** Explain why the late 1800s and early 1900s became known as the Age of Big Business.

To help you write your essay, review your answers to the Essential Questions in the section reviews and the chapter Foldables Study Organizer. Your essay should include:

- the effect of railroad expansion;
- the abundance of inventions in the late 1800s and their impact;
- factors of production and the business practices of industrial leaders; and
- government responses to labor unions.

GO ON ➡

History ONLINE

For additional test practice, use **Self-Check Quizzes**—Chapter 5 at <u>glencoe.com</u>.

Document-Based Questions

Directions: Analyze the documents and answer the short-answer questions that follow.

Document 1

The following words are from the workers' song "Drill, Ye Tarriers, Drill." "Tarrier" was the name given to Irish drillers who dug tunnels for the railroads.

> The new foreman is Dan McCann, / I'll tell you sure he's a blame mean man, / Last week a premature blast went off, / And a mile in the air went big Jim Goff.
>
> [Chorus:] Then drill, ye tarriers, drill, / Drill, ye tarriers, drill, / Oh it's work all day without sugar in your tay / When ye work beyant [beyond] on the railway, / And drill, ye tarriers, drill.
>
> When pay day next it came around, / Poor Jim's pay a dollar short he found, / "What for?" says he, then came this reply, / "You were docked for the time you were up in the sky."

Source: Norm Cohen, *Long Steel Rail: The Railroad in American Folksong*

7. How does the song reflect the challenges that railroad workers faced?

Document 2

Tall skyscrapers were built in the late 1800s. In 1879 Benjamin Oppenheimer submitted the drawing to the right with his patent application.

8. What do you think is the purpose of Oppenheimer's invention?

Source: A. E. Brown and H. A. Jeffcott, Jr., *World's Wackiest Inventions*

Document 3

John D. Rockefeller stated the following:

> God gave me my money. . . . Having been endowed with the gift I possess, I believe it is my duty to make money and still more money and to use the money I make for the good of my fellow man according to the dictates of my conscience.

Source: Suzy Platt, *Respectfully Quoted*

9. How did Rockefeller explain his own wealth? How do you think he might explain why some people are not wealthy?

Document 4

The following article, "Christianity and Wealth," is by Congregationalist minister Washington Gladden.

> During the past fourteen years the wealth of this nation has increased much faster than the population, but the people who work for wages are little if any better off than they were fourteen years ago. . . .
>
> But this is not saying that . . . the state [should] . . . take the property of the rich and distribute it among the poor. . . . There are, however, one or two things that [are] . . . the immediate duty of the state. Certain outrageous monopolies exist that the state is bound to crush. . . . Another gigantic public evil that the state must exterminate is that of gambling in stocks and produce.

Source: Washington Gladden, *Century Illustrated*

10. What problems does Gladden describe in the excerpt? What solution does he propose?

11. Expository Writing Using the information from the four documents and your knowledge of social studies, write an essay in which you:

- explain why this time period might be referred to as the beginning of modern America; and
- name at least one way American society today resembles the Industrial Age and one way it is different.

Need Extra Help?											
If you missed questions. . .	1	2	3	4	5	6	7	8	9	10	11
Go to page. . .	145	148	153	164	163	142–164	161	148	155	161	142–164

Chapter 6

An Urban Society 1865–1914

The Brooklyn Bridge with a view of the surrounding area, 1898

ANDREW
JOHNSON
1865–1869

ULYSSES S.
GRANT
1869–1877

RUTHERFORD
B. HAYES
1877–1881

JAMES
GARFIELD
1881

CHESTER
ARTHUR
1881–1885

GROVER
CLEVELAND
1885–1889

BENJAMIN
HARRISON
1889–1893

PRESIDENTS

U.S. Events

World Events

1865

1875

1885

★ **1866**
Transatlantic
telegraph line
successfully
completed

1882 ★
Robert Louis
Stevenson's
Treasure Island
published

1889 ★
Eiffel
Tower
erected

History ONLINE
Chapter Overview Visit glencoe.com
and click on **Chapter 6—Chapter
Overviews** to preview chapter information.

Section 1: The New Immigrants
Essential Question What were some characteristics of the new wave of immigrants that arrived after 1865?

Section 2: Moving to the City
Essential Question How did cities change during the late 1800s?

Section 3: A Changing Culture
Essential Question In what ways did American culture change in the late 1800s?

FOLDABLES®
Study Organizer

Organizing Information

Make this Foldable to help organize what you learn about changes to the culture of the United States.

Step 1 Place two sheets of paper on top of one another about one inch apart.

Step 2 Fold the papers to form four equal tabs.

Step 3 Staple the sheets, and label each tab as shown.

Reading and Writing As you read the chapter, write down key events and ideas that relate to the Essential Questions.

An Urban Society 1865–1914
Section 1: The New Immigrants Essential Question:
Section 2: Moving to the City Essential Question:
Section 3: A Changing Culture Essential Question:

◀ Ford factory, Detroit, Michigan

★ **1892**
Ellis Island admits immigrants

GROVER CLEVELAND 1893–1897

WILLIAM McKINLEY 1897–1901

THEODORE ROOSEVELT 1901–1909

1906 ★
San Francisco rocked by earthquake

WILLIAM HOWARD TAFT 1909–1913

★ **1913**
Ford develops first moving assembly line

1895   **1905**   **1915**

1895 ★
First complete performance of *Swan Lake*

1900 ★
First trial flight of Zeppelin

★ **1907**
Cubism arises in art

The New Immigrants

Reading Guide

Content Vocabulary

emigrate (p. 171)

sweatshop (p. 173)

ethnic group (p. 172)

assimilate (p. 174)

steerage (p. 172)

Academic Vocabulary

attitude (p. 175)   affect (p. 175)

Key People and Events

Emma Lazarus (p. 172)

Chinese Exclusion Act (p. 175)

Immigration Act of 1917 (p. 175)

Reading Strategy

Taking Notes As you read, place the immigration laws on a time line like the one below, and take notes on the purpose of each law.

1882	1892	1902	1907	1917

American Diary

At the end of a long ocean voyage, immigrants waited for entry into the United States. "The steerage passengers have before them more rigid examinations . . . so in spite of . . . the glad greetings shouted to and fro, they sink again into awe-struck and confused silence. When the last . . . passenger has disappeared from the dock, the immigrants with their baggage are loaded into barges and taken to Ellis Island for their final examination."

—*from* On the Trail of the Immigrant *by Edward A. Steiner*

Newly arrived immigrants at Ellis Island

A Flood of Immigrants

Main Idea New immigrants began to arrive in the late 1800s, seeking opportunities in the United States.

History and You Have you seen pictures of or visited the Statue of Liberty? Read to learn the statue's significance to millions of immigrants.

• •

Before 1865, most immigrants to the United States—except for enslaved Africans—came from northern and western Europe. After the Civil War, immigrants from other countries began making the journey to the United States.

New Immigration

In the mid-1880s, the pattern of immigration started to change. Large groups of "new" immigrants arrived from eastern and southern Europe. Greeks, Russians, Hungarians, Italians, Turks, and Poles were among the newcomers. At the same time, the number of "old" immigrants from northern and western Europe started to decrease. By 1907, 80 percent of immigrants came from southern and eastern Europe.

Many of these newcomers were Catholics or Jews. Few spoke English. Because of this, they did not blend into American society as easily as the "old" immigrants had. Often, they clustered together in neighborhoods made up of people of the same nationality.

After 1900, immigration from Mexico also increased. In addition, many people came to the United States from China and Japan. They, too, brought unfamiliar languages and religious beliefs and had difficulty blending into American society.

Leaving Troubles Behind

Why did so many people leave their homelands for the United States in the late 1800s and early 1900s? They were "pushed" away by difficult conditions at home. At the same time, many were "pulled" to the United States by new opportunities.

Many people **emigrated,** or left their homelands, because of economic troubles. In Italy and Hungary, overcrowding and poverty made jobs scarce. Farmers in Croatia and Serbia could not own enough land to support their families. Sweden suffered major crop failures. New machines such as looms put many craft workers out of work.

Primary Source / Responding to New Immigrants

Differing Opinions People had different opinions about immigration. Although some believed the United States should welcome immigrants with open arms, others saw the flood of people entering the country as a problem. These views were reflected in political cartoons of the day.

VOL 17 NO 440   MARCH 22 1890.   PRICE 10 CENTS

Judge

◄ This magazine cover demonstrates one reaction to making Ellis Island a new processing station for immigrants. The cartoon on the cover shows the Statue of Liberty frowning as immigrants are dumped at her feet.

Critical Thinking

Comparing and Contrasting What symbols does the artist use to represent the United States? What message is the artist trying to convey about new immigrants?

Seeking Fairness

Persecution also drove people from their homelands. Some countries passed laws or set policies against certain **ethnic groups**—minorities that spoke different languages or followed different customs from those of most people in a country. Members of these ethnic groups often emigrated to escape discrimination or unfair laws. Many Jews fled persecution in Russia in the 1880s and came to the United States.

Seeking Opportunity

Immigrants saw the United States as a place of jobs, plentiful land, and opportunities for a better life. Although some immigrants returned to their homelands after a few years, most came to America to stay.

Immigrants often had a difficult journey to America. Many had to first travel to a seaport to board a ship. Often they traveled for hundreds of miles and through foreign countries to get to port cities.

Then came the long ocean voyage to the United States—12 days across the Atlantic or several weeks across the Pacific. Immigrants usually could afford only the cheapest tickets and traveled in **steerage**—cramped quarters on the lower decks of the ships.

Entering America

Most immigrants landed at New York City. After 1886, the magnificent sight of the Statue of Liberty greeted immigrants as they sailed into New York Harbor. The statue, a gift from the people of France, seemed to promise hope for a better life in the new country. On its base, the stirring words of **Emma Lazarus,** an American poet, welcomed the many immigrants arriving in the country from Europe: "Give me your tired, your poor, Your huddled masses yearning to breathe free, The wretched refuse of your teeming shore. Send these, the homeless, tempest-tossed to me, I lift my lamp beside the golden door!"

Primary Source / Statue of Liberty

The statue, shown here under construction in Paris, was a gift of friendship from the people of France. The statue's full name is "Liberty Enlightening the World." ▼

The torch is a symbol of liberty. The crown's rays stand for the seven seas and seven continents of the world. ▶

Lady Liberty holds a tablet that represents the book of law. In Roman numerals it reads "July 4, 1776." ▼

Statue Facts	
Overall height, base to tip of torch	305 feet, 6 inches
Height from her heel to top of her head	111 feet, 6 inches
Height of face	8 feet
Width of waistline	35 feet
Total weight	225 tons
Number of steps from base to head	154

Source: Ellis Island Foundation.

◀ At her feet lies a broken chain, meaning freedom from tyranny.

Before the new arrivals could actually pass through the "golden door" to America, however, they had to register at government reception centers. In the East, immigrants were processed at Castle Garden, a former fort on Manhattan Island. After 1892, they went through Ellis Island in New York Harbor. Most Asian immigrants arrived in the United States on the West Coast in California and went through the processing center on Angel Island in San Francisco Bay.

Examiners at the centers recorded the immigrants' names—sometimes shortening or simplifying a name they found too difficult to write. The examiners asked the immigrants where they came from, their occupation, and whether they had relatives in the United States. New immigrants also were given health examinations. Immigrants with contagious illnesses could be refused permission to enter the United States.

Reading Check **Explaining** Why was the voyage to America often difficult?

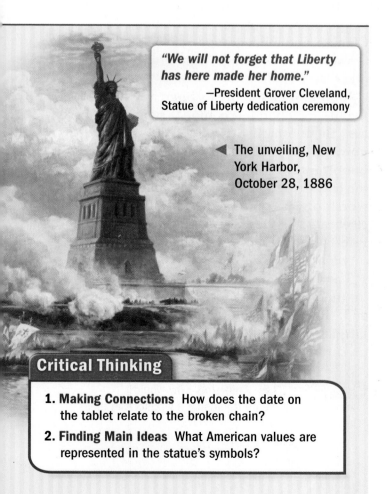

"We will not forget that Liberty has here made her home."
—President Grover Cleveland, Statue of Liberty dedication ceremony

◄ The unveiling, New York Harbor, October 28, 1886

Critical Thinking

1. **Making Connections** How does the date on the tablet relate to the broken chain?
2. **Finding Main Ideas** What American values are represented in the statue's symbols?

The Immigrant Experience

Main Idea Immigrants adjusted to life in America, finding work, forming communities, and adapting to a new culture.

History and You Are you familiar with parts of cities that are known as Little Italy or Chinatown? Read to learn how these neighborhoods might have formed.
. . . .

After passing through the reception centers, most immigrants gained entry to the United States. Where would they go? How would they live? Some had relatives or friends to stay with and to help them find jobs. Others knew no one and would have to strike out on their own.

Finding Work

An immigrant's greatest challenge was finding work. Sometimes organizations in his or her homeland recruited workers for jobs in the United States. These organizations supplied American employers with unskilled workers who worked unloading cargo or digging ditches.

Some of America's fastest-growing industries hired immigrant workers. In the steel mills of Pittsburgh, for example, most of the laborers in the early 1900s were immigrant men. They might work 12 hours per day, seven days per week.

Many immigrants, including women and children, worked in **sweatshops** in the garment industry. These were dark, crowded shops where workers made clothing. The work was repetitive and hazardous, the pay low, and the hours long.

Pauline Newman, who later became an official in the International Ladies' Garment Workers Union, worked in a New York sweatshop as a child. She recalled: "We started work at 7:30 [in the morning] and during the busy season we worked until nine o' clock in the evening. They didn't pay any overtime and didn't give you anything for supper money. At times they would give you . . . a little apple pie . . . for your supper."

This cartoon comments on successful Americans who wanted to limit immigration.

1. **Interpreting** How are the successful Americans treating the new immigrant?

2. **Analyzing** If the Americans looked backward, as the title suggests, what would they see? What is the cartoonist saying?

A. New, poor immigrant   B. Successful Americans
C. Immigrant forefathers of the Americans

LOOKING BACKWARD THEY WOULD CLOSE TO THE NEWCOMER THE BRIDGE THAT CARRIED THEM AND THEIR FATHERS OVER.

Adjusting to America

In their new homes, immigrants tried to preserve their own cultures. At the same time, most wanted to **assimilate,** or become part of the American culture. These two desires sometimes came into conflict.

Many immigrant parents continued to speak their native languages. Their children spoke English at school and with friends, but they spoke their native language at home. The grandchildren of many immigrants spoke only English.

Furthermore, in the United States, women generally had more freedom than women in European and Asian countries. New lifestyles conflicted with traditional ways and sometimes caused family friction.

Building Communities

Most of the new immigrants were from rural areas. Because they lacked the money to buy farmland in America, however, they often settled in industrial cities. With little or no education, they usually worked as unskilled laborers.

People of the same ethnic group tended to form separate communities. As a result, neighborhoods of Jewish, Italian, Polish, Chinese, and other groups quickly developed in New York, Chicago, San Francisco, and other large cities.

Immigrants sought to re-create some of the life they had left behind. The communities they established revolved around a number of traditional institutions. Most important were the houses of worship— the churches and the synagogues—where worship was conducted and holidays were celebrated as they were in their homelands. Priests and rabbis often acted as community leaders.

The immigrants published newspapers in their native languages, opened stores and theaters, and organized social clubs. Ethnic communities helped the immigrants preserve their cultural heritage.

✔ Reading Check **Analyzing** Why would immigrants re-create traditional institutions in their new land?

The Nativist Movement

Main Idea Some people opposed immigration, while others appreciated the positive contributions made by immigrants.

History and You Did any of your relatives immigrate to the United States from another country? If so, when? Read to find out how immigrants were regarded by American society.

. . . .

Assimilation also was slowed by the **attitudes**—ways of thinking and acting—of many native-born Americans, who resented the new wave of immigrants. They feared that the new immigrants would take away their jobs or drive down everyone's wages by accepting lower pay. These Americans also argued that the new immigrants—with their foreign languages, unfamiliar religions, and distinctive customs—would not fit into American society.

People found it easy to blame immigrants for increasing crime, unemployment, and other problems. The nativist movement, which had opposed immigration since the 1830s, gained strength during the late 1800s. Calls for restrictions on immigration mounted.

Lawmakers responded quickly to the tide of anti-immigrant feeling. In 1882 Congress passed the **Chinese Exclusion Act,** which prohibited Chinese workers from entering the United States for 10 years. Congress extended this law in 1892 and again in 1902. Similarly, in 1907 the federal government and Japan came to a "gentleman's agreement" that aimed to limit the number of Japanese immigrants.

Other legislation **affected,** or had an impact on, immigrants from all nations. In 1897 Congress passed a bill that required immigrants to be able to read and write in some language. Although the president vetoed the bill, Congress later passed the **Immigration Act of 1917,** which included a similar literacy requirement.

On the other hand, some Americans supported immigration. These people recognized that immigrants supplied the country's industries with workers. We now appreciate that immigrants also enriched the country with the culture of their homelands.

✓ **Reading Check** **Explaining** Why did some Americans blame immigrants for the nation's problems?

Section 1 Review

History ONLINE **Study Central™** To review this section, go to glencoe.com.

Vocabulary

1. Use each of these terms in a sentence that will help explain its meaning: emigrate, ethnic group, steerage, sweatshop, assimilate, attitude, affect.

Main Ideas

2. **Contrasting** How did immigration change after 1865?

3. **Describing** What were the working conditions in sweatshops?

4. **Evaluating** What is your opinion of the nativist movement?

Critical Thinking

5. **Determining Cause and Effect** What was the effect of each of the following immigration laws?

Chinese Exclusion Act	
"Gentleman's Agreement"	
Immigration Act of 1917	

6. **Speculating** What was an immigrant's greatest challenge upon arriving in the United States?

7. **Expository Writing** Write a paragraph explaining what happened at government reception centers for immigrants.

8. **Answer the Essential Question** What were some characteristics of the new wave of immigrants that arrived after 1865?

TIME NOTEBOOK

What were people's lives like in the past?

These two pages will give you some clues to everyday life in the United States as you step back in time with TIME Notebook.

AMERICA'S FIRST AUTO RACE
Built for Speed

BETTMANN / CORBIS

In 1893 two brothers, **CHARLES** and **FRANK DURYEA**, built the first American automobile in Springfield, Massachusetts. It could travel up to 7.5 miles per hour (mph). In 1895 the two bicycle mechanics held the first automobile race. The course was 54 miles (87 km), going from Chicago to Evanston, Illinois, and back again. Six cars started the race that snowy morning—the Duryea's second automobile, two electric cars, and three gas-powered Benzes from Germany. Here is how Frank Duryea describes the race:

The machine made good going of the soft unpacked snow in Jackson Park.... While still in the lead, the left front wheel struck a bad rut at such an angle that the steering arm was broken off.... We, fortunately, located a blacksmith shop where we forged down, threaded, and replaced the arm.... The Macy Benz passed us and held the lead as far as Evanston, where we regained it. Having made the turn at Evanston, elated at being in the lead again, we started on the home trip.

"... One of the two cylinders ceased firing.... This repair was completed in fifty-five minutes and we got going, feeling that the Macy Benz must surely be ahead of us, but learned later that the Macy did not get that far. After a stop for gasoline ... we continued on to the finish.... The motor had at all times shown ample power, and at no time were we compelled to get out and push."

Averaging 7.3 mph, Frank Duryea's car was the first to finish the race in just over 10 hours. He won the $2,000 prize.

CORBIS

The Eighth Wonder of the World

Fourteen years after construction began, the **BROOKLYN BRIDGE** —the largest suspension bridge in the world—opens in 1883. Schools and shops in Brooklyn are closed so everyone can celebrate.

With a span half again as long as that of any previous bridge, it hangs from steel cables. Its designer and builder, John Roebling, was killed on the job. His son, Washington, continued directing the work until he was injured. Then Washington's wife, Emily, completed the job, making her possibly the first woman field engineer.

The Well-Dressed Cowhand

These are prices from the Montgomery Ward catalogs of the 1880s.

Stetson hat	$10.00
Cotton shirt (no collar)	$1.25
Chaps and pants	$8.00
Leather boots	$20.00
Spurs	$0.70
Colt pistol	$12.20
Holster, cartridge belt	$2.00
Saddle	$40.00
Horse (usually provided by ranch)	$35.00
Lariat (lasso)	$7.75

BETTMANN / CORBIS

MILESTONES

EVENTS AND PEOPLE OF THE TIME

OFFERED. A "company of fifty lady sharpshooters" to President William McKinley in 1898 at the start of the Spanish-American War, by the famous sharpshooter and performer, Annie Oakley. She promised each would bring along her own rifle and ammunition—McKinley has yet to respond to the offer.

HULTON-DEUTSCH COLLECTION / CORBIS

ANNIE OAKLEY

CALLED. Government officials by President Rutherford B. Hayes, who took office in 1877; he was the first president to use the new telephone in the White House.

DRAWN. The first comic strip, *The Yellow Kid,* by R. F. Outcault in 1896—it has provided the name for dishonest reporting: "yellow journalism."

DEDICATED. The new Statue of Liberty in New York Harbor by President Cleveland in 1886.

SHOWN. First moving picture in 1896; featured are two girls dancing with umbrellas and two men boxing.

OPENED. Hull House in Chicago by Jane Addams in 1889—providing meals, health care, and education for the poor, including many immigrants.

NUMBERS

UNITED STATES AT THE TIME

5 The number of transcontinental railroads crisscrossing the country in 1900

10 The number of years Chinese people must wait after applying to immigrate to the United States, according to the Chinese Immigration Act passed by Congress in 1882

21 The age of Frances Folsom when she married President Cleveland in 1886, making her the youngest First Lady

27,000,000 The number of visitors to the Chicago Exposition—sometimes called the first world's fair—in 1893, where visitors rode G.W. Ferris's new 250-foot-high invention, the Ferris wheel

VISUAL ARTS LIBRARY (LONDON) / ALAMY

200 Approximate number of Sioux Indians, mostly women and children, killed at Wounded Knee, South Dakota, when they were attacked by the American 7th Cavalry

CRITICAL THINKING

Describing Name the inventions and structures mentioned in this Notebook. How did each change the lives of Americans?

Analyzing Primary Sources Based on Duryea's diary of the race, why was it considered a daring and unusual adventure to race, or even drive, a car in 1893?

Moving to the City

Essential Question ◄

How did cities change during the late 1800s?

Reading Guide

Content Vocabulary

tenement *(p. 180)*

slum *(p. 180)*

suburb *(p. 180)*

settlement house *(p. 181)*

Hull House *(p. 181)*

skyscraper *(p. 182)*

Academic Vocabulary

major *(p. 179)*

minor *(p. 181)*

Key People and Events

Gilded Age *(p. 180)*

Jane Addams *(p. 181)*

Louis Sullivan *(p. 182)*

Frederick Law Olmsted *(p. 183)*

Reading Strategy

Taking Notes As you read, describe three effects of the growth of cities.

Growth of Cities

American Diary

Americans across the United States were leaving farms and towns and moving to cities. Henry Fletcher wrote, "Undeniably the city has superior attractions as a place of residence for the well-to-do; even the poorest classes, who live in filthy tenements and are completely shut out from the enjoyments of nature, seem to find in the noises, the crowds, the excitements, even in the sleepless anxieties of the daily struggle for life, a charm they are powerless to resist."

—*from "The Drift of Population to Cities: Remedies"*

Chicago, Illinois, grew from 109,000 residents in 1860 to nearly 1.7 million in 1900.

Growth of Cities

Main Idea Immigrants and others flooded to American cities, where extremes of poverty and wealth existed.

History and You What is the largest city in your state? Read to learn how many American cities grew rapidly during the late 1800s.

. . . .

American cities grew rapidly after the Civil War. In 1870 one American in four lived in cities with 2,500 or more people. By 1910, nearly half of the American population were city dwellers. The United States was changing from a rural to an urban nation.

Immigrants played an enormous part in the growth of cities. In **major,** or larger, urban centers such as New York, Detroit, and Chicago, immigrants and their children made up 80 percent or more of the population in 1890. Native-born Americans also contributed to the urban growth, moving in huge numbers from farming areas to cities, looking for jobs.

The industrialization of America had changed work on farms. New farm machinery made it possible to produce crops using fewer farmworkers. In addition, women in rural areas no longer had to make clothing and household goods. These items, made by machine, could now be bought in stores or from catalogs. Freed from such chores, many women left farms to look for jobs in the cities.

African Americans also migrated to cities in large numbers. After the Civil War, many African Americans began moving to Southern cities in search of jobs. Beginning in 1914, a large number of African Americans moved to Northern cities, where they hoped to find less discrimination.

Transportation and Resources

America's expanding railroad network fed the growth of cities. Railroads helped people move, and they also transported the raw materials for industry. Trains carried cattle to Chicago and Kansas City, making these cities large meatpacking centers.

Some cities flourished because of nearby resources. Pittsburgh developed rapidly as a center for iron and steel manufacturing because both iron ore and coal—to fuel the industry's huge furnaces—were found in the area. Seaports such as New York and San Francisco developed as American trade with the rest of the world increased.

By the Numbers / **Urban and Rural Population Growth**

Urban and Rural Population Growth, 1860–1900

Population (in millions) / Urban Rural / Year

Source: *Historical Statistics of the United States.*

Critical Thinking

Analyzing Which year saw the least difference between urban and rural populations?

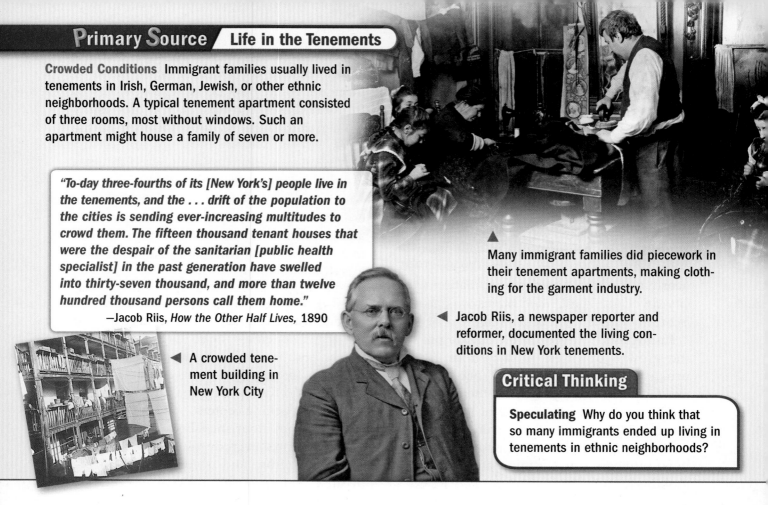

Crowded Conditions Immigrant families usually lived in tenements in Irish, German, Jewish, or other ethnic neighborhoods. A typical tenement apartment consisted of three rooms, most without windows. Such an apartment might house a family of seven or more.

"To-day three-fourths of its [New York's] people live in the tenements, and the . . . drift of the population to the cities is sending ever-increasing multitudes to crowd them. The fifteen thousand tenant houses that were the despair of the sanitarian [public health specialist] in the past generation have swelled into thirty-seven thousand, and more than twelve hundred thousand persons call them home."

—Jacob Riis, *How the Other Half Lives*, 1890

Many immigrant families did piecework in their tenement apartments, making clothing for the garment industry.

◄ A crowded tenement building in New York City

◄ Jacob Riis, a newspaper reporter and reformer, documented the living conditions in New York tenements.

Critical Thinking

Speculating Why do you think that so many immigrants ended up living in tenements in ethnic neighborhoods?

Tenement Living

In the biggest, most crowded cities, the poorest residents—including most immigrants—lived in **tenements.** Originally a tenement was simply a building in which several families rented rooms. By the late 1800s, however, a tenement had come to mean an apartment building in the **slums**—poor, run-down urban neighborhoods.

Several people lived in each room. Usually several families had to share a cold-water tap and a toilet. A government inspector wrote of the "filthy and rotten tenements" of the Chicago slums in 1896, where children filled "every nook, eating and sleeping in every windowsill, pouring in and out of every door."

The Middle Class

The cities also had a growing middle class, which included the families of doctors, lawyers, and ministers, as well as managers, salaried office clerks, and others. The middle class

enjoyed a comfortable life. Many families moved to the **suburbs,** residential areas that sprang up outside city centers. There they lived in houses with hot water, indoor toilets, and—by 1900—electricity. Middle-class families might have servants and the leisure time to enjoy music, art, and literature.

The Very Rich

At the top of the economic and social ladder were the very rich. They built enormous mansions in the cities and huge estates in the country. In these mansions, the rich lived lives of extreme luxury. Because of their extravagant wealth—and the terrible poverty that lay beneath it—this time period became known as the **Gilded Age.** The word *gilded* refers to something covered with a thin layer of gold.

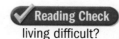 **Reading Check** **Describing** Why was tenement living difficult?

Cities in Crisis

Main Idea Growing cities suffered from health and sanitation problems, poverty, fire, and crime.

History and You How do cities handle health and sanitation today? Read to learn about the problems of city life in the 1800s.

The rapid growth of cities produced serious problems. Garbage and horse manure accumulated in city streets, and the sewers could not handle the flow of human waste. Fires were another ever-present threat.

Health problems were widespread in the cities, because the filth was a breeding ground for quickly spreading diseases. In one Chicago neighborhood in 1900, babies often died of whooping cough, diphtheria, or measles before reaching their first birthday. One section of New York City was called the "lung block" because so many of its residents were suffering from tuberculosis. In an effort to control the spread of disease, New York City began to screen schoolchildren for contagious diseases, provide visiting nurses to mothers with young children, and establish public health clinics.

Yet disease was not the only threat to city life. Poverty in the cities led to crime as well. Orphaned and homeless children sometimes resorted to committing **minor,** or less serious, crimes in order to survive. Gangs roamed the poor neighborhoods.

The problems of the cities did not go unnoticed. Many dedicated people worked to improve urban life and help the poor. Some of this help came from religious groups that ran orphanages, prisons, hospitals, and recreation centers. The poor also received assistance from establishments called **settlement houses.** One of the most famous settlement houses was Chicago's **Hull House,** founded by **Jane Addams** in 1889.

Reading Check Explaining Why did disease spread so rapidly in large cities?

Primary Source / Settlement Houses

An Approach to Social Reform During the late 1800s, reformers such as Jane Addams established settlement houses in poor neighborhoods. The women who ran settlement houses provided everything from medical care, recreation programs, and English classes to hot lunches for factory workers.

Hull House, begun in Chicago by Jane Addams and Ellen Gates Starr in 1889, was surrounded by tenements and factories. ▶

"The Settlement, then, is an experimental effort to aid in the solution of the social and industrial problems which are engendered by the modern conditions of life in a great city. . . . It is an attempt to relieve, at the same time, the over-accumulation at one end of society and the destitution at the other."
—Jane Addams, *Philanthropy and Social Progress*

Children at Hull House ▼

▼ The crowded areas of Chicago near Hull House had poor sanitation, and most residents lived in poverty.

Critical Thinking

Making Connections What kinds of organizations offer help to people today?

The Great Bridge To accommodate the growing population of New York City, the Brooklyn Bridge was built over the East River to connect Manhattan and Brooklyn. Its long, high span was designed to allow for the passage of ships beneath. The bridge took 14 years to build. When completed in 1883, it was the longest suspension bridge in the world.

Workers finish a cable on the Brooklyn Bridge during construction. ▶

◀ The Brooklyn Bridge was the first suspension bridge to use woven steel cable wire, a technology developed by John Roebling, chief engineer. Four suspension cables support the bridge, and each cable contains 5,434 wires.

"*The contemplated work [the bridge] ... will not only be the greatest bridge in existence, but it will be the greatest engineering work of this continent, and of the age. . . . [It will be] a great work of art, and . . . a successful specimen of advanced bridge engineering.*"

—John A. Roebling, quoted in *The Great Bridge*

◀ The Brooklyn Bridge, view from the Brooklyn side toward Manhattan, 1883

Critical Thinking

Explaining Why was it important for the Brooklyn Bridge to be a suspension bridge? What innovation made this possible?

The Changing City

Main Idea New technology in transportation and architecture reshaped cities.

History and You What is the tallest building you have ever visited? Read to learn how skyscrapers forever changed American cities.

Urban growth led to new developments. In the late 1800s, the look and feel of American cities changed with the introduction of skyscrapers, new kinds of public transportation, new bridges, and public parks.

Building Up—Not Out

Because of the limited space in cities, imaginative architects began building upward rather than outward. In the 1860s, architects started to use iron frames to strengthen the building walls. Iron supports—together with the safety elevator that Elisha Otis invented in 1852—made taller buildings possible.

In 1884 William LeBaron Jenney constructed a 10-story office building in Chicago. Supported by an iron-and-steel frame, it was the world's first **skyscraper**. **Louis Sullivan** was one of the first to design skyscrapers. Soon architects were designing higher structures. New York's Woolworth Building, completed in 1913, soared an incredible 55 stories—792 feet (241 m) high. People called the building the Cathedral of Commerce.

New Designs

Some people looked to reshape the urban landscape. A group known as the "City Beautiful" movement believed city dwellers should be able to enjoy the beauties of nature.

Frederick Law Olmsted, a leader in this movement, designed New York's Central Park as well as several parks in Boston.

Olmsted designed the fairgrounds for the World's Fair held in Chicago in 1892 and 1893. The fair revealed that American architecture was dynamic and original. The best architects thoroughly understood European styles and adapted them for modern use.

New Forms of Transportation

As cities grew, people needed new means of transportation. Streetcars, which horses pulled on tracks, provided public transportation at the time. In 1873 San Francisco began construction of cable-car lines. A large underground cable powered by a motor at one end of the rail line moved passengers along. In 1888 Richmond, Virginia, pioneered the use of the trolley car, a motorized train that was powered by electricity supplied through overhead cables. By 1900, the trolley was everywhere. In 1897 Boston opened the nation's first subway, or underground railway. In 1904 New York City opened the first section of what was to become the largest subway system in the world.

Building Bridges

Bridge construction also improved urban transportation. Many American cities were divided or bounded by rivers. Architects and engineers designed huge steel bridges to link sections of cities that were divided by rivers. The 520-foot (158-m) Eads Bridge across the Mississippi River in St. Louis opened in 1874. Nine years later, New York's majestic Brooklyn Bridge, with a main span of 1,600 feet (488 m) long, connected Manhattan and Brooklyn. Both bridges remain in use today.

New forms of transportation not only helped people travel within the cities, they also helped the cities grow. Middle-class suburbs developed along train or trolley lines stretching away from city centers. People who moved out of city centers could easily travel downtown to work, shop, or seek entertainment.

The increase in immigration and the growth of the cities went hand in hand with other changes in American life. Education, culture, and recreation were changing too.

✓ **Reading Check** **Summarizing** What were the new forms of urban transportation?

History ONLINE
Study Central™ To review this section, go to glencoe.com.

Section 2 Review

Vocabulary

1. Use each of these terms in a sentence that will help explain its meaning: major, tenement, slum, suburb, minor, settlement house, Hull House, skyscraper.

Main Ideas

2. Contrasting During the Gilded Age, how was life different for the poor, the middle class, and the very rich?

3. Listing What problems did cities face in the 1800s?

4. Describing How did American architecture change during this period?

Critical Thinking

5. Problem Solving How did Americans respond to the following problems in cities?

Disease	
Poverty	
Lack of Space	

6. Determining Cause and Effect What effect did the new forms of transportation have on city life?

7. Descriptive Writing As a settlement house worker in the 1800s, write a diary entry explaining the problems you see in cities.

8. Answer the Essential Question How did cities change during the late 1800s?

A Changing Culture

Essential Question ◄

In what ways did American culture change during the late 1800s?

Reading Guide

Content Vocabulary

land-grant college (p. 186)

spectator sport (p. 189)

realism (p. 187)

vaudeville (p. 189)

regionalism (p. 187)

jazz (p. 190)

yellow journalism (p. 188)

ragtime (p. 190)

Academic Vocabulary

philosophy (p. 185)   isolate (p. 186)

Key People

George Washington Carver (p. 186)

Mark Twain (p. 187)

Joseph Pulitzer (p. 188)

William Randolph Hearst (p. 188)

Reading Strategy

Taking Notes As you read, describe the achievements of the persons listed.

Individual	Achievement
Booker T. Washington	
Edith Wharton	
Paul Laurence Dunbar	

American Diary

New ideas about education were changing how people viewed physical education for girls. Gertrude Dudley wrote: "This matter of playing games is one to be determined, not by comparison of the sexes, but by an educational principle. If women can be trained well enough to make athletics beneficial . . . to themselves, then it is good for them to play; if athletics develop . . . qualities valuable to them as individuals . . . then also is it well for them to play."

—*from* Athletic Games in the Education of Women *by Gertrude Dudley*

A team of young Cherokee athletes, c. 1910

Expanding Education

Main Idea Educational opportunities were extended to many more Americans, as the system of public schools and colleges expanded.

History and You How would American life be different if people attended only four years of school? Read to learn how more Americans began attending school during this period.

. . . .

Most Americans in 1865 had attended school for an average of only four years. Government and business leaders as well as reformers believed that for the nation to progress, the people needed more schooling. Toward the end of the 1800s, the "treasure" of education became more widely available to Americans.

By 1914, most states required children to have at least some schooling. More than 80 percent of all children between the ages of 5 and 17 were enrolled in elementary and secondary schools.

Public Schools

The expansion of public education was particularly notable in high schools. The number of public high schools increased from 100 in 1860 to 6,000 in 1900 and increased to 12,000 in 1914. Despite this huge increase, however, many teenagers did not attend high school. Boys often went to work instead of attending school. The majority of high school students were girls.

The benefits of a public school education, however, were not shared equally by everyone. In the South, many African Americans received little or no education. In many parts of the country, African American children had no choice but to attend segregated elementary and secondary schools.

Progressive Education

Around 1900, a new **philosophy**—ideas and beliefs—of education emerged in the United States. Supporters of this "progressive education" wanted to shape the characters of the students and teach them good citizenship as well as facts. They also believed children should learn through the use of hands-on activities. These ideas had the greatest effect in elementary schools.

John Dewey, the leading spokesperson for progressive education, criticized schools for stressing too much memorization of facts. Instead, Dewey argued, schools should relate learning to the interests, problems, and concerns of students.

Primary Source / **First Day of School**

A Day to Remember Public education was important to newcomers to America. Mary Antin came to the United States in 1894 and described her first day of school this way: "That day I must always remember, even if I live to be so old that I cannot tell my name. To most people their first day at school is a memorable occasion. In my case the importance of the day was a hundred times magnified, on account of the years I had waited, the road I had come, and the conscious ambitions I entertained."

Critical Thinking

Speculating Why do you think going to school in America was such a memorable experience for an immigrant like Mary Antin?

Higher Education

Colleges and universities changed and expanded. The 1862 Morrill Act gave states federal land that could be sold to raise money for education. States used these funds to start schools called **land-grant colleges.**

In 1865 few American colleges admitted women. The new land-grant schools admitted women students, as did new women's colleges—Vassar, Smith, Wellesley, and Bryn Mawr. By 1910, almost 40 percent of all American college students were women.

Some new colleges, such as Hampton Institute in Virginia and Howard University in Washington, D.C., provided higher education for African Americans. Prominent Howard graduates of today include Supreme Court Justice Thurgood Marshall and author Toni Morrison. One Hampton Institute student, Booker T. Washington, became an educator. In 1881 he founded the Tuskegee Institute in Alabama to train teachers and provide practical education for African Americans. Then, in 1896, scientist **George Washington Carver** joined the Tuskegee faculty. His research transformed agriculture in the South. From the peanut, Carver developed hundreds of products, including plastics and paper.

Schools for Native Americans

Reservation schools and boarding schools also opened to train Native Americans for jobs. Although these schools provided Native Americans with training for jobs in industry, they also **isolated,** or cut off, Native Americans from their tribal traditions. Boarding schools were sometimes located hundreds of miles away from a student's family.

Reading Check **Comparing** What did Bryn Mawr, Vassar, and Smith have in common?

Primary Source — The Tuskegee Institute

Washington Founds a School In 1881 Booker T. Washington founded Tuskegee Institute, a school for the education of African American men and women. Tuskegee combined academics with vocational training and an emphasis on self-reliance. The school began in a one-room building with 30 students. By the time of Washington's death in 1915, the school had grown to 100 buildings, 200 faculty, and 1,500 students.

These students erecting a school building show Tuskegee's early emphasis on self-reliance and education in the trades. ▲

Tuskegee combined academics with vocational training. ▶

"If one thing more than another has taught me to have confidence in the masses of my own people it has been their willingness (and even eagerness) to learn and their disposition to help themselves."

—Booker T. Washington, *My Larger Education*, 1911

Critical Thinking

Predicting What effect do you think the Tuskegee Institute had on the lives of African Americans who went to school there?

People IN HISTORY

Paul Laurence Dunbar

Poet, playwright, and songwriter

Dunbar was the first African American poet to gain national attention. He was forced to make a living by writing for white audiences who preferred his black dialect poetry. For example, in *"Song of Summer,"* he portrayed the South as an idyllic and peaceful place: *"Sky all white wif streaks o' blue,/Sunshine softly gleamin',/D'ain't no wuk hit 's right to do,/Nothin' 's right but dreamin'."* In other writings, Dunbar was an advocate for civil rights and higher education for African Americans.

Edith Wharton

Pulitzer Prize–winning author

Edith Wharton was born into a rich family. However, she came to dislike the manners and lifestyle of the upper-class Americans she often wrote about. *"Such dreariness, such whining sallow [pale] women, such utter absence of the amenities [pleasantries], such crass [foul] food, crass manners, crass landscape!!"* . . . *"What a horror it is for a whole nation to be developing without the sense of beauty."*

CRITICAL Thinking

1. **Describing** Describe the attitudes of Wharton and Dunbar toward the people they wrote about.
2. **Evaluating** How do you think writing for a white audience affected Dunbar's poetry?

A Nation of Readers

Main Idea Educated Americans found new reading material in public libraries, a growing literary culture, and thriving newspapers.

History and You Do you ever borrow books from your public library? Read to learn which prominent industrialist gave support to libraries.

As opportunities for education grew, more Americans became interested in reading. New books, magazines, and newspapers were published, and more libraries opened. In 1881 Andrew Carnegie, the steel industrialist, pledged to build a public library in any city that would pay its operating costs. With gifts from Carnegie and others, and the efforts of state and local governments, every state in the Union established free public libraries.

Changes in Literature

Many writers of the era explored new themes and subjects. Their approach to literature was called **realism** because they sought to describe the lives of people. Related to realism was **regionalism,** writing that focused on a particular region of the country.

Mark Twain was a realist and a regionalist. Many of his books, including *Adventures of Huckleberry Finn* and *The Adventures of Tom Sawyer,* are set along the Mississippi River, where Twain grew up.

Stephen Crane wrote about city slums in *Maggie* and about the Civil War in *The Red Badge of Courage.* In books such as *The Call of the Wild* and *The Sea Wolf,* Jack London portrayed the lives of miners and hunters in the far Northwest. Edith Wharton described upper-class Easterners in *The House of Mirth* and *The Age of Innocence.*

Paul Laurence Dunbar, the son of former enslaved Africans, wrote books that used the dialects and folktales of Southern African Americans. Dunbar was one of the first African American writers to gain fame around the world.

Inexpensive paperback books appeared for the first time in the late 1800s. Horatio Alger wrote a series of young-adult books with titles such as *Work and Win* and *Luck and Pluck*. Based on themes of hard work and honesty, Alger's books sold millions of copies.

Spreading the News

Technological advances in printing, paper-making, and communications made it possible to publish a daily paper for a large number of readers. The growing cities provided readers for the newspapers.

In 1883 **Joseph Pulitzer** purchased the New York *World* and created a new kind of newspaper. The paper grabbed the reader's attention with illustrations, cartoons, and sensational stories with huge headlines—such as "ANOTHER MURDERER TO HANG." Under Pulitzer's management, the *World* had more than 1 million readers every day.

Other newspapers soon imitated Pulitzer's style. The New York *Morning Journal,* purchased by **William Randolph Hearst** in 1895, became even more successful than the *World* by exaggerating dramatic or gruesome aspects of stories. This sensational writing style became known as **yellow journalism.**

Ethnic and minority newspapers thrived as well. By 1900, six daily Jewish-language newspapers were operating in New York City. African Americans started more than 1,000 newspapers between 1865 and 1900.

More magazines took advantage of printing improvements and mass-circulation techniques to reach a national market. Between 1865 and 1900, the number of magazines in the United States rose from about 700 to 5,000. Some magazines of that era—the *Atlantic Monthly, Harper's Magazine,* and *Ladies' Home Journal*—are still published today.

Reading Check **Discussing** How did yellow journalism attract readers?

LINKING PAST TO PRESENT American Football

THEN Football began in 1869 as a soccer-style game between college teams. In the 1870s, the game became more like English rugby, with players carrying the ball and tackling. The game was brutal. Players did not even wear helmets at first. A new rule in 1894 banned projecting nails from shoes.

◀ Knute Rockne in 1913 was an all-American end for Notre Dame. Later, he coached Notre Dame to six national championships.

▲ College football scrimmage, c. 1905

Leisure and the Arts

Main Idea American culture moved away from European influence and became distinctively American.

History and You What are your favorite movies? Read to learn which famous inventor introduced the first "moving pictures."

. . . .

During this era, Americans enjoyed increasing amounts of leisure time. Unlike round-the-clock farmwork, professional and industrial jobs gave people hours and even days of free time. To fill their leisure time, Americans developed new forms of recreation, including sports, art, and music.

A Changing World of Sports

A favorite leisure-time activity for many people was watching and following sports. Baseball became the most popular **spectator sport** in America. By the early 1900s, the National and American Leagues were founded—each made up of teams from major cities. Their games drew large crowds of enthusiastic fans, and in 1903 the first World Series was held.

NOW Football has evolved into an exciting style of play. Rule changes and better protective gear have made the game safer. Each week millions watch high school, college, and pro teams in action.

Critical Thinking

Comparing What do you think is the biggest difference in football between the two eras?

Another popular spectator sport was football, which developed from the English game of rugby. The first college football game was played between Rutgers and Princeton in 1869. By the 1890s, college football games were drawing huge crowds.

Basketball, invented by Dr. James Naismith of Springfield, Massachusetts, also became popular. Naismith developed the game in the 1890s as an indoor winter sport for the students in his YMCA physical education classes. Considered the only major sport that is completely American in origin, basketball soon spread to other countries.

Americans not only watched but also participated in sports. The wealthy played tennis and golf, usually in exclusive private clubs. Bicycling grew in popularity after the "safety" bicycle was developed. Older bicycles had a large wheel in front and a small one in back, but the new ones had two air-filled rubber tires of the same size.

These improvements helped bicycle riding take the country by storm. One romantic song celebrated the bicycle: "It won't be a stylish marriage, I can't afford a carriage, But you'll look sweet upon the seat of a bicycle built for two."

Vaudeville and Movies

Not only did Americans watch sports, they also became eager fans of shows and movies. Large cities had many theaters. Plays performed ranged from serious dramas by Shakespeare to **vaudeville** shows, which were variety shows with dancing, singing, comedy, and magic acts.

Many people could afford the price of a ticket, and in the early 1900s, vaudeville offered the most popular shows in town. The circus was another popular attraction that brought large crowds. In 1910 the United States had about 80 traveling circuses that moved from town to town.

Prominent inventor Thomas Edison introduced "moving pictures" in the 1880s. The "movies" soon became enormously popular in the United States.

Theaters called nickelodeons got their name because they charged five cents to see short films. The nickelodeons marked the beginning of today's film industry.

American Artists and Musicians

For most of the 1800s, the work of American artists and musicians reflected a European influence. After the Civil War, Americans began to develop a distinctively American style.

Some American painters pursued realist themes in their works. Thomas Eakins of Philadelphia painted the human anatomy and surgical operations as well as rowers and other athletes. One of Eakins's students, Henry Tanner, depicted warm family scenes of Americans in the South. Frederic Remington portrayed the American West, focusing on subjects such as cowhands and Native Americans. Winslow Homer painted Southern farmers, Adirondack campers, and stormy sea scenes. James Whistler's *Arrangement in Grey and Black,* commonly known as *"Whistler's Mother,"* is one of the best-known American paintings. Mary Cassatt was influential in the Impressionist school of painting that arose during the late 1800s. Impressionists tried to capture the play of light, color, and patterns as they made immediate impressions on the senses.

Distinctively American kinds of music were also becoming popular. Bandleader John Philip Sousa composed many rousing marches, including "The Stars and Stripes Forever."

African American musicians in New Orleans in the late 1800s developed another entirely new kind of music—jazz. **Jazz** combined elements of work songs, gospel music, spirituals, and African rhythms. One of jazz's major characteristics was syncopation, a shifting of the usual musical accent. Related to jazz was **ragtime** music. One of the best ragtime composers was Scott Joplin. He wrote "Maple Leaf Rag" and many other well-known works.

The symphony orchestras of New York, Boston, and Philadelphia, all founded before 1900, were among the world's finest orchestras. Great singers and conductors from all over the world came to perform at New York's Metropolitan Opera House.

✔ **Reading Check** **Describing** What elements make up jazz music?

History ONLINE
Study Central™ To review this section, go to glencoe.com.

Section 3 Review

Vocabulary

1. Use each of these terms in a sentence that will help explain its meaning: philosophy, land-grant college, isolate, realism, regionalism, yellow journalism, spectator sport, vaudeville, jazz, ragtime.

Main Ideas

2. **Explaining** What was the goal of progressive education?

3. **Contrasting** How did realism and regionalism differ?

4. **Describing** What forms of entertainment were popular during this era?

Critical Thinking

5. **Making Connections** Identify the causes that sparked an increase in the number of publications in the late 1800s.

6. **Making Inferences** In what ways did schools have a negative effect on Native Americans?

7. **Creative Writing** Write a local newspaper article in the style of yellow journalism.

Answer the
8. **Essential Question**
In what ways did American culture change in the late 1800s?

City Life

- Industry and immigration lead to the growth of cities.
- In the poorest parts of crowded cities, people live in tenements and slums.
- Overcrowding leads to sanitation problems, disease, and crime.
- "The Gilded Age" refers to American riches overshadowing the poverty in many areas.

Immigration

- New groups of immigrants arrive in the U.S. from eastern and southern Europe.
- Reasons for immigration include: economic troubles, persecution in the native country, and better opportunities in the United States.
- New industries, such as steel and garment manufacturing, offer low-paying jobs for immigrant workers.
- Ethnic groups establish separate communities to re-create former lifestyles.
- Nativists fear immigration and call for restrictions.

Technology and Culture

- Architects address the lack of space in cities by building skyscrapers.
- Streetcars, trolleys, subways, and bridges all improve transportation in cities.
- The American educational system expands and offers new opportunities.
- Public libraries and new forms of literature and journalism add to culture in the cities.

Leisure Activities

- Middle-class Americans have newfound leisure time for sports, arts, and music.
- Sports, including baseball, football, and basketball, grow in popularity.
- Vaudeville shows, traveling circuses, and the first movies offer other new forms of entertainment.
- Distinctively American forms of music, including jazz and ragtime, become popular.

STUDY TO GO Study anywhere, anytime! Download quizzes and flash cards to your PDA from glencoe.com.

STANDARDIZED TEST PRACTICE

Consider carefully before changing your answer to a multiple-answer test question. Unless you misread the question, your first answer choice is often correct.

Reviewing Main Ideas

Directions: Choose the best answer for each of the following questions.

1. Most of the immigrants who arrived in the United States in the late 1800s

   A came from Latin America.

   B immediately blended into American society.

   C were from rural areas.

   D sought highly skilled technical jobs.

2. By the 1900s, where were middle-class Americans increasingly likely to live?

   A in rural areas

   B in the suburbs

   C in slums

   D in tenements

3. What was Frederick Law Olmsted's major contribution to American cities?

   A His safety elevator made taller buildings possible.

   B He founded settlement houses to help the urban poor.

   C He invented the electric trolley car, making city travel easier.

   D He led the "City Beautiful" movement, which promoted urban parks.

4. Supporters of "progressive education" emphasized which of the following?

   A character education

   B rote memorization of facts

   C the opening of libraries

   D land-grant schools for women

Short-Answer Question

Directions: Base your answer to question 5 on the table below and on your knowledge of social studies.

Family Characteristics of Major Immigrant Groups, 1909–1914

Group	Percentage Returning to Europe	Males per 100 Females	Percentage Under Age 14
Czechs	5	133	19
English	6	136	16
Finnish	7	181	8
Germans	7	132	18
Greeks	16	170	4
Hungarians	22	141	16
Italians	17	320	12
Poles	13	188	10
Slovaks	19	162	12

Source: "Immigrant America," Digital History

5. According to the table, which group was the most likely to return to Europe? Which group had the most uneven ratio between the sexes?

Review the Essential Questions

6. **Essay** Explain how immigration contributed to (a) the rise of the modern city; (b) the expansion of education; and (c) the development of a distinctly American culture by the early 1900s.

To help you write your essay, review your answers to the Essential Questions in the section reviews and the chapter Foldables Study Organizer. Your essay should include:

- characteristics and challenges of immigrants;
- changes and living conditions of cities;
- expansion of education and reading; and
- leisure activities and the arts.

GO ON ➤

History ONLINE

For additional test practice, use **Self-Check Quizzes**—Chapter 6 at glencoe.com.

Document-Based Questions

Directions: Analyze the documents and answer the short-answer questions that follow.

Document 1

> The immigrant of the former time came almost exclusively from western and northern Europe. . . . Immigrants from southern Italy, Hungary, Austria, and Russia . . . made up hardly more than one per cent of our immigration. To-day the proportion has risen to something like forty per cent. . . . These people . . . are beaten men from beaten races; representing the worst failures in the struggle for existence. . . . They have none of the ideas and [abilities] which fit men to take up readily and easily the problem of self-care and self-government.

Source: F. A. Walker, "Restriction of Immigration," 1907

7. Identify *two* reasons Walker opposed immigration from southern and eastern Europe.

Document 2

U.S. President Theodore Roosevelt stated the following.

> There is no room in this country for hyphenated Americanism. . . .
> . . . The one absolutely certain way of bringing the nation to ruin . . . would be to permit it to become a tangle of squabbling nationalities.

Source: address to Knights of Columbus, 1915

8. What did Roosevelt mean by "hyphenated Americanism"?

9. Based on the quote, did he favor or oppose the acceptance of immigrants into the American society? Explain your answer.

Document 3

This photo of three homeless boys sleeping in an alley appeared in Jacob Riis's *How the Other Half Lives: Studies Among the Tenements of New York*, 1890.

Source: Bettmann/CORBIS

10. Who was the "other half" referred to in the title of Riis's book? What did Riis hope to accomplish by publishing pictures such as this?

Document 4

In this passage, African American composer W. C. Handy—the "Father of the Blues"—explains what the blues are all about.

> My purpose was to capture in fixed form the highly distinctive music of my race. Everything I have written has its roots deep in the folk life of the South.

Source: "The Birth of the Blues," 1911

11. Based on the passage, what was the inspiration for Handy's music?

12. **Expository Writing** Using the information from the four documents and your knowledge of social studies, write an essay in which you:

- identify ways that American society by the early 1900s had become a true "melting pot" of assimilated cultures; and

- point out ways in which Americans remained separated in the early 1900s.

Need Extra Help?												
If you missed questions. . .	1	2	3	4	5	6	7	8	9	10	11	12
Go to page. . .	171	180	183	185	172	170–190	175	175	177	180–181	179	170–190

Unit 3

Reform and Empire
1865–1920

Program cover for women's right to vote demonstration, Washington, D.C., 1913

"Give me your tired,
your poor,
your huddled masses
yearning to
breathe free . . ."
—Emma Lazarus

Members of the famous 369th Colored
Infantry return from World War I.

Unit 3 Reading History

READING SKILL — **Paraphrasing**

Learn It!

When you paraphrase, you use your own words to retell the information. You can improve your understanding of difficult passages by rewording, or paraphrasing, them.

Paraphrased Version
As the army asks for your solid and steady support, think about the courage and strength of our ancestors. Your support will help ensure that America's democratic values will not be destroyed.

—from Chapter 9, p. 280
General John J. Pershing
"Invoking the spirit of our forefathers, the army asks for your unflinching support, to the end that the high ideals for which America stands may endure upon the earth."

Practice It!

Read the quote below. On another sheet of paper, paraphrase the passage by completing the sentences with your own words.

—from Chapter 7, p. 220
W.E.B. Du Bois
"Freedom . . . we still seek,—the freedom of life and limb, the freedom to work and think, the freedom to love and aspire. Work, culture, liberty,—all these we need, not singly but together, . . . all striving toward that vaster ideal . . . the ideal of human brotherhood, gained through the unifying ideal of Race."

Paraphrased Version
We still need _____
_____.

By making sure each of us has all these freedoms, together we _____
_____.

Academic Vocabulary Preview

Listed below are the academic vocabulary words and their definitions that you will come across as you study Unit 3. Practice It! will help you study the words and definitions.

Academic Vocabulary	Definition	Practice It!
Chapter 7 The Progressive Era		
behalf (bih · HAF) *p. 204*	in the interest of	**Identify** *the term from Chapter 7 that best completes each sentence.*
accurate (A · kyuh · ruht) *p. 205*	correct	
professional (pruh · FEHSH · nuhl) *p. 209*	a person in an occupation requiring special knowledge or education	**1.** U.S. laws make sure that food and drug labels are _____ .
intelligence (ihn · TEH · luh · juhnts) *p. 209*	the ability to understand and use knowledge	**2.** One goal of progressive reforms is to eliminate _____ against women and minorities.
inspect (ihn · SPEHKT) *p. 216*	to carefully examine	**3.** In the early 1900s, most _____ jobs for women were in teaching.
primary (PRY · MEHR · ee) *p. 218*	an election in which a political party chooses its candidate	
deny (dih · NY) *p. 222*	to not allow access to	
bias (BY · uhs) *p. 223*	an unbalanced view or consideration	
Chapter 8 Rise to World Power		
communicate (kuh · MYOO · nuh · KAYT) *p. 234*	to transmit information so it is received or understood	**Choose** *the word that best matches the meaning of each vocabulary term listed below.*
vision (VIH · zhuhn) *p. 234*	an imagined plan	**4. annual** **6. vision**
consult (kuhn · SUHLT) *p. 239*	to seek opinions or information from	**a.** always **a.** plan
exploit (ihk · SPLOYT) *p. 240*	to make use of	**b.** yearly **b.** work
trigger (TRIH · guhr) *p. 244*	to start	**c.** often **c.** process
eventual (ih · VEHNT · shuh · wuhl) *p. 247*	occurring later	**5. trigger** **7. eliminate**
eliminate (ih · LIH · muh · NAYT) *p. 249*	to end	**a.** stop **a.** include
annual (AN · yuh · wuhl) *p. 249*	yearly	**b.** tease **b.** end
		c. start **c.** explain
Chapter 9 World War I		
dimension (duh · MEHN · shuhn) *p. 267*	magnitude or extent	**Choose** *terms from Chapter 9 to complete the paragraph.*
equip (ih · KWIHP) *p. 267*	to provide with	During World War I, the plane added a new **8.** _____ to combat. Fighter
stress (STREHS) *p. 271*	to call particular attention to	planes were **9.** _____ with machine guns and flown by daring pilots. Airplanes,
revolution (REH · vuh · LOO · shuhn) *p. 274*	a war to overthrow a government	as well as other sophisticated weapons, helped the Allies **10.** _____ victory.
proceed (proh · SEED) *p. 278*	to continue on	
consent (kuhn · SEHNT) *p. 281*	to agree to	
consume (kuhn · SOOM) *p. 284*	to use	
perceive (puhr · SEEV) *p. 285*	to recognize; understand	
final (FY · nuhl) *p. 288*	last	
achieve (uh · CHEEV) *p. 288*	to accomplish; to gain by effort	

Chapter 7

The Progressive Era 1877-1920

Woman suffrage parade, New York City, 1915

Ferris wheel at Columbian Exposition ▶

PRESIDENTS

RUTHERFORD B. HAYES 1877–1881

JAMES GARFIELD 1881

CHESTER ARTHUR 1881–1885

GROVER CLEVELAND 1885–1889

BENJAMIN HARRISON 1889–1893

GROVER CLEVELAND 1893–1897

1893 ★
World's Columbian Exhibition held in Chicago

U.S. Events
World Events

1880

1890

★ 1879
British win Zulu War

★ 1889
Brazil becomes a republic

Japanese Parliament ▶

★ 1890
First general election in Japan

★ 1893
New Zealand grants woman suffrage

History ONLINE
Chapter Overview Visit glencoe.com
and click on **Chapter 7—Chapter Overviews**
to preview chapter information.

Section 1: The Progressive Movement

Essential Question How did the progressives fight corruption in business and in government?

Section 2: Women and Progressives

Essential Question How did reforms affect the lives of women and other groups in the late 1800s?

Section 3: Progressive Presidents

Essential Question Why were Theodore Roosevelt and William Howard Taft known as progressive presidents?

Section 4: Excluded From Reform

Essential Question How did minority groups react to discrimination?

FOLDABLES®
Study Organizer

Organizing Information

Make this Foldable to help you organize information about the Progressive Era.

Step 1 Fold an 11" x 17" sheet of paper length-wise to create five equal sections.

Step 2 Then fold it to form five columns.

Step 3 Label your Foldable as shown.

Chapter 21: The Progressive Era	The Progressive Movement	Women and Progressives	Progressive Presidents	Excluded From Reform
Essential Question				
Key Events and Dates				
1877–1920 Attitudes				
Current Attitudes				

Reading and Writing As you read the chapter, take notes about the people, places, and events related to the Progressive Era in the correct place on the chart.

WILLIAM McKINLEY 1897–1901

★ **1901** President McKinley is assassinated

THEODORE ROOSEVELT 1901–1909

★ **1909** The NAACP is formed

WILLIAM HOWARD TAFT 1909–1913

WOODROW WILSON 1913–1921

★ **1920** Nineteenth Amendment grants woman suffrage

1900   **1910**   **1920**

★ **1897** The Sultan of Zanzibar abolishes slavery

★ **1905** Einstein announces theory of relativity

★ **1911** Rutherford discovers structure of atom

The Progressive Movement

Essential Question

How did the progressives fight corruption in business and in government?

Reading Guide

Content Vocabulary

oligopoly *(p. 203)*   referendum *(p. 205)*
muckraker *(p. 205)*   recall *(p. 205)*
initiative *(p. 205)*

Academic Vocabulary

behalf *(p. 204)*   accurate *(p. 205)*

Key People and Events

Pendleton Act *(p. 202)*
Sherman Antitrust Act *(p. 203)*
Interstate Commerce Act *(p. 203)*
Eugene V. Debs *(p. 204)*
Ida Tarbell *(p. 205)*
Upton Sinclair *(p. 205)*

Reading Strategy

Taking Notes As you read, use a diagram like the one below to show how the Seventeenth Amendment reformed the political process.

Before ⟷ **Seventeenth Amendment** ⟷ After

American Diary

Boss Tweed was a dishonest but powerful political official in New York City in the late 1800s. During this time, bribery, fixed elections, and kickbacks were common practices in city government. Journalists and reformers, however, exposed these activities and tried to change the political system. Political cartoonist from the time, Thomas Nast, said: "I made up my mind not long ago to put some of those fellows behind bars, and I am going to put them there."

—quoted in **The Great Bridge** *by David McCullough*

The former New York County Courthouse, also known as Tweed Courthouse

Fighting Corruption

Main Idea Americans took action against corruption in business and government.

History and You How would you feel if the team members who paid the coach the most money got to be the starting players on your school's basketball team? Read to find out how reformers worked to fight corruption in city governments.

. . . .

Many Americans called for reform in the late 1800s. The reformers, called progressives, had many different goals. Progressives focused on urban problems, government, and business. They claimed that government and big business were taking advantage of the American people rather than serving them.

Fighting the Political Machines

Political machines were powerful organizations linked to political parties. These machines controlled local government in many cities. In each ward, or political district within a city, a machine representative controlled jobs and services. This person was the political boss. A political boss was often a citizen's closest link to local government. Although they helped people, many bosses were dishonest.

Corrupt politicians found different ways to make money. They accepted bribes from tenement landlords to overlook violations of city housing codes. They took campaign contributions from contractors who hoped to do business with the city. They also took kickbacks, or illegal payments. For example, a contractor would pad, or add to, the amount of the bill for city work. The contractor then paid, or "kicked back," a percentage of that amount to the bosses.

Some politicians profited illegally from city business. One corrupt city boss was William M. Tweed. Known as Boss Tweed, he headed New York City's Democratic political machine in the 1860s and 1870s. Boss Tweed led a network of city officials called the Tweed ring.

By the Numbers / Stealing From the People

Courthouse Corruption As the New York County Courthouse was built in the late 1800s, dishonest construction workers and city officials stole money from the city's treasury by submitting bills for fraudulent work. An investigation by the *New York Times* found that more than $12 million was billed for questionable work on the courthouse. Evidence about corrupt practices prompted a public outcry against Boss Tweed and his political machine. Some of the huge charges recorded by the city are listed in the chart below.

Payment for Work Completed on New Courthouse

To	For	Amount
Andrew Garvey	Plastering, Repairs	$2,870,464
Keyser & Co.	Plumbing	$1,200,000
Ingersoll	Chairs	$170,727.60
Ingersoll	Cabinets, Furniture	$2,817,469.19
George Miller	Carpentry	$360,751.61

▲ Cartoon showing Boss Tweed

Critical Thinking

Inferring How does the right of a free press contribute to a democracy?

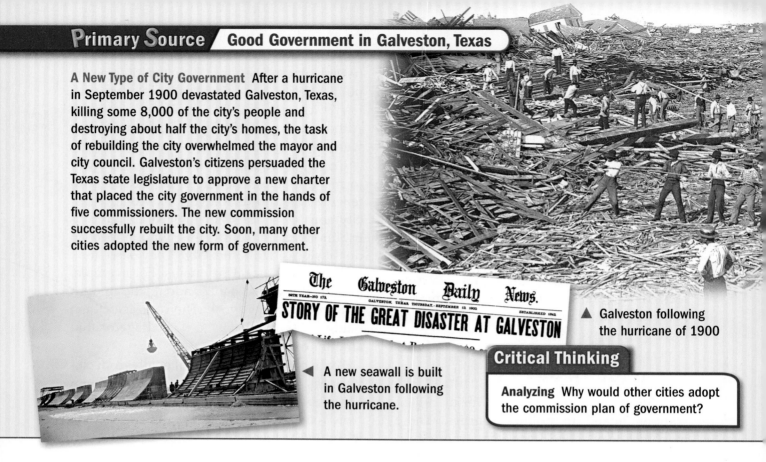

A New Type of City Government After a hurricane in September 1900 devastated Galveston, Texas, killing some 8,000 of the city's people and destroying about half the city's homes, the task of rebuilding the city overwhelmed the mayor and city council. Galveston's citizens persuaded the Texas state legislature to approve a new charter that placed the city government in the hands of five commissioners. The new commission successfully rebuilt the city. Soon, many other cities adopted the new form of government.

The Galveston Daily News.
66TH YEAR—NO 172   GALVESTON, TEXAS, THURSDAY, SEPTEMBER 13, 1900   ESTABLISHED 1842

STORY OF THE GREAT DISASTER AT GALVESTON

▲ Galveston following the hurricane of 1900

◄ A new seawall is built in Galveston following the hurricane.

Critical Thinking

Analyzing Why would other cities adopt the commission plan of government?

The Tweed ring controlled the city's police, the courts, and even some newspapers. They collected millions of dollars in illegal payments from companies doing business with the city. Political cartoonist Thomas Nast exposed the Tweed ring's operations in his cartoons for *Harper's Weekly.* Tweed was convicted and sentenced to prison.

Reformers wanted to break the power of political bosses. They founded organizations such as the National Municipal League in Philadelphia. They worked to make city governments more honest and efficient. Galveston, Texas, for example, changed to a government run by five commissioners. By 1917, commissioners governed nearly 400 cities.

Fighting the Spoils System

Since the presidency of Andrew Jackson, the spoils system had been common practice. Under this system, political supporters were rewarded with jobs and favors. When a new president came to power, job seekers flooded the nation's capital. Also called patronage, the spoils system could be found at all levels of government and led to abuses. Many people who received government jobs were not qualified, and some were dishonest.

Presidents Rutherford B. Hayes (1877–1881) and James Garfield (1881) tried to change the spoils system. Hayes tried to reform the civil service, the body of government workers who are not elected. Neither major political party backed his efforts. Before Garfield could launch his reforms, he was assassinated by an unsuccessful office seeker.

When Vice President Chester A. Arthur succeeded Garfield as president, he tried to end the spoils system. In 1883 Congress passed the **Pendleton Act,** which established the Civil Service Commission to give examinations for federal jobs. Job seekers had to demonstrate their skills in these tests. By 1900, the commission controlled the hiring of many federal workers.

Reading Check **Contrasting** How was the hiring of government employees under the Pendleton Act different from how people were hired in the spoils system?

Controlling Business

Main Idea The government passed acts to regulate businesses and transportation.

History and You Do you think the government should have a role in managing big businesses? Read to learn how the government became more involved in regulating businesses.

. . . .

Many Americans believed that trusts, or groups of companies, had too much control over the economy and the government. This concern led to new laws regulating big business. In 1890 Congress passed the **Sherman Antitrust Act,** the first federal law to control trusts and monopolies.

During the 1890s, however, the government rarely used the Sherman Act to curb business. Instead, it applied the act against labor unions. The government claimed that labor strikes hurt trade. It was not until the early 1900s that the Sherman Act was used to win cases against trusts.

Reining in the Railroads

The railroads formed an **oligopoly,** a few large companies that controlled prices for an entire industry. Reformers called for rules on railroad rates. In 1887 Congress passed the **Interstate Commerce Act,** requiring railroads to charge and publish "reasonable and just" rates. The act set up the Interstate Commerce Commission (ICC) to oversee the railroad and, later, trucking industries.

Lowering Tariffs

Reformers wanted to lower tariffs. They believed that higher tariffs increased the price of goods. In 1890 the Republicans raised tariffs sharply to protect U.S. businesses from foreign competition. Voters opposing high tariffs sent many Democrats to Congress. Grover Cleveland, who became president in 1893, also favored lower tariffs.

✓ **Reading Check** **Explaining** How did the government gain control over powerful businesses?

Primary Sources
INTERPRETING
POLITICAL CARTOONS

A quote by Andrew Carnegie inspired the cartoon below:
"The public may regard trusts or combinations with serene confidence."

—from the *New York Times,* October 9, 1888

1. **Analyzing** Why do you think the cartoonist chose to depict the trust as an animal with many heads?

2. **Interpreting** Does the beast look trustworthy to you? Why or why not?

A. Andrew Carnegie
B. Uncle Sam
C. Carnegie's steel trust

A TRUSTWORTHY BEAST

Exposing Corruption Between 1900 and 1910, muckrakers wrote articles for several popular magazines that exposed the social hardships caused by corrupt big business. Public outrage caused by the stories inspired some politicians to take the lead in passing some social reforms.

Samuel Hopkins Adams's articles in *Collier's* exposed patent medicines—sold as cure-alls—as frauds and led to the 1906 Pure Food and Drug Act. He wrote that without patent medicines, *"the nation would be richer not only in lives and money, but in drunkards and drug fiends saved."*

In order to be committed to an asylum for poor women, reporter Nellie Bly pretended to be insane. She later wrote about her experiences in *Ten Days in a Mad-House.* Her account shocked readers and led to improvements in the care of the insane. *"So I have at least the satisfaction of knowing that the poor unfortunates will be the better cared for because of my work."*

Lewis Hine's work for the National Child Labor Committee took him across the country to photograph children at work. His photographs of dirty coal miners, anemic mill workers, and tired oyster shuckers made the plight of working children real to Americans. *"My child labor photos have ... set the authorities to work to see 'if such things can be possible,'"* he wrote. *"They try to get around them by crying 'fake,' but therein lies the value of data & a witness."*

Critical Thinking

Analyzing What did the groups of people that Bly, Hine, and Adams tried to help have in common?

The New Reformers

Main Idea Writers exposed corruption in business and government, and voters gained more power in choosing candidates.

History and You What sorts of problems do your local TV investigative reporters try to resolve? Read how reporters brought about reforms in business and government.

• •

In the early 1900s, reformers in America had new ideas for ending injustice and solving social problems. These ideas included socialism and progressivism.

Socialists believed the government should own and operate resources and major industries on **behalf,** or in the interest, of all the people. **Eugene V. Debs** helped found the American Socialist Party in 1898. With Debs as its leader, the party gained some support in the early 1900s. Debs ran for president five times, but he never received more than 6 percent of the popular vote.

At the same time, progressives brought new energy to the reform movement. Like the socialists, many progressives were alarmed by the fact that only a few people held most of America's wealth and power. Unlike the socialists, they wanted government to regulate industry rather than own it. They also wanted government to be more efficient and less influenced by powerful businesses. Society, progressives believed, had a duty to protect and help all its members. Many of their reforms were aimed at helping people who did not have wealth or power.

Muckrakers Expose Problems

Journalists aided the reformers. Investigative reporters wrote newspaper and magazine stories that alerted people about problems.

Called **muckrakers,** these reporters "raked"—or exposed—the "muck"—dirt and corruption—underlying society.

One of the most effective muckrakers was Lincoln Steffens. Working for *McClure's Magazine,* Steffens exposed corrupt machine politics in New York and other cities. **Ida Tarbell,** also with *McClure's,* described the oil trust's unfair practices. Her articles increased public pressure for more government control over big business.

In his novel *The Jungle* (1906), **Upton Sinclair** described the horrors of the Chicago meatpacking industry. His vivid descriptions shocked people in America. In response, Congress passed the Meat Inspection Act and the Pure Food and Drug Act in 1906. Now food and medicine had to be **accurately** labeled, and harmful food could not be sold.

Progressives also backed many reforms designed to increase the people's direct control of government. Robert La Follette reformed Wisconsin's electoral system. He introduced the "Wisconsin idea," a direct primary election in which party candidates were chosen by voters instead of by party bosses and state conventions.

The Oregon System

Oregon also made important reforms. With the **initiative,** voters could place an issue on the ballot in a state election. Voters could accept or reject measures that the state legislature enacted with the **referendum.** The **recall** allowed voters to remove incompetent elected officials. These reforms, called the Oregon System, were adopted by other states.

The Seventeenth Amendment

Progressives also changed the way U.S. senators were elected. The Constitution gave state legislatures the responsibility of choosing senators. Party bosses and business interests, however, often controlled the process. Progressives wanted to give people the opportunity to vote for their senators directly. Support for this idea grew. In 1912 Congress passed the Seventeenth Amendment to the Constitution. This amendment set forth the direct election of senators. Ratified in 1913, the amendment gave the people a voice in choosing their representatives.

Reading Check **Summarizing** How did progressive reformers reinforce democratic ideas?

Section 1 Review

History ONLINE
Study Central™ To review this section, go to glencoe.com.

Vocabulary

1. Define each of the following terms in a sentence: oligopoly, behalf, muckraker, accurate, initiative, referendum, recall.

Main Ideas

2. Listing Identify some ways in which political machines were corrupt in the late 1800s.

3. Discussing Why did reformers want regulation of the railroads, and what was the government's response?

4. Identifying How did muckrakers bring about reform?

Critical Thinking

5. Determining Cause and Effect Use a diagram like the one below to show which problem reformers were trying to resolve with each legislation.

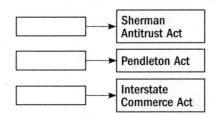

	Sherman Antitrust Act
	Pendleton Act
	Interstate Commerce Act

6. Persuasive Writing You are a muckraker. Choose something you think is unfair in your school or community and write a two- or three-paragraph article about it. Try to move your readers to improve the situation.

Answer the Essential Question

7. How did the progressives fight corruption in business and in government?

Meet the Author

Elizabeth Winthrop (1948–) was inspired to write *Counting on Grace* after seeing a photograph of a 12-year-old girl named Addie at work in a textile mill in Vermont. The photograph, taken by child labor photographer Lewis Hine in 1910, has been reprinted hundreds of times and has even appeared on a U.S. postage stamp.

Vocabulary

bobbin a small round device on which thread or yarn is wound

mumblety-peg game in which players throw or flip a jackknife in various ways so that the knife sticks in the ground

dawdles wastes time

This photograph of mill worker Addie Card inspired Elizabeth Winthrop to write the novel *Counting on Grace*. ▶

Building Background

In *Counting on Grace*, the main character is a 12-year-old girl who leaves school to work at the thread mill in a Vermont town in 1910. Grace had been in the mill "lots of times" before to play and bring lunch to her family. Now she works to help support her family. Her mother, Mamère, her father, and her sister, Delia, also work in the mill. French Johnny, a French-Canadian second hand in the mill, is in charge of the spinning rooms where Grace and her family work. As you read Grace's description, think about the difficulties that the workers had to endure.

COUNTING ON GRACE

Elizabeth Winthrop

I've been in the mill lots of times. Summers ever since I was nine, I've been cooking the hot meal for Mamère and Papa and Delia and taking in the dinner pails in the middle of the day. Delia let me push her **bobbin** dolly. I played **mumblety-peg** or roll the bobbin with Dougie and Bridget and Felix when he was

a summer sweeper boy in the spinning room. And grease skating. That's the best. Thomas invented that game. Too bad he can't play it no more with his twisted foot.

With all the oil dripping off the machines, bare feet slide around easy. The boys draw a line at the end of one alley, between the frames where French Johnny can't see us, and we run and set our legs into a long slide. I'm skinny for my age and I've got big feet, but I can go the farthest 'cause I know how to keep myself low to the floor. Sometimes you slip and fall. That's a chance you take.

But now I'm here to work, not play.

The air in the mill is stuffy and linty and sweaty at the same time 'cause all day long water sprays down on the frames from little hoses in the ceiling. Wet keeps the threads from breaking. The windows are shut tight even in the summer. You don't breathe too deep for fear of what you might be sucking down your throat.

People complain about the noise, but it's not so bad in the spinning room. The belts up above our heads slap and the big roll drives turn and the bobbins spin like a thousand bees buzzing. You get used to it so you almost miss it when you step outside. The world seems too quiet all of a sudden.

The weaving room is the worst. In there you get a pounding sound every time a beam slaps into place. And there are a hundred beams slapping at once and the whole floor shakes and jumps. Most of the people who work in weaving go deaf early on. That's why I say Delia should stay in the spinning room even if she won't make as much money.

You're not supposed to work in the mill until you're fourteen, but visiting is fine. French Johnny likes us kids going in and out all the time. He says, that way we get used to the work.

The only people you worry about are the state inspectors. When French Johnny blows the whistle, all the kids in the mill, even the ones just visiting, know to run as fast as we can so he can hide us in the elevator that carries the cotton between the floors. The inspector always stops in at the front office and **dawdles** around there for a while so us kids have time to hide. Seems to me he don't really want to find us. We skitter across the room like those big cockroaches that come up through the floorboards in the summertime. Our mothers make a wall out of themselves to hide us.

You don't breathe too deep for fear of what you might be sucking down your throat.

It gets hot in that old elevator and the inspector can take hours to look through the mill, top to bottom. A couple of kids fainted last August and French Johnny had to throw cold water on them when he slid open the metal doors.

I didn't feel so good myself, but I didn't say a word.

"You look kind of green," Pierre Gagnon said to me when we filed out.

"Green Grace, green Grace," Felix shouted, and everybody called me that for a while. When nobody was looking, I smacked Felix hard on the top of his head. By the time he turned around I was gone. I've got fast feet, fast hands, and fast fingers.

Now I'm really going to need them.

Analyzing Literature

1. **Respond** Describe the relationship between Grace and the other young workers.

2. **Recall and Interpret** Stories sometimes contain a symbol— an object that stands for something else, often an idea. What do you think the elevator in this story might symbolize?

3. **Evaluate** What conclusions can you draw from the reading about Grace's character? In your opinion, would she be a good friend? Is Grace a conscientious worker? Explain.

Women and Progressives

Essential Question ◄
How did reforms affect the lives of women and other groups in the late 1800s?

Reading Guide

Content Vocabulary
suffragist *(p. 210)*   prohibition *(p. 213)*

Academic Vocabulary
professional *(p. 209)*
intelligence *(p. 209)*

Key People and Events
Jane Addams   *(p. 209)*
Mother Cabrini   *(p. 209)*
Mary Church Terrell   *(p. 210)*
Frances Willard   *(p. 213)*

Reading Strategy
Taking Notes As you read, use a diagram like the one below to describe the two constitutional amendments.

Amendment		Description
Eighteenth		
Nineteenth		

American Diary

Progressive women formed clubs and organizations to socialize and to make a difference in people's lives. Women's leader, Mary Eastman, said: "We must learn sympathy, learn unity, learn the great lesson of organization. . . . This club and other clubs reach out into the new life for women. It is certainly a new life. These clubs have made a new world, and we have got to adapt ourselves to it and to educate the world around us."

—*quoted in* **History of the Woman's Club Movement in America**

By the end of the 1800s, middle-class women had more free time to organize clubs and to socialize.

Women's Roles Change

Main Idea Roles began to change for middle-class women in the late 1800s.

History and You Do you believe women today have unlimited career choices? Read to learn how women's career choices began to expand in the late 1800s.

. . . .

Many leaders of urban reform were women of the middle class. The lives of middle-class women changed during the late 1800s. As people moved from farms to cities, fewer children were needed to help a family survive. As a result, families became smaller. More children spent the day at school, and men worked away from home. Women also gained more free time as technology made housework easier. Because of these factors, women's lives became less centered around maintaining a home.

With more free time, more middle-class women began to pursue higher education. About 40 percent of all college students in 1910 were women.

Educated women were starting professional careers. Most **professional** women, those in occupations requiring special knowledge or education, were teachers, but others worked in nursing, medicine, and other fields. Between 1890 and 1910, the number of women in the workforce increased from 4 million to nearly 7.5 million.

The "New Woman"

These changes created the "new woman." This term was a popular way to refer to educated, modern women who pursued interests outside their homes. For example, **Jane Addams** set up Hull House, a settlement house, in Chicago. She became a pioneer in the emerging field of social work. Working with disadvantaged people gave Addams an outlet for her energy and **intelligence.**

Women became writers, public speakers, fund-raisers, and social or political reformers. Many young women followed the example of talented public figures such as Jane Addams. Others were inspired by the life of **Mother Cabrini,** an Italian nun who came to the United States to work with the poor.

Primary Source / Demonstrating for the Right to Vote

A Parade for Suffrage Women who fought for the right to vote were known as suffragists. Beatrice Forbes-Robertson Hale described a suffrage parade: "A little time ago I found myself in a great American city, where a Woman Suffrage Parade was to be held for the first time. . . . Some large stores had hung out the yellow suffrage flag, and yellow daffodils were being worn by many in the crowd. . . . Presently came the beat of a drum, then the fifes . . . they were here! Line upon line of white-clad figures with yellow badges, short-skirted, booted, and hatted in simple white. . . . Eyes front, earnest faces, marching feet, down the sunshine of the street they came."
—from *What Women Want*

Critical Thinking

Analyzing What types of issues are important to women today?

A Leader of Women Mary Church Terrell was well educated and was eventually appointed to the District of Columbia Board of Education, the first African American to hold such a position in the United States. Terrell also became active in the women's club movement.

"*With courage, born of success achieved in the past . . . we look forward to a future large with promise and hope. Seeking no favors because of our color, nor patronage because of our needs, we knock at the bar of justice, asking an equal chance.*"

In Washington, D.C., Terrell worked to establish kindergarten classes for African American children as well as a nursery for the children of working mothers. ▼

"*Free kindergartens in every city and hamlet of this broad land we must have, if the children are to receive from us what it is our duty to give.*"

▲ Terrell helped found the National Association of Colored Women in 1896. Members focused on education and community work as well as racial issues.

Critical Thinking

Evaluating How do the quotes from Mary Church Terrell show what social issues were important to her?

Women's Clubs

Women found another way to use their talents and energy in women's clubs. The number of women's clubs increased rapidly. At first the clubs focused on cultural activities, such as music and painting. Many clubs, however, became more concerned about social problems.

Some clubs refused to admit African Americans. In response, African American women set up their own network of clubs. Clubs such as the Phyllis Wheatley Club of New Orleans set up classes, recreational activities, and social services. In 1896 women from these clubs formed the National Association of Colored Women. Its founder and first president, **Mary Church Terrell,** was an active leader for women's rights. The association founded homes for orphans, established hospitals, and worked for woman suffrage. It fulfilled its motto "Lifting As We Climb."

✔ **Reading Check** **Identifying** Describe the characteristics of the "new woman" of the late 1800s.

The Fight for Suffrage

Main Idea Women in the United States gained the right to vote in 1920.

History and You Think about how your life might be different if only men were allowed to vote. Read to learn about some suffragists who fought for women's right to vote.

• •

Ratified after the Civil War in 1870, the Fifteenth Amendment gave voting rights to freed men but did not extend them to women. Women were excluded. Some leading abolitionists became **suffragists.** These men and women fought for woman suffrage, or women's right to vote.

Like other reformers, the suffragists formed organizations to promote their cause. Two woman suffrage associations merged in 1890 to form the National American Woman Suffrage Association.

Anna Howard Shaw, a minister and doctor, and Carrie Chapman Catt, an educator and newspaper editor, led the new group.

By 1917, the National American Woman Suffrage Association had more than 2 million members. In a speech to the association in 1902, Catt said:

PRIMARY SOURCE

"The whole aim of the [women's] movement has been to destroy the idea that obedience is necessary to women . . . and to train men to such comprehension of equity [fairness] they would not exact [demand] it."
—quoted in *The American Reader*

Opposition to Woman Suffrage

Groups protested the idea of giving women the vote. Some women, as well as men, supported these groups. They claimed that woman suffrage would upset society's "natural" balance and lead to divorce and neglect of children. As the progressive movement gained momentum, however, many middle-class women concluded that they needed the vote to promote the reforms they favored. Many working-class women also wanted the vote to pass labor laws protecting women. The suffrage movement also gained strength when respected people such as Jane Addams spoke out in support of the vote for women.

As the movement grew, women began lobbying lawmakers, organizing marches, and delivering speeches on street corners. On March 3, 1913, the day before President Woodrow Wilson's inauguration, suffragists marched on Washington, D.C.

The suffragists won their early victories in the West. First as a territory and then as a state, Wyoming led the nation in giving women the vote. Between 1910 and 1913, five other states adopted woman suffrage. By 1919, women could vote in at least some elections in most of the 48 states.

Continuing the Fight

Meanwhile, suffragists continued their struggle to win the vote everywhere. Alice Paul, a Quaker social worker, founded the National Woman's Party in 1916. She sought greater economic and legal equality, as well as suffrage, for women.

In 1917 Alice Paul met with President Woodrow Wilson but failed to win his support for woman suffrage. In response, Paul led women protesters in front of the White House. They were arrested for blocking the sidewalk.

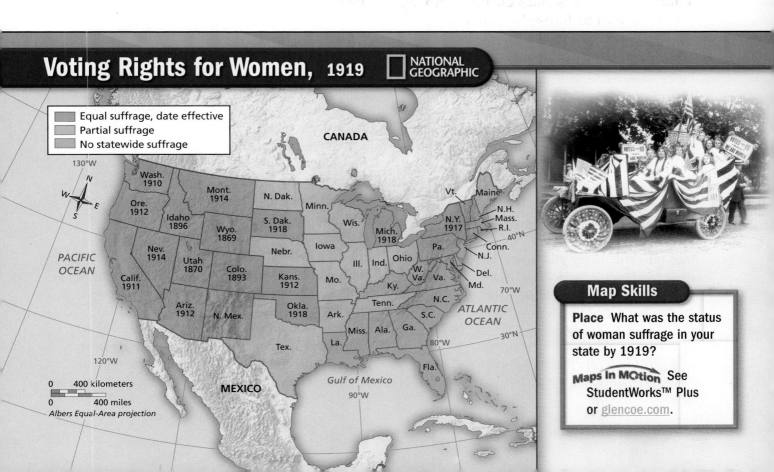

Voting Rights for Women, 1919   NATIONAL GEOGRAPHIC

- Equal suffrage, date effective
- Partial suffrage
- No statewide suffrage

CANADA

130°W

Wash. 1910
Mont. 1914
N. Dak.
Minn.
Ore. 1912
Idaho 1896
Wyo. 1869
S. Dak. 1918
Wis.
Mich. 1918
Vt.
Maine
N.H.
N.Y. 1917
Mass.
R.I.
40°N
Nev. 1914
Utah 1870
Nebr.
Iowa
Ill. Ind. Ohio
Pa.
Conn.
N.J.
PACIFIC OCEAN
Colo. 1893
Kans. 1912
Mo.
W. Va.
Va.
Del.
Md.
70°W
Calif. 1911
Ariz. 1912
N. Mex.
Okla. 1918
Ark.
Ky.
Tenn.
N.C.
S.C.
ATLANTIC OCEAN
Miss. Ala. Ga.
La.
Tex.
30°N
120°W
Fla.
80°W

0   400 kilometers
0   400 miles
Albers Equal-Area projection

MEXICO
Gulf of Mexico
90°W

Map Skills

Place What was the status of woman suffrage in your state by 1919?

Maps In Motion See StudentWorks™ Plus or glencoe.com.

Campaigning Against Alcohol The Woman's Christian Temperance Union (WCTU), founded in 1874, became the largest and most powerful women's organization in the country. To promote temperance, the WCTU used education on the dangers of alcohol.

Frances Willard, president of the WCTU, believed in the motto "Do Everything." She thought all social problems were connected and activists should embrace many social reforms. ▶

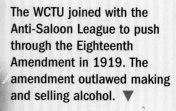

The WCTU joined with the Anti-Saloon League to push through the Eighteenth Amendment in 1919. The amendment outlawed making and selling alcohol. ▼

◀ The WCTU was founded after the successful Women's Crusade of the winter of 1873–1874. During the Crusade, women demonstrated outside saloons, praying and singing hymns.

Critical Thinking

Drawing Conclusions Do you agree with Frances Willard that all social problems are connected? Explain.

After their arrest, the women started a much-publicized hunger strike. Alva Belmont, one of the protesters, proudly said that all the women did was stand there "quietly, peacefully, lawfully, and gloriously."

Women Vote Nationally

By 1917, the national tide was turning in favor of woman suffrage. New York and, a year later, South Dakota and Oklahoma, granted equal suffrage. As more states granted women the right to vote, Congress debated the issue.

In 1918 the House of Representatives passed a woman suffrage amendment. The next year, the Senate also passed the amendment. After three-fourths of the states had ratified it, the Nineteenth Amendment went into effect in 1920. The amendment came in time for women to vote in that year's presidential election. For the first time, American women could take part in the election of their leaders on a national level.

✔ **Reading Check** **Explaining** Why were some groups against giving women the right to vote?

Women and Social Reform

Main Idea Women were active in many social reform efforts to improve the lives of others.

History and You Do you know anyone who has worked hard for a cause? Read to learn how women worked for reforms to help improve life for themselves and others.

During the Progressive Era, women became involved in many reform movements in addition to woman suffrage.

Working for a Better Life

Many middle-class women worked to improve the lives of others. They helped working-class people, immigrants, and society as a whole. The women supported and staffed libraries, schools, and settlement houses. They also raised money for various charities.

Some women worked for other causes. They sponsored laws to regulate the labor of both women and children and to require the regular inspection of workplaces by the government.

Their pressure on Congress helped create the Children's Bureau in the Labor Department. Women also worked for reforms in the food and medicine industries. They pressured state legislatures to provide pensions for widows and for abandoned mothers with children.

Working women also were active in the reform movement. In 1903 the Women's Trade Union League (WTUL) was formed. The WTUL urged working women to form labor unions. It also supported laws to protect the rights of women factory workers. WTUL members raised money to help striking workers pay bail for women who were arrested for striking.

The Temperance Crusade

The crusade against alcohol was led by the Woman's Christian Temperance Union (WCTU), founded in 1874, and the Anti-Saloon League, set up 20 years later. They called for temperance, urging individuals to stop drinking. They also supported **prohibition**—laws that would ban making or selling alcohol.

In 1879 **Frances Willard** became head of the WCTU. Willard educated the public about the dangers of alcohol abuse. The WCTU's goal was prohibition, but it also supported other causes, including prison reform, woman suffrage, improved working conditions, and world peace. Through state WCTU chapters, women combined their role as guardians of the home with social activism.

Carry Nation was a colorful crusader for temperance in the early 1900s. During her protests, she would enter saloons and destroy the bottles and kegs of alcohol there with an ax.

Progressive reformers also wanted to ban alcohol for social reasons. Other Americans opposed alcohol for moral reasons. In response, Congress in 1917 passed a constitutional amendment declaring it illegal to make, transport, or sell alcohol in the United States. The Eighteenth Amendment, known as the Prohibition Law, was ratified in 1919.

✔ Reading Check **Describing** What was the goal of the temperance movement?

History ONLINE
Study Central™ To review this section, go to glencoe.com.

Section 2 Review

Vocabulary

1. Use complete sentences to define the following terms: professional, intelligence, suffragist, prohibition.

Main Ideas

2. Summarizing In what ways did middle-class women's roles change near the end of the 1800s?

3. Explaining Why was 1920 a good year for the passage of the Nineteenth Amendment?

4. Identifying In what ways did reformers try to improve the lives of working women?

Critical Thinking

5. Drawing Conclusions Why was gaining the right to vote important to women?

6. Creative Writing Write a dialogue between a man and a woman before 1920 in which they discuss whether women should be allowed to vote for the president.

7. Sequencing Complete a time line like the one below to show important steps in woman suffrage.

1890	1896	1916	1920

Answer the

8.
How did reforms affect the lives of women and other groups in the late 1800s?

Essential Question ◀

Why were Theodore Roosevelt and William Howard Taft known as progressive presidents?

Reading Guide

Content Vocabulary

trustbuster *(p. 215)*   Square Deal *(p. 216)*

arbitration *(p. 216)*   conservation *(p. 217)*

Academic Vocabulary

inspect *(p. 216)*   primary *(p. 218)*

Key People and Events

Federal Reserve Act *(p. 219)*

Clayton Antitrust Act *(p. 219)*

Reading Strategy

Taking Notes As you read, use a diagram like the one below to identify how the beliefs of Theodore Roosevelt were similar to but different from William Howard Taft's.

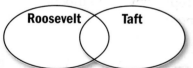

Roosevelt   Taft

American Diary

Progressive reformers wanted to protect America's wilderness and environment. President Theodore Roosevelt was an enthusiastic supporter of their cause. Describing his travels in California in 1903, he wrote: "The first night was clear and we lay down in the darkening aisles of the great sequoia grove. The majestic trunks, beautiful in symmetry [proportion], rose round us like the pillars of a mightier cathedral than ever was conceived."

—quoted in Roosevelt the Explorer

Theodore Roosevelt riding at a western ranch

Theodore Roosevelt

Main Idea Theodore Roosevelt believed that businesses must be regulated.

History and You Are there powerful businesses in your community? Read to learn how big business was regulated when Theodore Roosevelt was president.

. . . .

Theodore Roosevelt won the Republican vice presidential nomination in 1900. Mark Hanna, the Republican leader, called Roosevelt "that cowboy" and warned that only one life would stand between Roosevelt and the White House. When the Republicans won, Hanna told President McKinley, "Now it is up to you to live." Less than one year later, McKinley was assassinated. Suddenly 42-year-old Theodore Roosevelt became president. He was the youngest president in the nation's history. When Roosevelt moved into the White House in 1901, he brought progressive ideas with him.

The "Trustbuster"

President McKinley favored big business. President Roosevelt, in contrast, supported the regulation of business and other progressive reforms. During his term, Roosevelt tackled certain trusts that violated the Sherman Antitrust Act.

His first target was the Northern Securities Company. This railroad monopoly fought the accusations of illegal activity all the way to the Supreme Court. In 1904 the Supreme Court decided that Northern Securities had illegally limited trade. The Court ordered that the trust be taken apart.

During the rest of Roosevelt's term, he obtained indictments, or legal charges, against trusts in the beef, oil, and tobacco industries. Although called a **trustbuster,** Roosevelt did not want to break up all trusts. He thought trusts should be regulated, not destroyed. He grouped trusts into "good" and "bad" ones. Good trusts, he believed, were concerned with public welfare, but bad trusts were not.

Labor Crisis

In 1902 Roosevelt faced a major labor crisis. More than 100,000 Pennsylvania coal miners, members of the United Mine Workers, went on strike. They demanded better pay, an eight-hour workday, and recognition of the union's right to represent its members in discussions with mine owners.

By the Numbers / Protecting America's Wilds

Theodore Roosevelt is said ▶ to have remarked that "birds in the trees and on the beaches were much more beautiful than on women's hats."
—from Theodore Roosevelt: *The Naturalist*

Setting Aside American Lands While he was president, Roosevelt used his authority to create a number of parks, preserves, and monuments to protect birds, wildlife, and millions of acres of American land.

Lands Protected Under Theodore Roosevelt	
4	Federal Game Preserves
5	National Parks
18	National Monuments
51	Federal Bird Preserves
150	National Forests

Critical Thinking

Speculating What might happen if the federal government did not protect natural resources and wildlife?

The mine owners refused to negotiate with the workers. The coal strike dragged on for months. As winter approached, coal supplies dwindled. Public feeling began to turn against the owners. As public pressure mounted, Roosevelt invited representatives of the owners and miners to a meeting at the White House. He was angry when the owners refused to negotiate. Roosevelt threatened to send federal troops to work in the mines and produce the coal. The owners finally agreed to **arbitration**—settling the dispute by agreeing to accept the decision of a neutral outsider. Mine workers won a pay increase and a reduction in hours, but they did not gain recognition for their union.

Roosevelt's action marked a departure from normal patterns of labor relations at the time. Earlier presidents used troops against strikers. In contrast, Roosevelt used the government's power to force the company owners to negotiate. In other labor actions, however, Roosevelt supported employers in disputes with workers.

Square Deal

Roosevelt ran for president in 1904. He promised the people a **Square Deal**—fair and equal treatment for all. He easily won the election with more than 57 percent of the popular vote.

Roosevelt's Square Deal called for the government regulation of business. This attitude toward business differed from the presidency of Thomas Jefferson. That approach was called laissez-faire (LEH•say FEHR). This French term generally means "let people do as they choose." In economics, it refers to an economic policy in which there is little government involvement in the affairs of businesses.

Roosevelt introduced a new era of government regulation. He supported the Meat Inspection Act and the Pure Food and Drug Act. These acts gave the Department of Agriculture and the Food and Drug Administration the power to visit businesses and **inspect,** or carefully examine, the products that were produced there.

LINKING PAST TO PRESENT   Conserving Wild Places

THEN By the mid-1800s, Americans began to view wild places as more than obstacles to overcome or resources to use. The nation began setting aside areas of natural beauty for future generations. President Theodore Roosevelt greatly expanded the system of national parks and forests.

The conservation movement began partly as a response to uncontrolled logging. Roosevelt understood, though, that the nation also needed to use its resources: "Conservation means development as much as it does protection." ▼

"There are no words that can tell the hidden spirit of the wilderness, that can reveal its mystery . . . and its charm."
—Theodore Roosevelt

◀ Visitors enjoying Yosemite National Park, 1920

Conserving the Wilderness

Roosevelt had a lifelong enthusiasm for the great outdoors and the wilderness. He strongly believed in the need for **conservation,** the protection and preservation of the country's natural resources.

As president, Roosevelt took steps to conserve the country's forests, mineral deposits, and water resources. In 1905 he proposed the U.S. Forest Service. He pressured Congress to set aside millions of acres of national forests to create the nation's first wildlife sanctuaries. Roosevelt also formed the National Conservation Commission, which produced the first survey of the country's natural resources.

Roosevelt has been called America's first environmental president. He made conservation an important public issue. Roosevelt, however, also saw the need for economic growth and development. He tried to balance business interests with conservation.

✔ **Reading Check** **Describing** What was Roosevelt's approach to labor relations?

William Howard Taft

Main Idea Conflict between Roosevelt and Taft led to Woodrow Wilson's election as president.

History and You Has a friend ever disappointed you by an action he or she has taken? Read to learn about the conflict between Theodore Roosevelt and William Howard Taft.

· ·

No president had ever served more than two terms. In keeping with that tradition, Roosevelt decided not to run for reelection in 1908. Instead he chose William Howard Taft to run for president. Taft easily defeated Democrat William Jennings Bryan.

Taft lacked Roosevelt's flair. Still, he carried out—and went beyond—many of Roosevelt's policies. The Taft administration won more antitrust cases in four years than Roosevelt won in seven. Taft also favored safety standards for mines and railroads.

Taft supported the Sixteenth Amendment. It allowed Congress to tax citizens' incomes to collect money for the federal government.

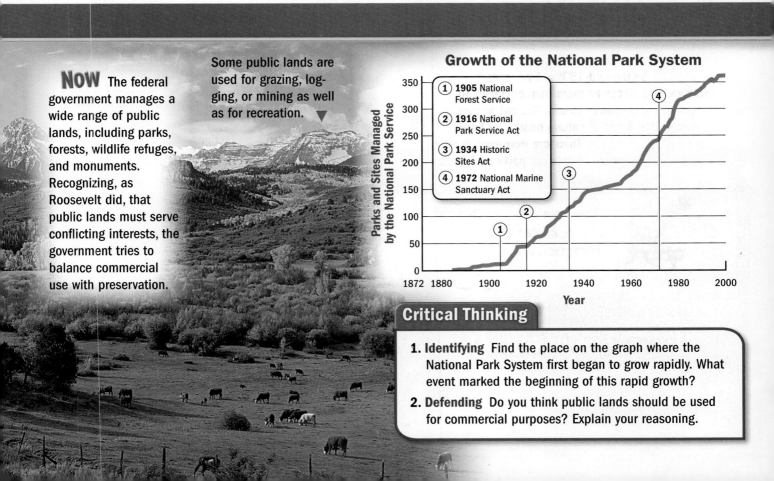

NOW The federal government manages a wide range of public lands, including parks, forests, wildlife refuges, and monuments. Recognizing, as Roosevelt did, that public lands must serve conflicting interests, the government tries to balance commercial use with preservation.

Some public lands are used for grazing, logging, or mining as well as for recreation. ▼

Growth of the National Park System

Parks and Sites Managed by the National Park Service

① 1905 National Forest Service
② 1916 National Park Service Act
③ 1934 Historic Sites Act
④ 1972 National Marine Sanctuary Act

Year

Critical Thinking

1. **Identifying** Find the place on the graph where the National Park System first began to grow rapidly. What event marked the beginning of this rapid growth?

2. **Defending** Do you think public lands should be used for commercial purposes? Explain your reasoning.

Progressives believed income taxes to be fairer and hoped the taxes would allow the government to lower tariffs and relieve the hardship of the poor. The Sixteenth Amendment, added to the Constitution in 1913, did not state how income would be taxed. Congress passed further laws so that higher incomes were taxed at a higher rate than lower incomes.

Taft made progressive reforms. Yet he disappointed many progressives such as Theodore Roosevelt. The two important areas where progressives believed Taft was weak were tariffs and conservation. Taft failed to fight for a lower tariff, and he altered a number of conservation policies so that they favored businesses.

Roosevelt Challenges Taft

By 1912, Roosevelt had become disappointed in Taft. Claiming that Taft "completely twisted around" his own policies, Roosevelt decided to challenge Taft for the Republican presidential nomination.

The showdown between Roosevelt and Taft came at the Republican national convention in Chicago in June. Roosevelt had won every **primary**—an election in which a political party chooses its candidates—and had many supporters. Taft, however, had the backing of party leaders. Taft also had the support of business interests that controlled the party machinery. Taft was nominated on the first ballot.

Roosevelt charged the Republican Party leaders with stealing the nomination from him. He led his supporters out of the convention hall. They formed a new party, the Progressive Party. In August the Progressives held their own convention in Chicago and nominated Roosevelt for president.

A reporter asked Roosevelt about his health. The candidate thumped himself on the chest and declared, "I feel as strong as a bull moose!" From then on, the Progressive Party was known as the Bull Moose Party.

Economics & History

Before the Civil War, the federal government received most of its funds from tariffs, or taxes on imported goods. During the Civil War, the government placed a tax on people's incomes. This type of tax, however, remained controversial for many years.

Federal Income Taxes		
	Earnings	**Tax Rate**
1864	$600-$5,000	5%
	over $10,000	10%
1894	**Earnings**	**Tax Rate**
	all	2%

★ **1872** Federal income tax repealed

★ **1895** Income tax ruled unconstitutional

★ **1862** First federal income tax passed

★ **1894** Everyone required to pay 2% of income

★ **1913** Income tax made permanent

Income taxes today are progressive—rates are based on ability to pay. People who earn more pay a larger percentage of their income in taxes than do people who earn less.

Sources of Funds for the Federal Government Today

Today, income taxes from individuals and businesses are the main source of funds for the federal government.

Retirement and unemployment taxes 36%

Borrowing 1%

Individual income taxes 43%

Other taxes 7%

Business income taxes 13%

Source: Internal Revenue Service

Critical Thinking

Calculating Suppose you earned $1,000 in 1894. How much income tax would you pay? Your friend earned $2,000. How much tax would he or she pay?

The Election of 1912

The split in the Republican Party hurt both Taft and Roosevelt. While Republicans and the Progressive Party battled at the polls, Democrat Woodrow Wilson, a progressive reformer and former governor of New Jersey, gathered enough support to win the election. Wilson received only 42 percent of the popular vote. Roosevelt received 27 percent, and Taft got 23 percent. Wilson, though, won the presidency by the largest electoral majority up to that time. He swept 435 of the 531 electoral votes.

Wilson in the White House

Woodrow Wilson had criticized big government, as well as big business, during his campaign. He called his program the "New Freedom."

In 1913 Wilson achieved a long-held progressive goal—tariff reform. He persuaded the Democrat-controlled Congress to adopt a lower tariff on imports. Wilson believed that foreign competition would force American manufacturers to improve their products and lower their prices. The government income that was lost by lowering tariffs would be replaced by the new income tax.

That same year Congress passed the **Federal Reserve Act** to regulate banking. The act created 12 regional banks supervised by a central board in Washington, D.C. Banks that operated nationally were required to join the Federal Reserve System and follow the rules established by the Reserve's board.

Wilson also worked to strengthen government control over business. In 1914 Congress established the Federal Trade Commission (FTC). The FTC was to investigate corporations for unfair trade practices. Wilson also supported the **Clayton Antitrust Act** of 1914. This act, like the Sherman Antitrust Act, was one of the government's chief weapons used against trusts. The government also tried to regulate child labor. The Keating-Owen Act of 1916 banned goods produced by child labor from being sold in interstate commerce. This legislation, however, was struck down as unconstitutional two years later.

By the end of Wilson's first term, progressive support was declining. Americans turned to world affairs—especially the war that began in Europe in 1914.

Reading Check **Analyzing** How did Roosevelt's run for the presidency affect the election of 1912?

Section 3 Review

History ONLINE
Study Central™ To review this section, go to glencoe.com.

Vocabulary

1. Define the following terms in sentences: trustbuster, arbitration, Square Deal, inspect, conservation, primary.

Main Ideas

2. Identifying Cause and Effect How did President Roosevelt's Square Deal affect American businesses?

3. Discussing On what issues did Roosevelt and Taft disagree by 1912?

Critical Thinking

4. Predicting How do you think Roosevelt might have felt about President Wilson's policies?

5. Organizing Use a diagram like the one below to show the legislation that President Roosevelt supported to further regulation and conservation.

Roosevelt's Square Deal

6. Expository Writing Write a paragraph summarizing the progressive reforms made during Woodrow Wilson's presidency.

7. Answer the **Essential Question** Why were Theodore Roosevelt and William Howard Taft known as progressive presidents?

Section 4 ★ Excluded From Reform

Essential Question ◀

How did minority groups react to discrimination?

Reading Guide

Content Vocabulary
discrimination *(p. 221)*
mutualista *(p. 226)*
barrio *(p. 226)*

Academic Vocabulary
deny *(p. 222)*   bias *(p. 223)*

Key People and Events
Ku Klux Klan *(p. 222)*
Booker T. Washington *(p. 224)*
W.E.B. Du Bois *(p. 224)*

Reading Strategy
Taking Notes As you read, use a diagram like the one below to show how Booker T. Washington and W.E.B. Du Bois differed in their beliefs for achieving equality.

	Beliefs
Booker T. Washington	
W.E.B Du Bois	

American Diary

Many people, such as African Americans, did not enjoy the benefits of progressive reforms. W.E.B. Du Bois spoke forcefully for equality for African Americans: "Freedom . . . we still seek,—the freedom of life and limb, the freedom to work and think, the freedom to love and aspire. Work, culture, liberty,— all these we need, not singly but together, . . . all striving toward that vaster ideal . . . the ideal of human brotherhood. . . ."

—*from* The Souls of Black Folk

Students at the Hampton Institute, Hampton, Virginia, 1899

Prejudice and Discrimination

Main Idea Many members of ethnic and religious minority groups in the United States faced discrimination and even violence.

History and You How would you feel if, after moving to a new land and hoping to start a new life, you were told that you could go only to certain schools or hold certain low-paying jobs? Read to learn about the challenges that some immigrants faced.

. . . .

During the 1800s, the majority of Americans were white Protestants who were born in the United States. Many believed that the United States should remain a white Protestant nation. Nonwhite, non-Protestant, and non-native residents often faced **discrimination.** People who face discrimination receive unequal treatment because of their race, religion, ethnic background, or place of birth. The government rarely addressed discrimination in the late 1880s.

Anti-Catholicism

Some Americans faced discrimination because of their religion. America's largely Protestant population feared that Catholic immigrants threatened the "American" way of life. Anti-Catholic Iowans formed the American Protective Association (APA) in 1887. Its members vowed not to hire or to vote for Catholics.

By the mid-1890s, the APA claimed to have 2 million members across the nation. Among other activities, the APA spread false rumors that Catholics were making plans to take over the country.

Anti-Semitism

Many Jewish immigrants came to the United States to escape discrimination in their homelands but found anti-Semitic, or anti-Jewish, attitudes in America as well. Landlords, employers, and even schools discriminated against Jews.

Eastern European Jews faced even more discrimination because they were Jewish and from eastern Europe. Many Americans regarded eastern Europeans as more "foreign" than western Europeans because their languages, customs, and traditions were so different from those of earlier immigrants.

Primary Source / Pursuing Reforms

Denouncing Discrimination In 1909 the National Negro Committee, a group of whites and African Americans, drafted a statement of opposition to discrimination. The Committee declared:

We denounce the ever-growing oppression of our 10,000,000 colored fellow citizens as the greatest menace that threatens the country. . . . We regard with grave concern the attempt . . . to deny black men the right to work and to enforce this demand by violence and bloodshed.

We demand of Congress and the Executive:

(1.) That the Constitution be strictly enforced and the civil rights guaranteed under the Fourteenth Amendment be secured impartially to all.

(2.) That there be equal educational opportunities for all and in all the States, and that public school expenditure be the same for the Negro and white child.

(3.) That in accordance with the Fifteenth Amendment the right of the Negro to the ballot on the same terms as other citizens be recognized in every part of the country.

Critical Thinking

Speculating How might whites and African Americans working together help end discrimination?

New Immigrants In the late 1800s, the character of immigration changed. Most "new" immigrants who entered the United States after 1880 were from southern and eastern Europe rather than from England, Ireland, and Germany. The new immigrants changed the ethnic makeup of the nation.

Prejudice against Catholic immigrants ▲ is presented in this cartoon, which shows a bishop forcing children to attend a Catholic school, rather than a public school.

◄ Some Americans urged the government to turn back the new wave of immigrants, fearing that the newcomers were criminals or of lower moral character.

Anti-Asian Policies

Discrimination also was based on race. In California and other Western states, Asians faced prejudice and resentment. White Americans claimed that Chinese immigrants, who worked for lower wages, took jobs away from them. Congress passed the Chinese Exclusion Act in 1882 to prevent Chinese immigrants from coming to the United States.

America's westward expansion created opportunities for thousands of Japanese immigrants. Many came to the United States to work on railroads or farms. Like the Chinese before them, Japanese immigrants met with prejudice. California would not allow them to become citizens and made it illegal for them to buy land. Other Western states passed similar laws.

President Theodore Roosevelt yielded to a rising tide of anti-Japanese feeling. He authorized the Gentlemen's Agreement with Japan in 1907. This accord restricted Japanese immigration to the United States, but it did not bring an end to anti-Japanese feeling.

Discrimination Against African Americans

African Americans faced discrimination in the North and the South. Although officially free, African Americans were continually **denied,** or refused, the basic rights held by white citizens.

Four-fifths of the nation's African Americans lived in the South. Most worked as rural sharecroppers or in low-paying jobs in the cities. African Americans were separated from white society. They had their own neighborhoods, schools, parks, restaurants, theaters, and even cemeteries. In 1896 the Supreme Court legalized segregation in the case of *Plessy* v. *Ferguson*. This case recognized "separate but equal" facilities for blacks and whites.

The **Ku Klux Klan,** which terrorized African Americans during Reconstruction, was reborn in Georgia in 1915. The new Klan wanted to restore white, Protestant America. The Klan lashed out against minorities, including Catholics, Jews, and immigrants, as well as African Americans.

Rebirth of the Ku Klux Klan The Ku Klux Klan (KKK) underwent a resurgence in the early 1900s following the release of D.W. Griffith's 1915 movie *The Birth of a Nation*, which presented a romantic vision of the KKK. Following a brief growth spurt, in which membership climbed into the millions, the Klan began to decline in 1924 after a series of scandals involving the group's leadership. Membership shrank and politicians who supported the Klan were voted out of office. The Klan declared bankruptcy and disbanded again in 1944.

Ku Klux Klan march in Washington, D.C. ▲

KKK Membership	
Year	Members
1915	5,000
1920	100,000
1924	4,000,000
1930	30,000

Critical Thinking

Analyzing Why were the late 1800s a time of fear and prejudice in the United States?

Calling for "100 percent Americanism," the number of Klan supporters continued to grow and even spread beyond the South. Many Klan members were from Northern as well as Southern cities and towns.

Racial Violence

Many people lost their jobs during the economic depressions of 1893 and 1907. Frustrated and desperate, they sometimes unleashed their anger against African Americans and other minorities. More than 2,600 African Americans were lynched between 1886 and 1916, mostly in the South. Lynching also was used to terrorize Chinese immigrants in the West.

Progressivism and Prejudice

In the late 1800s and the early 1900s, many Americans held **biased,** or prejudiced, views. They believed that white, male, native-born Americans had the right to make decisions for all of society.

Most of the progressive reformers came from the middle and upper classes. They saw themselves as moral leaders who worked to improve the lives of less fortunate people in their communities and throughout the nation. The reforms they supported, though, often discriminated against one group as they tried to help another group.

Trade unions often did not allow African Americans, women, or immigrants to join. The unions argued that skilled laborers could obtain better working conditions if they did not demand improved conditions for all workers.

Sometimes progressive reforms were really efforts to control a particular group. The temperance movement, for example, was partly an attempt to control the behavior of Irish Catholic immigrants. Civil service reforms required job applicants to be educated. This change reduced the political influence that immigrants, who were largely uneducated, began to achieve in some cities. In spite of their mixed results, though, progressive reforms did improve conditions for many Americans.

✓ **Reading Check** **Identifying** Which Supreme Court decision legalized segregation?

Struggle for Equal Opportunity

Main Idea Minority groups in the United States sought to end discrimination and obtain equal rights.

History and You Have you ever been part of a group that worked for a common cause? Read to find out how some groups fought discrimination.

. . . .

Minorities were often banned from joining progressive organizations because of prejudice. They had to battle for justice and opportunity on their own. African Americans, Native Americans, Mexican Americans, and Jewish Americans took steps to form organizations that would work to improve their lives.

Struggle for Equality

African Americans rose to the challenge of achieving equality. Born enslaved, **Booker T. Washington** taught himself to read. In 1881 he founded the Tuskegee Institute. The school taught African Americans farming and industrial skills.

Washington believed African Americans needed more economic power. With such power, they would be better able to demand social equality and civil rights. Washington founded the National Negro Business League. The League wanted to promote business development among African Americans.

In his autobiography, *Up from Slavery,* Washington advised African Americans to patiently work for equality. He argued that African Americans needed education and skills. These would help African Americans become more valuable members of their community and lead to equality.

W.E.B. Du Bois also worked for civil rights. He was the first African American to receive a doctoral degree from Harvard University. As an educator, Du Bois took a different approach than did Booker T. Washington. Du Bois rejected Washington's emphasis on job skills and argued that the right to vote was the way to end racial inequality, stop lynching, and gain better schools. "The power of the ballot we need in

People IN HISTORY

Booker T. Washington

African American educator and leader

Washington urged African Americans to work hard for economic security before looking for ways to end discrimination and segregation. In one speech, he said that the opportunity to

"earn a dollar in a factory" was worth much more than the opportunity to "spend a dollar in an opera house."

W.E.B. Du Bois

Sociologist and advocate of civil rights for African Americans

Du Bois believed that African Americans should protest their unequal treatment in American society. An African American, he wrote, "simply wishes to . . . be both a Negro and an American, without being cursed and spit upon by his fellows, without having the doors of Opportunity closed roughly in his face."

CRITICAL Thinking

1. **Making Inferences** What did Washington mean when he said the opportunity to earn a dollar was worth more than the opportunity to spend one in an opera house?

2. **Synthesizing** Which leader would be more likely to protest having separate schools for African Americans and whites? Explain your answer.

sheer self-defense," he said, "else what shall save us from a second slavery?" Du Bois helped start the Niagara Movement in 1905. This movement demanded equal economic and educational opportunity for African Americans and insisted on an end to legalized segregation and discrimination.

Although it never gained great support, the Niagara Movement led to the creation of the National Association for the Advancement of Colored People in 1910. This organization was greatly influential in the fight for African American civil rights throughout the twentieth century.

Some African Americans thought that they would be better off in separate societies. These societies could be located either in the United States or in Africa. To achieve this goal, groups were founded to establish African American towns. A back-to-Africa movement began, but its ideas were not popular. The goals of these movements gained few supporters among African Americans.

African American Women Take Action

African American women also formed groups to end discrimination. The National Association of Colored Women fought lynchings and other forms of racial violence. Ida B. Wells was editor of an African American newspaper in Memphis, Tennessee. She was forced to leave town after publishing the names of people involved in a lynching. Wells started a national crusade against the terrible practice of lynching.

In 1895 Wells published a book, *A Red Record*. She showed that lynching was used mainly against African Americans who became prosperous or who had competed with white businesses. "Can you remain silent and inactive when such things are done in your own community and country?" she asked. Although Congress rejected an anti-lynching bill, the number of lynchings declined significantly due in great part to the efforts of Wells and other activists.

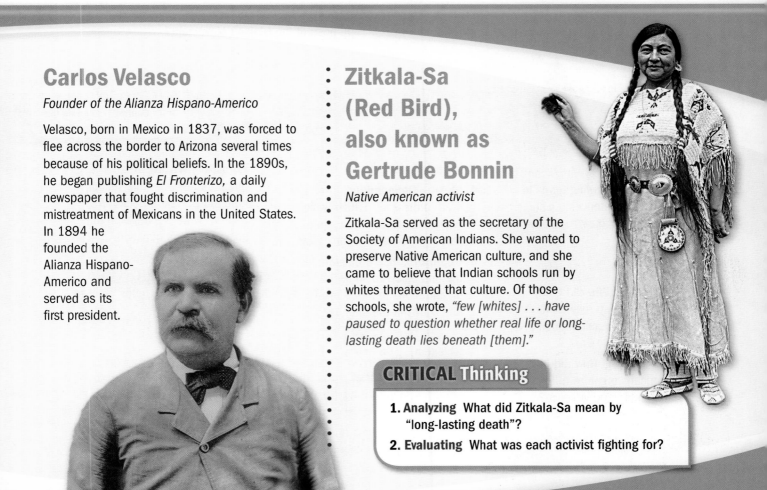

Carlos Velasco

Founder of the Alianza Hispano-Americo

Velasco, born in Mexico in 1837, was forced to flee across the border to Arizona several times because of his political beliefs. In the 1890s, he began publishing *El Fronterizo*, a daily newspaper that fought discrimination and mistreatment of Mexicans in the United States. In 1894 he founded the Alianza Hispano-Americo and served as its first president.

Zitkala-Sa (Red Bird), also known as Gertrude Bonnin

Native American activist

Zitkala-Sa served as the secretary of the Society of American Indians. She wanted to preserve Native American culture, and she came to believe that Indian schools run by whites threatened that culture. Of those schools, she wrote, *"few [whites] . . . have paused to question whether real life or long-lasting death lies beneath [them]."*

CRITICAL Thinking

1. **Analyzing** What did Zitkala-Sa mean by "long-lasting death"?

2. **Evaluating** What was each activist fighting for?

African American Successes

African Americans achieved success in many professions. George Washington Carver, a chemist at Tuskegee Institute, helped improve the South's economy through his research on plant products. Maggie Lena founded the St. Luke Penny Savings Bank in Richmond. She served as America's first woman bank president.

Other Groups

The federal government's efforts to blend Native Americans into white society threatened their traditional cultures. In 1911 Native American leaders formed the Society of American Indians to improve living conditions for Native Americans and to teach white America about native cultures. One society founder, Dr. Carlos Montezuma, revealed government abuses of Native American rights. Montezuma believed that Native Americans should leave the reservations and make their own way in white society.

In the early 1900s, the Mexican American population quickly grew. Many crossed the border to escape conflict and economic woes in Mexico. Like other groups, Mexican Americans faced discrimination and violence.

Mexican Americans often relied on their own efforts. Their **mutualistas**—self-defense groups—provided insurance and legal help. One of the first *mutualistas* was the *Alianza Hispano-Americo* (Hispanic American Alliance). Another, the *Orden Hijos de America* (Order of Sons of America), promoted Mexican American rights. In labor camps and Mexican neighborhoods called **barrios,** *mutualistas* handled issues such as overcrowding and poor public services.

Jewish Americans also faced prejudice during this period. A number of organizations, including the American Jewish Committee and the Anti-Defamation League, formed to fight anti-Semitism and other types of bigotry. Many of these groups continue their work today, addressing injustices both in America and around the world.

Reading Check **Identifying** What was the purpose of the Niagara Movement?

Section 4 Review

Vocabulary

1. Define the following terms in complete sentences: discrimination, deny, bias, *mutualista,* barrio.

Main Ideas

2. **Discussing** Why did many Americans and recent immigrants face discrimination in the Progressive Era?

3. **Summarizing** How did Mexican Americans organize to fight discrimination and violence?

Critical Thinking

4. **Making Connections** If you lived in the early 1900s, which organization would you join to help fight discrimination? Why?

5. **Organizing** Use a diagram like the one below to show the organizations founded by African Americans in the later 1800s.

Booker T. Washington	W.E.B. Du Bois	Maggie Lena

6. **Expository Writing** Read the quotation again in this section from Ida B. Wells's book *A Red Record.* Write a paragraph that answers Wells's question.

Answer the
7. **Essential Question**
How did minority groups react to discrimination?

Chapter 7

Visual Summary

Business and Politics

Target	Reform
Corrupt politics at all levels of government	• City commissioners • Civil Service Commission
More participation in government	• Seventeenth Amendment • Election reform
Trusts and big business	• Sherman Antitrust Act • Theodore Roosevelt's "Square Deal" • Federal Trade Commission • Clayton Antitrust Act
Railroad oligopoly	• Interstate Commerce Act/Commission
Conservation interests	• U.S. Forest Service • National Conservation Commission
High tariffs	• Sixteenth Amendment • "New Freedom" tariff reform
Banking regulation	• Federal Reserve Act

▲ Yosemite National Park

◄ Educator Booker T. Washington

Prohibition agents dump alcohol ►

Gender and Race

Target	Reform
Equal voting rights for women	• Woman suffrage movement • State-by-state voting rights • National Woman's Party • Nineteenth Amendment
Prejudice and discrimination	• Tuskegee Institute • National Negro Business League • Niagara Movement • National Association for the Advancement of Colored People • Society of American Indians • Mexican American *mutualistas*

Society

Target	Reform
Social problems related to alcohol	• Women's Christian Temperance Union • Anti-Saloon League • Eighteenth Amendment
Unsafe food and medicine	• Meat Inspection Act • Pure Food and Drug Act
Difficult working conditions	• Children's Bureau of Labor Department • Women's Trade Union League • Mine/railroad safety standards • Keating-Owen Act

STUDY TO GO Study anywhere, anytime! Download quizzes and flash cards to your PDA from glencoe.com.

STANDARDIZED TEST PRACTICE

TEST-TAKING TIP

Answer the questions you know first and go back to those for which you need more time.

Reviewing Main Ideas

Directions: Choose the best answer for each of the following questions.

1. The Interstate Commerce Act was an attempt to control

   A the spoils system.

   B excessive union activity.

   C railroad oligopoly.

   D the excessive influence of trusts.

2. For which cause was Carry Nation best known as a crusader?

   A labor rights

   B temperance

   C woman suffrage

   D immigration reform

3. Grouping trusts into "good" and "bad" ones was a characteristic of

   A Theodore Roosevelt's first term in office.

   B William Jennings Bryan's 1908 presidential campaign.

   C William Howard Taft's administration.

   D Woodrow Wilson's first term in office.

4. How did W.E.B. Du Bois differ from Booker T. Washington regarding racial discrimination?

   A Du Bois strongly promoted political involvement by African Americans.

   B Du Bois put the responsibility on the individual to gain employable skills.

   C Du Bois called for minorities to use violence against the Ku Klux Klan.

   D Du Bois encouraged *mutualistas* to help African Americans solve problems.

Short-Answer Question

Directions: Base your answer to question 5 on the excerpt below and on your knowledge of social studies.

> That woman's physical structure and the performance of maternal [motherly] functions place her at a disadvantage in the struggle for subsistence is obvious. This is especially true when the burdens of motherhood are upon her. Even when they are not, . . . continuance for a long time on her feet at work, repeating this from day to day, tends to injurious effects upon the body, and as healthy mothers are essential to vigorous offspring, the physical well-being of woman becomes an object of public interest.
>
> —Supreme Court Justice David J. Brewer, *Muller* v. *Oregon*, 1908

5. In this opinion, Justice Brewer upholds a law limiting women's workday to 10 hours. What reasons does Justice Brewer give for not striking down the law? Why might some equal-rights feminists have opposed Brewer's decision?

Review the Essential Questions

6. **Essay** Compare and contrast the role of government with the role of private citizens in the progressive movement.

To help you write your essay, review your answers to the Essential Questions in the section reviews and the chapter Foldables Study Organizer. Your essay should include:

- differences and similarities among progressives, socialists, and muckrakers;
- the role of women in reform;
- the policies and actions of Roosevelt, Taft, and Wilson; and
- attempts of minorities to effect change.

GO ON ▶

History ONLINE

For additional test practice, use **Self-Check Quizzes**—Chapter 7 at glencoe.com.

Document-Based Questions

Directions: Analyze the documents and answer the short-answer questions that follow.

Document 1

In 1916, Theodore Roosevelt stated the following about conservation.

> It is entirely in our power as a nation to preserve large tracts [areas] of wilderness, which are valueless for agricultural purposes and unfit for settlement . . . so that it shall continue to exist for the benefit of all lovers of nature. . . . But this end can only be achieved by wise laws. . . . Lack of such legislation and administration will result in harm to all of us, but most of all in harm to the nature lover who does not possess vast wealth. Already there have sprung up here and there through the country . . . large private preserves.

Source: Theodore Roosevelt, *Outdoor Pastimes of an American Hunter*

7. According to Roosevelt, why should wilderness areas be preserved?

Document 2

George Washington Plunkitt was a powerful state senator in New York. This is what he had to say about the political machine system.

> Have you ever thought what would become of the country if the bosses were put out of business, and their places were taken by a lot of cart-tail orators and college graduates? It would mean chaos. It would be just like takin' a lot of dry-goods clerks and settin' them to run express trains on the New York Central Railroad.

Source: William L. Riordon, *Plunkitt of Tammany Hall*

8. Based on the document, do you think Plunkitt favored or opposed reforms to the political machine system? Explain.

Document 3

This map shows the spread of woman suffrage in the United States from 1890 to 1920.

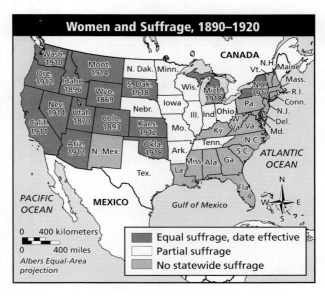

Women and Suffrage, 1890–1920

9. Based on the map, which area was most resistant to woman suffrage?

Document 4

This is an excerpt from *The Jungle,* a novel about the meatpacking industry.

> There would be meat that had tumbled out on the floor, in the dirt and sawdust, where the workers had tramped and spit. . . . There would be meat stored in great piles in rooms; . . . and thousands of rats would race about on it.

Source: Upton Sinclair, *The Jungle*

10. Why do you think *The Jungle* was written?

11. Creative Writing Using the information from the four documents and your knowledge of social studies, write an essay in which you:

- take on the role of a reformer for a cause of your choice; and
- describe the challenges you face and the tactics you will use to succeed.

Need Extra Help?											
If you missed questions . . .	1	2	3	4	5	6	7	8	9	10	11
Go to page . . .	203	213	215	224–225	209–212	200–226	217	201–202	210–212	205	200–226

8

Rise to World Power 1865–1917

When American Commodore Matthew Perry arrived in Tokyo in 1853–54, he presented the Japanese with a miniature steam locomotive.

PRESIDENTS

ANDREW JOHNSON 1865–1869

ULYSSES S. GRANT 1869–1877

RUTHERFORD B. HAYES 1877–1881

JAMES GARFIELD 1881

CHESTER ARTHUR 1881–1885

GROVER CLEVELAND 1885–1889

U.S. Events

World Events

1865

1875

1885

★ **1867** United States purchases Alaska

1867 ★ Japan ends shogun rule

St. Peter's Basilica in Vatican City ▶

★ **1871** Italian law gives pope possession of Vatican

★ **1875** British take control of Suez Canal

★ **1883** Vietnam becomes French protectorate

Section 1: Expanding Horizons

Essential Question Why did the United States extend its influence to other regions in the late 1800s?

Section 2: Imperialism in the Pacific

Essential Question Why did the United States expand its role in the Pacific?

Section 3: Spanish-American War

Essential Question How did the Spanish-American War help the United States become a world power?

Section 4: Latin American Policies

Essential Question How did the beliefs of the U.S. presidents shape Latin American foreign policies?

FOLDABLES Study Organizer

Organizing Information Make this four-tab Foldable to help you learn about how the United States expanded its influence around the world.

Step 1 Fold the sides of three pieces of paper into the middle to make a shutter fold.

Step 2 Cut each flap at the midpoint to form tabs.

Step 3 Label the tabs as shown.

Reading and Writing As you read the chapter, take notes about the role the United States played in each region. Use your Foldable to help you prepare for assessment.

 BENJAMIN HARRISON 1889–1893

 GROVER CLEVELAND 1893–1897

 ★ **1898** Spanish-American War erupts

 WILLIAM McKINLEY 1897–1901

 THEODORE ROOSEVELT 1901–1909

 WILLIAM HOWARD TAFT 1909–1913

 WOODROW WILSON 1913–1921

★ **1916** National Park Service established

1895

1905

1915

★ **1895** José Martí leads revolt in Cuba

 ★ **1900** Boxer uprising in China

★ **1907** Shackleton organizes expedition to Antarctica

 ★ **1911** Qing dynasty overthrown in China

Reading Guide

Content Vocabulary

isolationism *(p. 233)*   imperialism *(p. 234)*
expansionism *(p. 233)*

Academic Vocabulary

communicate *(p. 234)* vision *(p. 234)*

Key People and Events

Matthew Perry *(p. 233)*
William H. Seward *(p. 234)*
Pan-American Union *(p. 235)*

Reading Strategy

Taking Notes As you read, use a diagram like the one below to describe how the United States was able to expand its influence during the age of imperialism.

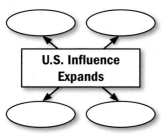

U.S. Influence Expands

American Diary

In 1899 Albert J. Beveridge was elected to the U.S. Senate as a Republican from Indiana. A brilliant speaker, Beveridge praised the new strength of the U.S. Navy and called on the country to expand its influence overseas. In a speech in 1900, Beveridge declared: "The Philippines are ours forever. . . . And just beyond the Philippines are China's [vast] markets. We will not retreat from either. . . . The Pacific is our ocean."

—from "In Support of an American Empire"

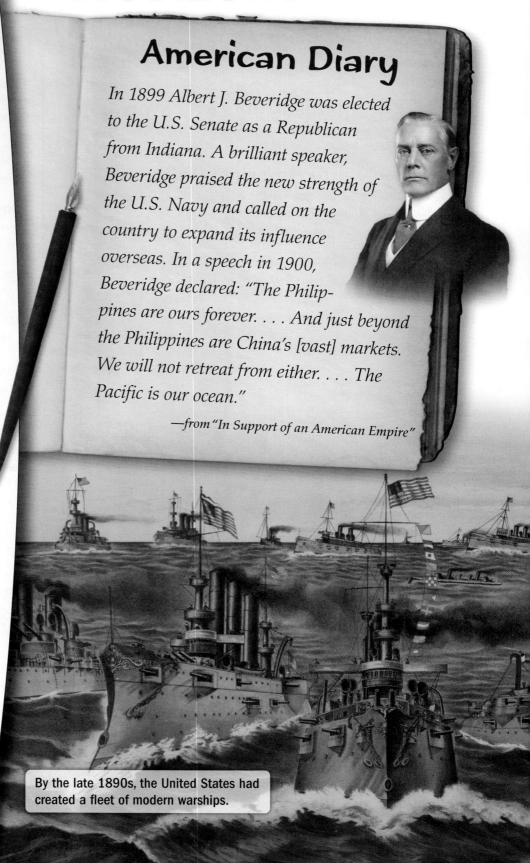

By the late 1890s, the United States had created a fleet of modern warships.

American Foreign Policy

Main Idea The influence of the United States began to extend to other world regions.

History and You How many products do you own that are made in Japan? Read to learn about the beginning of U.S. trade with Japan.

. . . .

Senator Albert Beveridge was not alone in his opinions. Many Americans yearned for an empire abroad. This idea greatly differed from earlier attitudes.

In his Farewell Address, George Washington warned Americans to "steer clear of permanent alliances with any portion of the foreign world." This principle guided American foreign policy for about 100 years. Some people, however, interpreted Washington's words differently. They said he supported a policy of **isolationism,** or non-involvement, in world affairs. Others said Washington supported trade with other countries and not complete isolation from the rest of the world.

Americans expanded their territory by moving west and south. This **expansionism** was a driving force in American history. Most of the land between the Atlantic Coast and the Pacific Coast was settled. The American "frontier" had ended.

Americans then looked beyond the nation's borders to frontiers overseas. American merchants already traded with China, but they also wanted to trade with Japan, which had long been isolated from the West.

In 1853 Commodore **Matthew Perry** traveled to Japan. He steamed into Tokyo Bay with four warships and asked the Japanese to open their ports to U.S. ships. He told them he would return in several months for their answer. When Perry returned in 1854, the Japanese signed the Treaty of Kanagawa. They opened two ports to American ships. Perry's mission marked the start of greater U.S. involvement in Asia.

Reading Check **Making Inferences** What effect do you think Perry's warships had on Japan's decision to trade with the United States?

Primary Source / **Modern Battleships**

A New Navy Moving away from wooden ships powered solely by the wind, the U.S. Navy built steel-hulled ships with steam-powered engines that included sails. One of the U.S. Navy's first armored battleships was the USS *Maine*.

1 **Torpedo tubes** are devices to launch torpedoes.
2 **Steam boilers** power the engines.
3 **Munitions** were stored in the **magazine**.
4 **Cowls** provided fresh air below deck.

Critical Thinking

Interpreting What do you think Senator Beveridge meant when he said "The Pacific is our ocean"?

Expanding Northward In 1867 Secretary of State William Seward negotiated a treaty to buy Alaska from Russia for $7.2 million. Congress approved his Alaska treaty because it eliminated the Russian presence from North America. Though Seward acquired the vast territory for only two cents per acre, many Americans ridiculed the purchase. Critics at the time called Alaska "a large lump of ice" and "Seward's Folly."

District of Alaska

"*I can see no good reason for adopting at this time the treaty with Russia for the purchase of 'Alaska,' a country which . . . we know but little about, and judging from its location, doubtful if any of it will . . . induce persons to settle there under a homestead law; and as to minerals, we have little or no reliable information.*"

—George Miller,
speech in the House of Representatives, July 14, 1868

◄ Seward and the president's Cabinet discussing the Alaska purchase

A gold miner in Alaska ►

Critical Thinking

Identifying Points of View Why did some Americans oppose the purchase of Alaska?

An Age of Imperialism

Main Idea The United States expanded its territory when it bought Alaska and extended its influence in Latin America.

History and You Think about what you have seen on TV and read about Alaska. Read to learn about how Alaska became a territory of the United States.

Other Western nations, in addition to the United States, also began to expand their trade and influence in Asia and other parts of the world. The late 1800s and the early 1900s were called an age of **imperialism.** During this time, powerful European nations created large empires by gaining economic and political control over weaker nations.

The search for materials and markets drove imperialism. The industrial nations of Europe needed raw materials and new markets for the goods they manufactured. This led to competition among European powers for influence in Asia and Africa.

Toward an Empire

After the Civil War, some Americans wanted the nation to build an empire. By annexing new lands, they argued, the United States would join the ranks of the world's great powers. Their country could take its rightful place at the center of power.

Secretary of State **William H. Seward,** appointed by Abraham Lincoln, supported this view. Seward pictured an American empire dominating the Caribbean, Central America, and the Pacific. This vast empire would be connected by a canal across Central America linking the Atlantic and Pacific Oceans, a transcontinental railroad system, and the telegraph, which would provide rapid **communication.**

The Purchase of Alaska

In 1867 Seward moved closer to making his **vision,** or imagined plan, a reality when he bought Alaska from Russia for $7.2 million. It was a great bargain for a territory twice the size of Texas.

Many people ridiculed Seward's actions. They mocked the purchase as "Seward's Ice Box" and a "polar bear garden." Alaska was viewed as an icy, barren place. However, after gold was discovered there in the 1890s, Seward's "folly" seemed like a wise purchase. In 1912 Alaska became a territory of the United States.

A Sense of Mission

Some Americans had another reason for favoring imperialism. They believed they could "lift up" the world's "uncivilized" people by sharing Christianity and Western civilization. Josiah Strong, a Congregational minister, proposed an "imperialism of righteousness." He thought Americans should bring their religion and culture to Africa, Asia, and Latin America.

American Interest in Latin America

The United States had a flourishing trade with Latin America. Taking advantage of the Monroe Doctrine, American merchants wanted to further extend U.S. economic influence in the region. In 1884 James G. Blaine, then the Republican nominee for president, declared that the United States should "improve and expand its trade with the nations of America."

As secretary of state in 1889, Blaine invited Latin American leaders to attend a Pan-American Conference in Washington, D.C. Blaine hoped to develop closer ties among the Latin American nations. The conference led to the **Pan-American Union,** which promoted cooperation among member nations.

Building Sea Power

As the United States expanded its influence overseas, Captain Alfred Thayer Mahan, president of the Naval War College, wanted to improve the navy. "Sea power," Mahan said, "is essential to the greatness of every splendid people." The United States would be able to use its colonies as bases to refuel its ships.

During the 1880s, the U.S. Navy shifted from sails to steam power and from wooden to steel hulls. By the early 1900s, the United States had the naval power needed to support its expanded role in foreign affairs.

Reading Check **Explaining** What factors led to imperialism?

Section 1 Review

Vocabulary

1. Define each of the following terms in a sentence: isolationism, expansionism, imperialism, communication, vision.

Main Ideas

2. Discussing Why did the U.S. begin to expand overseas?

3. Summarizing Summarize why many Americans favored imperialism in the late 1800s and early 1900s.

Critical Thinking

4. Predicting Do you think George Washington would support the Pan-American Union? Why or why not?

5. Determining Cause and Effect Use a diagram like the one below to discuss the causes and effects of the Treaty of Kanagawa.

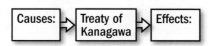

Causes: → Treaty of Kanagawa → Effects:

6. Persuasive Writing You are William H. Seward, and you have just read a newspaper article criticizing your purchase of Alaska. Write a letter to the paper defending your purchase.

Answer the Essential Question

7. Why did the United States extend its influence to other regions in the late 1800s?

History ONLINE
Study Central™ To review this section, go to glencoe.com.

Imperialism in the Pacific

Essential Question ◄

Why did the United States expand its role in the Pacific?

Reading Guide

Content Vocabulary
provisional government *(p. 238)*
spheres of influence *(p. 240)*

Academic Vocabulary
consult *(p. 239)*   exploit *(p. 240)*

Key People and Events
Liliuokalani *(p. 238)*
John Hay *(p. 240)*
Open Door policy *(p. 240)*
Russo-Japanese War *(p. 241)*
Treaty of Portsmouth *(p. 241)*

Reading Strategy
Taking Notes As you read, use a diagram like the one below to explain why these events strained relations between Japan and the United States.

| Treaty of Portsmouth | → | |
| 1906 San Francisco Board of Education Policy | → | |

American Diary

On a trip to England in 1887, Hawaii's Princess Liliuokalani heard about a "revolutionary movement, [begun] by those of . . . American birth" in her Pacific island homeland. The royal party set out by ship for Honolulu, Hawaii's capital. Later, the princess wrote: "As our vessel was entering the harbor . . . we knew, although no word was spoken, the changes which had . . . been forced upon the king. We were received by the members of the new [council] of the king . . . all men of foreign birth."

—from Hawaii's Story

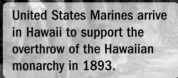

United States Marines arrive in Hawaii to support the overthrow of the Hawaiian monarchy in 1893.

Hawaii

Main Idea The United States strengthened its foothold in the Pacific by annexing Hawaii and part of Samoa.

History and You Has anyone ever taken something that belonged to you without your approval? Read to learn why the Hawaiians resisted American influence in their country.

· ·

Princess Liliuokalani (lih•LEE•uh•woh•kuh•LAH•nee) realized that time was running out for her people. American planters and businesspeople were tightening their control of Hawaii and threatening the much-loved monarchy.

Since the mid-1800s, many Americans had wanted to build an American trading empire in the Pacific. In 1867 Secretary of State William H. Seward acquired the Pacific islands of Midway. These islands were more than 3,000 miles (4,800 km) west of California. They would serve as an important stopping place for American ships en route to China. American merchants and the U.S. Navy, however, needed more than two islands to establish a firm foothold in the vast stretches of the Pacific.

The Hawaiian Islands

The Hawaiian Islands, a chain of eight large and about 100 smaller islands, lay about 2,000 miles (3,200 km) west of California. The Hawaiian people in the 1800s lived in independent communities, each with its own chieftain. The people depended on the lush environment for farming and fishing. American trading ships and whalers often stopped at the islands for supplies and water.

In the 1790s, Americans and Hawaiians began to trade with each other. About that same time, King Kamehameha I began to unify the islands. Because they had good ports, the villages of Honolulu and Lahaina (luh•HY•nuh) grew in importance. Trade continued to flourish.

American and European ships also brought infectious diseases to the islands. These diseases devastated the island population just as they had once devastated the Native Americans.

Primary Source / The Republic of Hawaii

Taking Control of the Islands On January 17, 1893, a group of American businesspeople overthrew Hawaii's monarchy. A temporary government was then set up that would "exist until terms of union with the United States . . . have been . . . agreed upon." Sanford B. Dole, an elderly judge, became its leader. U.S. president Grover Cleveland opposed the takeover. Dole, however, refused to hand power back to the Hawaiian queen, saying, "We do not recognize the right of the President of the United States to interfere in our domestic affairs." On July 4, 1894, Hawaii officially became an independent republic, with Dole as president.

—from *History of Later Years of the Hawaiian Monarchy and the Revolution of 1893*

▲ Sanford B. Dole

Critical Thinking

Explaining Why do you think Hawaii is important to the United States today?

Liliuokalani

Queen of Hawaii

After she was removed from power in 1893, Queen Liliuokalani continued her fight to take back the throne. She headed the Oni pa'a ("Stand Firm") movement, whose motto was "Hawaii for the Hawaiians." She appealed to the U.S. government to "do justice in this matter and to restore to me this property." In this 1898 letter to the U.S. House of Representatives, she wrote, *"I, Liliuokalani of Hawaii . . . do hereby earnestly and respectfully protest against the assertion [declaration] of ownership by the United States of America of the so-called Hawaiian Crown Islands. . . . I especially protest against such . . . taking of property without due process of law."*

CRITICAL Thinking

1. **Explaining** How did Liliuokalani fight the overthrow of the Hawaiian government?

2. **Evaluating** What did Liliuokalani mean when she wrote that she especially protested the taking of Hawaii without "due process of law"?

Missionaries and Sugar Growers

In 1820 Christian missionaries from the United States arrived in Hawaii. They established schools, created a written Hawaiian alphabet, and translated the Bible into Hawaiian. Many American merchants in the whaling trade also came to settle in the Hawaiian Islands.

An American firm introduced sugarcane in Hawaii in the 1830s. The missionaries and traders began buying land and establishing sugar plantations. The United States agreed not to impose tariffs on Hawaiian sugar. The sugar industry grew quickly, and American planters reaped huge profits. Gradually the Americans took control of most of the land and businesses. They also served as advisers to the Hawaiian ruling family. The United States recognized Hawaiian independence in 1842, but American influence remained strong.

Then, in the early 1890s, Congress began imposing tariffs on Hawaiian sugar. As a result, sugar exports to the United States dropped sharply. Facing ruin, the sugar planters plotted a way to avoid the new tariff. They argued that because the United States already had a naval base at Pearl Harbor, Hawaii could be made a territory of the United States.

American Planters' Revolt

The Hawaiians, meanwhile, had begun to resist the growing influence of the Americans. In 1891 the new ruler, Queen **Liliuokalani,** came to the throne. Wanting Hawaiians to regain economic control of their islands, she took away the powers of the American sugar planters. In response, the white planters overthrew Liliuokalani and set up their own **provisional government,** or temporary government, in 1893. The queen yielded:

PRIMARY SOURCE

"Now, to avoid any collision of armed forces, and perhaps the loss of life, I . . . yield my authority."
—Queen Liliuokalani

Annexation

The success of the planters' revolt was due in part to the support of John Stevens. Stevens was the chief American diplomat in Hawaii. He arranged for marines from the warship *Boston* to assist in the revolt. Stevens immediately recognized the new government. A delegation was sent to Washington to seek a treaty that would annex, or add, Hawaii to the United States. President Benjamin Harrison signed the treaty and sent it to the Senate for approval.

The Senate, however, did not ratify the treaty before President Harrison left office. The new president, Grover Cleveland, opposed annexation and withdrew the treaty from the Senate when he found out that Hawaiians did not support the revolt. Cleveland called American interference in the Hawaiian revolution "disgraceful."

Most Hawaiians opposed annexation, but a small, powerful group of sugar growers, traders, and missionaries, along with their allies and leaders in the United States, supported it. After William McKinley became president, Congress approved the annexation of Hawaii, and in 1900 it became a territory of the United States.

The Islands of Samoa

About 3,000 miles (4,800 km) south of Hawaii lay the Samoa Islands. Samoa allowed the Americans to build a naval station at Pago Pago. Samoa also granted special trading rights to the United States. Because Great Britain and Germany secured trading rights in the islands, tensions grew as the three powers competed for power in Samoa.

In 1899 the United States, Great Britain, and Germany met in Berlin. Without **consulting**— seeking an opinion from—the Samoans, the United States and Germany split Samoa, and the United States quickly annexed its portion. Great Britain withdrew from the area in return for rights to other Pacific islands.

✔ **Reading Check** **Explaining** Why did the planters want Hawaii as a U.S. territory?

United States Overseas Possessions, 1900 ▪ NATIONAL GEOGRAPHIC

0   2,000 kilometers
0   2,000 miles
Miller projection

- U.S. possessions with date acquired
- • Ports open to U.S. trade

RUSSIA

Alaska 1867

CANADA

Aleutian Islands 1867

NORTH AMERICA

ASIA

UNITED STATES

40°N

CHINA   JAPAN   PACIFIC OCEAN

ATLANTIC OCEAN

Shanghai •   • Nagasaki

Midway Islands 1867

Canton •

TROPIC OF CANCER

Puerto Rico 1898

Philippine Islands 1898   Wake Island 1899   Johnston Island 1858   Hawaiian Islands 1898   MEXICO

Guam 1898

Kingman Reef 1858

Howland Island 1857   Palmyra Island 1898

EQUATOR   0°

Baker Island 1857   Jarvis Island 1857

SOUTH AMERICA

American Samoa 1899

100°W

N W E S

AUSTRALIA

TROPIC OF CAPRICORN

Map Skills

Place When were the Hawaiian Islands acquired?

100°E   180°   140°W

Extending Influence At the turn of the century, the United States used diplomatic and military tactics to protect its economic interests in Asia. Maintaining access to the vast Chinese market was a major American foreign policy goal.

▼ American troops fighting in Peking during the Boxer Rebellion.

"The policy of the Government of the United States is to seek a solution which may bring about permanent safety and peace to China, preserve Chinese territorial and administrative entity [existence], protect all rights to friendly powers by treaty and international law, and safeguard for the world . . . trade with all parts of the Chinese Empire."

—John Hay

America's "Great White Fleet" helped convince Japan to reaffirm the Open Door policy in China and to maintain the status quo in the Pacific.

Critical Thinking

Making Inferences Based on the quote from John Hay, what were the United States's intentions in China?

China and the Open Door

Main Idea The Open Door policy protected and expanded U.S. trading interests in China.

History and You Do you remember reading about a trade agreement with Japan in the 1850s? Read to learn about trade between the U.S. and China.

• •

Pacific island territories were stepping-stones to a larger prize—China. Weakened by war, China also lacked industry. It could not resist the efforts of foreign powers that wanted to **exploit,** or make use of, its vast resources and markets.

Rivalries in China

By the late 1890s, Japan and European powers had carved out **spheres of influence** in China. These were sections of the country where each of the foreign nations enjoyed special rights and powers. Japan, Germany, Great Britain, France, and Russia all had spheres of influence in China.

An Open Door to China

Some U.S. government and business leaders worried about being left out of the profitable China trade. To protect and expand American trading interests, Secretary of State **John Hay** proposed an **Open Door policy.** It gave each foreign nation in China rights to trade freely in the other nations' spheres of influence. The other powers hesitated to accept the policy.

The Boxer Rebellion

In 1899 a secret Chinese society, the Boxers, revolted against the "foreign devils" in China, and many foreigners died. The next year, foreign troops defeated the Boxers.

The Boxer Rebellion led to a second Open Door proposal. This version stressed the importance of maintaining China's independence and respecting its borders. Alarmed by the revolt, the other foreign powers accepted Hay's policy.

Reading Check **Analyzing** Explain the purpose of the Open Door policy.

Japan

Main Idea The relations between Japan and the United States were strained in the early 1900s.

History and You Have you ever tried to help two friends agree on an issue? Read to learn how the United States helped settle the Russo-Japanese War.

Eager to expand its power in Asia, Japan began to ignore the Open Door policy. Japan's actions led to war with Russia and conflict with the United States.

In the early 1900s, Japan and Russia clashed over Manchuria, a Chinese province rich in natural resources. On February 8, 1904, Japan attacked the Russian fleet in Manchuria, starting the **Russo-Japanese War.** By the spring of 1905, both Japan's and Russia's resources were nearly exhausted. Both countries were eager to make peace.

Treaty of Portsmouth

President Theodore Roosevelt met with the Russian and Japanese leaders in Portsmouth, New Hampshire, to help settle the conflict. In September 1905, Japan and Russia signed the **Treaty of Portsmouth.** This recognized Japan's control of Korea in return for Japan's pledge to halt expansion. Roosevelt hoped the treaty would preserve a balance of power in Asia, but it failed. Japan became the strongest naval power in the Pacific and challenged the United States in the region.

Strained Relations

Many people in Japan immigrated to the United States during the Russo-Japanese War and settled in California. In 1906 the San Francisco Board of Education ordered all Asian students to attend separate schools. The Japanese government protested. President Roosevelt forced the school board to change its policies. In return, Japan promised to restrict emigration. The Japanese, however, resented the agreement, and relations between Japan and the United States worsened. Some Americans called for war.

President Roosevelt had no plan for war. He sent 16 gleaming white battleships on a cruise around the world. The "Great White Fleet" greatly impressed the Japanese. By 1909, the United States and Japan resolved many of their differences.

✔ **Reading Check** **Describing** What role did the U.S. play in the end of the Russo-Japanese War?

Section 2 Review

History ONLINE
Study Central™ To review this section, go to glencoe.com.

Vocabulary

1. Define each of the following terms in a sentence: provisional government, consult, exploit, spheres of influence.

Main Ideas

2. **Explaining** How did planters and missionaries become powerful in Hawaii?

3. **Identifying Cause and Effect** Explain the effect of the Boxer Rebellion on foreign powers in China.

4. **Making Inferences** Why did Japan want control of Manchuria?

Critical Thinking

5. **Organizing** Draw a diagram like the one below. In each oval, describe the relationship between the United States and the location listed.

6. **Persuasive Writing** Write a speech that Theodore Roosevelt might have delivered to the San Francisco Board of Education to convince it to reverse its decision of sending Asian students to different schools.

Answer the
7. **Essential Question**
Why did the United States expand its role in the Pacific?

Essential Question

How did the Spanish-American War help the United States become a world power?

Reading Guide

Content Vocabulary

yellow journalism (p. 244)

protectorate (p. 246)

armistice (p. 245)

territory (p. 246)

Academic Vocabulary

trigger (p. 244)

eventual (p. 247)

Key People and Events

Rough Riders (p. 245)

Battle of San Juan Hill (p. 245)

Platt Amendment (p. 246)

Reading Strategy

Taking Notes As you read, use a diagram like the one below to identify the lands that the United States acquired after the Spanish-American War.

Land Acquired

American Diary

Soldiers of the Ninth and Tenth Cavalry made the charge up San Juan Hill. In the face of enemy fire, Colonel Theodore Roosevelt on horseback encouraged his Rough Riders forward. He later recalled: "Some forty yards from the top [of the hill] I . . . jumped off [the horse]. . . . As I ran up to the hill, [my orderly] stopped to shoot, and two Spaniards fell. . . . Almost immediately afterward the hill was covered by the troops, both Rough Riders and the [African American] troopers of the Ninth [Cavalry]."

—*from* The Rough Riders

American artist Frederic Remington painted the Rough Riders' charge up San Juan Hill.

"A Splendid Little War"

Main Idea Events in Cuba led to war between the United States and Spain in 1898.

History and You Why do countries go to war? Read to learn why the United States declared war on Spain.

The charge of the Rough Riders took place in Cuba, a Caribbean island about 90 miles (145 km) from American shores. The Cubans had lived under Spanish rule for centuries. They rebelled several times in the late 1800s. Each time, however, the Spanish overpowered them and shattered their dreams of independence.

José Martí was one hero of the Cuban independence movement. He fled to the United States to gather money, arms, and troops. In 1895 Martí returned to Cuba to lead his people in a new revolt.

Martí's revolution led to huge losses in human life and property. The rebels burned sugarcane fields and destroyed buildings in hopes of forcing the Spanish to leave. In response, Spanish troops herded Cuban people into camps to separate them from the rebels and to destroy their morale. Thousands of Cubans died of starvation and disease in the conflict.

War Fever

The Cuban people's struggle caused great concern in the United States. Businesspeople worried about the loss of their investments and trade in Cuba. Government leaders were concerned about a rebellion taking place so close to the United States. Many Americans were horrified by the violence against Cuban citizens, and they called for the U.S. government to do something about it.

President Grover Cleveland opposed any American involvement in Cuba. In March 1897, William McKinley became president. He, too, hoped for a peaceful settlement.

The American press reported the tragedy in Cuba in graphic detail. Coverage fueled the debate over America's role in the crisis. Newspapers, including Joseph Pulitzer's *World* and William Randolph Hearst's *Journal*, tried to outdo one another. They printed shocking reports about the revolution.

Hearst, it is said, told an artist who was illustrating a news story on Cuba, "You furnish the pictures, and I'll furnish the war."

Primary Source / Sheet Music

Rallying Support During the 1890s, popular music was sold primarily as sheet music. Friends and families gathered around pianos in homes and sang to the latest music. The Spanish-American War was a popular theme in much of this sheet music. Many songwriters wrote patriotic marches and stirring songs to rally American support for the war. War heroes were celebrated in musical numbers, such as "The Charge of the Rough Riders." Patriotic music not only provided entertainment, it also shaped people's attitudes about the war.

Critical Thinking

Making Connections Do you think popular music shapes people's attitudes about major events today? Explain.

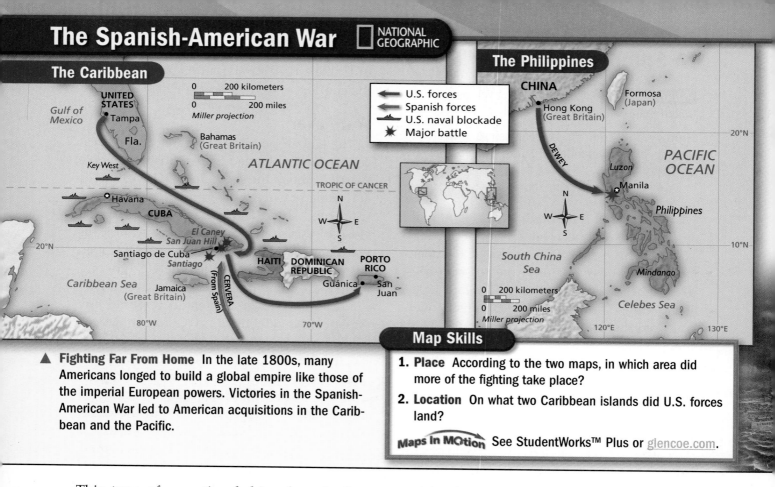

The Spanish-American War · NATIONAL GEOGRAPHIC

The Caribbean

200 kilometers
200 miles
Miller projection

UNITED STATES
Gulf of Mexico
Tampa
Fla.
Key West
Bahamas (Great Britain)
ATLANTIC OCEAN
TROPIC OF CANCER
Havana
CUBA
El Caney
San Juan Hill
Santiago de Cuba
Santiago
Caribbean Sea
Jamaica (Great Britain)
CERVERA (From Spain)
HAITI
DOMINICAN REPUBLIC
Guánica
PORTO RICO
San Juan
80°W
70°W
20°N

→ U.S. forces
← Spanish forces
⚓ U.S. naval blockade
✶ Major battle

The Philippines

CHINA
Hong Kong (Great Britain)
DEWEY
Formosa (Japan)
PACIFIC OCEAN
Luzon
Manila
Philippines
South China Sea
Mindanao
Celebes Sea
20°N
10°N
120°E
130°E
200 kilometers
200 miles
Miller projection

Map Skills

▲ **Fighting Far From Home** In the late 1800s, many Americans longed to build a global empire like those of the imperial European powers. Victories in the Spanish-American War led to American acquisitions in the Caribbean and the Pacific.

1. **Place** According to the two maps, in which area did more of the fighting take place?
2. **Location** On what two Caribbean islands did U.S. forces land?

Maps In MOtion See StudentWorks™ Plus or glencoe.com.

This type of sensational, biased, and often false reporting is called **yellow journalism.** It played a major role in the formation of pro-war opinion in the United States.

"Remember the *Maine*"

The pressure on President McKinley to take action seemed to grow by the hour. Rioting broke out in the Cuban capital of Havana in January 1898. McKinley responded by sending the battleship *Maine* to Havana to protect American citizens and property.

The ship remained quietly at anchor in Havana Harbor for three weeks. Then, on the night of February 15, 1898, a huge explosion shattered the *Maine,* killing 260 officers and crew members. American newspapers immediately blamed the Spanish. Spain denied responsibility for the explosion. Much later, evidence indicated that the explosion may have been accidental. At the time, however, Americans wanted war with Spain. The slogan "Remember the *Maine*" became a rallying cry for revenge.

After the *Maine* incident, President McKinley sent the Spanish a strong note. He demanded a truce and an end to brutality against the Cubans. The Spanish agreed to some American demands, but not enough to satisfy McKinley or Congress. On April 19 Congress recognized Cuban independence and it also demanded the withdrawal of Spanish forces from the island. McKinley was authorized to use the army and navy to enforce American aims. On April 25, 1898, Congress declared war on Spain.

War in the Philippines

Events in Cuba **triggered,** or started, the Spanish-American War. The war's first military actions, however, occurred thousands of miles away in the Spanish colony of the Philippines. These islands served as a base for part of the Spanish fleet.

In late February 1898, Assistant Secretary of the Navy Theodore Roosevelt had wired Commodore George Dewey to prepare for possible military action in the Philippines.

Articles and cartoons in American "yellow" newspapers highlighted Spanish atrocities in Cuba. Many Americans wanted to rescue Cuba from the "villainous" Spanish. ▶

▼ The U.S. battleship *Maine* blew up in Havana Harbor on February 15, 1898. The cause of the explosion was a mystery—the Spanish had little motive to destroy a U.S. ship, but Cuban rebels had much to gain by increasing hostilities between the United States and Spain.

In the early morning hours of May 1, Dewey launched a surprise attack on the Spanish fleet in Manila Bay. Dewey destroyed most of the Spanish ships.

American troops arrived in July, and Filipino rebels, led by Emilio Aguinaldo (AH•gee•NAHL•doh), helped the Americans capture the city of Manila. Using American weapons, the rebels then took the main island of Luzon and declared independence. They expected American support, but the United States debated what to do with the islands.

Fighting in Cuba

Meanwhile in the Caribbean, a Spanish fleet entered the harbor of Santiago in Cuba on May 19. American ships soon blockaded the coast, trapping the Spanish in the harbor.

About 17,000 American troops—nearly a quarter of them African American—then came ashore while forces under Cuban general Calixto García drove off the Spanish soldiers. As the Cuban and American forces advanced, heavy fighting followed.

History ONLINE
Student Web Activity Visit glencoe.com and complete the Chapter 8 Web Activity about the Rough Riders.

The Rough Riders

Theodore Roosevelt resigned his position as assistant secretary of the navy to join the fighting in Cuba. He led the First Regiment of U.S. Cavalry Volunteers. The regiment was an assorted group of former cowhands and college students, popularly known as the **Rough Riders.** On July 1, the Rough Riders, with African American soldiers of the Ninth and Tenth Cavalries, joined the **Battle of San Juan Hill.** "I waved my hat and we went up the hill with a rush," Roosevelt wrote later.

The Americans captured San Juan Hill after intense fighting. Two days later the Spanish fleet attempted to break out of the Santiago harbor. In a battle that lasted about four hours, the Spanish fleet was destroyed, ending Spanish resistance in Cuba.

The United States then turned to the Spanish colony of Puerto Rico. American troops landed on Puerto Rico in late July and quickly took control of the island. On August 12, the Spanish signed an **armistice,** or peace agreement, and the war ended.

Losses in the War

Secretary of State John Hay called the Spanish-American War "a splendid little war." The war lasted fewer than four months. About 400 Americans were killed in battle or died from wounds received in the fighting.

Yet the war had other aspects that were not at all "splendid." More than 2,000 Americans died of yellow fever, malaria, and other diseases found in the tropical climate. The African Americans who served during this war faced the additional burden of discrimination. They were placed in segregated units, but they fought alongside the Cuban rebel army, in which African American and white troops fought as equals.

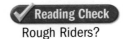 **Reading Check** **Identifying** Who were the Rough Riders?

Uncle Sam's menu includes "Cuba Steak," "Porto Rico Pig," "the Philippine Floating Islands," and "the Sandwich Islands."

1. **Interpreting** What does Uncle Sam's menu represent?

2. **Analyzing** Does the cartoon depict President McKinley as an imperialist or as an anti-imperialist? How do you know?

A. Uncle Sam (United States)
B. President William McKinley   C. Menu

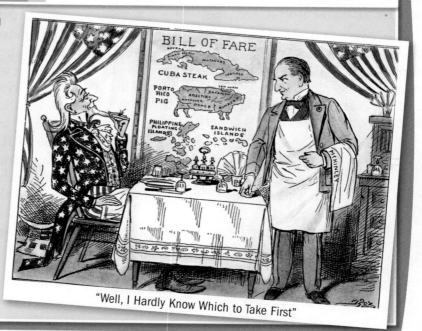

"Well, I Hardly Know Which to Take First"

Acquisitions

Main Idea The American empire became a reality after the Spanish-American War.

History and You Think about what it means to be independent. Read to learn how Cuba was ruled after the Spanish-American War.

· ·

The United States and Spain signed the Treaty of Paris on December 10, 1898, ending the war. The treaty dissolved most of the Spanish Empire.

Cuba became an American **protectorate.** A protectorate is technically an independent country, but it is under the control of another country. Puerto Rico and Guam became **territories** of the United States. A territory is an area that is completely controlled by another country. Spain also surrendered the Philippines to the United States in exchange for $20 million. The American empire became a reality despite criticism that it was contrary to the democratic values on which the country was based.

Cuban Protectorate

Americans debated what to do about Cuba. Finally, in 1901 the United States granted Cubans full independence, but only if their new constitution included clauses giving the United States certain rights. Known as the **Platt Amendment,** these conditions prohibited Cuba from making treaties with other nations. They gave the United States control of a naval base at Guantanamo Bay. The United States also could intervene in Cuban affairs if the country's independence was threatened.

New Government for Puerto Rico

After the war, Puerto Rico remained under direct military rule. In 1900 the United States set up a new Puerto Rican government under the Foraker Act. The American government controlled the new administration. In 1917 the Jones Act made Puerto Rico a territory of the United States. American citizenship was granted to all Puerto Ricans. Many Puerto Ricans, however, still wanted independence.

Acquiring the Philippines

The United States had gained possession of the Philippines in the treaty that ended the Spanish-American War. Acquisition of the Philippines, however, aroused fierce debate among American citizens.

During the 1890s, the anti-imperialists—people who opposed American foreign expansion—fought approval of the treaty. Some argued that American rule of the Philippines went against the democratic principles on which the United States was founded. Others opposed the large standing army that would be necessary to control the Philippines. Still others feared competition from Filipino laborers. Many Americans—including Andrew Carnegie, Carl Schurz, and Mark Twain—joined the anti-imperialist campaign.

The imperialists, however, led by Senators Henry Cabot Lodge and Albert Beveridge, eventually won out. They emphasized what they believed to be the benefits of taking the islands. Some argued that the Philippines would provide the United States with another Pacific naval base, a stopover on the way to China, and a large market for American goods. Others felt that the Americans had a duty to help "less civilized" peoples. As a result, the Senate ratified the Treaty of Paris on February 6, 1899.

Rebellion in the Philippines

The United States quickly learned that controlling its new empire would not be easy. In February 1899, Emilio Aguinaldo's forces began a fight for independence. This conflict became a gigantic undertaking for the United States. More than 4,000 Americans died. Filipinos suffered far greater casualties—at least 200,000 soldiers and civilians died.

When Aguinaldo was captured in March 1901, many Filipino military officers and soldiers surrendered. Others refused to give up even after Aguinaldo urged them to stop fighting.

In the summer of 1901, the United States transferred authority from a military to a civilian government headed by William Howard Taft. Taft set out to prepare the islands for **eventual,** or later, self-rule. The Philippines gained independence in 1946.

✔ **Reading Check** **Contrasting** What is the difference between a protectorate and a territory?

Section 3 Review

History ONLINE
Study Central™ To review this section, go to glencoe.com.

Vocabulary

1. Define each of the following terms in a sentence: yellow journalism, trigger, armistice, protectorate, territory, eventual.

Main Ideas

2. **Explaining** How did newspapers contribute to America's declaration of war against Spain in 1898?

3. **Discussing** Why did some Americans oppose empire building by the United States?

Critical Thinking

4. **Summarizing** Use a time line like the one below to summarize the events in the Philippines after the end of Spanish rule in 1898.

1898   1899   1901   1946

Filipino rebels create democratic republic

5. **Creative Writing** Write an account of the Battle of San Juan Hill from the point of view of an African American soldier of the Ninth Cavalry.

Answer the Essential Question

6. How did the Spanish-American War help the United States become a world power?

Essential Question

How did the beliefs of U.S. presidents shape Latin American foreign policies?

Reading Guide

Content Vocabulary

isthmus *(p. 249)*

anarchy *(p. 251)*

dollar diplomacy *(p. 252)*

Academic Vocabulary

eliminate *(p. 249)*   annual *(p. 249)*

Key People and Events

Roosevelt Corollary *(p. 252)*

Francisco "Pancho" Villa *(p. 254)*

John J. Pershing *(p. 254)*

Reading Strategy

Taking Notes As you read, use a diagram like the one below to compare the principles on which each American foreign policy was based.

Policy		Principle
Roosevelt Corollary	→	
Dollar Diplomacy	→	
Moral Diplomacy	→	

American Diary

On August 15, 1914, the Ancon, a cargo ship, made the first official trip through the Panama Canal. One traveler onboard the Ancon noted: "So quietly did [the ship] pursue [its] way that . . . a strange observer coming suddenly upon the scene would have thought that the canal had always been in operation, and that the Ancon was only doing what thousands of other vessels must have done before [it]."

—quoted in The Path Between the Seas

Since the *Ancon*'s voyage, more than 800,000 ships have passed through the Gaillard (Culebra) Cut, the narrowest channel of the Panama Canal.

Panama

Main Idea The United States negotiated with Panama to build the Panama Canal.

History and You Have you negotiated for better pay for lawn mowing or babysitting services? Read to learn how the United States negotiated in order to build the Panama Canal.

• •

The opening of the Panama Canal in 1914 was the fulfillment of a long-held dream. For hundreds of years, Americans and Europeans had wanted to build a canal across Central America to connect the Atlantic and Pacific Oceans. They wanted that connection to **eliminate** the long and dangerous sea voyage around South America. Now that the United States controlled territory in both oceans, it was even more important to have a canal that would allow easier access to American overseas territories.

Panama was an **isthmus**—a narrow strip of land connecting two larger bodies of land—about 50 miles (80 km) wide. Wedged between the Caribbean Sea and the Pacific Ocean, Panama seemed like the perfect site for the canal.

In 1879 a French company acquired a lease from Colombia to build a canal across Colombia's northern province of Panama. French efforts to build a canal failed, however, because of lack of funds and terrible losses from disease among the workers.

The United States had long considered two possible canal sites, one through Nicaragua and one through Panama. The French company eased this choice by offering to sell its rights and property in Panama to the United States.

In 1901 the United States bought the lease from the French for $40 million. Secretary of State John Hay negotiated a treaty with Colombia in 1903 that granted the United States a 99-year lease on a strip of land across Panama. That lease cost the United States a payment of $10 million with an **annual** rent of $250,000.

Revolution in Panama

The Colombian Senate, however, rejected the U.S. offer to lease the strip of land. President Roosevelt then looked for other ways to get land for the canal. He wrote that he would "be delighted if Panama were an independent state."

If You Were There | Working on the Panama Canal

Digging the "Big Ditch" With tropical diseases under control, you and thousands of workers begin digging. In grassy and swampy coastal areas, you struggle against the extreme heat, but your equipment works well. It is difficult work when you reach the rugged inland mountains, though. Heavy rains create mud and landslides. You also have to blast away solid rock with dynamite. After the blasts, giant steam shovels scoop up the rocks and dump them into nearby railroad cars. President Theodore Roosevelt is excited about the project, and he arrives at the site in 1906. He is photographed sitting at the controls of a steam shovel. With such presidential backing, how can you not succeed? In 1913 digging ends at last, and one of the greatest engineering projects of your time is almost complete.

Critical Thinking

Interpreting How does the phrase "The land divided, the world united" reflect the importance of the Panama Canal to the United States and the rest of the world?

The Panamanians had staged a number of revolts against Colombia in the past, but those uprisings had never met with success. This time, however, the Panamanians had reason to believe that the Americans would support them in a revolt against Colombia.

On November 2, 1903, the American warship *Nashville* steamed into the port of Colón on the Caribbean coast of Panama. Encouraged by this show of support, the Panamanians revolted the next day and declared their independence. Colombia sent forces to stop the revolt, but the United States intervened and turned them back.

The Panama Canal

On November 6, the United States recognized Panama's independence. Less than two weeks later, Hay signed a treaty with the new nation of Panama. It gave the United States a 10-mile (16-km) strip of land across the country for the same amount offered earlier to Colombia. The United States now had land to build a canal.

Roosevelt's actions did not meet with praise from everyone, however. Many Latin Americans, some Congress members, and other Americans were angered. The president, however, took great pride in his accomplishment. He later said: "I took the canal zone and let Congress debate, and while the debate goes on, the canal does also."

The United States could now start work on the canal—not an easy undertaking. Disease struck the workers. An English writer described Panama as "a damp, tropical jungle, intensely hot, swarming with mosquitoes." Those mosquitoes carried two deadly diseases—yellow fever and malaria.

The Grand Opening

The Panama Canal opened on August 15, 1914. A cargo ship named the *Ancon* made the first voyage through the new waterway.

Building the Panama Canal, 1900s

An Engineering Feat The Panama Canal was regarded as one of the great engineering feats of its day. Thousands of workers struggled to carve a path through the dense jungle and over mountains. Laborers dug out huge amounts of earth and rock and used the excavated materials to build a dam, which created a large lake. Workers also constructed giant locks to raise and lower ships from sea level, over the mountains, and then back to sea level again on the other side of the isthmus.

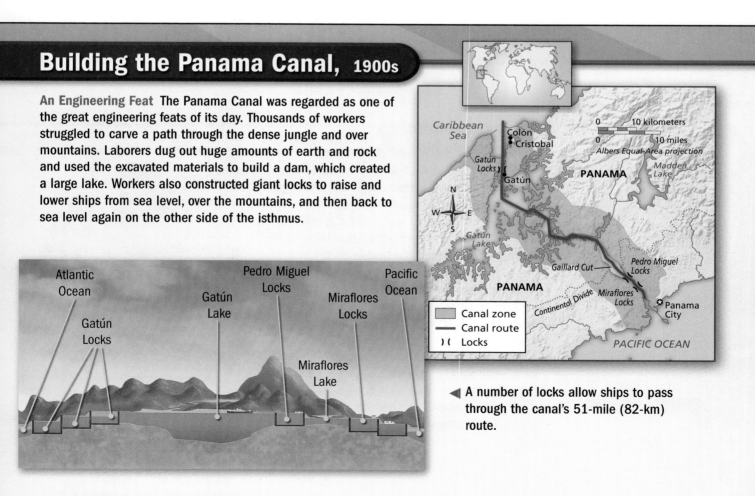

◀ A number of locks allow ships to pass through the canal's 51-mile (82-km) route.

From the start, the canal was a great success. Before the canal opened, ships sailing from New York to San Francisco traveled 12,600 miles (20,277 km) around the treacherous tip of South America. Afterwards, the trip was only 4,900 miles (7,886 km). It could be completed in less than half the time, significantly reducing shipping costs.

The Panama Canal also helped extend American naval power. The U.S. naval fleet could now move freely between the Atlantic and Pacific Oceans. The canal was a valuable property that the United States intended to protect. Thus, it guaranteed that there would be a strong American presence in Latin America. Yet many Latin Americans remained bitter over how the canal land had been acquired. This resentment soured relations between the United States and Latin America for years.

Reading Check **Identifying** What problem faced workers on the canal?

Policing the Western Hemisphere

Main Idea Using its economic and military power, the United States policed the Western Hemisphere.

History and You Have you ever heard the proverb "Speak softly and carry a big stick"? What does that mean? Read to learn about American foreign policies in Latin America.

President Roosevelt often quoted an African proverb, "Speak softly and carry a big stick." He believed the United States should respond to foreign crises not with threats but with military action. Roosevelt became known for his "big stick" approach to foreign affairs.

Roosevelt also believed that America must exercise "an international police power." He felt that this was necessary to preserve order and to prevent the world from falling into **anarchy**—disorder and lawlessness.

More than 6,000 men used shovels, explosives, and a system of railways to create the Gaillard (Culebra) Cut. Below, a sailing ship is towed through the finished passageway.

◄ Colonel William Gorgas

Eliminating Disease Colonel William Gorgas, an army doctor who helped eliminate yellow fever in Cuba, went to Panama to improve health conditions. Gorgas instructed workers to drain swamps, spray insecticides, spread oil on stagnant pools of water, and cut grassy marshes in order to destroy mosquito breeding places. Workers who did become ill were isolated in "pens" to stop the spread of the disease. By 1906, these measures eliminated yellow fever and greatly reduced the number of malaria cases. Without controlling disease, the United States could not have built the canal.

Critical Thinking

Making Inferences What do the efforts devoted to the construction of the Panama Canal reveal about how U.S. leaders felt about the project?

Primary Sources

INTERPRETING POLITICAL CARTOONS

When European powers threatened to send warships to the Dominican Republic to collect debts owed them, the United States applied the Roosevelt Corollary to stop them.

1. **Analyzing** How is the Dominican Republic portrayed? What does this suggest about American opinion of Latin Americans?

2. **Interpreting** According to the cartoon, how did the Monroe Doctrine prevent European intervention in Latin America?

A. President Theodore Roosevelt
B. European powers
C. Republic of Santo Domingo (Dominican Republic)

HANDS OFF!

Roosevelt Corollary

Theodore Roosevelt was worried about instability in the Caribbean region. He feared that European powers would try to intervene there. In 1904 Roosevelt asserted America's right to act as a "policeman" in Latin America and to intervene "however reluctantly . . . in cases of wrongdoing."

This policy, known as the **Roosevelt Corollary,** was an addition to the Monroe Doctrine. The United States used the Monroe Doctrine only to prevent European intervention in Latin America. Under the Roosevelt Corollary, the United States now claimed the right to intervene in the affairs of Latin American nations whenever those nations seemed unstable.

The United States first applied the Roosevelt Corollary in 1905 when it took control of the Dominican Republic's finances following a revolution that had toppled the country's government. Then in 1906, the United States used the policy again when troops were sent to Cuba to stop a revolution there.

Dollar Diplomacy

Theodore Roosevelt thought of American power mostly in military terms. His successor, William Howard Taft, had a different view. Taft hoped to change American foreign policy by "substituting dollars for bullets." That is, he was willing to intervene in other nations' affairs if they threatened American business interests.

Taft's policy was known as **dollar diplomacy.** This policy had some positive and some negative effects. First, American investments in Latin America grew. Roads, railroads, and harbors built with American investments helped increase trade and profits. Second, the United States played a stronger role overseas. When U.S. business interests in Latin America were threatened, military intervention often followed. Of course, such action led to increased anti-U.S. feelings throughout Latin America.

Reading Check **Contrasting** How were Taft's views about power different from Roosevelt's?

Relations With Mexico

Main Idea During the early 1900s, the United States and Mexico almost went to war with each other.

History and You Think about a country today that is experiencing a long civil war. Then read about the United States's involvement in the Mexican revolution.

In the early 1900s, Mexico was a poor country. A tiny group of rich landholders controlled the nation. Investors in the United States invested millions of dollars in Mexican oil wells and other businesses.

Then, in 1910, events in Mexico began to threaten American investments. This period also revealed the weaknesses of dollar diplomacy and forced the United States to use military intervention to protect its interests in the area.

In 1911 a popular Mexican reformer named Francisco Madero (muh•DEHR•oh) led a successful revolution. His goal was to overthrow Mexico's brutal dictator, Porfirio Díaz (DEE•ahs). Foreign businesses and some Mexican politicians and landowners prospered under the rule of Díaz. The lives of most Mexicans, however, had grown worse.

Just two years after taking power, Madero was overthrown and killed by General Victoriano Huerta (WEHR•tuh). Like Díaz, Huerta favored the wealthy and foreign interests. President Woodrow Wilson, who had just taken office, refused to recognize Huerta's "government of butchers."

Primary Source / Relations With Mexico

American Troops in Mexico In 1916 Mexican rebel Pancho Villa, angered by American support for a political rival, began attacking Americans. He killed 16 American miners in Mexico, then crossed the U.S. border and burned the town of Columbus, New Mexico, killing even more Americans. American president Woodrow Wilson sent 6,000 soldiers under the leadership of General John Pershing into Mexico to capture Villa. Though Mexican president Carranza also wanted to capture Villa, he opposed the presence of U.S. forces in Mexican territory.

▲ American soldiers used motorcycles, trucks, and horses in their unsuccessful search for Villa.

Pursuing Pancho Villa — NATIONAL GEOGRAPHIC

Arizona
New Mexico
UNITED STATES

Site of Villa's raid
Columbus
El Paso

30°N

Pershing's route

Texas
Rio Grande

N W E S

Gulf of California
MEXICO

0   200 kilometers
0   200 miles
Albers Equal-Area projection

110°W

Bold and ruthless, Villa commanded a strong rebel force in northern Mexico. ▶

"Villa is entirely familiar with every foot of Chihuahua, and the Mexican people, through friendship or fear, have always kept him advised of our every movement. He carries little food, lives off the country, rides his mounts hard and replaces them with fresh stock taken wherever found. Thus he has had the advantage since the end of the first twenty-four hours after the Columbus raid occurred."

—from a report by General John Pershing, April 1916

Critical Thinking

Drawing Conclusions Why do you think U.S. forces failed to capture Pancho Villa?

Wilson's "Moral Diplomacy"

In foreign affairs, Woodrow Wilson hoped to avoid further imperialism by the United States. He sought to promote democracy in other nations as a means of ensuring stability and preventing war and revolution. According to Wilson, the United States had a duty "to teach the South American republics to elect good men." Like Roosevelt and Taft, Wilson recognized the importance of military power and economic interests. Wilson however, wished to base his foreign policy on moral principles.

Wilson's "moral diplomacy" faced a serious challenge in Mexico. After Huerta took power, a civil war broke out in Mexico. Wilson hoped that the Huerta government, without American support, would fall. That did not happen. Wilson then authorized arms sales to Huerta's rival, Venustiano Carranza (kuh•RAN•zuh).

Problems came to a head in April 1914. When Huerta's troops arrested some American sailors, Wilson ordered U.S. troops to seize the port of Veracruz. This show of force strengthened Carranza's position. Huerta was forced to flee in August. Carranza took power, and American troops withdrew.

Francisco "Pancho" Villa

Huerta's departure did not end the civil war. Rebel leader **Francisco "Pancho" Villa** rose up against Carranza. In January 1916, Villa held and shot 16 Americans because of U.S. support for the Carranza government. Villa hoped to damage Mexican-American relations, but the United States did not act against Mexico. Then Villa and his rebels crossed into New Mexico, burning the town of Columbus and killing 18 Americans.

Villa's actions angered the United States. Troops led by General **John J. Pershing** crossed the border into Mexico and pursued Villa for almost a year. Many Mexicans protected Villa from capture. After America's attention turned to the war raging in Europe in 1917, Pershing's troops left Mexico. American actions had brought the countries close to war and led to great resentment in Mexico. As in the Caribbean, America's experience in Mexico showed other nations that the United States would willingly use its power when its interests or its honor was threatened.

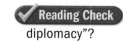 **Reading Check** **Defining** What was "moral diplomacy"?

History ONLINE
Study Central™ To review this section, go to glencoe.com.

Section 4 Review

Vocabulary

1. Define the following terms, using each one in a sentence: eliminate, isthmus, annual, anarchy, dollar diplomacy.

Main Ideas

2. Identifying How did the United States benefit from the construction of the Panama Canal? What were the drawbacks?

3. Explaining Why did President Roosevelt believe the United States should assert its military power in Latin America?

4. Discussing What event prevented an outbreak of war between the United States and Mexico in 1917? What did the United States prove by its actions in Mexico?

Critical Thinking

5. Evaluating Use a diagram like the one below to identify the positive and negative effects of Taft's dollar diplomacy in Latin America.

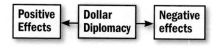

| Positive Effects | ← | Dollar Diplomacy | → | Negative effects |

6. Creative Writing You are a follower of Francisco "Pancho" Villa. Write a paragraph explaining why you support him.

Answer the
7. Essential Question
How did the beliefs of U.S. presidents shape Latin American foreign policies?

Main Idea	Supporting Details
American influence around the world expands in the late 1800s.	• After the closing of the frontier, the U.S. looks overseas to expand its territory. • Matthew Perry's expedition in 1854 opens Japan to U.S. trade. • The U.S. competes with European nations for overseas markets and resources. • Americans seek to spread Christianity and Western culture. • The United States purchases Alaska from Russia and seeks to develop friendly relations with Latin America. • U.S. Navy is strengthened to support overseas territories.
America seeks an empire in the Pacific.	• American sugar planters overthrow Hawaii's Queen Liliuokalani; Hawaii becomes a U.S. territory. • Germany and the United States divide the Samoa Islands. • The Open Door Policy protects and expands American trade in China. • Japan threatens U.S. power in the Pacific.
The Spanish-American War helps the United States become a world power.	• War erupts over concerns about Spanish rule in Cuba; explosion of the USS *Maine*. • U.S. defeats Spain; acquires Puerto Rico, Guam, and the Philippines.
U.S. involvement in Latin America increases in the early 1900s.	• U.S. seeks to build a canal across Central America to ease travel between the oceans. • U.S. supports Panama's revolt against Colombia to gain canal site. • The construction of the Panama Canal guarantees a strong American influence in the region.
The U.S. uses its military and economic power to maintain its interests in Latin America.	• The Roosevelt Corollary supports the use of American military force to prevent instability in Latin America. • Taft's "dollar diplomacy" calls for American intervention to protect U.S. business and economic interests. • Wilson's "moral diplomacy" supports the spread of democracy in Latin America.

▲ Queen Liliuokalani

◄ American troops in Mexico

STUDY TO GO ▷ Study anywhere, anytime! Download quizzes and flash cards to your PDA from glencoe.com.

Did the United States Have the Right to Build the Panama Canal?

Building Background

Theodore Roosevelt wanted the United States to be one of the world's great powers. He believed that the citizens of weaker countries were incapable of governing themselves. His beliefs guided him to help Panama secede from Colombia, enabling the United States to build a canal in the area.

Rubén Darío, an influential poet and journalist from Nicaragua, became increasingly concerned about the possibility of U.S. colonization of Latin America. In 1904 Darío wrote a poem entitled "To Roosevelt."

YES

THEODORE ROOSEVELT

I did not lift my finger to incite the revolutionists.... I simply ceased to stamp out the different revolutionary fuses that were already burning.... We gave to the people of Panama self-government, and freed them from subjection to alien oppressors.... When we did act and recognize Panama, Colombia at once acknowledged her own guilt by promptly offering to do what we had demanded, and what she had protested it was not in her power to do. But the offer came too late.... It would have necessitated our abandoning the people of Panama, our friends, and turning them over to their and our foes.... If, as representing the American people, I had not acted precisely as I did, I would have been an unfaithful or incompetent representative; and inaction at that crisis would have meant not only indefinite delay in building the canal, but also practical admission on our part that we were not fit to play the part on the Isthmus which we had arrogated[1] to ourselves....

I deeply regretted, and now deeply regret, the fact that the Colombian Government [forced] me to take the action I took; but I had no alternative, consistent with the full performance of my duty to my own people, and to the nations of mankind.

---

[1] **arrogated** claimed

NO

RUBÉN DARÍO

. . . .

You think that life is fire,
that progress is eruption,
that wherever you shoot
you hit the future.

. . . .

But our America, that has had poets
since the ancient times of Netzahualcoyotl,[2]

. . . .

has lived on light, on fire, on perfume, on love,
America of the great Montezuma, of the Inca,
the fragrant America of Christopher Columbus,
Catholic America, Spanish America,
the America in which noble Cuahtemoc[3] *said:*
"I'm not in a bed of roses"; that America
that trembles in hurricanes and lives on love,
it lives, you men of Saxon[4] *eyes and barbarous soul.*
And it dreams. And it loves, and it vibrates, and it is the
daughter of the Sun.
Be careful. Viva Spanish America!
There are a thousand cubs loosed from the Spanish lion.
Roosevelt, one would have to be, through God himself,
the-fearful Rifleman and strong Hunter,
to manage to grab us in your iron claws.

Building the Panama Canal

---

[2] **Netzahualcoyotl** ruler in 1400s Mexico
[3] **Cuahtemoc** last emperor of the Aztecs
[4] **Saxon** a person of English birth or descent

DBQ Document-Based Questions

1. **Interpreting** What did Roosevelt believe was his duty?

2. **Making Inferences** What do you think was more important to Roosevelt: Panamanian independence or the Panama Canal? Why?

3. **Analyzing** According to Darío, what are the differences between the United States and Latin America?

4. **Evaluating** In your opinion, which man made a stronger argument for his position? Explain your answer.

Reviewing Main Ideas

Directions: Choose the best answer for each of the following questions.

1. Commodore Matthew Perry is most associated with

  A the purchase of Alaska.

  B improving and expanding U.S. trade.

  C ending the Russo-Japanese War.

  D the opening of Japanese ports to U.S. ships.

2. What was the Boxer Rebellion?

  A a Chinese uprising against foreigners

  B a brief skirmish between the United States and Germany over the division of Samoa

  C a revolt of sugar planters in Hawaii

  D a clash between Japan and Russia

3. Which of the following became U.S. territories or protectorates following America's victory in the Spanish-American War?

  A Cuba, Puerto Rico, and Hawaii

  B Spain and Cuba

  C Cuba, Puerto Rico, and Guam

  D the Philippines and Hawaii

4. The Roosevelt Corollary stated that

  A all European nations had the right to trade freely in China.

  B the U.S. had the right to get involved in Latin America to preserve order.

  C the United States was destined to expand from the Atlantic to the Pacific Ocean.

  D no European nation should intervene in Latin American affairs.

Short-Answer Question

Directions: Base your answer to question 5 on the excerpt below and on your knowledge of social studies.

> The two great needs of mankind, that all men may be lifted up into the light of the highest Christian civilization, are, first, a pure, spiritual Christianity, and, second, civil liberty. . . . It follows, then, that the Anglo-Saxon, as the great representative of these two ideas, . . . is . . . to be, in a peculiar sense, his brother's keeper.
>
> —Josiah Strong, on imperialism and the Spanish-American War, 1885

5. Based on the document, explain why Josiah Strong supported American imperialism.

Review the Essential Questions

6. Essay Which do you believe was the *most important* factor in American imperialism from 1865 to 1914: economic gain, military-strategic interest, or ideology? Explain and defend your answer.

To help you write your essay, review your answers to the Essential Questions in the section reviews and the chapter Foldables Study Organizer. Your essay should include:

- the actions and ideas of James G. Blaine and Alfred Thayer Mahan;
- the annexation of Hawaii, division of Samoa, and Open Door policy;
- events before, during, and after the Spanish-American War;
- the Panama Canal; and
- the foreign policies of Roosevelt, Taft, and Wilson.

GO ON ▶

Document-Based Questions

Directions: Analyze the documents and answer the short-answer questions that follow.

Document 1

This is an excerpt from Alfred Thayer Mahan's 1890 book, *The Influence of Sea Power Upon History.*

> The government should . . . build up for the nation a navy which, if not capable of reaching distant countries, shall at least be able to keep clear the chief approaches to its own. . . . It is essential to the welfare of the whole country that the conditions of trade and commerce should remain, as far as possible, unaffected by an external war.

Source: Alfred Thayer Mahan, *The Influence of Sea Power Upon History*

7. Based on the excerpt, identify one reason why Mahan wanted the United States to strengthen its sea presence.

Document 2

The following is taken from a June 1897 letter from Hawaiian queen Liliuokalani to President McKinley concerning the proposed U.S. annexation of Hawaii.

> My people, about forty thousand in number, have in no way been consulted by those, . . . who claim the right to destroy the independence of Hawaii.
>
> [The] treaty ignores, not only the civic rights of my people, but, further, the hereditary property of their chiefs.
>
> [The] treaty ignores, . . . all treaties made by . . . sovereigns with other and friendly powers, and it is thereby in violation of international law.

Source: Queen Liliuokalani, *Hawaii's Story*

8. Use the document to explain Queen Liliuokalani's arguments against annexation.

Document 3

This cartoon shows Roosevelt "taking" Panama.

Source: Bettmann/CORBIS

9. What is this cartoon's message? Explain.

Document 4

Woodrow Wilson made these remarks in a speech in Mobile, Alabama, on October 27, 1913.

> It is a very [dangerous] thing to determine . . . foreign policy . . . in the terms of material interest. . . . Human rights, national integrity, and opportunity as against material interests—that, . . . is the issue which we now have to face. I want to . . . say that the United States will never again seek . . . territory by conquest.

Source: John Woolley and Gerhard Peters, *The American Presidency Project*

10. How do Wilson's remarks reflect his rejection of "dollar diplomacy"?

11. Persuasive Writing Using the information from the four documents and your knowledge of social studies, write an essay in which you:

- state the principles you think should govern American foreign policy; and
- explain when the United States is justified in interfering in a foreign nation.

Need Extra Help?											
If you missed questions. . .	1	2	3	4	5	6	7	8	9	10	11
Go to page. . .	233	240	246	252	234–235	232–256	235	236–239	249–251	252–254	232–256

Chapter 9

World War I
1914–1919

U.S. soldiers on the battlefront

EVEN A DOG ENLISTS
WHY NOT YOU?
660 MARKET ST. SAN FRANCISCO
or any U.S. Army Recruiting Station

WOODROW WILSON
1913–1921

PRESIDENTS

U.S. Events

World Events

1914
★ **1914**
Millions of immi-
grants from southern
and eastern Europe
enter U.S.

★ **1915**
Germany torpedoes
the *Lusitania*

1917 ★
• Zimmermann telegram angers
United States
• United States enters World War I
• Selective Service Act passed

1916

1914
Franz
Ferdinand
assassinated

★ **1914**
World War I
begins

★ **1915**
International
Congress of
Women held
at The Hague

Lenin
addresses
a crowd,
1917 ▶

1917 ★
Lenin leads
Bolshevik
Revolution

Section 1: War in Europe
Essential Question How did militarism contribute to the outbreak of World War I?

Section 2: America's Road to War
Essential Question Why did the United States enter World War I?

Section 3: Americans Join the Allies
Essential Question How did the United States help the Allies win the war?

Section 4: The War at Home
Essential Question How did the United States mobilize its resources to fight the war?

Section 5: Searching for Peace
Essential Question Why did Wilson's peace plan fail?

Study Organizer

Organizing Information

Make this Foldable to help organize what you learn about World War I.

Step 1 Place two sheets of paper on top of one another about one inch apart.

Step 2 Fold the papers to form four equal tabs.

Step 3 Staple the sheets and label each tab as shown.

> World War I
> 1914–1919
> War in Europe
> America in the War
> Searching for Peace

Reading and Writing As you read the chapter, list the key events of World War I in Europe and in the United States.

◀ President Woodrow Wilson on tour to promote the League of Nations

1918
National War Labor Board established

1919
President Woodrow Wilson wins Nobel Peace Prize

★ **1920**
Senate rejects League of Nations

1918

1920

1918
World War I ends

★ **1918**
Flu epidemic kills more than 20 million people

★ **1919**
Treaty of Versailles signed

1920
The Hague chosen as seat of International Court of Justice

★ **1920**
League of Nations headquarters moves to Geneva

War in Europe

Essential Question ◄

How did militarism contribute to the outbreak of World War I?

Reading Guide

Content Vocabulary

nationalism (p. 263)

alliance system (p. 264)

ethnic group (p. 263)

balance of power (p. 264)

militarism (p. 264)

U-boat (p. 267)

Academic Vocabulary

dimension (p. 267)   equip (p. 267)

Key People and Events

Archduke Franz Ferdinand (p. 263)

Battle of Verdun (p. 266)

Reading Strategy

Taking Notes As you read, use a diagram like the one below to list the new technologies used in World War I.

New Technologies in World War I

American Diary

In the spring of 1914, President Woodrow Wilson sent his chief adviser, Colonel E. M. House, to evaluate the political situation in Europe. Relations were hostile between Europe's nations and were growing worse. His attempt at maintaining peace, however, failed. Colonel House reported: "The situation is extraordinary. It is militarism run stark mad. . . . There is too much hatred, too many jealousies."

—*from* The Intimate Papers of Colonel House

German men march through the streets of Berlin in response to the call to mobilize.

Troubles in Europe

Main Idea Several factors led to the outbreak of World War I.

History and You Why might one country defend another country that was attacked? Read about why most European nations went to war in 1914.

. . . .

On the morning of June 28, 1914, the people of Sarajevo, Bosnia, crowded the city streets to see **Archduke Franz Ferdinand,** who was the next in line to the throne of the Austro-Hungarian Empire. The archduke and his wife were on a state visit to Bosnia, an Austrian province. Suddenly shots rang out. The royal couple were shot and died soon after.

The assassination destroyed the delicate balance of European stability. Within weeks Europe was at war. The tensions that led to World War I, however, went back many years. The conflicts grew as European nations pursued dreams of new empires, built up their armies, and formed alliances.

Nationalism

Nationalism, a feeling of intense loyalty to one's country or group, caused much of the tension in Europe. Nationalism encouraged new nations, such as Italy and Germany, to unify and establish their power in the world. Italy became a kingdom in the 1860s, and the German states united in the 1870s. Their actions threatened the power of older nations such as Great Britain and France.

Nationalism also inspired certain groups of people to break away from existing nations. Some of these **ethnic groups**—people who share a common language and traditions—demanded independent nations of their own.

Imperial Expansion

Tension in Europe increased as nations expanded their empires. Nations competed for colonies in Africa, Asia, and other parts of the world. These colonies not only provided new markets and raw materials, they also boosted a nation's status.

Primary Source / Forming Alliances

Taking Sides European nations made alliances with one another for mutual self-defense. Alliances were sometimes broken or dissolved and new ones created. This 1915 propaganda poster ridicules Italy for changing sides. Italy allied with Germany and Austria-Hungary at first, then formed an alliance with France, Russia, and Great Britain.

Critical Thinking

Making Inferences Should a country form military alliances with other nations? Explain.

Great Britain and France already had large overseas empires, but both nations wanted to expand them even more. Germany, Italy, and Russia wanted to increase their colonial holdings as well. Expansion by one European nation often brought it into conflict with another country.

Military Buildup

As European nations competed for colonies, they strengthened their armies and navies to protect their interests. If one nation increased its military strength, its rivals felt threatened and built up their military. In this atmosphere of **militarism,** Germany, France, and Russia developed huge armies in the early 1900s.

Great Britain had the world's largest and strongest navy. Germany began to challenge Britain's naval power in the early 1900s. A bitter rivalry grew between the two nations. The rivalry led to an arms race that threatened the peace of Europe.

Formation of Alliances

As a result of military buildups, an **alliance system** developed. When a country joined an alliance, it agreed to defend other alliance countries if they were attacked. By 1914, two major alliances were established. Germany, Austria-Hungary, and Italy formed the Triple Alliance. Great Britain, France, and Russia formed the Triple Entente. An entente is an understanding among nations.

The purpose of alliances was to keep peace by creating a **balance of power.** This system prevents any one country from dominating the others. However, the alliance system posed a great danger because an attack on one nation could easily trigger a war involving many countries.

Europe was like a keg of gunpowder. One American diplomat noted that it would take "only a spark to set the whole thing off." That spark was ignited in the Balkans.

Reading Check Describing What was the purpose of the alliance system?

Crisis in the Balkans

Main Idea War spread throughout Europe as a result of the alliance system.

History and You When your friends argue, is it difficult for you not to take sides? Read to learn how World War I began in Europe.
· ·

The Balkan Peninsula was a hotbed of nationalist and ethnic rivalries in the early 1900s. Several nations argued over territory. Slavic nationalists hoped to unite all Slavic peoples in the region. One conflict was especially bitter. The Slavic people in Austria-Hungary wanted independence, and Serbia supported them.

An Assassination Leads to War

Gavrilo Princip, Franz Ferdinand's assassin, belonged to a Serbian nationalist group. Princip and other terrorists plotted the mur-

Europe Goes to War

Time of Crisis Despite more than 40 years of general peace, tensions among European nations were building in 1914. Militarism was on the rise. Rival countries had formed alliances. Because of the way the alliances were set up, an attack on one nation by another was all that was needed to trigger a war.

◄ The assassination of Archduke Franz Ferdinand on June 28, 1914, provided the incident that ignited Europe into war.

der of Ferdinand to bring down the Austro-Hungarian Empire and unite the Slavs.

Austria-Hungary moved to crush Serbia. With Germany's support, it gave Serbia a list of harsh demands, which Serbia refused. Austria-Hungary declared war on Serbia on July 28, 1914.

Europe's alliance system caused the war to spread quickly. Russia, which was Serbia's protector, prepared for war. Germany then came to the side of its ally Austria-Hungary. Germany declared war on Russia on August 1, 1914, and then declared war on France, Russia's ally, on August 3.

A day later, Germany invaded Belgium, violating a treaty that guaranteed Belgium's neutrality. Great Britain, honoring a pledge to protect Belgium, declared war on Germany.

✓ **Reading Check** **Identifying Cause and Effect** How did nationalism contribute to the outbreak of World War I?

A World War Begins

Main Idea World War I was a long, deadly war as a result of new technologies and battle strategies.

History and You Think about the technology you use as you go about your everyday routines. Read to learn how new technology affected armies during World War I.

. . . .

The "Great War" had begun. On one side were the Allied Powers, or the Allies. They included Great Britain, France, and Russia. On the other side, Germany, Austria-Hungary, and the Ottoman (Turkish) Empire made up the Central Powers.

Japan, a rival of Germany in Asia, joined the Allies in late August 1914. Italy refused to honor its alliance with Germany and Austria-Hungary. Instead, it joined the Allies in 1915 after being promised territory in Austria after the war.

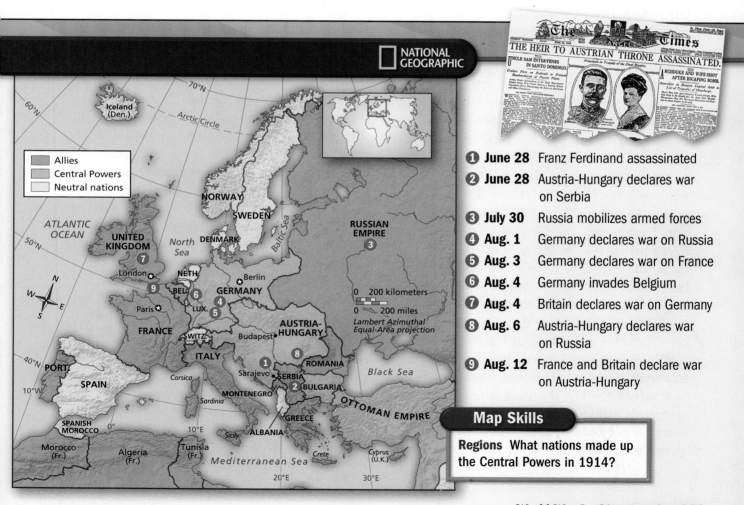

NATIONAL GEOGRAPHIC

Map legend:
- Allies
- Central Powers
- Neutral nations

❶ **June 28** Franz Ferdinand assassinated

❷ **June 28** Austria-Hungary declares war on Serbia

❸ **July 30** Russia mobilizes armed forces

❹ **Aug. 1** Germany declares war on Russia

❺ **Aug. 3** Germany declares war on France

❻ **Aug. 4** Germany invades Belgium

❼ **Aug. 4** Britain declares war on Germany

❽ **Aug. 6** Austria-Hungary declares war on Russia

❾ **Aug. 12** France and Britain declare war on Austria-Hungary

Map Skills

Regions What nations made up the Central Powers in 1914?

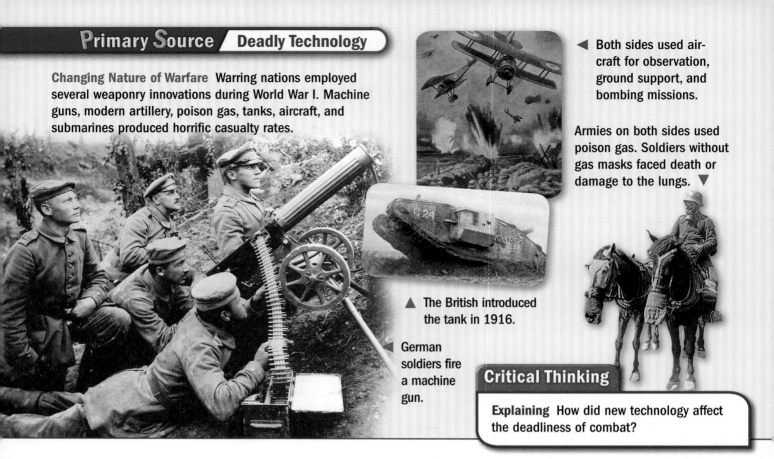

Changing Nature of Warfare Warring nations employed several weaponry innovations during World War I. Machine guns, modern artillery, poison gas, tanks, aircraft, and submarines produced horrific casualty rates.

◄ Both sides used aircraft for observation, ground support, and bombing missions.

Armies on both sides used poison gas. Soldiers without gas masks faced death or damage to the lungs. ▼

▲ The British introduced the tank in 1916.

◄ German soldiers fire a machine gun.

Critical Thinking

Explaining How did new technology affect the deadliness of combat?

Fighting on the Western Front

Germany launched its offensive through Belgium because it hoped to defeat France and then move troops east against Russia. The plan almost succeeded. The Belgians, however, held out for nearly three weeks against the powerful German army. This delay gave the French and British time to prepare their armies for war.

After defeating the Belgians, the Germans marched into France. They advanced to within 15 miles (24 km) of Paris. The British and French met the Germans at the Marne River just a few miles east of the city. The Battle of the Marne, fought between September 5 and 12, 1914, stopped the German advance and boosted French morale. The battle also made it clear that neither side was capable of winning the war quickly or easily.

The fighting in western Europe reached a stalemate, where neither side made any military advances. For the next three years, the opposing armies faced each other across a complex network of deep trenches. Trenches along the front lines provided protection from flying bullets and artillery shells. Trenches behind the lines served as first-aid stations, headquarters, and storage areas.

To break the standstill, both sides launched major offensives in 1916. The German offensive, the **Battle of Verdun** in northeastern France, began in February. It continued until December. At first the Germans made small gains, but these gains were lost after the French counterattacked. Verdun was one of the longest and bloodiest battles of the war. When it was over, more than 750,000 French and German soldiers had lost their lives.

While the Battle of Verdun raged, the Allies launched their own offensive in July. This was known as the Battle of the Somme. Again the number of casualties was high. The Allies gained only 7 miles (11.2 km) in the offensive.

Technology of War

New deadly weapons caused large numbers of injuries and deaths. Improved cannons and other artillery fired larger shells at great distances. Better rifles enabled soldiers to hit targets with greater accuracy.

The Germans first used poison gas against Allied troops in April 1915. The gas could kill or seriously injure anyone who breathed it. A British officer said:

PRIMARY SOURCE

"They fought with their terror, running blindly in the gas cloud, and dropping . . . in agony."
—quoted in *Avoiding Armageddon*

The Allies began to use poison gas as well. Soldiers started to carry gas masks.

The armored tank, first used in World War I in January 1916, could cross battle lines and fire on the enemy at close range. By crushing barbed wire, tanks also provided an easier route for advancing troops. After seeing the effectiveness of the Allies' tanks, the Germans produced them, too.

The most dramatic new weapon—the airplane—added a new **dimension**, or magnitude, to fighting in World War I. Both sides used airplanes to watch the movements of enemy troops and bomb targets. Daring pilots waged duels in the skies called "dogfights."

The first fighter planes were **equipped**, or outfitted, only with machine guns fastened to the top wing. The most famous pilots included Germany's Baron von Richthofen—the "Red Baron"—and Eddie Rickenbacker, an American who served in the French air force. The Germans used the zeppelin, or blimp, to bomb Allied cities.

On the Seas

With their land armies deadlocked in western Europe, both sides turned to the sea. Great Britain blockaded all ports under German control, eventually causing severe shortages. Many Germans went without food and other supplies.

Germany had an effective naval weapon of its own: the submarine. Known as **U-boats**—from the German word *Unterseeboot*—submarines sunk ships carrying supplies to Britain. U-boat attacks on ships at sea eventually brought the United States into the war.

Reading Check **Explaining** What did both sides realize after the Battle of the Marne?

Section 1 Review

History ONLINE
Study Central™ To review this section, go to glencoe.com.

Vocabulary

1. Define the following terms in a sentence: nationalism, ethnic group, militarism, alliance system, balance of power, dimension, equip, U-boat.

Main Ideas

2. **Stating** Why did nations form alliances with other nations?

3. **Discussing** Discuss the role of the Slavic nationalist movement in Austria-Hungary in the early 1900s.

4. **Explaining** How did the Central Powers and the Allies try to break the deadlock caused by trench warfare?

Critical Thinking

5. **Organizing** Use a diagram like the one below to identify the Allies and the Central Powers.

6. **Expository Writing** Write a paragraph to explain why the airplane became an important weapon during World War I.

Answer the
7. **Essential Question**
How did militarism contribute to the outbreak of World War I?

World War I and Trench Warfare

The Germans were determined to hold onto the parts of France and Belgium that they still occupied after the Battle of the Marne. They dug trenches for protection from the advancing French and British troops. The Allies could not break through the German trenches and began digging their own. For the next three years, neither side advanced more than a few miles along the line of trenches that became known as the Western Front.

How Did Geography Affect Trench Warfare?

The nature of trench warfare resulted in the development of its own unique form of geography. In the forward zone, traditional methods of transportation such as roads and rail were replaced by a network of trenches and light tramways. Occupying the high ground was critically important. Savage battles were fought just to gain possession of a small hill. Many farmhouses and groves of trees were fought over simply because they were the largest identifiable features of the landscape.

The Western Front

Legend:
- Line of trench warfare, 1915–1917
- Farthest advance of Central Powers, 1918
- Allied offensive
- Major battle involving U.S. forces
- German offensive
- Armistice Line, Nov. 11, 1918

▲ On the Western Front where Allied and German armies faced each other, the troops dug a network of trenches that stretched from the English Channel through parts of France and Germany.

◄ American artist Mal Thompson served in France as a lieutenant with the U.S. Army. After the war, he published a volume of his sketches of war life entitled *In France with the American Expeditionary Forces.*

War Poetry British soldier and poet Wilfred Owen became famous for his realistic verses about life in the trenches. He was killed just one week before the end of the war. This is an excerpt from his poem "Dulce et Decorum Est." The title is taken from a Latin phrase: *Dulce et decorum est pro patria mori* ("How sweet and lovely it is to die for your country").

Gas! Gas! Quick, boys!—An ecstasy of fumbling,
Fitting the clumsy helmets just in time;
But someone still was yelling out and stumbling
And flound'ring like a man in fire or lime . . .
Dim, through the misty panes and thick green light,
As under a green sea, I saw him drowning.

Aircraft were used to assess enemy troops before an attack.

Long range artillery 4–5 miles (6–8 km) behind the front line fired on advancing enemy troops.

Rows of barbed wire slowed down advancing troops.

Concrete block house for a machine gun

Reserve trench

Support trench

Front-line trench

A deep dugout could protect from artillery shells but could trap soldiers underground.

Front-line dugouts provided some protection but could be hit by an artillery shell from above.

No Man's Land was the area between the trenches of opposing sides. Churned mud and hardened ruts made it difficult for troops to cross.

American nurses in France make their way through a trench carrying gas masks. Poison gas attacks could cause vomiting, blindness, and suffocation. Gas masks were a necessary part of equipment for soldiers and nurses. ▶

Today the trenches at Vimy Ridge in northern France are preserved in a memorial park. ▼

▲ Soldiers set up living quarters in dugouts and caves that were joined to the trenches. This picture from 1915 shows makeshift beds lined up against the walls of a dugout. In many cases, soldiers tried to make dugouts as much like home as possible.

Analyzing Geography

1. **Location** Use the text and map to determine in which countries the Western Front of World War I was located.

2. **Human-Environment Interaction** Why was it a tactical advantage for troops in World War I to occupy the high ground?

America's Road to War

Essential Question ◀

Why did the United States enter World War I?

Reading Guide

Content Vocabulary
propaganda *(p. 271)*   autocracy *(p. 274)*

Academic Vocabulary
stress *(p. 271)*   revolution *(p. 274)*

Key People and Events
Lusitania *(p. 272)*
Selective Service Act *(p. 275)*

Reading Strategy
Taking Notes As you read, use a diagram like the one below to compare how Germany's policy on submarine warfare changed between 1915 and 1917.

Policy in 1915 → **Policy in 1917**

American Diary

In 1914 many Americans believed that the war in Europe was a European conflict in which the United States should not be involved. Mississippi Congressperson Percy E. Quin strongly opposed building an army just to be ready because "When our country really needs soldiers to defend it, millions of patriots will rush to arms and rally to the flag." That time was drawing near.

—*from* America's Great War: World War I and the American Experience

U.S. members of the Women's Peace Party arrive in Europe to call for negotiations to end the war.

American Neutrality

Main Idea The United States tried to remain neutral in the war in Europe.

History and You Do you think the newspaper in your city or town reports on national events accurately? Read how propaganda influenced people's ideas about the war in Europe.

. . . .

President Wilson had to make some difficult decisions. He declared that the United States would be neutral in the war in Europe. Most Americans did not think that the war concerned them. Many shared the view expressed in an editorial in a New York newspaper.

PRIMARY SOURCE

"There is nothing reasonable in such a war . . . and it would be [foolish] for this country to sacrifice itself to . . . a clash of ancient hatreds which is urging the Old World to destruction."

—from the *New York Sun*

Despite pleas for neutrality, Americans soon began to take sides. More than one-third of the nation's 92 million people were either foreign-born or the children of immigrants. Many naturally favored their countries of origin. Some of the 8 million Americans of German or Austrian descent and the 4.5 million Irish Americans—who hated the British because they ruled Ireland—favored the Central Powers.

Even more Americans, however, including President Wilson, favored the Allies. Ties of language, customs, and traditions linked the United States to Great Britain. President Wilson told the British ambassador: "Everything I love most in the world is at stake." A German victory "would be fatal to our form of government and American ideals."

Using Propaganda

To gain support, both sides in the war used **propaganda.** This term describes information used to influence opinion. Allied propaganda **stressed,** or called attention to, the German invasion of neutral Belgium and included horror stories of German atrocities. It called the Germans "Huns" and barbarians.

By the Numbers / Land Forces

Size of Armies, August 1914

Troops (in thousands)

Central Powers **Allied Powers**

*Although not yet involved in the war, American troops totaled about 119,250 enlisted men.

Source: *Encyclopaedia Britannica;* U.S. Census Bureau

German soldier, 1916 ▶

Critical Thinking

Analyzing How did the armies of the Central and Allied powers compare in size?

War at Sea: The Submarine

The United States began building its own submarine fleet during the war. The fastest American submarines reached a top surface speed of 14 knots (a little more than 16 miles per hour).

Captured German submarine on display in Hoboken, New Jersey, 1919 ▶

1 The **conning tower** is the attack center.

2 The **diving rudders** guide the submarine to different depths.

3 The **rudder** steers the vessel.

4 About 12 **torpedoes** could be carried at a time.

Periscope

Deck gun

Engine room   Control room   Crew's quarters

Critical Thinking

1. **Naming** What part of the craft guided the submarine up and down?
2. **Predicting** How might submarine warfare lead to U.S. entry into the war?

The propaganda from the Central Powers was equally horrible, but because of sympathy for the British, Allied propaganda was more effective in influencing Americans.

America's Early Involvement

Trade between the United States and the Allies helped build support for the Allied cause. As a neutral nation, America sought to trade with both sides. However, Britain's blockade of Germany made this difficult.

Stopping and searching American ships headed for German ports, the British navy often seized the ships' goods. The United States protested that its ships should be able to pass without interference. The British responded with the defense that they were fighting for their survival. "If the American shipper grumbles," wrote a London newspaper, "our reply is that this war is not being conducted for his pleasure or profit." The U.S. government could do nothing about the blockade. Barred from trading with Germany, it continued trading with Britain.

Indeed, American trade with the Allies soared. In addition, Great Britain and France borrowed billions of dollars from American banks to help pay for their war efforts. All this business caused an economic boom in the United States. It also upset the Germans, who watched the United States—supposedly a neutral nation—helping the Allies.

Submarine Warfare

To stop American aid to Britain, Germany stated in February 1915 that it would sink any vessels that entered or left British ports. President Wilson warned that the United States would hold Germany responsible for any American lives lost in submarine attacks. The Germans ignored Wilson's threat. On May 7, 1915, a German U-boat torpedoed the British passenger liner **_Lusitania_** near the coast of Ireland. The captain reported:

"I saw a torpedo speeding toward us, and immediately I tried to change our course, but was unable to [maneuver] out of the way. There was a terrible impact as the torpedo struck the starboard side of the vessel, and a second torpedo followed almost immediately."

—from W. T. Turner, captain of the *Lusitania*

More than 1,000 people died, including 128 American citizens, when the *Lusitania* sank. Americans were outraged, and President Wilson denounced the attack. Later it was learned that the ship carried war materials.

Within a few months, several Americans were injured when a German U-boat attacked the unarmed French passenger ship *Sussex*. Germany feared that the Americans might enter the war. To pardon itself, Germany offered money to people who were injured on the *Sussex* and promised to warn neutral ships and passenger vessels before attacking. The *Sussex* Pledge seemed to resolve the issue.

Reading Check **Describing** What is the purpose of propaganda?

The End of Neutrality

Main Idea Relations with Germany worsened, and the United States entered World War I.

History and You Why did the United States enter into a war with Iraq in 2003? Read to learn why the United States finally entered World War I.

. . . .

The crisis over submarine warfare led Congress, in the summer of 1916, to pass legislation to strengthen the military. Congress doubled the size of the army and provided funding for the construction of new navy warships. President Wilson still hoped, however, to stay out of the war.

Antiwar sentiment remained very strong. Some Americans saw the nation's military buildup as a step toward entering the war. The phrase "He [Wilson] Kept Us Out of War" became the Democrats' campaign slogan in 1916. Wilson, however, only narrowly defeated the Republican candidate, Charles Evans Hughes.

People IN HISTORY

Jeannette Rankin

First Female Member of the U.S. Congress

Rankin voted against the declaration of war on Germany just a few days after taking office in 1917. During the vote, she said, *"I want to stand by my country—but I cannot vote for war."* Her pacifism probably cost her the Republican Senate nomination in 1918. She was reelected to Congress in 1940 on an antiwar platform. She was the only member of Congress to vote against the declaration of war on Japan after the bombing of Pearl Harbor in December 1941. The vote met with wide disapproval, and Rankin did not seek reelection the following year.

CRITICAL Thinking

1. **Analyzing** Why do you think Rankin made the statement "I want to stand by my country" at the time she voted against a declaration of war on Germany?

2. **Synthesizing** Did voters agree or disagree with Rankin's position on war? How do you know?

What If the British Had Not Intercepted the Zimmermann Note?

In January 1917, German foreign minister Arthur Zimmermann proposed that Mexico help Germany if the United States entered the war. A British official intercepted Zimmermann's telegram.

The Telegram

"We shall endeavor . . . to keep the United States of America neutral. In the event of this not succeeding, we make Mexico a proposal of alliance on the following basis: make war together, make peace together, generous financial support and an understanding on our part that Mexico is to reconquer the lost territory in Texas, New Mexico, and Arizona."

Reaction to Telegram

The Zimmermann telegram angered Americans and helped build popular sentiment for the war. Then, in mid-March, four American merchant ships were sunk without warning. On April 2, 1917, President Wilson asked Congress to declare war on Germany.

Critical Thinking

Analyzing If there were no Zimmermann note, do you think the United States would have: (a) entered the war when it did in April; (b) entered the war at a later time; or (c) not been drawn into the war at all? Explain.

On the Brink of War

In January 1917, Germany announced that it would sink on sight all merchant vessels, armed or unarmed, sailing to Allied ports. The Germans knew they risked bringing Americans into the war. However, the Germans believed they could defeat the Allies before the United States became too involved. An angry President Wilson broke off diplomatic relations with Germany.

Then a few weeks later, British agents intercepted a secret telegram sent by the German foreign minister, Arthur Zimmermann. It offered an alliance with Mexico against the United States if war broke out. Newspapers published the Zimmermann telegram, and Americans reacted angrily to the German offer. The telegram set off a new wave of anti-German feeling.

Revolution in Russia

Dramatic events continued to push the United States into the war. First, in March 1917 a **revolution**—a war to overthrow the government—took place in Russia. The Russian people overthrew the monarchy and established a temporary government that promised free elections. The new Russian government also vowed to continue the fight to defeat Germany.

This change from an **autocracy,** in which one person with unlimited powers rules, to a more democratic government, raised Allies' hopes. Wilson could now argue that the Allies were fighting a war for democracy.

Other critical events took place at sea. In March 1917, within a few days' time, the Germans attacked and sank four American merchant ships. Thirty-six lives were lost.

President Wilson continued to struggle with his conscience. His cabinet, on the other hand, strongly favored war. One government official later explained:

PRIMARY SOURCE

"If we had stayed out of the war and Germany had won there would no longer have been a balance of power in Europe or a British fleet to support the Monroe Doctrine and protect America."
—from "The Duties of the Citizen," 1917

America Enters the War

President Wilson decided that the United States could no longer remain neutral. On the cold, rainy evening of April 2, 1917, he asked Congress for a declaration of war against Germany:

PRIMARY SOURCE

"The world must be made safe for democracy. . . . . . . It is a fearful thing to lead this great, peaceful people into war, into the most terrible and disastrous of all wars. . . . But the right is more precious than peace."

—from *Democracy Today: An American Interpretation*

Congress did not agree at once to a war resolution. In the end, however, most members agreed that the nation must defend its rights if it wished to remain a great world power. As a result, Congress passed a declaration of war, and Wilson signed it on April 6. Fifty-six members of the House and Senate voted against war. One of those 56 was Jeannette Rankin of Montana—the first woman to serve as a representative in Congress.

The United States had to raise an army quickly. On May 18, Congress passed the **Selective Service Act,** setting up a military draft. Men aged 21 to 30 registered by the millions. By war's end, some 24 million men had registered. Of them, about 3 million were called to serve. Another 2 million joined voluntarily. In addition, for the first time, women enlisted in the armed forces. They served in noncombat roles, such as radio operators, clerks, and nurses.

More than 300,000 African Americans joined the armed forces, but they faced discrimination and racism. Most held low-level jobs at military bases. Among the 140,000 African American soldiers sent to Europe, 40,000 fought in combat. Many served with honor, including a regiment that received medals for bravery from France. One of its members, Henry Johnson, was the first American to receive the French Croix de Guerre [Cross of War], a medal for bravery.

✔ **Reading Check** **Describing** What was the purpose of the Selective Service Act?

Section 2 Review

History ONLINE
Study Central™ To review this section, go to glencoe.com.

Vocabulary

1. Define each of the following terms in a sentence: propaganda, stress, revolution, autocracy.

Main Ideas

2. **Summarizing** Why did many Americans favor the Allies?

3. **Explaining** Why did the revolution in Russia push the United States toward entering the war?

Critical Thinking

4. **Analyzing** How is propaganda used as a "weapon" in war?

5. **Determining Cause and Effect** Use a diagram like the one below to show the consequences of Germany's attacks on various ships.

Ship Attacked	Consequence
Lusitania	
Sussex	
Four U.S. Merchant Ships	

6. **Persuasive Writing** Write a letter to President Wilson to persuade him to keep the United States out of the war.

Answer the Essential Question

7. Why did the United States enter World War I?

Americans Join the Allies

Essential Question ◄····

How did the United States help the Allies win the war?

Reading Guide

Content Vocabulary

convoy (p. 277)   kaiser (p. 281)

armistice (p. 281)

Academic Vocabulary

proceed (p. 278)   consent (p. 281)

Key People and Events

Bolsheviks (p. 277)

Vladimir Lenin (p. 277)

Treaty of Brest-Litovsk (p. 278)

John J. Pershing (p. 278)

Reading Strategy

Taking Notes As you read, use a diagram like the one below to describe how the U.S. Navy helped get much-needed supplies to Great Britain.

Supplies to Great Britain

American Diary

"Late one afternoon our captain . . . formed the company and, with great solemnity [seriousness], announced: 'This company is going to France. We are going right away. Is there a man here who does not want to go?' No one replied. He commanded: 'Dismissed.' I have often wondered if that company did not have a pack of silent liars."

—quoted in Doughboy War: The American Expeditionary Force in World War I

A French couple greets U.S. soldiers.

Supplying the Allies

Main Idea Russia withdrew from the war, but the American troops helped turn the tide in favor of the Allies.

History and You Can you complete a task more quickly by working alone or by working with a team? Read to learn how the American soldiers fought with the Allies in the war.

. . . .

In 1917 the Allies desperately needed the help of American soldiers. Years of trench warfare had exhausted the Allied armies. Some French troops refused to continue fighting after a failed offensive in 1917. The British started to run out of war supplies and food, so their people were starving. Furthermore, German submarines were taking a deadly toll on Allied shipping. They sank one of every four ships that left British ports.

American entry into the war made an immediate difference. To ensure that needed supplies reached Great Britain, the U.S. Navy helped the British destroy German submarines. Then **convoys,** or teams, of navy destroyers escorted groups of merchant ships across the Atlantic.

If German submarines wanted to attack a merchant ship, they had to get past the American ships protecting it. The convoy system worked well. In one year it reduced Allied shipping losses from 900,000 to 300,000 tons per month. With the convoy system, not one American soldier bound for Europe was lost to submarine attack.

Russian Withdrawal

The Allies also needed more troops because of a second revolution in Russia. In March 1917, Czar Nicholas II, leader of the Russian Empire, gave up his throne in the first revolution. Political leadership was handed to a temporary government that supported the war. This government, however, was unable to solve major problems, such as food shortages, that plagued the nation.

In November 1917, riots broke out over the government's handling of the war and over the scarcity of food and fuel. The **Bolsheviks,** a group of Communists, overthrew the democratic Russian government and established a Communist government. Led by **Vladimir Lenin,** the Bolsheviks wanted to pull out of the war so they could concentrate their efforts on setting up a new Communist state.

Primary Source | Soldiers' IDs

Dog Tags Before World War I, the U.S. military often had a difficult time identifying dead soldiers after a battle. By 1917, each American soldier was required to wear an identification badge around the neck. Soldiers nicknamed them "dog tags."

Critical Thinking

Making Inferences Why do you think identifying fallen soldiers was an important issue for soldiers and their families?

Lenin took Russia out of the war, and in March 1918, he signed the **Treaty of Brest-Litovsk** with Germany. As a result of this treaty, Russia lost substantial territory to the Germans. Russia's withdrawal from the war allowed the Germans to move thousands of troops from the Eastern Front, or line of battle, to the Western Front in France.

New German Offensive

In March 1918, the Germans launched a massive attack along the Western Front. German military leaders hoped to drive a wedge in the Allied lines. They wanted to capture the city of Amiens before proceeding to Paris. Between March and June 1918, the Germans hammered at Allied lines. They pushed the Allies back to within 40 miles (64 km) of

History ONLINE
Student Web Activity Visit glencoe.com and complete the Chapter 9 Web Activity about World War I.

Paris. After years of stalemate along the Western Front—the area along the French-German border—it looked as if Germany might win the war.

American Troops Arrive in France

In May 1917, General **John J. Pershing** was named supreme commander of the American Expeditionary Force (AEF), the American army in Europe. American correspondent Floyd Gibbons described the welcome for the first American troops to arrive in France:

PRIMARY SOURCE

"The sooty girders of the Gare du Nord [railroad station] shook with cheers when the special train pulled in. . . .
. . . A minute later, there was a terrific roar from beyond the walls of the station. The crowds outside had heard the cheering within. . . . Paris took Pershing by storm."

—from *"And They Thought We Wouldn't Fight"*

Europe During World War I, 1914–1918

NATIONAL GEOGRAPHIC

Legend
- Allies
- Central Powers
- Neutral nations
- Eastern Front
- Western Front

ATLANTIC OCEAN
NORWAY
SWEDEN
UNITED KINGDOM
Ireland
Great Britain
North Sea
DENMARK
Baltic Sea
RUSSIAN EMPIRE
NETH.
BEL.
GERMANY
LUX.
FRANCE
SWITZ.
AUSTRIA-HUNGARY
ITALY
ROMANIA
Black Sea
SERBIA
BULGARIA
MONTENEGRO
Corsica
Sardinia
ALBANIA
GREECE
Sicily
Mediterranean Sea
Crete
Cyprus (U.K.)
OTTOMAN EMPIRE
Aral Sea
Caspian Sea
PERSIA
SPAIN
PORT.
Morocco (Fr.)
SPANISH MOROCCO
Algeria (Fr.)
Tunisia (Fr.)

May, 1915 Germany sinks Lusitania

0   200 kilometers
0   200 miles
Lambert Azimuthal Equal-Area projection

Major Battles
- Tannenberg, Aug. 1914
- 1st Marne, Sept. 1914
- Gallipoli, Apr. 1915–Jan. 1916
- Verdun, Feb.–Dec. 1916
- Somme, July–Nov. 1916
- Château-Thierry and Belleau Wood, June 1918
- 2nd Marne, July 1918
- St. Mihiel, Sept. 1918
- Meuse-Argonne, Sept.–Nov. 1918

The AEF was ready for battle in Europe by the spring of 1918. The French and British wanted to use the American soldiers to build up their own troops. However, General Pershing refused. He preferred to keep the AEF a separate force.

Doughboys in Battle

American soldiers, or "doughboys," saw their first serious fighting in early June 1918. They were nicknamed "doughboys" because of their brass uniform buttons that resembled boiled dough dumplings, a popular food. In June, the AEF helped turn back a German offensive at Château-Thierry on the Marne River east of Paris. The American troops then advanced to nearby Belleau Wood. For 24 hours a day for the next three weeks, American forces fought their way through the forest against a solid wall of German machine-gun fire.

The Americans and the French fought back German attacks on Allied forces along the Marne and the Somme Rivers and stopped the German offensive. General Pershing wrote that the battles had "turned the tide of war."

The Battle of the Argonne Forest

The Allies now began an offensive of their own. In mid-September, about 500,000 American soldiers fought and defeated the Germans at Saint Mihiel, east of Verdun. Later that month, more than 1 million American troops joined the Allies in the Battle of the Argonne Forest. It became the most massive attack in American history.

The Battle of the Argonne Forest raged for nearly seven weeks. Soldiers struggled over the rugged, heavily forested ground. Rain, mud, barbed wire, and fire from German machine guns hindered the Allies' advance. Many lives were lost.

African Americans in World War I

World War I gave African Americans the opportunity to show their loyalty and patriotism. In 1917 the War Department created two divisions of primarily African American combat units. Discrimination remained, however. Units were forced to train separately. Four regiments fought alongside the French, where they were treated as equals and fought valiantly.

"These Negroes are American citizens. Naturally I cannot and will not discriminate against these soldiers."

—General John Pershing's response to British protest of using African American troops

The 369th regiment fought on the front lines for 191 days, five days longer than any other U.S. regiment. The entire unit received the French Croix de Guerre medal for bravery. ▶

Critical Thinking

Making Inferences Why do you think some African American soldiers wanted to stay in Europe after the war?

General John J. Pershing

Commander of the American Expeditionary Force during World War I

Pershing was a skillful military leader. He insisted that the American Expeditionary Force remain independent from the French and British armies. In a message he recorded for the American people during the battle of Picardy and Flanders in April 1918, he said, *"Three thousand miles from home, an American army is fighting for you. Everything you hold worthwhile is at stake. . . . Invoking the spirit of our forefathers, the army asks your unflinching support, to the end that the high ideals for which America stands may endure upon the earth."*

CRITICAL Thinking

1. **Analyzing** What was the purpose of Pershing's message?
2. **Evaluating** How does Pershing appeal to his listeners' emotions?

The Battle of the Argonne Forest ended in early November. The Allies had pushed back the Germans and broken through the enemy lines. The Germans now were faced with an invasion of their own country.

Although the war led to many acts of bravery, the actions of two Americans captured the nation's imagination. During the fighting at Argonne Forest, Corporal Alvin York killed several German soldiers, captured machine guns, and took 132 prisoners. Captain Eddie Rickenbacker was a member of the 94th Aero Squadron. He fought in 134 air battles and shot down 26 aircraft. Both York and Rickenbacker were awarded the Medal of Honor for their actions.

✓ Reading Check **Summarizing** Why was the Battle of the Argonne Forest important?

The End of the War

Main Idea By late 1918, Germany was losing the war and appealed for an armistice to end the fighting.

History and You Think about the reasons a nation decides to stop fighting a war. Read to learn why Germany asked for peace.

· ·

While fighting raged along the Western Front, Germany's allies faced certain defeat. In late 1918, the Ottoman Empire was on the brink of collapse, and a revolution engulfed Austria-Hungary. Street protests in Vienna, Budapest, and other cities led to the end of the centuries-old empire. In October 1918, the ethnic territories within the empire began to break away. Poland, Hungary, and Czechoslovakia, for example, declared independence.

By early in November, the governments of Austria-Hungary and the Ottoman Empire had surrendered to the Allied Powers.

Request for an Armistice

Meanwhile, military leaders in Germany realized they had little chance of winning the war. American troops and supplies had fortified and added new determination to the Allied war effort. In addition, the Germans on the home front were suffering greatly from severe shortages of food and other needed supplies.

On October 4, 1918, the German government appealed to President Wilson for an **armistice.** An armistice is an agreement to end the fighting. Wilson **consented,** or agreed, but only under certain conditions. Germany must accept his plan for peace and promise not to renew hostilities. All German troops must leave Belgium and France. Finally, Wilson would deal only with civilian leaders, not with the military.

While German leaders considered Wilson's demands, political unrest erupted in Germany. On November 3, sailors in Kiel, the main base of the German fleet, revolted. Within days,

groups of workers and soldiers seized power in other German towns. As the revolution spread, the German **kaiser,** or emperor, decided to step down. On November 9, Germany was declared a republic. The new leaders of Germany agreed to Wilson's terms for an armistice.

Peace Begins

The armistice began on November 11, 1918—the 11th hour on the 11th day of the 11th month. Germany agreed to withdraw all land forces west of the Rhine River, withdraw its fleet to the Baltic Sea, and surrender huge amounts of equipment. The fighting stopped, and the Great War ended. President Wilson said:

PRIMARY SOURCE

"Everything for which America fought has been accomplished. It will now be our fortunate duty to assist by example, by sober friendly counsel and by material aid in the establishment of a just democracy throughout the world."
—from "Proclamation of the Armistice with Germany"

✓ **Reading Check** **Describing** What conditions did Germany accept to end the fighting?

Section 3 Review

History ONLINE
Study Central™ To review this section, go to glencoe.com.

Vocabulary
Define the following terms in a sentence: convoy, proceed, armistice, consent, kaiser.

Main Ideas
2. **Explaining** Why did the war intensify on the Western Front after the second Russian revolution?

3. **Determining Cause and Effect** What factor led to Germany's acceptance of a peace agreement?

Critical Thinking
4. **Predicting** If the war had continued on the Eastern Front, do you think the Allies still could have won? Why or why not?

5. **Determining Cause and Effect** Draw a diagram like the one below to list three reasons the Allies needed the help of U.S. forces.

U.S. Help

6. **Creative Writing** Think about what it was like for a soldier serving on the front line in WWI. Write a letter home describing battle conditions.

Answer the
7. **Essential Question**
How did the United States help the Allies win the war?

The War at Home

Essential Question ◄

How did the United States mobilize its resources to fight the war?

Reading Guide

Content Vocabulary

mobilization (p. 283) pacifist (p. 285)
ration (p. 284) dissent (p. 285)
socialist (p. 285)

Academic Vocabulary

consume (p. 284) perceive (p. 285)

Key People and Events

Great Migration (p. 283)
Espionage Act (p. 285)
Sabotage Act (p. 285)
Sedition Act (p. 285)

Reading Strategy

Taking Notes As you read, use a chart like the one below to describe how these three acts controlled public opinion.

	Description
Espionage Act	
Sabotage Act	
Sedition Act	

American Diary

As American men left their homes for war, American women grabbed tools and went to work. Ella May Stumpe, in her early twenties, described her contribution: "When the harvest time came, there weren't enough young men left to work the fields. So an old bachelor organized a bunch of us, about a dozen young women, and came with a wagon and took us out to the fields to shuck grain. He told us we were helping the war effort."

—quoted in Centenarians: The Story of the 20th Century by the Americans Who Lived It

Workers prepare missiles in a factory.

Mobilizing the Nation

Main Idea The United States prepared to fight the war.

History and You If you have a summer job, do you manage the work for someone who is on vacation? Read to learn how the United States had to adjust its workforce during World War I.

. . . .

After the United States declared war on Germany in 1917, Americans began focusing their energies on getting ready to fight the war. **Mobilization,** or the gathering of resources and the preparation for war, affected almost every part of American life.

To ensure production of vital war materials, the government created the National War Labor Board in April 1918. The board pressured businesses to grant some of the most important demands of workers. As a result, workers won an eight-hour working day. They also received overtime pay, equal pay for women, and the right to form unions. In return, workers agreed not to go on strike.

Workers During the War

To pay for the war, the United States government sold war bonds and increased taxes. Then industries had to expand in order to produce war materials. During this time, however, there was a labor shortage. Millions of men left their jobs to serve in the armed forces. Also, immigration slowed during the war. Fewer immigrants were arriving to take on the jobs.

The labor shortage provided new job opportunities for women. Many women joined the workforce for the first time by taking on jobs previously held by men.

The prospect of finding good jobs also brought hundreds of thousands of African Americans to Northern cities from the rural South. From 1914 to 1920, between 300,000 and 500,000 African Americans left their homes in the rural South to settle in Northern cities and find jobs. This huge population movement was known as the **Great Migration.** In addition, thousands of Mexicans migrated to the United States in search of jobs.

Primary Source / Saving Resources

Make-Do Recipes
The Food Administration enlisted 20 million housewives to promote awareness of the need to follow the rules for conserving food. Eggs, butter, milk, and wheat flour were to be used sparingly so that enough food was available to feed the soldiers. In 1918 the Royal Baking Company even published a book of recipes that identified ingredients that could be substituted for those that were needed for the troops.

Barley or Oat Flour Biscuits

2 cups barley or oat flour

1 tablespoon sugar

4 teaspoons Royal Baking Powder

1 tablespoon shortening

1/2 teaspoon salt

2/3 cup milk

Sift dry ingredients together. Rub in shortening and add enough milk to make a soft dough. Roll out on board to about one-half inch thick and cut with biscuit cutter. Bake in very hot oven 15 to 20 minutes.

Critical Thinking

Analyzing If you lived in the United States during World War I, how could you have contributed to the war effort?

Building Support The Committee on Public Information launched a massive campaign to build support for the war. Posters were an important part of this campaign.

The government sold war bonds to help pay for the cost of the war. ▶

YOU
Buy a Liberty BOND
Lest I Perish!

With millions of men serving in the military, women were needed to take their places in the labor force. ▼

JOIN THE UNITED-STATES SCHOOL GARDEN ARMY

ENLIST NOW

Write to The United States School Garden Army. Bureau of Education, Department of Interior, Washington, D.C.

◀ The Food Administration urged people to observe "Wheatless Mondays," "Meatless Tuesdays," and "Porkless Thursdays," and to add to their own store of food by planting "victory gardens." Slogans such as "Serve Just Enough" and "Use All Leftovers" reminded Americans to conserve food.

I WANT YOU FOR U.S. ARMY
NEAREST RECRUITING STATION

▲ James Montgomery Flagg's depiction of Uncle Sam for the U.S. Army is the most famous American wartime poster.

For EVERY FIGHTER & WOMAN WORKER
UNITED WAR WORK CAMPAIGN
CARE for HER through The YWCA

Critical Thinking

Synthesizing What common message is found in all four posters?

Producing Supplies

The United States had to produce food not only for its own needs but also for the Allies. President Wilson appointed Herbert Hoover to head a new Food Administration. This agency's campaign encouraged American farmers to produce more and persuaded the public to eat less.

The Food Administration also put price controls on many agricultural products to encourage voluntary **rationing,** or the limitation of use. As a result of such efforts, Americans **consumed,** or used, less food, expanded food production, and increased food exports.

Another government agency, the War Industries Board, supervised the nation's industrial production. The board's responsibilities included overseeing the changeover of factories to produce war-related goods and setting prices for key consumer products. Finally, the Fuel Administration managed the nation's coal and oil. To save energy, the agency introduced daylight savings time and called for "Heatless Mondays."

Mobilizing Support

The federal government also needed to mobilize public support for the war. Antiwar sentiment remained strong even after the United States entered the war. The president appointed journalist George Creel to head the Committee on Public Information. The purpose of the committee was to promote the war as a battle for democracy and freedom.

The Committee on Public Information launched a massive propaganda campaign. The Committee distributed millions of pro-war pamphlets, posters, articles, and books, and it provided newspapers with government accounts of the war and advertisements. The committee hired speakers, writers, artists, and actors to build support for the war.

Reading Check **Explaining** Why did the United States face a labor shortage during the early days of World War I?

Public Opinion and the War

Main Idea During World War I, the American government approved legislation to control public opinion.

History and You Have you ever spoken out against a government action? Read to learn how the government tried to stop people from speaking out against the war.

· ·

World War I helped the American economy. Yet the war had harmful effects on American society. To create a sense of national unity, the government tried to silence opposition. Some Americans became intolerant of those who were different.

Controlling Public Opinion

Even after America entered the war, opposition to it remained strong. Some German Americans and Irish Americans sympathized with the Central Powers. Many **socialists**—people who believe industries should be publicly owned—opposed the war. They thought it would only help rich business owners and hurt working people. **Pacifists**—people who are opposed to the use of violence—were also against the war.

During the war, the Committee on Public Information began trying to silence **dissent.** Dissent is disagreement or opposition. It portrayed people who were against the war as unpatriotic. The **Espionage Act** of 1917 gave the government a new weapon to combat dissent to the war. The law provided stiff penalties for espionage, or spying. People who aided the enemy or interfered with army recruiting also could be penalized.

Congress passed even harsher measures in 1918—the **Sabotage Act** and the **Sedition Act.** These laws made it a crime to say, print, or write any criticism **perceived,** or recognized, as negative about the government. Such acts were considered sabotage—secret action to damage the war effort. Thousands of people were convicted under the laws.

Some people spoke out against these laws and the intolerance they produced. Most Americans, however, believed that in wartime no measure could be "too drastic" toward traitors and disloyal Americans.

✓ **Reading Check** **Making Inferences** Why do you think Congress passed laws to penalize people who criticized the government?

Section 4 Review

History ONLINE
Study Central™ To review this section, go to glencoe.com.

Vocabulary

1. Define the following terms in a sentence: mobilization, ration, consumed, socialist, pacifist, dissent, perceive.

Main Ideas

2. Identifying How did World War I benefit workers?

3. Explaining For what reasons did some people oppose the U.S. involvement in World War I?

Critical Thinking

4. Organizing Draw a diagram like the one below that explains why each organization was created.

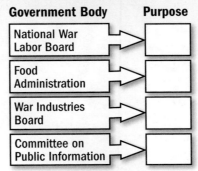

Government Body	Purpose
National War Labor Board	
Food Administration	
War Industries Board	
Committee on Public Information	

5. Persuasive Writing Make a poster to encourage the people in your town to eat less so more food can be given to the Allied troops.

Answer the Essential Question

6. How did the United States mobilize its resources to fight the war?

Searching for Peace

Essential Question ◄

Why did Wilson's Peace Plan fail?

Reading Guide

Content Vocabulary
national self-determination (p. 287)
reparations (p. 288)

Academic Vocabulary
final (p. 288)   achieve (p. 288)

Key People and Events
Fourteen Points (p. 287)
League of Nations (p. 288)
Treaty of Versailles (p. 289)
Henry Cabot Lodge (p. 290)

Reading Strategy
Taking Notes As you read, use a diagram like the one below to list the conditions that Germany agreed to under the Treaty of Versailles.

```
┌──────────┐  ┌──────────┐
│          │  │          │
└──────────┘  └──────────┘
        ╲      ╱
   ┌──────────────────┐
   │  Conditions of the │
   │ Treaty of Versailles │
   └──────────────────┘
        ╱      ╲
┌──────────┐  ┌──────────┐
│          │  │          │
└──────────┘  └──────────┘
```

American Diary

"We want Wilson," the war-weary crowd roared. "Long live Dr. Wilson!" British students with American flags smiled, tossing flowers in the president's path. Everywhere in Europe the Wilsons visited—Paris, Rome, Milan—the reception was jubilant. Boosted by the cheers of the European crowds, Wilson walked into the Paris Peace Conference at the Palace of Versailles with confidence. He was sure that his plan for a just and lasting peace would win swift approval in Europe and the United States.

President Woodrow Wilson leads the procession after the signing of the Treaty of Versailles.

Making a Peace

Main Idea World War I ended, but the Allies opposed Wilson's plan for peace.

History and You Think about the destruction caused by war. Read to learn why the Allies wanted to punish Germany.

. . . .

World leaders from 27 nations gathered in Paris, France, in January 1919. They met for the peace conference following World War I. When President Woodrow Wilson arrived in the city, huge crowds cheered him. With great hope, Europeans looked to Wilson to help build a better postwar world, but enormous problems lay ahead.

Europe was in ruins. Its landscape, farms, and towns were destroyed. The human losses were huge. France, Russia, Germany, and Austria-Hungary each lost between 1 million and 2 million people in the fighting. Millions more were wounded. More than 50,000 Americans were killed in battle, while another 60,000 soldiers died from disease. Estimates put the number of soldiers killed worldwide at nearly 9 million. Millions of civilians also lost their lives.

Europe faced social and political turmoil. Millions of people were homeless and hungry, and civil war raged in Russia. Poles, Czechs, and other peoples struggled to form their own nations. The search for peace and stability was difficult.

Wilson's Fourteen Points

Woodrow Wilson had a vision of a just and lasting peace. He outlined his peace plan in the **Fourteen Points.** Several of the proposals dealt with adjusting boundaries in Europe and creating new nations. These points reflected Wilson's belief in **"national self-determination"**—the right of the people to decide how they should be governed.

Wilson also proposed a number of principles for conducting international relations. They included calls for free trade and freedom of the seas.

By the Numbers / The Human Cost of War

Total Mobilized Forces

Allies
42 million

Central Powers
23 million

Military Deaths

Allies
5.1 million

Central Powers
3.4 million

Critical Thinking

Calculating What percent of the Allies' mobilized forces were killed in the war? The Central Powers?

The Postwar World

- Treaties changed the boundaries of Europe.
- Allied nations weakened the Central Powers by dividing their land.
- Germany's land area was greatly reduced.
- New nations emerged in Eastern Europe, including Poland, Czechoslovakia, and Yugoslavia.
- Economic depression aided the rise of dictatorships in Europe and Japan.

Map Skills

Regions Which new nations bordered Germany?

Maps In Motion See StudentWorks™ Plus or glencoe.com.

In addition, Wilson supported an end to secret treaties or agreements among nations. He also called for limits on arms and peaceful settlement of disputes over colonies.

League of Nations

Wilson's **final,** or last, point was the creation of a **League of Nations.** The League's member nations would help preserve peace and prevent future wars. They would respect and protect one another's independence.

At first, many Europeans welcomed Wilson's ideas, but problems developed when nations put their own interests first. Also, some of Wilson's points did not provide clear solutions to difficult questions, such as how to **achieve,** or accomplish, self-determination in regions where different ethnic groups lived closely together.

The Allies Disagree

The Allies did not invite either Germany or Russia to the peace talks. The major participants were called the Big Four. In this group was President Wilson; Prime Minister David Lloyd George of Great Britain; France's premier, Georges Clemenceau; and Italian prime minister Vittorio Orlando.

The European leaders showed little enthusiasm for the Fourteen Points. Wilson opposed punishing the defeated nations. In contrast, the Europeans sought revenge.

Clemenceau wanted to make sure that Germany could never invade France again. He believed that Germany should be broken up into smaller countries. Both he and Lloyd George demanded that Germany make large **reparations,** or payments, for the damage Germans caused in the war. Wilson struggled to uphold the principles of his Fourteen Points at the Paris meeting, yet he was forced to compromise or give in to the demands of the other Allies.

At the same time, the Allies had to decide how to deal with the new Bolshevik government of Russia. Fearing the spread of communism, France, Britain, and the United States supported anti-Bolshevik forces fighting in a civil war for control of Russia. All three countries sent troops to Russia.

The Treaty of Versailles

On June 28, 1919, the Allies and Germany signed the **Treaty of Versailles.** The treaty dealt harshly with the Germans but because they were defeated, they had no choice but to sign. Under the treaty's terms, Germany had to accept full responsibility for the conflict. It had to pay billions of dollars in reparations to the Allies. Also, Germany had to disarm completely and give up its overseas colonies and some territory in Europe.

The treaty carved up the Austro-Hungarian and Russian Empires as well. New nations were created and old nations restored. The new nations fulfilled Wilson's vision of national self-determination. Border disputes, however, would lead to future conflicts.

Wilson succeeded in having the League of Nations included in the treaty. He believed that the League would correct any mistakes in the rest of the treaty.

✓ **Reading Check** Identifying Cause and **Effect** Why didn't Great Britain, France, and Italy support Wilson's Fourteen Points?

Opposition at Home

Main Idea The U.S. Senate rejected the Treaty of Versailles and the League of Nations.

History and You Think about how Americans might have felt after World War I. Read to learn how the U.S. Senate reacted to the treaty and the League of Nations.

· ·

Wilson presented the Treaty of Versailles to the U.S. Senate for ratification in July 1919. "Dare we reject it and break the heart of the world?" he asked. In spite of Wilson's plea, a difficult struggle lay ahead.

Many Americans had doubts about the treaty. Some thought it dealt too harshly with Germany, while others worried that the League of Nations marked a permanent American commitment to international affairs.

In 1919 the Republicans controlled the Senate, which had to ratify the treaty. Some Republican senators saw the ratification issue as a chance to embarrass President Wilson.

Primary Sources

INTERPRETING POLITICAL CARTOONS

Under the Covenant (constitution) of the League of Nations, members pledged to defend any member nation attacked by any other nation. Many Americans, however, believed the Covenant violated national sovereignty. It would allow other nations to commit American troops to foreign conflicts.

1. **Interpreting** What is the League Covenant trying to do in the cartoon?

2. **Identifying Point of View** Does the cartoon express a view for or against joining the League of Nations? How do you know?

NOT ROOM FOR BOTH

Some Republicans viewed it as an opportunity to weaken the Democratic Party before the upcoming elections of 1920. Other senators had sincere concerns about the treaty, particularly the League of Nations. A few senators opposed signing any treaty.

Lodge vs. Wilson

The most powerful opponent of the treaty was **Henry Cabot Lodge** of Massachusetts. Lodge was head of the Senate Foreign Relations Committee and a longtime foe of President Wilson. Lodge said that membership in the League would mean that:

PRIMARY SOURCE

"American troops and American ships may be ordered to any part of the world by nations other than the United States, and that is a proposition to which I, for one, can never assent."
—from *Vital Forces in Current Events*, 1920

Lodge delayed a vote on the treaty so that opponents could present their cases. He then proposed a number of reservations that would limit America's obligations under the treaty.

Wilson went on a national tour in September to rally support for the treaty and League of Nations. When he returned to Washington, he suffered a stroke. During the president's illness, his wife, Edith Wilson, shielded him from pressures and took a major role in deciding which issues to raise with him.

The Treaty Is Rejected

In the months after Wilson's stroke, opposition to the treaty grew. In March 1920, the Senate voted on the treaty with Lodge's changes. Opposed by most Republicans and deserted by former supporters, the Treaty of Versailles was rejected in the Senate.

Wilson hoped the 1920 election would be a "great and solemn referendum" on the League. He even considered running for a third term. In the end, however, Wilson did not run. In 1921 the United States signed a separate peace treaty with each of the Central Powers. The United States never joined the League of Nations.

Reading Check Explaining Why did the Senate reject the Treaty of Versailles?

Section 5 Review

History ONLINE
Study Central™ To review this section, go to glencoe.com.

Vocabulary

1. Define the following terms in a sentence: national self-determination, final, achieve, reparation.

Main Ideas

2. **Explaining** Why did Woodrow Wilson think a lasting peace could be achieved in Europe?

3. **Identifying Cause and Effect** What effect did Wilson's illness have on the ratification of the Treaty of Versailles?

Critical Thinking

4. **Analyzing** Use a diagram like the one below to identify the challenges that the United States and Europe faced after the war.

Challenges Facing U.S. and Europe

5. **Expository Writing** If you were in Paris for the peace talks, do you think you would support Wilson's plan? Why or why not? Write a paragraph that explains your point of view.

Answer the
6. **Essential Question**
Why did Wilson's Peace Plan fail?

Visual Summary

1914

June Archduke Franz Ferdinand assassinated

July Austria-Hungary declares war on Serbia

Aug. Germany declares war on Russia and France, and invades Belgium; World War I begins

1915

May German U-boat torpedoes the British *Lusitania,* killing 128 Americans

1916

Feb. The Germans launch a major offensive at the Battle of Verdun

July Allies begin their offensive at the Battle of the Somme

Nov. Woodrow Wilson wins presidential reelection

1917

Jan. Germany requests an alliance with Mexico if the U.S. entered the war

March Germany attacks and sinks four American ships

April U.S. Congress declares war against Germany

May Selective Service Act sets up a military draft

Dec. Russia's new Communist government pulls out of the war

1918

March Treaty of Brest-Litovsk shifts German troops to the Western Front

Sept.– Nov. Battle of the Argonne Forest turns war in favor of Allies

Nov. Germany becomes a republic; armistice begins

1919

Jan. World leaders meet at Paris peace conference

June Germany and the Allies sign the Treaty of Versailles

1920

March U.S. Senate rejects the Treaty of Versailles and League of Nations

STUDY TO GO Study anywhere, anytime! Download quizzes and flash cards to your PDA from glencoe.com.

TIME NOTEBOOK

What were people's lives like in the past?

These two pages will give you some clues to everyday life in the United States as you step back in time with TIME Notebook.

FRANK COBB

American Voices

MEETING WITH A TROUBLED PRESIDENT

Just one day before President Wilson appeared before Congress in 1917 to ask for a declaration of war against Germany, he was struggling with whether or not it was the right thing to do. He sent for his friend, **FRANK COBB**, *editor of the* New York World *newspaper. Here is how Cobb remembers that late-night meeting at the White House:*

"[Wilson] was waiting for me sitting in his study. . . . I'd never seen him so worn down. He said he was probably going before Congress the next day to ask a declaration of war, and he'd never been so uncertain about anything in his life as about that decision. For nights, he said, he'd been lying awake going over the whole situation—over the provocation [outrage] given by Germany, over the probable feeling in the United States, over the consequences to the settlement to the world at large if we entered the [war].

"He said he couldn't see any alternative. . . . 'I think I know what war means,' he said, and he added that if there were any possibility of avoiding war he wanted to try it. 'What else can I do?' he asked. 'Is there anything else I can do?'

"I told him his hand had been forced by Germany, that so far as I could see we couldn't keep out."

AMERICAN SCENE
Average Life Spans in 1900

Average life expectancy: **47.3 YEARS**

Male life expectancy: **46.3 YEARS**

Female life expectancy: **48.3 YEARS**

White life expectancy: **47.6 YEARS**

Nonwhite life expectancy: **33.0 YEARS**

| 0 years | 10 | 20 | 30 | 40 | 50 |

VSTOCK / ALAMY

The Slang Game

Want to express yourself more clearly? Then test your knowledge of the latest slang of the early 1900s! Match the word or phrase with the correct description.

1. Big bug
2. Bully for you
3. Dude
4. Greased lightning
5. Full of grit
6. Into a pucker
7. Schoolmarm
8. Waking snakes

a. Well-dressed person
b. Causing a ruckus
c. Very important person
d. Female teacher
e. Upset
f. Brave
g. Quick speed
h. Good job!

Answers: 1. c; 2. h; 3. a; 4. g; 5. f; 6. e; 7. d; 8. b

MILESTONES

EVENTS AND PEOPLE OF THE TIME

BETTMANN / CORBIS

GRADUATED. Helen Keller from Radcliffe College in 1904. Deaf and blind from a childhood illness, Keller has been assisted by her lifelong friend and teacher, Anne Sullivan. Keller was introduced to Sullivan by none other than Alexander Graham Bell, inventor of the telephone and teacher of the hearing impaired.

NAMED. The "hot dog," after a drawing in 1906 showed a dachshund—a small, long dog—inside a frankfurter bun.

SUNG. The "Star-Spangled Banner" for the first time before a baseball game in 1918. The owner of the Boston Red Sox wanted to honor the many wounded veterans of World War I who were in the stands to watch the Sox take on the Chicago Cubs.

STRUCK. Oil in Spindletop, Texas, in 1901, triggering what many believe will be an oil boom in the American Southwest. Oil companies are springing up quickly as this new fuel is used to heat homes and run trains.

ESTABLISHED. Mother's Day, by President Woodrow Wilson in 1914—after all, it is only fair since Father's Day was created in 1910.

It Is the Law

Two laws were passed in 1902 to deal with the automobile.

1. Tennessee demands that all drivers give the public a week's notice before they start any trip.
2. Vermont states that an adult waving a red flag has to walk in front of any moving automobile.

NUMBERS

UNITED STATES AT THE TIME

12 cents
Price of a dozen eggs in 1910

$12 Price of a sewing machine in 1900

$12 Lowest price for a steamship ticket from Italy to America in 1905

$12 Average weekly salary (seven-day weeks/12-hour days) for arriving immigrants in 1907

12 seconds
Air time of Wright brothers' first flight in 1903

BETTMANN / CORBIS

1.2 million
Approximate number of immigrants who entered the United States in 1907

395,000 Approximate number of immigrants in 1908 who gave up on the American dream and returned to their homelands

CRITICAL THINKING

Creative Writing Write a story about how you would feel arriving in a strange land and starting a new life as an immigrant.

Contrasting Use the graph to determine who had the longest and shortest life expectancies in 1900. What do you think accounts for the differences in life expectancies?

STANDARDIZED TEST PRACTICE

When reviewing for a test, pay special attention to bold type, questions, and summary paragraphs in your text.

Reviewing Main Ideas

Directions: Choose the best answer for each of the following questions.

1. Nationalism caused much of the tension in Europe that led to World War I. *Nationalism* can best be defined as

   A the practice of one nation extending its control over another nation.

   B a feeling of intense loyalty to one's country or group.

   C a political system based on military strength.

   D a structure of defense agreements among nations.

2. In 1917 Germany offered Mexico an alliance against the United States in the

   A Treaty of Brest-Litovsk.

   B Selective Service Act.

   C Zimmermann telegram.

   D Triple Entente.

3. Russia's withdrawal from World War I in December 1917

   A convinced German military leaders that they had little chance of winning the war.

   B allowed the Germans to move hundreds of thousands of troops from the Eastern to the Western Front.

   C eliminated the Allies' need for help from American soldiers.

   D caused thousands of French and British soldiers to refuse to continue fighting.

Short-Answer Question

Directions Base your answer to question 4 on the excerpt below and on your knowledge of social studies.

> In what I have already said about other nations putting us into war I have covered one point of sovereignty [supreme power] which ought never to be yielded—the power to send American soldiers and sailors everywhere, which ought never to be taken from the American people.
>
> —Senator Henry Cabot Lodge, "The League of Nations Must Be Revised," 1919

4. According to the document, why did Senator Lodge oppose U.S. participation in the League of Nations?

Review the Essential Questions

5. **Essay** When World War I began, many Americans felt torn and personally involved. Why? How did Americans' attitudes toward the war change as the conflict progressed?

To help you write your essay, review your answers to the Essential Questions in the section reviews and the chapter Foldables Study Organizer. Your essay should include:

- the causes and start of World War I;
- American neutrality and the eventual entry of the United States into war;
- the impact of the American military on the war effort;
- mobilization of the war effort at home and the control of public opinion; and
- Wilson's Fourteen Points, the League of Nations, and the Treaty of Versailles.

GO ON

Document-Based Questions

Directions: Analyze the documents and answer the short-answer questions that follow.

Document 1

Theodore Roosevelt wrote the following about the American war effort in 1917.

> The German-language papers carry on a consistent campaign in favor of Germany against England. They should be put out of existence for the period of this war. . . . Every disloyal native-born American should be disfranchised [deprived of rights] and interned [confined]. It is time to strike our enemies at home heavily and quickly.

Source: *The Foes of Our Own Household*

6. How did Roosevelt think disloyal Americans should be treated during the war? Why?

Document 2

This American poster from 1917 was directed toward recent immigrants to the U.S.

Remember Your First Thrill of
AMERICAN LIBERTY

YOUR DUTY-Buy
United States Government Bonds
2nd Liberty Loan of 1917

Source: The Granger Collection, New York

7. Why does this poster encourage recent immigrants to remember their "first thrill of American liberty"? Name two goals the poster hoped to achieve.

Document 3

The following table shows the number of military deaths by country in World War I.

Country	Number of Deaths
Austria-Hungary	1,200,000
France	1,375,800
Germany	1,773,700
Great Britain	908,371
Italy	650,000
Russia	1,700,000
U.S.	126,000

Source: Susan Everett, *History of World War I*

8. Which two countries had the most deaths? Why were U.S. deaths comparatively low?

Document 4

Sir Harold Nicolson, a British delegate, described the signing of the Treaty of Versailles.

> Through the door at the end appear two huissiers [court officers] with silver chains. . . . After them come four officers of France, Great Britain, America and Italy. And then, isolated and pitiable, come the two German delegates. . . . They keep their eyes fixed away from those two thousand staring eyes [ceremony attendees], fixed upon the ceiling. They are deathly pale. They do not appear as representatives of a brutal militarism.

Source: Harold Nicolson, *Peacemaking 1919*

9. What is the tone of this passage? How does Nicolson seem to feel about events? Explain.

10. Expository Writing Using the information from the four documents and your knowledge of social studies, write an essay in which you:

- discuss the war's most important impact on American society; and

- compare this to its most important impact on Allied and Central Powers.

Need Extra Help?										
If you missed questions. . .	1	2	3	4	5	6	7	8	9	10
Go to page. . .	263	274	278	290	262–290	285	283	286	289	262–290

Unit 4

Change and Conflict
1920–1945

King Kong film poster, 1933

"The only thing we have to fear is fear itself."
—Franklin D. Roosevelt

Drought refugees with stalled truck on New Mexico highway, 1937

Unit 4

Reading History

Questioning

Learn It!   One way to understand what you are reading is to interact with the text by asking questions.

Practice asking questions by turning headings into questions. For instance, the heading "Government Action" can be turned into the question "What actions did the government take to deal with the Great Depression?"

As you read, you should be able to find the answer in the next paragraph or section.

—from Chapter 11, p. 335

Government Action

Eventually Hoover recognized that the federal government had to take steps to combat the Depression. In 1931 he authorized additional federal spending on public works—projects such as highways, parks, and libraries—to create new jobs.

Practice It!   Read the paragraph. Turn the heading into a question and write your answer on another sheet of paper.

—from Chapter 11, p. 354

Creating Jobs

Millions of people—20 percent of the workforce—were still unemployed in 1935. In April Congress created the Works Progress Administration (WPA) to give people jobs and help the country. Led by Harry Hopkins, the WPA kept about 2 million people employed between 1935 and 1941. WPA workers built or repaired airports, public buildings, bridges, and roads.

Question

Answer

Academic Vocabulary Preview

Listed below are the academic vocabulary words and their definitions that you will come across as you study Unit 4. Practice It! will help you study the words and definitions.

Academic Vocabulary	Definition	Practice It!
Chapter 10 The Jazz Age		
normal (NAWR · muhl) *p. 303*	typical; average	**Identify** *the term from Chapter 10 that best completes the sentence.*
dynamic (dy · NA · mihk) *p. 305*	active and energetic	1. Mass production _____ led to increased productivity and lower prices.
detect (dih · TEHKT) *p. 310*	to uncover or discover the true character of	2. Businesses hired _____ to help them develop new products.
intervene (IHN · tuhr · VEEN) *p. 311*	to involve oneself in the affairs of another	3. Most people did not want the United States to _____ in the affairs of other countries.
expert (EHK · spuhrt) *p. 313*	a person with advanced knowledge	
technique (tehk · NEEK) *p. 313*	a skillful method	
device (dih · VYS) *p. 317*	an instrument or piece of equipment	
enormous (ih · NAWR · muhs) *p. 318*	huge	
Chapter 11 The Depression and The New Deal		
decline (dih · KLYN) *p. 332*	to descend; drop	**Identify** *the word from Chapter 11 that best matches the underlined term.*
collapse (kuh · LAPS) *p. 333*	to break down	4. When prices <u>fall</u>, many investors sell their stock.
promote (pruh · MOHT) *p. 340*	to help advance	5. President Roosevelt's fireside chats were designed to <u>build</u> people's confidence.
generate (JEH · nuh · RAYT) *p. 340*	to create	6. Many Dust Bowl families had to leave their homes and <u>move</u> to California in search of work.
migrate (MY · GRAYT) *p. 346*	to relocate; move	
advocate (AD · vuh · KAYT) *p. 348*	to support	
scheme (SKEEM) *p. 353*	a plan	
welfare (WEHL · FEHR) *p. 355*	standard care; well-being	
Chapter 12 America and World War II		
obtain (uhb · TAYN) *p. 364*	to gain	**Choose** *the word that best matches the meaning of each vocabulary term listed below.*
unify (YOO · nuh · FY) *p. 365*	to join together	7. **obtain** 9. **tense**
target (TAHR · guht) *p. 367*	an object of attack	a. select a. anxious
fund (FUHND) *p. 371*	a reserve or source of money	b. acquire b. loose
shift (SHIHFT) *p. 373*	to move	c. remove c. colorful
overseas (OH · vuhr · SEEZ) *p. 374*	across the ocean	8. **shift** 10. **conflict**
concentrate (KAHN · suhn · TRAYT) *p. 379*	to focus	a. delay a. theory
tense (TEHNS) *p. 381*	anxious; nervous	b. create b. fight
secure (sih · KYUR) *p. 388*	to gain control	c. change c. plan
conflict (KAHN · FLIHKT) *p. 390*	a war; prolonged struggle	

The Jazz Age
1920-1929

After World War I, many Americans enjoyed a time of prosperity and confidence.

★ 1920
- Prohibition begins
- Nineteenth Amendment grants woman suffrage

WARREN G. HARDING

★ 1922
Teapot Dome Scandal

PRESIDENTS

U.S. Events

World Events

1918

1921

★ 1918
Flu pandemic kills millions worldwide

Gauze masks were worn to protect against the flu. ▶

★ 1921
- Ireland becomes an independent country
- Albert Einstein wins Nobel Prize for Physics

History ONLINE

Chapter Overview Visit glencoe.com and click on **Chapter 10—Chapter Overviews** to preview chapter information.

Section 1: Time of Turmoil

Essential Question How did prejudice and labor strife affect the nation following World War I?

Section 2: Desire for Normalcy

Essential Question In what ways did the election of Harding and Coolidge reflect America's changing mood?

Section 3: A Booming Economy

Essential Question How did new technology and forms of transportation change American life?

Section 4: The Roaring Twenties

Essential Question How did social change affect the arts, the role of women, and minorities?

FOLDABLES
Study Organizer

Organizing Information

Make this four-pocket Foldable to help organize what you learn about the 1920s.

Step 1 On an 11" x 17" sheet of paper, make a fold as shown.

Step 2 Fold the sheet into four equal parts. Staple or glue the ends of the paper to make four pockets.

Step 3 Label the pockets of your Foldable as shown.

Reading and Writing As you read the chapter, list key people and events on index cards. Place the cards in the appropriate pocket. Use your cards to help you study for quizzes and tests.

▶ Babe Ruth of the New York Yankees

CALVIN COOLIDGE

★ **1924**
• Wyoming and Texas elect female governors
• Model T sells for less than $300

◀ Nellie Tayloe Ross, governor of Wyoming

★ **1927**
• Lindbergh flies across Atlantic
• Babe Ruth hits 60 home runs

1924   **1927**   **1930**

★ **1924**
First Winter Olympics staged in Chamonix, France

★ **1928**
Kellogg-Briand Pact aims to outlaw war

Essential Question ◄

How did prejudice and labor strife affect the nation following World War I?

Reading Guide

Content Vocabulary

capitalism *(p. 303)*   deport *(p. 303)*
anarchist *(p. 303)*

Academic Vocabulary

normal *(p. 303)*   dynamic *(p. 305)*

Key People and Events

Red Scare *(p. 303)*
Calvin Coolidge *(p. 305)*
Marcus Garvey *(p. 305)*

Reading Strategy

Taking Notes On a diagram like the one below, list the ways the U.S. government dealt with people they thought were a threat to the government.

Government Action	

American Diary

A wave of strikes after World War I fueled fears that Communists were conspiring to start a revolution in the United States. Attorney General A. Mitchell Palmer viewed them as a threat to the American values of religion, private property, and democracy. Declaring that "the blaze of revolution [is] eating its way into the homes of the American workman," Palmer was ready to take action.

—*from* New World Coming

Fear of Radicalism

Main Idea Events after World War I made some Americans intolerant of immigrants and foreign ideas.

History and You How do you feel about ideas and practices that are different from your own? Read to find out how Americans responded to people who had new ideas about social change.

· ·

As the 1920s began, Americans were coping with the uncertainties that followed World War I. Tired of war and world responsibilities, Americans wanted to return to a **normal,** or typical, way of life. As a result, they grew more suspicious of foreigners and those holding views that were different from their own.

Some Americans were especially disturbed by the Russian Revolution. In 1917 the Bolsheviks set up a Communist state in Russia. They urged workers around the world to overthrow **capitalism**—an economic system based on private property and free enterprise. Many Americans feared that "bolshevism" threatened American society.

Fanning those fears were the actions of **anarchists**—people who believe there should be no government. A series of anarchist bombings in 1919 in New York City, Seattle, and other cities frightened Americans.

The Red Scare

This wave of fear led to the **Red Scare,** a period when the government went after "Reds"—as Communists were known—and others with radical views. In late 1919 and early 1920, Attorney General A. Mitchell Palmer and his deputy, J. Edgar Hoover, ordered the arrest of more than 10,000 people suspected of being Communists and anarchists. Palmer and Hoover also staged raids on the headquarters of "suspicious" groups. They did not find the large stockpiles of weapons and dynamite they claimed they were seeking.

The government **deported**—expelled from the United States—a few hundred of the aliens it arrested but quickly released many others for lack of evidence.

Boston police confiscate literature on a raid.

Primary Source / **The Alien Act**

Rights v. Security The Alien Act, passed by Congress in October 1918, stated that "any alien who, at any time after entering the United States, is found to have been at the time of entry, or to have become thereafter, a member of any anarchist organization" could be deported. Journalist and critic H. L. Mencken spoke out about the erosion of rights. "Government, today, is growing too strong to be safe. There are no longer any citizens in the world; there are only subjects."

Critical Thinking

Defending Do you think the federal government should have the power to curtail individual rights during times of war or during times of great crisis? Why or why not?

People IN HISTORY

A. Philip Randolph

Labor leader and civil rights activist

A. Philip Randolph worked tirelessly for more than a decade to win union recognition for the Brotherhood of Sleeping Car Porters. He said, *"Freedom is never given; it is won. And the Negro people must win their freedom. . . . This involves struggle, continuous struggle."* Years later, when President Kennedy's Civil Rights Bill stalled in Congress, Randolph helped organize the March on Washington. More than 250,000 people rallied near the Lincoln Memorial on August 28, 1963, to show their support for civil rights.

Robert Sengstacke Abbott

Newspaper publisher

By the beginning of World War I, the *Chicago Defender*, founded by Robert Sengstacke Abbott, was the nation's most influential African American weekly newspaper. The paper led the Great Migration, a movement that encouraged African Americans in the South to move to Northern cities to escape segregation and to fill a labor shortage in factories. His paper wrote, *"To die from the bite of frost is far more glorious than at the hands of a mob."*

CRITICAL Thinking

Explaining What was the Great Migration? What effect did it have on Northern cities?

Sacco and Vanzetti

An event that for many came to symbolize fear of immigrants and radical ideas was the trial of Nicola Sacco and Bartolomeo Vanzetti. These two Italian immigrants and anarchists were accused of killing two men during a robbery in Massachusetts. The two men were tried and convicted in July 1921 and were sentenced to death.

Many Americans demanded that the death sentence be carried out. In 1927 a special Massachusetts commission upheld the verdict. Sacco and Vanzetti—proclaiming their innocence—were executed.

✓ **Reading Check** **Synthesizing** What events of the 1920s might be cited as evidence of prejudice against immigrants?

Labor and Racial Strife

Main Idea The 1920s brought increased labor unrest and racial tensions, often marked by violence.

History and You Do you think people of very different backgrounds can live together peacefully? Read to see how this issue affected Americans during the 1920s.

⋯⋯⋯⋯⋯⋯⋯⋯⋯⋯⋯⋯⋯⋯⋯⋯⋯⋯

After World War I, industrial workers launched strikes to get wage increases that would keep up with rapidly rising prices. Many Americans believed that Bolsheviks and radicals were causing this labor unrest. At the same time, racial tensions increased. In the North, many whites resented African American competition for factory jobs.

Strikes Sweep Country

In September 1919, about 350,000 steelworkers went on strike, demanding an increase in wages and an eight-hour workday. The steel companies accused the strikers of being "Red agitators." This charge cost the strikers public support and forced them to end the strike—but not before 18 strikers died in a riot in Gary, Indiana.

That same month, Boston police officers went on strike for the right to form a union. This strike by public employees angered many Americans, and they applauded when Massachusetts governor **Calvin Coolidge** called out the National Guard. When the strike collapsed, the entire police force was fired.

Many workers did not join labor unions, linking them with radicalism. Distrust of unions, as well as pressure from employers and government, led to a sharp drop in union membership in the 1920s.

Despite the unions' decline, a **dynamic,** or energetic, African American, A. Philip Randolph, started the Brotherhood of Sleeping Car Porters. This union of railroad workers began to grow in the 1930s, when the government began to encourage unions.

Racial Unrest

In 1919 rising racial tensions led to violence. In the South, more than 70 African Americans were lynched. In Chicago a violent riot broke out after a group of whites stoned an African American youth who was swimming in Lake Michigan. The youth drowned and the incident set off rioting. For two weeks African American and white gangs roamed city streets, attacking each other and burning buildings. The riot left 15 whites and 23 African Americans dead and more than 500 people injured.

Many African Americans turned to **Marcus Garvey** for answers. Marcus Garvey was born to a poor family in Jamaica. A powerful leader with a magnetic personality, Garvey opposed integration. Instead he supported a "back-to-Africa" movement, urging African Americans to establish their own country in Africa. Garvey founded the Universal Negro Improvement Association (UNIA) in 1914 to promote African American pride. It also helped African Americans start businesses. Garvey gained a large following.

✔ **Reading Check** **Explaining** Did Marcus Garvey support or oppose integration? Explain.

History ONLINE
Study Central™ To review this section, go to glencoe.com.

Section 1 Review

Vocabulary

1. Use each of these words in a sentence that explains its meaning: normal, capitalism, anarchist, deport, dynamic.

Main Ideas

2. Explaining What was the outcome of the Boston police strike of 1919?

3. Describing What was the UNIA? What was its purpose?

Critical Thinking

4. Analyzing Why did Americans fear anarchists? What did Americans expect to happen?

5. Determining Cause and Effect Create a diagram like the one below to identify reasons why union membership dropped in the 1920s.

Drop in Union Membership

6. Expository Writing Write a news summary of the arrest and trial of Sacco and Vanzetti.

Answer the
7. Essential Question
How did prejudice and labor strife affect the nation following World War I?

The Great Migration

Before World War I, most African Americans lived in the rural South. Most were farmers or sharecroppers; almost all were poor. Racial barriers kept them from moving into better-paying jobs. Legal racial segregation and frequent harassment were facts of life.

How Did Geography Affect the Great Migration?

Employment opportunities in Northern cities spurred migration. Labor shortages and limits on immigration after World War I prompted Northern factory owners to actively recruit African American workers. By 1920, almost 500,000 African Americans had moved to industrial cities such as Chicago, Detroit, New York, and Philadelphia. Many hoped to escape the racial injustice and economic hardship they faced in the South. This massive population movement, which became known as the Great Migration, radically changed the racial makeup of the entire nation.

Southern states
Primary migration routes

0 400 kilometers
0 400 miles
Albers Equal-Area projection

Detroit
Chicago
Cleveland
Pittsburgh
New York City
Philadelphia
Indianapolis
Cincinnati
Ky.
Va.
Ark.
Tenn.
N.C.
S.C.
Miss.
Ala.
Ga.
Tex.
La.
Fla.
ATLANTIC OCEAN
Gulf of Mexico
40°N
70°W
30°N
90°W
80°W

◄ Many African American soldiers returning to the United States after World War I settled in the North, seeking better lives for themselves and their families.

The Harlem Renaissance

Painter Jacob Lawrence (1917–2000) moved from the South to Harlem in New York City. He was a member of the movement called the Harlem Renaissance, in which African American writers and artists began creating works grounded in their own experiences and culture. His work included the series of paintings called "The Migration of the Negro" (1940–1941). This panel from the series shows African Americans buying train tickets to Northern cities. ▶

During the Great Migration, entire families—and sometimes whole communities—moved north. ▶

If You are a Stranger in the City

If you want a job   If you want a place to live
If you are having trouble with your employer
If you want information or advice of any kind
CALL UPON
The CHICAGO LEAGUE ON URBAN
CONDITIONS AMONG NEGROES
3719 South State Street
T. ARNOLD HILL, Executive Secretary
Telephone Douglas 9098
No charges—no fees. We want to help YOU

▲ Advertisements like this one from the *Chicago Defender*—an African American newspaper published in Chicago that strongly urged Southern African Americans to move north—offered help to recent arrivals.

"The wash and rush of this human tide on the beach line of the Northern city centers is to be explained primarily in terms of a new vision of opportunity, of social and economic freedom, of a spirit to seize, even in the face of an [excessive] and heavy toll, a chance for the improvement of conditions. With each successive wave of it, the movement of the [African American] becomes more and more a mass movement toward the larger and the more democratic chance—in the [African American's] case a deliberate flight not only from countryside to city, but from medieval America to modern."

—Professor Alain Locke,
Howard University, 1925

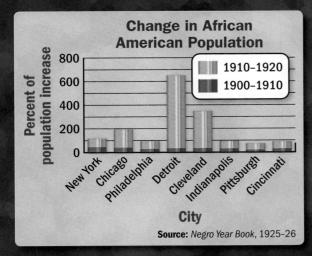

Change in African American Population

Percent of population increase

800
600
400
200
0

New York, Chicago, Philadelphia, Detroit, Cleveland, Indianapolis, Pittsburgh, Cincinnati

City

1910–1920
1900–1910

Source: *Negro Year Book*, 1925–26

Urban Growth In 1910, 75 percent of all African Americans lived on farms, and 90 percent lived in the South. The Great Migration changed that. Between 1900 and 1920, Chicago's African American population grew by nearly 200 percent; Cleveland's by 350 percent; Detroit's by more than 650 percent.

Analyzing Geography

1. **Human-Environment Interaction** How did World War I affect the migration of African Americans?

2. **Place** Which Northern cities saw the greatest increases in African American population as a result of the Great Migration?

Desire for Normalcy

Essential Question

In what ways did the election of Harding and Coolidge reflect America's changing mood?

Reading Guide

Content Vocabulary

lease *(p. 309)*   isolationism *(p. 311)*

Academic Vocabulary

detect *(p. 310)*   intervene *(p. 311)*

Key People and Events

Warren G. Harding *(p. 309)*

Teapot Dome *(p. 309)*

Reading Strategy

Taking Notes Re-create the Venn diagram below, and compare the characteristics of the presidencies of Harding and Coolidge.

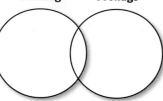

Harding   Coolidge

American Diary

In the summer of 1920, the Republicans gathered in Chicago to nominate a candidate for president. They had no outstanding leaders to head the party ticket. Senator Warren G. Harding of Ohio attracted attention with his friendly personality and fine voice. Harding had earned a reputation as a loyal Republican. Ohio political boss Harry Daugherty promoted Harding as a candidate for the nomination. "He looks like a president," Daugherty explained.

Harding's easygoing nature won the goodwill of the voters.

Harding and Coolidge

Main Idea The Harding and Coolidge administrations favored business and wanted a smaller government.

History and You Have you ever enjoyed a restful moment after working or playing hard? Read to find out about two presidents who tried to turn America from fast-paced change to quieter ways.

. . . .

In his campaign, **Warren G. Harding** promised a return to "normalcy." What Harding meant by "normalcy" was not really explicit, but the word sounded reassuring to Americans who wanted an end to foreign involvement and domestic turmoil.

Harding and his running mate, Massachusetts governor Calvin Coolidge, won a landslide victory in November 1920—the first presidential election in which women could vote. The Republican team easily defeated the Democratic candidate, Governor James Cox of Ohio, and his young running mate, Franklin Delano Roosevelt of New York. Harding named several talented people to his cabinet—Charles Evans Hughes, a former Supreme Court justice, as secretary of state; Andrew Mellon, a Pittsburgh banker and financier, to head the Treasury Department; and Herbert Hoover, a skilled organizer, as secretary of commerce.

Scandals

President Harding also gave government jobs to many of his political supporters— the so-called Ohio Gang. Many of these appointees were unqualified; some turned out to be corrupt. The biggest scandal of the administration involved Albert Fall, the secretary of the interior. In 1922 Fall secretly **leased,** or rented, government oil reserves in Elk Hills, California, and Teapot Dome, Wyoming, to the owners of two oil companies. In exchange, Fall received more than $400,000. Fall was convicted of bribery and became the first cabinet official ever to go to prison. **Teapot Dome** became a symbol of the corruption in the Harding administration.

Harding himself was not directly involved in any scandals, but as the rumors spread, he became troubled. In the summer of 1923, before the full story of the scandals came out, Harding took a trip west to escape the political troubles of Washington. During the trip, he became ill, suffered a heart attack, and died.

Primary Source / Campaign Items

Showing Support Political buttons and posters have long been used in campaigns to show support for a candidate.

Critical Thinking

Analyzing How do these campaign items portray the candidates? Which one do you think is more effective? Explain.

Primary Sources
INTERPRETING
POLITICAL CARTOONS

This cartoon was drawn by Daniel R. Fitzpatrick, who worked as the editorial cartoonist for the *St. Louis Post-Dispatch* in 1924. It shows business leaders gathered around a cash register singing about their friend, President Calvin Coolidge.

1. **Identifying** What does the cash register represent?

2. **Analyzing** What are the business leaders saying about President Coolidge? Why?

"Silent Cal" Takes Over

Vice President Calvin Coolidge was visiting his father in Vermont when he heard the news of Harding's death. Coolidge's father, a justice of the peace, administered the presidential oath of office. As president, Calvin Coolidge was in many ways the opposite of Harding. Harding loved to talk and meet people; in contrast, Coolidge said very little and earned the nickname "Silent Cal." In addition, Coolidge had a reputation for honesty. After becoming president, he allowed the investigations into the Harding scandals to proceed without interference. He replaced corrupt members of the Ohio Gang with honest officials.

Coolidge, like Harding, took a hands-off, or laissez-faire, approach to government. He once said, "If the federal government should go out of existence, the common run of the people would not **detect** the difference for a considerable length of time."

History ONLINE
Student Web Activity Visit glencoe.com and complete the Chapter 10 Web Activity about the Jazz Age.

A Friend to Business

The Coolidge administration and the Republican-controlled Congress held that support of business would aid prosperity. The government cut spending and lowered income tax rates on wealthy Americans and corporations. It also raised tariffs to protect business and overturned laws regulating child labor and women's wages.

A New Term

Coolidge seemed to be what the country wanted. At the 1924 Republican national convention, Coolidge was nominated without opposition. The Democrats named John W. Davis of West Virginia as their candidate. Wisconsin senator Robert La Follette was the choice of a third party, the Progressives. Coolidge swept the 1924 presidential race with 54 percent of the popular vote. For the first time in America's history, women won governors' races—Nellie Tayloe Ross in Wyoming and Miriam Ferguson in Texas.

Reading Check **Describing** Why was Harding's emphasis on "normalcy" an effective campaign strategy?

Foreign Policy

Main Idea Harding and Coolidge aimed to limit the role of the United States in foreign affairs.

History and You Have you ever wanted to stay out of an argument between two other people? Read on to see how the United States tried to avoid involvement in international disputes.

Harding and Coolidge both favored a limited role for the nation in world affairs. They desired world peace but did not want the nation to enter the League of Nations or join foreign alliances. Harding had promised the American people that he would not lead them into the League "by the side door, back door, or cellar door." Many Americans supported this policy of **isolationism.**

Promoting Peace

The Harding administration made serious efforts to promote peace. After the war the United States, Britain, and Japan began a naval arms race. In 1921 Secretary of State Hughes invited Japan and Britain to Washington, D.C., to discuss the problem. In February 1922, the three nations, along with France and Italy, signed the Five-Power Treaty to limit the size of the nations' navies. The treaty marked the first time in modern history that world powers agreed to disarm.

In August 1928 the United States joined 14 other nations in signing the Kellogg-Briand Pact, which called for outlawing war. Within a few years, 48 other nations signed the pact, but it lacked any means of enforcing peace.

A More Friendly Neighbor

The United States **intervened,** or got involved, in Latin America several times in the early 1900s to support American business interests. By 1920 American troops were stationed in the Dominican Republic and Nicaragua, and relations with Mexico were tense.

After the Dominican Republic and Nicaragua held elections in the mid-1920s, the United States withdrew its troops from those countries. American investors asked President Coolidge to send troops into Mexico when its government threatened to take over foreign-owned oil and mining companies. Coolidge chose to negotiate instead, and the United States reached a peaceful settlement with Mexico.

Reading Check **Explaining** Why would the Kellogg-Briand Pact prove to be ineffective?

Section 2 Review

History ONLINE
Study Central™ To review this section, go to glencoe.com.

Vocabulary

1. Use each of these terms in a complete sentence that will help explain its meaning: lease, detect, isolationism, intervene.

Main Ideas

2. **Analyzing** Why did President Harding give important government jobs to people who were unqualified for their positions? What happened as a result?

3. **Summarizing** What did the Harding and Coolidge administrations do to promote world peace?

Critical Thinking

4. **Explaining** How does an increase in tariffs help the business community?

5. **Comparing** Create a table and list reasons for and against American isolationism.

Isolationism	
For	Against

6. **Persuasive Writing** Neither Harding nor Coolidge wanted the United States to join the League of Nations. Do you agree with their position? Write a paragraph that explains your point of view.

7. **Answer the Essential Question** In what ways did the election of Harding and Coolidge reflect America's changing mood?

A Booming Economy

How did technology and new forms of transportation change American life?

Reading Guide

Content Vocabulary

recession *(p. 313)*

productivity *(p. 313)*

gross national product *(p. 313)*

installment buying *(p. 314)*

Academic Vocabulary

expert *(p. 313)*   technique *(p. 313)*

Key People and Events

Henry Ford *(p. 314)*

Reading Strategy

Taking Notes Re-create the chart below and record new American business management changes and what they were intended to achieve.

Business Practice	Goal

American Diary

After a brief decline, the American economy began to grow steadily; this lasted most of the 1920s. Higher wages and shorter workdays kept the economy booming. In a speech in 1925, President Calvin Coolidge said, "The chief business of the American people is business. . . . The accumulation of wealth means the multiplication of schools, the increase of knowledge, . . . the expansion of liberties."

—*from* Address to the American Society of Newspaper Editors

Growth in the 1920s

Main Idea The United States experienced amazing economic growth during the 1920s.

History and You As you get ready for school, think about all the ways that you use electricity. Read to find out how electricity improved the lives of people living in the 1920s.

• •

A **recession,** or economic downturn, lingered after World War I. The economy then began a steady growth that lasted most of the decade. In 1922 the nation's **gross national product** (GNP)—the total value of all goods and services produced—was $70 billion. By 1929 it rose to $100 billion.

Technology spurred, or stimulated, rapid industrial growth, and electricity powered American industry. Before World War I, only 30 percent of the nation's factories were run by electricity. By 1929, this figure had risen to 70 percent. Electricity was cheaper than steam power. By cutting the costs of production, businesses could lower prices and increase profits.

Management and Workers

New ways of managing businesses helped the economy grow. Many employers used scientific management—hiring **experts,** or people with advanced knowledge, to adopt more efficient work methods. These methods lowered costs and increased **productivity**—the amount of work each worker could do.

Many businesses adopted mass-production **techniques,** or skillfull methods, using the assembly line, which was first introduced in Henry Ford's automobile factories. Assembly lines increased productivity and cut production costs.

Businesses also tried to build better relations with workers. They set up safety programs that lowered the risk of death or injury on the job. Some provided health and accident insurance. Others encouraged workers to buy stock in the company. These steps—known as welfare capitalism—aimed to link workers more closely to the company they worked for. Businesses also adopted these steps to keep workers from joining independent unions.

By the Numbers / The 1920s Economy

Industry (Percentage Increase, 1922–28)	
Industrial production	70%
Gross national product	40%
Corporate profits	62%

Workers (Percentage Increase, 1922–28)	
Workers' incomes	11%
Average workweek	-4%

Source: Jules Tygiel, "The 1920s Economy: A Statistical Portrait"

TOASTMASTER Automatic Electric Toaster
You do not have to Watch it—The Toast can't Burn.
Study Carefully These INSTRUCTIONS

Invented in the 1920s
- Push-button elevators
- Electric razors
- Spiral-bound notebooks
- Pop-up toasters
- Car radios
- Adhesive tape
- Self-winding wristwatch
- Band-Aid™

Critical Thinking

Identifying Cause and Effect How did standardized mass production change the American economy?

*The Ford assembly line sped production and led to lower prices. Tires **A** are put on the wheels; gas tanks **B** slide onto the conveyor belt; and the engine **C**, the radiator **D**, and the auto body **E** are lowered onto the moving chassis.*

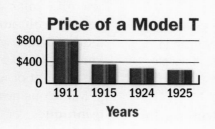

Price of a Model T

U.S. Auto Industry in 1914

Workers   Cars produced

84%   48%   52%
16%

Ford Motor Company
Other U.S. auto companies

Source: *Encyclopaedia Britannica.*

Graph Skills

Speculating Why was the Ford Motor Company able to produce and sell more cars than its competitors?

Graphs In MOtion See StudentWorks™ Plus or glencoe.com.

The Consumer Economy

By the 1920s, more than 60 percent of American households had electricity. Companies produced and consumers acquired electric appliances—refrigerators, stoves, vacuum cleaners, and radios. Using electric appliances meant less time on household chores.

Businesses spent more money on advertising to persuade people to buy a particular product. Newspapers and magazines were filled with ads, and with the spread of radio, a new advertising form—the commercial announcement—was born.

Spurred by ads to buy more, consumers found a new way to make those purchases—**installment buying.** Consumers could now buy products by promising to pay small, regular amounts over a period of time.

Reading Check **Explaining** Why did the price of some consumer goods decrease?

The Automobile Age

Main Idea The automobile industry stimulated the economy and transformed the ways Americans traveled and lived.

History and You Can you think of a recent invention that has greatly changed the way in which you live? Read on to find out how the automobile changed America during the 1920s.

D uring the 1920s, the car became an important part of American life. The nation's economy, too, revolved around the automobile. Almost 4 million Americans worked for auto companies or in related jobs. Detroit, Michigan, became the automobile manufacturing center of the world. **Henry Ford** was a pioneer in making affordable, dependable autos with his Model T, which was built using assembly-line methods.

The car was sturdy, reliable, and inexpensive. In 1914 Ford announced that he would pay his workers the high wage of $5 per day. Workers were happy, and Ford had more customers as he steadily dropped the price of his Model T. By the mid-1920s, other car makers, such as General Motors, cut into Ford's sales by offering autos with various improvements. Out of this competition came the practice of introducing new car models each year.

Effect on Other Industries

Americans' love of driving called for new roads and highways. Highways, in turn, needed gas stations and rest stops. Businesses along major roads profited from many people now traveling around the country by car.

The car boom affected industries that made products used in cars. For example, the steel, rubber, and glass industries grew.

Travel for pleasure became a regular part of daily life. People could now go wherever they wished. Cars also contributed to the spread of suburbs. Because people could now drive to work, they could live in a suburb and still hold a job in the city.

Those Left Behind

Despite this prosperity, many Americans did not share in the boom of the 1920s. Farmers especially had difficulties. During the war, the government had bought wheat, corn, and other products, and farmers prospered from higher prices. After the war, farmers had to compete with European agriculture again. Food prices fell, and farm income dropped. Unable to pay their debts, many farmers lost their farms.

Farmers were not alone in suffering. Railroad workers and coal miners had a difficult time as trucks took business from railroads and electricity replaced coal as a power source. Americans also were buying less cotton and more clothes made of synthetic fibers. As cotton prices plunged, many textile factories had to shut down. Workers' wages rose slightly, but the cost of living rose more. By 1929 nearly three-fourths of families had incomes below $2,500, the accepted level needed for a comfortable life.

Reading Check **Explaining** How did the automobile change life in the United States?

Section 3 Review

History ONLINE
Study Central™ To review this section, go to glencoe.com.

Vocabulary

1. Explain the meaning of the following terms by using each one in a sentence: recession, gross national product, expert, productivity, technique, installment buying.

Main Ideas

2. **Explaining** How did the availability of electricity change the habits of American consumers in the 1920s?

3. **Evaluating** Who benefited from the increased popularity of the automobile?

Critical Thinking

4. **Analyzing** Discuss the pros and cons of installment buying for the American consumer.

5. **Determining Cause and Effect** Create a chart like the one below. Record the major cause behind the invention of the automobile and add any additional causes and effects that occurred.

Cause	Effects	Effects

6. **Persuasive Writing** It is 1920 and you work for a company that manufactures and sells the latest home appliance—the refrigerator. Write a radio commercial explaining what a refrigerator does and the advantages of owning one.

Answer the Essential Question

7. How did new technology and forms of transportation change American life?

The Roaring Twenties

Essential Question

How did social change affect the arts, the role of women, and minorities?

Reading Guide

Content Vocabulary

flapper *(p. 317)*   nativism *(p. 320)*

mass media *(p. 317)*   quota system *(p. 320)*

expatriate *(p. 319)*   evolution *(p. 321)*

Prohibition *(p. 319)*

Academic Vocabulary

device *(p. 317)*   enormous *(p. 318)*

Key People and Events

Harlem Renaissance *(p. 318)*

Eighteenth Amendment *(p. 319)*

Twenty-first Amendment *(p. 320)*

Reading Strategy

Taking Notes On a diagram like the one below, list the major themes that appeared in the art, writing, and music of the 1920s.

American Diary

On the morning of May 20, 1927, a young pilot named Charles Lindbergh made the final preparations for takeoff. Shortly before 8:00 A.M., Lindbergh climbed into his aircraft and took off for Paris. The news of his departure "flashed along the wires," the American people were united in "the exaltation of a common emotion." All minds and hearts were focused on the brave pilot who was crossing the vast Atlantic Ocean.

Social and Cultural Change

Main Idea During the 1920s, social changes affected the role of women and led to new forms of entertainment and culture.

History and You Have you known anyone who has moved from the United States to reside in another country? Read to find out why many American writers and artists of the 1920s settled in Europe.

In May 1927 aviator Charles Lindbergh became the first person to fly alone across the Atlantic Ocean. Americans went wild and hailed Lindbergh as a hero. The national embrace of Lindbergh showed what one historian called a "delighted concern over things that were exciting but didn't matter profoundly."

Changes for Women

The 1920s brought changes for women. One important change was the ratification of the Nineteenth Amendment in 1920. The amendment guaranteed women in all states the right to vote. Women also ran for election to political offices.

The number of women working outside the home grew steadily. Most working women became teachers or office workers, but some college-educated women began professional careers. Still, most married women remained within the home, working as mothers and homemakers.

The symbol of the new "liberated" woman of the 1920s was the **flapper**—a carefree young woman with short "bobbed" hair, heavy makeup, and short skirts. Many people saw the behavior of flappers as a sign of changing morals and new freedoms.

Movies and Radio

Cultural changes spread quickly because of the growth of **mass media**—forms of communication, such as newspapers and radio, that reach millions of people. Laborsaving **devices,** or equipment, and fewer working hours gave Americans more leisure time to enjoy newspapers, magazines, phonograph records, the radio, and the movies.

In the 1920s the motion picture industry in Hollywood, California, became a major business. For millions of Americans, the movies offered entertainment and escape. The first movies were black and white and silent, with the actors' dialog printed on the screen. In 1927 Hollywood introduced movies with sound. The first "talkie," *The Jazz Singer,* created a sensation.

Primary Source | Bessie Coleman

A Flying Pioneer Bessie Coleman was the first female African American to receive a pilot's license and the first to become a stunt pilot. She championed the cause of equal rights, refusing to perform at shows that did not admit African Americans. Coleman's achievements inspired the founding of Chicago's Coffey School of Aeronautics. Its graduates helped train the U.S. military's first African American pilots, the Tuskegee airmen, who served with distinction in World War II. A Chicago, Illinois, city council resolution stated that "Bessie Coleman continues to inspire . . . young persons with her sense of adventure, her positive attitude and her determination to succeed."

Critical Thinking

Interpreting Why was Charles Lindbergh a symbol of modern America?

The radio brought entertainment into people's homes in the 1920s. Radio networks broadcast popular programs that included news, concerts, sporting events, and comedies. Businesses soon realized that the radio offered an **enormous,** or huge, audience for messages about their products, so they began to help finance radio programs. Radio stations sold spot advertisements, or commercials, to companies.

Sports and Fads

Radio added to the popularity of sports, such as baseball, football, and boxing, by allowing listeners to experience sporting events as they happened. Americans flocked to sporting events, and sports stars became heroes.

In the 1920s Americans took up new activities with enthusiasm, turning them into fads. Board games and crossword puzzles were all the rage. Contests such as flagpole sitting and dance marathons—often lasting three or four days—made headlines.

Jazz and the Harlem Renaissance

During the 1920s people danced to the beat of a new kind of music called jazz. Jazz captured the spirit of the era so well that the 1920s is often referred to as the Jazz Age. Rooted in African American music, jazz uses dynamic rhythms and improvisation—new rhythms and melodies created during a performance. Among the best-known African American jazz musicians were trumpeter Louis Armstrong, pianist and composer Duke Ellington, and singer Bessie Smith.

The rhythm and themes of jazz inspired a blossoming of culture in Harlem, an African American section of New York City. During this movement, called the **Harlem Renaissance,** writers such as Langston Hughes, James Weldon Johnson, and Zora Neale Hurston presented the African American experience in novels, poems, and short stories. In his autobiography, Langston Hughes described his arrival in Harlem:

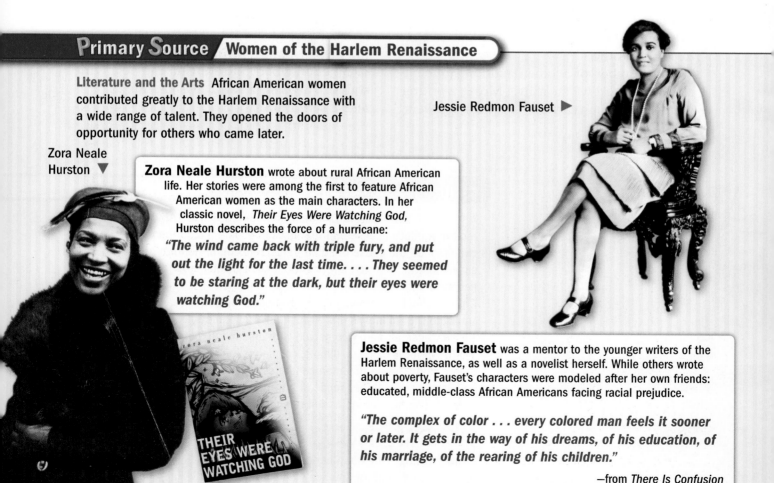

Primary Source | **Women of the Harlem Renaissance**

Literature and the Arts African American women contributed greatly to the Harlem Renaissance with a wide range of talent. They opened the doors of opportunity for others who came later.

Jessie Redmon Fauset ▶

Zora Neale Hurston ▼

Zora Neale Hurston wrote about rural African American life. Her stories were among the first to feature African American women as the main characters. In her classic novel, *Their Eyes Were Watching God,* Hurston describes the force of a hurricane:

"The wind came back with triple fury, and put out the light for the last time. . . . They seemed to be staring at the dark, but their eyes were watching God."

Jessie Redmon Fauset was a mentor to the younger writers of the Harlem Renaissance, as well as a novelist herself. While others wrote about poverty, Fauset's characters were modeled after her own friends: educated, middle-class African Americans facing racial prejudice.

"The complex of color . . . every colored man feels it sooner or later. It gets in the way of his dreams, of his education, of his marriage, of the rearing of his children."

—from *There Is Confusion*

"I can never put on paper the thrill of that underground ride to Harlem. . . . I went up the steps and out into the bright September sunlight. Harlem! I stood there, dropped my bags, took a deep breath and felt happy again."

—from *The Big Sea*

A Lost Generation of Writers

While the Harlem Renaissance thrived, other writers questioned American ideals. Some influential writers were **expatriates**—people who choose to live in another country. Writer Gertrude Stein called these rootless Americans "the lost generation."

Other writers remained at home and wrote about life in America. Novelist Sinclair Lewis presented a critical view of American culture. In *Winesburg, Ohio,* Sherwood Anderson explored small-town life in the Midwest.

✔ **Reading Check** **Comparing** What fads were popular in the 1920s? What are two comparable fads today?

Augusta Christine Savage was the seventh of 14 children. Because her family could not afford to buy toys, she molded small animals into playthings from the red-clay soil at her Florida home. Savage studied sculpture in France and eventually taught art in Harlem to young people.

Gamin by Augusta Christine Savage ▶

Critical Thinking

Analyzing Why do you think these women chose to write about the African American lifestyle and culture?

A Clash of Cultures

Main Idea During the 1920s, American society was divided by a clash between traditional and modern values.

History and You Think of an issue that is important to you. What would you be willing to do to stand up for that issue? Read to learn how various groups in the 1920s clashed over issues they considered important.

D uring the 1920s cities and industries grew. Many Americans, however, did not identify with this new, urban society. They believed that the America they knew and valued—a nation based on family, church, and tradition—was under attack. Disagreement arose between those who defended traditional beliefs and those who welcomed the new.

Prohibition

One issue that divided Americans was the use of alcoholic beverages. The temperance movement, the campaign against alcohol use, was rooted in religious objections to drinking alcohol and in the belief that society would benefit if alcohol were unavailable.

The movement reached its goal in 1919 with the ratification of the **Eighteenth Amendment** to the Constitution. This amendment established **Prohibition**—a total ban on the manufacture, sale, and transportation of liquor throughout the United States. In the rural South and Midwest, where the temperance movement was strong, Prohibition generally succeeded. In the cities, however, Prohibition had little support. The nation divided into two camps: the "drys"—those who supported Prohibition—and the "wets" —those who opposed it.

A continuing demand for alcohol led to widespread lawbreaking. Illegal bars and clubs, known as speakeasies, sprang up in cities. With only about 1,500 agents, the federal government could do little to enforce Prohibition. By the early 1920s, many states in the East stopped trying to enforce the laws.

Education in the 1920s

Going to School
Society was changing rapidly. Nowhere was change more evident than in education. Larger numbers of young people were in school than ever before. By 1930 a majority of children of high school age were in school.

1910 18%

1920 35%

1930 55%

■ Enrollment in grades 9–12 as a percentage of 14–17 year olds.

Source: U.S. Census Bureau, *Statistical Abstract of the United States*

Prohibition contributed to the rise of organized crime. Powerful gangsters, such as Chicago's Al Capone, made millions of dollars from bootlegging—producing and selling illegal alcohol. They used their profits to influence businesses, labor unions, and governments.

Over time many Americans realized that the "noble experiment," as Prohibition was called, had failed. Prohibition was repealed in 1933 with the **Twenty-first Amendment.** It is the only amendment ever passed to over-turn an earlier amendment.

Nativism

Many native-born Americans feared the rapid changes in society. Their concerns led to an upsurge of **nativism**—the belief that native-born Americans are superior to for-eigners. With this renewed nativism came a revival of the Ku Klux Klan.

The first Klan was founded in the 1860s in the South to deprive African Americans from exercising their rights. The second Klan, set up in 1915, still preyed on African Americans, but it also targeted Catholics, Jews, immi-grants, and other groups it believed to repre-sent "un-American" values. To get their way, Klan members used scare tactics, whipped or lynched people, and burned property. In the 1920s the Klan spread from the South to other areas of the country.

Nativism also arose because some Ameri-cans believed that foreigners would take away their jobs. This anti-immigrant preju-dice was directed mainly at southern and eastern Europeans and Asians.

In 1921 Congress responded to these Nativ-ist fears by passing the Emergency Quota Act. This law established a **quota system,** an arrangement that placed a limit on the number of immigrants from each country.

Trends in Public Education:

- High school attendance more than doubles during the 1920s.
- Minimum legal dropout age is raised.
- By 1930 every state has mandatory attendance laws.

Crowded Classrooms During the 1920s, many small schools were combined. Some consolidated schools grew to be very large. By 1930 the country had 29 high schools with more than 5,000 students. One school, DeWitt Clinton in New York City, had more than 10,000 students. A 1923 issue of *TIME* magazine described the crowded conditions:

"On the grand average, about one child in ten must join the overflow classes in basement or improvised classrooms."

Critical Thinking

Explaining What was one effect of the great increase in student enrollment?

Graphs In Motion See StudentWorks™ Plus or glencoe.com.

The act limited the number of immigrants to the United States in any one year to 3 percent of the total number of people in any national group that had been living in America in 1910. This policy favored immigration from northern and western Europe. In 1910 people from those regions were more numerous than those from other parts of Europe.

Congress revised the law in 1924. The National Origins Act reduced the annual country quota from 3 percent to 2 percent and based it on the census of 1890. The law also excluded Japanese immigrants completely. An earlier law passed in 1890 already excluded the Chinese.

Quotas did not apply to countries in the Western Hemisphere. As a result, immigration from Canada and Mexico increased. By 1930 more than 1 million Mexicans had come to live in the United States.

The Scopes Trial

Another cultural clash in the 1920s involved the role of religion in society. This conflict gained national attention in 1925 in one of the most famous trials of the era.

In 1925 the state of Tennessee passed a law making it illegal to teach **evolution**—the scientific theory that humans evolved over vast periods of time. The law was supported by Christian fundamentalists, who accepted the biblical story of creation. The fundamentalists saw evolution as a challenge to their values and their religious beliefs.

A young high school teacher named John Scopes deliberately broke the law against teaching evolution so that a trial could test its legality. Scopes acted with the support of the American Civil Liberties Union (ACLU). During the sweltering summer of 1925, the nation followed day-to-day developments in the Scopes trial with great interest. More than 100 journalists from around the country descended on Dayton, Tennessee, to report on the trial.

Two famous lawyers took opposing sides in the trial. William Jennings Bryan, Democratic candidate for president in 1896, 1900, and 1908 and a strong opponent of evolution, led the prosecution. Clarence Darrow, who had defended many radicals and labor union members, spoke for Scopes.

Although Scopes was convicted of breaking the law and fined $100, the fundamentalists lost the larger battle. Darrow's defense made it appear that Bryan wanted to impose his religious beliefs on the entire nation. The Tennessee Supreme Court overturned Scopes's conviction.

The Scopes case may have dealt a blow to fundamentalism, but the movement continued to thrive. Rural people, especially in the South and Midwest, remained faithful to their religious beliefs. When large numbers of farmers migrated to cities during the 1920s, they brought fundamentalism with them.

Reading Check **Analyzing** How did new laws limit immigration?

The Election of 1928

Main Idea Prosperity, prohibition, and religion were the major themes of the 1928 election.

History and You If you were choosing a president of the United States, what qualifications would you look for in a candidate? Read on to find out about the candidates who ran for president in 1928.

• •

In 1927 President Coolidge shocked people by announcing that he would not run for a second full term. Herbert Hoover declared his candidacy for the Republican nomination.

During World War I, Hoover won respect as the head of a committee providing food relief for Europe. He showed such a gift in this role that "to Hooverize" came to mean "to economize, to save and share." Later, Hoover served Presidents Harding and Coolidge as secretary of commerce.

Hoover worked tirelessly to promote cooperation between government and business. A symbol of the forward-looking middle class, he easily won the Republican nomination. Because he favored a ban on sales of alcohol, Hoover was considered the "dry" candidate.

The Democrats chose a far different kind of frontrunner—Alfred E. Smith, governor of New York. The son of immigrants and a man of the city, Smith opposed Prohibition and championed the poor and the working class. As the first Roman Catholic nominee for president, Smith was the target of anti-Catholic feeling. Many Protestants feared that the Catholic Church financed the Democrats and would rule the United States if Smith got into the White House. These attacks embarrassed Hoover, a Protestant Quaker, and he tried to stop them, but the charges seriously damaged Smith's candidacy.

Smith's bigger problem, however, was the prosperity of the 1920s, for which the Republicans took credit. Hoover won the election by a landslide due to the Republican prosperity and the religious prejudice against Smith. The contest reflected many of the tensions in American society—rural versus urban life, nativism versus foreign influences, "wets" versus "drys," Protestants versus Catholics, and traditional values versus modern values.

Reading Check **Identifying** Why was Hoover elected president by a landslide in 1928?

Section 4 Review

History ONLINE
Study Central™ To review this section, go to glencoe.com.

Vocabulary

1. Write a sentence to explain each term: flapper, mass media, device, enormous, expatriate, Prohibition, nativism, quota system, evolution.

Main Ideas

2. **Summarizing** What forms of art and entertainment became popular during the 1920s?

3. **Describing** What did reformers hope to accomplish with Prohibition in the 1920s?

4. **Explaining** How did the politics of the election of 1928 reflect the social changes of the 1920s?

Critical Thinking

5. **Identifying** On a diagram like the one below, identify some direct results of nativism in America in the 1920s.

Nativism

6. **Persuasive Writing** You are running for governor of your state in 1928. Write a campaign speech on the issues that will persuade your audience to vote for you.

Answer the
Essential Question

7. How did social change affect the arts, the role of women, and minorities?

Visual Summary

Economic Change

Business Innovation

- Mass production reduces prices
- New technology leads to new industries
- New consumer goods fuel a manufacturing boom

Charles Lindbergh

Government's Role

- Little interference with business
- Cut government spending and debt
- High tariffs

Effect: Prosperity for Some

The growth of new, urban industries fueled an economic boom during the 1920s. For the most part, farmers and minorities did not share in the prosperity.

Consumer Society

- Demand for product grows
- Installment buying boosts consumer spending
- Mass advertising

The 1920s was the age of the automobile.

Cultural and Social Change

Time of Turmoil

- Fear of communism grows
- Labor strikes occur
- Racial tension grows

The Jazz Age

- Women gain the right to vote
- The Harlem Renaissance reflects a new spirit of pride and protest
- Art, literature, and popular culture reflect the modern age

Effect: A Clash of Values

Major social and cultural achievements took place during the 1920s. For many Americans, however, these changes meant a loss of important traditional values.

Points of Conflict

- The Eighteenth Amendment establishes Prohibition
- The Twenty-first Amendment repeals Prohibition
- Nativism helps revive the Ku Klux Klan
- Congress passes quota laws to limit immigration
- Many fear the nation is losing its traditional values

Police confiscate literature

STUDY TO GO Study anywhere, anytime! Download quizzes and flash cards to your PDA from glencoe.com.

America's LITERATURE

Meet the Author

Langston Hughes (1902–1967) lived during a time of great racial turmoil in the United States. His grandmother raised him in Lawrence, Kansas, until he was a young teen. When she died, he lived with his grandmother's friends and then eventually with his mother in Ohio. Throughout his childhood, he turned to books to ease his loneliness.

Building Background

Hughes wrote poetry as a teenager, publishing "The Negro Speaks of Rivers" when he was 17 years old. That poem, along with "Mother to Son," exemplifies the pride Hughes had in his African American heritage. Hughes declared, "We younger Negro artists who create now intend to express our individual dark-skinned selves without fear or shame." As you read his poems, pay attention to how he uses words and symbols to relate the experiences of African Americans.

Vocabulary

dawns days

bosom chest

dusky dark

▲ "Jacobia Hotel" by William H. Johnson typifies the art of the Harlem Renaissance.

THE NEGRO SPEAKS OF RIVERS

Langston Hughes

I've known rivers:
I've known rivers ancient as the world and older than the
   flow of human blood in human veins.

My soul has grown deep like the rivers.

I bathed in the Euphrates when **dawns** were young.
I built my hut near the Congo and it lulled me to sleep.
I looked upon the Nile and raised the pyramids above it.
I heard the singing of the Mississippi when Abe Lincoln
   went down to New Orleans, and I've seen its muddy
   bosom turn all golden in the sunset.

I've known rivers:
Ancient, **dusky** rivers.

My soul has grown deep like the rivers.

MOTHER TO SON

Langston Hughes

Well, son, I'll tell you:
Life for me ain't been no crystal stair.
It's had tacks in it,
And splinters,
And boards torn up,
And places with no carpet on the floor—
Bare.
But all the time
I'se been a-climbin' on,
And reachin' landin's,
And turnin' corners,
And sometimes goin' in the dark
Where there ain't been no light.
So boy, don't you turn back.
Don't you set down on the steps
'Cause you finds it's kinder hard.
Don't you fall now—
For I'se still goin', honey,
I'se still climbin',
   And life for me ain't been no crystal stair.

Analyzing Literature

1. **Respond**
   (a) What is your impression about the lives of African Americans based on these poems?
   (b) What words and phrases in the poems give you that impression?

2. **Recall and Analyze**
   (a) What rivers does Hughes discuss in "The Negro Speaks of Rivers"?
   (b) How does Hughes use the rivers as a symbol for the African American experience?

3. **Evaluate** In what ways are the poems similar? How are they different?

STANDARDIZED TEST PRACTICE

TEST-TAKING TIP

If you are stuck on a question, temporarily skip it. Return to the question once you have answered those you are sure about. Come back to the question, and if you are still unsure, take a guess.

Reviewing Main Ideas

Directions: Choose the best answer for each of the following questions.

1. What contributed to the sharp drop in labor union membership in the 1920s?

   A rising prices

   B racial tensions

   C unchanged wages

   D government pressure

2. Who prospered under Coolidge and his Republican-controlled Congress?

   A the Ohio Gang

   B female workers

   C business interests

   D American children

3. Ford increased the sales of his automobiles by

   A building new highways.

   B establishing labor unions in his factories.

   C introducing the assembly line.

   D steadily dropping the price of the Model T.

4. A form of 1920s entertainment that was rooted in African American culture is

   A jazz.

   B movies.

   C football.

   D speakeasies.

Short-Answer Question

Directions: Base your answer to question 5 on the excerpt below and on your knowledge of social studies.

> An ostrich could assimilate a croquet ball or a cobble-stone with about the same ease that America assimilated her newcomers from Central and South-eastern Europe. Most of them seem to have been inoculated [vaccinated] against assimilation before leaving home. Their standard of living in their home countries was as low as any standard of living could possibly be. If it had been any lower, it would have ceased to be a standard, and would have become a hole or socket.
>
> —from *Why Europe Leaves Home*

5. What ideas about immigration are expressed in the above statement?

Review the Essential Questions

6. Essay How did changes after World War I affect American life?

To help you write your essay, review your answers to the Essential Questions in the section review and the chapter Foldables Study Organizer. Your essay should include:

   • examples illustrating fear of immigrants and persecution of unions;
   • evidence of American support for business and the policy of isolationism;
   • factors that led to economic growth;
   • changes in the arts; and
   • new roles for women and minorities.

GO ON

History ONLINE

For additional test practice, use **Self-Check Quizzes**—Chapter 10 at glencoe.com.

Document-Based Questions

Directions: Analyze the documents and answer the short-answer questions that follow.

Document 1

This excerpt, from a 1920 memoir by Evalyn McLean, talks about the kinds of friendships Warren G. Harding developed during his presidency.

> Unhappily, for many persons [Harding] had become something other than a friend; he was to all of these no less a thing than Opportunity.

Source: Henry Steele Commager, *Witness to America*

7. Based on this document, cite one reason that Harding's administration ended in scandal.

Document 2

First Lady Grace Coolidge describes her role.

> We New England women cling to the old way and being the President's wife isn't going to make me think less about the domestic duties I've always loved.

Source: Carl Sferrazza Anthony, *First Ladies: The Saga of Presidents' Wives and Their Power, 1789–1961*

8. Based on the document, did Grace Coolidge view herself as a liberated woman of the 1920s?

Document 3

This excerpt from *A Farewell to Arms* describes the Italian front during World War I.

> At the start of the winter came the permanent rain and with the rain came the cholera. But it was checked and in the end only seven thousand died of it in the army.

Source: Ernest Hemingway

9. How would you describe the mood of the speaker in Hemingway's story?

Document 4

This political cartoon shows President Coolidge making music while big business dances.

"YES, SIR, HE'S MY BABY!"

Source: Picture Research Consultants

10. Based on this cartoon, explain the relationship between government and business during the 1920s.

11. Persuasive Writing Using the information from the five documents and your knowledge of social studies, write an essay in which you:
- summarize the needs and goals of most Americans after World War I; and
- convince readers that Harding, Coolidge, and Hoover represented/did not represent most Americans.

Need Extra Help?											
If you missed questions...	1	2	3	4	5	6	7	8	9	10	11
Go to page...	305	310	314–315	318	320–321	312–322	309	310	319	310	303–311

The Depression and the New Deal 1929-1939

Pickers bring baskets of produce to be weighed.

BONUS

PRESIDENTS

HERBERT HOOVER

FRANKLIN D. ROOSEVELT

U.S. Events

World Events

1928

1931

1934

★ **1929**
Stock market crashes

★ **1932**
Bonus Marchers forced out of Washington, D.C.

★ **1930**
World population reaches 2 billion

★ **1933**
Hitler comes to power in Germany

History ONLINE
Chapter Overview Visit glencoe.com
and click on **Chapter 11—Chapter
Overviews** to preview chapter information.

Section 1: The Great Depression

Essential Question What were the factors that
brought about the Great Depression?

Section 2: Roosevelt's New Deal

Essential Question How did Franklin Roosevelt's
leadership bring about change in the U.S. economy?

Section 3: Life During the Depression

Essential Question How did the Great Depression
affect the economic and social traditions of Americans,
especially minorities?

Section 4: Effects of the New Deal

Essential Question Why did some
people support Roosevelt's New Deal
and some oppose it?

Organizing Information
Make this Foldable and use
it to help you study the chapter vocabulary.

Step 1 Use quarter sheets of
binder paper. Fold the sheets
in half.

Step 2 Cut a tab along the left
side of each sheet.

Step 3 Staple the multiple sections together on the left side.
Record the term on the front of
each tab.

Step 4 Record the definitions
and examples under each tab.

Reading and Writing Use this
Foldable as a self-checking
vocabulary study aid by reading
the word on the front of the tab,
mentally defining the word, and
then looking under the tab to
check your response.

★ **1935**
Social Security
Act passes

★ **1937**
Court-packing bill
defeated

★ **1938**
Fair Labor
Standards Act
passes

1937   **1940**

★ **1936**
American Jesse
Owens wins four
gold medals at
Berlin Olympic
Games

★ **1939**
World War II
begins

The Great Depression

Essential Question

What were the factors that brought about the Great Depression?

Reading Guide

Content Vocabulary

stock exchange (p. 331)

relief (p. 334)

default (p. 333)

public works (p. 335)

Academic Vocabulary

decline (p. 332)

collapse (p. 333)

Key People and Events

"Black Thursday" (p. 332)

Great Depression (p. 332)

Hoovervilles (p. 334)

Bonus Army (p. 335)

Reading Strategy

Taking Notes Re-create a time line like the one below to record the events that happened in September and October of 1929 that led to the stock market crash.

American Diary

The crash of the American stock market in 1929 sent shock waves through the country. Almost overnight, the country suffered financial disaster. Many people lost their savings, homes, and jobs. In 1932 humorist Will Rogers remarked: "We'll hold the distinction of being the only Nation in the history of the world that ever went to the poor house in an automobile."

—from the Will Rogers Memorial Archives

$100. WILL BUY THIS CAR. MUST HAVE CASH. LOST ALL ON THE STOCK MARKET

For many, the stock market crash of 1929 meant bankruptcy.

The Stock Market

Main Idea The stock market crash of 1929 signaled an end to the prosperity of the 1920s.

History and You You have probably heard statements on the news about the ups and downs of the stock market. Read to find out how a stock market collapse in 1929 ushered in the worst economic crisis in United States history.

• •

In the booming economy of the 1920s, confident business and government leaders said the nation had entered a new era of prosperity for all. The chair of General Motors advised people to invest money in the stock market every month—and many followed his advice. "Grocers, motormen, plumbers, seamstresses, and . . . waiters were in the market," reported writer Frederick Lewis Allen. The "market had become a national mania." Everyone, it seemed, was trying to get rich quickly.

Suddenly, in October 1929, everything changed. Almost overnight the value of stocks plunged. Millionaires lost fortunes, and thousands of less wealthy investors lost their savings. The stock market had crashed. The nation was about to enter its worst domestic crisis since the Civil War.

The Boom

A **stock exchange** is an organized system for buying and selling shares, or blocks of investments, in corporations. In the late 1920s, the value of stocks on the New York Stock Exchange climbed to dizzying heights. This long period of rising stock prices convinced many to invest heavily in stock. By 1929, 3 to 4 million Americans, or roughly 10 percent of all households, owned stocks.

Because many investors lacked the money to continue purchasing stock, they bought on margin. This means they paid only a fraction of the stock price and borrowed the rest from their brokers. Brokers, in turn, borrowed their money from banks. As long as the value of stocks continued to rise, the buyer could sell later, pay back what was borrowed, and make a profit. If that value fell, though, investors and brokers would not have enough cash to pay off the loans.

The Crash

Fearing that the boom market would end, some investors began selling their stocks in late September. These sales made stock prices fall. Brokers began to demand repayment of loans, forcing investors who had bought on margin to sell their stock.

By the Numbers / **Looking for Jobs**

No Work Following the stock market crash, many Americans wanted to work but could not find jobs.

— Total available to work
— Total employed

Number of workers* (in thousands)

55,000
50,000
45,000
40,000
35,000
30,000

1929   1930   1931   1932   1933

Years

*14 years and older   **Source:** Statistical Abstract of the United States

Critical Thinking

Analyzing What do the employment figures show about the financial health of America at this time?

Prices **declined**, or dropped, steadily until October 21, but most experts thought there was no need to worry. Then, for three straight days, stock prices plunged as investors sold millions of shares each day. Panicked traders sold almost 13 million shares on October 24, a day that became known as **"Black Thursday."** Following a few days of calm, the crisis worsened. On Tuesday, October 29, more than 16 million shares changed hands and stock prices plummeted. Journalist Jonathan Norton Leonard described the scene:

PRIMARY SOURCE

"The selling pressure was . . . coming from everywhere. The wires to other cities were jammed with frantic orders to sell. So were the cables, radio, and telephones to Europe and the rest of the world."
—from *Ordinary Americans*

The New York Stock Exchange closed for a few days to prevent more panic selling.

✔ **Reading Check** **Explaining** What is buying stock "on margin"?

The Great Depression

Main Idea The Great Depression, a worldwide economic slump, brought hardship to many Americans during the 1930s.

History and You If you were penniless and homeless, how would you try to survive? Read to find out how many Americans coped with the challenges of living through the Great Depression.

During the next two years, the nation slid into a severe economic crisis called the **Great Depression.** Total economic output dropped from $104 billion in 1929 to $58 billion in 1932. While the stock market crash shook confidence in the economy, it did not cause the Depression. Other factors, working together, sent the economy into a tailspin.

An Unbalanced Economy

The problems that led to the Great Depression began to surface in the early 1920s. Farm income shrank throughout the decade. Industries also declined.

Primary Source / **Surviving the Depression**

Hard Times During the Depression, the feelings of helplessness grew as the number of jobs dwindled and debts mounted. For many, surviving became a daily struggle.

Some people had little or no money to buy groceries. Some stores offered credit. In small farm towns, customers sometimes traded goods for groceries.

◄ Clerk and customer in small grocery store

A North Carolina woman hoped that a job for her husband meant better times lay ahead. *"After he gets his first pay check, we can get along. But we haven't had anything in the house to eat for a week now but two messes of flour and a peck of meal. The children has nothin' for breakfast but a biscuit or a slice of corn bread. They come home after school begging for food. But I can't give them but two meals a day."*
—from *American Life Histories*

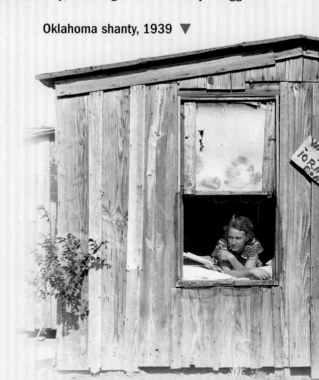

Oklahoma shanty, 1939 ▼

Factories began having trouble selling everything they produced. In the months before the stock market crash, the automobile and construction industries especially suffered from lagging orders. This overproduction of goods forced factory owners to slow production. Then they cut wages and laid off workers. Jobless or with reduced income, many Americans had to cut back on purchases, further reducing sales.

Another factor that fueled the Depression was the growing gap in wealth between rich people and most Americans. The prosperity of the 1920s did not help all Americans equally. In 1929 less than 1 percent of the population owned nearly one-third of the country's wealth. At the same time, about 75 percent of American families lived in poverty or on the very edge of it.

Credit Crisis

Borrowed money fueled much of the economy in the 1920s. Farmers bought land, equipment, and supplies on credit. Consumers used credit to buy cars. Investors borrowed to buy stocks. Many small banks

suffered when farmers **defaulted,** or failed to meet loan payments. Large banks, which had bought stocks as an investment, suffered huge losses in the crash. These losses forced thousands of banks across the nation to close between 1930 and 1933. At that time, the government did not insure bank deposits; therefore, when banks **collapsed,** or broke down, millions of depositors lost their money.

International Depression

Other countries also had crises. One problem was the lack of loans. During the 1920s, U.S. banks made loans to stock speculators instead of lending money to foreign countries. Without these loans from U.S. banks, foreign companies purchased fewer products from American manufacturers.

Matters grew worse after Congress passed the Hawley-Smoot Tariff in 1930. A tariff is a tax on imported goods. Because goods purchased from other countries now cost more, Americans bought fewer of them. Foreign countries responded by raising their own tariffs on American products. As a result, foreign countries purchased fewer American goods.

Joblessness and Poverty

As the Depression tightened its grip on the United States, millions lost their jobs. In 1932, 25 percent of American workers were out of work. The unemployment rate remained near 20 percent throughout the decade. Workers who managed to keep their jobs worked only part-time or for reduced wages.

The newly unemployed felt devastated. New Yorker Sidney Lens, who lost his job, wrote about developing "a feeling of worthlessness—and loneliness; I began to think of myself as a freak and misfit." Some tried to earn a few cents by shining shoes or selling apples on street corners.

Long lines of hungry people snaked through the streets of the nation's cities. They waited for hours to receive a slice of bread, a cup of coffee, or a bowl of soup from soup kitchens run by local governments or charities.

Average Prices, 1932–1934	
Sirloin steak (per pound)	29¢
Chicken (per pound)	22¢
Bread (20-ounce loaf)	5¢
Potatoes (per pound)	2¢
Bananas (per pound)	7¢
Milk (per quart)	10¢
Cheese (per pound)	29¢
Tomatoes (16-ounce can)	9¢
Oranges (per dozen)	27¢
Cornflakes (8 ounces)	8¢

Critical Thinking

Making Connections If your family had little or no income, how would you reduce expenses?

Growing Poverty The poverty of the 1930s was most visible in the number of shantytowns that popped up across the United States. The homeless clustered together shacks made from any materials they could find, including cardboard, wood, tar paper, and tin.

A Seattle man uses bricks to hold down a tar paper roof. ▼

A family evicted from its home ▼

Jesse Jackson, an out-of-work lumberjack, talks about the tasks the people performed in a Seattle Hooverville:

"Hooverville is a colony of industrious men, the most of whom are busy trying to hold their heads up and be self-supporting and respectable. A lot of work is required in order to stay here, consequently, the lazy man does not tarry [stay] long in this place."

—from "The Story of Hooverville, In Seattle"

DBQ Document-Based Questions

Analyzing Does anything about Jesse Jackson's description surprise you? Explain.

Peggy Terry, a young girl in Oklahoma City, told how each day after school her mother sent her to the soup kitchen:

PRIMARY SOURCE

"If you happened to be one of the first ones in line, you didn't get anything but water that was on top. So we'd ask the guy that was ladling out soup into the buckets—everybody had to bring their own bucket to get the soup—he'd dip the greasy, watery stuff off the top. So we'd ask him to please dip down to get some meat and potatoes from the bottom of the kettle. But he wouldn't do it."

—from *Hard Times*, by Studs Terkel

Families or individuals who had lost their homes built shelters out of old boxes and other debris, sometimes grouped together in pitiful "shantytowns." Some referred bitterly to the shantytowns as **Hoovervilles** because of President Hoover's failure to act. Across the country Americans wondered why the president did nothing to end the suffering.

✓ **Reading Check** **Describing** What effect did tariffs have on imports and exports?

Hoover and the Crisis

Main Idea Herbert Hoover gradually involved the federal government in the economic crisis.

History and You If you ran the government, how would you fix problems in your community? Read to find out how President Hoover tried to deal with the Great Depression.

· ·

President Hoover thought the economic crisis was temporary and that prosperity was "just around the corner." He also believed that the "depression cannot be cured by legislative action or executive pronouncement." Instead, Hoover called on business leaders not to cut wages or production of goods and on charities to do their best for the needy. Voluntary action by private citizens and local governments, Hoover thought, would pull the nation through tough times.

Charities, churches, and volunteers worked heroically to provide **relief**—aid for the needy. State and local governments did as well. But the number of people who needed help was simply overwhelming.

Government Action

Eventually Hoover recognized that the federal government had to take steps to combat the Depression. In 1931 he authorized additional federal spending on **public works**—projects such as highways, parks, and libraries—to create new jobs. State and local governments ran out of money, however, and the combined spending by all three levels of government declined.

In January 1932, Hoover asked Congress to create the Reconstruction Finance Corporation (RFC). The RFC lent money to businesses. It also provided funds for state and local programs. However, the RFC's directors were reluctant to make risky loans, and much of its budget remained unspent.

The Bonus Army

By 1932 Americans were growing increasingly discontented and began to take action. A march on Washington by World War I veterans turned many Americans, who were already blaming Hoover for the Depression, firmly against the president.

In 1924 Congress had agreed to give each veteran of World War I a bonus, to be distributed in 1945. Jobless veterans wanted the bonuses right away. In the summer of 1932, they formed the **Bonus Army** and marched to Washington, D.C., to demand their money. Once in Washington, the marchers camped in Hoovervilles. More veterans joined them.

When Congress voted against paying the bonus, many veterans left. About 2,000, however, vowed to remain. When the police tried to disband the veterans' camp, conflict broke out and two people were killed.

Hoover responded by calling in the army. Veterans and their families fled in terror as the troops burned their camp. Many Americans were horrified that the government had attacked its own citizens, particularly war veterans. Hoover seemed out of touch with ordinary people. Many people thought the time had come for a change in government.

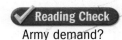 **Reading Check** **Explaining** What did the Bonus Army demand?

Section 1 Review

History ONLINE
Study Central™ To review this section, go to glencoe.com.

Vocabulary

1. Write a sentence for each of the following terms that explains its meaning: stock exchange, decline, default, collapse, relief, public works.

Main Ideas

2. **Summarizing** How did buying stocks on margin contribute to the stock market crash?

3. **Describing** What impact did the Great Depression have on employment?

4. **Explaining** How did President Hoover respond to the economic crisis?

Critical Thinking

5. **Sequencing** Re-create a flow chart like the one below to show the chain of Depression events caused by Congress agreeing to pay World War I veterans a bonus.

Bonus Approved

6. **Narrative Writing** You are a journalist. Write an article for your small-town newspaper that explains the stock market crash and the failure of the local bank in your community.

Answer the Essential Question

7. What were the factors that brought about the Great Depression?

Roosevelt's New Deal

Essential Question

How did Franklin Roosevelt's leadership bring about change in the U.S. economy?

Reading Guide

Content Vocabulary
work relief (p. 339)

Academic Vocabulary
promote (p. 340)   generate (p. 340)

Key People and Events
Franklin D. Roosevelt (p. 337)
Eleanor Roosevelt (p. 337)
Hundred Days (p. 339)
New Deal (p. 339)
Tennessee Valley Authority (p. 340)

Reading Strategy
Taking Notes As you read, complete a diagram like the one below to note what areas of American life and business were affected by Roosevelt's New Deal.

Banks

New Deal

American Diary

Americans huddled around their radios on March 12, 1933, to hear newly elected president, Franklin D. Roosevelt, in his first fireside chat: "Let us unite in banishing fear. We have provided the machinery to restore our financial system, and it is up to you to support and make it work. It is your problem my friends, your problem no less than it is mine. Together we cannot fail."

In the fireside chats, Roosevelt calmly but confidently explained in simple terms the nation's problems.

Families in the 1930s gathered around the radio to hear their favorite programs.

Franklin D. Roosevelt

Main Idea Franklin D. Roosevelt promised a "new deal" to get America out of the Great Depression.

History and You If you were out of work, would you vote for someone who promised to make your life better? Read to find out about the pledge that Roosevelt made to Americans in 1932.

· ·

With the nation's economy crumbling, the Democrats believed they had a good chance of winning the presidency. Meeting in Chicago in June 1932, the Democrats chose Governor **Franklin D. Roosevelt** of New York as their candidate. At the convention, Roosevelt —or FDR as he was called—told the Democrats and the nation, "I pledge you, I pledge myself, to a new deal for the American people."

The Republicans also met in Chicago and nominated President Hoover for reelection. With the country's economy worsening in 1932, Hoover's chances for being reelected seemed extremely slim. Delegates knew the Depression had turned many voters against Hoover.

Early Years of Promise

Franklin D. Roosevelt, a distant cousin of former president Theodore Roosevelt, came from a wealthy New York family. Ambitious and charming, FDR decided on a career in politics. In 1905 he married Theodore Roosevelt's niece, **Eleanor Roosevelt,** and she became a tireless partner in his public and political life.

FDR's political career began in 1910 with his election to the New York State senate. There, he was known as a forward-thinking leader who could persuade people to support his views. In 1913 Roosevelt became assistant secretary of the navy, and in 1920 the Democrats chose him as their candidate for vice president. The Democrats lost the election to Warren G. Harding, but Franklin Roosevelt's political future seemed bright.

Then in 1921 polio struck Roosevelt, paralyzing both his legs. Although there was no cure, FDR's will remained strong and he refused to give in. "Once I spent two years lying in bed trying to move my big toe," he said later. "After that, anything else seems easy."

If You Were There / America Tunes In

The Radio In the 1930s, you and your family and friends gathered around the radio for entertainment. In 1931, 2 out of every 5 families had a radio in their living rooms. By 1938, the number climbed to 4 out of 5 families. You could listen to musical shows, dramas, and comedies.

Bi-Acoustic Radio

It's "HIS MASTER'S VOICE" of the air!

RCA Victor Bi-Acoustic Radio

Radios in the United States, 1930

PACIFIC OCEAN

ATLANTIC OCEAN

Percentage of families owning radios
- 50 and over
- 40–49
- 30–39
- 20–29
- 10–19
- Less than 10

Source: U.S. Census Bureau

Critical Thinking

Interpreting How did the percentage of people who owned a radio differ in the North and in the South? What do you think was the reason for this difference?

Return to Politics

After a few years, FDR decided to return to politics. He never publicly mentioned his paralyzed legs, and he asked journalists not to photograph his leg braces or wheelchair. Elected governor of New York in 1928 and reelected in 1930, Roosevelt earned a national reputation as a reformer. He drew on the advice of a group of progressive lawyers, economists, and social workers—known as the Brain Trust—to develop relief programs for the state. When he decided to run for president, he counted on the Brain Trust to help him guide the nation out of the Great Depression.

During the 1932 campaign, Roosevelt declared that "the country needs and . . . demands bold, persistent experimentation." He also spoke of trying to help "the forgotten man at the bottom of the economic pyramid."

✔ **Reading Check** **Identifying** What was the Brain Trust? Why did Franklin Roosevelt rely on it?

FDR Takes Charge

Main Idea Roosevelt quickly launched programs to improve the American economy.

History and You Have you ever had to do something difficult? Who helped you gain the confidence to do it? Read to learn how Roosevelt reached out to Americans during the 1930s.
· ·

Drawn to Roosevelt's confidence, voters elected him in a landslide. Democrats also won important victories in Congress. People clearly wanted a change.

Restoring Confidence

In the months before Roosevelt took office, the economy worsened. People became desperately afraid. At his inauguration on March 4, 1933, Roosevelt told the nation that "the only thing we have to fear is fear itself." He reassured people and pointed out that the "greatest primary task is to put people to work." He also promised immediate action to help the nation's failed banks.

Primary Source / New Deal Programs

Relief and New Jobs In about 100 days, President Roosevelt and Congress gave hope to the nation with a number of programs designed to pull Americans out of the Depression and set the country on a path to prosperity.

New Deal Program	Initials	Purpose
Civilian Conservation Corps	CCC	Provided jobs for young men to plant trees and build bridges
Tennessee Valley Authority	TVA	Built dams to provide cheap electric power to seven Southern states; set up schools and health centers
Federal Emergency Relief Administration	FERA	Gave relief to unemployed and needy
Agricultural Adjustment Administration	AAA	Paid farmers not to grow certain crops
National Recovery Administration	NRA	Helped set standards for production, prices, and wages
Public Works Administration	PWA	Built ports, schools, and aircraft carriers
Federal Deposit Insurance Corporation	FDIC	Insured savings accounts in banks approved by the government

The CCC Beginning in March 1933, the CCC offered men ages 18 to 25 the opportunity to work. ▶

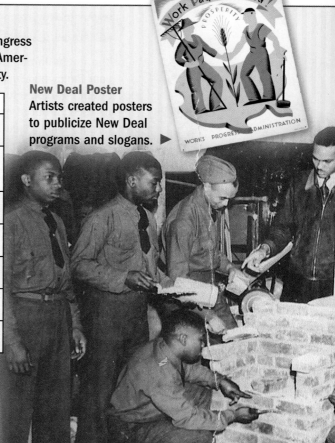

New Deal Poster Artists created posters to publicize New Deal programs and slogans. ▶

Roosevelt ordered all banks closed for four days. Congress passed the Emergency Banking Relief Act to help banks reorganize and open again. After a week in office, FDR assured Americans in a radio broadcast "that it is safer to keep your money in a . . . bank than under the mattress."

The president's radio talk was the first of many fireside chats—so called because he sat next to a fireplace in the White House as he spoke. These fireside chats helped FDR gain the public's confidence.

The Hundred Days

During a period that came to be called the **Hundred Days,** Roosevelt's proposals for new economic programs were quickly approved by Congress. It was an amazingly productive time. Optimism swept through the capital. Journalist Thomas Stokes recalled, "The gloom . . . of the closing months of the Hoover administration had vanished."

✔ **Reading Check** **Evaluating** Why did Roosevelt broadcast his fireside chats?

Tennessee Valley Authority

Ill.
Ohio R.
Kentucky
Missouri
Paducah
Cairo Kentucky Dam
Bowling Green
Green R.
Cumberland R.
Bristol Va.
Norris Dam
Cherokee Dam
Oak Ridge
Douglas Dam
Knoxville
Nashville
Watts Bar Dam
N.C.
Asheville
Ark.
Tennessee
Chickamauga Dam
Memphis
Wilson Dam
Elk R.
Little Tennessee R.
Corinth
Chattanooga
S.C.
Wheeler Dam
Huntsville
Guntersville Dam
Mississippi
Bear Cr.
Georgia
Mississippi
Alabama
N
0   100 kilometers
0   100 miles
Albers Equal-Area projection
W E S

Area supplied with power from the TVA
⬧ Dam
◼ Steam power plant

Map Skills

Place Why was the state of Tennessee a prime area to build the Tennessee Valley Authority Project?

Maps In MOtion See StudentWorks™ Plus or glencoe.com.

The New Deal Takes Shape

Main Idea Roosevelt's New Deal affected many areas of American life, including banking, the stock market, industry, agriculture, and welfare.

History and You Has a recent government action had an impact on your life? Read to learn how the New Deal changed the lives of many Americans during the 1930s.

• •

The new laws that Congress passed during the Hundred Days—and in the months and years that followed—came to be called the **New Deal.** New Deal laws and regulations affected banking, the stock market, industry, agriculture, public works, relief for the poor, and conservation of resources. These laws changed the face of America dramatically.

Frances Perkins, Roosevelt's secretary of labor, later recalled those early, exciting days of the New Deal:

PRIMARY SOURCE

"In March 1933, the New Deal was not a plan. . . . It was a happy phrase [FDR] had coined during the campaign. . . . It made people feel better, and in that terrible period of depression they needed to feel better."

—from *The Roosevelt I Knew*

Jobs and Relief

Roosevelt gave high priority to creating jobs. He planned to help the unemployed with **work relief** programs, giving needy people government jobs. During his first month in office, FDR asked Congress to create the Civilian Conservation Corps (CCC). Over the next 10 years, the CCC employed about 3 million young people to work on projects that benefited the public, including planting trees to reforest areas, building levees for flood control, and improving national parks.

The president made aid to the poor and suffering another priority. Roosevelt established the Federal Emergency Relief Administration (FERA) to give money to the states for use in helping people in need.

This cartoon is a takeoff on the children's nursery rhyme "Ring Around the Rosie." It shows President Roosevelt standing in the middle of a group of children playing the game and singing as they dance around him.

1. **Identifying** What do the letters on the children's clothes represent?

2. **Analyzing Visuals** Why did the cartoonist draw everyone in the picture, including Roosevelt, smiling and laughing?

Roosevelt appointed Harry Hopkins, a New York social worker, to lead the FERA. Hopkins became one of FDR's closest advisers and also became involved in several other New Deal programs.

Roosevelt did not forget agriculture. On May 12, Congress passed the Agricultural Adjustment Act (AAA). The act had two goals: to raise farm prices quickly and to control production so that farm prices would stay up over the long term.

In the AAA's first year, though, the supply of food outstripped demand. The AAA could raise prices only by paying farmers to destroy crops, milk, and livestock. To many, it seemed shocking to throw away food when millions of people went hungry. However, the New Dealers claimed the action was necessary to bring up prices.

To control production and farm prices, the AAA paid farmers to leave some of their land uncultivated. If market prices of key farm products such as wheat and cotton fell below a certain level, the AAA would pay farmers subsidies—grants of money—to make up the difference. In the first three years of the New Deal, farmers' incomes rose by about 50 percent. However, the Supreme Court ruled that the AAA was unconstitutional in *United States v. Butler* (1936) for invading the reserved powers of the states.

Rebuilding a Region

One of the boldest programs launched during the Hundred Days was the **Tennessee Valley Authority** (TVA). The TVA aimed to control flooding, **promote,** or help advance, conservation and development, and bring electricity to rural areas along the Tennessee River. By building new dams and improving others, the TVA ended the region's disastrous floods. And with hydroelectric power **generating,** or creating, affordable electricity, thousands of farms and homes in some Southern states were wired for electricity for the first time.

Some critics charged that funds for the TVA should be used to support programs nationwide. Power companies also attacked the program as unfair and communistic. When the spring rains came in 1937, however, the system worked—the dams prevented the Tennessee River from flooding. In the end, most observers agreed that the TVA was an example of successful social and economic planning.

Helping Business and Labor

On the last day of the Hundred Days, Congress passed the National Industrial Recovery Act (NIRA), which Roosevelt called "the most important and far-reaching legislation" ever passed in the United States. The goal of the NIRA was to boost the economy by helping business regulate itself.

The NIRA created the National Recovery Administration (NRA), which encouraged businesses to set a minimum wage and abolish child labor. The NRA also tried to set up codes governing pricing and other practices for every industry. To promote the agency, its blue eagle symbol and slogan—"We Do Our Part"—soon appeared everywhere.

Another program that the NIRA launched was the Public Works Administration (PWA). Its goal was to stimulate the economy through the building of huge public works projects. The PWA employed many people to work on the construction of roads, shipyards, hospitals, and schools. Many PWA projects—such as New York City's Lincoln Tunnel and Kentucky's Fort Knox—still stand. The PWA spent its funds slowly, though, and the impact on unemployment was not immediate.

To avoid future banking crises, Roosevelt called for reform of the nation's financial system. Congress established the Federal Deposit Insurance Corporation (FDIC) to insure bank deposits. The government guaranteed that money placed in a bank insured by the FDIC would not be lost if the bank failed.

Congress also passed a law regulating the sale of stocks and bonds and created the Securities and Exchange Commission (SEC). This law gave the SEC the power to punish dishonest stockbrokers and speculators.

Assessing the Early New Deal

The New Deal did not cure the nation's ills. The Depression dragged on, and hardships did not cease. Farmers continued to lose their land. Unemployment remained at high levels. Many people still struggled to survive and to make ends meet.

Yet the darkest days had passed. The panic of 1932 and 1933 had receded, and the flurry of activity from the nation's capital had restored some measure of confidence.

Reading Check **Describing** What was the goal of the Public Works Administration?

Section 2 Review

History ONLINE
Study Central™ To review this section, go to glencoe.com.

Vocabulary

1. Write a short paragraph using each of the following vocabulary terms: work relief, promote, generate.

Main Ideas

2. **Describing** How did Roosevelt's political experiences prepare him to face the challenges of being president?

3. **Summarizing** What steps did Roosevelt take to restore confidence in banks and in the stock exchange?

4. **Analyzing** Explain how work relief programs benefited the economy.

Critical Thinking

5. **Comparing** Re-create the diagram below to compare the arguments for and against the TVA dam-building project.

TVA Project

For	Against

6. **Descriptive Writing** Write a proposal from the mayor of your city to President Roosevelt that outlines a Public Works Administration project you would like him to authorize. Include specific information about the work as well as how it would benefit your community.

Answer the
Essential Question

7. How did Franklin Roosevelt's leadership bring about change in the U.S. economy?

Worker on a WPA project

YOU DECIDE

Was the New Deal an Abuse of Government Power?

Building Background

Roosevelt's New Deal program tried to regulate the American economy to ease the Great Depression. The New Deal differed from the traditional hands-off approach to the economy in American politics.

Herbert Hoover had refused to interfere in the economy. Hungry and jobless Americans blamed the Hoover administration for their suffering. As a result, Roosevelt easily beat Hoover in the 1932 presidential election. Hoover publicly opposed Roosevelt's New Deal. The New Deal was widely supported by Americans, however, because government agencies such as the Works Progress Administration (WPA) reduced the hardships of unemployed workers.

NO

RABBI SIMON COHEN

For about two years now I have been the supervisor of a project . . . under the Works Progress Administration. . . . I wish that those who are opposing such a program could meet these people. I could furnish instance after instance of old people who have worked hard all their lives, only to face desperate need in their old age; of middle-aged workers cast adrift not through their own incapability, but of those who employed them; of young people who have just completed their education and find that the working world has no place for them. I have found some shirkers[1] and cheaters, but they are a very small minority; and the thing that has impressed me is the eagerness with which the unemployed seek for work, even the most difficult, in order that they may do their part in the community.

It goes then without question that I heartily applaud the work that the government has done in this direction and that I feel that it must continue as long as the necessity exists. . . . There is a social need which private business cannot or will not meet, it must be met by the American people as a whole, as a worth-while investment in its own citizens.

—letter to President Roosevelt, October 27, 1935

---

[1] **shirker** person who avoids his or her responsibility

342

YES

HERBERT HOOVER

You cannot extend the mastery of government over the daily life of a people without somewhere making it master of people's souls and thoughts. . . . Every step in that direction poisons the very roots of liberalism. It poisons political equality, free speech, free press, and equality of opportunity. It is the road not to more liberty but to less liberty. True liberalism is found not in striving to spread bureaucracy,[2] but in striving to set bounds to it. True liberalism seeks all legitimate freedom first in the confident belief that without such freedom the pursuit of other blessings is in vain. . . .

Through four years of experience this New Deal attack upon free institutions has emerged as the transcendent[3] issue in America. . . .

Surely the NRA and the AAA alone, should prove what the New Deal philosophy of government means. . . .

But their illegal invasions of the Constitution are but the minor artillery with which this New Deal philosophy of government is being forced upon us. They are now . . . taking vast sums of the people's money and then manipulating its spending to build up personal power.

—*speech given October 30, 1936*

[2] **bureaucracy** system of government marked by many rules and regulations
[3] **transcendent** most important

DBQ Document-Based Questions

1. **Summarizing** According to Hoover, what is the danger of the New Deal?

2. **Analyzing** Why does Cohen think the Works Progress Administration should continue?

3. **Inferring** How do you think Hoover feels about the Works Progress Administration?

4. **Evaluating** With which position do you agree more? Explain your answer.

Homeless shelters in Seattle, Washington

Life During the Depression

Essential Question ◄

How did the Great Depression affect the economic and social traditions of Americans, especially minorities?

Reading Guide

Content Vocabulary

migrant worker (p. 346)

fascist (p. 348)

Academic Vocabulary

migrate (p. 346)   advocate (p. 348)

Key People and Events

Frances Perkins (p. 345)

Dust Bowl (p. 345)

Ralph Bunche (p. 347)

Mary McLeod Bethune (p. 347)

Indian Reorganization Act (p. 347)

Spanish Civil War (p. 348)

Reading Strategy

Taking Notes Re-create a diagram like the one below to record information about the various groups that were affected during the Depression.

Group	How Affected
Women	

American Diary

Dear Mrs. Roosevelt
I am writing to you for some of your old soiled dresses if you have any . . . . I am in the seventh grade in school but I have to stay out of school because I have no books or clothes to ware [wear] . . . . If you have any soiled clothes that you don't want to ware I would be very glad to get them.
Yours Truly

—*from* Dear Mrs. Roosevelt

Organized hunger marches, such as this one in Columbus, Ohio, were common during the years of the Great Depression.

Hard Times in America

Main Idea The Depression was a difficult time because many Americans faced unemployment and the loss of land and other property.

History and You Would you be willing to stay in an area that was damaged by a disaster? Read to find out what happened to people living on the Great Plains and what they did to find a better life.

. . . .

The letter in the American Diary is one of thousands of letters sent to first lady Eleanor Roosevelt. Many Americans—both young and old—sought relief from the pain brought about by the Depression.

Women Go to Work

Desperation drove a large number of women into the workforce, despite the fact that many people thought that women should not hold jobs as long as men were unemployed. Many families survived on a woman's income—even though American women earned less than men.

Women also worked harder at home to make ends meet. Instead of buying clothes or groceries, they sewed their own clothing, baked their own bread, and canned their own vegetables. Some women started home businesses such as laundries or boardinghouses.

The New Deal era also opened doors for women in public life. President Roosevelt appointed the first woman ever to serve in the cabinet, **Frances Perkins.** He also named more than 100 other women to federal posts. One—Ellen Sullivan Woodward—started a program to provide jobs for women.

Eleanor Roosevelt often acted as her husband's "eyes and ears." She made fact-finding trips for the president because polio had limited his mobility. Mrs. Roosevelt campaigned vigorously for women and families in need.

The Dust Bowl

During the 1930s, while people were struggling to make ends meet, the southern Great Plains suffered an environmental disaster. Hardest hit were western Kansas and Oklahoma, northern Texas, and eastern Colorado and New Mexico—the region dubbed the **Dust Bowl.**

Primary Source / Songs of Sorrow

"Brother Can You Spare a Dime?"

They used to tell me I was building a dream
And so I followed the mob.
When there was earth to plow or guns to bear
I was always there, right on the job.

They used to tell me I was building a dream
With peace and glory ahead.
Why should I be standing in line
Just waiting for bread?

Once I built a railroad, made it run,
Made it race against time.
Once I built a railroad, now it's done,
Brother, can you spare a dime?

Music of the Depression Many songs described Americans' feelings during the Great Depression. One of the more famous ballads describes the loss of hope by people who were unemployed.

Critical Thinking

Drawing Conclusions What do you think is meant by "building a dream" in the song?

Using new technology such as tractors and disc plows, farmers cleared millions of acres of sod for wheat farming. They did not realize that the roots of the grass held the soil in place. When a severe drought struck in 1931, the wheat crops died and the soil dried out. Strong prairie winds blew the soil away.

Each storm stripped away more soil. The drought—and the storms—continued for years. People called the storms "black blizzards" because the blowing dust reduced visibility to near zero. In some areas, sand drifts formed as high as 6 feet (1.8 m), burying roads and vehicles.

Thousands of Dust Bowl farmers went bankrupt and had to give up their farms. About 400,000 farmers **migrated,** or moved, to California and became **migrant workers,** moving from place to place to harvest fruits and vegetables. So many came from Oklahoma that people called them "Okies."

✓ **Reading Check** **Explaining** Why were dust storms called "black blizzards"?

The Plight of Minorities

Main Idea The Great Depression placed the hardest burden on minority groups. It also led to the growth of radical political movements.

History and You What might it be like to be poor but also to face prejudice? Read to find out about the challenges and gains of African Americans, Native Americans, and Hispanic Americans during the 1930s.
. . . .

The Depression fell especially hard on the minority groups who were already on the lower rungs of the American economic ladder. These groups included African Americans, Native Americans, and Hispanic Americans.

African Americans

In the South more than half of the African American population had no jobs. African Americans who lived and worked in Southern cities found their jobs taken by white people who had lost theirs. The collapse of farm prices crushed African American farmers.

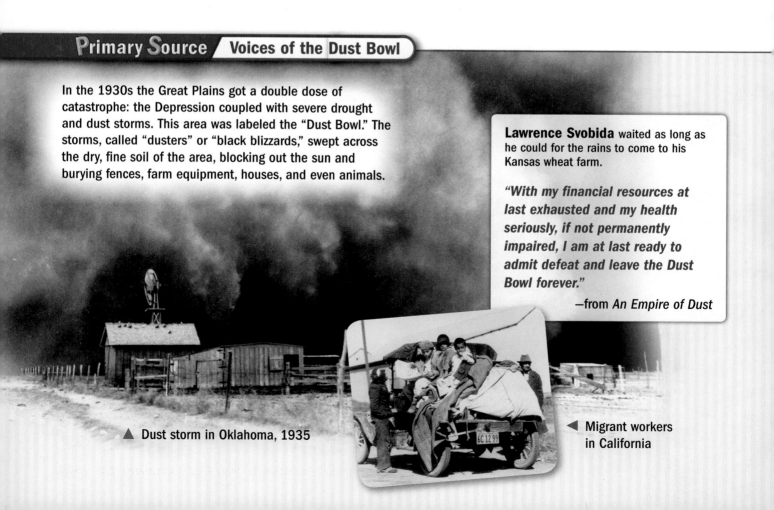

Primary Source / Voices of the Dust Bowl

In the 1930s the Great Plains got a double dose of catastrophe: the Depression coupled with severe drought and dust storms. This area was labeled the "Dust Bowl." The storms, called "dusters" or "black blizzards," swept across the dry, fine soil of the area, blocking out the sun and burying fences, farm equipment, houses, and even animals.

Lawrence Svobida waited as long as he could for the rains to come to his Kansas wheat farm.

"With my financial resources at last exhausted and my health seriously, if not permanently impaired, I am at last ready to admit defeat and leave the Dust Bowl forever."

—from *An Empire of Dust*

▲ Dust storm in Oklahoma, 1935

◄ Migrant workers in California

Seeking more opportunity, about 400,000 African American men, women, and children migrated to Northern cities during the 1930s. These migrants did not fare much better in the North, however. The jobless rate for African Americans remained high.

However, African Americans did make some social and political gains during the Depression. The National Association for the Advancement of Colored People (NAACP) worked to lessen discrimination in the labor movement. As a result, more than 500,000 African Americans were able to join labor unions. African Americans also won a greater voice in government. President Roosevelt appointed a number of African Americans to federal posts. He had a group of advisers, known as the Black Cabinet, that included Robert Weaver, a college professor, and **Ralph Bunche,** who later played an important role in the civil rights movement. **Mary McLeod Bethune,** who founded Bethune-Cookman College in Florida, also served as an adviser to the president.

African Americans continued to fight against prejudice. In 1939 opera singer Marian Anderson was denied permission to sing in Constitution Hall because she was African American. Mrs. Roosevelt helped arrange for Anderson to give a historic concert at the Lincoln Memorial.

Native Americans

The 1930s did provide some benefits to Native Americans. The head of the Bureau of Indian Affairs, John Collier, introduced a set of reforms known as the Indian New Deal. These changes would help restore Native American culture and heritage.

Collier halted the sale of reservation land, got jobs for 77,000 Native Americans in the Civilian Conservation Corps, and obtained Public Works Administration funds to build new reservation schools. Most importantly, he pushed Congress to pass the **Indian Reorganization Act** of 1934. This law restored traditional tribal government and provided money for land purchases to enlarge some reservations.

Latinos

By 1930, about 2 million people of Latino, or Hispanic, descent lived in the United States, mostly in California and the Southwest. Many had emigrated from Mexico. Some worked as farmers on small pieces of land. Others were laborers in industries or migrant workers, traveling from place to place harvesting crops.

As the Great Depression deepened, resentment against Mexican Americans grew, and many lost their jobs. Politicians and labor unions demanded that Mexican Americans be forced to leave the United States.

The government encouraged Mexican immigrants to return to Mexico. Authorities gave them one-way train tickets to Mexico or simply rounded them up and shipped them south across the border. More than 500,000 Mexican Americans left the United States during the early years of the Depression, often involuntarily.

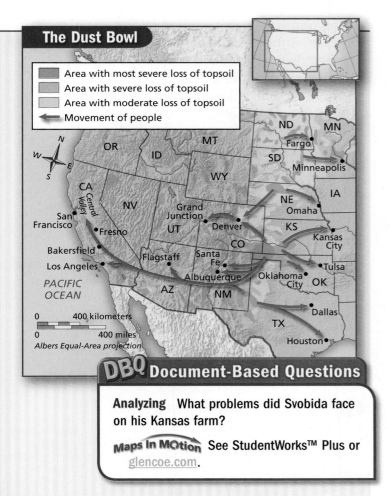

The Dust Bowl

- Area with most severe loss of topsoil
- Area with severe loss of topsoil
- Area with moderate loss of topsoil
- → Movement of people

0 400 kilometers
0 400 miles
Albers Equal-Area projection

DBQ Document-Based Questions

Analyzing What problems did Svobida face on his Kansas farm?

Maps In Motion See StudentWorks™ Plus or glencoe.com.

Riding the Rails During the Depression, at least 250,000 teenagers left home to ride the rails. They crisscrossed the country by hopping freight trains. Many went west to California or south to warmer states in search of jobs, a better life, or just plain adventure. The life of a hobo was often lonely and dangerous. In 1932 alone, nearly 6,000 hoboes were killed or injured when they attempted to jump on or off a train.

Symbol	Meaning
⌐_⌐	You can camp here
⊖	Leave quickly
⊗	Good place for food and money
‡ ‡‡	Danger, police
⌐·⌐	This water is dangerous to drink

▲ Hoboes developed their own symbols to communicate with other hoboes on the road.

"To be a hobo, you had to know how to get on a train while it is moving. Some hoboes got killed by trying to get on trains that were moving too fast."
—from Luther S. Head, National Heritage Museum

◄ Riding on trains was dangerous but free.

DBQ Document-Based Questions

Speculating How do you think the actions of these teenage hoboes reflected the effects of the Great Depression on American teenagers and families?

Those Mexican Americans who remained in the United States faced continued discrimination. They were kept from getting relief or were offered benefits far below those given to whites. Many hospitals and schools also turned away Mexican Americans. To resist job discrimination, some migrant workers tried to form labor unions, but local food producers and officials cracked down on these organizations.

Radical Political Movements

Hard times helped radical political groups gain ground in the United States during the 1930s. Radical groups **advocate,** or support, extreme and immediate change. Socialists and Communists viewed the Depression not as a temporary economic problem but as the death of a failed system. They proposed sweeping changes.

History ONLINE

Student Web Activity Visit glencoe.com and complete the Chapter 11 Web Activity about The Great Depression and the New Deal.

Communism attracted some Americans with promises to end economic and racial injustice. Although both socialism and communism had significant influence, neither became a political force in the United States.

Another political development was the rise of **fascists** in Germany and Italy. Fascism is a political philosophy that holds the individual second to the nation and advocates government by dictatorship. Although fascism never attracted many Americans, it drew enough attention to make it dangerous. During the Depression, fascists blamed Jews, Communists, and liberals for the country's troubles.

In 1936 the **Spanish Civil War** began. Germany and Italy supported fascists who were trying to take over the Spanish government. Although the United States remained neutral, more than 3,000 Americans went to Spain to fight the fascists.

✔ **Reading Check** **Explaining** What was the purpose of the Indian Reorganization Act?

Entertainment and the Arts

Main Idea The 1930s was a golden age of entertainment, literature, music, and art.

History and You What do you do for entertainment? Read to learn about the ways people sought fun or inspiration during the hard times of the Depression.

. . . .

The Depression produced two separate trends in entertainment and the arts. One was escapism—light or romantic entertainment that helped people forget about their problems. The other was social criticism—portraits of the injustice and suffering of Depression America.

Radio and the Movies

Radio became enormously popular during the 1930s. "Soap operas" were daytime dramas sponsored by laundry detergents. Adventure programs such as *Dick Tracy* and *Superman* had millions of listeners, as did variety shows featuring comedians George Burns and Gracie Allen and Jack Benny.

Every week about 85 million people went to movie theaters, usually to escape their cares and worries. Walt Disney produced the successful animated film *Snow White and the Seven Dwarfs* in 1937. Two years later, audiences flocked to see *The Wizard of Oz*, a colorful musical that lifted viewers' spirits.

Some movies did explore serious topics. For example, *The Grapes of Wrath* (1940) was a screen version of John Steinbeck's powerful novel about farm families fleeing the Dust Bowl. The 1939 film of Margaret Mitchell's novel *Gone With the Wind*, set in the Civil War era, also portrayed people coping with hard times.

Images of the Times

Many writers and painters portrayed the grim realities of Depression life. Richard Wright's novel *Native Son* told the story of an African American man growing up in Chicago. Writer James Agee and photographer Walker Evans depicted poor Southern farm families in *Let Us Now Praise Famous Men*.

Photographer Margaret Bourke-White also recorded the plight of American farmers, and Dorothea Lange took gripping photographs of migrant workers. Painters such as Grant Wood and Thomas Hart Benton showed ordinary people facing the hardships of Depression life.

✔ **Reading Check** **Analyzing** How is social criticism expressed in artwork?

Section 3 Review

History ONLINE
Study Central™ To review this section, go to glencoe.com.

Vocabulary

1. Write a paragraph in which you use all of the following vocabulary terms: migrate, migrant worker, advocate, fascist.

Main Ideas

2. Analyzing What was the Dust Bowl? How did advanced farming technology contribute to it?

3. Identifying What was the Black Cabinet, and why was it important?

4. Making Inferences Why was radio so popular?

Critical Thinking

5. Analyzing In a diagram like the one below, note some examples of social criticism found in 1930s art, movies, and writing.

6. Creative Writing Imagine you are an African American man who moved to a Northern city in 1935 to find work. Write a letter to a Southern relative about your experiences.

7. **Answer the Essential Question**
How did the Great Depression affect the economic and social traditions of Americans, especially minorities?

TIME NOTEBOOK

What were people's lives like in the past?

These two pages will give you some clues to everyday life in the United States as you step back in time with TIME Notebook.

Images of Our Nation

PICTURE OF THE PAST

In 1936 photographer **DOROTHEA LANGE** *took a picture called* Migrant Mother, Nipomo, California, *in a camp filled with seasonal agricultural workers. Shooting photos for the Farm Security Administration, Lange was trying to show how government programs might be improving the lives of people in the rural United States. However, Lange found something different from what she expected as she started to snap her photos.*

The woman in the photo was a pea-picker and the mother of seven children —all on the verge of starvation. Lange's photo ran in a San Francisco newspaper, capturing the desperation of the times perfectly. Thanks to the picture, the government immediately sent 20,000 pounds of food to the camp. Here's what Lange had to say about taking the picture:

DOROTHEA LANGE/THE LIBRARY OF CONGRESS

"I approached the hungry mother. She told me her age—that she was 32. She said that they had been living on frozen vegetables from the surrounding fields, and birds that the children killed. There she sat in that lean-to tent with her children huddled around her, and seemed to know that my pictures might help her, and so she helped me.... The pea crop ...had frozen and there was no work for anybody. I did not approach the tents...of other stranded pea-pickers.... I knew I had recorded the essence of my assignment."

HEADLINE FROM THE TIME

Lindbergh Baby Search Still On

Nearly two months have passed since famed flyer Charles Lindbergh and his wife Anne's baby boy was kidnapped in March 1932. A ladder leading up to the baby's window, muddy footprints, and a ransom note demanding $50,000 are the three clues that have been studied by more than 5,000 FBI agents. About 100,000 police and volunteers have combed the country, searching for the baby.

VERBATIM

WHAT PEOPLE ARE SAYING

❝ These storms were like rolling black smoke. We had to keep the lights on all day. We went to school with headlights on and with dust masks on. I saw a woman who thought the world was coming to an end. ❞

A BOY IN TEXAS,
during the devastating dust storms of 1936—with its churning storms called black blizzards that had winds up to 90 miles per hour

❝ While I still have got breath in my lungs, I will tell you what a dandy car you make. I [have driven] Fords exclusively when I could get away with one. ❞

CLYDE BARROW,
(half the team of bank robbers Bonnie and Clyde) in a 1934 letter to Henry Ford

❝ American history shall march along that skyline. ❞

GUTZON BORGLUM,
in 1924, standing near the Black Hills of South Dakota, where work on his Mount Rushmore sculptures would begin three years later

UNDERWOOD & UNDERWOOD / CORBIS

CHATTER OF THE DECADE

Can You Talk the Talk?

Sure, the Roaring Twenties are full of flappers and good times, but you cannot dance the Charleston forever. Sooner or later you are going to have to talk—will you know what to say? See if you can match the 1920s slang with the correct meaning.

1. sinker

2. speakeasy

3. flyboy

4. swanky

5. hoofer

6. clam

a. dancer

b. doughnut

c. place with illegal liquor

d. dollar

e. pilot

f. elegant

LORDPRICE COLLECTION / ALAMY

Answers: 1. b; 2. c; 3. e; 4. f; 5. a; 6. d

MILESTONES

EVENTS AND PEOPLE OF THE TIME

BETTMANN / CORBIS

FLOWN. The first helicopter in 1936, piloted by Russian-born Igor Sikorsky in Connecticut.

DIED. Harry Houdini in 1926. The world's most famous escape artist died after a trick went terribly wrong. The son of a poor Hungarian family who emigrated to the United States, he had a flair for the dramatic—escaping from tough spots, including a locked canister filled with water while in a straitjacket and hung upside down from a 50-foot-high (15 m) building.

SPACED OUT. In 1934 Wiley Post, wearing a pressurized suit, flew his plane to a height of nearly 9.5 miles (15.3 km), setting a new altitude record.

TUNED IN. 60,000 families who owned radios in 1922—that number jumps to 13,750,000 families in 1930.

CHILLED. Foods as they are cooled by the introduction of the first electric refrigerators in 1923. The new machines have quickly replaced the icebox, which uses huge blocks of ice to keep food cold.

NUMBERS

UNITED STATES AT THE TIME

Number One

Gone With the Wind wins the Pulitzer Prize for 1937. Millions of readers set aside their worries as they experienced the epic drama, defeat, and triumphs of Margaret Mitchell's cast of characters

Two is a charm for President Franklin Roosevelt, sworn in for the second time on January 20, 1937. FDR turned down a ride in a closed limousine—even though it was raining. He pointed toward the thousands of wet people who lined the streets of Washington, D.C., hoping to catch a glimpse of him, and said, "I'll ride in the open limo. If they can take it, I can!"

Four gold medals. Adolf Hitler, Germany's fascist leader, invited the world to Berlin for the 1936 Olympic Games. Hitler hoped to prove the supposed "inferiority" of non-Aryan races. No one told that to U.S. superstar Jesse Owens, an African American athlete who won four gold medals in track and field events

25¢ First federal minimum wage, signed into law as part of the Fair Labor Standards Act (FLSA) in 1938

CRITICAL THINKING

Analyzing Visuals Why did Lange's photo raise awareness of migrant workers' problems? What does the photo "say" to you?

Hypothesizing Why do you think Jesse Owens's victories at the Berlin Olympic Games thrilled Americans? What message did Owens's medals send to Hitler's Germany?

Effects of the New Deal

Essential Question ◀

Why did some people support Roosevelt's New Deal and some oppose it?

Reading Guide

Content Vocabulary

pension *(p. 353)*

unemployment insurance *(p. 355)*

Academic Vocabulary

scheme *(p. 353)*

welfare *(p. 355)*

Key People and Events

Second New Deal *(p. 354)*

Social Security Act *(p. 355)*

John L. Lewis *(p. 355)*

Fair Labor Standards Act *(p. 355)*

Reading Strategy

Taking Notes On a chart like the one below, record the major complaint or suggestion of each of the reformers who criticized Roosevelt's New Deal.

Reformer	Complaint/ suggestion
Charles Coughlin	
Francis Townsend	
Huey Long	

American Diary

Under Roosevelt's New Deal program, millions of Americans found jobs and a new sense of hope when the government created the Works Progress Administration (WPA). "Every time a man is taken from the demoralizing ranks of the jobless, every time a woman is removed from the humiliation of a breadline, and given work to do, a home somewhere becomes more secure."

—*from* "The Lasting Values of the WPA," a speech by Ellen Woodward

Critics of the New Deal

Main Idea During the mid-1930s, Roosevelt's New Deal programs faced growing opposition.

History and You When someone proposes or makes changes, why do other people often object or criticize? Think about this as you read about the people who opposed Roosevelt's New Deal.

· ·

In the early days of his presidency, FDR counted on big business to support his efforts to revive the economy. In general, however, the business world opposed the New Deal.

Business leaders accused Roosevelt of spending too much money. They viewed the government's expansion of power as a threat to individual liberty. These conservatives wanted the government to leave business alone and play a less active role in the economy.

Demanding More Reform

At the same time, Roosevelt drew fire from those who believed that the president had not gone far enough. Three men gained wide popularity with **schemes,** or plans, to help the average American.

Father Charles Coughlin, a Detroit priest, reached millions of listeners through his weekly radio program. Once a Roosevelt supporter, Coughlin called for heavy taxes on the wealthy and for the government to take over the nation's banks. Coughlin used his radio show to attack bankers, Jews, Communists, and labor unions, as well as the New Deal. In time Coughlin lost support because of his extreme views.

Francis Townsend, a California doctor, called for a monthly **pension,** or payment, for older, retired people. Townsend's plan received little support from Congress. It did, however, force many Americans to think about the needs of the elderly poor.

Of greatest concern to Roosevelt, however, was Senator Huey Long of Louisiana. As governor of Louisiana, Long won wide support with public works projects.

His "Share Our Wealth Plan" called for taxing the rich heavily, then using that money to give every American a home and $2,500 a year. Long's plans appealed to many Americans. Polls indicated that in 1936 he might receive as many as 4 million votes on a third-party ticket. But in 1935 he was assassinated by a political opponent.

✔ **Reading Check** **Identifying** What group was Townsend's pension plan designed to help?

WPA workers repair sidewalks, July 1936.

By the Numbers / WPA Projects

The projects completed by WPA workers were lasting and varied.

Total	Projects
651,087	Miles of highways, roads built
124,031	Bridges repaired
125,110	Public buildings erected
8,192	Public parks created
853	Airports built or improved
2,565	Murals painted
17,744	Sculptures created

Source: *The Depression and New Deal*

US 99

Critical Thinking

Explaining Why do you think WPA projects were considered beneficial to the entire nation?

The Second New Deal

Main Idea Roosevelt's Second New Deal introduced new programs to help jobless workers, the elderly, and labor unions.

History and You Do your grandparents receive a monthly social security check from the federal government? Read to find out about the origins of social security under the Second New Deal.

By the mid-1930s the economy had improved slightly, but the Depression was far from over. FDR took bolder steps.

To bring in more government funds, Roosevelt pushed Congress to pass the Revenue Act of 1935. The act raised taxes on wealthy people and corporations. Critics accused him of "soaking the rich" to pay for his programs, but many Americans cheered.

In 1935 President Roosevelt launched a new set of programs and reforms, often called the **Second New Deal.** The laws passed at this time changed American life even more than the Hundred Days had done.

Creating Jobs

Millions of people—20 percent of the workforce—were still unemployed in 1935. In April Congress created the Works Progress Administration (WPA) to give people jobs and help the country. Led by Harry Hopkins, the WPA kept about 2 million people employed between 1935 and 1941. WPA workers built or repaired airports, public buildings, bridges, and roads.

The WPA also found work for unemployed writers, artists, and musicians. WPA painters decorated the new public buildings with murals. WPA produced *Life in America,* 150 volumes that recorded folktales and songs, African American narratives, and Native American traditions.

Help for Those in Need

Before the Second New Deal, America was the only advanced industrial nation without a national government program to help the needy. In August 1935, Congress passed the Social Security Act.

LINKING PAST TO PRESENT — Women in Government

THEN As the nation's first woman cabinet member, Secretary of Labor **Frances Perkins** (large image, below) worked for safe working conditions. Since 1917, when **Jeannette Rankin** (top right) of Montana became the first woman to serve in Congress, more than 240 women have served in the U.S. Congress. In 1953 **Oveta Culp Hobby** (taking oath of office) became the second woman to serve in a presidential cabinet. In 1977 **Patricia Roberts Harris** (bottom right) became the first African American woman to serve in the cabinet. She is also the first woman to hold two different cabinet posts.

The **Social Security Act** created a tax on workers and employers. That money provided monthly pensions for retired people. Another tax, on employers alone, funded **unemployment insurance** payments to people who lost their jobs. In addition, Social Security helped people with disabilities, the elderly poor, and children of parents who could not support them.

With the Social Security Act, the federal government took responsibility for the **welfare** of all citizens. The act launched the American welfare system.

The Labor Movement

Labor unions grew stronger as workers battled the Depression. In 1937 workers at the General Motors plant in Flint, Michigan, used a new technique—the sit-down strike. Strikers continuously occupied the plant and refused to work until management agreed to negotiate with them about their demands. After 44 days, the Flint strikers won the right to organize their union.

Most unions in the American Federation of Labor (AFL) represented only skilled workers. **John L. Lewis** of the United Mine Workers helped form a new union, the Congress of Industrial Organizations (CIO). The CIO set out to organize unions that included all workers, skilled and unskilled, in a particular industry. By 1938, the CIO had 4 million members, including large numbers of women and African Americans.

Unions found support in the New Deal. The 1935 National Labor Relations Act—also called the Wagner Act after its sponsor, Senator Robert Wagner of New York—guaranteed workers the right to form unions to bargain collectively with employers. In 1938 Congress passed the **Fair Labor Standards Act** (FLSA), which banned child labor and set a minimum wage of 40 cents per hour. The FLSA and the Wagner Act form the basis of American labor rights today.

Reading Check **Comparing** How did the CIO differ from the AFL?

NOW More and more women play important roles in the national government. **Condoleezza Rice** (large image, far left) speaks at the Women of Courage ceremony in 2007. Rice is the first African American female secretary of state. In 1997 **Aída Álvarez** (top right) became the first Latina woman and Puerto Rican to serve in a presidential cabinet. In the 110th Congress beginning in 2007, 16 women serve in the Senate and 74 women serve in the House. **Nancy Pelosi** (sitting at desk) of California is the first woman to serve as Speaker of the House.

Critical Thinking

Analyzing Consider the statement "The number of women in important government positions will continue to grow." Do you agree or disagree? Explain.

The Supreme Court

Main Idea Roosevelt's Second New Deal was challenged by the Supreme Court.

History and You Think about a time when someone questioned what you said or did. How did you answer that person? Read to learn how Roosevelt responded to critics of the New Deal.

. . . .

Those opposed to the New Deal challenged many of its laws in the courts. Beginning in 1935, the Supreme Court began to declare New Deal legislation unconstitutional. The presidential campaign of 1936 focused on a single issue: Did the American people support FDR and the New Deal? On Election Day, FDR won 61 percent of the popular vote.

Roosevelt's "Court-Packing" Plan

After the election, FDR acted to keep the Supreme Court from undoing the New Deal. He asked Congress to increase the number of Court justices from 9 to 15. FDR planned to fill the six new positions with justices who would uphold the New Deal.

The proposal aroused bitter opposition. Critics accused the president of trying to "pack" the Court and ruin the system of checks and balances. The issue died when the Court ruled in favor of the Wagner Act and the Social Security Act. The New Deal was no longer in serious danger from the Court. The unpopularity of the court-packing plan, however, cost Roosevelt much support.

The End of the New Deal

FDR also ran into trouble with the economy. During 1937, an economic recovery seemed to be in full swing, so FDR cut spending on programs. An economic downturn, known to some as the Roosevelt Recession, took hold and lasted into 1938. Roosevelt helped reverse it with spending on public works. Still, it was clear that the economy had not fully recovered, despite wide-ranging New Deal programs. As the 1930s came to an end, however, dangerous events in Asia and Europe caused Americans to turn their attention from domestic to foreign affairs.

Reading Check Explaining Why was FDR's Supreme Court plan criticized?

Section 4 Review

History ONLINE
Study Central™ To review this section, go to glencoe.com.

Vocabulary

1. Use each of these terms in a complete sentence that will explain its meaning: scheme, pension, unemployment insurance, welfare.

Main Ideas

2. **Discussing** Why did many business leaders criticize Roosevelt?

3. **Stating** What was the intended dual purpose of the WPA?

4. **Analyzing** What did the 1936 election say about the public's opinion of the president's policies?

Critical Thinking

5. **Identifying** On a diagram like the one below, list the major labor legislative acts passed by Congress during the Second New Deal.

   Labor Legislation

6. **Explaining** What was the Social Security Act of 1935 and why was it a significant act for Congress to pass?

7. **Persuasive Writing** Imagine you were the unemployed head of your family in 1935. Would you have supported President Roosevelt's plan to add six more justices to the Supreme Court? Write a short essay explaining and supporting your view.

Answer the Essential Question

8. Why did some people support Roosevelt's New Deal and some oppose it?

Stock Market Helps Trigger Depression

- Investors buy stocks on margin
- Sharp drop in market prices leaves investors in debt
- International market falters
- Stock market crashes; financial panic

Causes of the Great Depression

- Uneven distribution of income leads to low demand for goods
- Overuse of credit to make purchases
- Supply exceeds demand in industry; leads to large inventories of unsold goods
- Farmers suffer from too much production, low prices, and large debts

Effects

- Businesses lay off workers, close plants
- Millions lose jobs
- Poverty is widespread
- Businesses and banks close
- New Deal legislation enacted
- Despite periods of economic upturn, the Depression remains

STUDY TO GO Study anywhere, anytime! Download quizzes and flash cards to your PDA from glencoe.com.

STANDARDIZED TEST PRACTICE

TEST-TAKING TIP

When you take a test, do not answer the questions right away. Look over the test first. How many questions are there? How many different sections? Are some questions worth more points than others? Pace yourself accordingly.

Reviewing Main Ideas

Directions: Choose the best answer for each of the following questions.

1. What hardship did more than 20 percent of Americans face during the Great Depression?

   A inflation

   B unemployment

   C scarcity of goods

   D high stock prices

2. The National Recovery Administration helped the economy by

   A providing jobs.

   B insuring bank deposits.

   C distributing food and cash.

   D encouraging businesses to set a minimum wage.

3. Whom did the government encourage to leave the country during the Great Depression?

   A Native Americans

   B African Americans

   C Dust Bowl families

   D Mexican Americans

4. Conservative critics wanted the Roosevelt administration to

   A give every American a house.

   B impose heavy taxes on the wealthy.

   C play a less active role in the economy.

   D pay older workers to quit their jobs.

Short-Answer Question

Directions: Base your answer to question 5 on the excerpt below and on your knowledge of social studies.

> Now a lot of people remember [the WPA] as boon-doggles and raking leaves. . . . But I can take you to our town and show you things, like a river front that I used to hike through once that was a swamp and is now a beautiful park place built by WPA.
>
> —Ronald Reagan, as quoted in *The New Deal*

5. What were some lasting effects of the New Deal?

Review the Essential Questions

6. **Essay** Did the New Deal correct the factors that caused the Great Depression? Explain.

To help you write your essay, review your answers to the Essential Questions in the section reviews and the chapter Foldables Study Organizer. Your essay should include:

- factors that caused the Great Depression;

- New Deal programs that addressed these factors;

- changes brought about by New Deal programs; and

- evaluation of the views of supporters and opponents of the New Deal.

GO ON ➡

History ONLINE

For additional test practice, use **Self-Check Quizzes**—Chapter 11 at glencoe.com.

Document-Based Questions

Directions: Analyze the documents and answer the questions that follow.

Document 1

Reverend Reinhold Niebuhr recorded his thoughts about Ford's new model car in 1927.

> The car cost [laid-off] Ford workers at least fifty million in lost wages during the past year. . . . We are now asked to believe that the whole idea of waiting a year after the old car [Model T] stopped selling before bringing out a new one was a great advertising scheme.

Source: Robert Sklar, *The Plastic Age (1917–1930)*

7. What phrases in the excerpt foreshadow the coming of the Great Depression?

Document 2

"Bread Line," a poem by Florence Converse, was first published in 1932.

> What if we should be destroyed
> By our patient unemployed?

Source: David A. Shannon, *The Great Depression*

8. How does the poet think that the unemployed might react to continued hard times?

Document 3

Langston Hughes recorded these observations while in Spain during the Spanish Civil War.

> I've met wide-awake Negroes [African Americans] from various parts of the world—New York, our Middle West . . . all of them here because they know that if Fascism creeps across Spain, across Europe, and then across the world, there will be no more place for intelligent young Negroes at all.

Source: Langston Hughes, "Negroes in Spain"

9. Why did African Americans volunteer in Spain?

Document 4

This cartoon by Cliff Berryman was published in 1938.

Source: Granger Collection

10. Based on the cartoon, explain the economic downturn of the late 1930s and Roosevelt's reaction.

11. Descriptive Writing Using the information from the four documents and your knowledge of social studies, write an essay in which you:

- illustrate, with examples, hardships suffered just before and during the Great Depression; and
- describe the feelings these hardships brought out in wealthy, middle-class, and poor Americans.

Need Extra Help?											
If you missed questions. . .	1	2	3	4	5	6	7	8	9	10	11
Go to page. . .	333	341	347	353	352–356	333	348	348	348	354	344–349

Chapter 12

America and World War II

1939–1945

American troops land in France, D-Day, June 6, 1944

FRANKLIN
DELANO
ROOSEVELT

PRESIDENTS

U.S. Events

★ **1937**
Neutrality Act
limits trade
with warring
nations

★ **1940**
Selective
Training and
Service Act
passes

1937

1939

World Events

★ **1937**
Mexico president
Lázaro Cárdenas
continues land,
railroad reform

★ **1939**
• Germany invades
  Austria and
  Czechoslovakia
• Hitler seizes Poland

Section 1: The Road to War

Essential Question How did dictators acquire and expand power in Europe in the 1930s?

Section 2: War Begins

Essential Question How did peaceful nations confront foreign aggressors in World War II?

Section 3: On the Home Front

Essential Question In what ways did American men, women, and minorities support the war effort at home?

Section 4: War in Europe and Africa

Essential Question What strategies did the Allies pursue in Europe and Africa to defeat the Axis powers in World War II?

Section 5: War in the Pacific

Essential Question What was the turning point in the war in the Pacific, and what led up to it?

FOLDABLES®
Study Organizer

Summarizing Information

Make the following Foldable to help you summarize information about the effects of the war on women and minorities.

Step 1 Collect three sheets of paper and place them on top of each other about an inch apart.

Step 2 Fold up the bottom edges of the paper to form six tabs. This makes all tabs the same size.

Step 3 When all the tabs are the same size, crease the paper to hold the tabs in place, and staple the sheets together. Label each tab as shown.

Women and Minorities in World War II
- Women
- African Americans
- Native Americans
- Latinos
- Japanese Americans

Reading and Writing As you read the chapter, write details about how the war affected women and minorities.

About 2,000 women were accepted into the Women's Air Force Service Pilots. ▶

"I've found the job where I fit best!"

FIND YOUR WAR JOB
In Industry – Agriculture – Business

★ **1940**
• German troops occupy Paris
• Hitler orders bombing of Britain

★ **1941**
• Lend-Lease Act passes
• U.S. declares war

1941

★ **1941**
• Germany attacks Soviet Union
• Japan bombs Pearl Harbor, Hawaii

★ **1942**
• Allies capture North Africa
• U.S. increases war effort on home front

1943

★ **1944**
Supreme Court upholds internment of Japanese American civilians

★ **1944**
D-Day, Allies invade France

◀ American cemetery, Normandy, France

★ **1945**
U.S. drops atomic bombs on Hiroshima and Nagasaki, Japan

1945

The Road to War

Essential Question ◄

How did dictators acquire and expand power in Europe in the 1930s?

Reading Guide

Content Vocabulary

dictator *(p. 363)*   totalitarian *(p. 364)*

fascism *(p. 363)*   appeasement *(p. 365)*

anti-Semitism *(p. 364)*

Academic Vocabulary

obtain *(p. 364)*   unify *(p. 365)*

Key People and Events

Benito Mussolini *(p. 363)*

Joseph Stalin *(p. 364)*

Munich Conference *(p. 365)*

Reading Strategy

Taking Notes Use a chart like the one below to list the dictator and country where each political party originated in the 1930s.

	Nazi Party	Fascist Party	Communist Party
Dictator			
Country			

American Diary

Many people underestimated Adolf Hitler's influence, but not American journalist William Shirer. He described a rally for Hitler at Nuremberg in September 1934: "Like a Roman emperor Hitler rode into this mediæval town. . . . When Hitler finally appeared on the balcony for a moment, . . . [people] looked up at him as if he were a Messiah, their faces transformed into something positively inhuman." The passion of the Nazis shocked Shirer, and soon it would shock the world.

—*from* Berlin Diary

Nazi rally in Nuremberg, Germany

The Rise of Dictators

Main Idea Bitterness over the outcome of World War I and serious economic problems led to the rise of dictators in several countries.

History and You Is it ever okay for people to steal something if they need it? Read to learn how dictators in Europe and Asia used that argument to justify invading other countries.

• •

In the 1920s, Adolf Hitler stated in his book *Mein Kampf* (My Struggle): "He who wants to live must fight, and he who does not want to fight in this world, where eternal struggle is the law of life, has no right to exist." When Hitler became Germany's leader, he put his strong words into action.

Hitler was among other ruthless leaders to rise to power in the 1920s and 1930s by taking advantage of people's anger and suffering. Some Europeans resented the Treaty of Versailles, which ended World War I. When a worldwide economic depression hit in the 1930s, frustration and fear added to this anger. Hitler and other leaders promised a better life and a glorious future. Once they won power, these men became **dictators**—leaders who control their nations by force.

Italy

Benito Mussolini won power by appealing to Italians who resented that Italy had won little in the Versailles treaty. Mussolini made **fascism**—government characterized by militarism and racism—popular. By 1922, his Fascist Party was able to force Italy's king to name Mussolini the head of government. Mussolini soon banned all other political parties.

Known as *Il Duce* (the leader), Mussolini quickly ended democratic rule in Italy. Civil liberties and the free press ceased to exist. Mussolini also built up the military and vowed to regain the glory of ancient Rome.

In 1935 Mussolini took over the African nation of Ethiopia. The League of Nations banned the trade of certain goods with Italy, but it lacked the power to enforce the ban. Italy left the League and continued its expansion, seizing its neighbor Albania in 1939.

Germany

The Great Depression hit Germany extremely hard. Businesses failed, and millions of people lost their jobs. Hitler won German support by appealing to fears about the economy and bitterness over the Versailles treaty.

Time Line / Rise of Nazism

Path to Power By 1933 the Nazis—once a small, obscure group—had become Germany's most powerful political party.

★ **1918** Germany defeated in World War I

★ **1921** Hitler becomes leader of Nazi party

★ **1923** Nazis try to seize power in Munich

★ **1925** Hitler writes *Mein Kampf* in prison

★ **1929** Great Depression begins

★ **1930** Many Nazis elected to Germany's parliament

★ **1933** Hitler named chancellor, or head of government

Drawing from 1941 Nazi textbook ▶

Critical Thinking

Drawing Conclusions Why do you think many Germans supported Hitler and the Nazis?

Economic problems brought dictators to power in many countries. This June 1941 cartoon comments on Hitler's strong influence.

1. **Analyzing Visuals** Why is Hitler cutting the hair of Inönü and Stalin? How are they reacting?
2. **Identifying Points of View** What commentary do you think the cartoonist is making about Hitler?

A. Russia's Stalin B. Germany's Hitler
C. Turkey's Inönü

Hitler was leader of the National Socialist Party, or the Nazi Party. Hitler and the Nazis believed the German people were superior to other groups of people. Hitler blamed the Jews, including Germans who were Jewish, for Germany's problems. His **anti-Semitism**—hatred of the Jews—would lead to unspeakable horrors.

After gaining power in 1933, Hitler ended democracy and set up totalitarian rule. In a **totalitarian** state, leaders crush all opposition and try to totally control all areas of society.

Hitler claimed that Germany had a right to expand. Germany's neighbors watched uneasily as he defied the Versailles treaty and rebuilt Germany's military. To win support, Hitler formed an alliance with Italy in 1936.

Growing Tension

During the Depression the Japanese suffered from lack of jobs and food shortages. Military leaders believed that Japan needed more land and resources. In September 1931, Japan's army invaded mineral-rich Manchuria, China's northeastern region.

The League of Nations condemned the Japanese invasion but did nothing about it. Japan then set up a government in Manchuria. In 1937 Japan invaded China. Three years later, Japan joined Germany and Italy in the "Axis" alliance.

In the late 1920s, **Joseph Stalin** rose to power as the Communist leader of the Soviet Union. Stalin used force to **obtain,** or gain, obedience from his people. He executed his rivals and sent millions of people suspected of disloyalty to labor camps.

American Neutrality

Most Americans wanted to avoid foreign troubles. To keep the nation out of wars, Congress passed the Neutrality Acts between 1935 and 1937. The Neutrality Acts banned weapons sales and loans to nations that were at war. Many countries had not paid back their World War I loans and Congress wanted to prevent more debts.

Reading Check **Comparing** What plans did Mussolini and Hitler share?

Germany on the March

Main Idea Other European countries stood by as Germany expanded its territory.

History and You Is it better to stand up to bullies or give them what they want? Read to learn how Europe's leaders dealt with Adolf Hitler's demands.

....

Hitler moved forward with his plans for expansion. In March 1936, he ordered German troops into the Rhineland. The Versailles treaty had made the Rhineland, German lands west of the Rhine River, a neutral area.

Next, Hitler insisted that German-speaking Austria should be **unified** with Germany. In March 1938, he sent troops into Austria.

Hitler then turned to the Sudetenland, an area of Czechoslovakia where many German-speaking people lived. Falsely claiming that these people were being mistreated, Hitler declared Germany's right to take the territory.

Czechoslovakia was ready to fight to keep the Sudetenland. Britain and France, fearing a major war, sought a peaceful solution. In September 1938, European leaders met in Munich, Germany.

Britain and France thought that they could avoid war by accepting Germany's demands—a policy known as **appeasement.** At the **Munich Conference,** British and French leaders agreed to give the Sudetenland to Germany. Czechoslovakia was told to give up the Sudetenland or fight Germany on its own. Hitler pledged not to further expand Germany's territory. British prime minister, Neville Chamberlain, returned home to cheers, declaring that the agreement had preserved "peace for our time."

Hopes for peace were soon dashed. In March 1939, Hitler's army took the rest of western Czechoslovakia and set up a pro-Nazi state in the eastern part.

Meanwhile, Hitler prepared to invade Poland. He worried, however, that such an attack would anger Stalin because Poland bordered the Soviet Union. Though bitter enemies, Hitler and Stalin signed the Soviet-German Non-Aggression Pact in August 1939. Hitler was now free to attack Poland without fear of Soviet intervention.

Reading Check **Explaining** Why was Germany able to invade Poland?

Section 1 Review

History ONLINE
Study Central™ To review this section, go to glencoe.com.

Vocabulary

1. Use each term in a sentence: dictator, fascism, anti-Semitism, totalitarian, obtain, unify, appeasement.

Main Ideas

2. **Explaining** What were some of the problems that led to the rise of dictators in Germany, Italy, and Japan?

3. **Theorizing** How did the policy of appeasement work in Hitler's favor?

Critical Thinking

4. **Interpreting** Why do you think fascism became popular in Europe in the years following World War I?

5. **Sequencing** Create a time line like the one below to track Hitler's actions in each of the months and years noted.

| Mar. 1936 | Mar. 1938 | Mar. 1939 | Aug. 1939 |

6. **Persuasive Writing** Write an editorial that defends or criticizes the policy of American neutrality in the 1930s. Make sure to include reasons that support your position.

Answer the
7. **Essential Question**
How did dictators acquire and expand power in Europe in the 1930s?

War Begins

Essential Question ◄

How did peaceful nations confront foreign aggressors in World War II?

Reading Guide

Content Vocabulary

blitzkrieg (p. 367)   disarmament (p. 370)

Academic Vocabulary

target (p. 367)   fund (p. 371)

Key People and Events

Allied Powers (p. 368)

Axis Powers (p. 368)

Winston Churchill (p. 368)

Atlantic Charter (p. 370)

Pearl Harbor (p. 371)

Reading Strategy

Taking Notes Use a diagram like the one below to record which countries belonged to the Allied Powers and which belonged to the Axis Powers in World War II.

Allied Powers

World War II

Axis Powers

American Diary

On the morning of September 1, 1939, President Roosevelt received an urgent phone call from Europe. The voice on the other end was that of William Bullitt, U.S. ambassador to France. Bullitt told the President, "Several German divisions are deep in Poland, and fighting is heavy. . . . There were reports of bombers over the city." Roosevelt responded, "Well, Bill, it's come at last. God help us all."

—*from* American White Paper

Military aircraft being made in American factory, 1941

War in Europe

Main Idea World War II began in September 1939, when Germany invaded Poland, and Great Britain and France declared war on Germany.

History and You Have you ever had to do something difficult? What helped you? Read to learn how the British endured defeats and German bombing.

. . . .

In a speech in 1937, President Franklin Roosevelt expressed the feeling of many Americans toward the growing "epidemic of world lawlessness. . . . We are determined to keep out of war, yet we cannot insure ourselves against the disastrous effects of war and the dangers of involvement."

On September 1, 1939, Hitler sent his armies into Poland. Two days later, Great Britain and France declared war on Germany. World War II had begun.

The German attack on Poland was swift and fierce. German planes bombed and machine-gunned **targets,** or objects for attack. German tanks blasted holes in Polish defenses, and thousands of soldiers poured into Poland. The Germans called the offensive a **blitzkrieg,** or "lightning war." Then Soviet troops moved into and occupied eastern Poland, acting on the Soviet agreement with Germany to divide Poland.

Great Britain and France could do little to help Poland because its defeat came so quickly. In late September 1939, the conquered country was split in half by Hitler and Stalin. Stalin also forced the Baltic republics of Latvia, Lithuania, and Estonia to accept Soviet military bases. When he tried to do the same with Finland, war broke out between the two nations. The Finns held out heroically until March 1940, when the Soviets forced them to surrender.

The War Expands

All through the winter of 1939–1940, the western front was quiet. British and French forces settled in at the Maginot Line, a string of steel-and-concrete bunkers along the German border from Belgium to Switzerland. Hitler and his generals decided to attack other nations before invading France.

By the Numbers / America Prepares for War

Military Increases After Hitler's invasion of Poland, the United States began to expand its armed forces and defense plants.

U.S. Military Personnel on Active Duty	
1939	334,473
1940	458,365
1941	1,801,101
1942	3,858,791
1943	9,044,745
1944	11,541,719
1945	12,123,455

Source: Bureau of the Census, *Historical Statistics of the United States.*

U.S. Military Aircraft Production

Number of Aircraft (units): 100,000 / 80,000 / 60,000 / 40,000 / 20,000 / 0

Year: 1939, 1940, 1941, 1942, 1943, 1944, 1945

Source: John Ellis, *World War II: A Statistical Survey*

Critical Thinking

Making Inferences Why do you think increases in the armed forces and military production rose greatly after 1941?

In April, Hitler attacked Denmark and Norway to the north, and the following month he turned west to invade the Netherlands and Belgium. The Netherlands and Belgium immediately asked for help from Great Britain and France—the **Allied Powers,** or the Allies. After bombing raids in the Netherlands, the Dutch surrendered. The Belgians fought courageously, but they too were overwhelmed.

With the collapse of Belgium, Allied troops retreated to the port of Dunkirk in the northwest corner of France on the English Channel. They were now trapped between the advancing Germans and the French coast. In a daring move, more than 800 British ships—warships, ferries, and fishing boats—joined an operation to rescue the troops. Crossing the channel again and again, the boats evacuated more than 300,000 French and British troops to safety.

In June the Germans crossed the Somme River and continued their sweep into France. Italy joined the war on the side of Germany and attacked France from the southeast. Germany and Italy—and later Japan—formed the **Axis Powers.** On June 14, 1940, German troops marched victoriously into Paris. The French surrendered a week later.

The Battle of Britain

All that kept Hitler from taking western Europe was Great Britain. In August 1940, the Germans bombed British air bases, shipyards, and industries. German planes also bombed cities, destroying entire areas of London and killing many civilians.

Hitler's goal was to break British morale before invading Britain. The British people endured, however, in part because of the inspiration of Prime Minister **Winston Churchill.** When Hitler called for Britain to surrender, Churchill responded defiantly:

PRIMARY SOURCE

"We shall defend our island, whatever the cost may be, we shall fight on the beaches, we shall fight on the landing grounds, we shall fight in the fields and in the streets, we shall fight in the hills; we shall never surrender."

—from a speech to the British House of Commons

Primary Source / The Battle of Britain

Bombing Britain In mid-August 1940, Hitler ordered the German air force to concentrate on bombing London. Hitler's goal was to terrorize the British people into surrendering. Despite the bombing of London and other major cities, the British people stood firm against the threat of a Nazi invasion.

"Gas masks have suddenly become part of everyday civilian equipment and everybody is carrying the square cardboard cartons that look as though they might contain a pound of grapes for a sick friend. . . . Although the summer holiday is still on, village schools have reopened as centers where the evacuated hordes from London can be rested, sorted out, . . . refreshed with tea and biscuits, and distributed to their new homes."

—English writer, Mollie Panter-Downes

"It was a night when London was ringed and stabbed with fire. They came just after dark. . . . About every two minutes a new wave of planes would be over. The motors seemed to grind rather than roar, and to have an angry pulsation, like a bee buzzing in blind fury."

—journalist Ernie Pyle

Although the Battle of Britain continued until October, the Germans never gained control of the skies over Britain. The British Royal Air Force mounted a heroic defense and inflicted heavy losses on the German air force. Finally, Hitler ended the air attacks.

Germany Turns East

Unable to defeat the British, Hitler decided that Germany needed the resources of the Soviet Union. He also believed that the Soviets' vast land area could provide "living space" for Germans.

In June 1941, German forces attacked the Soviet Union, destroying planes and tanks and capturing half a million Soviet soldiers. As the Germans advanced, Stalin ordered a scorched-earth policy. The Soviets burned their own cities, destroyed crops, and blew up dams that produced electric power. These actions made it harder for the Germans to supply their troops and to keep advancing.

Reading Check **Examining** Why did Hitler end plans to invade Britain?

DBQ Document-Based Questions

Analyzing What do the two documents and the photographs reveal about the British people's reaction to the German air strikes?

America and the War

Main Idea Wanting to defend democracy, the United States gradually became involved in the European conflict on the side of the Allies.

History and You Have you ever tried to stay out of a quarrel, only to find yourself being drawn into it? Read to learn how the United States responded to the war in Europe.

. . . .

The United States watched the war in Europe with concern. Most Americans leaned toward the Allies, but they did not want war. Isolationists set up the America First Committee to further the idea that the United States should stay out of Europe's problems.

Although he vowed to remain neutral, Roosevelt prepared for war. In 1938, at his request, Congress strengthened the navy. In 1939 the president also had Congress pass a new Neutrality Act. It let warring nations buy U.S. goods as long as they paid cash and carried the goods in their own ships. In 1940 Roosevelt signed the Selective Training and Service Act, the first peacetime draft in United States history. The law applied to U.S. men between the ages of 21 and 35.

The 1940 Election

With the world in crisis, President Roosevelt chose to run for a third term, ending the tradition of serving two terms set by George Washington. Roosevelt promised Americans, "Your boys are not going to be sent into any foreign wars." The Republican candidate Wendell L. Willkie generally agreed with Roosevelt's New Deal and foreign policy, but Americans preferred to keep a president they knew. Roosevelt won an easy victory.

U.S. Involvement Grows

With the election won, Roosevelt supported the Allies openly. At Roosevelt's urging, Congress passed the Lend-Lease Act in March 1941. This law allowed the United States to sell, lend, or lease weapons to any country "vital to the defense of the United States."

A Surprise Attack The Japanese succeeded in their surprise attack on Pearl Harbor. Sailor Charles Christensen describes the terrible scene on the USS *Arizona*:

"The oil was on fire, and they were trying to swim out of it. They'd come up and try to get their breath. The whites of their eyes were red. Their skin was coming off."

—from *Remember Pearl Harbor*

Rescue boats move in on burning battleships. ▶

U.S. Losses at Pearl Harbor

Human Casualties	Killed	Wounded
Navy	1,998	710
Marine Corps	109	69
Army	233	364
Civilian	48	35

Ships	
Sunk or beached	12
Damaged	9

Aircraft	
Destroyed	164
Damaged	159

Critical Thinking

Speculating If the Japanese attack on Pearl Harbor had not occurred, do you think the United States would have entered the war? Why or why not?

Isolationists opposed the law, arguing that it would bring America closer to war. Britain, short of cash, was the first to use lend-lease.

In mid-1941, Roosevelt also had the navy protect British ships when they were close to the United States. When the Germans fired on American destroyers, Roosevelt ordered American ships to "shoot-on-sight" German and Italian ships found in certain areas.

The Atlantic Charter

In August 1941, President Roosevelt and British prime minister Churchill met and drew up the **Atlantic Charter.** While Roosevelt made no military promises, he joined Churchill in setting goals for the world after "the final destruction of the Nazi tyranny." The two nations pledged that the people would be free to choose their own form of government and live free of "fear and want." They urged **disarmament**—giving up military weapons—and the creation of a "permanent system of general security."

✔ **Reading Check** Explaining Why did isolationists oppose the Lend-Lease Act?

The Japanese Threat

Main Idea The United States entered World War II as a result of Japan's attack on the Pearl Harbor military base in 1941.

History and You Do you remember how the terrorist attacks on September 11, 2001, led to a war? The same thing happened in 1941 when an attack on American soil drew the United States into World War II.

· ·

While Hitler and Mussolini waged war in Europe, the Japanese made military conquests in the Far East. After seizing much of China in the 1930s, the Japanese continued their expansion. After France's fall in 1940, they seized French-ruled Indochina in Southeast Asia. Japan also planned to take the Dutch East Indies, British Malaya, and the American territory of the Philippines, primarily to acquire badly needed rubber and oil.

The United States Responds

The United States responded to Japan's moves by applying economic pressure.

Roosevelt froze all Japanese **funds,** or reserves of money, in U.S. banks. He also stopped the sale of oil, gasoline, and other resources that Japan lacked. The action angered the Japanese.

In October 1941, the Japanese prime minister, Fumimaro Konoye, resigned. Konoye wanted to hold talks with the United States because he believed Japan could not defeat America in a war. The new leader, General Hideki Tōjō, did not share Konoye's views. Still, on November 20, talks began in Washington. Meanwhile, Tōjō's government began planning an attack on the United States.

Attack on Pearl Harbor

At 7:55 A.M. on Sunday, December 7, 1941, Japanese warplanes attacked the American military base at **Pearl Harbor,** Hawaii. Ships there were anchored in a neat row, and airplanes were grouped together on the airfield—easy targets for an air attack.

The attack destroyed many battleships, cruisers, and airplanes. More than 2,300 soldiers, sailors, and civilians were killed. Fortunately, at the time of the attack, the navy's three aircraft carriers were at sea.

The Americans at Pearl Harbor were taken completely by surprise. According to Lieutenant Commander Charles Coe:

PRIMARY SOURCE

"The capsizing of the *Oklahoma* was to me a sight beyond all belief. It was in fact the most awful thing I had ever seen. To watch this big battleship capsize and to see only her bottom sticking up out of the water like the back of a turtle and to realize that U.S. officers and men were still in there—well, I just couldn't believe it. It made me realize . . . that war had come to Hawaii."
—from *December 7, 1941*

The attack on Pearl Harbor united the country. The next day, Roosevelt asked Congress to declare war, calling December 7 "a date which will live in infamy."

On December 11, Germany and Italy—Japan's allies—declared war on the United States. Congress then declared war on them. The United States joined the Allied nations—including Great Britain, France, China, and the Soviet Union—against the Axis Powers—Germany, Italy, and Japan.

Reading Check **Explaining** Why did Japan attack Pearl Harbor?

Section 2 Review

Study Central™ To review this section, go to glencoe.com.

Vocabulary

1. Use each of these terms in a complete sentence that will help explain its meaning: target, blitzkrieg, disarmament, fund.

Main Ideas

2. **Analyzing** What was the blitzkrieg, and why was it so effective during the war?

3. **Identifying** What was the outcome of the presidential election in 1940?

4. **Analyzing** Explain why the attack on Pearl Harbor was successful.

Critical Thinking

5. **Listing** Re-create a diagram like the one below to list the main goals of the Atlantic Charter.

6. **Creative Writing** You are a teen living in London in September 1940. Write a journal entry explaining what it is like living in a city that is daily bombarded.

Answer the
7. **Essential Question**
How did peaceful nations confront foreign aggressors in World War II?

On the Home Front

Essential Question ◄

In what ways did American men, women, and minorities support the war effort at home?

Reading Guide

Content Vocabulary

mobilization (p. 373)   civil defense (p. 375)

ration (p. 375)   internment camp (p. 377)

Academic Vocabulary

shift (p. 373)   overseas (p. 374)

Key People and Events

WACs (p. 373)

WAVES (p. 373)

Tuskegee Airmen (p. 375)

bracero (p. 377)

Nisei (p. 377)

Reading Strategy

Taking Notes Re-create the diagram below, and describe the new roles adopted by American men and women during World War II.

New Roles

American Diary

Sybil Lewis, a riveter for Lockheed Aircraft in Los Angeles, gave this description of her wartime job: "The women worked in pairs. I was the riveter and this big, strong, white girl from a cotton farm in Arkansas worked as the bucker. The riveter used a gun to shoot rivets through the metal and fasten it together. The bucker used a bucking bar on the other side of the metal to smooth out the rivets. Bucking was harder than shooting rivets; it required more muscle. Riveting required more skill."

—*from "Rosie the Riveter"*

During the war years, women worked at jobs traditionally held by men.

America Prepares

Main Idea The United States had to refocus its economy to provide supplies for the war effort.

History and You Have you heard the expression "strength in numbers"? Read to find out how Americans joined together to fight World War II.

The Japanese attack on Pearl Harbor united the American people as nothing else could. With astonishing speed, the nation's economy and its people prepared to fight the war.

Building an Army

Even before Pearl Harbor, the United States had begun raising an army under the Selective Service Acts of 1940 and 1941. More than 15 million Americans joined the armed forces during the war, both as volunteers and as draftees.

New draftees were given physical exams and injections against smallpox and typhoid. The draftees were then issued uniforms, boots, and equipment. The clothing bore the label "G.I." meaning "Government Issue." As a result, American soldiers came to be known as "GIs."

Recruits were sent to basic training for eight weeks. They learned how to handle weapons, load backpacks, read maps, pitch tents, and dig trenches.

For the first time, large numbers of women served in the military. About 250,000 women served in the **WACs** (Women's Army Corps), the **WAVES** (Women Appointed for Volunteer Emergency Service in the Navy), and women's units in the marines, Coast Guard, and army air corps. These women did not fight in combat—most performed clerical tasks or worked as nurses—but they played important roles in the war effort.

Creating a War Economy

Equipping the troops required changes in the nation's economy. To speed up **mobilization**—military and civilian preparations for war—the government created new agencies. The War Production Board supervised the conversion of industries to war production. Under its guidance, automakers **shifted,** or moved away, from building cars to produce trucks, jeeps, and tanks. The Office of Price Administration established limits on consumer prices and rents to prevent inflation.

Primary Source / **Women on the Home Front Poster**

The more WOMEN at work the sooner we WIN!

WOMEN ARE NEEDED ALSO AS:

FARM WORKERS, WAITRESSES, TIMEKEEPERS, LAUNDRESSES, TYPISTS, BUS DRIVERS, ELEVATOR OPERATORS, TEACHERS, SALESPEOPLE, TAXI DRIVERS, MESSENGERS, CONDUCTORS
— and in hundreds of other war jobs!

SEE YOUR LOCAL U.S. EMPLOYMENT SERVICE

Aiding the War Effort As the war progressed, women found their roles changing. Women enlisted for non-combat duties in various branches of the military. Women also found work on the home front in the construction industry or on assembly lines turning out tanks and airplanes. Eventually 2.5 million women went to work in shipyards, aircraft factories, and other manufacturing plants. Although most women left the factories after the war, their success permanently changed American attitudes about women in the workplace.

Critical Thinking

Making Connections What adjectives would you use to describe the woman in the poster? What do you think the poster says about the role of women in World War II? Explain.

The National War Labor Board helped resolve labor disputes that might slow down war production. By the summer of 1942, almost all major industries and some 200,000 companies had converted to war production.

Financing the War

From 1941 to the end of the war, the U.S. spent more than $320 billion on the war effort—10 times the amount spent in World War I. Much of this money was raised through taxes. The Revenue Act of 1942 raised corporate taxes and required most Americans to pay income taxes. Congress approved a system for withholding taxes from workers' paychecks—a practice still in effect today.

The government also borrowed money to finance the war. As in World War I, the government sold war bonds. Movie stars and other celebrities urged people to buy bonds to support the war.

Reading Check **Explaining** What was the purpose of the Office of Price Administration?

Wartime America

Main Idea During World War II, Americans faced hardships but united to help the war effort.

History and You What would it be like to live in a country that is fighting a world war? Read to find out how American lives were shaped by World War II.
. . . .

Those who remained at home had to provide food and shelter for all those in uniform. Civilians also provided training, equipment, transportation, and medical care.

Making Sacrifices

With the war effort came many sacrifices. For many American families, the war meant separation from loved ones serving **overseas.** Those at home lived in dread of receiving a telegram announcing that a family member had been killed, wounded, or captured.

With industries geared to producing goods to fight the war, Americans faced shortages of many consumer goods.

The War and Social Change

Mexican Farmworkers ▶ In 1942 the federal government arranged for Mexican farmworkers to help with the harvest in the Southwest. The laborers were part of the Bracero Program. *Bracero* is a Spanish word meaning "worker." More than 200,000 Mexicans came to help harvest fruit and vegetables and to build and maintain railroads.

◀ **Women Take New Roles** The need for defense workers changed traditional patterns of American society. As millions of men joined the armed services, more women than ever before entered the labor force.

Many things needed for the war were **rationed**—consumers could buy only limited numbers or amounts of them. Americans used government-issued books of ration coupons to buy certain items, such as gasoline, tires, sugar, and meat.

Helping the War Effort

People found other ways to help the war effort. Many planted "victory gardens" to grow vegetables, which were in short supply. Children collected scrap metal for industry.

Many people joined in **civil defense**—protective measures taken in case of attack. For example, volunteer spotters scanned the skies for possible enemy aircraft. Coastal cities enforced blackouts at night so that lights could not serve as beacons for enemy pilots.

The Office of War Information promoted patriotism to keep Americans united behind the war effort.

Reading Check Explaining Why were many consumer goods in short supply?

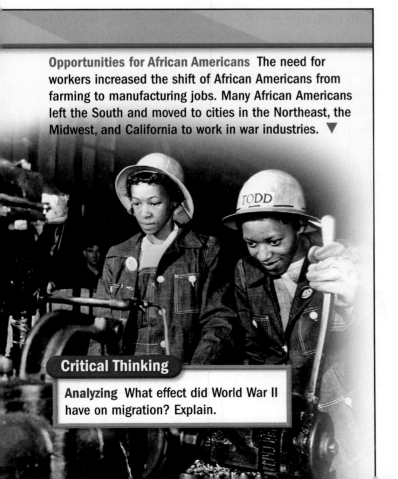

Opportunities for African Americans The need for workers increased the shift of African Americans from farming to manufacturing jobs. Many African Americans left the South and moved to cities in the Northeast, the Midwest, and California to work in war industries. ▼

Critical Thinking

Analyzing What effect did World War II have on migration? Explain.

Women and Minorities

Main Idea World War II brought new opportunities to women and minorities, but inequalities remained.

History and You Do you know anyone who has been discriminated against because of his or her gender or race? Read about the discrimination—and the opportunities—for women and minorities during the war.

The war had a tremendous impact on the lives of women and minorities. It created opportunities for new jobs and new roles in society.

As millions of men joined the armed forces, more women than ever before entered the labor force. In factories women worked in jobs previously held by men. An advertising campaign featuring a character called Rosie the Riveter encouraged women to take factory jobs. For many women, this was their first opportunity to work outside the home.

Although women had new job opportunities, they usually earned less than men. Moreover, when the war ended and the troops returned home, most women would lose their jobs. Still, the war changed public opinion about women's right to work.

African Americans

About one million African Americans served in the armed forces during the war. At first, most were given low-level assignments and kept in segregated units. Gradually, military leaders assigned African Americans to integrated units. In 1942 the army began training whites and African Americans together in officer candidate school. Eventually, African Americans were allowed to take combat assignments.

The 332nd Fighter Group, known as the **Tuskegee Airmen,** shot down more than 200 enemy planes. Benjamin Davis, Jr., who trained at the Tuskegee flying school, became the first African American general in the United States Air Force. His father, Benjamin Davis, Sr., was the first African American general in the army.

Serving With Honor

Tuskegee Airmen Although the nation's armed forces were segregated, minority groups served with courage. In early 1941, the air force created its first African American unit, the 99th Pursuit Squadron. The pilots trained in Tuskegee, Alabama and became known as the Tuskegee Airmen.

▲ Tuskegee Airmen in Italy

The Nisei Soldiers As the war progressed, second-generation Japanese Americans served in the 100th Infantry Battalion and the 442nd Regimental Combat team (right, fighting in Italy). Together, these units became the most decorated in the history of the U.S. military.

Critical Thinking

Speculating How do you think the efforts of the Tuskegee Airmen and Japanese American soldiers affected racial attitudes in America?

In civilian life, African Americans sought change. In the summer of 1941, labor leader A. Philip Randolph demanded that the government ban discrimination against African Americans in defense industries. He planned a large demonstration in Washington in support of his demands. President Roosevelt persuaded Randolph to call off the march by establishing the Fair Employment Practices Commission to combat discrimination in industries that held government contracts. The president announced that "there shall be no discrimination in the employment of workers in defense industries or government because of race, creed, color, or national origin."

The war accelerated the population shift that began during World War I. Large numbers of African Americans moved from the rural South to industrialized cities in the North and the West in search of work. In some cities, racial tensions erupted in violence. The riots inspired the African American poet Langston Hughes to write: "Yet you say we're fightin' for democracy. Then why don't democracy [i]nclude me?"

Native Americans

Thousands of Native Americans left reservations to work in defense industries and serve in the armed forces. Ira Hayes became a hero in the battle for Iwo Jima in the Pacific. A special group of Navajo formed the "code talkers." Many of the American radio communications about troop movements and battle plans were intercepted by the Japanese. The "code talkers" used a special code based on the Navajo language to send messages—a code that the Japanese never broke.

Latinos

More than 250,000 Latinos, also called Hispanic Americans, served in the armed forces. The Medal of Honor, the nation's highest military medal, was awarded to 12 Mexican Americans.

History ONLINE

Student Web Activity Visit glencoe.com and complete the Chapter 12 Web Activity about the Tuskegee Airmen.

Mercedes Cubría of Cuba became the first Latina woman officer in the Women's Army Corps. Horacio Rivero of Puerto Rico became the first Latino four-star admiral since David Farragut to serve in the United States Navy.

Prompted by the wartime need for labor, United States labor agents recruited thousands of farm and railroad workers from Mexico. This program, called the *bracero* program, stimulated emigration from Mexico.

Like African Americans, Mexican Americans suffered from discrimination, and their presence created tensions in some cities. In 1943, for example, a four-day riot started in Los Angeles when white sailors attacked Mexican American teens.

Japanese Americans

After the Japanese bombed Pearl Harbor, Japanese Americans were feared and hated by many other Americans. About two-thirds of Japanese Americans were **Nisei**—American citizens who were born in the United States. But this fact made little difference to people who questioned their loyalty.

Military and political leaders also worried about the loyalty of Japanese Americans if Japanese forces invaded the United States. President Roosevelt directed the army to relocate more than 100,000 Japanese Americans who were living on the West Coast to detention centers. Located mostly in desert areas, these **internment camps** were crowded and uncomfortable. Conditions were harsh.

With only days to prepare for the move, most Japanese Americans left valuable possessions behind. Many abandoned their homes and businesses or sold them at a loss. Most had to stay in internment camps for the next three years. Detainee Peter Ota remembered how his father suffered. "After all those years, having worked his whole life to build a dream—having it all taken away. . . . He died a broken man."

In 1944 in *Korematsu* v. *United States*, the Supreme Court upheld the order providing for the relocation of Japanese Americans. In 1988 Americans acknowledged the injustice of relocation. The United States Congress issued a formal apology and agreed to give each survivor $20,000 as a token of the nation's regret.

✔ **Reading Check** **Explaining** What was the purpose of the *bracero* program?

Section 3 Review

History ONLINE
Study Central™ To review this section, go to glencoe.com.

Vocabulary

1. Explain the significance of each of the following terms: mobilization, shift, overseas, ration, civil defense, internment camp.

Main Ideas

2. **Discussing** What kinds of sacrifices did American civilians make during wartime?

3. **Explaining** What legal action was taken against many Japanese Americans?

Critical Thinking

4. **Comparing** Make a chart like the one below to record major challenges faced by each of these minority groups during the war.

Japanese Americans	
African Americans	
Native Americans	
Latinos	

5. **Persuasive Writing** Decide how you feel about the detention of Japanese Americans during the war. Then write a persuasive paragraph to convince a reader to agree with your point of view about this issue.

6. **Answer the Essential Question**
In what ways did American men, women, and minorities support the war effort at home?

War in Europe and Africa

Essential Question ◀

What strategies did the Allies pursue in Europe and Africa to defeat the Axis Powers in World War II?

Reading Guide

Content Vocabulary

siege (p. 380)   Holocaust (p. 383)
genocide   concentration
(p. 383)   camp (p. 383)

Academic Vocabulary

concentrate (p. 379)   tense (p. 381)

Key People and Events

Dwight D. Eisenhower (p. 379)
George Patton (p. 380)
Operation Overlord (p. 381)
D-Day (p. 381)
V-E Day (p. 382)
Harry S. Truman (p. 382)

Reading Strategy

Taking Notes Fill in a pyramid like the one below with events that led to the Allied victory in North Africa.

Allied Victory

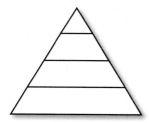

American Diary

Ernie Pyle, a war correspondent, described the life of the World War II American soldier: "In the magazine the war seemed romantic and exciting, full of heroics and vitality. . . . I saw instead: men . . . suffering and wishing they were somewhere else, . . . all of them desperately hungry for somebody to talk to besides themselves, . . . cold and fairly dirty, just toiling from day to day in a world full of insecurity, discomfort, homesickness, and a dulled sense of danger."

—from Here Is Your War

Soldiers in a foxhole during the Allied invasion of Normandy, France, July 1944

North African Campaign

Main Idea Allied armies fought a successful campaign against Axis forces in North Africa.

History and You What challenges do soldiers face when they go to battle in unfamiliar territory? Read to find out about American and other Allied forces involved in desert warfare during World War II.

• •

On January 1, 1942—three weeks after Pearl Harbor—the United States joined Britain, the Soviet Union, and 23 other Allied nations in vowing to defeat the Axis Powers. Although the Japanese were conquering vast areas in the Pacific, the Allied leaders decided to **concentrate,** or focus, first on defeating Hitler before dealing with Japan. The situation in Europe was desperate. German forces occupied almost all of Europe and much of North Africa. If the Germans defeated the Soviets, Germany might prove unstoppable.

Setting a Strategy

Stalin wanted the western Allies to launch a major attack on continental Europe across the English Channel. Churchill, however, argued that the United States and Britain were not yet ready to fight strong German forces in Europe. Instead he wanted to attack the edges of Germany's empire.

Roosevelt agreed, and the Allies made plans to invade North Africa. The invasion would give untested American troops combat experience. Also, once the Americans were in North Africa, they would be able to help British forces in Egypt.

The Struggle for North Africa

The Axis forces in North Africa were led by German general Erwin Rommel, known as the "Desert Fox" because of his success in desert warfare. In November 1942, the British defeated Rommel at the battle of El Alamein. The victory prevented the Germans from capturing the Suez Canal, linking the Mediterranean and Red Seas. Rommel's forces, however, remained a serious threat.

Later that year, British and American forces under American general **Dwight D. Eisenhower** landed in Morocco and Algeria. Moving swiftly eastward, they joined British forces advancing west from Egypt to close in on Rommel. The Allies drove the Germans out of North Africa in May 1943.

Primary Source / Reporting the War

The *Stars and Stripes* For printed news, American soldiers fighting overseas relied on an eight-page newspaper called *Stars and Stripes.* Produced daily, editions of the paper were put together close to the front so that the latest news could reach as many troops as possible. Experienced journalists in uniform and young soldiers hoping to be journalists made up the staffs of *Stars and Stripes.* Among the paper's contributors were correspondent Ernie Pyle, writer Ernest Hemingway, and cartoonist Bill Mauldin. Today, a much-expanded *Stars and Stripes* still serves as the "hometown" newspaper of the U.S. military.

Critical Thinking

Making Inferences What effect might *Stars and Stripes* have had on the morale of soldiers during World War II?

The Invasion of Italy

Allied troops then moved into southern Europe. They took the island of Sicily in the summer of 1943 and landed on Italy's mainland in September. Eisenhower directed the invasion. Another American general, **George Patton,** and British general Bernard Montgomery actually led the troops.

As the Allies advanced, the Italians overthrew dictator Benito Mussolini and surrendered. German forces in Italy fought on but failed to stop the Allied move into central Italy. In June 1944, the Allies finally took Rome, Italy's capital.

Meanwhile, the Allies launched an air war on Germany. Day and night, bombs battered German factories and cities and killed thousands. Yet the attacks failed to crack Germany's determination to win the war.

✓ Reading Check **Explaining** Why did the Allies invade North Africa first instead of Europe?

The Tide Turns in Europe

Main Idea From 1944 to 1945, the Allies fought a two-front war in Europe to defeat the Nazis.

History and You What is one memory you have that you will never forget? For many Americans who lived through World War II, June 6, 1944, stands out in their memory. Read to find out why.

. . . .

During the time of the North African campaign, the Soviets and the Germans were locked in ferocious combat on Soviet territory. For months the Soviet Union bore the main brunt of Germany's European war effort.

The Eastern Front

After invading the Soviet Union in June 1941, German troops advanced into the country's interior. They began a **siege,** or military blockade, of the city of Leningrad that lasted nearly 900 days. As food ran out, thousands

World War II in Europe and Africa NATIONAL GEOGRAPHIC

People of Palermo, Italy, welcome U.S. troops, 1943 ▼

Major Axis powers
Greatest extent of Axis control
Allied or Ally-controlled
Neutral nations

0   400 kilometers
0   400 miles
Lambert Azimuthal Equal-Area projection

of people died. Still the Germans could not take the city, and in early 1944 the siege was broken.

German forces also attacked other Soviet cities. In 1941 the Germans tried to take Moscow, the Soviet capital. Heavy losses and wintry weather slowed them, but the Germans reached Moscow by December. When all seemed lost, the Soviets counterattacked and forced a German retreat.

In the spring of 1942, the Germans tried to take Stalingrad, a major industrial city. No sooner had the Germans won Stalingrad than Soviet forces surrounded the city, cutting off the German supply lines. Cold and starving, the Germans at Stalingrad finally surrendered in February 1943.

After Stalingrad, the Soviets drove the Germands back hundreds of miles. The Germans struck back the following summer, but their defeat at Stalingrad marked a major turning point in the war.

Invasion of France

As the Soviets pushed toward Germany from the east, Allied forces under General Eisenhower were getting ready for **Operation Overlord,** the invasion of occupied Europe. Eisenhower later wrote of the **tense,** or anxious, days of preparation: "All southern England was one vast military camp, crowded with soldiers awaiting final word to go."

On June 6, 1944, or **D-Day**—the day of the invasion—ships carried troops and equipment across the English Channel to the French province of Normandy. At the same time, paratroopers were dropped inland, east and west of the coastal beaches.

As dawn broke, the warships in the Allied fleet let loose with a tremendous barrage of fire. Thousands of shells rained down on the beaches, code-named "Utah," "Omaha," "Gold," "Sword," and "Juno." After wading ashore the troops faced land mines and fierce fire from the Germans.

Audie Murphy (1924–1971)
He wanted to join the Marines, but at 5 feet 5 inches tall, he was too short. The Navy also turned him down. Reluctantly, Audie Murphy, the orphaned son of Texas sharecroppers, enlisted in the Army. By the end of the war, Murphy was the most decorated combat soldier of World War II. When victory was declared in Europe in May 1945, Murphy had still not reached his 21st birthday. Today, through the Audie Murphy Club, the Army honors noncommissioned officers who best represent Audie Murphy's motto:

"You lead from the front."

Ruby Bradley (1907–2002)
About 440 American women serving in the military were killed during World War II. Eighty-eight were taken as prisoners of war. Colonel Ruby Bradley (left) is the nation's most decorated military woman. During World War II, she was a prisoner of war for 37 months. The experience of living in a Japanese prison camp taught her a lesson she could not have learned any other way:

"The many privileges, normally enjoyed every day, become very cherished when they no longer exist: Freedom to speak without censorship, freedom to communicate in writing without censorship . . ."

Critical Thinking

Comparing Compare the lives of American men and women on the battlefront.

Maps in Motion See StudentWorks™ Plus or glencoe.com.

Many Allied troops were hit as they stormed across the beaches to establish a foothold on high ground. By the end of the day, nearly 35,000 American troops had landed at Omaha, and another 23,000 had landed at Utah. More than 75,000 British and Canadian troops were on shore as well. The invasion succeeded.

Within a few weeks, the Allies landed a million troops in France. From Normandy the Allies pushed across France. On August 25, French and American soldiers marched through joyful crowds and liberated Paris.

Victory in Europe

Germany fought for survival as Soviet forces pushed from the east and American and British forces from the west. The advance across France was so rapid that many believed the war would soon end. In December of that year, however, the Germans counterattacked along a 50-mile front in Belgium. As their troops advanced, they pushed back the Allied lines, creating a bulge. The attack later became known as the Battle of the Bulge. After weeks of fighting, the Americans won the battle and headed into Germany.

By late 1944, the Soviets had driven the Germans from Russia to Poland. By February 1945, Soviet troops were just outside Berlin. Realizing the situation was hopeless, Hitler committed suicide in Berlin on April 30. Germany signed an unconditional surrender on May 7, ending the war in Europe. The Allies declared May 8 **V-E Day** for "Victory in Europe."

President Roosevelt did not share in the celebration. On vacation in Warm Springs, Georgia, Roosevelt died suddenly on April 12, 1945. Americans were greatly saddened by the death of the man who had led them for 12 difficult years. Vice President **Harry S. Truman** became president.

✔ **Reading Check** **Explaining** Why was the Battle of the Bulge an important Allied victory?

D-Day, June 6, 1944 ▪ NATIONAL GEOGRAPHIC

The Allies Invade Europe The D-Day invasion marked a turning point in the war in Europe. Paris soon fell to the Allies, and, early in 1945, the final Allied assault in Europe began. D-Day was the beginning of the end of the war.

- Allied territory
- Axis territory
- British troops
- Canadian troops
- U.S. troops
- Airborne and glider landing zone
- Major German fortification

General Dwight Eisenhower talks to paratroopers before the invasion of Normandy. ▶

UNITED KINGDOM

Southampton • Portsmouth • Shoreham-by-Sea • Dover 2°E • Calais • Boulogne

Strait of Dover

Portland •

Dartmouth 4°W

Channel

English Channel

Juno Gold Sword

Utah Omaha

50°N

0°

Cherbourg

Dieppe

Le Havre

Rouen

Seine River

Scale varies in this perspective view.

N W E S

Saint-Lô • Caen

2°W

Normandy

FRANCE

The Holocaust

Main Idea The Nazis increased their persecution of the Jews and set up death camps in an effort to kill all of Europe's Jewish population.

History and You Today many people use the word *Nazi* to mean "someone very evil." The main reason is the Holocaust. Read on to learn about this dark chapter in human history.

A s the Allies freed German-held areas, they discovered numerous instances of Nazi cruelty. During World War II, the Nazis developed what they called "the final solution." Their "solution" was **genocide**—wiping out an entire group of people. About 6 million Jews were killed in what is known as the **Holocaust.** Millions of others—Slavs, Roma (Gypsies), communists, homosexuals, and people with handicaps—were also killed, though Jews were the only group singled out for total extermination.

Persecution of Germany's Jews

Ever since Hitler gained power in 1933, the Nazis had persecuted the Jews of Germany. They first quickly deprived Jews of many rights that all Germans had long taken for granted. In September 1935, the Nuremberg laws removed citizenship from Jewish Germans and banned marriage between Jews and other Germans. Other laws kept Jews from voting, holding public office, and employing non-Jewish Germans. Later, Jews were banned from owning businesses and practicing law and medicine. With no source of income, life became difficult for Jews in Germany.

By the end of the decade, Nazi actions against the Jews became more violent. On the night of November 9, 1938, the Nazis burned Jewish places of worship, destroyed Jewish shops, and killed many Jews. About 30,000 Jewish men were sent to **concentration camps,** large prison camps used to hold people for political reasons.

Numbers	
Allied Forces	**Casualties**
· 15,000 troops (11 divisions)	By the end of the day, 2,500 Allied soldiers were killed.
· 1,500 tanks	
· 5,300 ships and landing craft	
· 12,000 airplanes	D-Day planners had forecast 10,000 dead.
· 20,000 airborne troops	

"I could not swim when we jumped off the [landing craft]. I was tied to my platoon sergeant with a nylon rope. . . . I was too scared to even know my name."
—Dale L. Shrop, 1st Engineer Combat Battalion

Critical Thinking

Speculating What might have happened if the German forces had pushed the Allied forces back when they tried to establish a beachhead at Normandy? How might such an outcome have affected the war?

The Final Solution Before and during World War II, many Jewish young people in Europe suffered terrible persecution and eventual death at the hands of the Nazis.

Auschwitz, 1940 At death camps like Auschwitz (right), Jews were the Nazis' main victims. Alexander Ehrmann, a 17-year-old from Czechoslovakia, experienced a nightmarish scene when he reached one of the death camps:

"The doors flung open and we saw strange uniformed men. . . . Sentries and dogs were there, and they yelled at us . . . as they beat us out of the wagon."

—from *Children With A Star*

Hungary, 1944 Thirteen-year-old Èva Heyman described her fears as the Nazis forced her family to leave their home in Hungary:

"We are allowed to take along . . . the clothes on our bodies, and the shoes on our feet. . . . All the while I thought I was just having a bad dream. . . . I have never been so afraid."

—from *We Are Witnesses*

Critical Thinking

Analyzing What was life like for Jewish young people during the years of the Holocaust?

This event became known as *Kristallnacht,* or the "night of the shattered glass," because of the Jewish shop windows that were broken by Nazi mobs.

The Persecution Spreads

During World War II, the Nazis mistreated the Jews in the lands they conquered. They forced Jews to wear a yellow, six-pointed star on their clothing. The mass killing of Jews began when the German army invaded the Soviet Union in 1941. Special Nazi forces carried out these murders. They rounded up thousands of Jews, shooting them and throwing them into mass graves. Josef Perl, who survived a massacre of Czech Jews, wrote of the act:

PRIMARY SOURCE

"We marched into a forest where a huge long ditch was already dug. . . . I could hear . . . a machine gun going . . . . All of a sudden, . . . I saw my mother and four sisters lined up and before I had a chance to say,

'Mother!' they were already dead. Somehow time stands still. . . . But what woke me was the sight of my five nieces and nephews being marched, and the murderers had the audacity to ask them to hold hands. . . . I would have been almost the next one but all of a sudden the bombers came over, we were ordered to lay face downwards, but everyone started running . . . and I . . . ran deep into the forest.

—from *Remembering: Voices of the Holocaust*

Nazi troops crammed thousands more into railroad cars like cattle, depositing them in concentration camps, such as Buchenwald in Germany. Guards took the prisoners' belongings, shaved their heads, and tattooed camp numbers on their arms. Prisoners often had only a crust of bread or watery soup to eat. Thousands became sick and died.

The Final Solution

In January 1942, the Nazis agreed on what they called the "final solution" to destroy the Jews. They built death camps, such as those at Auschwitz and Treblinka in Poland.

At these camps, many people died in poison gas chambers. Others died of starvation. Still others were victims of cruel experiments carried out by Nazi doctors. Of the estimated 1.6 million people who died at Auschwitz, about 1.3 million were Jews.

Upon arrival at a death camp, healthy prisoners were chosen for slave labor. The elderly, disabled, sick, and mothers and children were sent to the gas chambers, after which their bodies were burned in giant furnaces.

Although information about the unfolding Holocaust had reached western leaders well before 1945, Allied forces moving through Germany and Poland after V-E Day saw the unspeakable horrors of the camps firsthand. British soldier Peter Coombs described the condition of the survivors in a camp:

PRIMARY SOURCE

"One has to take a tour round and see their faces, their slow staggering gait and feeble movements. The state of their minds is plainly written on their faces, as starvation had reduced their bodies to skeletons."

—from *The Holocaust*

People around the world were stunned by this terrible result of Nazi tyranny. Allied governments, however, had evidence of the death camps as early as 1942. Historians today debate why and how an event as horrifying as the Holocaust could have occurred. They also discuss why so relatively little was done to stop it.

In Remembrance

The United States Holocaust Memorial Museum is located near the National Mall in Washington, D.C. This memorial provides a national mark of respect for all victims of Nazi persecution.

In 2004 the National World War II Memorial opened on a site on the National Mall. The Memorial is dedicated to the 16 million who served in the military during World War II, the more than 400,000 who died, and the men and women who supported the war effort on the home front.

Reading Check **Identifying** What groups did the Nazi government victimize?

History ONLINE
Study Central™ To review this section, go to glencoe.com.

Section 4 Review

Vocabulary

1. Write a sentence for each of the following terms that explains its meaning: concentrate, siege, tense, genocide, Holocaust, concentration camp.

Main Ideas

2. **Explaining** When the United States joined the Allies, why did the Allies concentrate first on defeating Hitler?

3. **Identifying** What was the significance of Operation Overlord?

4. **Describing** What was the Nazis' "final solution"?

Critical Thinking

5. **Determining Cause and Effect** Create a cause-and-effect chart like the one below to describe the two fronts fought in Europe to defeat the Nazis.

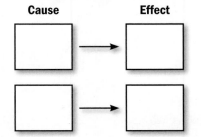

Cause → Effect

6. **Persuasive Writing** Take the role of an American relative of a Polish Jew. Write a letter to the editor of your local newspaper explaining what you know about the Nazi persecution of the Jews and urging the United States to take action.

7. **Answer the Essential Question**
What strategies did the Allies pursue in Europe and Africa to defeat the Axis Powers in World War II?

War in the Pacific

What was the turning point in the war in the Pacific, and what led up to it?

Reading Guide

Content Vocabulary

island hopping   kamikaze
    (p. 388)   (p. 388)

Academic Vocabulary

secure (p. 388)   conflict (p. 390)

Key People and Events

Douglas MacArthur (p. 387)

Bataan Death March (p. 387)

Battle of Midway (p. 388)

Guadalcanal (p. 388)

Battle of Leyte Gulf (p. 388)

V-J Day (p. 390)

Reading Strategy

Taking Notes On a time line like the one below, track the important events on the Pacific front in 1945.

Mar.	July	Aug.	Sept.
1945	1945	1945	1945

American Diary

Marine Private Newman Baird was a machine gunner on a tracked landing vehicle. As the Marines hit the beaches on the island of Tarawa, he recalls: "'They [the Japanese] were knocking out [boats] left and right. A tractor'd get hit, stop, and burst into flames, with men jumping out like torches.' Baird's own vehicle was then hit by a shell, . . . killing many of the troops. . . . 'I didn't want to put my head up. The bullets were pouring at us like a sheet of rain.'"

—*from* Across the Reef

American Marines in battle on the Pacific island of Tarawa, November 21, 1943

The Pacific Front

Main Idea The Allies fought the Japanese for four long years in the Pacific.

History and You Have you ever had to follow a step-by-step plan to finish a project? Read to learn how step-by-step, the Allies pushed back Japan on the Pacific front.

• •

On December 7, 1941, the same day Japan attacked Pearl Harbor, Japanese bombers struck American airfields in the Philippines and on the islands of Wake and Guam—key American bases in the Pacific. In the following days, the Japanese intensified their campaign in the Pacific. They invaded Thailand and Malaya and captured Guam, Wake Island, and Hong Kong.

Japanese troops landed in the Philippines in mid-December and had quickly took the capital of Manila. The defending forces—Filipino and American troops commanded by American general **Douglas MacArthur**— were forced to retreat to the rugged Bataan Peninsula west of Manila and the small island fortress of Corregidor.

The Philippines Fall

After months of fierce fighting, the exhausted Allied troops defending Bataan surrendered on April 9, 1942. The forces on Corregidor held out for another month. The Japanese forced their Bataan prisoners—many sick and near starvation—to march to a prison camp more than 60 miles away. About 76,000 prisoners started out, but only about 54,000 of those on the **Bataan Death March** reached the camp. As survivor Marion Lawton recalled:

PRIMARY SOURCE

"We'd march all day, a continuous plodding along, just trying to keep up. I always tried to stay in the middle of the column rather than on the flanks. That way I was further away . . . and might avoid a . . . beating. I don't know how to explain a typical day except that it was brutal, exhausting, hot, and your feet and legs just ached."

—from *Death March: The Survivors of Bataan*

Two months before the surrender, General MacArthur left for Australia to command Allied forces in the Pacific. MacArthur told the Filipinos, "I shall return."

Island Hopping

With Japan's victories, American morale was low. Then in April 1942, 16 American bombers, launched from an aircraft carrier in the Pacific, bombed Tokyo. This daring raid led by James Doolittle had little military importance, but it lifted Americans' spirits.

Primary Source — Amphibious Warfare

The LVT "Amphtrac" In the invasion of Tarawa, only one vehicle—the LVT, or amphibious tractor "amphtrac"—was able to cross hazardous coral reefs and deliver troops onto the beaches. The "amphtrac" is like a boat with tank tracks. A true amphibian is capable of movement afloat and ashore.

A Armor-plated pontoon (float)
B Tracks
C Machine guns

Critical Thinking

Making Connections How did physical geography affect U.S. military strategy on the Pacific front during the war?

In May 1942 American warships defeated a Japanese fleet in the Battle of the Coral Sea. An even greater victory followed in June 1942. In the **Battle of Midway,** northwest of Hawaii, the navy destroyed four Japanese aircraft carriers and hundreds of airplanes.

The United States was now ready to go on the offensive against Japan. The commanders—General MacArthur and Admiral Chester Nimitz—adopted a strategy known as island hopping. This called for attacking and capturing certain key islands. The United States then used these islands as bases for leapfrogging to others, moving ever closer to the Philippines—and to Japan.

Between August 1942 and February 1943, American forces engaged in a campaign for control of **Guadalcanal,** one of the Solomon Islands. The Japanese put up stiff resistance, but the Americans finally secured the island.

In June 1944, American forces captured Guam and other islands nearby. Guam provided a base for launching bombing strikes on Japan. In October, American ships destroyed most of the Japanese fleet at the **Battle of Leyte Gulf** in the Philippines.

The Advance on Japan

American forces then closed in on Japan. In March 1945, they seized the island of Iwo Jima and in June the island of Okinawa. The Japanese fought fiercely to defend these islands so near Japan. Thousands of Americans died in the battles, and many thousands more were wounded.

With most of the Japanese air force and navy destroyed, American bombers pounded Tokyo and other major cities of Japan. In desperation, the Japanese unleashed suicide pilots known as **kamikazes.** They crashed planes loaded with explosives into American ships. Kamikaze pilots sank several destroyers during the battle for Okinawa.

Reading Check **Explaining** What is significant about the Battle of Midway?

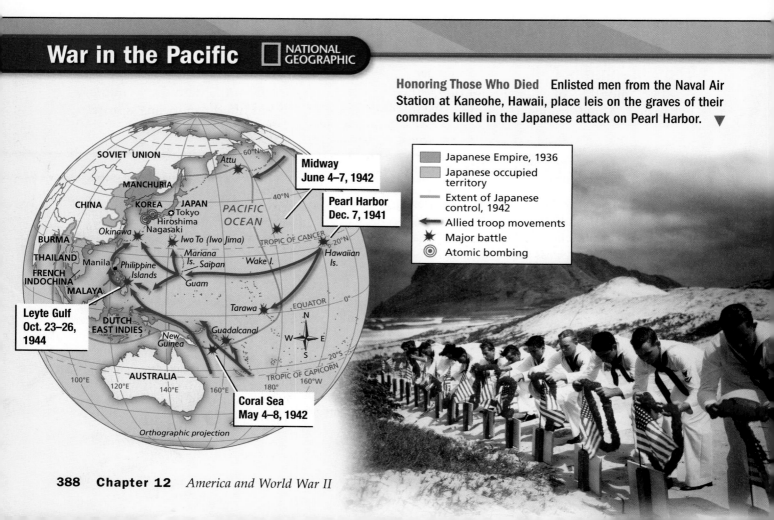

War in the Pacific   NATIONAL GEOGRAPHIC

Honoring Those Who Died Enlisted men from the Naval Air Station at Kaneohe, Hawaii, place leis on the graves of their comrades killed in the Japanese attack on Pearl Harbor. ▼

Midway
June 4–7, 1942

Pearl Harbor
Dec. 7, 1941

Leyte Gulf
Oct. 23–26,
1944

Coral Sea
May 4–8, 1942

SOVIET UNION
Attu
MANCHURIA
CHINA   KOREA   JAPAN   PACIFIC
Tokyo   OCEAN
Hiroshima
Okinawa   Nagasaki
BURMA
Iwo To (Iwo Jima)   TROPIC OF CANCER
Mariana
THAILAND   Manila   Is.   Saipan   Wake I.   Hawaiian
Philippine   Is.
FRENCH   Islands
INDOCHINA
MALAYA   Guam
EQUATOR
Tarawa
DUTCH
EAST INDIES   Guadalcanal
New
Guinea
AUSTRALIA
TROPIC OF CAPRICORN
Orthographic projection

Japanese Empire, 1936
Japanese occupied territory
Extent of Japanese control, 1942
Allied troop movements
Major battle
Atomic bombing

The End of the War

Main Idea American use of the atomic bomb brought about Japan's surrender in the Pacific conflict.

History and You What challenges in your life have forced you to make changes? Read to find out how Japanese leaders were forced to make changes as a result of a powerful new weapon.

. . . .

Although the Japanese faced certain defeat, they continued to fight. Their refusal to surrender led the United States to use a powerful new weapon: the atomic bomb.

In 1939 the German-born physicist Albert Einstein wrote to President Roosevelt warning him that the Nazis might try to use the energy of the atom to build "extremely powerful bombs." Roosevelt then organized a committee of scientists to study the issue. In 1941, the committee members met with British scientists who already were working on a similar bomb. The Americans were impressed with the British research. They then urged Roosevelt to start a program so that the U.S. could develop its own atomic bomb.

President Roosevelt created a top-secret operation, the Manhattan Project. In 1942 scientists at the University of Chicago built the world's first nuclear reactor, a device that splits apart atoms and releases energy. Later, another team of scientists and engineers built an atomic bomb at a secret laboratory in Los Alamos, New Mexico. On July 16, 1945, the first atomic bomb went off in a test near Alamogordo in the New Mexico desert.

Dropping the Atomic Bomb

Even before the bomb was tested, American officials began to debate how to use it. The final decision rested with President Harry Truman. Truman had taken office after President Roosevelt's death on April 12, 1945. Truman did not know the bomb existed until a few weeks before he had to make the decision to use it.

Pearl Harbor Hero

Doris "Dorie" Miller (1919–1943), Mess attendant, USS *West Virginia*

Doris Miller was one of the first heroes of the war in the Pacific. He was awarded the Navy Cross for his actions during the attack on Pearl Harbor. Less than two years later, Miller was killed when the USS *Liscome Bay* was torpedoed and sunk in the Pacific Ocean. A navy ship, the USS *Miller*, was named in his honor in 1973.

◀ **Raising the Flag at Iwo Jima** Five Marines and one sailor raise the flag on Mount Suribachi on Iwo Jima. For many Americans, the image remains a symbol of courage and patriotism.

Iwo Jima

Ira Hayes (1923–1955), Corporal, 2nd Battalion, 28th Marines

Born and raised on a Pima Indian Reservation in Arizona, Ira Hayes enlisted in the Marine Corps at the age of 19. He was one of the six who raised the flag at Iwo Jima, but Hayes did not feel like a hero:

How could I feel like a hero when only five men in my platoon of 45 survived?

Map Skills

Place What strategic importance does the map show for Iwo Jima and Okinawa?

Maps In MOtion See StudentWorks™ Plus or glencoe.com.

President Truman later wrote that he "regarded the bomb as a military weapon and never had any doubts that it should be used." His advisers warned him to expect large numbers of casualties if American soldiers invaded Japan. Truman believed it was his duty as president to use every weapon available to save American lives.

The Allies then issued the Potsdam Declaration, warning that if Japan did not surrender, it faced "prompt and utter destruction." The Japanese did not surrender, and Truman ordered the use of the bomb.

Japan's Surrender

On August 6, 1945, an American B-29 bomber, the *Enola Gay,* dropped an atomic bomb on the Japanese city of Hiroshima. Three days later, a second bomb was dropped on the city of Nagasaki. The atomic bombs caused immense destruction. The first bomb leveled Hiroshima and killed between 80,000 and 120,000 people; the Nagasaki bomb killed between 35,000 and 74,000. Thousands more were injured, and many died later from burns and radiation sickness.

Faced with such destruction, the Japanese emperor said that "the unendurable must be endured" and ordered his government to surrender. August 15, 1945, was proclaimed **V-J Day** for "Victory over Japan." All around America, people expressed happiness and relief. Japan signed the formal surrender on September 2 aboard the battleship USS *Missouri.* World War II had finally ended.

In the years immediately after the war, Allied authorities put the top Nazi and Japanese leaders on trial. They were accused of war crimes and crimes against humanity. The Allies held the trials in Nuremberg, Germany, and in Tokyo.

The Cost of the War

World War II was the most destructive **conflict** in history. More than 55 million people died during the war; more than half of these were civilians killed by bombing, starvation, disease, torture, and murder. American casualties—about 322,000 dead and 800,000 injured—were high, but light compared with those of other nations. The Soviet Union suffered more than 22 million deaths. Those who survived faced the huge task of trying to rebuild their lives and their countries.

Reading Check **Describing** What was the goal of the Manhattan Project?

Section 5 Review

Vocabulary

1. Write a sentence for each key term that demonstrates its meaning: island hopping, secure, kamikaze, conflict.

Main Ideas

2. **Explaining** What was the strategy of island hopping, and what was its purpose?

3. **Describing** What was the Manhattan Project?

Critical Thinking

4. **Comparing** Create a chart like the one below in which you note the reasons for and against using the atomic bomb in World War II.

For	Against

5. **Analyzing** Why were the battles on the islands of Iwo Jima and Okinawa important to the Americans?

6. **Evaluating** What was significant about the cost of World War II?

7. **Answer the Essential Question**
What was the turning point in the war in the Pacific, and what led up to it?

1939

Sept. 1	Germany invades Poland.
Sept. 3	Britain and France declare war on Germany.

▼ Japanese American soldiers fighting in Italy

1940

June	German troops enter Paris.

July	German air force launches Battle of Britain.
Sept.	Germany, Japan, and Italy sign a pact.

1941

March	U.S. passes the Lend-Lease Act.
June	Hitler attacks the Soviet Union.
Dec. 7	Japan bombs Pearl Harbor.
Dec. 11	U.S. and Britain declare war on Japan. Germany and Italy declare war on the U.S.

1942

April	Japan captures Bataan, leading to Death March.
May	United States defeats Japan in the Battle of Coral Sea.
June	U.S. defeats Japan at Midway.

The more WOMEN at work the sooner we WIN!

WOMEN ARE NEEDED ALSO AS:

SEE YOUR LOCAL U.S. EMPLOYMENT SERVICE

1943

Feb.	Germans are defeated at Stalingrad.
July	Allies invade Sicily; Mussolini resigns.
Aug.	Women Air Force Service Pilots is formed.
Sept.	Allies invade mainland Italy; Italy surrenders.

1944

June 6	D-Day: Allies launch an invasion of Europe.
Aug.	Paris is liberated from German control.

1945

Jan.	U.S. forces invade Luzon, Philippines.
Feb.	U.S. flag is raised over Iwo Jima.
April	Franklin Roosevelt dies; Harry Truman becomes president.
May 8	Germany surrenders, victory in Europe.

June	U.S. troops capture Okinawa, liberate Philippines.
Aug.	Atomic bombs are dropped on Hiroshima and Nagasaki.
Sept. 2	Japan signs unconditional surrender, ending World War II.

◄ Raising the flag on Iwo Jima

Tuskegee Airmen ▶

STUDY TO GO Study anywhere, anytime! Download quizzes and flash cards to your PDA from glencoe.com.

STANDARDIZED TEST PRACTICE

TEST-TAKING TIP

When answering multiple-choice questions, your first answer is usually correct. Do not change the answer unless you are absolutely certain your first answer is wrong.

Reviewing Main Ideas

Directions: Choose the best answer for each of the following questions.

1. One of the factors that contributed to the rise of European dictators was

  A American neutrality.

  B the Nazi-Soviet pact.

  C a policy of appeasement.

  D joblessness and resentment.

2. The United States entered World War II because

  A the Japanese seized Manchuria.

  B German soldiers invaded Poland.

  C Japanese planes bombed Pearl Harbor.

  D German subs fired on American destroyers.

3. How did the American economy change when the U.S. entered World War II?

  A Many women lost their jobs.

  B Factories shifted to producing tanks.

  C African American workers faced discrimination.

  D The military began drafting workers.

4. Who fought the Axis Powers on the Eastern Front?

  A Soviets   **C** Japanese

  B Italians   **D** Americans

5. The war with Japan ended when the U.S.

  A unleashed suicide pilots.

  B imposed an economic blockade.

  C offered concessions for surrender.

  D dropped atomic bombs on Japanese cities.

Short-Answer Question

Directions: Base your answer to question 6 on the excerpt below and on your knowledge of social studies.

> We Americans will contribute unified production and unified acceptance of sacrifice and of effort. That means a national unity that can know no limitations of race or creed or selfish politics. The American people expect that much from themselves.
>
> —quoted from Roosevelt's fireside chat on February 23, 1942

6. Did the American people live up to Roosevelt's ideals? Give examples to support your answer.

Review the Essential Questions

7. Essay How did the Allies defeat Axis ideas and armies in World War II?

To help you write your essay, review your answers to the Essential Questions in the section reviews and the chapter Foldables Study Organizer. Your essay should include:

* the ideas and acts of aggression by Axis Powers;
* the responses of the Allied Powers to these ideas and acts;
* reasons the Allies were able to cast doubt on fascist ideas and defeat the Axis armies; and
* the costs of the war.

GO ON

History ONLINE

For additional test practice, use **Self-Check Quizzes**—Chapter 12 at glencoe.com.

Document-Based Questions

Directions: Analyze the documents and answer the short-answer questions that follow.

Document 1

Gunnar Myrdal wrote the following excerpt in *American Dilemma: The Negro Problem and Modern Democracy* published in 1944.

> Fascism and nazism . . . came to power by means of racial persecution and oppression.

Source: Ronald Takaki, *A Different Mirror*

8. Give two examples from the chapter that support Myrdal's claim.

Document 2

Jan Karski, a leader in the Polish resistance, gave this report to Roosevelt in 1943.

> Our underground authorities are absolutely sure that the Germans are out to exterminate the entire Jewish population of Europe.

Source: Doris Kearns Goodwin, *No Ordinary Time*

9. What events were occurring in European cities that support this statement?

Document 3

For a full week, Allied planes bombed the German city of Hamburg in 1943. Journalist Gwynne Dyer described what the bombing was like.

> Practically all the apartment blocks in the firestorm area had underground shelters, but nobody who stayed in them survived; those who were not cremated died of carbon monoxide poisoning. But to venture into the streets was to risk being swept by the wind into the very heart of the firestorm.

Gwynne Dyer, *War: The Lethal Custom*

10. How much longer did it take for Allied forces to defeat Hitler's army? Describe the effectiveness of the Allied bombing raids using this quote, as well as other facts, to support your opinion.

Document 4

Pearl Harbor was a naval base in Hawaii. The Japanese attacked it early in the morning on December 7, 1941.

Pearl Harbor, December 7, 1941

11. Using the information shown on the map, explain how the attack on Pearl Harbor impacted the U.S. Navy and American military readiness.

12. Creative Writing Using the information from the four documents and your knowledge of social studies, write an essay in which you:

- create a fictional character—soldier, pilot, diplomat, or leader—who participated in one or more events described in the documents; and

- include details about the person's hardships and reactions.

Need Extra Help?												
If You Missed Questions...	1	2	3	4	5	6	7	8	9	10	11	12
Go to Page...	363	371	373–377	369–381	389–390	375–377	365–370	363–364	383–385	380	371	369–390

Unit 5

Challenges at Home and Abroad
1945–1975

Peace movement button, 1970

"*I had been pushed as far as I could stand to be pushed.*"
—Rosa Parks

Leaders of March on Washington for Jobs and Freedom, August 28, 1963

Reading History

Identifying Problems and Solutions

Learn It!

Textbooks often describe problems that people face and how they try to solve them. Read the passage below. Ask yourself these questions: What is the problem? How did the president try to solve this problem?

Problem
the nation's economic problems

Solutions
raise the minimum wage, expand Social Security benefits, increase federal spending to create jobs, build new public housing, and create a system of national health insurance

—from Chapter 13, p. 410

In September 1945, President Truman presented a plan of **domestic**—or home-based—reforms aimed at solving some of the nation's economic problems. Truman later called this program the **Fair Deal.**

Truman proposed to raise the minimum wage, expand Social Security benefits, increase federal spending to create jobs, build new public housing, and create a system of national health insurance.

Practice It!

Read the paragraphs and write down the problem and solution(s) on another sheet of paper.

—from Chapter 14, p. 456

People with physical disabilities also sought equal treatment in the 1960s and the 1970s. Congress responded by passing a number of laws.

One law concerned the removal of barriers that prevented some people from gaining access to public facilities. Another required employers to offer more opportunities for disabled people in the workplace.

Problem

Solution

Academic Vocabulary Preview

Listed below are the academic vocabulary words and their definitions that you will come across as you study Unit 5. Practice It! will help you study the words and definitions.

Academic Vocabulary	Definition	Practice It!
Chapter 13 The Cold War Era		
cooperate (koh · AH · puh · RAYT) *p. 402*	to work together	**Identify** *the term from Chapter 13 that best completes the sentence.*
pose (POHZ) *p. 403*	to present; assert	1. Joseph Stalin believed a reunited Germany would _____ a threat to the Soviet Union.
stable (STAY · buhl) *p. 409*	unchanging	
domestic (duh · MEHS · tihk) *p. 410*	home-based; internal	2. During the war, government controls kept prices _____ .
assure (uh · SHUR) *p. 416*	to promise	3. The Federal Highway Act is an example of a successful _____ program.
conclude (kuhn · KLOOD) *p. 417*	to decide	
nuclear (NOO · klee · uhr) *p. 420*	atomic	
economy (ih · KAH · nuh · MEE) *p. 421*	a system of production, distribution, and consumption	
Chapter 14 The Civil Rights Era		
discriminate (dihs · KRIH · muh · NAYT) *p. 433*	to treat unfairly	**Identify** *the term from Chapter 14 that best matches the underlined term or terms.*
civil (SIH · vuhl) *p. 433*	relating to citizens as individuals	4. Kennedy and Nixon came from <u>different</u> backgrounds.
assign (uh · SYN) *p. 439*	to appoint	
consist (KUHN · SIHST) *p. 441*	to make up	5. A new labor movement <u>rose up</u> in the Southwest.
register (REH · juh · stuhr) *p. 447*	to enroll	6. One <u>goal</u> of the civil rights movement was to include all Americans in the voting process.
emerge (ih · MUHRJ) *p. 448*	to rise up	
aspect (AS · PEHKT) *p. 453*	a category, feature, or part	
diverse (dy · VUHRZ) *p. 454*	differing from one another	
Chapter 15 The Vietnam Era		
respond (rih · SPAHND) *p. 463*	to reply	**Choose** *the word that best matches the meaning of each vocabulary term listed below.*
occur (uh · KUHR) *p. 465*	to take place	
trace (TRAYS) *p. 469*	to follow back to	7. **occur** 9. **exclude**
regime (ray · ZHEEM) *p. 470*	a governing authority	a. start a. shut out
conduct (KAHN · DUHKT) *p. 478*	to direct the course of	b. disturb b. move beside
exclude (ihks · KLOOD) *p. 481*	to shut out	c. happen c. invite in
authority (uh · THAHR · uh · tee) *p. 485*	the power to give orders and make decisions	8. **regime** 10. **demonstration**
demonstration (DEH · muhn · STRAY · shuhn) *p. 486*	a march in protest	a. tool a. a failure
		b. rule b. a protest
		c. plan c. an embrace

Chapter 13

The Cold War Era 1945–1960

Beginning in the 1950s, television was the primary source of entertainment.

Whatever the weather
We only reach welfare
together

HARRY TRUMAN

★ **1945**
Franklin Roosevelt dies

★ **1948**
Marshall Plan is enacted

PRESIDENTS

U.S. Events

World Events

1944

1948

★ **1945**
Yalta Conference sets plans for postwar world

★ **1948**
• Soviets block-ade West Berlin
• State of Israel is created

★ **1950**
Korean War begins

Section 1: Cold War Origins

Essential Question How and why did America aid European nations after World War II?

Section 2: Postwar Politics

Essential Question What economic, social, and political challenges did Americans face after World War II?

Section 3: The Korean War

Essential Question How and why did America involve itself in the Korean conflict of the 1950s?

Section 4: America in the 1950s

Essential Question How did the American prosperity of the 1950s affect the country's economy and culture?

History ONLINE
Chapter Overview Visit glencoe.com and click on **Chapter 13—Chapter Overviews** to preview chapter information.

FOLDABLES Study Organizer

Organizing Information
Make this Foldable to help you learn about the superpowers.

Step 1 Fold a sheet of paper as shown.

Step 2 Turn the paper and fold it into thirds.

Step 3 Unfold and cut along the two inside fold lines.

Step 4 Label your Foldable as shown.

USA as a Superpower | Both | Soviet Union as a Superpower

Reading and Writing As you read the chapter, describe under the appropriate tabs how the superpowers were similar and how they were different.

Students are vaccinated for polio in 1955. ▶

DWIGHT EISENHOWER

★ 1954 Senator Joe McCarthy is censured

1955
• Polio vaccine becomes available
• Minimum wage increases to $1 an hour

★ 1956 Federal Highway Act passes

1952 ——————— **1956** ——————— **1960**

★ 1954 Roger Bannister breaks the four-minute mile barrier

★ 1957 Soviet Union launches *Sputnik*

Essential Question

How and why did America aid European nations after World War II?

Reading Guide

Content Vocabulary

iron curtain *(p. 402)*   espionage *(p. 406)*

containment *(p. 402)*   blacklist *(p. 406)*

airlift *(p. 404)*   perjury *(p. 407)*

cold war *(p. 404)*   censure *(p. 407)*

subversion *(p. 406)*

Academic Vocabulary

cooperate *(p. 402)*   pose *(p. 403)*

Key People and Events

Harry S. Truman *(p. 401)*

Mao Zedong *(p. 405)*

Reading Strategy

Taking Notes On a chart like the one below, record the major purposes of each of these postwar plans.

Plan	Purpose
Truman Doctrine	
Marshall Plan	

American Diary

The three most powerful men in the world met in Yalta to discuss the fate of the postwar world. President Roosevelt hoped to promote his vision of postwar cooperation. Prime Minister Churchill spoke elegantly and forcefully. Soviet leader Stalin stubbornly opposed much of what was proposed. Stalin stated to his aides: "They want to force us to accept their plans on questions affecting Europe and the world. Well, that's not going to happen!" As the Allies discovered, Stalin had his own plans.

—*quoted in* Memoirs *by Andrei Gromyko*

Churchill, Roosevelt, and Stalin meet at the Yalta Conference.

Wartime Diplomacy

Main Idea During World War II, the United States, the Soviet Union, and Great Britain worked out plans for the organization of the postwar world.

History and You Have you ever attended a meeting at which there was a lot of disagreement? How were the disagreements handled? Read to learn how the Allies tried to deal with their disagreements about the world's future.

In February 1945, the "Big Three" Allied leaders—Franklin D. Roosevelt, Winston Churchill, and Joseph Stalin—met at Yalta, a Soviet port on the Black Sea. They came to discuss issues affecting the postwar world. Out of this meeting came the Yalta agreement, in which the Soviet Union agreed to enter the war against Japan. In return, the Soviets received some territories in Asia.

Agreeing on other arrangements proved more difficult. Roosevelt and Churchill feared the spread of communism and Soviet control in Eastern Europe. Stalin, on the other hand, wanted this area as a shield to protect the Soviet Union from the West. Germany was a special problem. The Allies finally agreed to divide Germany into four zones, with each zone run by an Allied power.

Stalin agreed to free elections in Soviet-occupied Eastern Europe and to help in planning a new international organization. Roosevelt and Churchill felt encouraged about a peaceful postwar world. Their hopes went unfulfilled.

The United Nations

President Roosevelt died suddenly on April 12, 1945. Vice President **Harry S. Truman** succeeded him. Facing the enormous tasks of the presidency, Truman told reporters, "When they told me [of Roosevelt's death], I felt like the moon, the stars, and all the planets had fallen on me."

Truman decided to go ahead with the formation of the new international organization discussed at Yalta. On June 26, in San Francisco, California, 50 nations signed the charter creating the United Nations (UN). They hoped the UN could settle international disputes and prevent future wars.

Reading Check **Describing** How did the Allies agree to divide Germany?

Primary Source | Compromise at Yalta

Agreement Among the Allies At Yalta, the Allies issued the Declaration of Liberated Europe, which contained the following commitments:

◄ German refugee in Nuremberg, 1945

The Declaration of Liberated Europe

✔ The peoples of Europe can create their own democratic institutions but must rid their societies of Nazism and fascism.

✔ The United States, Great Britain, and the Soviet Union will help the peoples of Europe:

1. Establish peace in their countries.
2. Provide aid to people who need it.
3. Form temporary governments that represent the essentials of a democratic society and hold free elections.

Critical Thinking

Speculating Tensions between the United States and the Soviet Union grew after World War II. Why do you think this happened?

Soviet Expansion in Europe

Main Idea Soviet efforts to spread communism in Europe led to tense relations with the United States, which wanted to contain communism.

History and You Have you ever wanted to stop someone from doing something without having a fight? Read to learn how the United States wanted to stop communism without going to war.

· ·

Distrust soon arose between the West and the Soviets. Stalin set up Communist governments and kept Soviet forces in Eastern Europe. Europe eventually split into two armed camps—Communist Eastern Europe and democratic Western Europe.

Winston Churchill believed that the division between East and West was permanent. In 1946 he stated in a speech in Fulton, Missouri, that an **"iron curtain"** had descended on Europe. Churchill meant that the Soviets had cut off Eastern Europe from the West. He warned that the Soviets would eventually try to gain control of other parts of the world.

To halt Soviet expansion, Truman turned to George F. Kennan, an American diplomat. Kennan believed that the United States and the Soviet Union could not **cooperate,** or work together. Therefore, the United States had to be firm. Kennan's policy, called **containment,** stated that the United States had to "contain," or hold back, the Soviets, using military as well as nonmilitary ways.

The Truman Doctrine

The policy of containment soon went into effect. Civil war raged in Greece, as Communists attempted to overthrow the country's pro-Western government. At the same time, the Soviets pressured Turkey to give them naval bases on the straits leading to the Mediterranean Sea.

In March 1947, Truman asked Congress for money to help Greece and Turkey. The Truman Doctrine, as it came to be called,

Europe After World War II

NATIONAL GEOGRAPHIC

Legend:
- Communist countries
- Non-communist countries
- Iron Curtain

0   400 kilometers
0   400 miles
Lambert Azimuthal Equal-Area projection

"An iron curtain has descended across the Continent. Behind that line lie all the capitals of the ancient states of Central and Eastern Europe. . . . All these famous cities and the populations around them lie in what I might call the Soviet sphere, and all are subject, in one form or another, not only to Soviet influence but to a very high and in some cases increasing measure of control from Moscow."
—Winston Churchill, March 5, 1946

Critical Thinking

1. **Analyzing Primary Sources** Why do you think Churchill described Soviet domination as an "iron curtain"?

2. **Interpreting** What does the cartoon say about the attitude of Secretary of State Byrnes toward the Soviet leaders?

provided immediate aid to the Greeks and the Turks. In the long run, the doctrine pledged that the United States would fight the spread of communism worldwide.

The Marshall Plan

In June 1947, George Marshall, the U.S. secretary of state, proposed that the United States give massive economic aid to Western European countries. Their economies were in ruins, and people were starving. After Communists took over the Eastern European country of Czechoslovakia in 1948, Congress approved the plan. From 1948 to 1951, the Marshall Plan pumped $13 billion worth of supplies, machinery, and food into Western Europe. The economic recovery that followed weakened the appeal of communism.

Reading Check **Summarizing** What were the goals of the Truman Doctrine and the Marshall Plan?

▲ U.S. Secretary of State Byrnes calls on Soviet leader Joseph Stalin and government official Vyacheslav Molotov.

Crisis in Berlin

Main Idea The Western Allies successfully resisted Soviet attempts to halt the Allies' plans for uniting West Germany.

History and You Suppose you are trapped on an island without food or water. How might help reach you? Read to learn how the people of West Berlin were helped by the Western Allies when their city was cut off by the Soviets.

● ●

The Allied leaders at Yalta divided Germany into four occupation zones. The Soviet Union controlled the eastern part of the country, while the United States, Britain, and France held zones in the western part. The German capital of Berlin, located deep within Soviet-controlled East Germany, also was divided among the four nations.

President Truman believed that a reunited Germany was essential to the future of Europe. Stalin, on the other hand, feared that a reunited Germany would once again **pose,** or present, a threat to the Soviet Union. He sought to maintain Soviet influence in a divided Germany. Tensions over the German issue led to a serious crisis in 1948.

The Berlin Blockade

On June 7, 1948, the United States, Britain, and France stated their plan to unite their zones to form a new West German republic. Each nation's section of Berlin would be included in this republic as well, even though the city of Berlin lay within Soviet-held East Germany.

The Berlin blockade was Stalin's answer to the West's plans. On June 24, 1948, Soviet troops rushed into position around the edge of West Berlin. Almost overnight they created a blockade, stopping traffic on all highway, rail, and water routes through East Germany to West Berlin. As a result, West Berlin's 2.2 million citizens were cut off from needed supplies. The Soviets hoped this blockade would force the Americans, British, and French to reconsider their plan.

The Berlin Airlift

Believing that the Soviets wanted the West out of the city, President Truman made U.S. intentions clear: "We stay in Berlin, period." The president, however, did not want to risk war by using military force to end the blockade. Instead he organized a large **airlift** to save the city. American and British planes began flying food, fuel, and other supplies into West Berlin.

The airlift continued day and night for more than 10 months, delivering supplies to West Berlin. In May 1949, Stalin finally ended the blockade, realizing that the West was still intent on uniting their zones. Despite the airlift's success, Berlin and Germany remained divided. By the end of 1949, there were two German states—the Federal Republic of Germany (West Germany), allied with the United States, and the German Democratic Republic (East Germany), a Communist state tied to the Soviet Union.

✓ **Reading Check** **Analyzing** How did the West respond to the blockade of Berlin?

Two Armed Camps

Main Idea The United States and the Soviet Union formed rival alliances, and their competition for influence spread to other parts of the world.

History and You Does your school compete with a nearby school in sports or another activity? Read to learn how the United States and the Soviet Union sought support from other nations in their rivalry with each other.

. . . .

The Berlin crisis showed that the United States and the Soviet Union were locked in a **cold war**—a war in which the two enemies did not actually fight each other. Instead each side began building up its military forces and arms to intimidate the other.

The United States and other Western democracies agreed that military cooperation was the best way to contain the Soviets. In 1949 the United States, Canada, and 10 Western European nations formed the North Atlantic Treaty Organization. Member states agreed to aid any member that was attacked.

Primary Source / Berlin Airlift

Allied Assistance In June 1948, the Soviet Union stopped all land and water traffic from entering or exiting Western-controlled Berlin. The Soviets wanted the Allies to pull out of Berlin, leaving the entire city under their control. Instead, the Allies took to the air. For more than 10 months, British and U.S. cargo planes flew medicine, food, clothing, and even coal to the city's more than 2 million residents. The Berlin airlift involved some 278,000 flights delivering 2 million tons of supplies. Finally in May 1949, the Soviet Union lifted its blockade. Not only did the airlift succeed in stopping the Soviets' European expansion, it created a new bond between the Americans and Germans.

German children wave to a U.S. cargo plane as it flies over Berlin. ▼

▲ Berliners watch as sacks of flour are unloaded.

A 15-year-old girl living near one of the airports where a plane landed every three minutes, said,

"The noise of the planes didn't bother us at all. As a matter of fact, we felt secure. As long as we heard those planes flying, we felt like everything was all right."
—from *Berlin in the Balance*

Six years later, West Germany was allowed to form an army and join NATO. In response, the Soviets in 1955 set up a military alliance—the Warsaw Pact—with the Communist governments of Eastern Europe. The formation of NATO and the Warsaw Pact divided Europe into two armed camps.

The United States Rearms

After World War II, some of President Truman's foreign policy advisers in the National Security Council (NSC) argued that America could not rely on other nations to contain the Soviets. Unlike the supporters of the containment policy, these NSC advisers believed the United States needed to take a more active stand against communism everywhere—not just in strategic locations.

In 1950 the NSC released a report, known as NSC-68, which said that the United States must actively "foster the seeds of destruction within the Soviet Union" and fight Communist movements wherever they arose. The United States vowed to combat communist expansion everywhere in the world.

Independence Movements

As the Cold War deepened, many nations experienced dramatic change. Many areas broke free of colonial rule and became independent. The Philippines gained independence from the United States in 1946. For years afterward, Filipinos struggled with poverty, government corruption, and civil war. In the late 1940s, the South Asian countries of India, Pakistan, and Burma won freedom from British rule. During the 1950s and 1960s, more than 25 African nations gained independence from European powers. The path to freedom in Africa was often bloody. New nations faced the difficult task of building modern societies.

In the Middle East, Jews and Arabs both claimed Palestine, an area the British had controlled. In 1947 the United Nations divided Palestine into independent Jewish and Arab states. The Jews accepted the plan, but the Arabs did not. After declaring independence, the Jewish state of Israel was attacked by the armies of neighboring Arab countries in the first of six major wars between the Arabs and Israelis.

Communism in China

Meanwhile, significant change came to China, Asia's largest country. In 1949 Communist forces under **Mao Zedong** (MOW DZUH·DUNG) defeated armies led by China's leader Chiang Kai-shek (CHAHNG KY·SHEHK). Mao Zedong formed a new Communist state, the People's Republic of China. Chiang Kai-shek retreated with his forces to the island of Taiwan off the southeastern coast of China. The United States recognized the government in Taiwan as the legitimate government of all China.

With Communists ruling mainland China, the Soviet Union had a powerful ally in Asia. It appeared to many people that the entire continent of Asia was in danger of falling to communism.

✔ Reading Check **Evaluating** What do you think was the main cause of the cold war? Why?

West Berlin, located in the middle of Soviet-controlled Germany, was isolated when Soviet leader Joseph Stalin blockaded all roads, railways, and waterways into the city. All planes were streamed along one of three 20-mile-wide air corridors. ▼

Divided Germany

0   100 kilometers
0   100 miles
Lambert Azimuthal
Equal-Area projection

Soviet Zone
British Zone
Berlin
EAST GERMANY
WEST GERMANY
American Zone
French Zone

Air corridor

50°N
10°E   15°E   20°E

Critical Thinking

Speculating What might have happened to Germany and other parts of Europe if the Allies had not conducted the airlift?

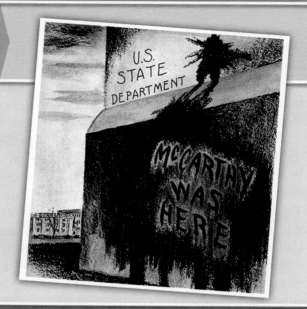

Cartoonist Herblock comments on the evidence provided by Senator Joe McCarthy for the 1954 Army-McCarthy hearings.

1. **Analyzing Visuals** What does the cartoon imply about McCarthy's tactics?
2. **Evaluating** What were the effects of McCarthyism?

Cold War Fears

Main Idea The Cold War heightened Americans' fears about communism in American society.

History and You Have you ever heard unproven charges made against a friend? How did you react? Read to find out how fear of communism caused some Americans to distrust other Americans in the late 1940s and early 1950s.

• •

The Cold War increased Americans' fears of communist **subversion,** or sabotage. Many Americans worried that Communists—"Reds"—had penetrated all levels of American society and were weakening the government. This Red Scare led to a massive hunt to uncover Communists. In 1947 President Truman ordered an investigation into the loyalty of all federal employees. Although little evidence of **espionage** was found, many federal workers lost their jobs.

Congressional Investigations

During the Red Scare, both houses of Congress set up investigation committees. In 1947 the House Un-American Activities Committee (HUAC) held hearings on alleged, or suspected, Communist influence in the entertainment industry. As a result, several screenwriters and film directors—the "Hollywood Ten"—went to jail for refusing to answer questions about their political beliefs or those of their colleagues. Reacting to pressure, film companies created **blacklists**—lists of individuals whose loyalty was suspect—that kept people from working in films.

In 1950 Congress passed the McCarran Act, which required all Communist groups to register with the government and to provide lists of members. Truman vetoed the act. "In a free country, we punish men for crimes they commit," he said, "but never for the opinions they hold." Congress overrode his veto.

American Spies Revealed

Meanwhile, stories of spies gripped the country. In 1948 Whittaker Chambers, a magazine editor, told the HUAC that he had spied for the Soviets in the 1930s. He accused Alger Hiss, a former government official, of giving him secret documents to pass on to the Soviets. To support this claim, Chambers showed copies of secret information that he said came from Hiss. Investigators could not prosecute Hiss for spying because too much time had passed since the events occurred. He was found guilty, however, of **perjury,** or lying under oath, and sent to prison.

The most dramatic spy case involved the atomic bomb, which the Soviets had acquired by 1949. Julius and Ethel Rosenberg, a New York couple who were Communist Party members, were accused of passing secrets about the atomic bomb to the Soviet Union. The Rosenbergs denied the charges but were sentenced to death for spying. Many people believed that the Rosenbergs were not spies but victims caught up in the Red Scare. Public appeals for mercy failed, however, and the couple was executed in June 1953.

McCarthyism

From 1950 to 1954, the hunt for Communists was led by Republican Senator Joseph McCarthy of Wisconsin. McCarthy claimed that a vast Communist network existed within the government. He called government employees to defend themselves before his committee. His unfounded charges ruined the careers of many innocent Americans. The word "McCarthyism" emerged to describe "the use of unproven charges to discredit people."

Millions of Americans, however, believed McCarthy. As a result, even the most powerful government officials hesitated to oppose him. In 1954 McCarthy made claims that Communists had infiltrated the U.S. Army. In a series of televised hearings, McCarthy hurled wild accusations at highly respected army officials. Toward the end of the hearings, Joseph Welch, an attorney for the army, said to McCarthy: "Until this moment, Senator, I think I never really gauged your cruelty or your recklessness. . . . Have you left no sense of decency?"

Many Americans now came to view McCarthy as a cruel bully who had little basis for his accusations. Congress also turned against McCarthy. In December 1954, the Senate voted to **censure,** or formally criticize, him for "conduct unbecoming a senator."

✔ **Reading Check** **Describing** What claims did McCarthy make against the U.S. Army?

History ONLINE
Study Central™ To review this section, go to glencoe.com.

Section 1 Review

Vocabulary

1. Write a paragraph using each of the following terms: iron curtain, cooperate, containment, pose, airlift, cold war, subversion, espionage, blacklist, perjury, censure.

Main Ideas

2. **Explaining** Who met at Yalta in 1945, and why did they meet?

3. **Analyzing** Was the Berlin airlift in 1948 successful? Explain why or why not.

4. **Determining Cause and Effect** How did the creation of NATO and the Warsaw Pact eventually affect the relations among European nations?

Critical Thinking

5. **Specifying** On a web diagram like the one below, list some of the direct results in America of the Red Scare.

Red Scare

6. **Persuasive Writing** What do you think about the conviction and execution of the Rosenbergs? Write a paragraph that supports your point of view.

Answer the
7. **Essential Question**
How and why did America aid European nations after World War II?

Section 2 Postwar Politics

Essential Question ◄

What economic, social, and political challenges did Americans face after World War II?

Reading Guide

Content Vocabulary

inflation *(p. 409)*   desegregate *(p. 413)*
closed shop *(p. 411)*

Academic Vocabulary

stable *(p. 409)*
domestic *(p. 410)*

Key People and Events

Fair Deal *(p. 410)*
Taft-Hartley Act *(p. 411)*

Reading Strategy

Taking Notes Create a diagram to describe social and economic change in postwar America.

American Diary

When soldiers returned home after World War II, they came back to a nation facing the difficult task of changing from wartime to peacetime. Would the economy collapse again and another depression sweep the country? President Truman was optimistic: "We are having our little troubles now . . . just a blowup after the letdown from war." Public fears, however, forced the nation's leaders into a debate over how best to deal with America's economic problems.

—Harry S. Truman, October 10, 1945

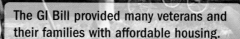

The GI Bill provided many veterans and their families with affordable housing.

The Postwar Economy

Main Idea Americans faced rising prices and labor unrest during the late 1940s.

History and You How difficult is it for you to adjust to major changes? Read to learn about how Americans tried to adjust to a peacetime economy after World War II.

· ·

After World War II, the United States had to adjust its economy to peacetime life. Industries shifted from producing war materials to making consumer goods, such as cars and appliances. Defense workers had to be retrained to work in consumer industries, and returning soldiers needed jobs.

During the war, government price controls kept the cost of consumer goods **stable,** or unchanging. When the government lifted these controls, prices began to climb. This rise in prices, or **inflation,** also came from a huge increase in consumer demand and spending. During the war years, Americans saved their money because many consumer goods were unavailable or rationed. Now they were eager for new consumer products and services.

Because of inflation, prices rose much faster than wages. During the war, workers had accepted government controls on wages and agreed not to strike. Now they would no longer be put off. When employers refused to raise wages, labor strikes broke out and disrupted the economy. In 1946 a miners' strike raised fears about fewer coal supplies. Meanwhile, a strike by railroad workers led to a shutdown of the nation's railroads.

Alarmed by the labor unrest, President Truman pressured the striking miners and railroad workers to go back to their jobs. In May 1946, he threatened to draft them into the army if they did not return to work. The president insisted he had the right to take such steps to keep vital industries operating.

President Truman finally forced striking miners back to work. He did this by having the government take over the mines. At the same time, he persuaded mine owners to grant many of the workers' demands. Truman also pressured railroad workers to return to work.

✓ Reading Check **Describing** What happened to prices when demand grew after the war?

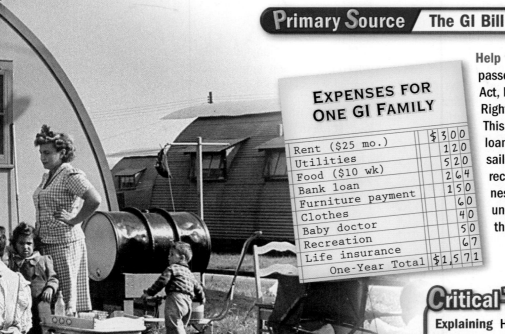

Primary Source / The GI Bill

EXPENSES FOR ONE GI FAMILY

Rent ($25 mo.)	$300
Utilities	120
Food ($10 wk)	520
Bank loan	264
Furniture payment	150
Clothes	60
Baby doctor	40
Recreation	50
Life insurance	67
One-Year Total	$1,571

Help for Veterans In 1944 Congress passed the Servicemen's Readjustment Act, better known as the GI Bill of Rights. GI stands for "government issue." This law provided billions of dollars in loans to help returning GIs—soldiers, sailors, and marines—attend college, receive special training, set up businesses, or buy homes. It also provided unemployment and health benefits for the GIs as they looked for jobs.

Critical Thinking

Explaining How did the GI Bill help war veterans?

Truman Faces the Republicans

Main Idea President Truman and the Republican-controlled Congress disagreed over how to solve the nation's economic problems.

History and You Have you ever been at a game in which a team that was predicted to lose won a stunning victory? Read to find out how Truman beat the odds in the 1948 presidential race.

· ·

In September 1945, President Truman presented a plan of **domestic**—or home-based—reforms aimed at solving some of the nation's economic problems. Truman later called this program the **Fair Deal.**

Truman proposed to raise the minimum wage, expand Social Security benefits, increase federal spending to create jobs, build new public housing, and create a system of national health insurance. However, because of opposition by a coalition of Republicans and Southern Democrats, these measures failed to pass in Congress.

Republicans Control Congress

Many Americans blamed Truman and the Democrats for the nation's problems and called for change. The Republicans seized upon this discontent in the congressional elections of 1946. The slogan "Had Enough?" helped the Republican Party win control of both houses of Congress.

The new Republican Congress set out to limit government spending, control labor unions, and reverse New Deal policies. Conservative Republicans especially favored big business and wanted to limit the power of labor unions.

People IN HISTORY

Hiram Fong

U.S. Senator, Hawaii

On March 12, 1959, Congress voted to admit the territory of Hawaii as a state. One of the two senators elected was Hiram Fong, who had served 14 years in the territorial legislature. As the first person of Chinese descent to hold a seat in the Senate, Fong supported civil rights. He also supported immigration reform that removed discrimination against Asian-Pacific people. Hawaii Senator Daniel Inouye described Fong as *"a legend in his time. He was a patriot . . . a most revered Asian-American leader."*

Margaret Chase Smith

U.S. Senator, Maine

In 1950 Senator Margaret Chase Smith and six other senators issued the Declaration of Conscience condemning "hate and character assassination."

"Those of us who shout the loudest about Americanism . . . are all too frequently those who, by our own words and acts, ignore some of the basic principles of Americanism—The right to criticize. The right to hold unpopular belief. The right to protest. The right of independent thought."

In the spring of 1947, Republican legislators introduced a measure that became known as the **Taft-Hartley Act.** This measure limited the actions workers could take against their employers. It outlawed the closed shop, or the practice of forcing business owners to hire only union members.

The Taft-Hartley Act also allowed the government to temporarily stop any strike that endangered public health or safety. This provision was intended to prevent any future strikes like those of the miners and the railroad workers the year before.

Labor unions sharply criticized the Taft-Hartley Act. They claimed that the measure erased many of the gains that labor had made since 1933. Truman, realizing that the Democrats needed the support of labor, vetoed the act. The Republican-controlled Congress, however, overrode Truman's veto.

Dennis Chavez

U.S. Senator, New Mexico

Dennis Chavez represented New Mexico in the U.S. Senate from May 11, 1935, until his death in 1962. He was the first American-born Latino senator. A lifelong supporter of civil rights, he cowrote one of the first Senate bills to stop discrimination in employment. He declared, *"I have been fighting for the so-called underprivileged all my days because I was one of them."*

CRITICAL Thinking

Speculating If Fong, Smith, and Chavez were in the Senate today, what issues do you think they might be addressing? Why?

Government Reorganization

Truman and Congress agreed on improving the efficiency of the federal government, which had grown considerably since the New Deal. In 1947 Congress passed the National Security Act. It unified the armed services under the Department of Defense. The act also set up a permanent Joint Chiefs of Staff, made up of the heads of each of the armed forces, to coordinate military policy. A National Security Council, located within the White House, would advise the president on foreign and military matters.

The National Security Act also set up another institution, the Central Intelligence Agency (CIA). The CIA aids American foreign policy by collecting information about what is going on in other countries, evaluating it, and passing it on to the president and other foreign-policy decision makers.

Many Americans feared that the CIA would be used to spy on American citizens. Truman, however, promised that the new agency would operate only in foreign lands and would not bring "police state methods" into American society.

The Election of 1948

As the 1948 presidential race neared, Truman seemed to have little chance of winning. Continuing economic problems made the president unpopular with many voters. Truman's failure to get U.S. domestic reforms passed made him look weak and ineffective.

Divisions within the Democratic Party also increased the chances of a Republican victory. At the Democratic national convention, two groups left the party altogether. Reacting angrily to Truman's support of civil rights, a group of Southern Democrats formed the States' Rights Democratic Party, or Dixiecrats. They nominated South Carolina's governor Strom Thurmond for president. At the same time, some Democrats left to form the Progressive Party, with Henry Wallace as their nominee for president. Wallace opposed Truman's foreign policy and called for closer American-Soviet ties.

Candidate	Electoral Vote	Popular Vote	Political Party
Truman	303	24,105,812	Democrat
Dewey	189	21,970,065	Republican
Thurmond	39	1,169,021	States' Rights

"We were getting good crowds despite the newspaper reports that Mr. Dewey was a 10-to-1 bet to win the election."
—William J. Bray, assistant on the 1948 presidential campaign train

Map Skills

1. **Comparing** From which region did Thurmond receive the most support?

2. **Calculating** By how many electoral votes did Truman win over Dewey?

Maps In Motion See StudentWorks™ Plus or glencoe.com.

Dewey Leads Polls

With the Democrats badly divided, it looked as though Governor Thomas Dewey of New York, the Republican nominee, would surely win the election. A dignified and popular candidate, Dewey seemed unbeatable. Opinion polls showed him with a huge lead. One pollster remarked: "Mr. Dewey is still so clearly ahead that we might just as well get ready to listen to his inaugural."

Perhaps the only one who gave Truman a chance to win was Truman himself. Ignoring the polls, the determined president poured his efforts into an energetic campaign. Traveling more than 21,000 miles (33,800 km) by train on a "whistle-stop" tour of the country, he gave some 300 speeches along the way. In town after town, he sharply attacked what he called "that do-nothing, good-for-nothing, worst Congress" for rejecting his Fair Deal legislation.

Truman Stages an Upset

On Election Day experts still expected Dewey to win. Expectations for a Republican victory were so great that on the evening of the election—before many votes were counted—the *Chicago Daily Tribune* newspaper issued a special edition announcing "Dewey Defeats Truman."

The nation was in for a great surprise. When all the ballots were counted, Truman had edged out Dewey by more than 2 million votes. The president's narrow victory was based largely on support from workers, African Americans, and farmers. Almost as remarkable as Truman's victory was the new popularity of the Democratic Party. In the election, Democrats regained control of both houses of Congress.

Reading Check **Analyzing** Why was the outcome of the 1948 presidential election a surprise?

A Fair Deal for Americans

Main Idea The Truman administration pushed for civil rights reforms.

History and You Have you ever put all your energy into making something important happen? Read to learn why President Truman wanted Congress to pass his legislation.

Truman took the election results as a sign that Americans wanted reform. He quickly reintroduced the Fair Deal legislation he presented to Congress in 1945. Some of these reform measures passed, but his plan lacked broad support, and Congress defeated most of the measures. Congress did pass laws to raise the minimum wage, expand Social Security benefits for senior citizens, and provide funds for housing for low-income families.

In a message to Congress in 1948, Truman called for an end to discrimination based on race, religion, or ethnic origins. He tried to persuade Congress to protect the voting rights of African Americans, abolish the poll tax, and make lynching a federal crime. Despite failing to get these measures passed, the president did take steps to advance the civil rights of African Americans. He ordered federal agencies to end job discrimination against African Americans and ordered the armed forces to **desegregate**—to end the separation of races. The president also instructed the Justice Department to enforce existing civil rights laws.

When Truman proposed his domestic agenda to Congress in 1949, he proclaimed that "every segment of our population and every individual has a right to expect from our government a fair deal." Truman asked for the clearance of slums, government-backed medical insurance, higher minimum wages, and more federal money for public schools. Although much of the president's Fair Deal vision went unfulfilled, he made an important start toward improving the lives of millions of Americans.

Reading Check Analyzing Why did President Truman call his proposed reforms a "fair deal"?

Section 2 Review

History ONLINE
Study Central™ To review this section, go to glencoe.com.

Vocabulary

1. Use each of the following terms in a complete sentence that will explain its meaning: stable, inflation, domestic, closed shop, desegregate.

Main Ideas

2. **Explaining** What happened to the price of American consumer goods after World War II? Why did this happen?

3. **Discussing** Why was Truman given little chance of winning the 1948 presidential election?

4. **Analyzing** What steps did President Truman take to end discrimination and segregation during his term in office? Was he successful?

Critical Thinking

5. **Explaining** Why was the CIA formed, and why were some Americans suspicious of the organization?

6. **Interpreting** Create a diagram like the one below that lists the main goals of the Fair Deal.

Fair Deal

7. **Persuasive Writing** President Truman threatened to draft striking coal miners into the army. Write a paragraph in which you explain whether you agree or disagree that a president should have this power.

Answer the
8. **Essential Question**
What economic, social, and political challenges did Americans face after World War II?

Section 3 ★ The Korean War

Essential Question ◄

How and why did America involve itself in the Korean conflict of the 1950s?

Reading Guide

Content Vocabulary

stalemate
(p. 416)

demilitarized
zone (p. 417)

Academic Vocabulary

assure (p. 416)   conclude (p. 417)

Key People and Events

Douglas MacArthur (p. 415)

Reading Strategy

Taking Notes On a sequencing chart like the one below, list a major event during the Korean conflict in each month and year.

June 1950

↓

Sept. 1950

↓

Nov. 1950

American Diary

Twelve U.S. Marines had just led their troops out of a trap. They listened to the words of their commander:
"We will come out as Marines, and not as stragglers. We're going to take our dead, wounded, and equipment when we leave. We're coming out . . . as Marines, or not at all." Two days of fighting followed. With the arrival of air cover, the Marines pushed back the Chinese and made their escape.

—*from* Chosin: Heroic Ordeal of the Korean War

A U.S. machine gun crew prepares for combat, November 1950.

Conflict in Korea

Main Idea Americans under the United Nations' flag fought a war in Korea during the early 1950s.

History and You How do you deal with people who use force to get what they want? Read to find out how the United States responded to Communist expansion in the Korean Peninsula.

· ·

At the end of World War II, the Americans and the Soviets divided the east Asian country of Korea at the 38th parallel of latitude. The Communists set up a government in North Korea, and an American-backed government took over South Korea.

On June 25, 1950, North Korean troops invaded South Korea in an attempt to take over that country. Poorly armed, the South Koreans were no match for the North. By September, the Communist forces gained control over much of South Korea, including Seoul, the capital city. Only a small area in the southeast around the port city of Pusan was still held by the South Korean army.

Early Phase of the War

President Truman reacted quickly to the Korean invasion, which he believed was supported by the Soviet Union. Without asking Congress to declare war, Truman ordered the use of limited American air and armed forces in Korea. Truman said:

PRIMARY SOURCE

"Korea is the Greece of the Far East. If we are tough enough now, if we stand up to them like we did in Greece three years ago, they won't take any next steps."
—from *Presidential Decisions for War*

Truman persuaded the United Nations to send troops. Most of these UN troops were American and under the command of U.S. general **Douglas MacArthur,** a hero of World War II. General MacArthur and the UN forces made a daring landing in the middle of the Korean Peninsula near the port of Inch'ŏn. They took that strategic city and then moved north to push the North Koreans back across the 38th parallel. South Korea now came under the control of UN forces.

Primary Source / The Korean War 1950–1953

— Truce line, July 1953

SOVIET UNION

PEOPLE'S REPUBLIC OF CHINA

NORTH KOREA
P'yŏngyang

P'anmunjŏm

Seoul

Inch'ŏn

SOUTH KOREA

Pusan

Sea of Japan (East Sea)

JAPAN

124°E 128°E 132°E 42°N 38°N

1 Farthest advance of North Koreans Sept. 1950
2 UN landing Sept. 1950
3 Farthest advance of UN forces Nov. 1950
4 Farthest advance of North Koreans and Chinese Jan. 1951

0 200 kilometers
0 200 miles
Two-Point Equidistant projection

Critical Thinking

Analyzing When did UN forces make their farthest advance?

Primary Source | Truman vs. MacArthur

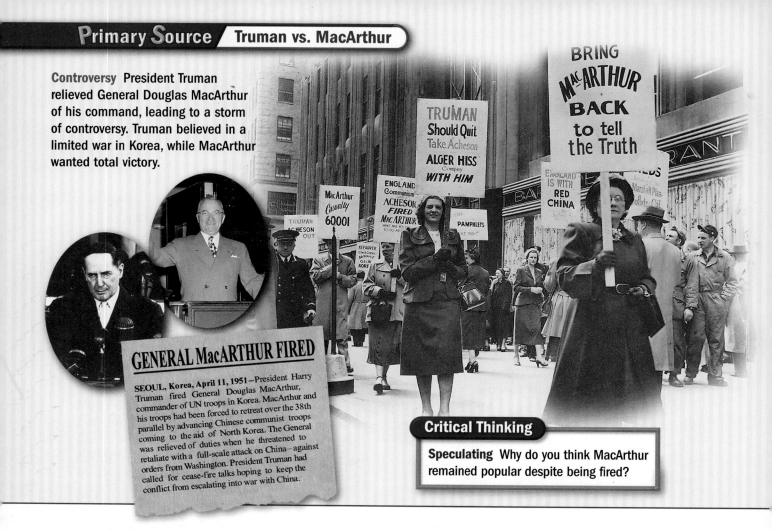

Controversy President Truman relieved General Douglas MacArthur of his command, leading to a storm of controversy. Truman believed in a limited war in Korea, while MacArthur wanted total victory.

GENERAL MacARTHUR FIRED

SEOUL, Korea, April 11, 1951—President Harry Truman fired General Douglas MacArthur, commander of UN troops in Korea. MacArthur and his troops had been forced to retreat over the 38th parallel by advancing Chinese communist troops coming to the aid of North Korea. The General was relieved of duties when he threatened to retaliate with a full-scale attack on China—against orders from Washington. President Truman had called for cease-fire talks hoping to keep the conflict from escalating into war with China.

Critical Thinking

Speculating Why do you think MacArthur remained popular despite being fired?

Taking the Offensive

Encouraged by this success, General Mac-Arthur urged President Truman to order the invasion of North Korea. He **assured,** or promised, Truman that neither China nor the Soviet Union would enter the war, and he pledged that he would have troops "home by Christmas." Truman sought UN approval for an invasion of the North to create a unified and democratic Korea.

After receiving these new orders, Mac-Arthur moved into North Korea and advanced toward the Chinese border. The Chinese Communists saw the advancing troops as a threat. Hundreds of thousands of Chinese troops crossed the border and drove the UN forces back to South Korea. Within weeks, the Communists held Seoul, South Korea's capital.

Reading Check **Describing** What line separated North Korea from South Korea?

American Leadership Divided

Main Idea President Truman and General Mac-Arthur disagreed over how to fight the Korean War.

History and You Have you ever been forced to give up something that you liked? Read to find out why General MacArthur had to resign his command of UN forces during the Korean War.

By January 1951, United Nations forces managed to stop their retreat. Launching a counteroffensive, they retook Seoul and pushed the Communists back across the 38th parallel. The war now became a **stalemate,** a situation in which neither side is able to gain much ground or achieve a decisive victory. The stalemate lasted for almost two years, with much bitter fighting along the 38th parallel.

Truman and MacArthur Disagree

As the stalemate continued, Truman thought about negotiating an end to the fighting. MacArthur, however, argued that dropping atomic bombs on Chinese bases and supply lines would bring a quick victory. Truman opposed MacArthur's plan, fearing that it would lead to a larger war with China or develop into another world war.

MacArthur publically criticized the president. In a letter to a member of Congress, MacArthur complained that he was being kept from doing his job. "We must win," he wrote. "There is no substitute for victory."

On April 11, 1951, President Truman relieved General MacArthur of his command in Korea. He **concluded,** or decided, that it was the only action he could take and "still be president of the United States." Truman wrote: "If I allowed him to defy the civil authorities in this manner, I myself would be violating my oath to uphold and defend the Constitution."

MacArthur's firing created a storm of protest in the United States. The general was popular, and polls showed that most Americans supported him against the president. Moreover, MacArthur did not go quietly. He returned home to a hero's welcome. MacArthur also delivered a farewell speech before Congress. "Old soldiers never die," he said, "they just fade away."

Ending the Conflict

The two sides in the Korean War began talks in July 1951. A cease-fire agreement ending the fighting was finally signed in July 1953 during the presidency of Dwight D. Eisenhower. It set up a **demilitarized zone**—a region barring military forces—between the two Koreas. The zone stretched along the border near the 38th parallel.

The Korean War ended with no victory for either side and almost no change in territory. More than 36,000 Americans died, and another 103,000 were wounded. Nearly two million Koreans and Chinese were killed.

By fighting in Korea, the United States showed the Soviets that it was willing to use force, if necessary, to block the spread of communism. At the same time, the lack of a clear victory led to uncertainty at home about America's foreign policy.

✓ Reading Check **Comparing** How did Truman's view on Korea differ from General MacArthur's view?

Section 3 Review

History ONLINE
Study Central™ To review this section, go to glencoe.com.

Vocabulary

1. Explain the significance of each of these terms: assure, stalemate, conclude, demilitarized zone.

Main Ideas

2. Explaining How did the Korean conflict begin?

3. Discussing Why did Truman relieve General MacArthur of his command in Korea?

4. Identifying What is a demilitarized zone, and where was it located in Korea?

Critical Thinking

5. Comparing and Contrasting Re-create a chart like the one below to compare the stalemate solutions of Truman and MacArthur.

Stalemate Solution	Stalemate Solution
Truman	MacArthur

6. Expository Writing Explain in a paragraph the major events that led directly to the stalemate in Korea.

Answer the
7. Essential Question How and why did America involve itself in the Korean conflict of the 1950s?

America in the 1950s

Essential Question ◄

How did the American prosperity of the 1950s affect the country's economy and culture?

Reading Guide

Content Vocabulary

surplus (p. 419)   affluence (p. 421)

arms race (p. 420)   materialism (p. 424)

summit (p. 420)

Academic Vocabulary

nuclear (p. 420)   economy (p. 421)

Key People and Events

Dwight D. Eisenhower (p. 419)

Nikita Khrushchev (p. 420)

Reading Strategy

Taking Notes Re-create a diagram like the one below to identify two Cold War crises that occurred in 1956 and how each was resolved.

American Diary

"Trust was the bedrock of Ike's presidency," one reporter said, adding, "We knew what was in his heart." These words were used to describe Dwight D. Eisenhower, Republican presidential candidate in 1952. Eisenhower's appeal went far beyond party label. His role in World War II made him an unquestioned hero. Above all, his personality made many people feel safe, comfortable, and confident.

—*from Hugh Sidey,*
TIME *magazine reporter*

Eisenhower supporters in Shreveport, Louisiana, during the 1952 campaign

The Eisenhower Years

Main Idea President Eisenhower promoted policies to maintain prosperity at home and to compete with the Soviets abroad.

History and You Have you ever taken part in an exciting contest to win first prize? Read to learn how the United States and the Soviet Union were rivals in a "contest" for world leadership.

• •

In November 1952, Americans elected **Dwight D. Eisenhower** to the presidency in a landslide victory—the first Republican to win the White House since 1928. Eisenhower collected more than 6 million popular votes over Illinois Governor Adlai E. Stevenson, his Democratic opponent, and carried the electoral college 442 to 89. The Republicans also won control of Congress.

Born in Texas and raised in rural Kansas, Dwight D. Eisenhower rose steadily through the army to become supreme commander of the Allied forces in Europe during World War II. People called him "Ike"—and voters trusted him. He won wide support with his pledge to bring the Korean War to an "early and honorable end."

Domestic Policy

During his two terms in office, Eisenhower followed a moderate, or middle-of-the-road, approach to domestic policy. He avoided ambitious new government programs but resisted the pressure to end popular older ones, and sometimes he even expanded them. As he once told reporters: "I feel pretty good when I'm attacked from both sides. It makes me more certain I'm on the right track."

President Eisenhower wanted to make the federal government "smaller rather than bigger." He backed free enterprise, shifted some financial powers to the states, and cut federal spending. When Eisenhower completed his second term in 1961, the federal budget had a **surplus,** or excess, of $300 million.

The greatest domestic program of the Eisenhower years involved building a network of interstate highways. In 1956 Congress passed the Federal Highway Act. The law funded the building of more than 40,000 miles (64,000 km) of highways that tied the nation together. The highway program spurred economic growth, especially in the automobile and oil industries, while improving military mobility in case of an attack.

Primary Source — Election of 1952

Electoral Vote

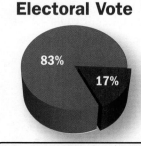

83%

17%

■ Dwight D. Eisenhower (R)
■ Adlai E. Stevenson (D)

Popular Vote

0.5% (Other)

55.1% 44.4%

■ Dwight D. Eisenhower (R)
■ Adlai E. Stevenson (D)

Critical Thinking

1. **Interpreting** Which candidate won a majority of the popular vote?

2. **Applying** What is a landslide victory? Would you consider Eisenhower's election a landslide? Explain.

United States–Soviet Rivalry

During the 1950s, the United States and the Soviet Union engaged in a nuclear **arms race.** Both sides built more and more **nuclear,** or atomic, warheads and guided missiles that could destroy the other side many times over. With the threat of nuclear destruction so great, the United States and the Soviet Union had to act carefully. A crisis, badly managed, could lead to all-out war.

In 1956 two crises tested the superpowers. First, trouble arose in the Middle East when Egypt's president Gamal Abdel Nasser seized the Suez Canal from its European owners. In October, Britain and France joined Israel in invading Egypt. Britain and France hoped to get rid of Nasser, and Israel wanted to end Egypt's military threat. American and Soviet opposition finally forced the three nations to pull out of Egypt.

The second crisis erupted in Hungary, when students and workers demonstrated to demand changes in the government. A new government called for Soviet troops to withdraw. In early November 1956, Soviet leader Nikita Khrushchev (kroosh·CHAWF) ordered Soviet forces to crush the revolt. President Eisenhower condemned the Soviet crackdown but did not intervene.

By the mid-1950s, the superpowers were interested in easing Cold War tensions. In July 1955, Eisenhower, NATO leaders, and Soviet officials met at a summit conference in Geneva, Switzerland. A **summit** is a meeting of heads of government. The leaders discussed major issues, raising hopes for peace.

After the Geneva summit, a policy of peaceful coexistence emerged. This meant the two superpowers would compete but avoid war. For example, the U.S. and the Soviet Union began competing in a space race. In October 1957, the Soviets sent into space the world's first artificial satellite, called *Sputnik*. The United States set up its own space program headed by the National Aeronautics and Space Administration (NASA).

✔ **Reading Check** **Describing** How did relations between the superpowers change after the Geneva summit?

LINKING PAST TO PRESENT Computers

THEN In the mid-1940s, the earliest computers were built specifically for scientific calculations in military use. Unveiled in 1946, ENIAC (Electronic Numerical Integrator and Computer) was the first programmable, general-purpose digital computer. It could take workers days, using punch cards, plug boards, and switches, to program the machine for each new task.

★ **1940s** ENIAC
Weight—30 tons
(27 metric tons)
Area—1,800 sq. feet
(167 sq. m)

★ **1990** Microsoft Windows 3.0 software introduced

★ **1977** First preassembled desktop, personal computer with color graphics; called "Apple II"

★ **1991** World Wide Web available to general public

Prosperity and Change

Main Idea A booming economy changed the social and cultural life of Americans during the 1950s.

History and You You probably have heard this expression: "Those were the good old days." For some older Americans, this expression describes the 1950s. Read to find out why the 1950s has this appeal for them.

· ·

During the 1950s, the American **economy** —the system of production, distribution, and consumption—grew rapidly. Americans earned higher wages and bought more consumer goods than ever before. As a result, factory production soared. A "baby boom," or increased birthrate, promised even more economic growth in the future.

Many women left the workforce to stay home and raise children. The demand for baby products and services grew. School enrollment soared as the "baby boomers" reached school age, putting a strain on the educational system.

The Consumer Society

Americans of the 1950s went on a buying spree. **Affluence,** the growing variety and quantity of products available, and expanded advertising all played a role in the increased demand for consumer goods. Buying goods became easier, too. Many Americans used credit cards, charge accounts, and easy-payment plans to purchase goods.

Consumers sought the latest products— dishwashers, washing machines, television sets, stereos, and clothes made from synthetic fabrics. The growing market for cars prompted automakers to outdo one another by manufacturing bigger, faster, and flashier cars. New models added stylish features such as chrome-plated bumpers and soaring tail fins.

The advertising and marketing of products on television, on radio, and in magazines created consumer fads and crazes that swept the nation. In the late 1950s, Americans bought millions of hula hoops—large plastic rings they twirled around their waists. Other popular fads included crew cuts for boys, poodle skirts for girls, and a new snack—pizza.

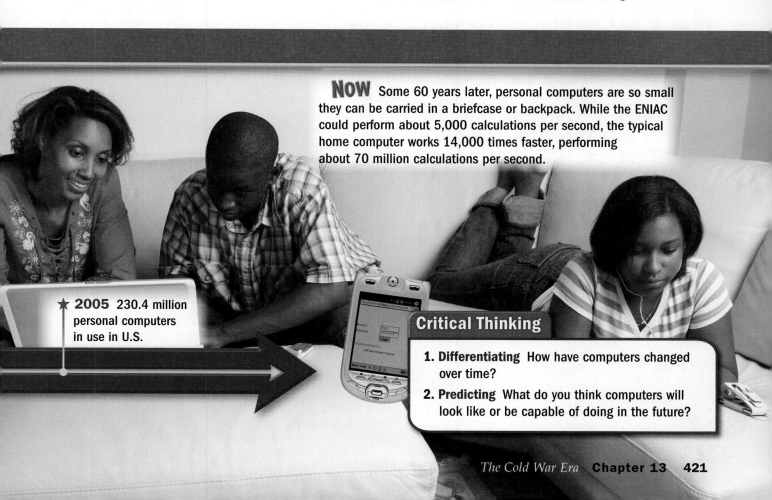

NOW Some 60 years later, personal computers are so small they can be carried in a briefcase or backpack. While the ENIAC could perform about 5,000 calculations per second, the typical home computer works 14,000 times faster, performing about 70 million calculations per second.

★ **2005** 230.4 million personal computers in use in U.S.

Critical Thinking

1. **Differentiating** How have computers changed over time?
2. **Predicting** What do you think computers will look like or be capable of doing in the future?

An American Culture

By 1949 more than 900,000 American households had television sets. The sets, in large wooden cabinets, had small screens that displayed grainy black-and-white images. During the 1950s, an average of 6.5 million sets were produced annually. By the end of the decade, most American families had television.

Television changed American life. It became the main form of entertainment as well as an important source of news and information. Millions of Americans gathered to watch weekly episodes of programs such as *I Love Lucy* and *Father Knows Best*. The images shown in many programs—of happy families in neat, middle-class homes—helped shape Americans' expectations for their own lives.

A new form of music—rock 'n' roll—achieved great popularity among teenagers. Rock 'n' roll grew from the rhythm and blues music that African American musicians cre-ated years before. It often had some elements of country music. In rock 'n' roll, the tempo was quicker, and electrically amplified instru-ments—mostly guitars—were used.

One of the first rock hits, reaching number one in 1955, was Bill Haley and the Comets' *Rock Around the Clock*. Adapting the style of African American performers such as Chuck Berry and Little Richard, Elvis Presley burst on the national scene in 1956. Presley quickly became an idol to millions of young Ameri-cans. Many young men copied his ducktail haircut and swaggering mannerisms.

For teenagers, the shared experience of lis-tening to the music helped forge a common identity. The differing attitudes of the older and younger generations toward music and other forms of popular culture later came to be known as the generation gap.

✔ **Reading Check** Analyzing How did television change American life in the 1950s?

Economics & History

Bread 180 loaves

Oranges 2 crates

Eggs 131 dz.

31 Chickens

Milk 698 qts.

Food for a Year *How far would a weekly grocery budget of $25 go to feed a family of four in 1951?*

Problems in a Time of Plenty

Main Idea Many Americans did not share in the prosperity of the 1950s.

History and You Can you recall hard times in your life? Read on to learn what groups considered the 1950s to be hard times.

. . . .

In the 1950s, more than 20 percent of Americans lived in poverty. Millions more struggled to survive on incomes that were only slightly above the poverty level. Such poverty marred the landscape of the affluent society.

Many farmers did not share in the prosperity of the 1950s. Business enterprises created large profitable farms that used new technology to produce an abundance of food for American and foreign consumers. Small farms, however, could not compete with large farms, so many small-farm families sold their land and migrated to urban areas. Small farmers who continued to farm struggled.

Rural poverty did not always come from agricultural problems. In Appalachia—a region stretching along the Appalachian Mountains—the decline of the coal industry plunged thousands of rural mountain people into desperate poverty. During the 1950s, about 1.5 million people abandoned Appalachia to seek a better life in the nation's cities.

Urban Poverty

As increasing numbers of middle-class Americans moved to the suburbs in the 1950s, they left the poor behind. The inner cities became islands of poverty. Still, people came to cities looking for work. Continuing their migration from rural areas of the South, more than 3 million African Americans moved to cities in the North and the Midwest between 1940 and 1960. For many, however, life proved to be little better in Northern cities. Many poor Latinos—Puerto Ricans in the East and Mexicans in the Southwest and the West—also moved to American cities.

The migration of poor African Americans and Latinos to Northern cities hastened the departure of whites to the suburbs. This "white flight" turned some areas of cities into ghettos—neighborhoods that were inhabited mainly by poor minority groups.

Few good job opportunities existed for the urban poor. Many factories and businesses relocated to suburban areas. In addition, automation—producing goods using mechanical and electronic devices—reduced jobs in the industries that remained. It became more and more difficult for the urban poor to rise from poverty and improve their lives.

The urban poor struggled not only with poverty but also with racial discrimination in employment, housing, and education. Crime and violence often grew out of inner-city poverty, especially among young people who saw no hope for escape from life in the ghetto.

By the Numbers

1951	Comparing by Cost	2007
$0.92	Milk, per gallon	$3.07
$0.75	Eggs, per dozen	$1.54
$0.15	Loaf of bread	$1.15
$0.49	Oranges, per dozen	$1.09
$0.60	Chicken, per pound	$1.03
$0.03	Cost of first-class postage stamp	$0.41
$0.49	Movie ticket	$6.50
$1.45	Average hourly wage	$17.30
$1,995	Average cost of a new car	$27,800
$3,709	Median income for a family of four	$59,000
$299	Television set, 16-inch screen	$299

—from various sources

Critical Thinking

Calculating What percentage of a family's income in 1951 was needed to buy a new car? In 2007?

History ONLINE

Student Web Activity Visit glencoe.com and complete the Chapter 13 Web Activity about life in the 1950s.

Social Critics

Changes in American society in the 1950s caused some people to question the values that were emerging. Some critics charged that the sameness of corporate and suburban life had a cost—the loss of individuality. Others condemned American materialism—a focus on accumulating money and possessions rather than an interest in personal and spiritual matters.

Leading social critics examined the complexity of modern society. Many wrote about its effects on individual behavior. William H. Whyte, Jr., studied American business life in *The Organization Man*. He drew a picture of young executives as "organization men" who "have left home spiritually as well as physically." He concluded that businesses discouraged independent thinking and considered the person with new ideas "a threat." Young executives who abandoned their own views were the ones most likely to fit in.

In his book, *The Affluent Society*, economist John Kenneth Galbraith wrote of the prosperous American society of the 1950s. However, not all Americans shared in this prosperity. Galbraith described a suburban family, comfortably installed in an "air-conditioned, power-steered and power-braked automobile, driven through cities that are badly paved, made hideous by litter, blighted buildings, and billboards." Prosperous Americans, Galbraith claimed, often ignored the hardships faced by the rural and urban poor.

Changing Times

A group of writers called the Beats had even sharper criticism of American society. The term "Beat," said novelist Jack Kerouac, meant "weariness with all forms of the modern industrial state." Many young Americans read the works of Kerouac, poet Allen Ginsberg, and other Beat writers. Some adopted Beat attitudes of rebellion against middle-class America.

With American society changing, women and African Americans began questioning their roles. They became increasingly impatient for change and less willing to accept their status as second-class citizens. In the 1950s both groups launched efforts to gain greater freedom and equality.

Reading Check **Describing** What criticisms were made about American society in the 1950s?

Section 4 Review

History ONLINE **Study Central™** To review this section, go to glencoe.com.

Vocabulary

1. Write each of the terms and a definition of each in your own words: surplus, arms race, nuclear, summit, economy, affluence, materialism.

Main Ideas

2. **Discussing** While president, what was Eisenhower's greatest domestic achievement, and why was it important?

3. **Explaining** What does it mean to say that Americans became a consumer society in the 1950s?

4. **Summarizing** Why did urban poverty increase during the 1950s?

Critical Thinking

5. **Determining Cause and Effect** On a chart like the one below, identify the direct effects of the 1950s baby boom.

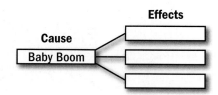

Cause → Effects

Baby Boom

6. **Descriptive Writing** Write a brief description of the types of music that were popular in the 1950s.

7. **Answer the Essential Question** How did the American prosperity of the 1950s affect the country's economy and culture?

Chapter 13

Visual Summary

The Cold War

- Soviets occupy much of Eastern and Central Europe
- Truman doctrine proposed
- Congress approves Marshall Plan
- Berlin airlift
- With United Nations, U.S. fights in Korea
- Crisis in the Middle East
- Uprising in Hungary
- War in Southeast Asia
- Troubles in Latin America
- Geneva summit encourages peaceful coexistence
- Space race

Berlin airlift (above);
Senator Margaret Chase Smith (right)

Prosperity

- Productivity increases
- Per-capita income and the standard of living increases
- The baby boom increases population
- Suburban housing developments boom
- Car culture grows
- Consumerism grows
- Television viewing increases

Problems and Issues

- Growing competition hurts small farmers
- Decline in coal industry increases poverty in rural areas
- Inner cities decay as businesses and residents relocate
- Social critics question conformity
- Women question their roles in society
- African Americans challenge segregation

THE IRON CURTAIN

Eisenhower's Domestic Policy

- Attempts to limit government spending
- Federal Highway Act
- Extends social programs

Students receive polio vaccine

Whatever the weather
We only reach welfare
together

Changing Settlement Patterns

Shortly after World War II, suburbs sprang up around American cities. By 1960 a majority of Americans lived in suburban areas rather than in cities. Meanwhile, many people were moving from older cities in the Northeast and Midwest toward newer centers in the South and West, the so-called Sunbelt. In most cases, people were going to where the jobs were.

How Did Geography Affect Changing Settlement Patterns?

The open spaces of the Sunbelt were well-suited for population growth. The economy of this area expanded as government defense spending created many jobs. A relatively cheap, nonunion workforce also drew industries from other parts of the nation. Additional factors in the Sunbelt's growth were low housing costs, lower taxes, improved public health, and milder climates. Some of the greatest growth occurred in Florida, Texas, and California.

Over the past several decades, population growth has been greatest in Southern and Western states.
▼

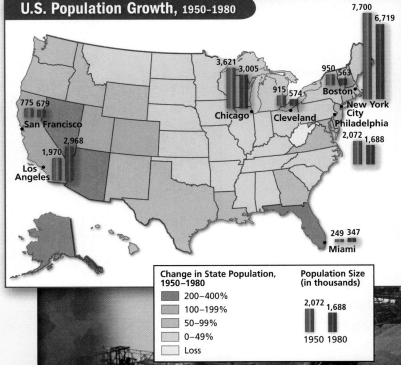

U.S. Population Growth, 1950–1980

7,700
6,719
3,621
3,005
950
563
915
574
Boston
Chicago
Cleveland
New York City
Philadelphia
775 679
San Francisco
2,968
1,970
Los Angeles
2,072 1,688
249 347
Miami

Change in State Population, 1950–1980
- 200–400%
- 100–199%
- 50–99%
- 0–49%
- Loss

Population Size (in thousands)
2,072 1,688
1950   1980

HISTORIC US 66

Increasing Mobility
Automobiles were essential to the development of the Sunbelt. The Interstate Highway Act of 1956 authorized the construction of a national highway system linking the entire country with roads that were at least four lanes wide. The highways made it easier for Americans to travel west and south.

A Changing Economy In the 1960s, the U.S. economy began to change from a manufacturing-based economy to a service economy or information economy. Many U.S. firms relocated overseas—partly to take advantage of cheaper labor and production costs. Older industrial regions of the Northeast and Midwest started to decline, and these areas came to be known as the Rust Belt, in contrast to the thriving Sunbelt.

Resources As people moved to the dry Southwest, they needed water and electricity. Hoover Dam, on the Colorado River, was built in the 1930s to control flooding and provide electric power. Today, the electricity produced is shared by Arizona, Nevada, and California.

Growing Cities The population of Sunbelt cities such as Las Vegas, Nevada, has exploded in recent decades. Urban sprawl—unplanned development across the landscape— has become common. Destruction of natural habitats and increased traffic and pollution are some effects of urban sprawl.

Analyzing Geography

1. **Movement** Between 1950 and 1980, which states had the largest percentage of population growth?

2. **Human-Environment Interaction** What kinds of challenges do you think the Sunbelt faces as a result of rapid growth?

STANDARDIZED TEST PRACTICE

TEST-TAKING **TIP**

When answering essay questions, organize your thoughts before you begin writing. This will help reduce the time you need to revise.

Reviewing Main Ideas

Directions: Choose the best answers for each of the following questions.

1. Which group formed to stop the spread of Soviet influence in Western Europe?

  A United Nations

  B Warsaw Pact nations

  C North Atlantic Treaty Organization

  D House Un-American Activities Committee

2. What proposal was part of Truman's program to solve the nation's economic problems?

  A the closed shop

  B the Taft-Hartley Act

  C abolition of the poll tax

  D national health insurance

3. Truman tried to contain communism on the Korean Peninsula by

  A dividing Korea.

  B attacking China.

  C defending South Korea.

  D bombing the Soviet Union.

4. Eisenhower established the National Aeronautics and Space Administration (NASA) to

  A conduct U.S. space activities.

  B create jobs for the urban poor.

  C make the federal government smaller.

  D increase demand for consumer goods.

Short-Answer Question

Directions: Base your answer to question 5 on the excerpt below and on your knowledge of social studies.

> More than any single action by the government since the end of the war, this one [the interstate highway system] would change the face of America. . . . Its impact on the American economy—the jobs it would produce in manufacturing and construction, the rural areas it would open up—was beyond calculation.
>
> —Dwight Eisenhower in *Mandate for Change, 1953–1956*

5. Why did Eisenhower think an interstate highway system was so important to the nation?

Review the Essential Questions

6. Essay How did the economies in the United States and Europe change after World War II?

To help you write your essay, review your answers to the Essential Questions in the section reviews and the chapter Foldables Study Organizer. Your essay should include:

- how and why America gave aid to Europe;
- economic challenges Americans faced;
- how you think the Korean War affected the American economy; and
- how American prosperity affected the economy.

GO ON

History ONLINE

For additional test practice, use **Self-Check Quizzes**—Chapter 13 at glencoe.com.

Document-Based Questions

Directions: Analyze the documents and answer the short-answer questions that follow.

Document 1

Julius and Ethel Rosenberg were on trial for espionage. The Rosenbergs' lawyer, Emanuel Bloch, made the following plea.

> Through you [Judge Kaufman] the rest of the world will either believe that we are a compassionate nation, a nation built upon the ideals of humanity and justice, or a nation that has been gripped in panic and fear and is embarked upon mad acts.

Source: Emanuel Bloch, NCRRC Letters

7. Was Bloch's plea successful? Explain.

Document 2

President Truman summed up a major economic problem in postwar America during his address to the nation in 1947.

> We all know that recent price increases have denied to many of our workers much of the value of recent wage increases.

Source: Harry S. Truman, *State of the Union Address*

8. What good and bad news did Truman deliver in this excerpt from his speech?

Document 3

President Truman explained why he was relieving General Douglas MacArthur of his command in South Korea.

> The free nations have united their strength in an effort to prevent a third world war. That war can come if the Communist rulers want it to come. This Nation and its allies will not be responsible for its coming.

Source: *Department of State Bulletin*, April 16, 1951

9. What strategy did Truman reject because he thought it could start another world war?

Document 4

This graph shows labor union membership.

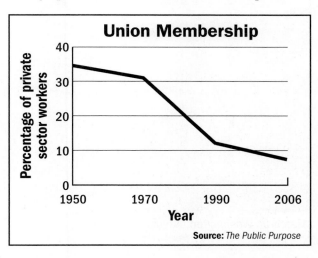

Union Membership

(y-axis: Percentage of private sector workers, 0 to 40)
(x-axis: Year — 1950, 1970, 1990, 2006)

Source: *The Public Purpose*

10. Describe the trend in union membership.

Document 5

This excerpt comes from the novel *On the Road*.

> The only people for me are the mad ones, the ones who are mad to live, mad to talk, mad to be saved, desirous of everything at the same time, the ones who never yawn or say a commonplace thing, but burn, burn, burn like fabulous yellow roman candles.

Source: Jack Kerouac, *On the Road*

11. Kerouac uses the term "mad ones." To whom do you think he is referring?

12. Expository Writing Using the information from the five documents and your knowledge of social studies, write an essay in which you:

- describe social and economic changes in the 1950s; and
- describe political changes in the 1950s.

Need Extra Help?												
If you missed questions. . .	1	2	3	4	5	6	7	8	9	10	11	12
Go to page. . .	404	410	415	420	419	402–405	407	409	417	410–411	424	403–408

Chapter 14

The Civil Rights Era 1954-1974

March on Washington, August 28, 1963

Linda Brown ▶

★ **1954**
Brown v. Board of Education ruling

★ **1955**
Montgomery bus boycott begins

DWIGHT EISENHOWER
1953-1961

JOHN F. KENNEDY
1961–1963

LYNDON JOHNSON
1963–1969

Dr. Martin Luther King, Jr. ▶

★ **1964**
Civil Rights Act passes

PRESIDENTS

U.S. Events

World Events

1954

1959

1964

★ **1959**
Fidel Castro seizes power in Cuba

★ **1964**
Nelson Mandela receives life sentence in South Africa

History ONLINE

Chapter Overview Visit glencoe.com and click on **Chapter 14—Chapter Overviews** to preview chapter information.

Section 1: The Civil Rights Movement

Essential Question What were the legal and social challenges to racial segregation in the 1940s and 1950s?

Section 2: Kennedy and Johnson

Essential Question How were Kennedy and Johnson alike and different as presidents of the United States?

Section 3: The Struggle Continues

Essential Question What areas of civil rights did groups try to improve in the 1960s, and what methods did those groups use?

Section 4: Other Groups Seek Rights

Essential Question How did the civil rights movement affect minorities other than African Americans?

FOLDABLES®
Study Organizer

Organizing Information
Make this Foldable to help organize what you learn about how the courts addressed civil rights issues.

Step 1 Fold a sheet of paper in half from side to side so that the left edge lies about 1/2 inch from the right edge.

Step 2 Cut the top layer only to make four tabs.

Step 3 Label the tab as shown.

Reading and Writing As you read the chapter, list key court decisions about civil rights on the outside of the Foldable. Summarize important details on the inside of the Foldable.

César Chávez was a leading voice for migrant farmworkers. ▶

1968
- Martin Luther King, Jr., assassinated
- Indian Civil Rights Act passes

RICHARD NIXON
1969–1974

★ **1970**
Grape workers gain better pay and working conditions

GERALD FORD
1974–1977

1969

1974

★ **1967**
First heart transplant performed in South Africa

1972
Britain imposes direct rule on Northern Ireland

★ **1972**
Terrorists kill Olympic athletes

The Civil Rights Movement

Essential Question ◄

What were the legal and social challenges to racial segregation in the 1940s and 1950s?

Reading Guide

Content Vocabulary
segregation *(p. 433)*
integrate *(p. 434)*
boycott *(p. 436)*
civil disobedience *(p. 437)*

Academic Vocabulary
discriminate *(p. 433)*   civil *(p. 433)*

Key People and Events
NAACP *(p. 433)*
Thurgood Marshall *(p. 434)*
Brown v. Board of Education of Topeka, Kansas *(p. 434)*
Rosa Parks *(p. 436)*
Dr. Martin Luther King, Jr. *(p. 436)*

Reading Strategy
Taking Notes Create a time line like the one below to record important events in the early struggle for equal rights.

1909   1954   1955   1957

American Diary

Howard Bailey remembers that when the white high school got new textbooks, the old ones would be dropped off at his African American school. "I can remember that occasionally they would shovel the books out of the pickup trucks with coal shovels and just . . . dump them on the ground outside of the school building. So our teachers and principals would . . . gather them up and tape up . . . the books that were in real bad shape."

—Kentucky Civil Rights Oral History Commission

In *Brown v. Board of Education*, the Supreme Court found that segregated classrooms denied children like Linda Brown (first row, far right) equal education.

Equality in Education

Main Idea After World War II, African Americans and other supporters of civil rights challenged discrimination in the nation's public schools.

History and You What might it have been like to be told that you could go only to certain schools because of your racial or ethnic background? Read to learn about the struggle to achieve equal rights for African American students in the 1950s.

• •

African Americans had suffered from racism and **discrimination,** or unfair treatment, since colonial times. By the mid-1900s, many African Americans believed that the time had come for them to enjoy an equal place in American life. They fought for equal opportunities in jobs, housing, and education. They also fought against **segregation**—the separation of people of different races.

The Push for Equal Rights

During World War II, African Americans demanded more rights. Their efforts helped end discrimination in factories that held government contracts and increased opportunities for African Americans in the military.

In Chicago in 1942, James Farmer and George Houser founded the Congress of Racial Equality (CORE). A year later, CORE carried out protests against public places that refused to admit or serve African Americans. CORE protesters successfully ended segregation in many restaurants, theaters, and other public places in Chicago, Detroit, Denver, and Syracuse.

When World War II ended, many African American soldiers returned home hopeful that their country would appreciate their loyalty and sacrifice. In the 1950s, when change did not come as quickly as desired, their determination to end injustices in the United States led to protests and marches—and to the rise of the **civil** (meaning, citizens as individuals) rights movement.

The **NAACP** (National Association for the Advancement of Colored People) had worked on behalf of African Americans since its founding in 1909. In the 1950s, NAACP lawyers searched for cases they could use to challenge the laws allowing the segregation of public schools.

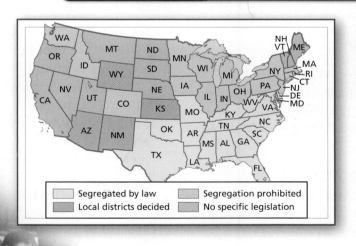

When and Where / School Segregation, 1950

Segregated by law
Local districts decided
Segregation prohibited
No specific legislation

Regional Differences
School segregation was treated differently in various parts of the United States.

Critical Thinking

1. **Identifying** In which category did more states belong: those where the law ordered segregation or those where the law prohibited segregation?
2. **Theorizing** Why do you think segregation was widespread in the South and prohibited in the North?

The *Brown* Decision

The Supreme Court had upheld segregation laws in the past. In 1896 in *Plessy* v. *Ferguson,* it ruled that "separate but equal" public facilities were legal. **Thurgood Marshall,** the chief lawyer for the NAACP, decided to challenge the idea of "separate but equal." Seven-year-old African American Linda Brown was not permitted to attend an all–white elementary school just blocks from her house. She was told to attend an all–African American school across town. The Brown family sued the school system but lost. Marshall and the NAACP appealed the case all the way to the Supreme Court.

The case of ***Brown* v. *Board of Education of Topeka, Kansas,*** combined with similar cases, reached the Supreme Court in December 1952. Marshall argued that segregated schools were not and could not be equal to white schools. Thus segregated schools violated the Fourteenth Amendment.

On May 17, 1954, the Court unanimously ruled in *Brown* v. *Board of Education of Topeka, Kansas,* that it was unconstitutional to separate schoolchildren by race. The *Brown* decision reversed the Court's decision in the earlier *Plessy* v. *Ferguson* case. Chief Justice Earl Warren summed up the Court's new ruling when he wrote:

PRIMARY SOURCE

"In the field of public education, the doctrine of 'separate but equal' has no place. Separate educational facilities are inherently [essentially] unequal."
—from *Brown* v. *Board of Education of Topeka, Kansas*

Integrating the Schools

The Court's decision in *Brown* v. *Board of Education* applied only to public schools. However, it had the much greater effect of threatening the entire system of segregation. The ruling convinced many African Americans that the time had come to oppose other forms of discrimination as well. At the same time, the Court's decision angered many

"In these days, it is doubtful that any child may reasonably be expected to succeed in life if he is denied the opportunity of an education. Such an opportunity, . . . must be made available to all on equal terms."

—*Brown v. Board of Education*

The Supreme Court ruled in *Brown* v. *Board of Education* that segregation in public schools was unconstitutional. Some segregated school districts integrated their schools quickly and with no incident. Other attempts to integrate led to anger and opposition. Many schools kept their schools segregated for many years.

◄ Linda Brown was at the center of the *Brown* decision.

white Southerners, who became more determined to defend segregation, no matter what the Supreme Court ruled.

In 1955 the Supreme Court followed up its decision in *Brown* v. *Board of Education* with another ruling. It called on school authorities to make plans for **integrating**—bringing races together—in public schools. The Court also ordered that integration was to be carried out "with all deliberate speed"—as fast as reasonably possible.

Some schools integrated quickly. However, in parts of the South, local leaders vowed to keep African American children out of white schools. A clash between the federal government and these states seemed likely.

Confrontation in Little Rock

In 1957 a federal judge ordered all-white Central High School in Little Rock, Arkansas, to admit African American students. Arkansas governor Orval Faubus opposed integration. In September he called out the state's National Guard to prevent African Americans from entering the high school.

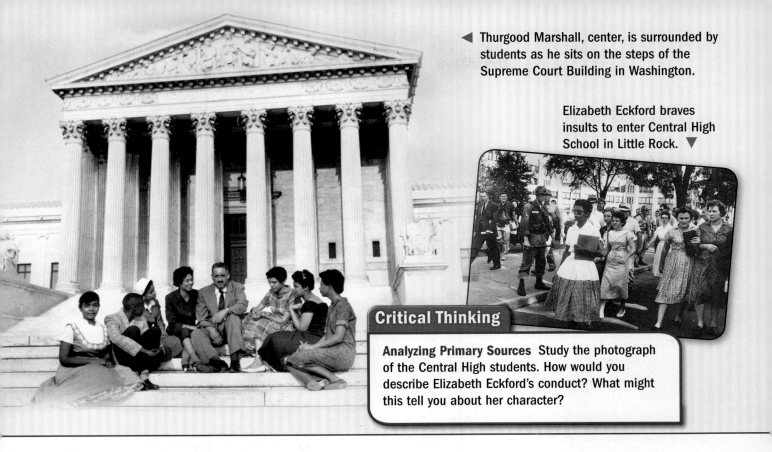

◀ Thurgood Marshall, center, is surrounded by students as he sits on the steps of the Supreme Court Building in Washington.

Elizabeth Eckford braves insults to enter Central High School in Little Rock. ▼

Critical Thinking

Analyzing Primary Sources Study the photograph of the Central High students. How would you describe Elizabeth Eckford's conduct? What might this tell you about her character?

On the first day of classes, armed members of the National Guard blocked the school's entrance and turned away nine African American students. One of them, 15-year-old Elizabeth Eckford, recalled that when she tried to squeeze past a member of the guard, "He raised his bayonet, and then the other guards moved in and raised their bayonets."

For the first time since the Civil War, a Southern state defied the federal government. Although Eisenhower had doubts about the *Brown* decision, he believed he had to enforce the law. The president warned Faubus that if the students were not admitted, the federal government would act.

When a federal judge ruled that the governor had violated the law, Faubus removed the National Guard. Eisenhower sent hundreds of soldiers to Little Rock to patrol the school and protect the students. Shielded by federal troops, the African American students entered the school.

✔ **Reading Check** **Explaining** How had the *Plessy* ruling contributed to segregation?

Gains on Other Fronts

Main Idea The success of the Montgomery bus boycott showed that nonviolent protest could help African Americans secure their rights.

History and You Have you ever tried hard to win over someone to your point of view? Read to learn how African Americans convinced officials in Montgomery, Alabama, to end segregation on city buses.

While school integration continued, African Americans made other advances in securing their rights. More and more took part in a movement dedicated to securing fair and equal treatment. In 1955, events in Montgomery, Alabama, sparked a chain reaction—the beginning of a mass movement that would change American society over the next 20 years.

History ONLINE
Student Web Activity Visit glencoe.com and complete the Chapter 14 Web Activity about school integration.

Rosa Parks

1913–2005
Civil Rights Activist

Parks was a civil rights activist as early as the 1940s, but it was her role in the Montgomery bus boycott that ushered in an era of real change for African Americans. Late in life she said: *"I do the very best I can to look upon life with optimism and hope and looking forward to a better day. . . . [yet] It pains me that there is still a lot of Klan activity and racism."* In 1999 Parks was awarded the highest civilian award in the country, the Congressional Gold Medal.

Dr. Martin Luther King, Jr.

1929–1968
Minister, Civil Rights Activist

In the 1950s, Dr. Martin Luther King, Jr., established himself as one of the main leaders of the civil rights movement. A Baptist minister and stirring speaker, King organized marches, boycotts, and demonstrations that opened many people's eyes to the need for change. In 1964 he was awarded the Nobel Prize for Peace. He said, *"I have the audacity [boldness] to believe that peoples everywhere can have three meals a day for their bodies, education and culture for their minds, and dignity, equality, and freedom for their spirits."* Dr. King was assassinated in 1968 in Memphis, Tennessee.

CRITICAL Thinking

Inferring What do the statements by Parks and King have in common?

The Montgomery Bus Boycott

On the evening of December 1, 1955, **Rosa Parks,** an African American, boarded a bus in downtown Montgomery, Alabama. Parks, a seamstress, was secretary of the local chapter of the NAACP. She found an empty seat in the section reserved for whites.

When white passengers entered the bus, the driver told Parks to move to the rear of the bus. Parks refused. At the next bus stop, she was taken off the bus by police, arrested for breaking the law, and fined $10. The episode could have ended there—but it did not.

Rosa Parks's arrest led African Americans in Montgomery to organize a **boycott**—a refusal to use—the city's buses. The boycott organizers hoped to hurt the city financially and force it to alter its policies. They had strength in numbers—almost 75 percent of the bus company's riders were African American.

At a boycott meeting, a young Baptist minister came forward to speak. Not widely known at the time, **Dr. Martin Luther King, Jr.,** made an impact on the crowd. He declared:

PRIMARY SOURCE

"We are here . . . because first and foremost we are American citizens and we are determined to apply our citizenship to the fullness of its meaning. . . . And you know, . . . there comes a time when people get tired of being trampled over by the iron feet of oppression."
—from *The Papers of Martin Luther King, Jr.*

The boycott upset many people's daily lives, but the African Americans of Montgomery pulled together to make it work.

Students hitchhiked to school; workers walked or rode bikes to their jobs. Dr. King helped organize car pools to shuttle people from place to place.

The bus boycott lasted for more than a year. City officials arrested Dr. King and other leaders at different times, but African Americans held firm. The local bus company lost thousands of dollars in fares, and downtown businesses lost customers. Finally, the Supreme Court settled the matter by ruling that the Montgomery bus segregation law was unconstitutional. In December 1956, the boycott ended.

Nonviolent Protest

With the victory in Montgomery, Dr. King became a leader of the civil rights movement. He followed the tactics of A. Philip Randolph, the nation's most prominent African American labor leader. Dr. King was also strongly influenced by Mohandas Gandhi, who used nonviolent protest to help India gain independence from Great Britain. In keeping with his beliefs, Gandhi used protest methods based on **civil disobedience,** or the refusal to obey laws that are considered unjust. Like Gandhi, Dr. King encouraged his followers to disobey unjust laws without using violence. Believing in people's ability to change themselves, he was certain that the American people would eventually convince the government to end segregation.

Dr. Martin Luther King, Jr., was not the only prominent minister in the bus boycott. Many of the other leaders were African American ministers. The boycott could not have succeeded without the support of the African American churches in the city.

In January 1957, Dr. King and 60 other ministers started a new organization called the Southern Christian Leadership Conference (SCLC). SCLC leaders also emphasized nonviolent protest. They showed civil rights workers how to protect themselves from violent attacks. The SCLC also discussed how to identify targets for protests and how to organize people for support. In taking these steps, the SCLC prepared African Americans for the struggle for equal rights.

Reading Check **Describing** How did the Montgomery bus boycott lead to a change in policy?

Section 1 Review

History ONLINE
Study Central™ To review this section, go to glencoe.com.

Vocabulary

1. Write a paragraph using each of the following terms: discriminate, segregation, civil, integrate, boycott, civil disobedience.

Main Ideas

2. **Comparing** What was the major difference in the ruling of *Plessy* v. *Ferguson* and *Brown* v. *Board of Education*?

3. **Describing** What impact did the Montgomery bus boycott have on securing equal rights for African Americans?

Critical Thinking

4. **Sequencing** On a time line like the one below, sequence the events that led to integration in Little Rock.

5. **Analyzing** What effect did Dr. Martin Luther King, Jr., have on the growth of the civil rights movement?

6. **Persuasive Writing** Take the role of a newspaper editor. Write an editorial that persuades the residents of your city to reject racial segregation.

Answer the Essential Question

7. What were the legal and social challenges to racial segregation in the 1940s and 1950s?

Kennedy and Johnson

Essential Question ◄

How were Kennedy and Johnson alike and different as presidents of the United States?

Reading Guide

Content Vocabulary

poverty line (p. 441)   Medicare (p. 441)

Medicaid (p. 441)

Academic Vocabulary

assign (p. 439)   consist (p. 441)

Key People and Events

John F. Kennedy (p. 439)

New Frontier (p. 440)

Lyndon B. Johnson (p. 440)

Great Society (p. 441)

Job Corps (p. 441)

Civil Rights Act of 1964 (p. 441)

Reading Strategy

Taking Notes On a chart like the one below, list the major aspects of each of these plans.

New Frontier	Great Society

American Diary

The Democratic nominee for president in 1960 was John F. Kennedy. Some people were concerned that, because of his Catholic faith, Kennedy could be influenced by the Pope. Kennedy confronted this issue openly. "I believe in an America where the separation of church and state is absolute," he said, "where no Catholic prelate [church leader] would tell the president (should he be a Catholic) how to act."

—from an address to Southern Baptist leaders

Kennedy campaigns at a July 1960 rally in Los Angeles.

Kennedy and the New Frontier

Main Idea John F. Kennedy's presidency appealed to many Americans who wanted change.

History and You Do you think that one person has the power to change things for the better? Read on to learn how many Americans welcomed the election of a young president in 1960.

In 1960 the nation prepared for a presidential election. The Republican candidate, Vice President Richard M. Nixon, pledged to continue the policies of President Eisenhower. The Democratic candidate, **John F. Kennedy,** promised new programs to "get the country moving again."

For much of the campaign, polls showed Nixon in the lead. One reason for this was the fact that Kennedy was Roman Catholic. No Catholic had ever been president, and many Americans feared that if Kennedy won he might show more loyalty to his church than to his country. Kennedy stressed to the country his belief in the separation of church and state.

A War Hero

Kennedy came from one of the country's wealthiest and most powerful families. His father, Joseph P. Kennedy, was a successful business leader and the American ambassador to Britain at the start of World War II.

John Kennedy joined the United States Navy during World War II and was **assigned,** or appointed, to active duty in the Pacific. When the Japanese sank the PT (patrol torpedo) boat he commanded, Kennedy saved the life of a crew member by swimming to shore with the injured man on his back.

Kennedy's political career began in 1946 when he won a seat in Congress from Massachusetts. Six years later, he was elected to the United States Senate. After easily winning reelection to the Senate in 1958, Kennedy ran for the presidency in 1960.

A New President

The turning point in the 1960 election came when the candidates took part in the first televised presidential debates. Nixon, who was recovering from an illness, looked tired and sick. Kennedy appeared handsome and youthful.

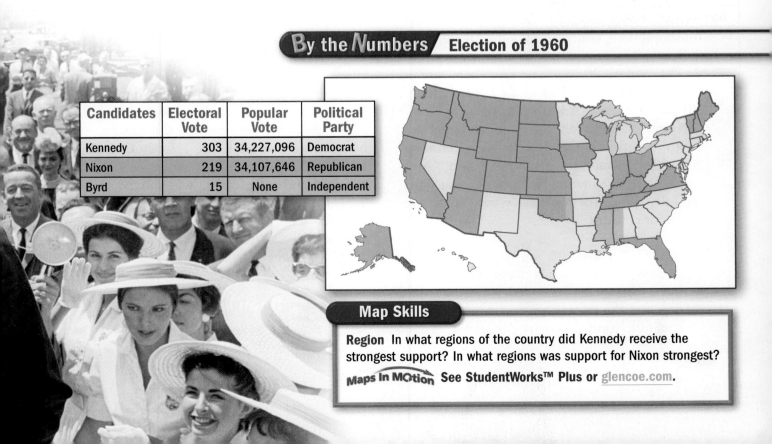

By the Numbers / Election of 1960

Candidates	Electoral Vote	Popular Vote	Political Party
Kennedy	303	34,227,096	Democrat
Nixon	219	34,107,646	Republican
Byrd	15	None	Independent

Map Skills

Region In what regions of the country did Kennedy receive the strongest support? In what regions was support for Nixon strongest?

Maps In Motion See StudentWorks™ Plus or glencoe.com.

Presidential Policies Presidents Kennedy and Johnson expanded civil rights by issuing executive orders and approving laws that affected many areas of African Americans' daily lives.

President Kennedy

- Expanded African American voting
- Increased job opportunities
- Outlawed discrimination in federal housing
- Established Committee on Equal Employment Opportunity

> "We are confronted primarily with a moral issue. . . . The heart of the question is—whether all Americans are to be afforded equal rights and equal opportunities. Whether we are going to treat our fellow Americans as we want to be treated."

President Johnson

- Provided funds to poorer states for education
- Gave federal funding to poor African American colleges
- Signed legislation that outlawed discrimination in registering voters

> "These are the enemies: poverty, ignorance, disease. They are the enemies and not our fellow man, not our neighbor. And these enemies too, poverty, disease and ignorance, we shall overcome."

Critical Thinking

Analyzing How was President Johnson's quote related to civil rights?

During the debate, he spoke with confidence about the future. Many viewers thought that Kennedy made a better impression.

In November, nearly 70 million voters turned out to choose between Nixon and Kennedy. The results were extremely close. In the popular vote, Kennedy won 49.7 percent, while Nixon received 49.5 percent. In the electoral vote, Kennedy gained a greater margin over Nixon—303 to 219 votes.

On January 20, 1961, Kennedy was sworn in as the 35th president of the United States. In his Inaugural Address, the young president promised to face the nation's challenges with determination. In closing, Kennedy roused the American people to action: "And so, my fellow Americans: ask not what your country can do for you—ask what you can do for your country."

Domestic Policies

Kennedy called for a **New Frontier** of social reforms. He backed federal aid for education and the poor. Congress, however, did not want to fund expensive programs.

Kennedy also supported civil rights but feared that moving too quickly would anger Southern Democrats whose support he needed. In 1963 Kennedy's civil rights bill passed in the House but stalled in the Senate.

Kennedy Assassinated

On November 22, 1963, Kennedy arrived in Dallas with his wife, Jacqueline. As the presidential motorcade rode through the streets, shots rang out. Kennedy was shot and later pronounced dead. Vice President **Lyndon B. Johnson** became president.

The assassination stunned the nation. In the midst of the grief, Lee Harvey Oswald, the man charged with the president's killing, was shot and killed as he was moved from one jail to another. A commission, headed by Supreme Court Chief Justice Earl Warren, later stated that Oswald had acted alone. Many people believed that the assassination was a plot.

Reading Check **Describing** What was the turning point in the 1960 election?

The Great Society

Main Idea The Johnson administration expanded Kennedy's domestic plans with far-reaching programs in many areas.

History and You What sort of problems do cities have today? Read to find out about efforts by the federal government to solve these problems.

· ·

President Lyndon B. Johnson outlined a set of programs known as the **"Great Society."** His plan was to reduce poverty, promote equality, improve education, and rebuild decaying cities. Johnson had served 22 years in Congress. He used his legislative skills to persuade Congress to pass these programs.

War on Poverty

In 1964 President Johnson declared the War on Poverty as part of his plan for a Great Society. It **consisted,** or was made up, of programs to help people who lived below the **poverty line**—the minimum income needed to live. For example, Head Start provided preschool education for poor children, and the **Job Corps** trained young people seeking work.

Among the most important laws passed under Johnson were **Medicare** and **Medicaid,** both passed in 1965. Medicare established a health insurance program for all elderly people, financed through the Social Security system. Medicaid provided health and medical assistance to low-income families.

Other parts of the Great Society targeted cities and education. In 1966 the Department of Housing and Urban Development (HUD) was created to fund public housing projects. Another program, Model Cities, provided money to rebuild cities. Schools were helped by the Elementary and Secondary Education Act of 1965.

Although a Southerner, Johnson was not a segregationist and supported civil rights for all Americans. With Johnson's backing, Congress passed the **Civil Rights Act of 1964.** The act banned discrimination against African Americans in employment, voting, and public places. It forbade discrimination not only by race but also by gender, religion, and national origin.

✓ **Reading Check** **Explaining** What was the purpose of the Job Corps?

History ONLINE
Study Central™ To review this section, go to glencoe.com.

Section 2 Review

Vocabulary

1. Write a sentence for each of the following terms that explains its meaning: assign, consist, poverty line, Medicare, Medicaid.

Main Ideas

2. Summarizing What did the Civil Rights Act of 1964 accomplish?

3. Explaining What message did President Kennedy send with his Inaugural Address when he said "ask what you can do for your country"?

Critical Thinking

4. Analyzing Why do you think John F. Kennedy won the 1960 presidential election over Richard M. Nixon?

5. Identifying On a diagram like the one below, list the government plans that were part of Johnson's War on Poverty.

War on Poverty

6. Expository Writing Take the role of an adviser to President Johnson. Write an essay that explains which of the president's domestic policies had the most impact on American citizens.

Answer the
Essential Question

7. How were Kennedy and Johnson alike and different as presidents of the United States?

The Struggle Continues

Essential Question ◄

What areas of civil rights did groups try to improve in the 1960s and what methods did those groups use?

Reading Guide

Content Vocabulary

sit-in (p. 443)   interstate (p. 444)

Academic Vocabulary

register (p. 447)   emerge (p. 448)

Key People and Events

Ella Baker (p. 443)

Robert Kennedy (p. 443)

James Meredith (p. 444)

George Wallace (p. 444)

Medgar Evers (p. 444)

Voting Rights Act of 1965 (p. 447)

Malcolm X (p. 448)

Reading Strategy

Taking Notes Create a diagram to show the major chain of events for the Freedom Riders in 1961.

Freedom Riders

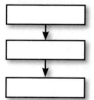

American Diary

On February 1, 1960, four African American students walked into a store in Greensboro, North Carolina. Sitting down at a "whites-only" lunch counter, they were refused service. The students stayed at the counter until the store closed, then stated that they would sit at the counter every day until they were given the same service as white customers. News of the sit-ins spread rapidly. Other students followed their example. Starting with just four students, a new American mass movement for civil rights began.

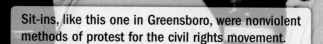
Sit-ins, like this one in Greensboro, were nonviolent methods of protest for the civil rights movement.

The Movement Grows

Main Idea New leaders and groups emerged as the civil rights movement took on new causes.

History and You What do you do if you think you are not being treated fairly? How do you speak out? Read on to learn what actions African Americans took in the 1960s to secure their rights.

. . . .

A new wave of civil rights activity swept across the nation during the Kennedy and Johnson administrations. Early activity targeted segregation in the South. Segregation existed in the North as well.

In Northern urban areas, African Americans and whites often lived in different neighborhoods; as a result, their children often attended different schools. Soon African Americans expanded their goal to fighting discrimination and racism in the North as well as in the South.

High school and college students staged sit-ins in nearly 80 cities. A **sit-in** is the act of protesting by sitting down. Sit-ins were held throughout the nation against stores that practiced segregation. Store managers wanted to end the disturbances and loss of business. Gradually many stores agreed to integrate.

The sit-ins launched a new civil rights group, the Student Nonviolent Coordinating Committee (SNCC). Civil rights activist **Ella Baker** was a guiding spirit behind SNCC and one of its organizers. Earlier, Baker played major roles in both the NAACP and the SCLC. SNCC was a key player in the civil rights cause for several years.

Freedom Rides

The Supreme Court had ruled in 1960 against segregated bus facilities. Another civil rights group, the Congress of Racial Equality (CORE), decided to see if the ruling was being enforced. On May 4, 1961, a group of African Americans and white CORE members left Washington, D.C., on two buses bound for New Orleans. They called themselves Freedom Riders. The trip went smoothly until it reached Alabama, where angry whites stoned and beat the Freedom Riders.

Television and newspapers reported the beatings. The president's brother, **Robert Kennedy,** the United States attorney general, asked CORE to stop the Freedom Rides for a "cooling-off period." CORE leader James Farmer responded: "We have been cooling off for 350 years. If we cool off anymore, we will be in a deep freeze."

Primary Source | **Birth of the SNCC**

Students Organize As the sit-ins spread, student leaders in different states realized they needed to coordinate their efforts. The person who brought them together was Ella Baker, the executive director of the Southern Christian Leadership Conference (SCLC). At a meeting in 1960, Baker urged students to create their own organization instead of joining the NAACP or the SCLC. Baker told them that students had "the right to direct their own affairs and even make their own mistakes." From this beginning was born the Student Nonviolent Coordinating Committee (SNCC).

Ella Baker ▶

Critical Thinking

Explaining What was the purpose of sit-ins?

Violence and Arrests

The Freedom Riders pressed on, only to meet more violence in Birmingham and Montgomery, Alabama. No mobs were waiting for the Freedom Riders in Jackson, Mississippi. However, police, state troopers, and Mississippi National Guard units were everywhere. As the Riders stepped off the bus and tried to enter the whites-only waiting room at the bus station, they were arrested for trespassing and jailed.

Despite the violence and the jail sentences, more Freedom Riders kept coming all summer. In the fall, the Interstate Commerce Commission enforced the Supreme Court ruling, issuing new regulations that banned segregation on **interstate** buses—those that crossed state lines—and in bus stations.

Integrating Universities

African Americans continued to apply pressure to secure their civil rights. They spurred President Kennedy to take a more active role in the civil rights struggle.

In 1962 a federal court ordered the University of Mississippi to enroll its first African American student, **James Meredith.** However, Mississippi Governor Ross Barnett, with the aid of state police, kept Meredith from registering. When President Kennedy sent federal marshals to escort Meredith to the campus, riots erupted. A mob armed with guns and rocks stormed the administration building. The marshals fought back with tear gas and nightsticks. Meredith succeeded in registering, but two people were killed. Federal troops remained at the university to protect him until he graduated in 1963.

Another clash between state and federal power took place in June 1963 in Alabama. Governor **George Wallace** vowed he would "stand in the schoolhouse door" to block the integration of the University of Alabama in Tuscaloosa. President Kennedy, acting on the advice of his brother, Robert, sent the Alabama National Guard to ensure the entry of African Americans to the university. As a result, Wallace backed down.

Birmingham

In the spring of 1963, Dr. Martin Luther King, Jr., and the SCLC targeted Birmingham, Alabama, for a desegregation protest. Police arrested hundreds of demonstrators, including Dr. King, but the demonstrations continued. During Dr. King's two weeks in jail, he wrote the eloquent "Letter from Birmingham Jail," in which he wrote: "We must come to see . . . that justice too long delayed is justice denied."

National television carried vivid pictures of police setting snarling police dogs on unarmed demonstrators and pushing small children across streets with the powerful impact of fire hoses. President Kennedy sent 3,000 troops to restore peace. On June 11, 1963, in Jackson, Mississippi, **Medgar Evers,** the state field secretary for the NAACP, was murdered. The murder and the events in Alabama forced President Kennedy to make a decision. Appearing on national television, Kennedy spoke of the "moral issue" facing the nation:

PRIMARY SOURCE

"It is not enough to pin the blame on others, to say this is a problem of one section of the country or another, or deplore the fact that we face. A great change is at hand, and our task, our obligation, is to make that revolution, that change, peaceful and constructive for all. Those who do nothing are inviting shame as well as violence. Those who act boldly are recognizing right."

—Kennedy's address to the nation, June 1963

Days later, the president introduced new legislation giving all Americans the right to be served in public places and barring discrimination in employment.

March on Washington

To rally support for the civil rights bill, Dr. King and the SCLC organized a massive march on Washington, D.C., on August 28, 1963. More than 200,000 people of all colors and from all over the country arrived to take part in the event.

Primary Source

Letter from Birmingham Jail

On April 16, 1963, from his jail cell in Birmingham, Alabama, Dr. Martin Luther King, Jr., used the margins of a newspaper and scraps of paper to craft a letter. The letter was in response to criticism from a group of white clergy, who wanted him to stop his nonviolent protests and his desegregation efforts. Dr. King's letter, which has been translated into more than 40 languages, serves as a stirring record of the Civil Rights Movement.

▲ Dr. King in jail

"We have waited for more than 340 years for our constitutional and God given rights. . . . We still creep at horse and buggy pace toward gaining a cup of coffee at a lunch counter. Perhaps it is easy for those who have never felt the stinging darts of segregation to say, 'Wait.' But when you have seen vicious mobs lynch your mothers and fathers at will and drown your sisters and brothers at whim; when you have seen hate filled policemen curse, kick and even kill your black brothers and sisters; when you see the vast majority of your twenty million Negro brothers smothering in an airtight cage of poverty in the midst of an **affluent** society; when you suddenly find your tongue twisted and your speech stammering as you seek to explain to your six year old daughter why she can't go to the public amusement park that has just been advertised on television, . . . then you will understand why we find it difficult to wait. . . .

. . . Let us all hope that the dark clouds of racial prejudice will soon pass away and the deep fog of misunderstanding will be lifted from our fear drenched communities, and in some not too distant tomorrow the radiant stars of love and brotherhood will shine over our great nation with all their **scintillating** beauty.

Yours for the cause of Peace and Brotherhood,
Martin Luther King, Jr."

Dr. King is referring to the settlers who arrived, in what would become the United States, in the 1600s.

He was responding to those who said that African Americans needed to move more slowly in their efforts to desegregate.

Unequal opportunities, when it came to jobs and education, trapped many African Americans in a state of poverty. The frustration was increased by the fact that many whites had opportunities that African Americans were not given.

VOCABULARY

affluent (A•FLOO•uhnt): wealthy
scintillating SIHN•tuhl•AYT•ihng: sparkling, dazzling

Critical Thinking

Interpreting King's letter was seen as a source of hope for African Americans fighting for equality. How does the letter convey that hope? Give examples.

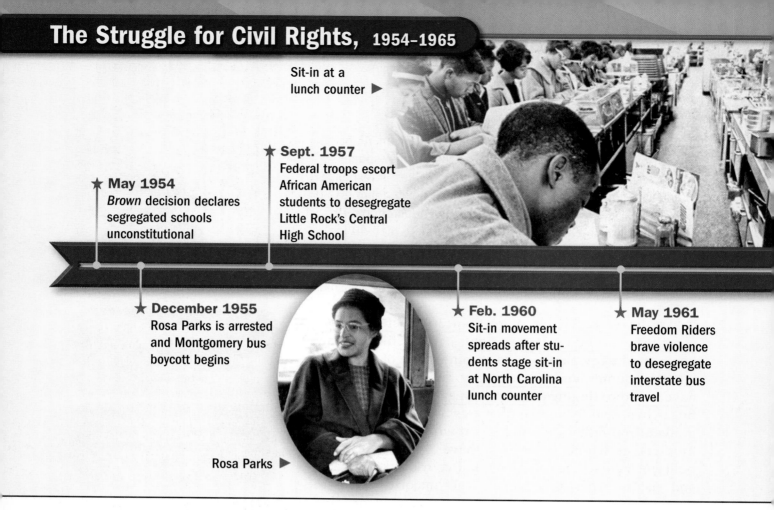

The Struggle for Civil Rights, 1954–1965

Sit-in at a lunch counter ▶

May 1954
Brown decision declares segregated schools unconstitutional

Sept. 1957
Federal troops escort African American students to desegregate Little Rock's Central High School

December 1955
Rosa Parks is arrested and Montgomery bus boycott begins

Feb. 1960
Sit-in movement spreads after students stage sit-in at North Carolina lunch counter

May 1961
Freedom Riders brave violence to desegregate interstate bus travel

Rosa Parks ▶

Nan Grogan Orrock has served in the Georgia Senate and House of Representatives. As a college student in 1963, Orrock describes how she felt at the march on Washington:

Primary Source

"You couldn't help but get swept up in the feeling of the March. It was an incredible experience of this mass of humanity with one mind moving down the street. It was like being part of a glacier. You could feel the sense of collective [united] will and effort in the air."

—from *Like a Mighty Stream*

About 6,000 police officers stood nearby, but they had nothing to do but direct traffic. There was no trouble. Proceeding peacefully through Washington with great dignity and joy, the marchers carried signs urging Congress to act. They sang songs, including the one that became the anthem of the civil

rights movement: "We Shall Overcome." Late in the afternoon, Dr. King delivered a powerful speech. He spoke to the crowd of his desire to see America transformed:

Primary Source

"I have a dream that one day this nation will rise up and live out the true meaning of its creed: 'We hold these truths to be self-evident; that all men are created equal.' . . . When we [let] freedom ring, . . . we will be able to speed up that day when all of God's children, . . . [will] join hands and sing in the words of the old . . . spiritual: Free at last! Free at last! Thank God Almighty, we are free at last!"

—from the "I Have a Dream" speech

Freedom Summer

Congress did not pass Kennedy's civil rights bill until after his death. President Lyndon B. Johnson persuaded Congress to pass the bill after he had taken over the office.

Birmingham police use hoses to force civil rights protestors to stop their marches. ▶

★ **Sept. 1962**
James Meredith tries to register at University of Mississippi

★ **Aug. 1963**
King delivers "I Have a Dream" speech during March on Washington

★ **March 1965**
King leads march in Selma, Alabama, to build support for new voting rights law

★ **May 1963** Police use force to stop Birmingham marchers

★ **July 1964**
President Johnson signs Civil Rights Act of 1964 into law

★ **Aug. 1965**
Congress passes Voting Rights Act of 1965

◀ National Guard escorts Freedom Riders

Critical Thinking

Analyzing What action did African Americans take in 1960 in the struggle for equal rights?

The Civil Rights Act of 1964 outlawed discrimination in hiring and ended segregation in stores, restaurants, theaters, and hotels. Yet, in many states, poll taxes and other discriminatory laws prevented African Americans from exercising their right to vote.

During the summer of 1964, thousands of civil rights workers spread throughout the South to help African Americans **register,** or enroll, to vote. They called the campaign Freedom Summer, but the workers faced strong, sometimes violent, opposition.

The Right to Vote

The next year SNCC organized a major demonstration in Selma, Alabama, to protest the continued denial of African Americans' right to vote. Police attacked and beat many of the demonstrators.

President Johnson stepped in. On March 15, 1965, in a televised speech, the president urged passage of a voting rights bill. "About this there can be no argument," he said. "Every American citizen must have an equal right to vote." In August, Johnson signed the **Voting Rights Act of 1965** into law. The act gave the federal government the power to force local officials to allow African Americans to register to vote.

The act led to dramatic changes in the political life of the South. In 1966 about 100 African Americans held elective office in Southern states. By 1972 that number had increased 10 times.

After passage of the Voting Rights Act, the civil rights movement shifted its focus. It began to pay more attention to the problems of African Americans trapped in poverty and living in major cities.

✔ **Reading Check** **Explaining** What was the goal of the Freedom Riders?

The Civil Rights Era **Chapter 14** **447**

"The common goal of 22 million Afro-Americans is respect as human beings, the God-given right to be a human being. Our common goal is to obtain the human rights that America has been denying us. We can never get civil rights in America until our human rights are first restored. We will never be recognized as citizens there until we are first recognized as humans."

—from "Racism: the Cancer that is Destroying America"

Critical Thinking

Interpreting What did Malcolm X mean when he said, "We can never get civil rights in America until our human rights are first restored"?

Other Voices

Main Idea Some African American leaders differed with Dr. King's strategy of nonviolent protest.

History and You What causes people to act violently? Read to find out why some African Americans took radical, even violent, stands during the mid-1960s.

By the mid-1960s, the civil rights movement had won numerous victories. Yet a growing number of African Americans grew tired of the slow pace of change and bitter over white attacks.

Malcolm X, born Malcolm Little in Omaha, Nebraska, **emerged**—rose up—as an important new voice for some African Americans. He was a leader in the Nation of Islam, commonly known as the Black Muslims. Malcolm X criticized the civil rights goal of integration, declaring that the best way for African Americans to achieve justice was to separate themselves from whites.

Malcolm X gained increasing support. By 1965, however, he began to change his ideas.

Instead of racial separation, he called for "a society in which there could exist honest white-black brotherhood." Soon afterwards he was killed by a rival group among the Black Muslims. His fiery words and passionate ideas, contained in his writings, continued to influence the civil rights movement after his death.

Black Power

Other African American leaders embraced more radical approaches. Stokely Carmichael, who became the leader of SNCC, advanced the idea of Black Power. This was a philosophy of racial pride that said African Americans should create their own culture and political institutions. Carmichael and other radicals called at times for revolution, a complete transformation of society. Although rejected by groups such as the NAACP, the idea of Black Power had a great impact on the civil rights movement. It became popular in the poor urban neighborhoods where many African Americans lived.

In Oakland, California, young radicals formed the Black Panther Party. The Panthers symbolized growing tension between African Americans and urban police. Large numbers of urban African Americans felt frustrated about poverty and a lack of jobs. The Panthers demanded reforms and armed themselves. Several clashes with the police occurred.

Violence Erupts

The first major urban riots since the 1940s took place in the summer of 1965 in the Watts section of Los Angeles. In a week of rioting, 34 people died and much of Watts burned to the ground. National Guard troops were called in to end the uprising.

The Watts riot was the first of a series of racial disorders that hit cities in the summers of 1965, 1966, and 1967. In July 1967, five days of protests, looting, and burning in Newark, New Jersey, ended with the deaths of 26 people and more than $10 million in damage. The next week, an uprising in Detroit shut down the city for several days. The governor of Michigan, who viewed the burning city from a helicopter, remarked that Detroit looked like "a city that had been bombed." President Johnson named a commission to study the causes of the riots and to suggest steps to improve conditions. The report of this group, the Kerner Commission, warned that "our nation is moving toward two societies, one black, one white—separate and unequal."

Dr. King Is Assassinated

On April 4, 1968, racial tension in the United States took another tragic turn. On that night in Memphis, Tennessee, an assassin shot and killed Dr. Martin Luther King, Jr. His murder set off riots in more than 100 cities. Fires burned in the nation's capital, just blocks from the White House.

Thousands of people attended Dr. King's funeral in Atlanta. Millions more watched on television. All mourned the death of an American hero who, the night before his death, said God "has allowed me to go up to the mountain, and I've seen the promised land. I may not get there with you. But I want you to know tonight, that we, as a people, will get to the promised land!"

Reading Check **Explaining** Why did some African Americans criticize integration?

Section 3 Review

Vocabulary

1. Use each of the terms in a sentence that will help explain its meaning: sit-in, interstate, register, emerge.

Main Ideas

2. **Discussing** What did the organizers of the 1963 march on Washington hope to accomplish?

3. **Identifying** Who was Malcolm X, and what was his philosophy?

Critical Thinking

4. **Analyzing** On a chart like the one below, list what each act was meant to achieve.

Civil Rights Act of 1964	
Voting Rights Act of 1965	

5. **Speculating** How would the civil rights struggle have been different if violence across America had not played a part in it?

6. **Descriptive Writing** Describe what happened across the nation when Dr. Martin Luther King, Jr., was assassinated.

Answer the
7. **Essential Question**
What areas of civil rights did groups try to improve in the 1960s, and what methods did those groups use?

America's LITERATURE

Meet the Author

Christopher Paul Curtis (1953–) was born and raised in Flint, Michigan, the setting for much of *The Watsons Go to Birmingham—1963*. Though the story is not autobiographical, Curtis admits that the characters are composites of his own family. Curtis was ten years old and living in Flint in 1963, when four African American girls were killed in a Birmingham church bombing.

Building Background

Nine-year-old Kenny and his family have driven from Flint, Michigan, to Birmingham, Alabama, to visit Kenny's grandmother. During their visit, white men bomb an African American church filled with worshippers. After the bombing, Kenny searches for his sister, Joetta, who was attending services that morning. Several days before the bombing, Kenny swam in dangerous waters and was saved from a whirlpool by his brother. In the rubble of the bombed church, Kenny faces the monstrous "Wool Pooh."

Vocabulary

bobby pin hair clip

wall socket electrical plug

THE WATSONS GO TO BIRMINGHAM—1963

Christopher Paul Curtis

I started going to sleep under the tree and thought I was dreaming when the noise came.

I felt it more than heard it. The giant old magnolia tree shook one time like something had given it a hard snatch by the roots. Then there was a sound like a far-off thunderstorm coming. Except it only thundered one long time.

It seemed like every animal and bird and bug in Birmingham stopped making noise for about two seconds. It seemed like everything that was alive stopped whatever it was doing and was wondering the same thing: What was that noise?

Doors opened in the neighborhood and people came out and looked up in the sky but there was nothing there, not one cloud, nothing to give a clue to what the big hollow sound was, nothing but bright, hot, stupid Alabama sun. . . .

I leaned back against the tree and closed my eyes. I don't know if I got to sleep or not but Momma's scream made me jump nearly to the magnolia's top branch. I'd never heard Momma's voice sound so bad. I felt like I did that time I stuck a **bobby pin** in a **wall socket.**

I ran to the door and into the house and By almost knocked me over running back toward the bedroom.

"What's wrong with Momma?" I asked.

I looked in the living room but Momma and Dad weren't there. I ran back to the bedroom, where Byron was trying to wrestle into a pair of pants.

"By! What happened?"

He got the pants up and said, "A guy just came by and said somebody dropped a bomb on Joey's church." And he was gone, exploding out of the front door trying to zip up his pants at the same time he ran off the porch. . . .

. . . It looked like a river of scared brown bodies was being jerked in the same direction that By had gone, so I followed.

I guess my ears couldn't take it so they just stopped listening. I could see people everywhere making their mouths go like they were screaming and pointing and yelling but I didn't hear anything. I saw Momma and Dad and Byron holding on to each other, all three of them looking like they were crazy and trying to keep each other away from the pile of rocks that used to be the front of the church. . . .

I got right next to where the door used to be when the guy came out with a little girl in his arms. He had on the same thing Dad did, a T-shirt and pajama pants, but it looked like he'd been painting with red, red paint. The little girl had on a blue dress and little blue frilly socks and black shiny, shiny shoes.

I looked into the church and saw smoke and dust flying around like a tornado was in there. One light from the ceiling was still hanging down by a wire, flickering and swinging back and forth, and every once in a while I could see stuff inside. . . . I could see a shiny, shiny black shoe lying halfway underneath some concrete, then it got covered with smoke, and then the lightbulb flickered out again.

I bent down to pull the shoe from under the concrete and tugged and pulled at it but it felt like something was pulling it back.

All the hair on my head jumped up to attention. The light flickered back on and the smoke cleared and I could see that hanging on to the other end of the shoe was a giant gray hand with cold, hard square fingers.

Oh-oh. . . . The Wool Pooh.

Analyzing Literature

1. **Respond** What descriptions in the scene remind you that the narrator is a child?

2. **Recall and Analyze**
   (a) What is the "red, red paint" on the man's pajamas?
   (b) Who is pulling on the shoe besides Kenny?

3. **Evaluate**
   (a) What does the Wool Pooh symbolize in this scene?
   (b) Why might the author use the Wool Pooh, which almost took Kenny's life in the water, as a symbol at the church bombing?

Other Groups Seek Rights

How did the civil rights movement affect minorities other than African Americans?

Reading Guide

Content Vocabulary

feminist *(p. 453)*   Latino *(p. 454)*

Academic Vocabulary

aspect *(p. 453)*   diverse *(p. 454)*

Key People and Events

National Organization for Women *(p. 453)*

Equal Rights Amendment *(p. 453)*

Sandra Day O'Connor *(p. 453)*

César Chávez *(p. 454)*

American Indian Movement *(p. 456)*

Reading Strategy

Taking Notes In a diagram like the one below, list the early successes of the NOW organization.

American Diary

By the early 1960s, many women had grown dissatisfied with their roles. Those who worked outside the home had fewer opportunities. Many women were increasingly resentful of a world where newspaper ads were separated into "Help Wanted—Women" and "Help Wanted—Men." Married women could not get credit cards in their own names. Worst of all, women were paid less than men for the same work. As more women entered the workforce, protests for equal treatment grew louder.

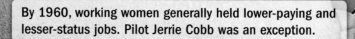

By 1960, working women generally held lower-paying and lesser-status jobs. Pilot Jerrie Cobb was an exception.

Women's Rights

Main Idea The influence of the civil rights movement led many American women to organize and push for greater rights and opportunities.

History and You Policies are supposed to ensure that people are treated fairly. How would you feel about policies that kept women from having the same rights as men? Read to find out how women in the 1960s and 1970s worked for change.

. . . .

During the 1960s, the movement for civil rights reached women, Latinos, Native Americans, and people with disabilities. Women were the first to benefit. In 1963 Congress passed the Equal Pay Act, which prohibited employers from paying women less than men for the same work.

That same year, in a book called *The Feminine Mystique*, Betty Friedan, herself a wife and mother, described the hopes of many women for greater opportunities in society. In 1966 **feminists**—activists for women's rights—created the **National Organization for Women** (NOW). NOW fought for equal rights for women in all aspects, or categories, of life—jobs, education, and marriage.

In the early 1970s, NOW began a campaign for an **Equal Rights Amendment** (ERA) to the Constitution. The amendment stated that "equality of rights under the law shall not be denied or abridged by the United States or by any state on account of sex." Phyllis Schlafly and other foes of the ERA warned that the amendment would upset traditional social roles and lead to the breakdown of the family. In the end, not enough states ratified the amendment to make it law.

Despite the ERA's defeat, progress was made. Women gained more job opportunities, and more women rose to higher-level jobs in their companies. More women than ever became doctors and lawyers.

Women also filled local and state political offices. Women won seats in Congress and were named to the president's Cabinet. In 1981 President Ronald Reagan appointed **Sandra Day O'Connor** as the first female justice of the U.S. Supreme Court.

Reading Check **Explaining** What was the purpose of the Equal Pay Act?

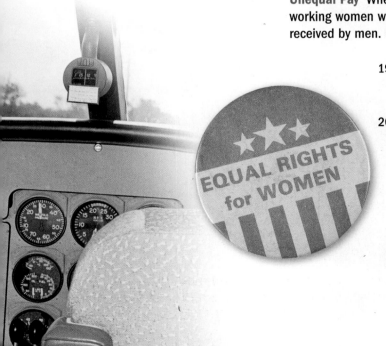

By the Numbers / Women's Pay

Unequal Pay When the Equal Pay Act was passed in 1963, full-time working women were paid 59 cents an hour on average for every dollar received by men. How do these figures compare some 40 years later?

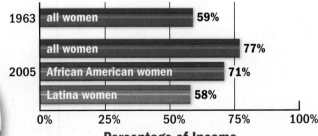

Year	Group	Percentage
1963	all women	59%
2005	all women	77%
2005	African American women	71%
2005	Latina women	58%

Percentage of Income Compared to That of Men

Source: U.S. Census Bureau, American Community Survey

Critical Thinking

Explaining What challenges did women face in the workforce in the early 1960s?

Seeking Greater Opportunity

Main Idea In the 1960s and 1970s, Hispanic Americans, Native Americans, and disabled Americans entered the struggle for equality.

History and You Have you ever refused to buy something in order to protest a certain price or policy? Read to find out how migrant farmworkers, fighting for better wages and working conditions, urged people to use this method.

• •

In the 1960s, the **Latino** (often called Hispanic) population sought equal rights. The term *Hispanic American* refers to Americans who have come, or are descended from others who have come, to the United States from the countries of Latin America and Spain.

Americans of Mexican heritage have lived in the United States since before the nation was founded. In the twentieth century, immigration from Mexico and Latin America rose dramatically. The Latino population in the United States rose from 3 million in 1960 to 42.7 million by 2005. Although they share the heritage of the Spanish culture and language, Latinos are a **diverse** (differing from one another) group with different histories.

Farmworkers Organize

By far the largest Latino group in the United States comes from Mexico. By 2005 more than 21 million Mexican Americans were living in the United States.

The fight for rights started among Mexican American migrant farmworkers, who faced great hardships. The migrant farmworkers did backbreaking work, laboring from dawn until dusk for low wages. When one job ended, they had to travel from farm to farm in search of the next job.

In the early 1960s, migrant workers formed unions to fight for better wages and working conditions. Their leader, **César Chávez,** organized thousands of farmworkers into the United Farm Workers (UFW). The union went on strike and organized boycotts. Consumers across the country supported the UFW by refusing to buy grapes, lettuce, and other farm produce under boycott. The success of the boycotts enabled the UFW to win higher

Primary Source / Protests and Progress

Organizing for Rights From the early 1960s into the 1970s, minorities in America began to organize into groups to voice their concerns to the government over fair treatment and better opportunities. Each group made different demands, but ultimately their goal was the same: a better quality of life.

Beginning in the 1960s, UFW cofounder César Chávez organized successful nationwide boycotts of non-union-picked produce. ▶

In the 1973 takeover of Wounded Knee, American Indian Movement (AIM) leaders Russell Means and Dennis Banks, along with others, protested the living conditions and treatment of Native Americans.

wages and shorter working hours for many farmworkers.

After the union boycott, Latinos made other gains. They joined together in an organization called La Raza Unida to fight discrimination and to elect Latinos to government posts. The League of United Latin American Citizens (LULAC) won lawsuits to guarantee Latinos the right to serve on juries and to send their children to integrated schools.

Puerto Ricans and Cubans

Puerto Ricans, another Latino group, come from the Caribbean island of Puerto Rico, a commonwealth of the United States. They are American citizens who have made major contributions to the United States.

In 1970 the first representative to Congress of Puerto Rican origin, Herman Badillo, was elected from New York City. Badillo later served as the city's deputy mayor. Baseball great Roberto Clemente was a hero on and off the baseball diamond. In 1972 he died in a plane crash while delivering relief supplies to earthquake victims in Nicaragua.

▲ Beginning in the 1960s, people with physical disabilities demanded—sometimes through protest—better access to stadiums, restaurants, and other public buildings.

Critical Thinking

Making Inferences How did boycotts and protests help minority groups better their lives?

Because Puerto Rico is not a wealthy island, many Puerto Ricans have migrated to American cities, such as New York City, in search of jobs. As with African Americans, Puerto Ricans have often faced discrimination in the job market.

After Cuba's revolution in 1959, dictator Fidel Castro set up a Communist government. More than 200,000 people opposed to Castro fled to the United States in the 1960s. Thousands more came in the 1980s. These immigrants settled all over the United States. The largest number of Cubans settled in southern Florida, where they have established a thriving community.

Native Americans Organize

After World War II, Native Americans experienced many changes. In the 1950s, the federal government began urging Native Americans to leave the reservations and to work in cities. Federal policy also tried to weaken the power of tribal government.

These efforts did not improve the lives of Native Americans. Many could not find jobs in the cities. Those still crowded on reservations had few jobs or other opportunities. More than one-third of Native Americans lived below the poverty line.

In the 1960s, Native Americans organized to improve their lives. They demanded political power and independence from the U.S. government. Native Americans emphasized their own histories, languages, and cultures in their schools. The National Congress of American Indians (NCAI) sought more control over Native American affairs.

The federal government responded to these issues. Congress passed the Indian Civil Rights Act of 1968, which protected the constitutional rights of all Native Americans. The new law also recognized the right of Native American nations to make laws on their reservations.

Supreme Court decisions in the 1970s reaffirmed the independence of tribal governments. They also confirmed Native Americans' rights to land granted in treaties.

American Indian Movement

Believing change was too slow, some younger Native Americans took stronger actions. In 1968 a group set up the **American Indian Movement** (AIM), which worked for equal rights and improved living conditions. AIM was founded by Clyde Bellecourt, Dennis Banks, and others. Later Russell Means became a leader. AIM carried out several protests. In November 1969, AIM was one of the Native American groups that took over Alcatraz Island, a former prison in San Francisco Bay. AIM wanted the island to serve as a cultural center. The incident ended in June 1971 when the groups surrendered.

In the fall of 1972, AIM occupied the Bureau of Indian Affairs in Washington, D.C. They demanded the lands and rights guaranteed under treaties with the United States. They surrendered the building after officials agreed to review their complaints.

In February 1973, AIM occupied Wounded Knee, South Dakota, the site of the 1890 massacre of Sioux by federal troops. In the early 1970s, Wounded Knee was part of a Sioux reservation. The people there suffered from terrible poverty and ill health.

AIM leaders vowed to stay until the government investigated the treatment of Native Americans. The siege ended, but it focused attention on the conditions under which Native Americans lived.

Americans With Disabilities

People with physical disabilities also sought equal treatment in the 1960s and the 1970s. Congress responded by passing a number of laws.

One law concerned the removal of barriers that prevented some people from gaining access to public facilities. Another required employers to offer more opportunities for disabled people in the workplace. The Education for All Handicapped Children Act (1975) asserted the right of children with disabilities to equal educational opportunity. Schools must also provide special services to meet their needs. As a result of these actions, people with disabilities enjoy more job opportunities, better access to public facilities, and a greater role in society.

Reading Check **Analyzing** Why did the American Indian Movement form?

History ONLINE
Study Central™ To review this section, go to glencoe.com.

Section 4 Review

Vocabulary

1. Use each of these terms in a sentence that tells how it relates to the civil rights movement: feminist, aspect, Latino, diverse.

Main Ideas

2. Discussing What was the Equal Rights Amendment, and why was it challenged by some?

3. Explaining What did César Chávez achieve for Latinos?

Critical Thinking

4. Contrasting Contrast the experiences of Puerto Rican and Cuban immigrants.

5. Sequencing On a time line like the one below, sequence important events of the AIM group in these years.

1968   1969   1972   1973

6. Creative Writing Imagine you are a physically disabled person who has been denied a job because of your disability. Write a letter to your U.S. representative in which you explain how you feel about this situation and what should be done about it.

Answer the
7. Essential Question
How did the civil rights movement affect minorities other than African Americans?

African Americans and Civil Rights

Changes brought about by the civil rights movement are still with us.

- *Brown* v. *Board of Education of Topeka, Kansas* attacks school segregation.
- Rosa Parks inspires Montgomery bus boycott.
- Freedom rides, the Birmingham demonstrations, and the march on Washington help build support for the civil rights movement.
- The Civil Rights Act (1964) outlaws discrimination based on race, gender, and religion, and gives equal access to public facilities.
- The Voting Rights Act (1965) ensures African Americans of the right to vote.

Latino and Native American Advances

Minority groups developed new ways to improve their status in the United States.

- La Raza Unida and the LULAC fight for education, employment, and government participation rights.
- César Chávez leads farm workers to gain better wages and improve working conditions.
- The Indian Civil Rights Act of 1968 recognizes the laws the Native American nations make on their own lands.
- The American Indian Movement works for improved equal rights and living conditions.

Women Fight for Equal Rights

During the 1960s and 1970s, a large number of American women organized to push for greater rights and opportunities.

- Equal Pay Act (1963)
- National Organization for Women (NOW) forms
- Equal Rights Amendment (ERA) proposed but failed to pass

Americans With Disabilities

People with disabilities sought equal rights and treatment in the 1960s and 1970s.

- Gain access to public facilities
- Gain more opportunities in the workplace
- Claim right of children with disabilities to equal education

STUDY TO GO Study anywhere, anytime! Download quizzes and flash cards to your PDA from glencoe.com.

STANDARDIZED TEST PRACTICE

Reviewing Main Ideas

Directions: Choose the best answers for each of the following questions.

1. Who argued against "separate but equal" schools before the Supreme Court?

A Earl Warren

B James Farmer

C George Houser

D Thurgood Marshall

2. How did Johnson expand on Kennedy's plans to help people with low incomes?

A by establishing Medicare

B by setting up Model Cities

C by introducing the Job Corps

D by pushing through the Civil Rights Act

3. What cause did civil rights workers take on during Freedom Summer in 1964?

A voter registration in the South

B enforcement of bus desegregation

C integration of Southern universities

D discrimination in employment and housing

4. La Raza Unida was formed to

A organize farmworkers.

B demand equal pay for equal work.

C elect Latinos to government office.

D extend voting rights to Spanish speakers.

Short-Answer Question

Directions: Base your answer to question 5 on the graph below and on your knowledge of social studies.

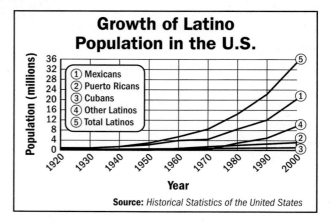

Growth of Latino Population in the U.S.

① Mexicans
② Puerto Ricans
③ Cubans
④ Other Latinos
⑤ Total Latinos

Population (millions) / Year

Source: *Historical Statistics of the United States*

5. Why have Latinos experienced a growing political influence in recent years?

Review the Essential Questions

6. Essay How did political, student, and labor leaders respond to different groups' demands for more rights and opportunities?

To help you write your essay, review your answers to the Essential Questions in the section reviews and the chapter Foldables Study Organizer. Your essay should include:

- names of political, student, and labor leaders during the 1940s, 1950s, and 1960s;
- names of organizations formed to meet the demands of struggling Americans; and
- descriptions of the interaction between leaders and organizations.

GO ON

History ONLINE

For additional test practice, use **Self-Check Quizzes**—Chapter 14 at glencoe.com.

Document-Based Questions

Directions: Analyze the documents and answer the short-answer questions that follow.

Document 1

James Baldwin wrote about the experiences of African Americans in novels such as *Go Tell It on the Mountain* and *If Beale Street Could Talk.*

> I love America more than any other country in the world, and, exactly for this reason, I insist on the right to criticize her perpetually.

Source: James Baldwin, "Notes of a Native Son"

7. What were two major reasons that Americans like James Baldwin criticized the United States?

Document 2

President Kennedy made the following remark in a speech given on May 18, 1963.

> Liberty without learning is always in peril, and learning without liberty is always in vain.

Source: John F. Kennedy Presidential Library & Museum

8. Which of Kennedy's proposals for the New Frontier addressed the concerns in this quote?

Document 3

Malcolm X explained his view on racism in a speech entitled, "Prospects for Freedom in 1965."

> My religion makes me against all forms of racism. It keeps me from judging any man by the color of his skin. It teaches me to judge him by his deeds and conscious behavior. And it teaches me to be for the rights of all human beings.

Source: John Bartlett, *Familiar Quotations*

9. Compare the views Malcolm X held before 1965 with the view expressed in the quote.

Document 4

Voter Registration Before and After the Voting Rights Act

7% of African American adults registered to vote in Mississippi before passage of the Voting Rights Act of 1965

▼

67% of African American adults in Mississippi registered to vote in 1969

70% of white adults registered to vote nationwide in 1964

▼

90% of white adults registered to vote nationwide in 1969

Source: *TIME* magazine

10. Do you think the Voting Rights Act was strongly enforced in Mississippi? Why or why not?

Document 5

Betty Friedan wrote about the effects of a high birthrate.

> By the end of the fifties, the United States birthrate was overtaking India's. . . . Where once [college women] had two children, now they had four, five, six. Women who had once wanted careers were now making careers out of having babies.

Source: Betty Friedan, *The Feminine Mystique*

11. Did Friedan approve or disapprove of the trend she described in this quote? Explain.

12. Descriptive Writing Using the information from the five documents and your knowledge of social studies, write an essay in which you:

• describe a vision of American life that all the people quoted would approve of; and

• compare this vision with your observations of life in the United States today.

Need Extra Help?												
If you missed questions...	1	2	3	4	5	6	7	8	9	10	11	12
Go to page...	434	441	446	455	454–455	433–437	433	440	448	447	453	442–456

The Vietnam Era 1960-1975

After spending five years as a prisoner of war in North Vietnam, Air Force Lt. Col. Robert Stirm is reunited with his family.

PRESIDENTS

U.S. Events

World Events

JOHN F. KENNEDY

★ 1962
Cuban missile crisis erupts

LYNDON B. JOHNSON

★ 1964
• Gulf of Tonkin resolution passes
• Johnson elected president

★ 1965
U.S. sends troops to Vietnam

1960

1964

★ 1961
Berlin Wall erected

1966 ★
Mao Zedong launches Cultural Revolution

Section 1: Kennedy's Foreign Policy

Essential Question What were the key foreign policy challenges the United States faced during the Kennedy administration?

Section 2: War in Vietnam

Essential Question How and why did America involve itself in the war in Vietnam?

Section 3: The Vietnam Years at Home

Essential Question How did the Vietnam War affect the political and social climate in the United States?

Section 4: Nixon and Vietnam

Essential Question How did President Nixon remove the United States from the Vietnam War?

History ONLINE
Chapter Overview Visit glencoe.com and click on **Chapter 15—Chapter Overviews** to preview chapter information.

FOLDABLES Study Organizer

Organizing Information

Make this Foldable to help organize what you learn about foreign policy challenges during the Vietnam years.

Step 1 Fold the sides of a piece of paper into the middle to make a shutterfold.

Step 2 Cut each flap at the midpoint to form four tabs.

Step 3 Label the tabs as shown.

| Bay of Pigs | Berlin Wall |
| Cuban Missile Crisis | Vietnam Conflict |

Reading and Writing As you read the chapter, list key people, events, and outcomes for each of these foreign policy issues.

American soldier equipped for battle ▶

1968 ★
Martin Luther King, Jr., assassinated

1968 ★
Robert Kennedy assassinated; Nixon elected president

RICHARD M. NIXON

★ 1969
Neil Armstrong becomes first human on the moon

★ 1973
Last U.S. troops leave Vietnam

1968　　　**1972**　　　**1976**

★ 1967
Arab-Israeli Six-Day War fought

1971 ★
Idi Amin seizes power in Uganda

★ 1972
11 Israeli athletes killed at Munich Olympic Games

★ 1975
Vietnam War ends after fall of Saigon

Essential Question

What were the key foreign policy challenges the United States faced during the Kennedy administration?

Reading Guide

Content Vocabulary

guerrilla warfare (p. 463)

executive order (p. 464)

flexible response (p. 463)

blockade (p. 466)

Academic Vocabulary

respond (p. 463)

occur (p. 465)

Key People and Events

Fidel Castro (p. 464)

Bay of Pigs (p. 465)

Berlin Wall (p. 465)

Cuban missile crisis (p. 466)

Reading Strategy

Taking Notes On a diagram like the one below, note the different areas of work in which Peace Corps volunteers were involved.

Peace Corps Work

American Diary

"In the long history of the world, only a few generations have been granted the role of defending freedom in its hour of maximum danger. I do not shrink from this responsibility—I welcome it." Although President Kennedy talked of approaching this responsibility with "energy" and "devotion," events unfolding around the world—in Cuba, Eastern Europe, and Vietnam—would challenge his determination. The new president and the nation soon faced a series of crises.

—from Kennedy's Inaugural Address

President Kennedy called the green beret worn by one of the nation's special military forces "a symbol of excellence, a badge of courage, a mark of distinction in the fight for freedom."

New Directions

Main Idea President John F. Kennedy sought new ways to deal with the challenges and fears of the Cold War.

History and You Have you ever heard the phrase "winning hearts and minds"? It means convincing people to support you rather than just forcing them to obey. Read on to learn how the United States used "good works" to convince the world's poor countries to reject communism.

. . . .

When Kennedy became president in 1961, America's dangerous rivalry with the Soviets continued to be a major challenge. As a result, the new president had to devote much of his energy in foreign policy to guiding the nation through the deepening Cold War. President Kennedy continued the anti-Communist foreign policy begun under Presidents Truman and Eisenhower. In pursuing that policy, though, Kennedy tried some new approaches.

During the presidential campaign, Kennedy led Americans to believe that the nation had fewer nuclear missiles than the Soviet Union. As president, Kennedy increased spending on nuclear arms. At the same time, he tried to convince Nikita Khrushchev, the Soviet leader, to agree to a ban on nuclear testing.

Strength Through Flexibility

Kennedy also worked to improve America's ability to **respond**—or reply with action— to threats abroad. In certain areas of the world, Communist groups fought to take control of their nations' governments. Many of these groups received aid from the Soviet Union. They employed **guerrilla warfare,** or fighting with small bands of soldiers who use tactics such as sudden ambushes.

The United States needed a new approach for fighting guerrilla wars. Kennedy introduced a plan called **flexible response,** to provide help to nations fighting Communist movements. This plan relied on special military units trained to fight guerrilla wars. One of these units was the Special Forces, known as the Green Berets. The Special Forces provided the president with troops that were ready to fight guerrilla warfare anywhere around the world.

Primary Source / U.S.–Soviet Relations

In a letter to Premier Nikita Khrushchev of the Soviet Union, President Kennedy expressed the need for direct communication between the leaders. "I think we should recognize, in honesty to each other, that there are problems on which we may not be able to agree."

Kennedy suggested a "hot line" to communicate quickly and directly between the United States and the Soviet Union in times of crisis. The original hot line was a teletypewriter. The hot line today uses two satellite systems and an undersea cable link. The American end of the hot line is located in the Pentagon, the headquarters of the U.S. Department of Defense.

Teletype used for hot line ▶

Critical Thinking

Speculating In what ways might use of the hot line lessen a crisis?

Strength Through Aid

President Kennedy understood that the poverty in Latin America, Asia, and Africa made the Communist promises of economic equality seem attractive. He decided to provide aid to countries in those areas to counteract the appeal of communism. For example, to help Latin America's economic growth, Kennedy set up a 10-year development plan called the Alliance for Progress.

In 1961 the president signed an **executive order,** or presidential directive, creating an organization called the Peace Corps. Peace Corps volunteers worked in other countries as teachers, health workers, and advisers in farming, industry, and government. Volunteers spent two years in countries that had asked for assistance. By 1963 some 5,000 volunteers were working in more than 40 countries around the world. Today, the Peace Corps is still active and remains one of Kennedy's most lasting legacies.

✓ Reading Check **Describing** What was the purpose of the Alliance for Progress?

Cold War Confrontations

Main Idea The Kennedy administration responded to Cold War crises in Cuba and Berlin.

History and You How do you think the U.S. government should deal with threats from other countries? Read to learn how the Kennedy administration dealt with Soviet threats in various parts of the world during the early 1960s.

. . . .

In 1961, just a few months after taking office, President Kennedy had to deal with a foreign policy crisis in Latin America. That same year, tensions between the United States and the Soviet Union arose in Europe.

Cuba

The United States faced a new challenge in Cuba, an island country in the Caribbean Sea. This challenge had begun during the last months of the Eisenhower administration. In January 1959, rebel leader **Fidel Castro** seized power and formed a new Cuban government. He soon set up a Communist dictatorship.

Primary Source / **Soviet Influence**

Footholds and Fences The United States began to see the influence of communism spreading around the world. The U.S. tried to shut down the threat closest to home with the invasion of the Bay of Pigs in Cuba. Half a world away, the U.S. could only watch as Communist East Germany isolated Democratic West Berlin with a cinder block and barbed wire wall.

Invasion of Cuba CIA-trained Cuban exiles landed at the Bay of Pigs on April 17, 1961. Within two days, Cuban President Fidel Castro's troops had captured more than 1,000 of the exiles and stopped the attempt at overthrowing his government.

Armed militia of the Castro government ▶

The Berlin Wall ▶

◀ Exiles taken prisoner

Cuba also became an ally of the Soviet Union. These actions worried many Americans because Cuba lies only 90 miles (145 km) south of Florida.

Late in Eisenhower's presidency, the Central Intelligence Agency (CIA) forged a plan to overthrow Castro. The CIA recruited Cuban refugees who had settled in the United States. The plan called for them to land in Cuba and spark an uprising that would overthrow Castro's rule. When Kennedy became president, he learned about the plan and had doubts about it. However, he accepted the advice of military advisers and the CIA and allowed the plan to go forward.

On April 17, 1961, about 1,500 CIA-trained Cuban exiles landed at the **Bay of Pigs** on the south coast of Cuba. Many blunders occurred, and at a crucial moment, Kennedy refused to provide American air support. Within days Cuban forces crushed the invasion and captured the survivors.

The Bay of Pigs embarrassed Kennedy, who took the blame for the failure. The disaster had three effects. First, Kennedy never again completely trusted military and intelligence advice. Second, nations in Latin America lost trust in Kennedy. Third, Soviet premier Khrushchev concluded that Kennedy was not a strong leader and could be bullied.

The Berlin Wall

Although 16 years had passed since the end of World War II, the wartime Allies had still not settled the status of Germany. West Germany became a full member of the Western alliance, and the Soviet Union continued to control East Germany.

The location of Berlin—fully within East Germany—posed special problems. American, British, and French troops still remained in the western part of the city, and they sometimes had difficulty getting into West Berlin and maintaining control there. Meanwhile a steady flow of people fled to West Berlin from Communist East Berlin, hoping to escape economic hardship and find freedom.

At a June 1961 summit conference in Vienna, Austria, Premier Khrushchev told President Kennedy that the West must move out of Berlin, and he insisted on an agreement by the end of the year. Kennedy rejected Khrushchev's demand. To emphasize the West's right to stay in West Berlin, the United States later sent more troops to the city.

Later that summer, a large number of East Germans fled to the West. On August 13, the East German government, with Soviet backing, closed the border between East and West Berlin and built a wall of concrete blocks with barbed wire along it. The Soviets posted armed guards along the wall to stop more East Germans from fleeing to the West. The **Berlin Wall** cut communications between the two parts of the city.

The Western Allies remained in West Berlin. They could do little, however, to stop the building of the wall, which came to symbolize Communist repression.

Reading Check Explaining What kind of government did Fidel Castro establish in Cuba?

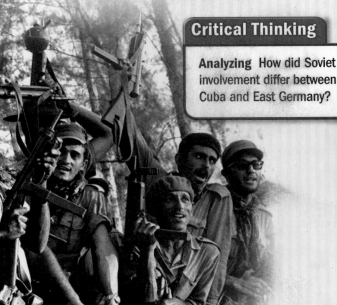

August 1961 To stop the flow of skilled workers, professionals, and intellectuals from leaving East Germany, the Communist country began building the Berlin Wall on August 13. By the 1980s, it had been made taller and wider and stretched 28 miles (45 km) through the middle of Berlin and another 75 miles (120 km) around West Berlin.

Critical Thinking

Analyzing How did Soviet involvement differ between Cuba and East Germany?

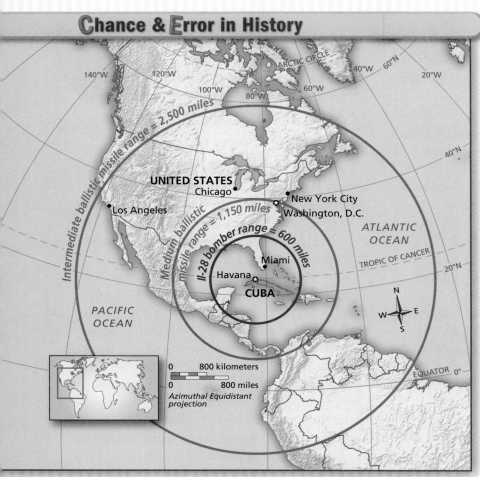

UNITED STATES
Chicago
Los Angeles
New York City
Washington, D.C.
ATLANTIC OCEAN
Miami
Havana
CUBA
TROPIC OF CANCER
PACIFIC OCEAN
EQUATOR 0°

Intermediate ballistic missile range = 2,500 miles
Medium ballistic missile range = 1,150 miles
Il-28 bomber range = 600 miles

0   800 kilometers
0   800 miles
Azimuthal Equidistant projection

What if the Soviets Had Ignored the Blockade?

Just days after President Kennedy ordered a U.S. blockade to prevent Soviet deliveries of missiles to Cuba, Soviet ships abruptly turned away. When the Soviets offered a deal, Kennedy took it. The Soviets would withdraw their missiles in exchange for a U.S. pledge to never invade Cuba. While it seemed like a victory at the time, it left a Communist government intact just miles from the U.S. coastline. The humiliation of giving in also prompted the Soviets to begin the largest peacetime military buildup in history.

Critical Thinking

Theorizing What might have happened if the Soviets had chosen to ignore the blockade and steamed forward to Cuba?

Maps In Motion See StudentWorks™ Plus or glencoe.com.

The Cuban Missile Crisis

Main Idea The United States forced the Soviet Union to withdraw Soviet missiles that had been placed in Cuba.

History and You Have you ever been in a situation that was so scary, you thought that you would never get through it alive? Read to learn how another crisis in Cuba left Americans and people in many other nations wondering whether the world would survive.

• •

The most dangerous Cold War dispute between the Americans and Soviets came in 1962. Once again the dispute involved Cuba.

In mid-October 1962, an American spy plane flying over Cuba made a disturbing discovery. Photographs revealed that the Soviets were building launching sites for nuclear missiles. These missiles could easily reach the United States in a matter of minutes.

For the next week, President Kennedy met secretly with advisers to determine how to deal with the **Cuban missile crisis.** They explored several options, including invading Cuba and bombing the missile sites. New spy photographs showed the bases nearing completion much faster than expected. Kennedy and his advisers needed to reach a decision quickly.

On October 22, President Kennedy, speaking on national television, revealed the "secret, swift, and extraordinary buildup" of Soviet missiles in Cuba. Kennedy ordered the navy to **blockade,** or close off, Cuba until the Soviets removed the missiles. He threatened to destroy any Soviet ship that tried to break through the blockade and reach the island. The president declared: "It shall be the policy of this nation to regard any nuclear missile launched from Cuba against any nation in the Western Hemisphere as an attack by the Soviet Union on the United States."

The United States would respond, he warned, with a nuclear attack against the Soviet Union.

As the two superpowers neared the brink of nuclear war, people all over the world waited nervously. After five agonizing days, the Soviet ships turned back. Soviet leaders also agreed to withdraw their missiles from Cuba. The United States agreed not to invade Cuba. Nuclear war had been avoided.

Having come so close to nuclear disaster, the two nations worked to establish better relations. In the summer of 1963, Kennedy and Khrushchev created the hot line between Moscow and Washington to allow the leaders to communicate instantly in times of crisis. That same summer, the two nations signed a treaty banning nuclear tests aboveground and underwater.

Rivalry in Space

Americans and Soviets continued their rivalry in space. In April 1961, Soviet cosmonaut Yuri Gagarin (guh•GAHR•uhn) became the first person to orbit the Earth. One month later, Alan Shepard, Jr., became the first American to make a spaceflight.

Shortly after Shepard's spaceflight, Kennedy committed the nation to the goal of landing a man on the moon by the end of the decade. He asked Congress for more money for NASA (National Aeronautics and Space Administration), which ran the space program. NASA expanded its launching facility in Florida and built a control center in Houston, Texas.

Astronaut John Glenn thrilled the country in February 1962 when he orbited the Earth in a spacecraft, the first American to do so. An even greater triumph for the space program came on July 20, 1969, with the Apollo project. Awestruck television viewers around the world watched the spacecraft *Eagle* land on the surface of the moon.

Hours later, with millions still watching, astronaut Neil Armstrong took the first human step on the moon and announced: "That's one small step for a man, one giant leap for mankind." By the end of the Apollo project in 1972, 10 more Americans had landed on the moon.

✓ Reading Check **Explaining** How was the Cuban missile crisis resolved?

Section 1 Review

History ONLINE
Study Central™ To review this section, go to glencoe.com.

Vocabulary

1. Write a sentence that explains the meaning of each of the following terms: respond, guerrilla warfare, flexible response, executive order, occur, blockade.

Main Ideas

2. **Describing** What was the relationship between guerrilla warfare and Kennedy's flexible response plan?

3. **Explaining** Why did the Soviet Union build the Berlin Wall?

4. **Summarizing** What was the responsibility of NASA?

Critical Thinking

5. **Analyzing** Re-create the diagram below and identify strategies that the Kennedy administration considered to stop the buildup of missiles in Cuba.

6. **Expository Writing** Take the role of a recruiter for the Peace Corps. Write a speech that describes the creation and mission of the Peace Corps and encourages people to apply.

Answer the
7. **Essential Question**
What were the key foreign policy challenges the United States faced during the Kennedy administration?

Section 2 · War in Vietnam

Essential Question ◄

How and why did America involve itself in the war in Vietnam?

Reading Guide

Content Vocabulary

escalate *(p. 471)* napalm *(p. 472)*
search-and-destroy mission *(p. 472)* Agent Orange *(p. 472)*

Academic Vocabulary

trace *(p. 469)* regime *(p. 470)*

Key People and Events

Ho Chi Minh *(p. 469)*
Vietcong *(p. 470)*
Gulf of Tonkin Resolution *(p. 471)*

Reading Strategy

Taking Notes On a chart like the one below, identify each president's main philosophy about America's involvement in Vietnam.

President	Philosophy
Eisenhower	
Kennedy	
Johnson	

American Diary

American efforts to stop the spread of communism led to U.S. involvement in Vietnam. President Eisenhower believed that "the loss of all Vietnam, together with Laos on the west and Cambodia in the southwest, would have meant the surrender to Communist enslavement of millions." In the late 1950s, President Eisenhower sent military supplies and advisers to pro-Western South Vietnam in support of its fight against Communist North Vietnam. President Kennedy continued this policy.

—from *American Policy Toward Laos*

Vietnamese women work in a rice field.

The U.S. and Vietnam

Main Idea Vietnam became a divided country as a result of conflict between Communist and non-Communist groups.

History and You What would it be like to live in a country where a civil war was raging? Read to learn how a civil war affected the people of Vietnam.

In the early 1960s, the United States became involved in a fight against the spread of communism in Southeast Asia. The war in Vietnam did not unfold as Americans hoped, however. General Maxwell Taylor, who served as U.S. ambassador to South Vietnam, reflected on the problems of the war years after it had ended:

PRIMARY SOURCE

"First, we didn't know ourselves. We thought that we were going into another Korean war, but this was a different country. Secondly, we didn't know our South Vietnamese allies. We never understood them, and that was another surprise. And we knew even less about North Vietnam."

—from *Vietnam: A History*

Origins of the War

The roots of the Vietnam conflict can be **traced,** or followed, back to World War II, when Japanese forces captured the French colony of Indochina in Southeast Asia. Vietnamese forces led by Communist **Ho Chi Minh** (HOH CHEE MIHN) fought against the Japanese.

When Japan surrendered at the end of World War II, Ho Chi Minh declared Vietnam's independence. The French, however, were unwilling to give up their empire. Their Indochina colony—the present-day nations of Cambodia, Laos, and Vietnam—was among the richest of France's colonies, supplying resources such as rice, rubber, and tin. Ho Chi Minh and his forces fought the French in a long, bloody war, finally defeating the French in 1954 at Dien Bien Phu.

The Geneva Accords

That same year, diplomats from the United States, France, Great Britain, the Soviet Union, China, and Vietnam met in Geneva, Switzerland, to work out a peace agreement. According to the Geneva Accords, Vietnam would be divided temporarily.

When and Where Indochina in 1959

In 1959 North Vietnam began to deliver supplies to its forces in South Vietnam through a network of paths and roads through the countries of Laos and Cambodia. This network became known as the Ho Chi Minh Trail. ▶

← Ho Chi Minh Trail

CHINA

BURMA

Hanoi

20°N

LAOS

NORTH VIETNAM

Vientiane

Rangoon

THAILAND

Bangkok

CAMBODIA

SOUTH VIETNAM

South China Sea

Gulf of Thailand

Phnom Penh

Saigon

10°N

0   200 kilometers

0   200 miles

Miller projection

100°E

110°E

Critical Thinking

Explaining According to President Eisenhower, why was it important for the United States to help South Vietnam?

The agreement also stated that Ho Chi Minh's Communist nationalists would control the North. Hanoi served as its capital. Non-Communist forces—supported by the United States—would control the South, with Saigon as the capital. Vietnam would be unified in 1956 after national elections.

Neither the United States nor South Vietnam signed the agreement, but they did not oppose its provisions. At the same time, the U.S. emphasized that it would act if Communist North Vietnam moved aggressively against the South.

In 1955 Ngo Dinh Diem (NGOH DIHN deh•EHM), with American support, became South Vietnam's leader. He refused to hold elections and cracked down on Communists in the South. In response the Communists set up the National Liberation Front (NLF), or the **Vietcong.** In 1959 the Vietcong, on orders from Ho Chi Minh, began a war against the Diem **regime,** or governing authority.

A Growing American Role

The United States had replaced the French as the dominant foreign power in the South in 1955. If Communists took South Vietnam, President Eisenhower once said, the other countries of Southeast Asia would fall to communism like a row of dominoes—one right after the other. This domino theory helped shape American policy in Vietnam for the next 20 years.

To support South Vietnam, the Eisenhower administration sent the country billions of dollars in aid. It also dispatched a few hundred soldiers, who acted as advisers to the South Vietnamese government and army.

Like Eisenhower, President Kennedy saw Vietnam as part of the global struggle against communism. Kennedy sent more Special Forces—the Green Berets—to train and advise South Vietnamese troops. Kennedy also pressured Diem to make reforms that would undercut the appeal of communism.

The Vietnam Conflict 1941–1954

Japanese troops advance into Indochina. ▶

Ho Chi Minh ▶

★ **July 1941**
Japan captures French colony of Indochina (Vietnam, Laos, Cambodia)

★ **September 1945**
- Japan surrenders to Allies
- Communist Ho Chi Minh declares Vietnam independent

★ **December 1941**
Japanese bomb Pearl Harbor, Hawaii

★ **Late 1943** Vietnamese battle Japanese

Japanese planes on a bombing mission ▶

Americans urged him to create a more democratic government and to help Vietnam's peasants. Diem introduced some limited reforms, but they had little effect.

Diem took away rights from the majority Buddhist population and favored Catholics, like himself. Buddhists responded with protests, including Buddhist monks setting themselves on fire on busy streets. As a result of these protests, Kennedy found it difficult to continue to support Diem.

In November 1963, the South Vietnamese army overthrew the government and assassinated Diem. The Kennedy administration had supported the takeover, but not Diem's killing. After President Kennedy's assassination later that month, the question of what to do in Vietnam fell on the shoulders of President Lyndon B. Johnson.

✔ **Reading Check** **Analyzing** What were the Geneva Accords?

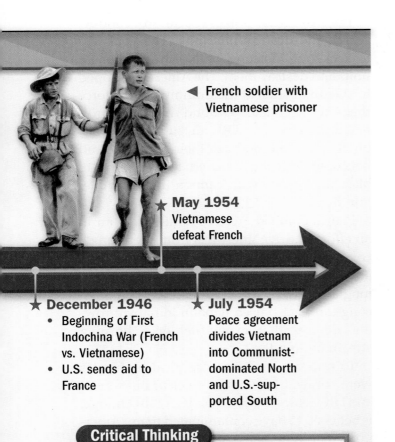

◄ **French soldier with Vietnamese prisoner**

★ **May 1954**
Vietnamese defeat French

★ **December 1946**
- Beginning of First Indochina War (French vs. Vietnamese)
- U.S. sends aid to France

★ **July 1954**
Peace agreement divides Vietnam into Communist-dominated North and U.S.-supported South

Critical Thinking

Making Connections Why do you think the United States sent aid to France in its battle to keep Vietnam under French rule?

The Conflict Deepens

Main Idea To stop the spread of communism in Southeast Asia, the United States became involved in a war in Vietnam.

History and You What sacrifices must a country make if it becomes involved in a war? Read to learn how the U.S. was affected by its involvement in the Vietnam War.

· ·

At the time of Kennedy's death, the United States had nearly 16,000 American troops in Vietnam as advisers. Secretary of Defense Robert McNamara told the president that South Vietnam could not resist the Vietcong rebels without more help from the United States. In a May 1964 conversation, taped but not made public until 1997, Johnson himself expressed doubts about American commitment. "I don't think it's worth fighting for," he said, "but I don't think we can get out." As Vietcong attacks continued, the United States moved toward deeper involvement in the region.

President Johnson wanted congressional support for expanding the American role in Vietnam. The opportunity to get that support came in August 1964, when North Vietnamese patrol boats allegedly attacked American destroyers in the Gulf of Tonkin near North Vietnam. Congress quickly passed a resolution that allowed the president to "take all necessary measures to repel any armed attack against the forces of the United States." The **Gulf of Tonkin Resolution** gave Johnson broad authority to use American forces.

In 1965 President Johnson began to **escalate**—gradually increase—U.S. involvement in Vietnam. The buildup included both ground troops and an air campaign. United States Marines landed near Da Nang, South Vietnam, on March 8, 1965. During the next three years, the number of American troops in Vietnam rose sharply. About 180,000 U.S. soldiers were in Vietnam by the end of 1965, almost 400,000 by the end of 1966, and more than 500,000 by 1968.

Primary Source — A Day in the Life of a Soldier

"My hands are covered with cuts. The jungles have thousands of leeches and mosquitoes of which I think I have gotten bitten almost all over my body. . . . Actually the fighting is not heavy yet, but the rumor is we're moving south."

—from *Dear America: Letters Home from Vietnam*

◄ American soldier in Vietnam

What would a foot soldier carry?

Typical Gear	Typical Pack
Rifle	Poncho
Web belt with ammo pouches	Poncho liner
Hand grenades	Five C-ration meals
Smoke grenades	Rain jacket
First aid pouch	Sweater shirt
Canteen	Extra canteen
Two bandoliers of ammo	Extra ammo
	Gun-cleaning kit
	Extra smoke grenade
	Extra rifle bolt
	Camera

Critical Thinking

Contrasting How were the experiences of a soldier in Vietnam different from a soldier during the U.S. Civil War?

In March 1965, the United States unleashed an intense bombing campaign called Operation Rolling Thunder. Some planes attacked the Ho Chi Minh Trail, a network of roads, paths, and bridges that wound from North Vietnam through Cambodia and Laos into South Vietnam. North Vietnamese troops used this route to bring equipment south. Other planes targeted bridges, docks, factories, and military bases in the North.

The bombing increased in intensity from 1965 through 1968. By then American planes had dropped more bombs on North Vietnam than they dropped on Germany, Italy, and Japan during World War II.

Fighting the War

The American troops found fighting a ground war in Vietnam difficult. Dense jungles, muddy trails, and swampy rice paddies hampered troop movement. The South Vietnamese army did not always fight effectively. As the Vietcong guerrillas blended with the population, American soldiers found it hard to tell friends and enemies apart.

The American forces began to conduct **search-and-destroy missions.** The goal was to seek out Vietcong or North Vietnamese units and destroy them. The Americans hoped to eventually defeat the Communists or force them to negotiate. Ground troops coordinated their moves with air support. Patrols on the ground radioed their location, and helicopter gunships roared to the scene to blast the enemy with cannon and machine-gun fire.

Planes bombed areas of South Vietnam in an effort to drive guerrillas from their jungle cover. Both sides used planes to drop **napalm,** an explosive that burned intensely, to destroy jungle growth. North Vietnamese and Vietcong forces also used napalm in flamethrowers, devices that expel fuel or a burning stream of liquids.

To improve visibility, chemical herbicides were sprayed in Vietnam to clear out forests and tall grasses. One herbicide, **Agent Orange,** is believed to have contaminated many Americans and Vietnamese, causing serious health problems.

Frustration Grows

The bombing of the Ho Chi Minh Trail and the North did not stop the constant flow of troops and equipment south. Neither did it break the morale of the North Vietnamese. As one of their leaders later said:

PRIMARY SOURCE

"[We survived] because of our courage and determination, together with wisdom, tactics, and intelligence. . . . We had to resort to different measures, some of which are quite simple, like hiding in man-holes and evacuating to the countryside. And we fought back with all our forces and with every kind of weapon."

—from an interview with General Vo Nguyen Giap

The search-and-destroy missions killed thousands of North Vietnamese and Vietcong troops—but the troops always seemed to be replaced. What Ho Chi Minh had said to the French became true again: "You can kill ten of my men for every one I kill of yours. But even at those odds, you will lose and I will win."

American troops advanced into rice paddies, jungles, and small villages and killed scores of Vietcong. Yet the next day, the same area often had to be attacked again. American soldiers grew frustrated. Philip Caputo, a young marine lieutenant, recalled the changing attitude:

PRIMARY SOURCE

"When we marched into the rice paddies on that damp March afternoon, we carried, along with our packs and rifles, the implicit convictions that the Viet Cong would be quickly beaten. . . . We kept the packs and rifles; the convictions, we lost."

—from A Rumor of War

Debate in the White House

Officials in the Johnson administration saw the mounting Communist losses and believed at first that the United States could succeed. As the war dragged on, however, some officials saw a gloomier situation. Secretary of Defense McNamara began to argue that the ground war and the air attacks had failed and that the war could not be won. Outside the nation's capital, opposition to U.S. involvement in Vietnam grew.

Reading Check Identifying By what means did President Johnson escalate the U.S. presence in Vietnam?

Section 2 Review

History ONLINE
Study Central™ To review this section, go to glencoe.com.

Vocabulary

1. Write a paragraph using each of the following terms: trace, regime, escalate, search-and-destroy mission, napalm, Agent Orange.

Main Ideas

2. **Describing** What was the domino theory, and how did it shape American policy in Vietnam?

3. **Summarizing** How large was the American troop increase in Vietnam between 1963 and the end of 1965?

Critical Thinking

4. **Explaining** What was the Gulf of Tonkin Resolution, and why was it important?

5. **Organizing Information** Re-create the diagram below to show the different warfare techniques used in search-and-destroy missions.

6. **Descriptive Writing** Imagine you are an American soldier arriving in Vietnam. In one or two paragraphs, describe the terrain you find yourself fighting in and how it affects your abilities as a soldier.

Answer the
7. **Essential Question**
How and why did America involve itself in the war in Vietnam?

Should We Be Fighting the Vietnam War?

Building Background

Government officials urged Americans to support the war's goals of spreading freedom and democracy. President Lyndon B. Johnson responded to criticism of his management of the war by defending the struggle as an idealistic cause.

As U.S. involvement in the war increased, so did opposition to it. The mainstream media, which had tried to remain balanced in their war coverage, now openly criticized the effort. Walter Cronkite, then the nation's most respected newscaster, supported the war effort at first. After traveling to Vietnam to report on the fighting, Cronkite's stories began to include his disappointments with the status of the war.

NO

WALTER CRONKITE,
after the Tet Offensive, February 27, 1968

We have been too often disappointed by the optimism of the American leaders, both in Vietnam and Washington, to have faith any longer in the silver linings they find in the darkest clouds. . . .

To say that we are closer to victory today is to believe, in the face of the evidence, the optimists who have been wrong in the past. To suggest we are on the edge of defeat is to yield to unreasonable pessimism. To say that we are mired[1] in stalemate seems the only realistic, yet unsatisfactory, conclusion. . . . It is increasingly clear to this reporter that the only rational way out then will be to negotiate, not as victors, but as an honorable people who lived up to their pledge to defend democracy, and did the best they could.

Fighting in Saigon during the Tet Offensive, May 1968

---

[1] **mired** stuck

YES

PRESIDENT JOHNSON

Addresses Johns Hopkins University, April 7, 1965

We fight because we must fight if we are to live in a world where every country can shape its own destiny. And only in such a world will our own freedom be finally secure.

This kind of world will never be built by bombs or bullets. Yet the infirmities[2] of man are such that force must often precede reason, and the waste of war, the works of peace. . . .

. . . To abandon this small and brave nation [Vietnam] to its enemies, and to the terror that must follow, would be an unforgivable wrong. . . .

We are also there because there are great stakes in the balance. Let no one think for a moment that retreat from Viet-Nam would bring an end to conflict. The battle would be renewed in one country and then another. The central lesson of our time is that the appetite of aggression is never satisfied.

---

[2] infirmities weaknesses

DBQ Document-Based Questions

1. **Interpreting** Why does Johnson believe the United States should be fighting the war in Vietnam?

2. **Making Inferences** What does Cronkite believe the result will be if the United States continues fighting in Vietnam?

3. **Analyzing** How do Johnson and Cronkite differ in their views on achieving peace?

4. **Synthesizing** Why might Americans, such as Walter Cronkite, be frustrated with the war?

Antiwar rally at Queens College in New York City

Essential Question ◄

How did the Vietnam War affect the political and social climate in the United States?

Reading Guide

Content Vocabulary

counterculture (p. 477)

conscientious objector (p. 478)

deferment (p. 478)

credibility gap (p. 479)

Academic Vocabulary

conduct (p. 478)

exclude (p. 481)

Key People and Events

Tet Offensive (p. 479)

Robert F. Kennedy (p. 479)

Dr. Martin Luther King, Jr. (p. 480)

Hubert H. Humphrey (p. 480)

George C. Wallace (p. 481)

Richard M. Nixon (p. 481)

Reading Strategy

Taking Notes On a diagram like the one below, record characteristics of the counterculture in America during the war.

Counterculture

American Diary

As casualties mounted in Vietnam, many people began to protest against the war. Jeff Sharlet was a Vietnam veteran who opposed the war but was disgusted by the attitudes and actions of the protesters. He decided to start a newspaper, Vietnam GI, *written entirely by veterans and soldiers. The soldiers, whether they supported or opposed the war effort, always knew they could express their views in its pages.*

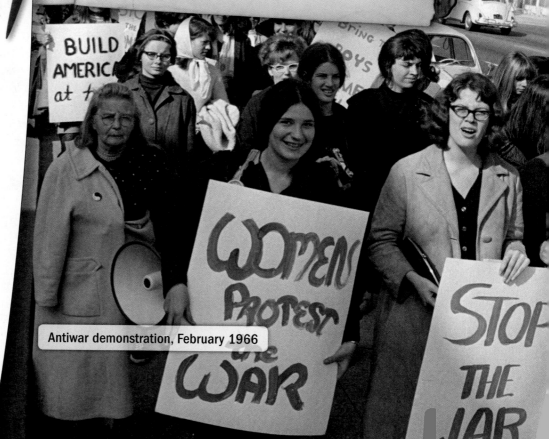

Antiwar demonstration, February 1966

The Youth Protest

Main Idea The war in Vietnam led to sharp divisions between Americans who supported the war and those who did not.

History and You Have members of your family heatedly disagreed over certain issues? Read to learn how the war in Vietnam affected American society.

. . . .

While fighting raged in Vietnam, the American people disagreed sharply over the war. Pro-war and antiwar groups attacked each other with mounting anger. Antiwar demonstrators called President Johnson and his supporters "killers." Supporters of the war referred to the protesters as "traitors." The war seemed to split America—and much of the division resulted from what people called the generation gap.

As United States involvement in the war increased, so did opposition to it. Some Americans felt that the conflict in Vietnam was a civil war and should not involve the United States. Others were concerned that the cost of America's commitment to Vietnam was hurting domestic programs. Still others viewed South Vietnam as a corrupt dictatorship and insisted that defending the country was immoral and unjust. All condemned the devastation of the countryside and the lives lost during the course of the war.

Many who opposed the war were part of the **counterculture,** a movement that rejected traditional American values. Some common symbols of the counterculture—torn blue jeans and long hair for males—aroused opposition from parents. Popular music played a role in communicating the ideas of the counterculture.

Other parts of the counterculture represented a more serious challenge to traditional middle-class values. Some young people refused to follow customary social roles of work and family. They aimed to reject aspects of American society such as the competition for material goods and personal success.

Opposition to the Draft

Student protests targeted the selective service system—the draft that supplied soldiers for the war. The law required all men to register for the draft when they reached age 18. Opposition to the draft had two sources.

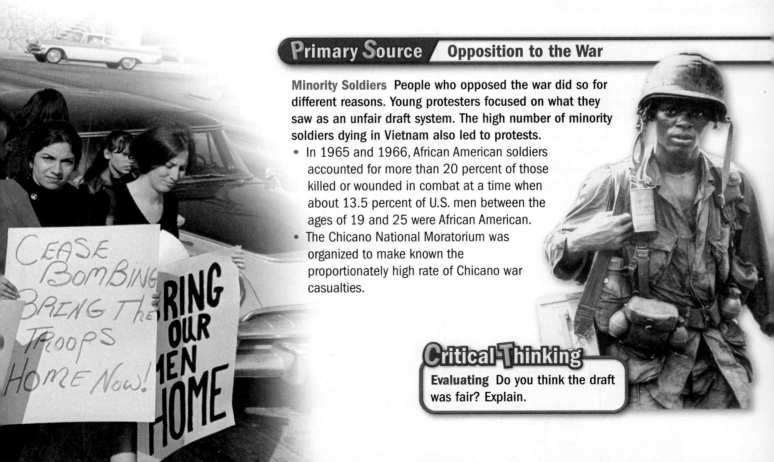

Primary Source / **Opposition to the War**

Minority Soldiers People who opposed the war did so for different reasons. Young protesters focused on what they saw as an unfair draft system. The high number of minority soldiers dying in Vietnam also led to protests.

- In 1965 and 1966, African American soldiers accounted for more than 20 percent of those killed or wounded in combat at a time when about 13.5 percent of U.S. men between the ages of 19 and 25 were African American.
- The Chicano National Moratorium was organized to make known the proportionately high rate of Chicano war casualties.

CEASE BOMBING BRING THE TROOPS HOME NOW!

BRING OUR MEN HOME

Critical Thinking

Evaluating Do you think the draft was fair? Explain.

History ONLINE

Student Web Activity Visit glencoe.com and complete the Chapter 15 Web Activity about young people and the draft.

Those who were strongly opposed to American involvement in Vietnam believed that by ending the draft, they could halt the supply of soldiers needed to fight there. Others called the draft unfair. Draft boards had the power to give people **deferments** that excused them from the draft for various reasons. Full-time students attending college—mostly from the middle class—received such deferments. As a result, a large percentage of soldiers came from poor or working-class families. Many argued that deferments discriminated against these families.

Some protesters became **conscientious objectors,** claiming that their moral or religious beliefs prevented them from fighting in the war. Other protesters showed their opposition by burning their draft cards—their military registration forms.

Doves and Hawks

Students and other opponents of the Vietnam War came to be called doves. Supporters of the war became known as hawks.

Across the nation more and more Americans came to view the war unfavorably. Some thought the United States should not be fighting in Vietnam. Others opposed the way the government **conducted,** or directed the course of, the war. Both hawks and doves criticized the president for his handling of the war in Vietnam, and his approval rating greatly declined.

As the opposition to the war mounted, the opponents staged larger demonstrations. In October 1967, more than 50,000 people marched to the Pentagon—headquarters of the Defense Department—to protest the war. Of those Americans who supported the war, many openly criticized the protesters for a lack of patriotism.

✓ Reading Check **Describing** How did some Americans protest the draft in the 1960s?

Primary Source / **Wounded in War**

Rapid Rescue The helicopter ambulance sped up the time in which wounded soldiers received medical treatment. Crews were able to shuttle the injured to a medical facility within one to two hours of a soldier being hurt. And because of the rapid transport, nurses in Vietnam saw more critically injured soldiers. Nurses usually worked 12 hours per day, 6 days per week. The average age of an American nurse in Vietnam was 23.6 years.

"Some days you felt you'd lived a lifetime in just a week. Because Vietnam was not John Wayne on the beach at Iwo Jima. It was not ketchup on make-believe wounds. It was more like a grotesque form of 'can you top this,' because each time you thought you'd seen the ultimate, something else would come along."

—Nurse Ruth Sidisin, USAF

A wounded soldier is loaded onto a helicopter. ▶

1968—Year of Crisis

Main Idea The year 1968 was a turning point in the Vietnam War that greatly affected the nation's political life.

History and You Do you recall a year that is meaningful to you because of the particular events that occurred during that time? Read to learn why 1968 became a significant year for Americans.

. . . .

The year 1968 opened with a shock for the American people. North Vietnam launched a major series of attacks in South Vietnam. As Americans soon learned, 1968 would be a long, dramatic, and very difficult year.

The Tet Offensive

On January 31, 1968, the North Vietnamese and Vietcong launched a series of attacks, which began on Tet—the Vietnamese New Year. This **Tet Offensive** marked a turning point in the Vietnam War. The Communist attacks targeted American military bases and South Vietnam's cities. Vietcong troops raided the United States embassy in Saigon, the capital. They also struck in Hue, the ancient capital of Vietnam.

Militarily, Tet turned out to be a disaster for the Communist forces. After a month of fighting, the American and South Vietnamese soldiers drove back the enemy troops, inflicting heavy losses. In the United States, however, the Tet Offensive turned many more Americans against the war—and President Johnson. The American people were shocked that an enemy supposedly close to defeat could launch such a large-scale attack.

Major newspapers and magazines openly criticized the Johnson administration's conduct of the war. Most Americans seemed to agree, believing that the army was losing ground. The Johnson administration developed a **credibility gap**—fewer people trusted its statements about the war.

Political Opposition

As opposition to the war grew, President Johnson faced challenges in his own party. In late 1967, Democratic senator Eugene McCarthy of Minnesota announced that he would run for the party's nomination for the presidency as a protest against the war. Not well known, McCarthy seemed to have little chance of winning. In the March 12 primary in New Hampshire, however, McCarthy surprised everyone by taking 42 percent of the popular vote. Although Johnson won the primary, McCarthy's strong showing indicated widespread opposition to the war.

Later, another antiwar candidate entered the race. **Robert F. Kennedy,** attorney general during his brother's presidency and now a senator from New York, announced that he, too, would seek the Democratic nomination.

The President Responds

Events in Vietnam and the growing antiwar movement disturbed President Johnson. After the Tet Offensive, the American commander in Vietnam, General William Westmoreland, requested still more troops.

Critical Thinking

Speculating How do you think young nurses reacted after working such long hours and seeing such horrific injuries?

Events of 1968

- President Johnson does not run for reelection.
- Martin Luther King, Jr., and Robert Kennedy are shot and killed.
- Antiwar demonstrations disrupt the Democratic convention in Chicago.
- Demonstrations spread to many college campuses.
- Third-party candidate George Wallace makes a strong showing.
- With Richard Nixon's victory in 1968, Republicans hold a near monopoly on the presidency for the next 20 years.

Election of 1968

◀ Robert Kennedy

Candidate*	Electoral Vote	Popular Vote	Political Party
Nixon	301	31,785,480	Republican
Humphrey	191	31,275,166	Democrat
Wallace	46	9,906,473	Independent

*One North Carolina elector voted for Wallace

Richard Nixon ▶

Map Skills

1. **Region** In what area of the nation did Wallace receive the most votes?
2. **Region** Explain why you agree or disagree with the following: The Northeast was Nixon's strongest region in 1968.

Maps In Motion See StudentWorks™ Plus or glencoe.com.

Instead of agreeing with Westmoreland's request for more troops, the president ordered a reevaluation of the war. He also reevaluated his own campaign for reelection.

On March 31, 1968, President Johnson appeared on television to announce a "new step toward peace"—he would halt the bombing of North Vietnam's cities. He asked North Vietnam for a comparable action so that peace talks could begin. The president concluded his speech with a startling announcement: "I shall not seek, and I will not accept, the nomination of my party for another term as your president."

Violence Erupts

A few days after Johnson withdrew from the presidential race, tragedy struck the nation. On the evening of April 4, a sniper in Memphis, Tennessee, shot and killed **Dr. Martin Luther King, Jr.,** the leading activist in the civil rights movement.

The assassination of Dr. King set off riots across the country. Army troops were called on to control unruly crowds in various cities. Already saddened by Dr. King's death, Americans worried about urban violence.

While the nation agonized over unrest at home and war abroad, the race for president picked up speed. Vice President **Hubert H. Humphrey** joined Eugene McCarthy and Robert Kennedy in seeking the Democratic nomination. Kennedy edged out McCarthy in a number of primary elections, but McCarthy rebounded and scored a victory in Oregon. Humphrey, meanwhile, avoided primaries. He won support among Democratic Party leaders, who in some states chose delegates.

In June 1968, Kennedy and McCarthy faced each other in the primary election in California, the state with the most delegates. That night, after Kennedy won, an assassin shot and killed him. The nation reeled with the shock of yet another assassination.

The Democratic Convention

By the time the Democrats held their convention in Chicago, Humphrey seemed to have enough votes to win the nomination. As a supporter of civil rights and labor causes, Humphrey had much backing in the party. As a supporter of Johnson's Vietnam policy, however, Humphrey was linked to the party's pro-war wing. Antiwar Democrats felt angry and **excluded,** or shut out, from the convention.

Meanwhile, thousands of antiwar activists flocked to Chicago to protest Humphrey's almost certain victory. Chicago's mayor, Richard J. Daley, feared violence and had the police out in force. When antiwar protesters tried to march to the convention site, police blocked the marchers, who began to pelt the officers with sticks and bottles. The police threw tear gas and charged in, wielding nightsticks. They pursued those who fled, beating some and arresting many.

Humphrey won the Democratic nomination, but the violence—all shown on television—damaged his candidacy. Humphrey admitted, "Chicago was a catastrophe."

The Election of 1968

Most Americans opposed the violence and longed for a return to law and order. As Election Day neared, third-party candidate Governor **George C. Wallace** of Alabama criticized protesters and efforts to integrate schools by busing. His tough stand on law and order and his appeal to racial fears won many voters. Republican nominee, former vice president **Richard M. Nixon,** claimed to stand for the conservative "silent majority" who wanted law and order and did not protest or demonstrate. He also offered "peace with honor" in Vietnam, but gave no details.

In the election, the popular vote was close. Nixon edged Humphrey by about 500,000 votes. In the electoral vote, however, Nixon won a solid majority—301 votes to Humphrey's 191. Nixon became president with the votes of only 43.4 percent of the people, but he and Wallace together won about 57 percent. It seemed that a sizeable majority of Americans wanted the government to restore order.

Reading Check **Identifying** What two popular leaders were assassinated in 1968?

Section 3 Review

History ONLINE
Study Central™ To review this section, go to glencoe.com.

Vocabulary

1. Use each of these terms in a complete sentence that will explain its meaning: counterculture, deferment, conscientious objector, conduct, credibility gap, exclude.

Main Ideas

2. Explaining What were draft deferments, and who received them?

3. Summarizing What was the Tet Offensive? Why was it significant to the course of the war?

4. Analyzing Why did President Lyndon B. Johnson decide not to seek reelection?

Critical Thinking

5. Identifying On a diagram like the one below, list the major points that Nixon campaigned on in 1968.

6. Analyzing Who were the "silent majority," and how did their votes affect the outcome of the 1968 presidential election?

7. Persuasive Writing Write a short essay to convince the reader to agree with your point of view on this question: *Should America use a draft system with the armed services?*

8. Answer the Essential Question
How did the Vietnam War affect the political and social climate in the United States?

TIME NOTEBOOK

What were people's lives like in the past?

These two pages will give you some clues to everyday life in the United States as you step back in time with TIME Notebook.

NASA

Profile

On July 20, 1969, **NEIL ARMSTRONG** *became the first human to walk on the moon. There he spoke the famous words, "That's one small step for a man, one giant leap for mankind." Later, Armstrong reflected on his voyage and the "spaceship" we call Earth.*

"From our position here on Earth, it is difficult to observe where the Earth is, and where it's going, or what its future course might be. Hopefully by getting a little farther away, both in the real sense and the figurative sense, we'll be able to make some people step back and reconsider their mission in the universe, to think of themselves as a group of people who constitute [make up] the crew of a spaceship going through the universe. If you're going to run a spaceship you've got to be pretty cautious about how you use your resources, how you use your crew, and how you treat your spacecraft."

—*from the book* First on the Moon

The Peace Corps

Established by President Kennedy in 1961, the Peace Corps sends trained Americans as "goodwill ambassadors" to developing nations. Once there, these volunteers help with agriculture, education, and health projects—as well as with small businesses and rural engineering. Here is what one volunteer said about working with the Peace Corps from 1963–1965:

BETTMANN / CORBIS

"I was in college when JFK created the Peace Corps, and I thought it was a great idea. I was inspired by his question, 'Ask not what your country can do for you; ask what you can do for your country.' I wanted to travel and experience a different culture, and I admired President Kennedy's idealism, so I applied. Living in another country, I learned to appreciate my own country more."

African American Firsts

Many African Americans are making a mark on United States history. Match these famous people with their achievements as the first African Americans to hold these positions.

1. Beverly Johnson
2. Arthur Ashe
3. Constance Baker Motley
4. Shirley Chisholm
5. Thurgood Marshall

a. in 1968, elected to Congress, and in 1972, first woman and first African American to run for United States president

b. in 1964, New York state senator who became a federal judge in 1966

c. in 1975, tennis champ at Wimbledon

d. in 1974, cover model on *Vogue* magazine

e. in 1967, sworn in as justice of the United States Supreme Court

PHOTODISC; (BALL) COMSTOCK

Answers: 1. d; 2. c; 3. b; 4. a; 5. e

MILESTONES

EVENTS OF THE TIME

PUBLISHED. *Silent Spring* by Rachel Carson in 1961, helping to start a new environmental movement in America.

ENROLLED. James Meredith at the University of Mississippi in 1962. The Supreme Court ordered his admission to the previously segregated school.

BROKEN. 25-day fast by César Chávez, labor organizer in 1965. His protest led others to join his nonviolent strike against the grape growers.

TAKEN AWAY. Boxer Muhammad Ali's heavyweight championship title in 1967 after refusing induction into military service. He was found guilty in federal court of violating the Selective Service Act. In 1971 the U.S. Supreme Court overturned his draft conviction.

AIRED. *Sesame Street* for the first time in 1969.

OPENED. Walt Disney World in Orlando, Florida, in 1971.

EVACUATED. The last of American soldiers from Vietnam in 1975.

AL FRENI / TIME LIFE PICTURES / GETTY IMAGES

GIFTED. The Pet Rock was 1975's hot holiday gift. For $3.95 you received a small, obedient "pet" and an owner's manual with housebreaking tips and tricks any rock could learn. A million rocks sold in just a few months.

NUMBERS

WHAT HAPPENED IN 1969

3 Days Duration of the Woodstock Music and Art Fair that attracted hundreds of thousands of young people to a 600-acre (243 ha) farm in New York to celebrate peace and music

7 Baseball player Mickey Mantle's team number, which the Yankees retired when Mantle stopped playing

747 The model number of Boeing's "Jumbo" jet launched this year; the world's largest and heaviest aircraft, it can carry at least 362 passengers, twice as many as an ordinary jet

ANDREAS MANOLIS / REUTERS / CORBIS

250,000 Number of people who marched from the United States Capitol to the Washington Monument in the largest demonstration in Washington's history—all to protest the U.S. involvement in the Vietnam War; President Nixon vowed to ignore the demonstration

CRITICAL THINKING

Making Generalizations How did African Americans who were first in their fields help move the civil rights movement forward?

Speculating What do you think programs such as the Peace Corps and landing a person on the moon did for the image of the United States around the world?

Nixon and Vietnam

Essential Question ◄
How did President Nixon remove the United States from the Vietnam War?

Reading Guide

Content Vocabulary
Vietnamization (p. 486)
martial law (p. 487)
MIA (p. 490)

Academic Vocabulary
authority (p. 485)
demonstration (p. 486)

Key People and Events
Henry Kissinger (p. 485)
Pentagon Papers (p. 488)

Reading Strategy
Taking Notes On a diagram like the one below, list the major points of Nixon's "peace with honor" strategy to end the war.

Nixon Strategy

American Diary

Speaking to reporters after his election, the new president, Richard Nixon, recalled seeing a young girl carrying a hand-lettered sign at one of his rallies that read: "Bring Us Together Again." This, he promised, would be his chief goal as president. Nixon also vowed to implement his plan to end the Vietnam War. Even though the United States began scaling back its involvement in Vietnam, the American home front remained divided.

Crowds lined the streets for the Inaugural parade following the swearing in of President Richard Nixon, in January 1969.

Up with People

A New Strategy

Main Idea Nixon took steps to bring American forces home and end the war in Vietnam.

History and You Have you ever worked long and hard on a project and wished that someone could come and replace you so that you could take a rest? Read to find out about a "changing of the guard" during the war in Vietnam.

· ·

In his Inaugural Address in January 1969, Richard M. Nixon appealed to the American people for calm: "We cannot learn from one another until we stop shouting at one another—until we speak quietly enough so that our words can be heard as well as our voices."

Nixon had campaigned on a pledge of "peace with honor" in Vietnam. Shortly after taking office, Nixon began taking steps to end the nation's involvement in the war. As a first step, the president appointed Harvard professor **Henry Kissinger** as his national security adviser. Kissinger was given wide **authority**—the power to give orders and make decisions—to use his diplomatic skills to end the conflict. Kissinger launched a policy he called "linkage." This policy aimed at improving relations with the Soviet Union and China—suppliers of aid to North Vietnam. Kissinger hoped to persuade the two Communist nations to cut back on their aid and help end the war.

At the same time, Nixon wanted to begin pulling American forces out of Vietnam. However, he did not want American withdrawal to be seen as a sign of defeat. Nixon's strategy of "peace with honor" had three parts—reforming the selective service system, giving South Vietnam more responsibility in fighting the war, and expanding the bombing campaign.

Changes in the Draft

Under President Nixon, the selective service system changed. College students could no longer obtain draft deferments, only 19-year-olds could be called for service in Vietnam, and draftees would be chosen by lottery on the basis of their birthdays. Protests against the draft faded with these reforms because the government began calling up fewer young men and because President Nixon promised to eliminate the selective service in the future.

Primary Source / A Changing Foreign Policy

The Nixon Doctrine Nixon and national security adviser Henry Kissinger shared views on many issues. The Nixon Doctrine spelled out a change in the nation's foreign policy. The United States would continue to provide military aid and training to allies. Nixon, however, set limits:

"America cannot—and will not—conceive all the plans, design all the programs, execute all the decisions and undertake all the defense of the free nations of the world."

Critical Thinking

Theorizing Do you think the Nixon Doctrine would change the role of the U.S. in Vietnam? Why or why not?

Troop Withdrawal

Meanwhile, President Nixon cut back the number of American troops in Vietnam. Known as **Vietnamization,** this plan called for the South Vietnamese to take a more active role in fighting—and for Americans to become less involved. As South Vietnamese soldiers took over, American troops would gradually withdraw from the country. In June 1969, Nixon announced the withdrawal of the first 25,000 American soldiers.

Increased Bombing

In the third part of his Vietnam policy, Nixon expanded the bombing campaign. Hoping to relieve pressure on troops in South Vietnam, Nixon ordered the bombing of enemy supply routes and hideouts in neighboring Cambodia and Laos. Although the president announced the changes to the draft and the troop withdrawals, he kept the bombing of Cambodia secret.

Reading Check **Identifying** To what position did President Nixon appoint Henry Kissinger?

Renewed Opposition at Home

Main Idea As Vietnamization moved forward, a new wave of antiwar protests gripped the nation.

History and You What would make you want to write an angry letter to a newspaper editor, join a protest march, or boycott a film producer? Read to learn why protests against the war in Vietnam resumed in 1969.

. . . .

A new round of antiwar **demonstrations,** or protest marches, began in late 1969, reflecting the growing sentiment for ending the war. In October more than 300,000 people took part in an antiwar protest in Washington, D.C.

The government also tried to end the war through peace talks with North Vietnam. Henry Kissinger, the president's national security adviser, represented the United States in the Paris talks. The United States had launched the bombing campaign to persuade the North Vietnamese to agree to peace terms.

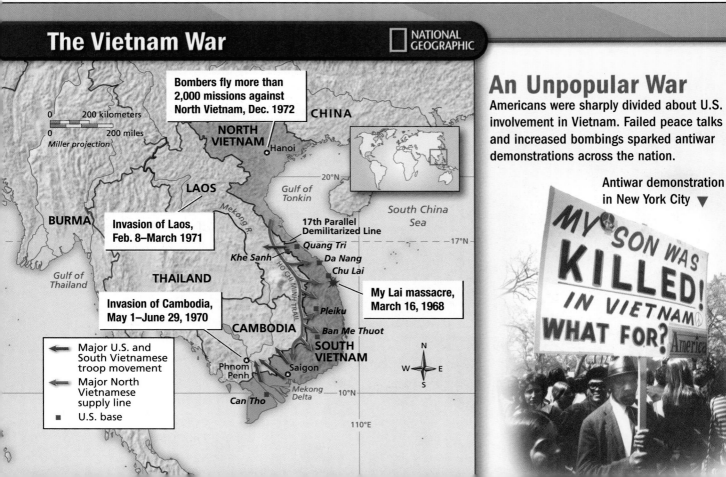

The Vietnam War

NATIONAL GEOGRAPHIC

Bombers fly more than 2,000 missions against North Vietnam, Dec. 1972

0   200 kilometers
0   200 miles
Miller projection

CHINA

NORTH VIETNAM
○ Hanoi

LAOS

20°N

Gulf of Tonkin

South China Sea

BURMA

Invasion of Laos, Feb. 8–March 1971

Mekong R.

17th Parallel Demilitarized Line

—17°N—

Quang Tri

Khe Sanh

Da Nang

Chu Lai

Gulf of Thailand

THAILAND

Invasion of Cambodia, May 1–June 29, 1970

HO CHI MINH TRAIL

My Lai massacre, March 16, 1968

Pleiku

CAMBODIA

Ban Me Thuot

SOUTH VIETNAM

Phnom Penh

Saigon

N
W   E
S

Mekong Delta

—10°N

Can Tho

110°E

← Major U.S. and South Vietnamese troop movement
← Major North Vietnamese supply line
■ U.S. base

An Unpopular War

Americans were sharply divided about U.S. involvement in Vietnam. Failed peace talks and increased bombings sparked antiwar demonstrations across the nation.

Antiwar demonstration in New York City ▼

MY SON WAS KILLED! IN VIETNAM WHAT FOR? America

The North Vietnamese, however, adopted a wait-and-see attitude. They believed that the growing strength of the antiwar movement in the United States would force the Americans to withdraw.

The new antiwar protests and North Vietnam's unyielding attitude alarmed President Nixon. In a speech in November, he appealed to the "silent majority" of Americans for support for his policy. "North Vietnam cannot defeat or humiliate the United States," he said. "Only Americans can do that."

Expanding the War

Further conflict gripped Southeast Asia when Cambodia plunged into a civil war between Communist and non-Communist forces. In April 1970, Nixon decided to send American troops to destroy Communist bases in Cambodia.

The attack aroused outrage throughout the nation. By sending U.S. troops to Cambodia, critics charged, Nixon invaded a neutral country and overstepped his constitutional authority as president.

Campus Protests

Many Americans viewed the Cambodian invasion as a widening of the Vietnam War. Nixon's action provoked a storm of antiwar protests on campuses across the nation. Most proceeded peacefully. Two protests, however, ended in tragedy.

At a protest at Kent State University in Kent, Ohio, students burned a military building on campus. Ohio's governor declared **martial law**—emergency military rule—on the campus and ordered 3,000 National Guard troops to Kent State.

At noon on May 4, students gathered for a protest rally on the campus lawn. The National Guard, young, inexperienced, and nervous, told the protesters to leave. When some students threw rocks at Guard members, the troops shot tear gas toward the students, and many students ran.

One National Guard unit chased some students between two buildings. Then—for reasons that are unclear—the troops opened fire. Four students were dead, and at least nine more were wounded.

By the Numbers

United States Troops in Vietnam, 1965–1973

Source: *Statistical Abstract of the United States*

Opposition to the War

1965 U.S. escalates involvement
1968 Tet offensive
1969 First withdrawal of U.S. troops
1973 Cease-fire signed

Source: *The Gallup Poll: Public Opinion*

Graph Skills

1. **Identifying** What percentage of Americans were against the war in 1965?

2. **Analyzing** In what year was opposition to the war the highest? The lowest? Why?

Violence flared again on May 15 at the nearly all-African American Jackson State University in Mississippi. Following a night of campus protests, two students were shot and killed. Witnesses charged that the police had recklessly blasted a residence hall with gunfire. The police claimed they were protecting themselves from sniper fire. A wave of student strikes followed the tragedies at Kent State and Jackson State. Hundreds of colleges and universities suspended classes.

The Pentagon Papers

In addition to sparking violence on campuses, the Cambodian invasion cost Nixon much support in Congress. Numerous lawmakers expressed outrage over the president's failure to tell them about the action. In December 1970, an angry Congress repealed the Gulf of Tonkin Resolution, which had given the president near-complete power in directing the war in Vietnam.

Support of the war weakened further that year when Daniel Ellsberg, a disillusioned former Defense Department worker, leaked documents to the *New York Times.* These documents, which became known as the **Pentagon Papers,** revealed that many government officials during the Johnson administration privately questioned the war while publicly supporting it.

The documents contained details of decisions that were made by presidents and their advisors without the approval of Congress. They also showed how various administrations acted to deceive Congress, the press, and the public about the situation in Vietnam. The Pentagon Papers backed up what many Americans had long believed: The government had not been honest with them.

 Reading Check **Describing** What tragedies occurred at Kent State and Jackson State Universities?

Legacy of the War NATIONAL GEOGRAPHIC

A Monument to the Fallen The war took a heavy toll on America's soldiers and their families. Post-Traumatic Stress Disorder, once called "shell shock," caused hallucinations, nightmares, and depression. In 1982 the Vietnam Veterans' Memorial Wall was dedicated in Washington, D.C. The names of those who were killed or missing in the war are engraved into two black granite walls.

United States . . .

- 58,000 American military personnel were killed
- 75,000 were severely disabled
- 2,338 were listed as Missing in Action (MIA) and 766 were Prisoners of War (POW)
- 725,000 Vietnamese resettled in U.S.
- 6.7 million tons of bombs were dropped on Vietnam (compared with 2.7 million tons dropped on Germany during World War II)

"Dear Michael: Your name is here but you are not. I made a rubbing of it, thinking if I rubbed hard enough I would rub your name off the wall. And you would come back to me. I miss you so."
—from an anonymous note left at the Vietnam Veterans' Memorial

Peace and the War's Legacy

Main Idea Peace talks led to the withdrawal of all American forces from Vietnam.

History and You Have you ever visited or seen pictures of the Vietnam War Memorial in Washington, D.C.? What effect did the memorial have on you? Read to find out about the end of the war and its impact on Americans.

• •

While antiwar feelings swelled at home—1971 polls showed that nearly two-thirds of Americans wanted the war to end quickly—the Nixon administration negotiated with representatives of the North Vietnamese government. These talks stalled, however.

In March 1972, the North Vietnamese launched another major offensive in the South. Because the United States had few troops left in Vietnam, Nixon resumed bombing. Nixon ordered American planes to bomb targets near Hanoi, the capital of North Vietnam. He also ordered the navy to plant mines in North Vietnamese harbors.

The president, however, stopped insisting that North Vietnam remove all its troops from South Vietnam before a full American withdrawal. Nixon sent Henry Kissinger to negotiate. In the fall of 1972 an agreement seemed ready, but South Vietnam opposed allowing North Vietnamese forces to remain in its territory. As a result the agreement collapsed.

Paris Peace Accords

After his reelection, Nixon unleashed American airpower against North Vietnam. In December 1972, the heaviest bombardment of the war fell on North Vietnam's cities. Nixon stood firm and North Vietnam returned to the talks. Meanwhile, the Americans pressured the South Vietnamese to accept the peace terms. On January 27, 1973, the negotiators signed the peace agreement.

Vietnam . . .
- 1.5 million Vietnamese soldiers and civilians were killed
- 362,000 were severely disabled
- 800,000 children were orphaned
- at least 1 million people fled the country
- 3.5 million acres of Vietnamese land were sprayed with chemicals that could impact the area for up to 100 years

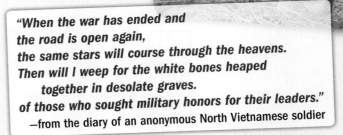

The effects of the Vietnam War still linger. Since the end of the war, more than 40,000 people in Vietnam have been killed by land mines or bombs that did not explode on impact. Agent Orange, a chemical sprayed by Americans to defoliate forests during the war, has been blamed for many birth defects.

"When the war has ended and
the road is open again,
the same stars will course through the heavens.
Then will I weep for the white bones heaped
        together in desolate graves.
of those who sought military honors for their leaders."
—from the diary of an anonymous North Vietnamese soldier

Critical Thinking

Making Inferences Although the countries and soldiers went into battle for different reasons, what did all people involved in the Vietnam War experience?

The War Ends

The United States agreed to pull its remaining troops out of the country. The North Vietnamese agreed to return all American prisoners of war. American involvement in Vietnam ended, but the conflict did not.

The North Vietnamese never gave up their goal of unifying Vietnam under their rule. In early 1975 they began a major offensive. The weakened South Vietnamese army collapsed on all fronts. Within a few weeks, North Vietnamese tanks approached Saigon. As North Vietnamese forces advanced, the last Americans left the country, some by helicopter from the roof of the U.S. embassy. Thousands of Vietnamese who had supported the Americans also fled to the United States. Many more could not escape. On April 30, 1975, Saigon fell to the Communists. Soon after, South Vietnam surrendered. The long war was over.

The Human Toll

The Vietnam War took a staggering toll. More than one million Vietnamese soldiers and civilians died, and Vietnam lay in ruins with many villages destroyed. More than 58,000 Americans were dead; 300,000 were wounded, many of them permanently disabled. The United States had poured more than $150 billion into the war.

Impact of the War

About 2.7 million Americans had served in Vietnam. Unlike the veterans of World War II, they found no hero's welcome when they returned home. Many Americans simply wanted to forget the war. They paid little attention to those who had fought and sacrificed in Vietnam.

The relatives of the American soldiers who had been classified as missing in action, or as **MIAs,** continued to demand that the government press the Vietnamese for information. The Vietnamese did allow a number of American groups to search the countryside. As the years passed, however, the likelihood of finding anyone alive faded.

Reading Check **Identifying** Who was in control of Vietnam when the war ended?

Section 4 Review

History ONLINE
Study Central™ To review this section, go to glencoe.com.

Vocabulary

1. Write a sentence for each of the following terms, explaining its significance in the Vietnam War era: authority, Vietnamization, demonstration, martial law, MIA.

Main Ideas

2. **Summarizing** What were the results of Nixon's Vietnamization plan?

3. **Explaining** What did Americans realize about the government after the release of the Pentagon Papers?

4. **Discussing** What did the Paris Peace Accords achieve?

Critical Thinking

5. **Categorizing** On a chart like the one below, list the major results from the Vietnam War in each category.

	Numbers of/ Results to
Vietnamese civilians and soldiers killed	
American soldiers killed	
American soldiers wounded	
U.S. cost in dollars	
Vietnamese countryside	

6. **Descriptive Writing** In a paragraph, describe how you feel about Nixon's actions during the Vietnam War and whether they were successful.

Answer the
7. **Essential Question** How did President Nixon remove the United States from the Vietnam War?

1954–1962

1954

July Geneva Accords divide Vietnam

1957

Oct. Soviet Union launches *Sputnik*

1961

April Bay of Pigs invasion fails

Aug. Berlin Wall is erected

▲ Berlin Wall

1962

Oct. Cuban missile crisis occurs

1963–1967

1963

Nov. John F. Kennedy is assassinated

Nov. Lyndon B. Johnson sworn in as president

1964

Aug. Gulf of Tonkin Resolution passes

1965

Dec. U.S. troop levels reach 180,000

1967

March War protesters march on Pentagon

Vietnamese village ▶

1968–1969

1968

Jan. North Korea captures USS *Pueblo*

Jan. North Vietnamese launch Tet offensive

April Dr. Martin Luther King, Jr., is assassinated

June Robert Kennedy is assassinated

Aug. Violence erupts at Democratic convention in Chicago

Nov. Richard Nixon wins presidency

1969

July Neil Armstrong walks on the moon

◀ Richard M. Nixon

1970–1975

1970

May Nixon sends troops to Cambodia

May Six students killed at Kent State and Jackson State

1973

Jan. Paris peace accords end U.S. involvement in Vietnam

1975

April South Vietnam surrenders to North Vietnam

Vietnam War protest ▼

STUDY TO GO
Study anywhere, anytime! Download quizzes and flash cards to your PDA from glencoe.com.

TEST-TAKING TIP

To understand the questions better, rewrite them in your own words, if you have time. Be careful not to change the meaning.

Reviewing Main Ideas

Directions: Choose the best answer for each of the following questions.

1. President Kennedy counteracted the appeal of communism in poor areas of Asia, Africa, and Latin America by
   - **A** creating the Peace Corps.
   - **B** introducing Green Berets.
   - **C** employing guerrilla warfare.
   - **D** spending more on nuclear arms.

2. Communism took root in South Vietnam because
   - **A** President Diem persecuted Buddhists.
   - **B** North Vietnam supported the Vietcong.
   - **C** Eisenhower sent billions in aid to Diem.
   - **D** many Vietnamese lacked land and services.

3. When did President Johnson halt the bombing of North Vietnam's cities?
   - **A** after the Tet Offensive
   - **B** after Nixon's election
   - **C** before the march on the Pentagon
   - **D** during the Democratic Convention

4. Nixon provoked protests on campuses by
   - **A** leaking the Pentagon Papers.
   - **B** sending troops to Cambodia.
   - **C** ending draft deferments for students.
   - **D** having Kissinger seek a peace settlement.

Short-Answer Question

Directions: Base your answer to question 5 on the excerpt below and on your knowledge of social studies.

> He was now in Ward 1-C with fifty other men who had all been recently wounded in the [Vietnam] war— twenty-year-old blind men and amputees, men without intestines, men who limped, men who were in wheelchairs, men in pain. He noticed they all had strange smiles on their faces and he had one too, he thought. They were men who had played with death and cheated it at a very young age.
>
> —Ron Kovic, *Born on the Fourth of July*

5. What was the human cost of the Vietnam War?

Review the Essential Questions

6. **Essay** What roles did Presidents Kennedy, Johnson, and Nixon play in the Vietnam War?

To help you write your essay, review your answers to the Essential Questions in the section reviews and the chapter Foldables Study Organizer. Your essay should include:
- why and how Americans became involved in the Vietnam War;
- presidential decisions that kept the war going; and
- how citizen protests influenced Johnson's and Nixon's policies.

GO ON ➡

Document-Based Questions

Directions: Analyze the documents and answer the short-answer questions that follow.

Document 1

Four days before the Bay of Pigs invasion, Kennedy responded to press reports of CIA-trained invaders.

> There will not be, under any conditions, any intervention in Cuba by United States armed forces.

Source: Howard Zinn, *A People's History of the United States*

7. Why do you think President Kennedy did not tell reporters about the planned invasion?

Document 2

Madame Nhu, a member of President Diem's family, commented on the monks who protested Diem's policies by setting themselves on fire.

> "Let them burn," she said. "We shall clap our hands."

Source: Stephen Kinzer, *Overthrow*

8. What impact did the monks' protests have on Diem and others?

Document 3

The author of this excerpt talks about the beginning of the Tet Offensive.

> When the assault . . . first began we didn't know what was going on. . . . All the towns of the Delta . . . were full of [Vietcong]. Every town and city in the country was under siege. Every airfield had been hit. Every road cut. They were in the streets of Saigon, in the American embassy. All in one night.

Source: Tobias Wolff, *In Pharoah's Army*

9. Why did Americans criticize the conduct of the war after the Tet Offensive?

Document 4

This political cartoon, titled "Our Position Hasn't Changed At All," appeared in the *Washington Post* on June 17, 1965.

Source: The Herb Block Foundation

10. What does this cartoon say about President Johnson's policy in Vietnam?

Document 5

General James Carroll defended his son's decision to seek conscientious objector status in 1972.

> All I know for sure is this: if human beings don't drastically change the way they resolve their conflicts, we won't survive this century. My son . . . certainly represents a drastic change from the way we were brought up. And that may be just the change we need.

Source: James Carroll, *An American Requiem*

11. What did Carroll's son decide to do? What options did the young man have regarding going to war?

12. Expository Writing Using the information from the five documents and your knowledge of social studies, write an essay in which you:
- explain why the Vietnam War was difficult for Vietnamese and American soldiers and civilians; and
- describe how support for U.S. involvement in Vietnam changed over time.

Need Extra Help?												
If you missed questions. . .	1	2	3	4	5	6	7	8	9	10	11	12
Go to page. . .	464	470	480	487	490	468–490	464–465	471	479	471–480	477–478	468–490

Unit 6

America in a Modern Era
1968 to Present

The iPhone is a multi-media mobile phone.

494

"We have every right to dream heroic dreams. . . . You can see heroes every day going in and out of factory gates."
—Ronald Reagan

Melissa Etheridge performs at Live Earth, the Concerts for a Climate in Crisis, 2007.

495

Unit 6

Reading History

Monitoring and Clarifying

Learn It!

Monitoring is the ability to know whether you understand what you have read. If you do not understand the information, then you must try to identify why you do not understand it. You must *clarify,* or clear up, the parts that are confusing. Read the following paragraph. Use the "Ways to Clarify" column for tips about how you can clarify your reading.

Monitor	Ways to Clarify
Are there any words that are unfamiliar?	Use the glossary, a dictionary, or context clues.
What is the main idea of the paragraph?	Try to summarize the information into one sentence to create a main idea.
Is it helpful to use what I already know about democracy to understand the text?	Think about what you have learned about democracy. Then think about how this relates to Iraq.
What questions do I still have after reading this text?	Write the questions and continue to read to find the answers.

—from Chapter 17, p. 552

The United States set out to create a democracy in Iraq. . . . The United States and its allies trained more Iraqis to serve in the police and the military. They also attempted to provide electricity, clean water, schools, and improved health care for Iraq's people.

Practice It!

Read the following paragraph. Draw a chart like the one below to help you monitor and clarify your reading.

—from Chapter 17, p. 562

Because pollution crosses international borders, many experts believe that nations have to work together to find solutions. In 1987, for example, 23 nations agreed to ban chemicals suspected of harming the ozone layer—a part of the atmosphere that shields Earth from the sun's radiation.

Monitor	Ways to Clarify
1. _____	1. _____
2. _____	2. _____
3. _____	3. _____

Academic Vocabulary Preview

Listed below are the academic vocabulary words and their definitions that you will come across as you study Unit 6. Practice It! will help you study the words and definitions.

Academic Vocabulary	Definition	Practice It!
Chapter 16 America in the 1970s		
relax (rih · LAKS) *p. 501*	to ease	**Identify** *the term from Chapter 16 that best completes the sentence.*
technology (tehk · NAH · luh · jee) *p. 503*	scientific tools and material	**1.** Diplomatic negotiations can dramatically _____ tensions and improve relations between countries.
energy (EH · nuhr · jee) *p. 510*	sources of usable power	**2.** The Soviet Union hoped détente with the United States would give them access to American _____.
controversy (KAHN · truh · VUHR · see) *p. 512*	arguments between opposing viewpoints	**3.** The 1973 oil embargo forced Americans to conserve _____.
integrity (ihn · TEH · gruh · tee) *p. 517*	moral character	**4.** A _____ erupted because Nixon would not give White House tapes to the special prosecutors.
exceed (ihk · SEED) *p. 517*	to be greater; go beyond	**5.** Most candidates for public office talk about their personal _____.
Chapter 17 New Challenges		
quote (KWOHT) *p. 531*	to repeat the words of another	**Identify** *the term from Chapter 17 that best matches the underlined term or terms.*
theme (THEEM) *p. 532*	a subject	**6.** The United States wants to <u>keep</u> its position as a leader in world trade.
retain (rih · TAYN) *p. 535*	to hold on to	**7.** Many scientists believe that changes in weather patterns due to global warming are <u>certain</u>.
site (SYT) *p. 537*	a location	**8.** Terrorists gave no <u>earlier</u> notice of their attack on the United States.
adequate (A · dih · kwuht) *p. 541*	enough	**Choose** *the word that best matches the meaning of each vocabulary term listed below.*
scope (SKOHP) *p. 543*	a range; area	
prior (PRY · uhr) *p. 551*	earlier	**9. quote** **11. decade**
definite (DEH · fuh · niht) *p. 555*	precise; well-defined	**a.** comment **a.** one hundred
decade (DEH · KAYD) *p. 559*	a period of ten years	**b.** punctuation **b.** ten
aware (uh · WEHR) *p. 561*	to be mindful; have knowledge of	**c.** guess **c.** lifetime
		10. site **12. adequate**
		a. location **a.** good
		b. vision **b.** too much
		c. spirit **c.** enough

Chapter 16

America in the 1970s 1968–1981

One goal of space exploration was reached on July 20, 1969, when U.S. astronauts set foot on the moon.

RICHARD
NIXON
1969–1974

PRESIDENTS

U.S. Events

World Events

1968

1971

★ 1967
Six-Day
Arab-Israeli
War

★ 1971
People's Republic
of China is admit-
ted to UN

1972 ★
Nixon
visits
Beijing

1972
SALT I is
signed

★ 1973
Watergate
hearings
begin

★ 1973
OPEC
imposes
embargo of
oil to U.S.

Section 1: Nixon's Foreign Policy

Essential Question What were President Nixon's main goals in foreign policy, and how did he work to achieve them?

Section 2: Nixon and Watergate

Essential Question What were President Nixon's major domestic challenges in the 1970s?

Section 3: The Carter Presidency

Essential Question What major foreign affairs issues did President Carter face during his presidency, and how did he deal with them?

American hostages are paraded by their Iranian captors, 1979. ▼

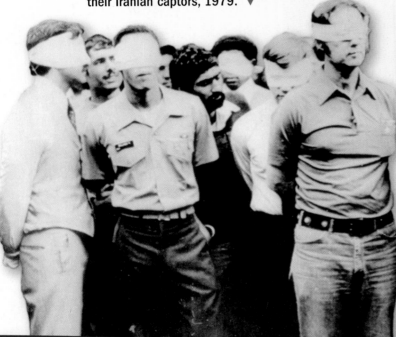

History ONLINE
Chapter Overview Visit glencoe.com and click on **Chapter 16—Chapter Overviews** to preview chapter information.

FOLDABLES Study Organizer

Organizing Information

Make this Foldable to organize what you learn about the presidents and their policies during the 1970s.

Step 1 Fold a 2 1/2 inch tab along the long edge of a sheet of paper.

Step 2 Fold the paper in thirds.

Step 3 Open the paper pocket Foldable. Staple the ends of the pockets together.

Step 4 Label the pockets as shown.

Reading and Writing

As you read the chapter, summarize key facts on note cards or on quarter sheets of notebook paper. Organize your notes by placing them in your pocket Foldable inside the appropriate pockets.

★ **1974** President Nixon resigns

GERALD FORD 1974–1977

JIMMY CARTER 1977–1981

★ **1979** Iranians take Americans hostages

★ **1980** U.S. boycotts Moscow Olympics

★ **1981** Iranians release U.S. hostages

RONALD REAGAN 1981–1989

1974   **1977**   **1980**

◄ Fluctuating prices and supplies of gas meant long lines at gas pumps.

★ **1979** Soviet troops invade Afghanistan

★ **1981** Scientists identify AIDS

Nixon's Foreign Policy

Essential Question ◄

What were President Nixon's main goals in foreign policy, and how did he work to achieve them?

Reading Guide

Content Vocabulary

détente (p. 501)   embargo (p. 504)
balance of power (p. 501)

Academic Vocabulary

relax (p. 501)   technology (p. 503)

Key People

Henry Kissinger (p. 501)

Zhou Enlai (p. 502)

Leonid Brezhnev (p. 503)

Golda Meir (p. 504)

Anwar el-Sadat (p. 504)

Reading Strategy

Taking Notes Re-create a diagram like the one below to show the countries that were the focus of Nixon's foreign policy.

Countries <

American Diary

Richard Nixon was long known for his anticommunist views. Thus, many people were surprised when Nixon set out to improve relations with the nation's main rivals—China and the Soviet Union—in the interests of world peace. Nixon announced: "We seek an open world—open to ideas, open to the exchange of goods and people—a world in which no people, great or small, will live in angry isolation."

—from Nixon's Inaugural Address,
January 1969

President Nixon's visit to China in 1972 was the first step in establishing better relations between the U.S. and the People's Republic of China.

Easing the Cold War

Main Idea President Nixon sought to ease Cold War tensions by improving relations with the Soviet Union and China.

History and You Have you ever tried to "mend fences" with somebody after a long disagreement? Read to learn about the changing relationships between the United States and Communist nations in the 1970s.

. . . .

In his Inaugural Address, President Nixon told the American people, "The greatest honor . . . is the title of peacemaker." Many Americans wondered whether Nixon fit the role of peacemaker. During his years in Congress, he gained a reputation as a fierce enemy of communism. Few people imagined that Nixon, the anti-Communist crusader, would introduce policies to improve America's relations with the Communist world.

Behind the Iron Curtain

President Nixon intended to leave his mark on foreign policy. He hoped to build a more stable, peaceful world by reaching out to the Soviet Union and the People's Republic of China. In the summer of 1969, Nixon visited several countries, including Romania—the first time an American president went behind the iron curtain. Nixon wanted to find areas of common interest and cooperation with these Cold War opponents.

Détente

To help him in this task, Nixon appointed **Henry Kissinger,** a Harvard University professor, as his national security adviser. Kissinger and Nixon shared a belief in *realpolitik*—policies based on national interests rather than political beliefs. They believed that peace among nations would come through negotiation rather than through threats or force. Nixon followed a policy of détente—attempts at **relaxing,** or easing, international tensions. As détente replaced confrontation, the United States and Communist states could begin working together to resolve issues that divided them.

Nixon realized that détente would work only if a **balance of power** existed. A balance of power is a distribution of power among nations that prevents any one nation from becoming too powerful. "It will be a safer world and a better world," he declared, "if we have a strong, healthy United States, Europe, Soviet Union, China, Japan—each balancing the other, not playing one against the other."

Primary Source — "Ping-Pong" Diplomacy

One of the first steps in improving relationships between China and the United States was the visit of the U.S. table-tennis team to China. *TIME* magazine called it "the ping heard round the world."

Pat Oliphant. *The Denver Post,* 1971.

Critical Thinking

Analyzing Do you think sports can help improve relations between nations? Explain.

Détente in Space

Détente led to the first cooperative space mission between the United States and the Soviet Union. The U.S. *Apollo* and the Soviet *Soyuz* linked up in Earth's orbit on July 17, 1975.

▲ Astronauts and cosmonauts share a meal inside the *Soyuz* mock-up during training at the Johnson Space Center in Houston.

▲ A view of the *Soyuz* space capsule from the *Apollo* command module

China

Détente began with improved American-Chinese relations. Since 1949, when a Communist government came to power in China, the United States had refused to recognize the People's Republic of China. Instead it recognized the anti-Communist Chinese government under Chiang Kai-shek in exile on the island of Taiwan.

By the time of Nixon's presidency, however, each side had good reasons for wanting to improve relations. China distrusted the Soviet Union. Since the 1960s, disagreements had developed between them that divided the Communist world. Chinese and Soviet troops occasionally clashed along their borders. The United States hoped that recognition of China would help end the war in Vietnam and drive a deeper wedge between the two Communist powers.

The winds of change began to blow in the fall of 1970 when Nixon told reporters that he wanted to go to China. Noting this change in tone, the Chinese responded by inviting an American table tennis team to visit the country in April 1971. A week later the United States announced the opening of trade with China.

"Ping-Pong diplomacy" was accompanied by secret talks between American and Chinese officials about forging closer ties between the two nations. After Kissinger made a secret trip to China in July 1971, President Nixon announced that he would visit Beijing, the Chinese capital, "to seek the normalization of relations."

In February 1972, Nixon arrived in China for a weeklong visit. Nixon and China's premier **Zhou Enlai** agreed to allow greater scientific and cultural exchange and to resume trade. Although formal diplomatic relations were not established until 1979, Nixon's trip marked the first formal contact with China in more than 25 years.

What Is Détente?

The Nixon administration developed a policy called détente, or relaxation of tensions, between the United States and the Soviet Union and China.

Goals of Détente
- Reduce risk of nuclear war
- Cut back on military budget
- Forge better relations with rivals

Apollo-Soyuz patch ▲

Détente at Work
- President Nixon visits China, Soviet Union
- 1972 SALT I agreement signed
- U.S.-Soviet joint venture in space
- 1975 Helsinki Accords promote rights, trade

Critical Thinking

Analyzing The *Apollo-Soyuz* mission provided an opportunity for scientific research. According to U.S. pilot Vance Brand, the mission also had another goal: "to open the door a little bit between East and West." What do you think Brand meant?

The Soviet Union

Nixon followed his trip to China with a visit to Moscow, the Soviet capital, in May 1972. The Soviets welcomed a Cold War thaw. They wanted to prevent a Chinese-American alliance. They also hoped to buy United States **technology,** or scientific tools and material. Soviet leader **Leonid Brezhnev** remarked, "There must be room in this world for two great nations with different systems to live together and work together."

While in Moscow, Nixon signed the Strategic Arms Limitation Treaty (SALT I). This treaty restricted the number of certain types of nuclear missiles. The United States and the Soviet Union also agreed to work together in trade and science. Nixon—and the world—hoped that a new era of cooperation would bring greater stability to world affairs.

 Reading Check **Identifying** What is détente?

The Middle East

Main Idea Nixon's foreign policy included easing Arab-Israeli tensions in the Middle East.

History and You Do you think that people of very different backgrounds can live together peacefully? Read to find out how the United States set out to achieve peace between the Arabs and the Israelis.

President Nixon's foreign policy aimed to maintain world stability without being drawn into regional disputes. The president stated that the United States would help other nations but would not take "basic responsibility" for the future of those nations. A crisis soon arose in the Middle East that tested this policy.

Arab-Israeli Tensions

Since the founding of the Jewish state of Israel in 1948, the U.S. had supported Israel in its struggles against its Arab neighbors. Tensions between Israel and the Arab states erupted in war in 1948 and 1956.

After Egypt closed a key waterway and massed its troops near Israel's border, Israel bombed Egyptian airfields on June 5, 1967. Within six days, Israel wiped out the air forces of its Arab neighbors. Israeli troops moved west into the Gaza Strip and Egypt's Sinai Peninsula and north into the Golan Heights, which were part of Syria. Israel also captured the old city of Jerusalem and the territory west of the Jordan River that Jordan had absorbed.

The "Six-Day War" of 1967 left Israel in control of these areas. When the fighting ended, the United Nations asked the Israelis to leave the captured territories. It asked the Arab nations to accept Israel's right to exist. Both sides refused.

The 1967 war also increased the number of Arab refugees, or displaced people. Thousands of Palestinians now lived in Israeli-held territory, and thousands more lived in neighboring Arab states. The Palestinians' demand for their own homeland became another source of instability.

The fuel shortages caused by the 1973 oil embargo plunged the nation into a state of emergency. The Department of Energy considered different plans to save fuel. One plan was to close gas stations on Sundays.

1. **Identifying** What is the event or issue that inspired this cartoon?

2. **Analyzing Visuals** What message is the author trying to convey in this cartoon?

"My text this morning is taken from Paragraph 15 of the President's message in regard to Sunday driving."

Yom Kippur War

Tensions remained high between Arabs and Israelis. As a result, war erupted again in 1973. Egypt and Syria attacked Israel to regain land lost in the 1967 War. Because this attack occurred on Yom Kippur, a major Jewish holiday, the conflict became known as the Yom Kippur War.

Egypt's forces attacked Israel, hoping to recapture the Sinai Peninsula. In early battles, many Israeli planes were shot down. Egypt's troops crossed into the Sinai, and Syria moved into the Golan Heights. With an American airlift of weapons, Israel struck back. The fighting raged until the United Nations negotiated a cease-fire. By this time, the Israelis had regained the land lost in the initial Arab advance. Israel also took additional territory from Syria and Egypt.

Angered by the U.S. support of Israel, Arab oil-producing states placed an **embargo**—a ban on shipments—of oil to the United States and other "non-friendly" nations.

The embargo led to an oil shortage in the United States. Long lines of cars formed at gas pumps as gas prices skyrocketed.

Shuttle Diplomacy

President Nixon sent Kissinger, now secretary of state, to the region to gain Arab trust and to negotiate an agreement between Israel and its Arab neighbors. Kissinger engaged in shuttle diplomacy—traveling back and forth among Middle Eastern capitals trying to resolve the oil crisis and forge a lasting peace.

Early in 1974, **Golda Meir,** the prime minister of Israel, and **Anwar el-Sadat,** the president of Egypt, agreed to separate Israeli and Egyptian forces in the Sinai Peninsula. Then in March 1974, Kissinger persuaded the Arab nations to end the oil embargo. Kissinger also improved U.S. ties with Egypt, the most powerful Arab state, by promising large amounts of foreign aid.

 ONLINE

Student Web Activity Visit glencoe.com and complete the Chapter 16 Web Activity about shuttle diplomacy.

Reading Check **Summarizing** What happened in the United States because of the oil embargo?

Latin America

Main Idea The Nixon administration continued the effort to halt the spread of communism in Latin America.

History and You Do you believe one country has the right to interfere in the affairs of another country? Read to find out how concerns about communism shaped the Nixon administration's policies in Latin America.

· ·

The Nixon administration sought to prevent the spread of communism in Latin America. In 1970 the country of Chile elected Salvador Allende president. Allende was a follower of Karl Marx, the founder of communism. He became the first Marxist, or supporter of Marx, to rise to power in the Americas through peaceful means.

To boost Chile's economy, Allende's government took over large businesses, gave land to the poor, and raised workers' wages. The economy grew, and the jobless rate declined. Not all of Allende's policies were successful, however. His breakup of large farms led to a decline in food production, which in turn caused food shortages. Also, increased wages led businesses to raise prices.

More important, Allende's policies made him enemies. Wealthy Chileans, frightened by Allende's Marxist views, took their money out of the country and invested it abroad. The United States, angered by Allende's takeover of American companies, decided to undermine the Allende government. It gave money to Allende's political opponents and promoted strikes. It also convinced foreign investors to stop loaning money to Chile. By 1972, Chile's economy was near collapse.

In 1973 Chile's military decided to take action. With the backing of the Central Intelligence Agency (CIA), a group of Chilean military leaders under General Augusto Pinochet overthrew the government and killed Allende. The United States immediately recognized the new military dictatorship and restored foreign aid to Chile.

Reading Check **Explaining** Why did the United States oppose Salvador Allende?

Section 1 Review

History ONLINE
Study Central™ To review this section, go to glencoe.com.

Vocabulary

1. Use each of the following terms in a paragraph about U.S. foreign policy: détente, relax, balance of power, technology, embargo.

Main Ideas

2. **Analyzing** What did the United States hope recognition of China would achieve?

3. **Discussing** What was the purpose of shuttle diplomacy?

4. **Explaining** How did the United States combat President Allende in Chile?

Critical Thinking

5. **Determining Cause and Effect** On a chart like the one below, list a major effect in each country caused by Nixon's foreign policy.

6. **Expository Writing** In a short essay, discuss Kissinger's achievements during the crisis in the Middle East.

Answer the
7. **Essential Question**
What were President Nixon's main goals in foreign policy, and how did he work to achieve them?

Section 2 ★ Nixon and Watergate

Essential Question ◄

What were President Nixon's major domestic challenges in the 1970s?

Reading Guide

Content Vocabulary

revenue sharing *(p. 507)*

affirmative action *(p. 508)*

tight money policy *(p. 508)*

deficit *(p. 509)*

executive privilege *(p. 511)*

impeach *(p. 511)*

amnesty *(p. 512)*

Academic Vocabulary

energy *(p. 510)*   controversy *(p. 512)*

Key People and Events

New Federalism *(p. 507)*

Watergate *(p. 510)*

Sam Ervin *(p. 511)*

Gerald R. Ford *(p. 511)*

Reading Strategy

Taking Notes On a diagram like the one below, record the factors that led to stagflation.

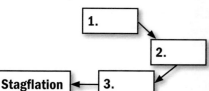

1.

2.

Stagflation ◄ 3.

American Diary

President Nixon believed that the national government had grown cumbersome and inefficient, and that too many people were dependent on it. In August 1969, he announced a policy called "New Federalism" in a speech to the nation:

"After a third of a century of power flowing from the people and the States to Washington it is time for a New Federalism in which power, funds, and responsibility will flow from Washington to the States and to the people."

—Richard Nixon's address to the nation,
August 8, 1969

President Nixon called for stiffer law enforcement measures and more aid for state and local law enforcement agencies.

Nixon's Domestic Program

Main Idea The Nixon administration sought to reduce the role of the federal government in American life.

History and You If you were on a group project and found that you had too much to do, how would you solve the problem? Read to find out how the Nixon administration tried to reduce the federal government's workload by shifting more tasks to state and local governments.

. . . .

In his 1968 presidential campaign, Nixon pledged to bring back "law and order" to American society. He also vowed to reduce government's role in people's lives.

Nixon's drive to restore law and order involved "cracking down on crime" and imposing stiffer penalties on lawbreakers. To strengthen police powers, Nixon used federal funds to help state and city police forces.

The Courts

Nixon thought the federal courts should be tougher on criminals. "As a judicial conservative," he said, "I believe some Court decisions have gone too far in weakening the peace forces against the criminal forces in our society." During his presidency, four

vacancies arose on the Supreme Court. Nixon hoped that the justices he appointed—Warren Burger as chief justice, and Harry Blackmun, Lewis Powell, and William Rehnquist —would shift the Court to a more conservative position. The decisions of the new justices did not fully meet the president's conservative goals, however.

New Federalism

Nixon wanted to reduce federal involvement in people's lives and to cut federal spending. He pledged to "reverse the flow of power and resources from the states and communities to Washington and start power and resources flowing back . . . to the people." To accomplish this goal, he introduced a program called the **New Federalism.** One part of the New Federalism called for giving the states some of the revenue earned from federal taxes for use at the state and local levels. This **revenue sharing** became law in 1972.

Nixon also sought to end or scale back many Great Society programs begun under President Johnson. He promised to "quit pouring billions of dollars into programs that have failed." He abolished the Office of Economic Opportunity, the agency that led Johnson's War on Poverty.

Primary Source / New Federalism

A New Approach President Nixon rejected the idea that "government in Washington, D.C., is inevitably more wise . . . than government at the local or State level." He called for turning over to state and local governments many of the responsibilities of the federal government. New Federalism would make government more effective by:

- reducing big government programs
- restoring political authority to the local level
- directing tax money away from federal bureaucracy
- directing money toward state and local governments

Critical Thinking

Explaining What was the goal of New Federalism policies?

Busing To end segregation in public schools, state courts ordered the busing of children to schools outside their neighborhoods.

Some civil rights leaders and some parents favored the use of busing. Many parents, however, did not want their children attending distant schools.

Diane Joyce kept her job when the Court ruled that gender can be a factor in hiring. ▶

Affirmative Action Opponents of affirmative action argue that merit is the only basis for making decisions on jobs, promotions, and school admissions. Supporters contend that affirmative action programs are needed to encourage the hiring and promotion of minorities and women in fields that were traditionally closed to them.

▲ Columbus, Georgia, students arrive for school, September 7, 1971.

On civil rights issues, Nixon took a conservative position aimed at appealing to white voters. For example, Nixon opposed busing. Busing was used to promote racial integration by transporting students from mostly white or African American neighborhoods to racially mixed schools.

At the same time, his administration worked to carry out federal court orders to integrate schools. The Nixon administration also promoted **affirmative action,** or preference to minorities in jobs where they previously were excluded. A practical politician, President Nixon did accept new government programs that had popular support. He approved the creation of two new agencies—the Occupational Safety and Health Administration (OSHA) to ensure workers' safety and the Environmental Protection Agency (EPA) to protect the environment.

Economic Troubles

While attempting to change the direction of government, President Nixon had to deal with serious economic problems. Industry and manufacturing were declining because of foreign competition. Businesses and consumers struggled with inflation—a general rise in the prices of goods and services. This was fueled by international competition for raw materials and the increasing cost of oil. The United States also faced slow economic growth and high unemployment.

President Nixon tried several approaches to reduce inflation. He began by cutting federal spending. At the same time, he called for a **tight money policy.** Interest rates were raised so that people would borrow less and spend less. With less money in circulation, prices dropped. However, as demand slowed, businesses began to cut back and output fell.

Disability Rights The Rehabilitation Act of 1973 was the first major legislation to prohibit discrimination against people with disabilities. The act applied to programs that receive federal financial assistance.

▼ Disabled Americans protest for equal rights.

Critical Thinking

1. **Explaining** What were the goals of affirmative action policies?
2. **Speculating** What accommodations can be made for people with disabilities, such as those in the photo above?

These steps slowed economic growth and led to stagflation—a combination of rising prices and a sluggish economy.

Nixon then switched tactics. He temporarily froze wages and prices and issued guidelines for any future increases. This put a brake on inflation, but the economy remained in a recession.

Later, Nixon tried a third approach—increasing federal spending to stimulate the economy. Although this policy helped revive the economy for a short time, it also created a budget **deficit** in which government spending was greater than government revenue. None of Nixon's policies restored the economy to its previous strength, and economic problems continued to trouble his administration.

✔ **Reading Check** **Analyzing** What is the outcome of a tight-money policy?

Reelection and Watergate

Main Idea During his second term, President Nixon was involved in a political scandal that forced him to resign.

History and You What would officials do if someone broke into your school and stole something? Read to learn how an attempted burglary shook the presidency and the nation.

. . . .

As the 1972 presidential election neared, Nixon had doubts about his chances for reelection. The war in Vietnam had not yet ended, and the nation was facing economic problems. The president and his supporters wanted to ensure his reelection.

A Campaign Against Enemies

To carry out his campaign, Nixon relied on a small group of aides, including John Ehrlichman, his chief domestic adviser, and H.R. Haldeman, his chief of staff. In their efforts to win the election, the president and his advisers, it was later revealed, sometimes crossed the boundaries of the law. In 1971, for example, Nixon asked his aides for an "enemies list" of people considered unfriendly to the administration. He then ordered the FBI and the Internal Revenue Service (IRS) to investigate some of these people. Nixon believed that those who opposed his policies posed a danger to the nation's security.

Nixon's campaign committee collected millions of dollars. It used some of this money to create a secret group to stop leaks of information that might hurt the administration. Some campaign money also paid for operations against Nixon's Democratic foes, but that party had many problems of its own.

Landslide Victory

The Democratic Party was split. Candidates seeking the nomination included former vice president Hubert Humphrey, Senators Edmund Muskie of Maine and George McGovern of South Dakota, and former governor of Alabama George Wallace.

Muskie and Humphrey could not gain enough support. Wallace's campaign was cut short in May 1972 by a would-be assassin's bullet that left him paralyzed.

McGovern, the most liberal of the four candidates, won the nomination. Many Democrats and labor union leaders were cool toward McGovern's candidacy.

The Democrats' lack of unity as well as an upsurge in the economy and the prospect of peace in Vietnam led to a landslide victory for Nixon. He won 60.7 percent of the popular vote. The Republican victory in the electoral college was even more lopsided—520 to 17.

The Energy Crisis

During Nixon's second term, severe economic problems confronted the nation. The U.S. economy depended heavily on foreign oil. In 1973 the Organization of Petroleum Exporting Countries (OPEC), placed an embargo on all oil shipments to the United States. As a result, many American companies had to lay off workers, while others raised their prices. Consumers complained about the high prices and the long lines at gas stations.

The president imposed measures to save oil. Nixon also urged Americans to conserve energy—sources of usable power—voluntarily. Congress reduced speed limits on highways because a vehicle burns less fuel at lower speeds. To deal with the problem of reliance on imported oil, Nixon urged development of domestic oil, especially in Alaska, which possessed vast, untapped oil reserves.

Watergate

During Nixon's second term, what seemed like a small scandal turned into a presidential crisis. In June 1972, Nixon's reelection committee had five men break into the Democratic Party's office at the **Watergate** apartment-office complex in Washington, D.C. The burglars set out to get information about the Democrats' campaign and to place listening devices—bugs—on the office telephones. A security guard caught them, and the police later arrested the men. Reports soon surfaced that the burglars were linked to the Nixon campaign and were paid from White House funds. The White House denied any involvement.

The Path of Watergate

The Watergate scandal rocked the nation's trust in its elected officials but ultimately illustrated that America's system of government works.

Security guard Frank Willis discovered the Watergate break-in ▶

June 1972 ★
Watergate break-in reported

June 1973 ★
John Dean implicates Nixon in cover-up

1972

1973

1974

Nov. 1972 ★
Nixon reelected

May 1973 ★
Senate hearings begin

Oct. 1973 ★
Saturday Night Massacre

April 1974 ★
Nixon releases edited tapes

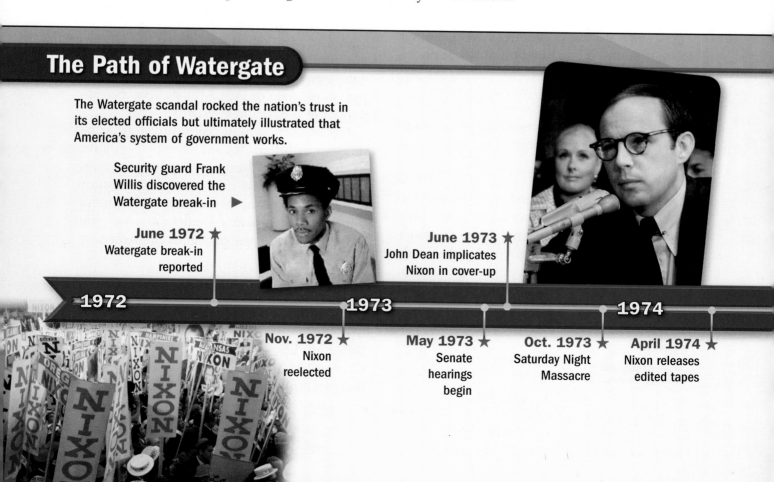

Investigation

Meanwhile, a series of newspaper articles in the *Washington Post* linked the burglary to the Nixon campaign. Eventually, one of the burglars admitted that White House aides had lied about their involvement and had pressured the burglars to plead guilty and remain silent.

In May 1973, the Senate began holding hearings on Watergate. Chaired by Senator **Sam Ervin** of North Carolina, the hearings slowly revealed the inner workings of the Nixon White House. John Dean, a White House official, testified that a cover-up occurred and that Nixon directed it, but he had no evidence to support his claim.

In July investigators learned that a secret taping system had recorded all of the president's office conversations. President Nixon refused to hand over the tapes. He claimed executive privilege, the principle that White House conversations should remain secret to protect national security.

Meanwhile, the special prosecutor—someone independent of the Justice Department—requested a court order to get the tapes. Nixon tried to have this official fired, but the attorney general and the attorney general's deputy both refused to carry out Nixon's order. In what became known as the Saturday Night Massacre, Nixon fired these officials and had the special prosecutor removed from office.

In the middle of the turmoil, another scandal struck the Nixon administration. Vice President Spiro Agnew was charged with taking bribes while governor of Maryland. In October 1973, he resigned. **Gerald R. Ford** of Michigan, the Republican leader of the House, became the new vice president.

The President Resigns

To quiet mounting public outrage, Nixon named a new special prosecutor, who was determined to get the tapes. After Nixon had released only edited versions of some of the tapes, the Supreme Court ruled that the president had to turn over all of the tapes, and Nixon complied.

Several days later, the House Judiciary Committee voted to **impeach** Nixon, or officially charge him with misconduct in office. Before the House of Representatives could vote on whether Nixon should be impeached, investigators found clear evidence against the president. One of the tapes revealed that Nixon had ordered a cover-up of the Watergate break-in just a few days after it happened.

With this news, even Nixon's strongest supporters admitted that an impeachment trial now seemed unavoidable. On August 9, 1974, Nixon resigned his office in disgrace. Gerald Ford took the oath of office and became the nation's 38th president.

The Watergate crisis revealed that the system of checks and balances worked to remove a president who had abused his power. Congress passed laws to correct some of the abuses. However, the scandal damaged the public's faith in its political leaders.

Reading Check Explaining How did Gerald Ford become president?

"I would say only that if some of my judgments were wrong—and some were wrong—they were made in what I believed at the time to be the best interest of the Nation."
—Nixon's resignation speech, August 8, 1974

★ **August 1974**
Nixon releases tapes and resigns

1975

Critical Thinking

Analyzing Visuals Look at the photo above. What thoughts or feelings do you think President Nixon was having at the time he left the White House?

A Time for Healing

Main Idea President Ford set out to unite the nation after the Watergate scandal.

History and You Whom do you turn to for advice when times are difficult? Read to find out how the nation responded to Gerald Ford's leadership.

. . . .

After becoming president, Gerald Ford assured Americans, "Our long national nightmare is over." To fill the office of vice president, Ford selected Nelson Rockefeller, a highly respected Republican and former governor of New York.

Domestic Controversies

Most Americans welcomed the new president and vice president as a fresh start for the nation. One of Ford's first acts, however, destroyed much of this confidence. On September 8, 1974, Ford granted Richard Nixon a pardon for any crimes he may have committed as president. This meant that the former president could not be prosecuted for his part in the cover-up.

Ford hoped that the pardon would help heal the wounds of Watergate. Instead, the pardon stirred **controversy,** or arguments between opposing viewpoints. Many Americans questioned why Nixon should escape punishment when others involved in the scandal went to jail. Some even accused Ford of striking a bargain with Nixon in advance—the promise of a pardon in exchange for Nixon's resignation. Although Ford defended his action, the new president never fully regained the trust and popularity he enjoyed in his first weeks in office.

Yet another controversy arose when President Ford offered **amnesty,** or protection from prosecution, to men who illegally avoided military service during the Vietnam War.

Primary Source / Congress vs. The White House

The Watergate crisis brought the president into direct conflict with the Congress. Over the course of several months, the Senate Watergate Committee held hearings to investigate the president's staff.

Barbara Jordan was a member of the House Judiciary Committee. ▶

Sam Ervin [1896–1985]
As chair of the Senate committee, Ervin rejected the White House claim of executive privilege as reason to withhold records and evidence.

"Divine right went out with the American Revolution and doesn't belong to White House aides. . . . That is not executive privilege. That is executive poppycock."

—April 1973

Fred Thompson [1942–]
Serving as chief legal counsel to the minority Republicans on the Senate committee, Thompson's team chanced upon critical evidence during an interview with Nixon's appointment secretary, Alexander Butterfield. They called him to testify before the whole committee, and Thompson asked:

"Mr. Butterfield, are you aware of any installation of any listening devices in the Oval Office of the President?"

—July 1973

Barbara Jordan [1936–1996]
Jordan delivered a passionate speech before the House Judiciary Committee on whether to introduce articles of impeachment against President Nixon. It was seen on TV by millions of Americans.

"If the impeachment provision in the Constitution of the United States will not reach the offenses charged here, then perhaps that 18th century Constitution should be abandoned to a 20th century paper shredder."

—July 1974

Counsel Fred Thompson and Senators Lowell Weicker and Sam Ervin during the Senate Watergate hearings ▶

Critical Thinking

Analyzing Why was the Watergate scandal also a constitutional crisis?

Ford promised that these people would not be punished if they pledged loyalty to the United States and performed some type of national service. Although many people approved of amnesty, others thought it was too lenient. Supporters of the Vietnam War argued that draft dodgers and deserters should be punished.

Ford and Foreign Affairs

Ford continued Nixon's foreign policies, relying on Secretary of State Henry Kissinger. Ford and Kissinger extended the policy of détente with the Soviet Union. In late 1974, Ford met with Soviet leader Leonid Brezhnev to discuss arms control. A year later, he traveled to Helsinki, Finland, where he signed the Helsinki Accords with the Soviet Union and other nations. The countries pledged to respect the human rights of their citizens. The accords also set new trade agreements.

The Ford administration also worked to improve relations with China. When Chinese leader Mao Zedong died in 1976, a more moderate government came to power. China's new leaders wanted to increase trade with the United States.

A Troubled Economy

Like Nixon, Ford had to face economic troubles. Inflation and unemployment remained high. By the 1970s, Europe and Japan challenged American world economic dominance. Foreign competition led to factory closings and worker layoffs in the United States. It also contributed to underemployment, people working in jobs that did not fully use their skills. OPEC also kept oil prices high, adding to inflation.

To fight inflation, Ford launched voluntary wage and price controls. He called on Americans to save rather than spend money and to plant their own gardens to counter rising food prices. Despite a small drop in inflation, the economy continued its decline.

Ford also tried to cut government spending to control inflation. When this failed, the president then had Congress pass a tax cut. Some economic growth was achieved, but the cut led to large budget deficits. Despite his efforts, Ford could not solve the nation's economic woes.

Reading Check Evaluating How did Ford attempt to fight inflation? Did the efforts work?

Section 2 Review

History ONLINE
Study Central™ To review this section, go to glencoe.com.

Vocabulary

1. Use each of these terms in a sentence that explains its meaning: revenue sharing, affirmative action, tight money policy, deficit, energy, executive privilege, impeach, controversy, amnesty.

Main Ideas

2. **Explaining** What was Nixon's New Federalism program?

3. **Analyzing** What three things led to Nixon's landslide victory in the 1972 presidential election?

4. **Summarizing** What problems with the economy did President Ford face?

Critical Thinking

5. **Sequencing** On a time line like the one below, note major events that occurred during the Watergate crisis.

June 1972	May 1973	Oct. 1973	Aug. 1974

6. **Creative Writing** Imagine you write for your school's newspaper. Write an editorial column expressing your opinion of President Ford's plan to offer amnesty to those who avoided the draft.

Answer the
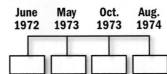
7. **Essential Question**

What were President Nixon's major domestic challenges in the 1970s?

What were people's lives like in the past?

These two pages will give you some clues to everyday life in the United States as you step back in time with TIME Notebook.

ALLSTAR PICTURE LIBRARY / ALAMY

Profile

In 1998 TIME *magazine put together a list called the* TIME *100—profiles of the 100 most influential people on the planet. It included world leaders, heads of industry—and* **OPRAH WINFREY.** *Here is part of what Oprah's profile said:*

"Oprah stands as a beacon, not only in the worlds of media and entertainment but also in many other ways. At 44, she has a personal fortune estimated at more than half a billion dollars. She owns her own production company which creates feature films, TV specials, and home videos. An accomplished actress, she won an Academy Award nomination for her role in *The Color Purple.*

"But it is through her talk show, *The Oprah Winfrey Show,* that first aired nationally in 1986, that her influence has been greatest. When Winfrey talks, her viewers—an estimated 14 million daily in the U.S. and millions more in 132 other countries—listen. Any book she chooses for her book club becomes an instant best seller. When she established the 'world's largest piggy bank,' people all over the country contributed spare change to raise more than $1 million (matched by Oprah) to send disadvantaged kids to college.

"Oprah exhorts viewers to improve their lives and the world. She makes people care because she cares. That is Winfrey's genius, and will be her legacy, as the changes she has wrought in the talk show continue to permeate our culture and shape our lives."

FASHION OF THE NATION

The Long & Short of It

In the early 1990s, five college freshmen at the University of Michigan changed basketball fashion. They wore long, baggy shorts instead of the kind with high hemlines like other basketball players wore. Thanks to the "Fab Five," most teams—from high school to the pros—dropped the "high on the thigh" shorts and adopted the long "jams" style.

STOCKDISC CLASSIC / ALAMY

TALK OF THE TIMES

"Ten-Four, Good Buddy"

CB radios (or Citizen Band radios) were a huge hit in the mid-1970s. More than 15 million of these two-way devices, which communicate over short distances, were in trucks, cars, and homes. There was even a special radio language. Do you think you have what it takes to chat on the air? Match the CB slang word or phrase with the correct meaning.

1. ten-four
2. ten-twenty
3. bear
4. saltshaker
5. bandage buggy
6. handle
7. go-go juice

a. police officer
b. fuel
c. snowplow
d. "I heard you"
e. user's nickname
f. location
g. ambulance

Answers: 1. d; 2. f; 3. a; 4. c; 5. g; 6. e; 7. b

INDEX STOCK / ALAMY

MILESTONES

EVENTS OF THE TIME

In the last quarter of the 1900s, the American people were introduced to inventions, places, and new ideas. Here are just a few examples and when they were introduced:

1976 Call waiting—it is now available for home phones

1979 Rubik's Cube—a habit-forming puzzle created by Hungarian professor Erno Rubik

LIBERTY · IN GOD WE TRUST · 1979
U.S. MINT

1979 Susan B. Anthony silver dollar

1980 In-line skates

1983 The computer mouse

1984 PG-13 movie rating

1992 Mall of America—world's largest mall opens in Minnesota

1996 "Dolly"—first lamb cloned from the cell of a fully grown sheep

1999 New heights in trading—the Dow Jones stock indicator breaks 10,000

2000 Census

According to the United States Census, our country's population was 281,421,906 in 2000—having grown by 32.7 million people in the 1990s. Here is how that growth averaged out:

One person was added to the population every 14 seconds
That means 6,300 people were added every day
4,400 of those added were from births (10,600 daily births less 6,200 daily deaths)
1,900 were from immigration
One immigrant was added every 35 seconds
One person left the U.S. to live in another country every 3 minutes

NUMBERS

UNITED STATES AT THE TIME

21 Age of Tiger Woods in 1997 when he set golfing records by winning the Masters Tournament—the youngest and the first of African American or Asian heritage to do so

$229,000,000 Ticket sales from the movie, *E.T., the Extra-Terrestrial*, released in 1982—one of the highest-grossing films ever

0 The number of cases of smallpox reported in 1979; the following year the World Health Organization said the disease had been wiped out thanks to vaccinations

1,920 The number of panels on the NAMES Project Foundation AIDS Memorial Quilt displayed for the first time in Washington, D.C., in 1987—in one weekend more than 500,000 people visited the quilt, which honored individuals who had died of AIDS

HISHAM IBRAHIM / PHOTOV.COM / ALAMY

CRITICAL THINKING

Hypothesizing Why do you think a recommendation from a celebrity (such as Oprah Winfrey) can influence what Americans read or buy? Is this justified? Explain your answer.

Evaluating Rank the items listed in Milestones in importance to you. Have the items impacted your life for better or worse? How?

The Carter Presidency

Essential Question ◄

What major foreign affairs issues did President Carter face during his presidency, and how did he deal with them?

Reading Guide

Content Vocabulary

trade deficit *(p. 517)*   apartheid *(p. 518)*

human rights   fundamentalist
    (p. 518)   *(p. 520)*

Academic Vocabulary

integrity *(p. 517)*   exceed *(p. 517)*

Key People and Events

Ronald Reagan *(p. 517)*

Jimmy Carter *(p. 517)*

Three Mile Island *(p. 518)*

Camp David Accords *(p. 519)*

Reading Strategy

Taking Notes On a diagram like the one below, identify the major points of Carter's National Energy Plan.

National Energy Plan

American Diary

In the 1976 Democratic presidential campaign, James Earl "Jimmy" Carter, Jr., a former governor of Georgia, made a virtue of his lack of experience in the federal government: "We have been shaken by a tragic war abroad and by scandals . . . at home. Our people are seeking new voices, new ideas and new leaders."

Many voters found Carter's down-home style refreshing after the ordeals of the Watergate scandal.

—Jimmy Carter's acceptance speech at the Democratic National Convention, July 15, 1976

Jimmy Carter, with his wife Rosalynn, addresses a crowd following his election victory in 1976.

An Informal Presidency

Main Idea President Carter faced a weakened economy and a growing energy crisis.

History and You If you had a choice, would you like to "dress up" or wear casual clothes to an event? Read to find out how Carter wanted to create a more informal presidency.

. . . .

As the 1976 elections neared, President Ford struggled to gain the Republican nomination. He faced a challenge from the former governor of California, **Ronald Reagan,** who was favored by party conservatives. Ford chose Senator Bob Dole of Kansas as his running mate. **Jimmy Carter** ran as the Democratic candidate, stressing his **integrity,** or moral character, his religious faith, and his standing as an outsider. Senator Walter Mondale of Minnesota ran as vice president.

During the campaign, Ford tried to stress his achievements as president. Carter ran as much against the memory of Nixon and government corruption as against Ford. Carter won in a close election, gaining 50.1 percent of the popular vote. He owed his margin of victory to support from African American Southern voters.

As president, Carter set a down-to-earth tone. At his inauguration, he wore an ordinary business suit rather than formal clothing. After the ceremony, Carter and his family walked from the Capitol to the White House instead of riding in a limousine, as earlier presidents had done.

Struggling With the Economy

After taking office, Carter cut taxes and increased spending to revive the economy. Unemployment decreased, but inflation rose. Carter then proposed spending cuts and a delayed tax cut. Carter's reversal made him seem weak and uncertain. As an outsider, the president had trouble gaining support in Congress.

Carter made energy policy a priority. High energy costs added to inflation. Also, as American money paid for overseas oil, the nation faced a growing **trade deficit**—the value of foreign imports **exceeded,** or was greater than, the value of American exports. In April 1977, Carter presented a National Energy Plan to resolve the energy crisis.

By the Numbers / Election of 1976

A Southern President Jimmy Carter's election marked the first time since 1844 that a candidate from the Deep South was elected president.

Electoral Votes

1 (Reagan)
240
297

Jimmy Carter (D)
Gerald Ford (R)

Popular Vote

1.9% (Other)
48%
50.1%

Jimmy Carter (D)
Gerald Ford (R)

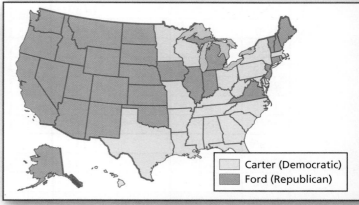

Carter (Democratic)
Ford (Republican)

Critical Thinking

Analyzing Explain how Carter's election in 1976 was partly a result of Watergate.

Carter's plan included creating a Department of Energy to oversee energy policy, explore alternative energy sources, and collect taxes to further domestic oil production and energy conservation. Congress passed a weakened version of the plan in 1978.

Nuclear Power

In the late 1970s, nuclear power became a major issue. In March 1979, a major accident occurred at the **Three Mile Island** nuclear power plant near Harrisburg, Pennsylvania. An antinuclear protest movement soon spread. President Carter, however, did not want to halt nuclear energy which provided more than 10 percent of the nation's energy. At the same time, supporters of nuclear power argued that, with safeguards, nuclear power did not harm the environment.

✔ **Reading Check** **Identifying** What economic problems did Carter face?

Foreign Affairs

Main Idea President Carter had some foreign policy successes but faced a growing crisis in the Middle Eastern country of Iran.

History and You How do you keep from getting discouraged when you fail to reach a goal? Read to find out about the long and difficult effort to release the Americans who were held captive in Iran.

· ·

Carter based his foreign policy on **human rights**—a belief that governments ought to respect the human dignity and liberties of their citizens. He proposed that any nation that violated human rights should not receive support from the United States. For example, Carter condemned South Africa for its policy of **apartheid,** racial separation and discrimination against nonwhites.

Carter's human rights diplomacy sometimes caused challenges for the United States.

Economics & History

Average Gas Prices, 1950–2007

Year	Price Per Gallon	Price Per Gallon (adjusted for inflation)
1950	$0.23	$1.91
1955	$0.24	$1.85
1960	$0.26	$1.79
1965	$0.26	$1.68
1970	$0.30	$1.59
1975	$0.48	$1.80
1980	$1.05	$2.59
1985	$1.01	$1.90
1990	$0.97	$1.51
1995	$0.96	$1.28
2001	$1.45	$1.66
2002	$1.31	$1.31
2003	$1.38	$1.52
2004	$1.67	$1.78
2005	$2.20	$2.28
2006	$3.03	$3.09
2007*	$3.26	$3.26

*June 2007   Source: U.S. Department of Energy

If gas cost 23 cents a gallon in 1950, what would be its equivalent price in today's prices? The table to the left shows the price of gas adjusted for inflation.

Car Wash

Gasoline	Self Serve
REGULAR LEADED	1.09 9/10
REGULAR UNLEADED	1.19 9/10
SUPREME UNLEADED	1.34 9/10

▲ Gas prices in 1991

◄ Gas prices in 2007

Critical Thinking

1. **Calculating** Which year shows the biggest increase in actual price? In price adjusted for inflation?

2. **Analyzing** What, if anything, surprises you about the average price of gasoline over time?

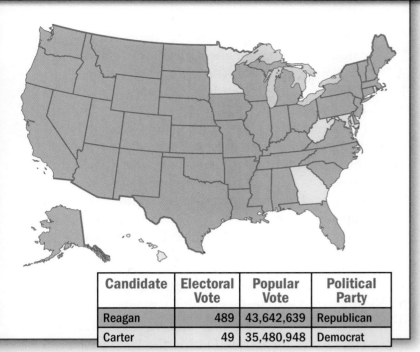

A Landslide for Reagan President Jimmy Carter lost his 1980 reelection bid by a landslide to Republican challenger Ronald Reagan. An important factor was Carter's inability to resolve the Iran hostage crisis. Soon after the inauguration of President Reagan on January 20, 1981, Iran agreed to release the 52 hostages.

WELCOME BACK TO FREEDOM

Freed American hostages ▶

Candidate	Electoral Vote	Popular Vote	Political Party
Reagan	489	43,642,639	Republican
Carter	49	35,480,948	Democrat

Critical Thinking

Drawing Conclusions Why would American voters believe Ronald Reagan could negotiate the hostages' release when President Carter was not able to?

In 1980 Cuban dictator Fidel Castro allowed thousands of Cubans, including criminals and political prisoners, to leave Cuba by boat for Florida. The United States, however, had trouble absorbing such large numbers of people. By the time Castro ended the boatlift, about 125,000 people entered the United States. Carter had learned that a foreign policy based on a single issue, human rights, had many limitations. Even so, the president continued to speak out on the issue.

The Panama Canal

Carter also acted to end Latin American bitterness over the Panama Canal. Over the years, U.S. control of the canal caused friction between the United States and Panama. Carter signed two treaties with Panama in 1977. The treaties turned the Panama Canal over to Panama by the year 2000 but ensured that the canal would remain a neutral waterway open to all shipping. Some Republicans in the Senate tried to block ratification of the treaties, charging that Carter was giving away U.S. property. The Senate approved the treaties in 1978.

The Middle East

President Carter sought to bring peace to the Middle East. When talks between Israel and Egypt stalled in 1978, Carter invited Israeli prime minister Menachem Begin and Egyptian president Anwar el-Sadat to Camp David, Maryland, for a summit meeting. The three leaders reached an agreement known as the **Camp David Accords.** The agreement led to an Egyptian-Israeli peace treaty signed at the White House in March 1979. The treaty marked the first time that Israel and an Arab nation had made peace.

The Soviet Union

Carter criticized Soviet human-rights abuses, but he also continued talks on arms control. In June 1979, the president signed a second Strategic Arms Limitation Treaty, or SALT II. Critics in the Senate claimed that the treaty gave the Soviets an advantage, and the Senate delayed ratification.

Any hope of Senate approval ended in December 1979, when the Soviets invaded the southwest Asian nation of Afghanistan. Carter ordered sanctions against the Soviets.

The United States and other nations refused to take part in the Olympic Games in Moscow.

Crisis in Iran

In the 1970s, Iran was a major U.S. ally in the oil-rich Persian Gulf region. Iran's ruler, Shah Mohammed Reza Pahlavi, built a powerful military with U.S. aid. Many Iranians criticized corruption in his government. Others opposed Western influences, which they felt weakened traditional Muslim values.

In January 1979, Islamic **fundamentalists** —people who believe in strict obedience to religious laws—forced the shah to flee Iran. The new ruler, Muslim leader Ayatollah Khomeini, was hostile to the United States for its support of the shah.

In November 1979, Iranian students, with government support, stormed the American embassy in Tehran, the capital of Iran, and held 52 Americans hostage. The United States was outraged. Attempts to negotiate the release of the hostages failed, and a daring desert rescue attempt ended in tragedy with the death of eight American soldiers. The hostage crisis dragged on and became a major issue in the presidential election of 1980.

The Election of 1980

The months before the 1980 election were difficult for President Carter. Many Americans blamed him for a weak economy and for not gaining the release of the American hostages. Carter's popularity among voters greatly declined.

Despite opposition, Carter gained the Democratic nomination, but the party was deeply divided. The Republicans nominated Ronald Reagan as their candidate. Reagan—a former actor and former governor of California—appealed to many voters with his conservative message of lower taxes, less spending, strong defense, and national pride.

Reagan swept to victory, with an electoral vote margin of 489 to 49. Republicans also gained control of the Senate for the first time since 1954. The election and its aftermath were bitter for Carter. During the last weeks of his presidency, Carter worked to free the hostages. The Iranians finally did release them—after Ronald Reagan took the oath of office.

Reading Check Summarizing Why did the United States boycott the 1980 Olympics?

Section 3 Review

History ONLINE
Study Central™ To review this section, go to glencoe.com.

Vocabulary

1. Use each of the following words in a paragraph: integrity, trade deficit, exceed, human rights, apartheid, fundamentalist.

Main Ideas

2. **Discussing** What was President Carter's position on nuclear energy?

3. **Explaining** What part did human rights play in Carter's foreign policies?

4. **Analyzing** What were the major reasons Carter lost the election of 1980?

Critical Thinking

5. **Drawing Conclusions** On a chart like the one below, record the major result of each prominent issue of the Carter presidency.

Issue	Result
Panama Canal	
Camp David Accords	
Crisis in Iran	

6. **Persuasive Writing** Write a letter to the editor expressing your opinion about the United States' decision not to take part in the 1980 Olympic Games in Moscow.

Answer the
7. **Essential Question**
What major foreign affairs issues did President Carter face during his presidency, and how did he deal with them?

Foreign Policy

- President Nixon formulates foreign policy plan of détente, easing international tensions with China and the Soviet Union.
- U.S. signs a treaty limiting nuclear arms.
- War between Israel and its Arab neighbors breaks out in 1973; violence in the Middle East is ongoing.
- U.S. supports the overthrow of Marxist government in Chile.

John Dean testifies during Watergate hearing. ▼

Nixon and Watergate

- Nixon introduces New Federalism.
- U.S. economy suffers under inflation.
- White House involvement with Watergate break-in is revealed.
- Vice President Agnew resigns.
- Nixon appoints Gerald Ford as his new vice president.
- Nixon resigns the presidency.

▲ President Nixon reviews troops during his visit to China.

President-elect Jimmy Carter and Rosalyn Carter ▼

Ford and Carter

- President Ford grants a pardon to Nixon.
- Ford continues détente with the Soviet Union.
- Inflation rises.
- President Carter makes energy policy a priority.
- Carter bases foreign policy on human rights.
- Carter works to bring peace in Middle East.
- Islamic fundamentalists take Americans hostage in Iran.
- Carter loses the 1980 presidential election to Ronald Reagan.

American hostages held in Iran ▼

STUDY TO GO Study anywhere, anytime! Download quizzes and flash cards to your PDA from glencoe.com.

America's LITERATURE

Meet the Author

Gary Soto (1952–), the son of Mexican American parents, was born and raised in California. Though much of his writing features Latino boys and girls, young people of all ethnic groups experience many of the same feelings and challenges. Soto's ability to depict real-life situations facing young people makes him one of the country's most influential authors.

Building Background

In *Taking Sides,* Lincoln moves from a poor neighborhood, Franklin, to the affluent suburb of Columbus, after his parents' breakup. A star basketball player, Lincoln feels like a traitor when Columbus is set to play Franklin in an upcoming game. As game day approaches, Lincoln struggles with who he is— a Mexican American from the barrio or a student from the suburbs. As you read the excerpt, think about the contrasting social and cultural rules experienced by Lincoln as the new kid in school.

Vocabulary

sycamores trees

scrawny small

stucco hardened sand and cement

opted chose

harangued nagged

splotched stained

Young boys learn the game of basketball on the playground. ▶

TAKING SIDES

Gary Soto

When he had arrived in the new neighborhood, Lincoln had liked the peacefulness of sprinklers hissing on green lawns and the **sycamores** that lined the street. He liked the splashes of flowers and neatly piled firewood. He liked the hedges where jays built **scrawny** nests and bickered when cats slith-ered too close. The people seemed distant, but that was fine with him. It was better than the loud cars that raced up and down his old block. It was better than littered streets and graffiti-covered walls that called out *"Con safos"* and "F-14."

Now, three months later, Lincoln was having second thoughts.

* * *

Columbus Junior High was a **stucco** group of pink and green buildings and a track the color of rust. The grass, like the grass at other schools, was mostly brown. The trash cans were buckled, but no candy wrappers or potato-chip bags scuttled across the campus. . . .

The kids dressed stylishly. When they smiled, their teeth gleamed with braces. It would never enter their minds to shop at K-mart or tote a bologna sandwich in a twice-used paper bag. Lincoln **opted** to live a simple life. His bologna sandwich, along with an apple and some chips, sat in his backpack, crushed between his geography and math books.

His mother **harangued** him about his clothes, but he wore jeans, busted at the knees, and his coat was a hand-me-down from an uncle. The front of Lincoln's shirt was **splotched** blue where he once let his Bic pen ride in the pocket during a wash.

Lincoln sighed and entered the school grounds. Just two more days to the weekend. . . .

At lunch he ate alone, scribbling out his homework for English, which was mostly recognizing the parts of speech. He thought it was funny how the teacher, Mrs. Baker, said the same things over and over. "A chair is a noun; a beach umbrella is a noun. . . ."

Lincoln bit into his sandwich roughly. He opened his geography book and once again the guy on the camel was smiling his lined face at him. He's like me, Lincoln thought. Brown as earth and no one knows his name. He closed the book when a basketball play came to his mind. . . .

He took another bite of his bologna sandwich and looked up to see James with a girl. Lincoln wiped his mouth, cleared his throat, and said to James, "Hey, homes." To the girl, he said, "Hi." . . .

He's like me, Lincoln thought.
Brown as earth
and no one knows his name.

James said, "This is Monica Torres. Monica, this is Lincoln, ah, let me see. What's your last name, Linc?"

"Mendoza."

"That's right, Linc Mendoza, star basketball player."

Monica smiled as she sat down. "James said you went to Franklin. I used to go there."

"Really?" Lincoln asked, curious, his eyebrows raised. "I don't remember you."

"Well, I did, for two months," she said. "But we moved here. My dad didn't like me going to school in the city."

"But your dad didn't have to go to school."

"It's true. But you know how Franklin is."

"You mean nasty."

"That's one way of putting it."

"That's the only way of putting it."

Lincoln wanted to tell her about the Franklin he knew, but how could he keep the conversation polite?

Analyzing Literature

1. **Respond** With which of Lincoln's experiences do you identify?

2. **Recall and Analyze** In what ways is Columbus Junior High different from Franklin?

3. **Evaluate** Lincoln says the man on the camel is like him: "Brown as earth and no one knows his name." What is Lincoln's view of himself?

STANDARDIZED TEST PRACTICE

TEST-TAKING TIP

On a multiple-choice test, remember that you are looking for the best, or most accurate, answer. It might not necessarily be the only answer that applies.

Reviewing Main Ideas

Directions: Choose the best answer for each of the following questions.

1. Nixon improved U.S. relations with China by

   A promising aid.

   B resuming trade.

   C signing SALT I.

   D sharing technology.

2. What was an outcome of the 1967 Six-Day War?

   A more Arab refugees

   B long lines at U.S. gas pumps

   C improved U.S. relations with Egypt

   D Egyptian control of the Sinai Peninsula

3. Nixon reduced the involvement of the federal government in people's lives by

   A introducing revenue sharing.

   B promoting affirmative action.

   C approving the creation of the EPA.

   D enforcing orders to integrate schools.

4. Why were the Ayatollah Khomeini and his supporters hostile to the United States?

   A Carter ordered sanctions against Iran.

   B U.S. policies were based on human rights.

   C American leaders supported the shah.

   D Carter condemned the practice of apartheid.

Short-Answer Question

Directions: Base your answer to question 5 on the excerpt below and on your knowledge of social studies.

> Finally, I feel that Richard Nixon and his loved ones have suffered enough and will continue to suffer, no matter what I do, no matter what we, as a great and good nation, can do together to make his goal of peace come true.
>
> —President Gerald R. Ford, September 8, 1974

5. Do you think this is a valid reason for pardoning President Nixon? Explain.

Review the Essential Questions

6. Essay Compare and contrast U.S.-Soviet relations in the Nixon and Carter administrations.

To help you write your essay, review your answers to the Essential Questions in the section reviews and the chapter Foldables Study Organizer. Your essay should include:

- an analysis of Nixon's relationship with the Soviets;
- an analysis of Carter's relationship with the Soviets; and
- similarities and differences in the leadership roles the presidents played in an international setting.

GO ON

History ONLINE

For additional test practice, use **Self-Check Quizzes**—Chapter 16 at glencoe.com.

Document-Based Questions

Directions: Analyze the documents and answer the short-answer questions that follow.

Document 1

Kissinger made this comment about the U.S. role in the overthrow of Chile's elected leader.

> I don't see why we need to stand by and watch a country go communist due to the irresponsibility of its own people.

Source: Tarak Barkawi, *War Inside the Free World*

7. What can you infer about Kissinger's attitude toward communism?

Document 2

In a 1977 interview, former President Nixon was asked about his views on the presidency and the law.

> Well, when the president does it that means that it is not illegal.

Source: Richard Nixon, from an interview with David Frost

8. What does Nixon's statement reflect about how he views the relationship of the president to the laws of the United States?

Document 3

In the following statement, Carter criticized the rise in oil imports during the Ford administration.

> We now import about 44 percent of our oil. . . . We need to shift very strongly toward solar energy and have strict conservation measures.

Source: The First Carter-Ford Presidential Debate, 1976

9. Why was the rise in oil imports a campaign issue in 1976?

Document 4

The graph shows President Nixon's approval rating during parts of 1973 and 1974.

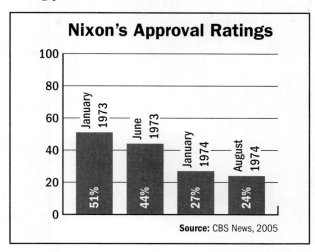

Nixon's Approval Ratings

January 1973: 51%
June 1973: 44%
January 1974: 27%
August 1974: 24%

Source: CBS News, 2005

10. What was Nixon's approval rating before he resigned in August 1974? What was the rating in January of that year?

Document 5

Senator William Proxmire objected to billions in military aid authorized by the Camp David Accords.

> The notion that we must provide military assistance to [these] nations . . . is precisely what has led us down this long and bloody and reprehensible road of providing the weapons of death and destruction in the name of peace.

Source: Barbara Hinckley, *Less Than Meets the Eye*

11. What does Senator Proxmire suggest Carter used to persuade Begin and Sadat to sign a peace treaty?

12. Expository Writing Using the information from the five documents and your knowledge of social studies, write an essay in which you:
- discuss the goals of federal policies in the 1970s; and
- discuss how the Watergate scandal affected Americans' view of the presidency.

Need Extra Help?												
If you missed questions. . .	1	2	3	4	5	6	7	8	9	10	11	12
Go to page. . .	502	503	507	520	510	501–520	501	511	518	511	519	501–513

Chapter 17

New Challenges
1981 to Present

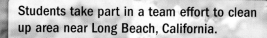

Students take part in a team effort to clean up area near Long Beach, California.

PRESIDENTS

U.S. Events

World Events

RONALD REAGAN

★ **1983**
U.S. troops invade Grenada

★ **1986**
Space shuttle *Challenger* explodes

GEORGE H.W. BUSH

★ **1990**
Americans with Disabilities Act passes

1980

1987

1981 ★
Egypt's president Anwar el-Sadat assassinated

★ **1985**
Mikhail Gorbachev becomes leader of Soviet Union

★ **1989**
Students protest in Tiananmen Square, China

★ **1990**
Nelson Mandela released from South African prison

History ONLINE

Chapter Overview Visit glencoe.com and click on **Chapter 17—Chapter Overviews** to preview chapter information.

Section 1: The Reagan Presidency

Essential Question How was President Reagan's attitude about communism reflected in his actions and policies?

Section 2: The Bush Presidency

Essential Question How did President Bush deal with the domestic challenges facing his presidency?

Section 3: A New Century

Essential Question How did the Clinton presidency change the U.S. domestic scene in the 1990s?

Section 4: The War on Terror

Essential Question How has the war on terror changed the way Americans live?

Section 5: Challenges Ahead

Essential Question How have economic and environmental developments led to the world's nations becoming more interdependent?

FOLDABLES
Study Organizer

Organizing Information

Make this Foldable to organize what you learn about the challenges faced by the United States.

Step 1 Place three sheets of paper on top of one another about 1 inch apart.

Step 2 Fold the papers to form six equal tabs.

Step 3 Staple the sheets and label each tab as shown.

New Challenges 1981–Present
The Reagan Presidency
The Bush Presidency
A New Century
The War on Terror
Challenges Ahead

Reading and Writing As you read the chapter, record notes, collect terms, note important dates and events, and answer the Essential Questions beneath the tabs.

A family in Mississippi is rescued from flood waters caused by Hurricane Katrina.
▶

BILL CLINTON

1995 Bomb kills 168 at Oklahoma City federal building

1998 President Clinton impeached

GEORGE W. BUSH

2001 War on terror begins

2005 Hurricane Katrina strikes Louisiana and Mississippi

2007 Nancy Pelosi becomes first female Speaker of the House

1994

2001

2008

1991
• Operation Desert Storm
• Breakup of Soviet Union

1994 U.S., Mexico, and Canada found NAFTA

2004 Tsunami devastates Indonesia and surrounding regions

2005 Terrorists bomb London subway system

Woman surveys destruction after hurricane. ▶

The Reagan Presidency

Essential Question ◄

How was President Reagan's attitude about communism reflected in his actions and policies?

Reading Guide

Content Vocabulary

deregulation *(p. 530)*   federal debt *(p. 531)*
supply-side economics *(p. 530)*

Academic Vocabulary

quote *(p. 531)*   theme *(p. 532)*

Key People and Events

Sandra Day O'Connor *(p. 530)*
George H.W. Bush *(p. 532)*
Geraldine Ferraro *(p. 532)*
Mikhail Gorbachev *(p. 533)*

Reading Strategy

Taking Notes On a diagram like the one below, identify the building blocks of President Reagan's conservative federal government.

Reagan Conservatism

American Diary

On March 30, 1981, President Ronald Reagan left a Washington, D.C., hotel after giving a speech. As he passed press photographers and TV cameras, six gunshots rang out. Secret Service agents rushed the president into his limousine and sped toward the hospital. A bullet had punctured his lung and lodged just an inch from his heart. Despite the seriousness of the situation, the president joked on the way into the operating room, telling his doctors, "I hope you're all Republicans."

President Reagan waves to the crowd moments before the assassination attempt.

The Reagan Revolution

Main Idea President Reagan brought a new conservative approach to government.

History and You What are principles? What principles do you live by? Read to discover the principles that guided the policies of the Reagan presidency.

. . . .

Ronald Reagan's election to the presidency in 1980 marked a significant conservative shift in America. During the 1970s, the conservative movement had grown throughout the country, most particularly in the South and Southwest.

Many Americans now wanted a return to what Ronald Reagan, a former actor with Illinois small-town roots, called "traditional American values"—an emphasis on family life, hard work, respect for law, and patriotism. They shared the conservative view that the federal government made too many rules, collected too much in taxes, and spent too much money on social programs.

Reagan believed that the key to restoring America's strength and influence was to get Americans to believe in themselves again. He expressed this idea in his Inaugural Address:

PRIMARY SOURCE

"We have every right to dream heroic dreams. . . . You can see heroes every day going in and out of factory gates. Others, a handful in number, produce enough food to feed all of us. . . . You meet heroes across a counter. . . . Their patriotism is quiet, but deep. Their values sustain our national life."
—*Ronald Reagan's First Inaugural Address, January 1981*

Air Traffic Controllers' Strike

A few months after Ronald Reagan became president, the nation's air traffic controllers went on strike. They refused to go back to work despite the president's orders to do so. President Reagan acted at once, firing the controllers and ordering military staff to oversee air traffic while new controllers were trained to do the work.

Critics of former president Carter felt he lacked leadership and was indecisive. With this action, Ronald Reagan showed that he would stand firm and use his presidency to carry out the policies in which he believed.

Primary Source / The Great Communicator

In His Own Words Ronald W. Reagan was nicknamed "the Great Communicator" because of his extraordinary skill as an orator. He appeared in more than 50 films as a Hollywood actor, which helped him polish his speaking skills.

"Honey, I forgot to duck."
—March 30, 1981, from www.pbs.org (said to Nancy Reagan when she arrived at the hospital following the assassination attempt)

"I've always believed that a lot of the trouble in the world would disappear if we were talking to each other instead of about each other."
—April 11, 1984, from www.reaganfoundation.org

Critical Thinking

Evaluating Why do you think Ronald Reagan was such a popular president?

Deregulation

As part of his promise to reduce government and "get the government off the backs of the American people," Reagan pursued a policy of **deregulation.** This meant cutting the rules and regulations that government agencies placed on businesses. The Department of Transportation, for example, wrote new rules for automobile exhaust systems and safety measures that were easier for car manufacturers to meet.

The Supreme Court

Reagan also put a conservative stamp on the Supreme Court by naming justices to the Court who shared his views. He wanted justices who favored a stricter interpretation of the Constitution. When the president appointed **Sandra Day O'Connor** in 1981, she became the first woman ever appointed to the Court. Reagan later appointed Antonin Scalia and Anthony Kennedy as Supreme Court justices.

Reaganomics

Economic policy formed the core of the "Reagan Revolution." The president believed that lower taxes would allow individuals and corporations to invest in new businesses. Because a tax cut would mean less government income, Reagan also called for less government spending.

Supporters called President Reagan's policy **supply-side economics** because it aimed to boost the economy by increasing the supply of goods and services. Critics labeled the policy "Reaganomics." They held that Reagan's policy would help corporations and wealthy Americans, while only a little prosperity would "trickle down" to average Americans.

In 1981 Congress lowered taxes and reduced federal programs such as student aid, welfare, and low-income housing. Supporters argued that Reaganomics would stimulate the economy, helping everybody in the long run.

People IN HISTORY

Sally Kristen Ride

First American woman in space

In 1983 Sally Ride became the first American woman in space when she orbited the Earth aboard the space shuttle *Challenger*. A strong advocate for improved science education, Ride has written several books for young readers. She says, *"Our future lies with today's kids and tomorrow's space exploration."*

Sandra Day O'Connor

First woman to serve on the Supreme Court

When a Supreme Court vacancy opened in 1981, President Reagan decided to fulfill his campaign promise to name the first woman justice. He chose Sandra Day O'Connor, an Arizona appeals court judge. O'Connor served until 2006. In an interview, she discussed the increased opportunities for women: *"When I went to law school, about 1 percent of all law students were women. And last year, over 50 percent were."*

While Reagan cut domestic programs, he sharply increased military spending. The president declared that the Soviet threat made a military buildup necessary. With higher defense spending and lower taxes, the government spent more money than it collected in revenue. It had to borrow money to make up the difference. This borrowing increased the **federal debt**—the amount of money owed by the government. Between 1970 and 1980, the federal debt grew from $381 billion to $909 billion. By 1990, the debt had jumped to $3.2 trillion.

President Reagan's economic policy seemed to falter when a recession began early in his first term. However, the economy recovered a year later and began to grow. Businesses expanded, and the high jobless rate declined. Investors showed confidence in the economy with a boom in stock trading.

Reading Check Explaining What caused the federal debt to grow significantly in the 1980s?

Teachers in Space

On January 28, 1986, the space shuttle *Challenger* exploded in space, killing all seven aboard. Among the seven was Christa McAuliffe (below right), a teacher and the first civilian passenger in space. McAuliffe was to teach lessons from space that would be beamed live back to Earth. Barbara Morgan (left) had been McAuliffe's backup in 1986. In 2007 Morgan taught lessons from the space shuttle *Endeavor.*

CRITICAL Thinking

Making Generalizations What special qualities are shared by all these individuals?

Reagan's Foreign Policy

Main Idea The Reagan administration believed that the United States should take strong action to resist Communist influences overseas.

History and You Have you ever heard a politician say that "a strong military helps keep the peace"? Read to learn how President Reagan used the military to check Communist activities abroad.

Ronald Reagan pledged in his campaign to wage a tough fight against communism. As president, he adopted a new Cold War foreign policy that rejected both containment and détente. Reagan called the Soviet Union "the focus of evil in the modern world" and an "evil empire." He believed that the United States should use strength to defeat it.

Military Buildup

To carry out his policy, President Reagan launched a massive buildup of the military. He expanded the American arsenal of tanks, ships, aircraft, and nuclear missiles. He defended these actions by **quoting**—repeating the words of—George Washington's advice: "To be prepared for war is one of the most effective means of preserving peace." The Reagan military buildup was the largest peacetime buildup in American history, costing about $1.5 trillion over five years.

Reagan also proposed an antimissile defense system, the Strategic Defense Initiative (SDI). Nicknamed "Star Wars," the SDI would thwart incoming enemy missiles. However, scientists were unable to develop the technology for the SDI.

Latin America

Besides building up the military, Reagan also committed U.S. forces and aid to the fight against communism, especially in nearby Latin America. Late in the Carter presidency, Sandinista rebels overthrew the government in Nicaragua. The rebels set up a socialist system, and accepted aid from both Cuba and the Soviet Union.

President Reagan held 42 presidential news conferences and gave 47 major presidential speeches during his 2 terms in office. He also made nearly 400 public appearances in the United States outside Washington, D.C.

1. **Identifying** What is President Reagan doing, and what does it mean?

2. **Making Connections** What is the cartoonist expressing about Reagan's communications to Americans?

"CONSTANT DRUMBEAT"

REAGAN ON TV REAGAN ON RADIO REAGAN QUOTES IN PRESS

©1983 HERBLOCK

◀ Presidents answer questions from the press at the official podium.

In the early 1980s, Reagan sent aid to the contras, a group battling the Sandinistas. The fighting in Nicaragua sparked disagreement between President Reagan and Congress.

In October 1983, President Reagan took direct military action in the Caribbean. Marxist rebels on the Caribbean island of Grenada staged an uprising. Concerned about the fate of 800 American medical students on the island, Reagan sent troops to rescue them and to set up an anticommunist government.

The Middle East

Reagan's policies were less successful in the Middle East. In 1982 he sent marines to keep the peace in Lebanon. However, a car bomb blast killed more than 60 people at the U.S. embassy in April 1983. Then in October, 241 Americans and 58 French died in attacks on U.S. and French military centers. Rather than deepen U.S. involvement, Reagan withdrew all U.S. forces from Lebanon.

Reading Check **Synthesizing** Why did Reagan take action in Grenada?

Reagan's Second Term

Main Idea During Reagan's second term, the United States continued to act against communism but also held talks with a new Soviet leadership.

History and You What would you do if someone who disliked you decided to change course and become your friend? Read to find out what happened to American-Soviet relations during Reagan's second term.

By 1984, the American economy was booming. In his State of the Union address, President Reagan declared: "America is back— standing tall, looking [toward the future] with courage, confidence, and hope."

President Reagan and Vice President **George H.W. Bush** continued this optimistic **theme,** or subject, in their campaign for reelection. The Democrats chose Walter Mondale, vice president under Jimmy Carter, and **Geraldine Ferraro,** a member of Congress from New York. Ferraro became the first woman to run for vice president on a major political party ticket.

Reagan won the electoral votes in 49 out of the 50 states. It was one of the most lopsided presidential elections in American history. Spurred on by high employment, a strong economy, and low interest rates, Reagan enjoyed high popularity ratings early in his second term.

The Iran-Contra Scandal

Despite his popularity, a scandal cast a shadow over part of President Reagan's second term. Terrorists, with ties to the Iranian government, held Americans hostage in Lebanon. Hoping to secure the hostages' release, Reagan officials made a deal with Iran's Islamic leaders.

Marine Lieutenant Colonel Oliver North and Navy Vice Admiral John Poindexter were both assigned to the White House National Security Council. They arranged for the sale of weapons to Iran in return for help in freeing American hostages. North and Poindexter decided to funnel money from this secret arms sale to help the Nicaraguan contras.

News of these deals—which became known as the Iran-Contra scandal—created an uproar. Critics charged that these deals violated federal laws that barred officials from aiding the contras. Congress held hearings to determine whether the president took part in breaking the law, but no proof of the president's involvement was ever found.

A Changing Soviet Policy

A remarkable shift in Soviet-American relations took shape during Reagan's second term. In 1985 **Mikhail Gorbachev** became the new Soviet leader. Gorbachev was committed to reforming the Soviet government. He called for a policy of glasnost—opening Soviet society to new ideas. Gorbachev also reduced government control of the economy and allowed local decision making. This new policy, perestroika, encouraged the Soviets to seek more changes.

In 1987 Reagan and Gorbachev signed an agreement, the Intermediate-Range Nuclear Forces (INF) Treaty. The treaty aimed to reduce the number of nuclear missiles in each superpower's arsenal. Both nations still held vast nuclear arsenals, but they had taken a major step toward reducing the threat of nuclear war.

Reading Check **Summarizing** What change in Soviet domestic policy took place in the 1980s?

Section 1 Review

History ONLINE
Study Central™ To review this section, go to glencoe.com.

Vocabulary

1. Use each of the following terms correctly in a sentence: deregulation, supply-side economics, federal debt, quote, theme.

Main Ideas

2. **Discussing** What did Reagan hope his supply-side economics would accomplish?

3. **Analyzing** What military stand did Reagan take in Nicaragua, and why did he take it?

4. **Explaining** What was the INF treaty?

Critical Thinking

5. **Describing** On a chart like the one below, describe the actions taken by the Reagan administration in the following areas:

Area	Action
Supreme Court	
Domestic Program	
U.S.–Soviet Relations	
Latin America	

6. **Expository Writing** In a paragraph, explain the main philosophy of Reaganomics and what it was supposed to achieve.

Answer the
7. **Essential Question**
How was President Reagan's attitude about communism reflected in his actions and policies?

Section 2

The Bush Presidency

Essential Question ◄

How did President Bush deal with the domestic challenges facing his presidency?

Reading Guide

Content Vocabulary

coalition (p. 537)   downsize (p. 539)
bankruptcy (p. 539)

Academic Vocabulary

retain (p. 535)   site (p. 537)

Key People and Events

Tiananmen Square (p. 537)
Saddam Hussein (p. 537)
Colin Powell (p. 537)
Norman Schwarzkopf (p. 537)
Operation Desert Storm (p. 537)

Reading Strategy

Taking Notes On a diagram like the one below, determine the effects of the revolt that took place in the Soviet Union at the time of the Bush presidency.

Cause		Effects
Soviet Revolt	→	

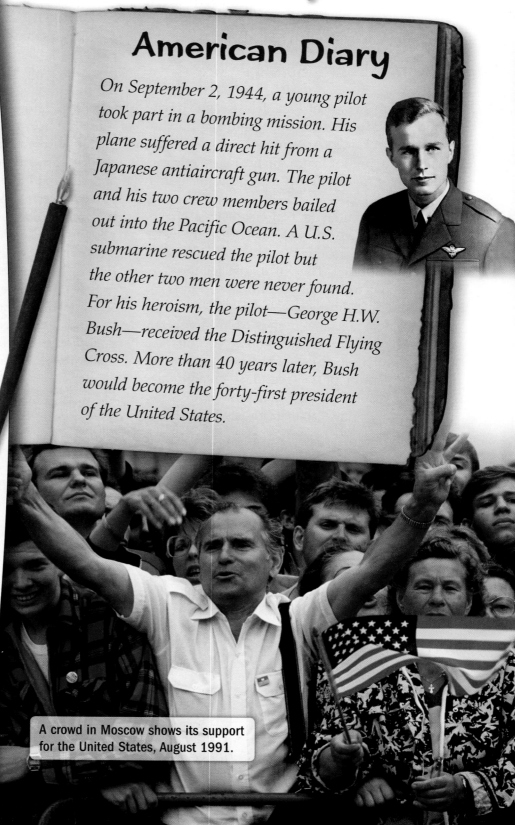

American Diary

On September 2, 1944, a young pilot took part in a bombing mission. His plane suffered a direct hit from a Japanese antiaircraft gun. The pilot and his two crew members bailed out into the Pacific Ocean. A U.S. submarine rescued the pilot but the other two men were never found. For his heroism, the pilot—George H.W. Bush—received the Distinguished Flying Cross. More than 40 years later, Bush would become the forty-first president of the United States.

A crowd in Moscow shows its support for the United States, August 1991.

The End of the Cold War

Main Idea During Bush's presidency, significant global events led to the end of the Cold War.

History and You Why do things change in the world? Do you think people make a difference, or are big events and developments responsible? Read to learn why the Soviet Union collapsed.

. . . .

In 1988 Vice President George H.W. Bush was elected president. Bush carried 40 states, giving him 426 electoral votes to 112 for the Democratic Party candidate, Michael Dukakis. However, Bush's victory did not extend to Congress. The Democrats **retained,** or held onto, control of the House and the Senate.

A Changing Soviet Union

Bush's presidency was during a time of sweeping change in world affairs. Soviet leader Gorbachev wanted to end the arms race so he could focus on reforms within his country. In 1990 Gorbachev and President Bush achieved a breakthrough with the Strategic Arms Reduction Treaty (START). For the first time, two nuclear powers agreed to destroy existing nuclear weapons.

Most Soviet citizens, however, were more concerned about their own problems than about arms control. For years they had endured shortages of food and basic items such as shoes and soap because of government mismanagement and heavy defense spending. Gorbachev's policies aimed to solve the economic problems, but changes came slowly. With Gorbachev's policy of glasnost, Soviet citizens began to express their dissatisfaction openly.

A Rising Tide of Freedom

With reforms underway in the Soviet Union, the peoples of Eastern Europe felt free to demand change in their countries. In Poland, shipyard workers won the right to form an independent labor union—called Solidarity—in August 1980. Lech Walesa, the leader of Solidarity, emerged as a symbol of resistance to Communist rule. Solidarity forced the government to hold open elections in June 1989.

Elsewhere in Eastern Europe, demonstrators filled the streets of major cities. As public pressure increased and Soviet controls relaxed, long-sealed national borders were opened and Communist governments toppled.

Primary Source / A New Era

Openness As president, Bush continued Reagan's policy of cooperation with Soviet leader Mikhail Gorbachev. Early in his presidency, Bush said, *"a new breeze is blowing across the steppes and cities of the Soviet Union. Why not, then, let this spirit of openness grow, let more barriers come down.*

—from Remarks at the Texas A&M University Commencement Ceremony, 1989

Critical Thinking

Explaining President Bush also called on the Soviet Union to follow policies of "open emigration" and "open air-waves." What did he mean by this?

Gorbachev, President Reagan, and ▲ President-Elect George Bush view the Statue of Liberty after meeting in New York City, December 1988.

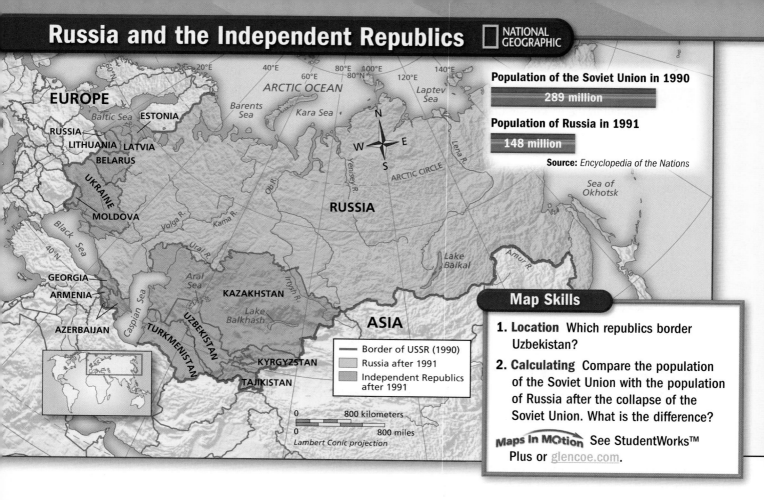

Population of the Soviet Union in 1990
289 million

Population of Russia in 1991
148 million

Source: *Encyclopedia of the Nations*

Border of USSR (1990)
Russia after 1991
Independent Republics after 1991

0   800 kilometers
0   800 miles
Lambert Conic projection

Map Skills

1. **Location** Which republics border Uzbekistan?

2. **Calculating** Compare the population of the Soviet Union with the population of Russia after the collapse of the Soviet Union. What is the difference?

Maps In Motion See StudentWorks™ Plus or glencoe.com.

In late 1989, the iron curtain that had divided Eastern and Western Europe for more than 40 years began to crumble. During this time, Gorbachev encouraged reform.

Freedom also came to East Germany. With protests raging and thousands of citizens fleeing to West Germany, the Communist government opened the Berlin Wall on November 9, 1989. Germans brought hammers and chisels to chop away at the Berlin Wall, long the symbol of the barrier to the West. In 1990 East Germany and West Germany were finally reunited.

Collapse of the Soviet Union

As Eastern Europe was changing, Gorbachev faced opposition from political rivals within the Soviet Union. Some reformers demanded that he move quickly to establish democratic and free enterprise reforms. Hard-line Communists in the military and secret police resisted his changes and feared the collapse of the Soviet empire.

In August 1991, a group of hard-line Communist officials and army generals staged a coup, or an overthrow of the government. They arrested Gorbachev and ordered soldiers to seize the parliament building.

As the world anxiously waited, about 50,000 people surrounded the parliament building to protect it from the soldiers. Boris Yeltsin, president of the Russian Republic and a reformer, stood on top of a tank and declared, "Democracy will win!" President Bush telephoned Yeltsin to express America's support. On August 22, the coup collapsed. Freed, Gorbachev returned to Moscow.

The defeat of the coup brought a tidal wave of democracy. Soon all 15 republics had declared their independence from the Soviet Union. Yeltsin outlawed the Communist Party in Russia. On December 25, 1991, Gorbachev announced the end of the Soviet Union.

Reading Check **Cause and Effect** What did Solidarity accomplish in Poland?

A New Foreign Policy

Main Idea After the Cold War's end, Bush administration officials set out to develop a new foreign policy.

History and You Have you ever had to handle several problems at once? Read to learn about the foreign crises that the United States faced in the late 1980s and early 1990s.

. . . .

The end of the Cold War brought both hope and new challenges. While redefining U.S. foreign policy goals, President Bush faced crises in various parts of the world.

In 1989 Bush sent U.S. troops to Panama to overthrow dictator Manuel Noriega. Under Noriega's rule, political repression and corruption had become widespread. The troops seized Noriega and sent him to the United States to stand trial for drug trafficking. Panama then held elections and organized a new government.

Bush also was interested in China. In 1974 he had served as the U.S. diplomatic representative to China. During the 1980s, China's Communist government began to reform the economy, but it refused to make political changes. In May 1989, students and workers in China held protests calling for democracy. On June 4, 1989, troops sent by the government killed several hundred protesters in **Tiananmen Square** in the center of Beijing. Bush and other world leaders condemned the killings.

The Persian Gulf War

President Bush faced perhaps his most serious crisis in the Middle East. In August 1990, Iraq's dictator, **Saddam Hussein** (hoo·SAYN), sent his army into Kuwait, a small neighboring country rich in oil.

Vowing to "draw a line in the sand," President Bush persuaded other nations to join the United States in a **coalition,** or a group united for action. The U.S. forces were commanded by General **Colin Powell,** chairman of the Joint Chiefs of Staff, and General **Norman Schwarzkopf.** Hussein was ordered to withdraw his troops from Kuwait, but he refused.

In January 1991 coalition forces launched **Operation Desert Storm.** Missiles and bombs fell on Iraq, destroying military and civilian **sites,** or locations. Six weeks later, the coalition began a short ground war that freed Kuwait and forced Iraq to accept a cease fire. American troops returned home to cheering crowds.

Primary Source / The Spirit of Freedom

The Barrier Falls In November 1989, crowds tore down the Berlin Wall that had divided Germany and symbolized the "iron curtain" that separated Eastern Europe and Western Europe. ▼

Tragedy in Tiananmen Square In the spring of 1989, Chinese students held demonstrations for democracy. Government tanks and soldiers crushed their protests in Tiananmen Square in Beijing. Many people were killed, and hundreds of pro-democracy activists were arrested. ▶

Critical Thinking

1. **Analyzing** Why was the fall of communism in East Germany significant?

2. **Assessing** How did the United States react to the Chinese government's actions at Tiananmen Square? Was the reaction appropriate? Explain.

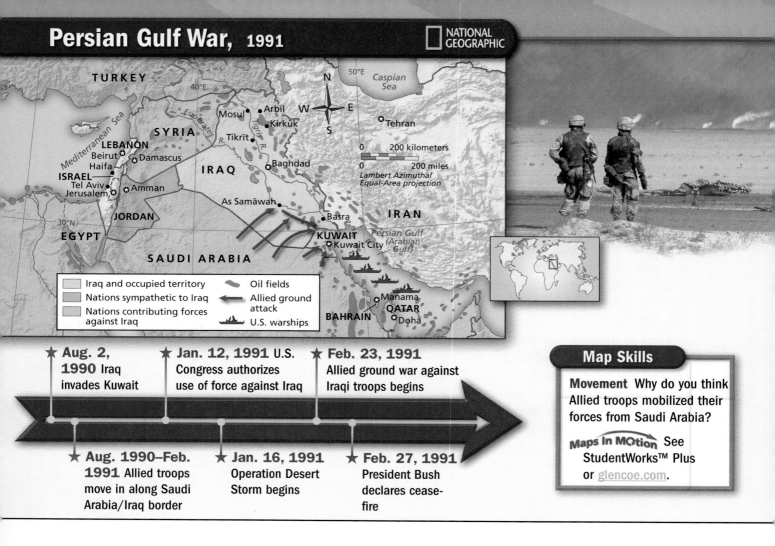

Persian Gulf War, 1991

NATIONAL GEOGRAPHIC

Legend:
- Iraq and occupied territory
- Nations sympathetic to Iraq
- Nations contributing forces against Iraq
- Oil fields
- Allied ground attack
- U.S. warships

Timeline:

★ Aug. 2, 1990 Iraq invades Kuwait

★ Jan. 12, 1991 U.S. Congress authorizes use of force against Iraq

★ Feb. 23, 1991 Allied ground war against Iraqi troops begins

★ Aug. 1990–Feb. 1991 Allied troops move in along Saudi Arabia/Iraq border

★ Jan. 16, 1991 Operation Desert Storm begins

★ Feb. 27, 1991 President Bush declares cease-fire

Map Skills

Movement Why do you think Allied troops mobilized their forces from Saudi Arabia?

Maps In Motion See StudentWorks™ Plus or glencoe.com.

War in the Balkans

Another conflict occurred in Yugoslavia. Yugoslavia had been made up of several republics. After the collapse of Yugoslavia's government, the republics of Slovenia, Croatia, and Bosnia-Herzegovina declared their independence in 1991.

The people of Croatia and Bosnia included many Serbs—people from the Yugoslav republic of Serbia. These Serbs, backed by Serbia's government, fought to hold on to parts of Croatia and Bosnia. A terrible civil war followed, and thousands died. Reports of killings committed by the Serbs angered world leaders. After NATO took military action, the participants signed a peace plan in 1995 known as the Dayton Accords.

Reading Check **Describing** What political event took place in Tiananmen Square, Beijing?

Domestic Issues

Main Idea The federal debt and an economic slowdown were challenges for the Bush administration.

History and You Have you ever come up with a plan to raise money when you wanted to make an expensive purchase? Read to find out how the federal government had to meet financial challenges during the Bush administration.

President Bush spent much of his time dealing with foreign policy, but he also faced major domestic challenges. From the Reagan years, Bush inherited a growing federal debt and a slowing economy.

Early in his presidency, Bush faced a serious crisis. During the 1980s, the Reagan administration cut regulations in many industries. New laws eased limits on savings and loan associations (S&Ls)—financial institutions that specialized in making loans to home buyers.

Banking Crisis

The new laws allowed S&Ls to pay very high interest rates to attract deposits and to make far too many risky loans and investments. When many borrowers could not repay their loans and real estate values declined, S&Ls lost millions of dollars. Individual S&L deposits were insured by the government, which now had to pay out billions of dollars to customers of failed S&Ls. To limit the crisis, the government bailed out other struggling S&Ls, a move costing taxpayers almost $500 billion.

Economic Downturn

The heavy borrowing of the 1980s brought trouble to the economy. As the federal debt reached new highs, business and personal debt grew. In 1990 the economy slowed to a recession, partly caused by the end of the Cold War. Cuts in military spending led to job losses in defense-related businesses.

Companies also began to **downsize**—lay off workers—to become more efficient. The nation's debt burden made the recession worse. Individuals and businesses had borrowed heavily and now could not meet loan payments. Some had to declare **bankruptcy,** selling off what they owned to pay debts.

Many people urged the government to stimulate the economy. President Bush refused to increase federal spending. He did agree to extend benefits to the jobless, but he opposed further government involvement.

Accomplishments

Despite disagreements, the president and Congress cooperated on updating the Clean Air Act and pushing forward on civil rights. The Americans with Disabilities Act of 1990 banned job discrimination against people with disabilities. It also opened ways for disabled people to gain easier access to workplaces, transportation, and housing.

Bush also carried out a war on illegal drugs. In 1989 President Bush created the Office of National Drug Control Policy. This department oversees more than 50 federal agencies involved in the war on drugs.

Reading Check **Analyzing** Why did so many S&Ls fail in the 1980s?

Section 2 Review

History ONLINE
Study Central™ To review this section, go to glencoe.com.

Vocabulary

1. Use each of these terms correctly in a sentence: retain, coalition, site, downsize, bankruptcy.

Main Ideas

2. **Analyzing** Why was START so important?

3. **Explaining** What action did Bush take in Panama using U.S. troops?

4. **Discussing** Why did the government lose so much money through the failure of S&L banks?

Critical Thinking

5. **Sequencing** Using a diagram like the one below, generally sequence the events that led to the country's deep recession during the 1990s.

6. **Creative Writing** Take a stand on how you feel about U.S. participation in Operation Desert Storm. Write a short protest or support song about your feelings.

Answer the
7. **Essential Question**
How did President Bush deal with the domestic challenges facing his presidency?

Essential Question ◄

How did the Clinton presidency change the U.S. domestic scene in the 1990s?

Reading Guide

Content Vocabulary

grassroots movement (p. 541)

deficit spending (p. 541)

budget deficit (p. 541)

gross domestic product (p. 543)

perjury (p. 543)

Academic Vocabulary

adequate (p. 541)   scope (p. 543)

Key People and Events

Bill Clinton (p. 541)

Al Gore (p. 541)

George W. Bush (p. 545)

Richard Cheney (p. 545)

Condoleezza Rice (p. 547)

Reading Strategy

Taking Notes On a diagram like the one below, identify early Clinton-sponsored legislation that passed into law.

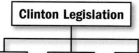

Clinton Legislation

American Diary

At 16 years old, Bill Clinton heard the "I Have a Dream" speech by Dr. Martin Luther King, Jr., for the first time. It inspired him to find common ground in politics for the benefit of all citizens. After becoming president in 1993, he still held his vision of people working together for the common good. He said, "We have got to move beyond division and resentment to common ground. We've got to go beyond cynicism to a sense of possibility."

—from Remarks at Georgetown University, July 1995

Candidate Bill Clinton greets supporters at a campaign rally in 1992.

The Clinton Administration

Main Idea President Clinton struggled with Republicans in Congress and faced impeachment, but he achieved several major economic and social reforms.

History and You Have you ever visited our closest neighbors—Canada and Mexico? Read to find out how the United States and these two nations drew closer together in the 1990s.

• •

After victory in the Persian Gulf War, President Bush's popularity with Americans soared. A troubled economy, however, hurt Bush's reelection chances for 1992 and encouraged challengers to enter the presidential race. The Democrats nominated Arkansas governor **Bill Clinton** to run against President Bush. Clinton chose Tennessee senator **Al Gore** as his running mate. The Clinton campaign focused on the economy and the high unemployment rate.

Unhappy with "politics as usual," many Americans did not want to vote for either Bush or Clinton. A **grassroots movement**—people around the nation organizing at the local level—put Texas business leader H. Ross Perot on the ballot as a third-party candidate.

Perot called for an end to the government's **deficit spending,** or spending more money than it takes in.

Voters elected Clinton, the first president born after World War II. Clinton received 43 percent of the popular vote, Bush 38 percent, and Perot 19 percent. Clinton received less than a majority of the votes because of Perot's strong showing, the highest percentage of popular votes for any third-party candidate since Theodore Roosevelt in 1912.

Domestic Program

One of the new president's goals was reducing the **budget deficit**—the amount by which spending exceeds revenue. Clinton proposed cutting government spending, raising taxes for middle-and upper-income Americans, and providing tax credits to the poorest. Most Republicans in Congress opposed this plan, but it narrowly passed.

Clinton faced even stronger opposition to his plan for health-care reform. His goal was to control rising health-care costs and provide **adequate,** or enough,health insurance for every American. The president named the First Lady, Hillary Rodham Clinton, to head the task force.

By the Numbers / The 1992 Election

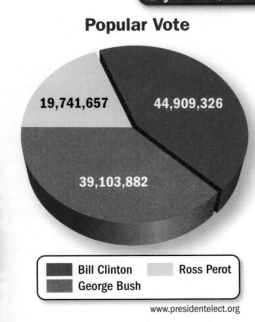

Popular Vote

19,741,657

44,909,326

39,103,882

Bill Clinton | Ross Perot
George Bush

www.presidentelect.org

Three-Way Race Democratic candidate Bill Clinton won the electoral vote by more than a 2-to-1 margin over incumbent President George H.W. Bush. Clinton, however, did not win a majority of the nation's popular vote, but he did beat Bush by six percentage points.

Critical Thinking

Evaluating How can a third-party candidate for the presidency like Perot affect an election?

Voting for Impeachment The House of Representatives accused President Clinton of lying under oath and obstructing justice, and voted to impeach him. Now it was up to the Senate to convict and remove him from office. Passionate voices cried out for and against conviction.

For Conviction *"As the youngest member of this body, I believe we must hold firm to the oldest truths. . . . I vote as I do because I will not stand for the proposition that a President can, with premeditation and deliberation, obstruct justice and commit perjury before a grand jury. It cannot be."*

Senator Peter Fitzgerald (R–Illinois) ▲

	GUILTY	NOT GUILTY
GOP	30	3
DEM	0	31
TOTAL	30	34

CLINTON ACQUITTED

SENATE VOTE

67 VOTES TO CONVICT

IMPEACHMENT ARTICLE 2 OBSTRUCTION OF JUSTICE

LIEBERMAN D

Against Conviction *"Impeachment is a power singularly lacking any of the checks and balances on which the Framers depended. It is solely a power of the Congress. Do not doubt that it could bring radical instability to American government."*

▲ Senator Daniel Moynihan (D–New York)

Congress rejected the Clinton plan, calling it too expensive and too reliant on government control. Later, Congress did pass measures that provided more health-care protection for the elderly, children, and other groups that were not previously covered.

During his first term, President Clinton won some legislative battles. Despite strong opposition, the president succeeded in passing the Brady Bill of 1993. The law imposed a waiting period and background checks for handgun purchases. The 1994 crime bill banned 19 kinds of assault weapons and provided for 100,000 new police officers.

Another Clinton proposal that became law was the Family and Medical Leave Act of 1993. It permitted workers to take time off from their jobs for special family situations.

Contract With America

Before the 1994 mid-term elections, House Republicans led by Newt Gingrich of Georgia created a new plan. Known as the Contract with America, it called for a "return to the basic values that had built the country: work and family and the recognition of a higher moral authority."

In the contract, the Republicans promised to reduce the federal government, balance the budget, lower taxes, and reform how Congress operates. They also pledged to pass laws to reduce crime, reform welfare, and strengthen the family. The result was a strong Republican victory in the 1994 elections. For the first time in 40 years, the Republicans controlled both houses of Congress. In their first hundred days in office, the Republicans passed much of the Contract with America.

In 1995, however, the Republicans lost ground when they clashed with President Clinton over the new federal budget. This dispute caused the federal government to run out of money. The government shut down nonessential services twice for a total of 27 days. Congress and the president recognized that compromise was needed.

The Power to Impeach If a majority of the House votes to impeach, the Senate then has the power to try the official. Only two presidents have been impeached: Andrew Johnson in 1868 and Bill Clinton in 1998. Both were tried by the Senate and acquitted (not removed from office).

Critical Thinking

1. **Analyzing** Why did Senator Fitzgerald believe that the president should be removed from office?

2. **Explaining** What reasons does Senator Moynihan give for his vote not to remove President Clinton from office?

Soon afterward, the Republicans in Congress and President Clinton reached an agreement to balance the budget. The president pushed for an increase in the minimum wage and supported a welfare reform act. This measure set a work requirement for people receiving benefits and put a five-year time limit on benefits.

Clinton Wins a Second Term

The Republicans hoped to regain the White House in 1996. However, the economy was healthy and unemployment was at a 30-year low. President Clinton easily won reelection, beating the Republican candidate, former Senate majority leader Robert Dole.

During Clinton's second term, the economy continued to grow. One measure of economic growth is the **gross domestic product** (GDP), the value of all the goods and services produced in a nation in a year. In 1996 and 1997, the GDP grew by about 4 percent per year—one of the highest rates of growth since the post-World War II boom.

The economy's growth increased the amount of tax money the government received. At the same time, the president and Congress cut back the size of the federal budget. The federal budget is prepared for a fiscal year—a 12-month planning period. The 1998 fiscal year ended with a federal budget surplus—the amount of money remaining after all expenditures—of about $80 billion, the first surplus in three decades.

Scandals and Impeachment

The strong economy kept Clinton's popularity high, but scandals threatened his presidency. Clinton was accused of arranging illegal loans for a real estate company while he was governor of Arkansas. Former judge Kenneth Starr led the investigation. A new scandal emerged involving a personal relationship between the president and a White House intern. Evidence suggested that the president may have committed **perjury,** or lied under oath, about the relationship. Starr widened the **scope,** or range, of the investigation. In September 1998, Starr sent a report to Congress claiming that President Clinton had committed perjury and obstructed justice.

The House of Representatives then began hearings to decide whether to impeach the president. To impeach is to make a formal accusation of wrongdoing against a public official. Despite general agreement that the president had lied, the House was split over whether his actions justified impeachment. Clinton's supporters argued that his offenses did not qualify as "high crimes and misdemeanors," as stated in the Constitution. Clinton's accusers insisted that the president was accountable if his actions were illegal.

In December 1998, the House passed two impeachment articles—for perjury and for obstruction of justice. The case moved to the Senate for trial. A two-thirds majority vote is needed to convict and remove a president from office. In February 1999, the Senate acquitted the president of both charges.

Foreign Policy

Even as the nation struggled with domestic issues, foreign affairs presented new challenges. Important decisions faced American policy makers on defining the nation's role in the post–Cold War world.

In 1993 Clinton persuaded Congress to ratify the North American Free Trade Agreement, or NAFTA. Under NAFTA the United States, Canada, and Mexico agreed to eliminate trade barriers among the three nations. NAFTA opponents feared a loss of U.S. jobs. Farmers also feared NAFTA, saying that low-priced Mexican produce would undercut American goods. Supporters argued that the treaty would lower prices for American consumers and expand markets.

The Middle East was also a major concern. In September 1993, President Clinton invited Israeli prime minister Yitzhak Rabin and Yassir Arafat, head of the Palestine Liberation Organization (PLO), to the White House for the signing of a historic agreement between the two leaders. Israel recognized the PLO as the representative of the Palestinians, and the PLO recognized Israel's right to exist. The agreement created a plan for limited Palestinian self-government in certain areas.

Opposition to the plan emerged on both sides, and violence in the area continued. In 1995 an Israeli extremist assassinated Prime Minister Rabin. During the remainder of his term, Clinton continued peace efforts, but little success was achieved.

As you read in Section 2, civil war had erupted in the former Yugoslavia. In Bosnia, Serbs engaged in ethnic cleansing—forcibly removing or killing members—of the Muslim population. In 1998 Serbian leader Slobodan Milošević tried to drive Muslims out of the Kosovo region. U.S. and NATO air strikes against Serbia finally forced the Serbs to leave Kosovo and agree to negotiate. Clinton then led peace talks, which produced the Dayton Accords in late 1995.

Reading Check **Identifying** What major trade agreement did Clinton make in 1993?

National Defense, Selected Nations

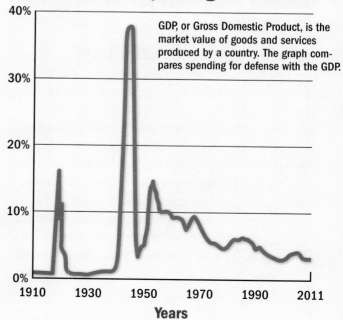

Defense Spending, 2006 (% of world total)

Britain 5.1
France 4.6
China 4.3
Japan 3.8
Germany 3.2
Russia 3.0
India 2.1
U.S. 45.7
Total: $1.2 trillion
Rest of world 28.3

Sources: Stockholm International Peace Research Institute (SIPRI); Center for Strategic and Budgetary Assessments; International Institute for Strategic Studies

U.S. Defense Spending as % of GDP

GDP, or Gross Domestic Product, is the market value of goods and services produced by a country. The graph compares spending for defense with the GDP.

40%
30%
20%
10%
0%

1910   1930   1950   1970   1990   2011
Years

A New President for a New Century

Main Idea As the 2000s began, the United States enjoyed economic prosperity but was deeply divided politically.

History and You Have you seen or taken part in a race in which the outcome was so close that it was difficult to declare a winner? Read to find out how the winner of the 2000 presidential race—one of the closest in American history—was determined.

. . . .

As Clinton prepared to leave office, his legacy was uncertain. He had balanced the budget and succeeded in turning around the nation's economy. The impeachment trial during Clinton's second term, however, had left the country divided. Many Americans were pleased with his accomplishments but were disappointed with the president's personal conduct. As the 2000 election approached, the major parties looked for candidates who appealed to a wide cross section of voters.

Comparing the Military, Selected Nations The U.S. military has about 1.5 million personnel on active duty. An additional 1.3 million men and women serve in the reserves.

	Armed forces* in millions	Nuclear warheads, est.	Aircraft carriers
U.S.	1.5	5,163	12
Britain	0.2	200	3
China	2.3	400	0
France	0.3	350	2
India	1.3	50	1
Japan	0.2	0	0
Russia	1.0	5,830	1

*Not including reservists

Graph Skills

Analyzing Explain any trends apparent in U.S. defense spending as a percentage of GDP. **Graphs In Motion**

The Candidates

The Democrats nominated Vice President Al Gore for president, hoping that the popularity of Clinton's policies would mean votes for Gore. The large Republican field eventually came down to two men: Governor **George W. Bush** of Texas and Senator John McCain of Arizona. Ultimately, the Republicans chose Bush, the son of former President George H.W. Bush, as their nominee.

Gore made history by naming Senator Joseph Lieberman, from Connecticut, as his running mate. This marked the first time in U.S. history that a Jewish American ran on a national ticket. George W. Bush chose **Richard Cheney** as his running mate. Cheney had served as chief of staff to President Gerald Ford and defense secretary to former President Bush in 1989.

During the campaign, Gore stressed protecting the environment and improving education. Bush also supported educational reform. Calling himself a "compassionate conservative," Bush favored local "grassroots" efforts to help the disadvantaged without large and costly government programs. A major campaign issue was what to do with the budget surplus. Gore and Bush agreed that Social Security and Medicare needed reform, but they disagreed on the details. Both also supported tax cuts and plans to help seniors pay for prescription drugs.

Claiming that there was little difference between Bush and Gore, activist Ralph Nader entered the race. Noting that "too much power in the hands of the few has further weakened our democracy," Nader ran as the nominee of the Green Party, which was known for its strong environmental views.

The Election of 2000

The 2000 election was extraordinarily close between Bush and Gore. For five weeks after the race, the outcome remained undecided. The key state was Florida, where Bush had a slim lead. Without Florida's 25 electoral votes, neither Bush nor Gore had the 270 electoral votes needed to win.

Election of 2000

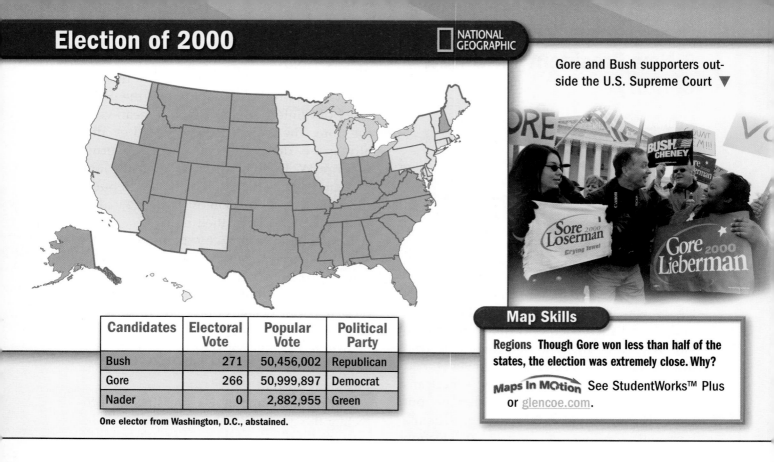

Gore and Bush supporters outside the U.S. Supreme Court ▼

Candidates	Electoral Vote	Popular Vote	Political Party
Bush	271	50,456,002	Republican
Gore	266	50,999,897	Democrat
Nader	0	2,882,955	Green

One elector from Washington, D.C., abstained.

Map Skills

Regions Though Gore won less than half of the states, the election was extremely close. Why?

Maps In Motion See StudentWorks™ Plus or glencoe.com.

Because the results in Florida were so close, state law required a recount of the ballots using vote-counting machines. Gore also asked for hand recounts in several counties, and a battle began over whether and how to conduct them. Lawsuits were filed in state and federal courts. The issue ultimately reached the U.S. Supreme Court.

On December 12, in *Bush* v. *Gore,* the Court ruled that the hand recounts of selected votes in Florida ordered by the Florida Supreme Court violated the equal protection clause of the Constitution. It further held that there was not enough time to conduct a recount that would pass constitutional standards. This ruling left Bush the winner in Florida. The next day, Gore conceded the election.

Bush Becomes President

On January 20, 2001, Bush became the 43rd president of the United States. In his Inaugural Address, President Bush called for "inclusion, not division," saying that America should be united. The need for unity and cooperation was important in Congress as well. After the election the Senate was evenly split—50 Republicans and 50 Democrats.

In May 2001 Vermont senator James Jeffords left the Republican Party and became an independent. This led to a historic switch in power, transferring control to the Democrats in mid-session. However, in the midterm elections of 2002, the Republicans regained control of the Senate and increased their majority in the House.

When assembling his cabinet, President Bush sought people from different career backgrounds. He appointed popular retired Army general Colin Powell as secretary of state. He also named Donald Rumsfeld as secretary of defense. Rumsfeld previously served as secretary of defense during the Ford adminstration. The Bush cabinet also reflected much of the country's diversity, including three African Americans, two Asians, and one Latino.

In addition, five women served in President Bush's cabinet. Elaine Chao, the secretary of labor, was the first Asian American woman to serve in a president's cabinet.

Other women played leading roles in the new administration. **Condoleezza Rice,** the first woman in history to hold the job of national security adviser, was instrumental in shaping foreign policy. First Lady Laura Bush promoted education. She called attention to the need for recruiting more teachers and improving reading skills.

Domestic Policy

Once in office, President Bush focused on his domestic plans: cutting taxes, improving public education, reforming Social Security and Medicare, and strengthening the nation's defenses. Bush's first task was to carry out his campaign pledge to cut taxes. Some politicians argued that the tax money lost could be used more responsibly, for example, to pay off the national debt. Supporters claimed the cut would help the economy, which had gone into a slump during the election campaign. In June 2001, Congress passed and Bush signed into law the 10-year, $1.3 trillion tax-cut bill.

After passage of the tax-cut plan, Bush proposed reforms in education. He called for public schools to hold yearly tests to measure student performance. He also wanted to allow parents to use federal funds to pay for private schools if their public schools were doing a poor job. Congress refused to give federal funds to private schools, but it did vote in favor of annual testing in public schools for grades 3 to 8. This law became known as the No Child Left Behind Act.

Foreign Policy

In foreign affairs, Bush pushed for new military programs. One was a National Missile Defense System designed to shoot down incoming missiles before they reached the United States. The president argued that missile defense was needed because many hostile nations were developing long-range missiles.

Meanwhile, a horrifying event took place on September 11, 2001,that changed everything. A stunned nation realized that it was not immune to the dangers of a violent world. A new kind of war had begun.

✔ **Reading Check** **Summarizing** What was George W. Bush's policy on education?

Section 3 Review

History ONLINE
Study Central™ To review this section, go to glencoe.com.

Vocabulary

1. Write a sentence using each of the following terms correctly: grassroots movement, deficit spending, budget deficit, adequate, gross domestic product, perjury, scope.

Main Ideas

2. **Analyzing** What was Clinton's plan for health-care reform, and who did he name to administer it?

3. **Explaining** What were the main goals of the Contract with America?

4. **Discussing** What caused the confusion over the outcome of the 2000 presidential election?

Critical Thinking

5. **Interpreting** What did George W. Bush mean when he called himself a compassionate conservative?

6. **Identifying** On a diagram like the one below, identify the main goals in Bush's domestic plans.

Bush Domestic Plans

7. **Persuasive Writing** Decide the answer to this question: *Should a president be protected from impeachment because the presidency is the highest office in America?* Write a one-page persuasive paper describing your opinion on this topic.

8. **Answer the Essential Question** How did the Clinton presidency change the U.S. domestic scene in the 1990s?

The War on Terror

Reading Guide

Content Vocabulary

terrorism (p. 549)　　insurgent (p. 552)
fundamentalist　　levee
　(p. 550)　　　　　　(p. 555)
counterterrorism (p. 551)

Academic Vocabulary

prior (p. 551)　　definite (p. 555)

Key People and Events

Osama bin Laden (p. 549)
USA Patriot Act (p. 551)
Hurricane Katrina (p. 555)
Nancy Pelosi (p. 555)

Reading Strategy

Taking Notes On a diagram like the one below, identify the American sites of the September 11 terrorist attacks.

```
┌──────┐          ┌──────┐
└──────┘          └──────┘
    ┌──────────────────┐
    │   September 11   │
    │      Sites       │
    └──────────────────┘
┌──────┐          ┌──────┐
└──────┘          └──────┘
```

American Diary

On September 11, New York City firefighter John Breen had orders to search for trapped people on the top floor of a hotel, nestled between the towers of the World Trade Center. Once inside, Breen felt the hotel begin to sway as the first tower collapsed. "I heard it getting louder and louder like an approaching train. You could hear the floors one on top of each other like dominoes." After the second tower collapsed, it was reported that at least 41 firefighters had been killed inside the hotel.

—*from* Firehouse Magazine

A man walks amid the rubble of the World Trade Center looking for victims to help.

The Events of 9/11

Main Idea On September 11, 2001, the United States suffered the worst terrorist attack in its history.

History and You How did people react when they heard about the attacks of September 11, 2001? Read to learn about what effect the attacks had on the nation and the world.

. . . .

On September 11, 2001, the nation witnessed horrifying acts of terrorism. **Terrorism** is the use of violence against civilians to reach a political goal. Early that morning, terrorists seized four U.S. passenger planes. Two planes were deliberately crashed into New York City's World Trade Center. A third plane was flown into the Pentagon, the U.S. military headquarters in Washington, D.C. A fourth plane was seized, but the passengers heroically fought back. This plane crashed in Pennsylvania. More Americans died in the attacks of September 11, 2001, than died at Pearl Harbor or on D-Day in World War II.

The Spirit of America

The 9/11 attacks shocked Americans, but they responded rapidly to the crisis. Firefighters and medical workers from throughout the nation headed to New York City to help. Across the nation, Americans lined up to donate blood and to collect food, blankets, and other supplies. From coast to coast, people put up flags to show their unity. They held candlelight vigils and prayer services as they searched for ways to help.

The U.S. government also responded quickly to the attacks. The Air National Guard patrolled the skies over major cities. Army National Guard troops were sent to airports to strengthen security. On September 14, President Bush declared a national emergency. Congress approved the use of force to fight whoever had attacked the United States. The U.S. government quickly identified the attacks as the work of a Saudi Arabian man named **Osama bin Laden** and his terrorist organization, al-Qaeda (al KY·duh).

Primary Source / America Is Attacked

World Trade Center

110 floors

110 floors

1 8:45 A.M. American Airlines Flight 11 crashes into North Tower.

2 9:05 A.M. United Airlines Flight 175 crashes into South Tower.

U.S. Customs House
8 floors

WTC 7
47 floors

Marriott Hotel
22 floors

South Plaza Building
9 floors

North Plaza Building
9 floors

Critical Thinking

Analyzing What were some of the obstacles firefighters faced in trying to rescue people from the burning buildings?

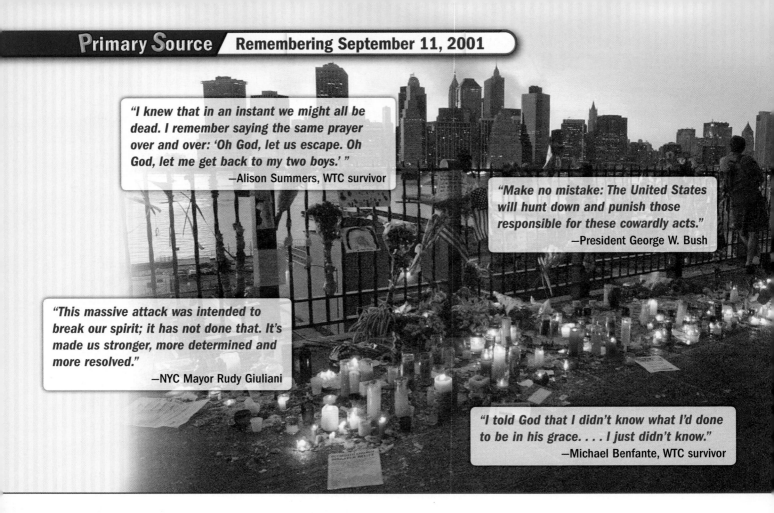

"I knew that in an instant we might all be dead. I remember saying the same prayer over and over: 'Oh God, let us escape. Oh God, let me get back to my two boys.' "
—Alison Summers, WTC survivor

"Make no mistake: The United States will hunt down and punish those responsible for these cowardly acts."
—President George W. Bush

"This massive attack was intended to break our spirit; it has not done that. It's made us stronger, more determined and more resolved."
—NYC Mayor Rudy Giuliani

"I told God that I didn't know what I'd done to be in his grace. . . . I just didn't know."
—Michael Benfante, WTC survivor

The Roots of Terrorism

Terrorist groups act on their own and are usually not part of a government. Today, most terrorist acts against Americans have been carried out by groups from the Middle East. Those groups often object to the presence of American military on the Arabian Peninsula, the spread of Western culture, which they believe undermines traditional Islamic values, and American support of Israel. In the 1970s, several Middle Eastern nations realized that supporting terrorist organizations—helping arm and train them— was a means to fight Israel and the United States.

Although the vast majority of the 1 billion Muslims worldwide reject terrorism, some **fundamentalists** like bin Laden do not. Muslim fundamentalists call for a return to traditional Muslim ways. Those who favor bin Laden's methods believe that any action is justified to create a pure Muslim society.

The Rise of al-Qaeda

Al-Qaeda grew out of the Muslim struggle against the Soviet Union in the Southwest Asian country of Afghanistan. Bin Laden formed al-Qaeda, or "the Base," to recruit new fighters.

When the Soviets left Afghanistan, bin Laden decided that all Westerners should be pushed out of the Muslim world. Bin Laden then turned al-Qaeda into a terrorist group. He won the support of the Taliban, a Muslim fundamentalist group that took power in Afghanistan. Bin Laden's followers set off bombs at U.S. embassies in Kenya and Tanzania in 1998. They also attacked a U.S. navy ship in Yemen in 2000. Then, on September 11, 2001, al-Qaeda struck again, seizing four American passenger planes and carrying out the most deadly terrorist attack in history.

Reading Check **Analyzing** What caused the rise of al-Qaeda in the Middle East?

The Victims and Heroes

World Trade Center	
Total Injured	2,261
Total Deaths (ground, including firefighters and police)	2,752
American Airlines Flight 11 Deaths—WTC North Tower	92
United Airlines Flight 175 Deaths—WTC South Tower	65

Washington, D.C., and Pennsylvania	
Total Injured—The Pentagon	76
Total Deaths—The Pentagon (ground)	124
American Airlines Flight 77—The Pentagon	64
United Airlines Flight 93—Shanksville, Pennsylvania	40

Critical Thinking

Evaluating How do you think these acts of terrorism brought Americans together?

Fighting Terrorism

Main Idea After the 9/11 attacks, the United States launched a massive effort to eliminate international terrorism.

History and You What steps does your family take to protect your home from crime? Read to find out what actions the United States and other countries took to fight against terrorism.

. . . .

After the attacks on September 11, the United States declared war on terrorism. In an address to Congress on September 20, the president demanded that the Taliban in Afghanistan turn over bin Laden and his followers and shut down all terrorist camps. The war against terrorism, President Bush told Americans, would be global in its reach. It would not end quickly, but it was a war the people of the United States were now called to fight:

PRIMARY SOURCE

"Great harm has been done to us. We have suffered great loss. And in our grief and anger, we have found our mission and our moment. . . . We will not tire; we will not falter; and we will not fail."

—from President Bush, *Address to Joint Session of Congress*, September 20, 2001

Protecting America

President Bush took steps to protect Americans from terrorist attacks. On September 24, he issued an executive order blocking the use of funds by individuals and groups suspected of supporting terrorism. The president also created a new federal agency—the Office of Homeland Security—to coordinate **counterterrorism** efforts. Counterterrorism involves military or political activities intended to combat terrorism. In June 2002, President Bush asked Congress to combine all of the agencies responsible for the public's safety into a new department called the Department of Homeland Security.

In late October 2001, Congress passed and the president signed into law new measures to combat terrorism. The **USA Patriot Act** of 2001 gave federal prosecutors and FBI agents new powers to investigate those who plot or carry out acts of terrorism. The law expanded the power of federal agents to tap telephones and track Internet usage in the hunt for terrorists. It also permitted agents to conduct secret searches of a suspect's home or office without giving **prior,** or earlier, notice to the owner of the property.

The War in Afghanistan

The war on terrorism first focused on Afghanistan, where Taliban leaders refused to hand over bin Laden. On October 7, the U.S. military began bombing Taliban and al-Qaeda forces. In December, the Taliban government collapsed, and surviving Taliban members fled to Afghanistan's mountains. Fighting continues between NATO and Taliban forces. Meanwhile, bin Laden remains at large, possibly hiding in the neighboring country of Pakistan.

The Iraq War

The attacks of 9/11 raised fears that terrorist groups might acquire nuclear, chemical, or biological weapons. These weapons of mass destruction could kill tens of thousands of people at a time. President Bush believed that Iraq's government was hiding these deadly weapons and was an immediate threat.

In the summer of 2002, Bush increased pressure on Iraq's dictator, Saddam Hussein. When questions arose over whether Iraq was cooperating with UN weapons inspectors, the president asked the UN to call for the use of force in Iraq. Although some UN members opposed the use of force, the United States prepared for war.

On March 20, 2003, the American military, aided by soldiers from Britain and some other countries, attacked Iraq. The Iraqi army was quickly defeated, and Saddam Hussein was overthrown. He was later captured, tried, and executed for crimes against his people.

The United States set out to create a democracy in Iraq. In 2005, Iraqi voters elected a parliament and approved a new constitution. The United States and its allies trained more Iraqis to serve in the police and the military. They also attempted to provide electricity, clean water, schools, and improved health care for Iraq's people.

These efforts were more difficult than winning the war. **Insurgents,** or rebel groups, battled U.S. forces. Iraq also was torn apart by disputes among Iraq's Muslim communities.

Between 2003 and 2007, more than 3,700 American and British soldiers and 70,000 Iraqis died. As the fighting dragged on, support for the war began to decline. The failure to find weapons of mass destruction also caused many people to wonder if the war in Iraq was a mistake. President Bush, however, was determined to stay the course in Iraq.

Reading Check Describing In 2002, what did the U.S. accuse Iraq of hiding?

Global Terrorism

NATIONAL GEOGRAPHIC

7	1996 U.S. complex in Saudi Arabia bombed, 19 U.S. soldiers killed
8	1998 U.S. embassies in Kenya and Tanzania bombed, 200 killed
9	1999 Chechen separatists bomb apartments in Russia, 300 killed
10	2000 USS *Cole* bombed in Persian Gulf, 17 U.S. soldiers killed
11	2001 Hijacked airliners crash into the World Trade Center, the Pentagon, and in rural Pennsylvania
12	2002 Bomb explodes at resort in Bali, Indonesia, more than 200 killed
13	2002–present Attacks in Afghanistan against troops and civilians
14	2003–present Attacks in Iraq against coalition troops and civilians
15	2004 Beslan school hostage crisis, 344 killed, mostly children
16	2004 Train system in Madrid, Spain, bombed, 191 killed
17	2004 U.S. Consulate in Jeddah, Saudi Arabia, attacked, 5 killed
18	2005 London subway bombed, 52 killed
19	2007 Car bomb attempt at Glasgow, Scotland, airport

1	1979 Fifty-two Americans held hostage in Iran
2	1983 U.S. Marine barracks in Lebanon bombed, 241 killed
3	1985 TWA flight hijacked; hostages held in Lebanon
4	1988 Pan Am flight explodes over Scotland, 270 killed
5	1993 World Trade Center bombed in New York, 6 killed
6	1995 Bombing of federal office building in Oklahoma City, 168 killed, more than 500 injured

Bush's Second Term

Main Idea During his second term, President Bush lost much support as a result of the Iraq war and difficult challenges at home.

History and You Have you ever taken part in an election at your school? Read to learn about the election of 2004, in which more voters turned out than had voted in other recent elections.

· ·

As the Iraq war dragged on, Bush's popularity began to shrink. The growing national debt fueled by the war sapped the country's economic strength. The failure to find any weapons of mass destruction undermined the president's support. In addition, Bush's standing was hurt by a scandal at the Iraqi prison of Abu Ghraib. There, some Iraqi prisoners of war were abused by their American guards.

Disrupting Terror Plots

Law-enforcement officials such as the officer watching the banks of monitors (above) work to uncover threats from terrorist activity. Highlights of their success:

- **December 2001** Would-be bomber stopped by passengers while on trans-Atlantic flight
- **2003** Disrupted a plot to use hijacked commercial airplanes to attack Heathrow Airport in London
- **2004** Disrupted plot to conduct large-scale bombings in cities in the United Kingdom
- **July 2005** Attempt to bomb the London subway is stopped
- **August 2006** Uncovered plot to smuggle liquid explosives onto trans-Atlantic airline flights
- **June 2007** Vehicles packed with explosives are discovered in London; suspects arrested

Critical Thinking

Analyzing Which attack took place in the U.S. Southwest?

Election of 2004

All of these setbacks gave the Democrats a chance to mount a serious challenge in the 2004 election. The Democratic Party chose Massachusetts senator John Kerry for president and North Carolina senator John Edwards for vice president. The Republicans renominated President Bush and Vice President Cheney.

On domestic issues, the candidates offered the nation a clear choice. Bush pledged to continue to cut taxes while building a strong national defense. Kerry promised to raise taxes on the wealthy to fund wider health-care coverage. Both candidates focused their efforts on a few key states where voters were narrowly divided.

Election Day saw the highest voter turnout since 1968—nearly 61 percent of eligible voters went to the polls. Nationwide, President Bush won a majority of the popular vote. His victory helped increase the Republican hold on Congress.

Security and Civil Liberties

The war on terrorism raised questions about the nation's security and civil liberties. A major issue concerned what to do with captured terrorists. The Bush administration decided to hold them at the U.S. military base in Guantanamo Bay, Cuba. Administration officials claimed that the prisoners were illegal enemy fighters, not suspects charged with a crime. As such, they did not have the right of appeal to an American court.

The U.S. Supreme Court disagreed. In 2004 it ruled in *Rasul* v. *Bush* that foreign prisoners who claimed they were unlawfully held had the right to appeal to a court. In response, the Bush administration set up special military courts to hear each prisoner's case.

However, in 2006, in *Hamdan* v. *Rumsfeld,* the Court struck down this plan. It argued that President Bush's military courts violated U.S. military law and international laws. Bush then asked Congress to pass legislation setting up courts that met the Supreme Court's guidelines.

Monday, August 29:

✔ Katrina, a Category 4 hurricane with 145 mph winds, makes landfall near Buras, LA, at 6:10 A.M. CDT (7:10 A.M. EDT).

✔ President Bush makes emergency disaster declarations for Louisiana and Mississippi, freeing up federal funds for aid.

✔ Katrina rips two holes in the Superdome's roof. Some 10,000 storm refugees are inside.

✔ At least eight Gulf Coast refineries shut down or reduce operations.

✔ Airports close in New Orleans, Baton Rouge, Biloxi, Mobile, and Pensacola. Hundreds of flights are canceled or diverted.

Hurricane Katrina hit the Gulf Coast as a Category 4 storm with 145 mph winds on August 29, 2005. ▼

◄ Levees in New Orleans failed when the storm surge hit, flooding low-lying areas and trapping many people who did not evacuate.

DBQ Document-Based Questions

1. **Analyzing Visuals** What do these photographs tell you about the effects of Hurricane Katrina?

2. **Making Decisions** When documenting a tragic event, should a news photographer help a person in need or photograph the scene?

After Bush agreed to protect certain prisoner rights, Congress passed a law stating that anyone declared an illegal enemy fighter by a court could be held indefinitely without trial.

In addition to prisoners' rights, the Bush administration faced challenges about citizens' rights. As part of the war on terror, U.S. security officials had secretly expanded their practice of monitoring, or tracking, international calls and e-mails.

In 2005 word leaked out about this program, creating a controversy. Civil rights groups protested that it would be abused and used to violate citizens' constitutional rights. President Bush argued that he needed to expand this activity without legal approval. In this way, the government would be able to deal more quickly with terrorist threats. After a federal judge ruled the program was not constitutional, Bush officials stated in 2007 that they would carry out the program only with court approval.

Supreme Court Appointments

Early in Bush's second term, he had to fill two vacancies on the U.S. Supreme Court. As a result, the president was able to move the Court in a more conservative direction. First, Bush named federal judge John G. Roberts, Jr., to replace retiring justice Sandra Day O'Connor. Before the Senate could act, however, Chief Justice William Rehnquist died, and the president named Roberts to replace him. Roberts easily won Senate confirmation as chief justice.

Next, Bush tried to fill the O'Connor court vacancy. After Senate opposition to Bush's first nominee, the president named federal judge Samuel Alito, Jr. Although some Democrats expressed concern about Alito's conservative views, the Senate voted 58–42 to confirm Alito.

History ONLINE

Student Web Activity Visit glencoe.com and complete the Chapter 17 Web Activity about America and the war on terror.

Hurricane Katrina

A major natural disaster as well as political storms affected Bush's second term. On August 29, 2005, **Hurricane Katrina** struck the Gulf of Mexico coast. Storm conditions raged from Florida to Louisiana. The hurricane destroyed buildings, roads, and electrical lines. Thousands of people were left homeless, and at least 1,800 people died.

The city of New Orleans suffered extensive damage. After the hurricane had passed, rising waters broke through the levees, or high walls, that protected the low-lying city. As water flooded neighborhoods, residents who stayed behind during the hurricane were forced to await rescue or to flee. Many waited for days without much food, clean water, or information. Eventually troops and transportation arrived and moved flood survivors to other cities.

News broadcasts of the disaster, however, caused many Americans to wonder why national, state, and local governments were failing to respond more quickly. President Bush fired the head of the federal government's emergency relief agency. He also pledged federal funds to rebuild the city.

The 2006 Midterm Elections

American voters expressed their unhappiness with Bush administration policies in the 2006 mid-term elections. The Democrats won control of both houses of Congress for the first time since 1992. House Democrats then elected **Nancy Pelosi** to be the first female Speaker of the House of Representatives.

The day after the election, Secretary of Defense Donald Rumsfeld—a chief planner of the Iraq war—resigned. Bush chose Robert Gates to replace Rumsfeld and put a new commander—General David Patraeus—in charge of the forces in Iraq. The president then announced a "surge," or rapid increase, of some 20,000 more troops to Iraq.

House Democrats criticized the president's plan. They called for the president to set a definite, or precise, timetable for pulling U.S. troops out of Iraq. Whether or not the surge could work was unclear. However, by the autumn of 2007, what was clear was that Americans were divided over the Iraq war and that its outcome remained uncertain.

 Reading Check **Summarizing** What did the Supreme Court rule in *Hamdan* v. *Rumsfeld?*

Section 4 Review

History ONLINE
Study Central™ To review this section, go to glencoe.com.

Vocabulary

1. Use each of these terms correctly in a sentence: terrorism, fundamentalist, counterterrorism, prior, insurgent, levee, definite.

Main Ideas

2. Describing How did Osama bin Laden become so strong in Afghanistan?

3. Explaining What powers did the USA Patriot Act give to federal officers?

4. Analyzing Why was the Supreme Court ruling in *Rasul* v.*Bush* important?

Critical Thinking

5. Sequencing On a time line like the one below, name the events in the war on terror that took place on these dates:

| Sept. 2001 | Oct. 2001 | June 2002 | March 2003 |

6. Descriptive Writing In a paragraph, describe how Hurricane Katrina affected specific areas as well as the entire United States.

Answer the
7. Essential Question
How has the war on terror changed the way Americans live?

Public protests of the Patriot Act

Should the Patriot Act Be Reauthorized?

Building Background

The USA Patriot Act gave federal law officials the power to track personal communications and check personal records. Federal officials can tap telephones and computers and get legal access to voice mail and e-mail messages. They could also obtain personal medical, financial, educational, and even library records without proof that a crime has been committed.

Congress passed the USA Patriot Act in 2001 and renewed it in 2006. Americans who supported it said it was an important part of the war on terror. Others, however, argued that the act represents a threat to civil liberties and privacy.

NO

CONGRESSWOMAN LOUISE McINTOSH SLAUGHTER

Mr. Speaker, I rise today in defense of nothing less than our national security, but national security is not just about protecting our borders. It is also about protecting our freedoms.

All of my colleagues understand that the PATRIOT Act has provided the law enforcement agencies with many valuable tools which facilitate[1] their work in the struggle against terrorism. But with these new tools comes a very real danger that the liberty we seek to protect could be easily compromised. . . .

We have evidence which suggests, in contrast to information coming out of the Justice Department, that many of these measures have resulted in the violation of the civil liberties of American citizens. In addition, we understand that some of the extended search and seizure powers used by the law enforcement are apparently not being used for their intended purpose, which is strictly to fight terrorism, and that is unacceptable.

---

[1] **facilitate** to make easy

YES

ATTORNEY GENERAL JOHN ASHCROFT

Our responsibility was to reorganize our justice system from a backward-looking system focused on prosecution,[2] to a forward-looking system first focused on prevention. Our response was to track down and dismantle highly compartmentalized[3] terrorist networks. To forge new relationships of cooperation with other nations. To mobilize a frightened citizenry. To fight for new and needed tools for law enforcement. To do anything and everything we could under the Constitution to prevent further acts of terrorism. . . .

Congress provided these tools in the USA Patriot Act, . . . and while our job is not finished, we have used the tools provided in the Patriot Act to fulfill our first responsibility to protect the American people. We have used these tools to prevent terrorists from unleashing more death and destruction on our soil. We have used these tools to save innocent American lives. We have used these tools to provide the security that ensures liberty. . . .

America MUST remember. It is my commitment to you that we WILL remember. In the war against terror, we will not falter and we will not fail.

---

[2] **prosecution** the pursuit of legal action
[3] **compartmentalized** divided into separate sections

Firefighter in New York City on September 11, 2001

DBQ Document-Based Questions

1. **Interpreting** What does Ashcroft mean when he states, "We have used these tools to provide the security that ensures liberty"?

2. **Analyzing** What do Ashcroft and Slaughter agree about?

3. **Analyzing** What do Ashcroft and Slaughter disagree about?

4. **Evaluating** Who do you think makes the stronger argument: Ashcroft or Slaughter? Explain your answer.

Challenges Ahead

Essential Question

How have economic and environmental developments led to the world's nations becoming more interdependent?

Reading Guide

Content Vocabulary

interdependent
(p. 559)

acid rain
(p. 561)

globalism
(p. 559)

global warming
(p. 562)

trade deficit (p. 560)

deport (p. 563)

free trade (p. 560)

amnesty (p. 563)

urban sprawl (p. 561)

Academic Vocabulary

decade (p. 559)

aware (p. 561)

Reading Strategy

Taking Notes Complete a diagram like the one below by identifying three global challenges. Then explain why each of these is a problem.

Global Challenges

American Diary

In the 1960s, educator Marshall McLuhan used the phrase "the global village" to express the idea that electronic communication would unite the world. The Internet, for example, allows us to communicate with one another regardless of distance. Soon half the people of the world will access the Web, many through wireless devices. Already, more than 25 billion e-mails are sent internationally each day— that adds up to more than 9 trillion e-mails each year!

Students with learning disabilities in Brooklyn, New York, use laptop computers to work on reading skills.

The New Global Economy

Main Idea Advances in technology now link the United States to a global economy.

History and You Describe something you know about the way people live in another part of the world. How do you know what you know? Read to find out why the world has become more connected during the last 30 years.

In recent years, the United States and other nations of the world have developed a global economy. This means that they are **interdependent**, or rely on one another for raw materials to make goods and for markets in which to sell goods. When the economies of countries are linked, a drought or a war in one region can cause price increases or shortages in another region far away.

The Technology Revolution

A major reason for the rise of the global economy is the technology revolution. Today we take for granted computers, cell phones, cable television, and compact discs. A few **decades**—periods of 10 years—ago, these things had either not been invented or were not widely available.

The invention that drives this revolution is the computer. In the 1960s, scientists developed the integrated circuit, a small electronic device. A decade later, more powerful circuits called microprocessors were developed. They made it possible to make smaller, faster computers that could store a lot of information.

Through their personal computers, people are now able to go on the Internet. This is a huge web of linked computer networks. The Internet has made global communications almost instantaneous.

Global Trade and the U.S.

The technology revolution has tied together people and nations more closely than before. It has contributed to the rise of **globalism.** This is the idea that the world's economies and societies are all part of one big system. Interaction is no longer limited by physical distance.

The United States is a key player in the global economy. Its large, productive economy, based on the free enterprise system, has made it a leader in world trade. The United States exports chemicals, farm products, and manufactured goods, as well as raw materials such as metals and cotton fiber.

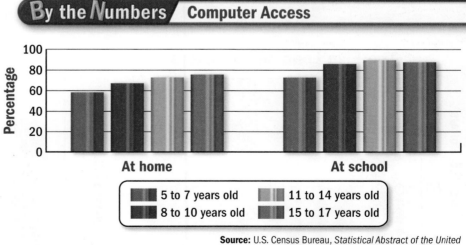

By the Numbers / **Computer Access**

Legend:
- 5 to 7 years old
- 8 to 10 years old
- 11 to 14 years old
- 15 to 17 years old

(Bar graph: Percentage on y-axis from 0 to 100; categories "At home" and "At school")

Source: U.S. Census Bureau, *Statistical Abstract of the United States: 2006*; U.S. National Center for Education Statistics

Critical Thinking

Calculating Which age group has the highest percentage of computer use at home? At school?

The nation imports most of its energy resources, however. The suppliers include Canada, Mexico, Saudi Arabia, and Nigeria.

The United States also buys many additional products from other countries. In fact, the United States spends hundreds of billions of dollars more on imports than it earns from exports. The result is a massive **trade deficit.** A trade deficit occurs when a country spends more on imports than it earns from exports. A trade deficit that lasts over a long period can cause economic troubles for a country.

Therefore, selling American-made goods has long been important to the prosperity of the United States. To further American economic growth, Republican and Democratic administrations since World War II have supported **free trade.** This means the removal of trade barriers so that goods flow freely among countries. In 2001 President Bush called for a world trading system that is dramatically open and more free:

PRIMARY SOURCE

"We know that nations that open their economies to the benefits of trade are more successful in climbing out of poverty. . . . We also know that free trade encourages the habits of liberty that sustain freedom."
—**President George W. Bush in a speech to the World Bank**

Since its formation in 1995, the World Trade Organization (WTO) has arranged numerous trade agreements and settled trade disputes among the nations of the world. Today, the WTO has more than 140 member countries.

Debate on Free Trade

As the world economy becomes more interconnected, Americans debate whether ending trade barriers helps or hinders the United States. Supporters claim that free trade generally helps the American economy. Those supporters say that American businesses make money selling more goods around the world.

Economics & History

The United States imports many manufactured goods from Japan. Automobiles are the largest single category. ▶

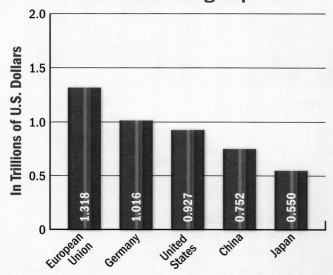

The Five Leading Exporters

In Trillions of U.S. Dollars

- European Union: 1.318
- Germany: 1.016
- United States: 0.927
- China: 0.752
- Japan: 0.550

Source: CIA World Factbook, 2006

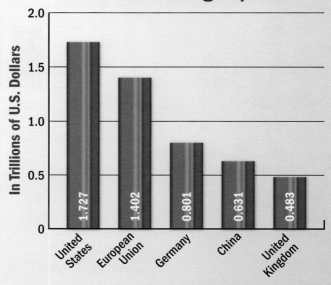

The Five Leading Importers

In Trillions of U.S. Dollars

- United States: 1.727
- European Union: 1.402
- Germany: 0.801
- China: 0.631
- United Kingdom: 0.483

Source: CIA World Factbook, 2006

They also claim that American consumers benefit by being able to buy foreign goods that are less expensive than those made in the United States. Supporters of free trade also state that importing low-cost goods keeps inflation and interest rates low.

Opponents, however, charge that free trade has caused manufacturing jobs to move from the United States to nations where wages are low and where there are fewer regulations. They state that having cheap imports available to buy does not help those Americans who can no longer find work because their industries have moved overseas. This transfer of work to other countries is called outsourcing. Because free trade affects jobs—and votes—the debate between supporters and opponents of free trade has become an important part of American politics.

Reading Check **Explaining** What does the World Trade Organization (WTO) do?

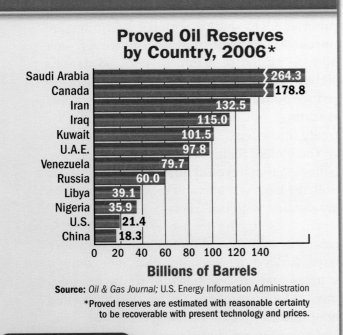

Proved Oil Reserves by Country, 2006*

Country	Billions of Barrels
Saudi Arabia	264.3
Canada	178.8
Iran	132.5
Iraq	115.0
Kuwait	101.5
U.A.E.	97.8
Venezuela	79.7
Russia	60.0
Libya	39.1
Nigeria	35.9
U.S.	21.4
China	18.3

0   20   40   60   80   100 120 140
Billions of Barrels

Source: *Oil & Gas Journal;* U.S. Energy Information Administration

*Proved reserves are estimated with reasonable certainty to be recoverable with present technology and prices.

Graph Skills

1. **Calculating** What is the difference in dollar amounts between U.S. exports and U.S. imports?

2. **Classifying** Which of the 12 nations shown on this graph are in South America? In Africa?

The Environment

Main Idea Concern about the environment has become a serious political issue in recent years.

History and You Have you seen instances of air or water pollution in your area? Read to learn about challenges to the nation's environment.

Globalism has made people **aware,** or mindful, of issues that affect the world as a whole. In recent years, people have become aware of dangers to the world environment. For example, many people fear that the Earth's resources will soon be unable to support a rapidly rising world population, especially in cities.

Urban sprawl, or the spread of human settlements into natural areas, has created many problems. Urban growth leads to the loss of farmland and wilderness areas. The building of homes and roadways also can produce traffic jams and increase air pollution. Growing populations put strains on water supplies, food supplies, and other resources as well. People in some areas that are growing rapidly want to slow the rate of growth. They fear that having too many people will destroy the wide-open spaces and scenery that attracted them.

Air and Water Pollution

The United States faces several environmental challenges. Air and water pollution remains a problem. Americans burn coal, oil, and natural gas to power their factories and run their cars. Burning these fossil fuels pollutes the air. The pollution mixes with water vapor in the air to make **acid rain,** or rain containing high amounts of chemical pollutants. Acid rain damages trees and harms rivers, lakes, and the stone used in buildings. The United States has acted to reduce the amount of chemicals that are released into the air. Climate experts are particularly concerned about damage to some areas in the eastern United States.

How Much Do We Recycle?

Recycling Rates

Paper & Cardboard
- 1990
- 2003

Glass
- 1990
- 2003

United States
Spain
Germany
Britain
Italy
Japan

0% 20% 40% 60% 80% 100%

Source: Organisation for Economic Co-operation and Development; UN Statistical Division

Why Recycle? What happens to trash? Most ends up in landfills. Some is burned in incinerators. Some is dumped into lakes, rivers, and oceans. All of these methods create pollution and harm living things. Recycling your trash can help. About 80 percent of household trash can be recycled.

Critical Thinking

Comparing Which nation had the highest percentage of paper and cardboard recycling in 2003?

Because pollution crosses international borders, many experts believe that nations have to work together to find solutions. In 1987, for example, 23 nations agreed to ban chemicals suspected of harming the ozone layer—a part of the atmosphere that shields Earth from the sun's radiation.

Global Warming

Many scientists also think that Earth is getting warmer and are worried that this might be caused by pollution. They claim that the increased burning of coal, oil, and natural gas has released more gases into the atmosphere. These gases have trapped more of the sun's heat near the Earth's surface, raising temperatures around the planet.

Such **global warming,** these scientists claim, will lead to changing weather patterns. For example, a warmer climate could lead to drought conditions in some areas and could melt the polar ice caps. Melting would raise ocean levels and flood low-lying coasts.

The issue of global warming has become very controversial. Critics argue that computer models showing global warming are unrealistic. Many nations, however, are addressing the problem. In 1997, 38 nations signed the Kyoto Protocol promising to reduce pollution that might be causing global warming, but few countries have put the treaty into effect.

The United States has not signed the treaty, believing that it would hurt economic growth. Still, the United States and many other nations are dealing with pollution.

They are trying to use energy more efficiently and burn coal more cleanly. They also have funded research to find new energy sources that are less harmful to the environment. Many countries already have adopted nonpolluting forms of energy such as wind and solar power.

Reading Check **Describing** How does acid rain affect the environment?

A Changing Society

Main Idea As the 2000s begin, immigrants and the elderly make up a larger share of the American population.

History and You Do you remember the reasons why some Americans objected to immigration in the 1800s? Read to find out how the debate on immigration continues today.

. . . .

As America enters the twenty-first century, its population is changing significantly. The number of older Americans has risen. Ways of living and working have changed as a result of new technologies. Above all, changes in U.S. laws and unstable conditions worldwide have led to a dramatic rise in the number of immigrants to the United States.

By 2007, nearly half of all the country's immigrants came from Latin America and Canada, and another third from various parts of Asia. Less than 15 percent came from Europe, the place of origin of most immigrants throughout U.S. history.

Illegal Immigration

Many immigrants have entered the United States legally, but an estimated 12 million of them have arrived without official permission. Today, most Americans view this illegal immigration as a serious challenge to the country. However, people are deeply divided about how to solve the problem.

Some Americans believe that letting illegal immigrants stay in the country undermines respect for the rule of law. They often call for illegal immigrants to be **deported,** or sent out of the country. Others are willing to grant **amnesty,** or a pardon, to people who are already here illegally so that they can take steps toward becoming citizens. To stop further illegal immigration, some people favor allowing potential immigrants to apply for temporary work permits and earn permanent residence if they learn English, pay back taxes, and have no criminal record.

Many Americans on both sides of the issue agree on the need for more border patrols. Some propose building a continuous wall from Texas to California.

U.S. Foreign-Born Population, 1850–2005

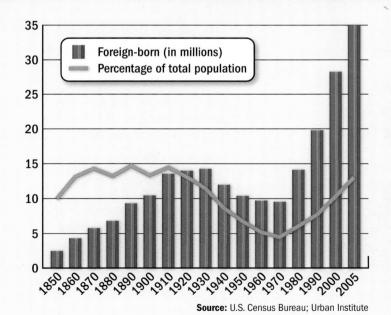

Legend:
- Foreign-born (in millions)
- Percentage of total population

Source: U.S. Census Bureau; Urban Institute

Three generations of the Solano family from San Antonio, Texas ▶

Graph Skills

1. **Identifying** In what year did the foreign-born population reach its all-time high?

2. **Calculating** In what year did the foreign-born population reach its all-time numeric high? Percentage high?

Graphs In MOtion See StudentWorks™ Plus or glencoe.com.

They believe the wall is needed to prevent illegal immigration from Mexico. Critics of the wall-building proposal, however, claim that this would not stop people who are determined to enter the country illegally. Instead, it would force them to take more dangerous risks.

Health Issues

Immigration contributes to population growth. Another factor is natural population increase, or the surplus of births over deaths. Today, the United States has a larger percentage of young people than do other developed countries. Yet, the overall population of the country is aging. This aging is due to a rising birthrate and a declining death rate as well as to the effects of better health care.

Despite health advances, the rates of cancer have risen. Today, cancer and heart disease are the leading causes of death in the United States. This is because of an aging population, pollution, and the unhealthy lifestyle of many Americans who eat high-fat foods and do not exercise enough.

The United States devotes many resources to health care. Still, many Americans are unable to buy health insurance, and others cannot afford health care even with insurance. The high cost of health care also places a burden on businesses that provide health care to employees.

America on the Move

Being mobile, or moving from place to place, has always been a characteristic of American life. Widespread use of the automobile has given people a greater choice of where to live and work.

In recent decades, most of the nation's population growth has taken place in the West and South. These two regions attract residents because of their mild climates and growing industries. Meanwhile, areas of the North, East, and Midwest have lost population. There, heavy manufacturing has declined, although efforts are being made to build more high-tech businesses.

Reading Check **Summarizing** What factors have led to population growth?

Section 5 Review

History ONLINE
Study Central™ To review this section, go to glencoe.com.

Vocabulary

1. Use each of the following terms correctly in a sentence: interdependent, decade, globalism, trade deficit, free trade, aware, urban sprawl, acid rain, global warming, deport, amnesty.

Main Ideas

2. Analyzing How did international trade change the world economy?

3. Explaining What is the goal of the Kyoto Protocol?

4. Summarizing What proposals have been made to stop illegal immigration?

Critical Thinking

5. Organizing Complete a diagram like the one below to describe the characteristics of the global economy.

6. Expository Writing Identify the issue of global concern that you think is the most serious. In an essay, explain why you think it is the most serious problem. Include some possible solutions.

Answer the
7. Essential Question
How have economic and environmental developments led to the world's nations becoming more interdependent?

Visual Summary

Reagan's Agenda

- Supply-side economics to boost the economy
- Military buildup to fight communism
- Treaty with Soviets to reduce nuclear arms

World Change

- Communism collapses in Eastern Europe and the Soviet Union
- Persian Gulf War/Operation Desert Storm
- Economic recession weakens President Bush's reelection campaign

The Clinton Years

- Clinton and Congress cut spending; reform welfare and health care
- U.S. economy grows; federal budget is balanced
- Scandal and impeachment tarnish the Clinton administration

Bush Takes Office

- Supreme Court resolves 2000 election results dispute; George W. Bush becomes president
- Bush focuses on cutting taxes and reforming education
- Terrorists destroy the World Trade Center and attack the Pentagon
- Bush launches war on terror

Toward the Future

- World trade plays major part in global interdependence
- Global community faces serious environmental problems
- Population increases due to immigration and aging Americans

▲ First section of Berlin Wall torn down, November 10, 1989

Presidential candidate Bill Clinton at campaign rally ▼

California teens clean up trash and litter ▼

▲ Worker walks through the rubble of the World Trade Center, September 11, 2001

STUDY TO GO
Study anywhere, anytime! Download quizzes and flash cards to your PDA from glencoe.com.

▼ Mexican American celebration

Immigration

The United States is undergoing its fourth great period of immigration. According to the Census Bureau, the number of foreign-born in the United States increased from 19.8 million in 1990 to 31.1 million in 2000. Never before have so many people immigrated to America.

How Does Geography Affect Immigration?

In recent years, most immigrants to the United States have come from Latin America and Asia. By far the greatest number is from Mexico. While immigration has increased, its effects have not been felt in equal measure throughout the country. Immigrants have tended to settle in the more densely populated areas of the United States: California, Florida, Texas, and the Northeast. The foreign-born population of the United States is growing four times faster than the native-born population. Over the next 50 years, immigrants will account for two-thirds of U.S. population growth.

U.S. Immigration: Place of Origin, 2004

Canada
Europe
Asia
Caribbean
Africa
Central & S. America
Mexico
ATLANTIC OCEAN
INDIAN OCEAN
PACIFIC OCEAN

0   4,000 kilometers
0   4,000 miles
Miller Cylindrical projection

Percentage of Population Immigrating to the U.S.

- >15%
- 5–15%
- 3–4.9%
- 1–2.9%
- <1%

California road signs in English and Spanish ▼

DANGER
STAY OUT STAY ALIVE
216
LIVES LOST IN KERN RIVER SINCE 1968

PELIGRO
POR FAVOR NO NADE
216
VIDAS PERDIDAS EN EL RIO KERN DESDE 1968

◀ **Becoming Citizens**
Immigrants to America can apply to become U.S. citizens. Applicants must offer proof of residence; evidence of good moral character; and knowledge of the history and government of the United States. In most cases, applicants must have a basic knowledge of the English language.

Asian seafood shop in New York City's Chinatown ▶

▲ Sign in English and Arabic urging people to vote

U.S. Foreign-Born Population

Foreign-born population as a percentage of county population, 2000

- 23.4–50%
- 11.2–23.3%
- 7.1–11.1%
- 3.0–7.0%
- 0–2.9%

Illegal Immigration

Americans are divided over what to do about the illegal population living in the United States. Solutions have ranged from finding and deporting all illegals, to granting various forms of legalization and naturalization, to building a wall along the 2,000-mile (3,219 km) border with Mexico.

As recently as 1960, almost three-quarters of all immigrants to America came from Europe. Today, eight of every ten immigrants to the U.S. come from Asia or Latin America. ▶

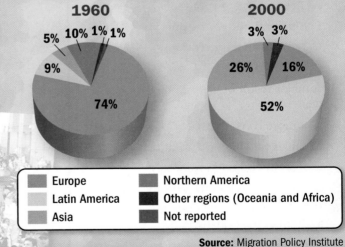

Foreign-Born Population by Region of Birth

1960
- 5%
- 10%
- 1%
- 1%
- 9%
- 74%

2000
- 3%
- 3%
- 26%
- 16%
- 52%

- Europe
- Latin America
- Asia
- Northern America
- Other regions (Oceania and Africa)
- Not reported

Source: Migration Policy Institute

Analyzing Geography

1. **Location** Use the map on the previous page to identify the part of the world that provided the most U.S. immigrants.

2. **Movement** How do you think the United States will be different in 2050 because of current immigration patterns? Explain.

STANDARDIZED TEST PRACTICE

TEST-TAKING TIP

Answer the questions you know first and go back to those for which you need more time.

Reviewing Main Ideas

Directions: **Choose the best answers for each of the following questions.**

1. One result of Reagan's approach to government was

    A safe, environmentally friendly cars.

    B more housing for low-income families.

    C a tripling of the 1980 federal debt.

    D a reduction in troop levels.

2. How did the federal government deal with the failures of S&Ls during the late 1980s?

    A bailouts

    B deregulation

    C spending cuts

    D supply-side economics

3. Which of Clinton's goals went unrealized?

    A stricter gun control

    B a federal budget surplus

    C family leave for workers

    D health care for all Americans

4. A major result of George W. Bush's presidency was

    A a more conservative Supreme Court.

    B the expansion of U.S. citizens' rights.

    C federal budget surpluses.

    D improved relations with the Middle East.

5. Which pair of environmental terms has a cause-and-effect relationship?

    A chemicals and urban sprawl

    B acid rain and solar radiation

    C global warming and rising seas

    D water pollution and the ozone layer

Short-Answer Question

Directions: **Base your answer to question 6 on the excerpt below and on your knowledge of social studies.**

> A few months ago I told the American people I did not trade arms for hostages. My heart and my best intentions still tell me that's true, but the facts and the evidence tell me it is not. . . . [N]o one kept proper records of meetings or decisions. This led to my failure to recollect whether I approved an arms shipment before or after the fact. I did approve it; I just can't say specifically when.
>
> —from President Reagan's address to the nation about Iran-Contra

6. Why do you think the Iran-Contra hearings never produced any proof of the president's involvement?

Review the Essential Questions

7. **Essay** How are the U.S. economy and environment today linked to the policies of Reagan, Clinton, and the Bushes?

To help you write your essay, review your answers to the Essential Questions in the section reviews and the chapter Foldables Study Organizer. Your essay should include:

- the effects of military spending on the economy;
- the effects of deregulation on the environment;
- the effects of NAFTA on American jobs; and
- the effects of spending on the war in Iraq on the economy.

GO ON ➡

Document-Based Questions

Directions: Analyze the documents and answer the short-answer questions that follow each document.

Document 1

Joseph Hatcher entered army basic training the day before September 11, 2001. Here he comments on his later mission in Iraq.

> There was no mention of a noble cause. At no point through any one of my chain of command was there a noble cause placed on the table. We were given a job, and our job was to go to Iraq for a year and to provide safety and security operations for our area of control.

Source: Trish Wood, *What Was Asked of Us*

8. Explain what Hatcher meant by "a noble cause."

Document 2

The chart shows the value of U.S. imports and exports in two separate years.

U.S. International Trade, 2000 and 2005 (in millions of dollars)		
Exports	**2000**	**2005**
Goods	$771,994	$894,631
Services	$298,603	$380,614
Imports	**2000**	**2005**
Goods	$1,224,408	$1,677,371
Services	$223,748	$314,604

Source: U.S. Census Bureau, *U.S. International Trade in Goods and Services*

9. Based on the chart, how did the value of exports change from 2000 to 2005? During that same time period, how did the value of imports change?

Document 3

This political cartoon comments on present-day election campaigns.

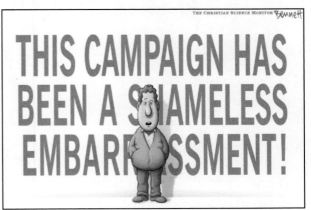

THE CHRISTIAN SCIENCE MONITOR Bennett

THIS CAMPAIGN HAS BEEN A SHAMELESS EMBARRASSMENT!

'I'm an American voter and I approve this message.'

10. What does this cartoon say about election campaigns? Why would a voter approve of it?

Document 4

In 2006 New Mexico Governor Bill Richardson urged Congress to help illegal immigrants as well as American businesses.

> Most [illegal] immigrants come to the United States to work low-wage jobs which few Americans want, such as picking crops or cleaning toilets. Our economy creates demand for at least 400,000 new low-skill illegal immigrants per year, but only about 140,000 are allowed to enter legally. When demand and legal supply are so out of line, the pressures for illegal immigration are enormous.

Source: Bill Richardson, speech on comprehensive immigration reform

11. What pressures does Richardson refer to?

12. Expository Writing Using the information from the four documents and your knowledge of social studies, write an essay in which you:

- identify two issues the U.S. faces; and
- explain why the U.S. must address these issues, and what might happen if it does not.

Need Extra Help?												
If you missed questions. . .	1	2	3	4	5	6	7	8	9	10	11	12
Go to page. . .	531	539	542	554	562	533	528–563	552	560	546	563	559–564

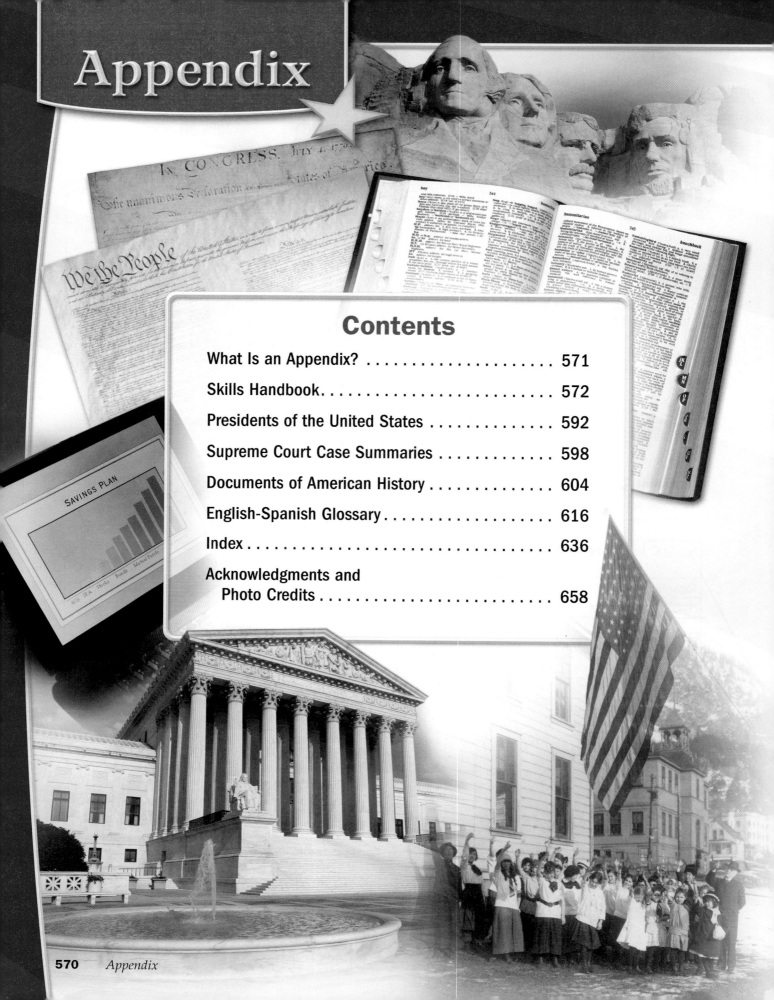

Appendix

Contents

What Is an Appendix?

An appendix is the additional material you often find at the end of books. The following information will help you learn how to use the appendix in The American Journey.

Skills Handbook

The Skills Handbook offers you information and practice using critical thinking and social studies skills. Mastering these skills will help you in all your courses.

Presidents of the United States

The presidents have served as our nation's leaders. In this resource you will find information of interest on each of the nation's presidents, including their term in office, their political affiliation, and their occupations before they became president.

Supreme Court Case Summaries

The Supreme Court Case Summaries provide readable discussions of important Supreme Court cases. The summaries are listed in alphabetical order and include a summary of the facts of the case and its impact.

Documents of American History

This is a collection of some of the most important writings and speeches in American history. Each document begins with an introduction describing the author and placing the selection within its historical context.

English-Spanish Glossary

A glossary is a list of important or difficult terms found in a textbook. The glossary gives a definition of each term as it is used in the book. The glossary also includes page numbers telling you where in the textbook the term is used. Since words sometimes have other meanings, you may wish to consult a dictionary to find other uses for the term.

In *The American Journey*, the Spanish glossary is included with the English glossary. The Spanish term is located directly across from the English term. A Spanish glossary is especially important to bilingual students or those Spanish-speaking students who are learning the English language.

Index

An index is an alphabetical listing that includes the subjects of the book and the page numbers where those subjects can be found. The index in this book also lets you know that certain pages contain maps, graphs, charts, photos, paintings, or cartoons about the subject.

Acknowledgments and Photo Credits

This section lists photo credits and literary credits for the book. You can look at this section to find out where the publisher obtained the permission to use a photograph or to use excerpts from other books.

Test Yourself

Find the answers to these questions by using the Appendix on the following pages.

1. What does *ironclad* mean?
2. Who was the sixth president of the United States?
3. Which section of the Appendix would help you find out about "bleeding Kansas"?
4. What was the purpose of issuing the Seneca Falls Declaration?
5. What was the Supreme Court's decision in *Marbury* v. *Madison*?

Skills Handbook

Contents

Critical Thinking Skills

Social Studies Skills

Understanding Cause and Effect

Why Learn This Skill?

Cause-and-effect relationships are important in the study of history. To understand cause and effect, consider *why* an event occurred. A *cause* is an action or situation that produces an event. What happens as a result of a cause is an *effect*.

Marco Polo ▶

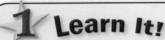

Learn It!

To identify cause-and-effect relationships, follow these steps:

1. Identify two or more events or developments.

2. Decide whether one event caused the other. Look for "clue words" such as *because, led to, brought about, so that, after that, produced, as a result of, since,* or *in the wake of.*

3. Identify the outcomes of events. Remember that some effects have more than one cause, and some causes lead to more than one effect. Also, an effect can become the cause of yet another effect.

> *The Crusades brought western Europeans into contact with the Middle East. Arab merchants sold spices, sugar, silk, and other goods from China and India to Europeans. As a result, European interest in Asia grew.*
>
> *That interest grew even more after Marco Polo returned from China. In 1296 he began writing an account of his trip. He described Asia's marvels in his book* Travels, *which was widely read in Europe. Little did Marco Polo realize that 200 years later* Travels *would inspire Christopher Columbus to sail in the opposite direction to reach the East.*

Practice It!

Categorize the items below as either *cause, effect,* or *both.*

1. The Crusades brought western Europeans to the Middle East.

2. European interest in Asia grew.

3. Marco Polo wrote *Travels,* an account of his trip to China.

4. *Travels* inspired Christopher Columbus to sail in the opposite direction to reach the East.

Apply It!

In a newspaper, read an article describing a current event. Determine at least one cause and one effect of that event, and complete a flowchart like the one below.

Cause	→	Event	→	Effect

Classifying and Categorizing Information

Why Learn This Skill?

As a student, it is important to know how to organize large quantities of information in an understandable way. *Classifying* helps you to arrange facts into broad groups. *Categorizing* helps you to organize that information into more detailed groups according to common characteristics.

Rudolph Valentino movie poster (left) and King Kong movie poster (right) ►

Learn It!

Follow these steps to learn how to classify and categorize:

1. To classify information, look for topics and facts that have common broad characteristics. In the first paragraph, a broad topic might be *Reasons for Cultural Change in America.* Under this topic, further classifications might be *The Growth of Mass Media* and *Increase in Leisure Time.*

2. Divide the information further into categories, based on more specific characteristics. For example, under *Mass Media,* categories could be *Movies* and *Radio.* Each of those categories could contain more examples and details and could become column heads in a chart.

3. As you read, look for examples that fit into the categories you created.

Cultural changes spread quickly because of the growth of mass media—forms of communication, such as newspapers and radio, that reach millions of people. Laborsaving devices and fewer working hours gave Americans more leisure time to enjoy newspapers, magazines, phonograph records, the radio, and the movies.

In the 1920s, the motion picture industry in Hollywood, California, became a major business. For millions of Americans the movies offered entertainment and escape. The first movies were black and white and silent, with the actor's dialogue printed on the screen. In 1927 Hollywood introduced movies with sound. The first "talkie," The Jazz Singer, *created a sensation.*

The radio brought entertainment into people's homes in the 1920s. Radio networks broadcast popular programs that included news, concerts, sporting events, and comedies.

Practice It!

1. What are two further classifications for the topic *Increase in Leisure Time?*

2. What details/examples from the paragraphs above could you place under the categories *Movies* and *Radio?*

Apply It!

Look at the Geographic Dictionary on pages Ref 30–Ref 31. In a chart, list the terms that would fall into the classifications "Landforms" or "Bodies of Water." Can you identify other categories in which to group the information?

Making Comparisons

Why Learn This Skill?

When you make comparisons, you determine similarities among ideas, objects, or events. You should also examine qualities that make each of the ideas, objects, or events unique. Making comparisons is an important skill because it can help you to choose among several possible alternatives.

1 Learn It!

To make comparisons, follow these steps:

1. Select the items to compare.

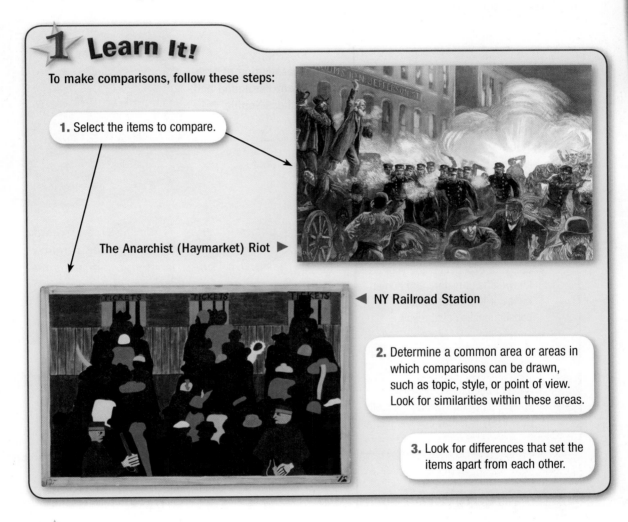

◀ The Anarchist (Haymarket) Riot ▶

◀ NY Railroad Station

2. Determine a common area or areas in which comparisons can be drawn, such as topic, style, or point of view. Look for similarities within these areas.

3. Look for differences that set the items apart from each other.

2 Practice It!

After studying the paintings above, answer the following questions:

1. How are the subjects of the paintings similar?

2. How are they different?

3. What can you tell about the two artists' attitudes toward their subject?

3 Apply It!

Survey 10 of your classmates about an issue in the news, and summarize their responses. Then write a paragraph or two comparing their opinions.

Predicting Consequences

Why Learn This Skill?

Predicting future events is difficult, but the more information you have, the more accurate your predictions will be. Making good predictions will help you to make better decisions. Using these skills can also help you to understand the consequences of historical events.

The assassination of Archduke Franz Ferdinand and Archduchess Sophie ▶

Learn It!

To help you make predictions, follow these steps:

1. Gather information about the topic.

2. Use your experience and your knowledge of history and human behavior to predict what consequences could result.

3. Analyze each of the possible consequences by asking yourself: How likely is it that this will happen?

On the morning of June 28, 1914, Archduke Franz Ferdinand, the heir to the throne of the Austro-Hungarian Empire, and his wife Sophie were assassinated while visiting Bosnia, an Austrian province.

Gavrilo Princip, Franz Ferdinand's assassin, belonged to a Serbian nationalist group that had plotted Ferdinand's murder to bring down the Austro-Hungarian Empire and unite the Slavs.

Practice It!

Read the excerpt above and answer the following questions:

1. What outcome is most likely to occur between Austria-Hungary and Serbia?

2. On what do you base your prediction?

3. Do you think a situation similar to the one described in the passage is likely to occur again?

Apply It!

Analyze three newspaper articles about an event affecting your community or the nation. Make an educated prediction about what will happen, and explain your reasoning. Then write a few paragraphs summarizing your prediction. You may want to check back later to see if your prediction came true.

Analyzing and Interpreting Information

Why Learn This Skill?

Have you ever heard someone say, "Don't believe everything you read"? To be an informed citizen, you have to analyze and interpret information carefully as you read to make sure you understand the meaning and the intent of the writer. Doing so helps you decide what you think about a subject.

Andrew Carnegie ▶

1 Learn It!

To analyze and interpret information, use the following steps:

1. Identify the topic being discussed.

2. Examine how the information is organized. What are the main points?

3. Think about how reliable the source of the information is.

4. Summarize the information in your own words. Does the information agree with or contradict something you believe?

[T]he surplus wealth of the few will become, in the best sense, the property of the many. . . . [T]his wealth, passing through the hands of the few, can be made a much more potent [strong] force for the elevation of our race than if it had been distributed in small sums to the people themselves. Even the poorest can be made to see this, and to agree that great sums gathered by some of their fellow-citizens and spent for public purposes, from which the masses reap the principal benefit, are more valuable to them than if scattered among them through the course of many years in trifling amounts.

—Andrew Carnegie, "Wealth"

2 Practice It!

Read the excerpt above and answer the following questions:

1. What topic is being discussed?

2. What is the main point?

3. Summarize the information in this excerpt, and then provide your analysis, based on this information and what you already know about the subject.

3 Apply It!

Select an issue that is currently in the news, such as gasoline prices, global warming, or taxation. Read an article or watch a news segment about the issue. Analyze the information and make a brief statement of your own about the topic. Explain your thinking.

Distinguishing Fact From Opinion

Why Learn This Skill?

To make reasonable judgments about what others say or write, it is important to distinguish facts from opinions. Facts can be checked for accuracy and proven. They answer specific questions such as: What happened? Who did it? When and where did it happen? Opinions are based on people's differing values and beliefs. Opinions often begin with phrases such as *I believe* or *It seems to me*. They also frequently contain words such as *should* or *ought* or judgment words such as *best, worst,* or *greatest*.

Louise Slaughter speaks at National Press Club June 2007 ▶

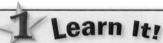 **Learn It!**

To learn how to separate facts from opinions, follow these steps:

1. Identify the facts. Ask: which statements can be proved? Where would I find information to verify this statement? If the information is a statistic, it may sound impressive, but you won't know if it's accurate unless you check the source.

2. Identify opinions by looking for statements of feelings or beliefs. Opinions sometimes contain words like *should, would, could, best, greatest, all, every,* or *always*.

All of my colleagues understand that the PATRIOT Act has provided the law enforcement agencies with many valuable tools which facilitate their work in the struggle against terrorism. But with these new tools comes a very real danger that the liberty we seek to protect could be easily compromised in the overzealous pursuit of greater security. . . .

We have evidence which suggests, in contrast to information coming out of the Justice Department, that many of these measures have resulted in the violation of the civil liberties of American citizens. In addition, we understand that some of the extended search and seizure powers used by the law enforcement are apparently not being used for their intended purpose, which is strictly to fight terrorism, and that is unacceptable.

—Congresswoman Louise McIntosh Slaughter, July 21, 2005

 Practice It!

The excerpt above is from a speech delivered to Congress by U.S. Representative Louise McIntosh Slaughter concerning the reauthorization, or renewal, of the Patriot Act. Reread the excerpt and answer the questions that follow.

1. Which statements in the passage are factual?

2. Which statements are opinions? Explain.

 Apply It!

Watch a television interview. Then list three facts and three opinions that you hear.

Skills Handbook

Drawing Inferences and Conclusions

Why Learn This Skill?

When you make an *inference,* you "read between the lines," or use clues to figure something out that is not stated directly in the text. A *conclusion* is a logical understanding that you reach based on details or facts that you read or hear. By drawing inferences and conclusions you can formulate ideas and make decisions.

Jefferson Davis ▶

 Learn It!

Follow these steps to draw inferences and conclusions:

1. Read carefully for facts and ideas, and list them.

2. Summarize the information.

3. Consider what you may already know about the topic.

4. Use your knowledge and insight to develop some logical conclusions based on the facts.

There can be but little rivalry between ours and any manufacturing or navigating community, such as the Northeastern States of the American Union. It must follow, therefore, that a mutual interest would invite good will and kind offices. If, however, passion or the lust of dominion [power] should cloud the judgment or inflame the ambition of those States, we must prepare to meet the emergency and to maintain, by the final [deciding power] of the sword, the position which we have assumed among the nations of the earth. We have entered upon the career of independence, and it must be inflexibly pursued. . . . As a necessity, not a choice, we have resorted to the remedy of separation; and henceforth our energies must be directed to the conduct of our own affairs, and the [lasting life] of the Confederacy which we have formed.

—Jefferson Davis's inaugural speech,
February 18, 1861

 Practice It!

After reading the passage above, answer the following questions:

1. What points does the author make?
2. Which point does your experience contradict?
3. What inference can you make about the Confederate states' reasons for declaring their independence?
4. What conclusions can you draw about Davis' beliefs about a possible war?

 Apply It!

Read an editorial printed in today's newspaper. What can you infer about the importance of the topic being addressed? Can you tell how the writer feels about the topic? Explain your answer.

Writing a Paragraph

Why Learn This Skill?

Paragraphs are the building blocks of an essay or other composition. Each paragraph is a unit—a group of sentences about a single topic or idea.

Washington observes Von Steuben drilling troops at Valley Forge ▶

Learn It!

Most well-written paragraphs share four characteristics:

At first glance the British had an overwhelming advantage in the war. They had the strongest navy in the world. They also had an experienced, well-trained army and the wealth of a worldwide empire. Britain also had a much larger population than the United States. There were over 8 million people in Britain, compared with only 2.5 million in the United States.

1. A paragraph expresses one main idea or is about one subject. A topic sentence states the main idea, and may be located at the beginning, middle, or end of the paragraph.

2. The rest of the sentences support the main idea. The main idea may be developed by facts, examples, or reasons.

3. The sentences are arranged in a logical order.

4. Transitional words link sentences within the paragraph. Examples include *next, then, finally, also, because, however,* and *as a result.*

Practice It!

Use the following sentences to build a paragraph containing a topic sentence and other sentences that give supporting details. Put the sentences in a logical order and add transitional words if you need to. Underline your topic sentence.

1. They were forced to ship soldiers and supplies thousands of miles across the Atlantic.

2. They were fighting on their own ground and fought with great determination to protect it.

3. The Americans possessed some advantages.

4. The British, in contrast, had to wage war in a faraway land.

Apply It!

Choose a topic from the era of the Revolutionary War and write a paragraph about it. Then rewrite the paragraph with its sentences out of order. Exchange papers with a classmate. Can he or she find the topic sentence? Does it read logically?

Taking Notes and Outlining

Why Learn This Skill?

Taking notes and outlining are ways of recording important information about what you read. Both methods also help you recall information. Writing down information in a brief and orderly form helps you remember key points and makes it easier to study.

Outlining is similar to sketching a scene. First, you draw the rough shape, or outline, of the picture. Then you fill in the details. Outlining helps you identify main ideas and group related facts.

Learn It!

To learn how to take notes, use the following steps:

1. **Identify** the subject and write it at the top of your page.

2. **Select** specific details that support the main subject and include them in your notes. Look for topic sentences of paragraphs and words in bold or italics.

3. **Paraphrase** the information. Putting it in your own words helps you understand the meaning of the information.

4. **Condense** words into a personal shorthand, such as dropping vowels ("develop" becomes "dvlp"), and use symbols ("and" becomes "+") to save time.

In 1776 the Second Continental Congress appointed a committee to draw up a plan for a new government. After much debate the Congress adopted the **Articles of Confederation** *in November 1777. The Articles, America's first constitution, provided for a new central government under which the states kept most of their power. For the states, the Articles of Confederation were "a firm league of friendship" in which each state retained "its sovereignty, freedom and independence." Under the Articles of Confederation, Congress had the authority to conduct foreign affairs, maintain armed forces, borrow money, and issue currency.*

Practice It!

Read the excerpt above. Then, on a separate sheet of paper, take notes on the paragraph. Be sure to consider the following questions.

1. What is the subject of the paragraph?
2. What is the main point of the paragraph?
3. What details are especially important to write down?

Apply It!

Read a short article from a local newspaper about a governmental issue. Outline the important information. Write a short summary of the article using only your outline.

Summarizing Information

Why Learn This Skill?

Imagine you have been assigned a long chapter to read. How can you remember the important facts? Summarizing information means that you reduce large amounts of information to a few key phrases. Being able to summarize can help you remember the main ideas and key details.

Statue of Liberty ▶

 Learn It!

To summarize information, follow these guidelines when you read:

1. Read through the selection. Determine the main idea and the most important supporting details.

2. A summary can be a sentence or a short paragraph that includes the main ideas. In your summary, restate the text using your own words. Be brief—do not include many supporting details.

3. For the first paragraph, a summary statement might be: By the early 1900s, immigration patterns were changing and most new immigrants came from southern and eastern Europe.

In the mid-1880s, the pattern of immigration started to change. Large groups of "new" immigrants arrived from eastern and southern Europe. Greeks, Russians, Hungarians, Italians, Turks, and Poles were among the newcomers. At the same time, the number of "old" immigrants from northern and western Europe started to decrease. By 1907, 80 percent of immigrants came from southern and eastern Europe.

Many of these newcomers were Catholics or Jews. Few spoke English. Because of this, they did not blend into American society as easily as the "old" immigrants had. Often, they clustered together in neighborhoods made up of people of the same nationality.

 Practice It!

After reading the excerpt above, answer the following questions:

1. In a summary of the first paragraph, would you include the statement, "The number of 'old' immigrants decreased"? Why or why not?

2. Write a summary statement for the second paragraph.

 Apply It!

Read the section titled "Citizen Participation" of the Constitution Handbook of this book. Summarize the information in two or three sentences.

Reading a Time Line

Why Learn This Skill?

Knowing the relationship of time to events is important in studying history. A time line is a visual way to show the flow of dates and events in the correct order that they occurred. On many time lines, the years are evenly spaced. For example, a time line showing 1,000 years might be divided into ten 100-year intervals. Each event on a time line is described beside the date when the event took place.

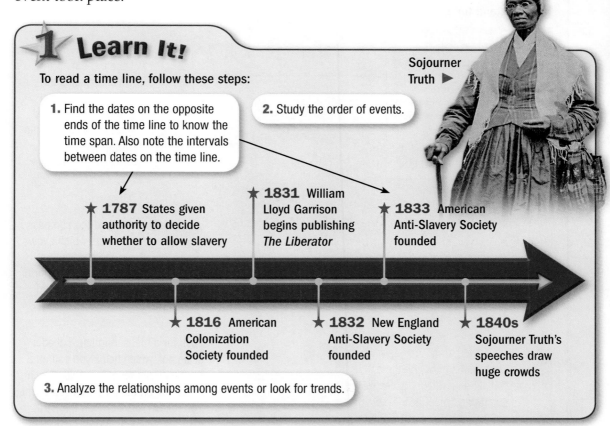

1 Learn It!

To read a time line, follow these steps:

Sojourner Truth ▶

1. Find the dates on the opposite ends of the time line to know the time span. Also note the intervals between dates on the time line.

2. Study the order of events.

★ **1787** States given authority to decide whether to allow slavery

★ **1831** William Lloyd Garrison begins publishing *The Liberator*

★ **1833** American Anti-Slavery Society founded

★ **1816** American Colonization Society founded

★ **1832** New England Anti-Slavery Society founded

★ **1840s** Sojourner Truth's speeches draw huge crowds

3. Analyze the relationships among events or look for trends.

2 Practice It!

Analyze the time line about the Abolition movement. Use it to answer the questions that follow.

1. What time span is represented?

2. Which occurred first: the founding of the American Colonization Society or the founding of the American Anti-Slavery Society?

3. How many years after states were allowed to decide the issue of slavery did William Lloyd Garrison begin publishing *The Liberator*?

3 Apply It!

List 10 key events that have occurred in your life and the dates on which these events occurred. Write the events in chronological order on a time line.

Understanding Parts of a Map

Why Learn This Skill?

Maps can direct you down the street or around the world. There are as many different kinds of maps as there are uses for them. Being able to read a map begins with learning about its parts.

1 Learn It!

To understand the parts of a map, follow these steps:

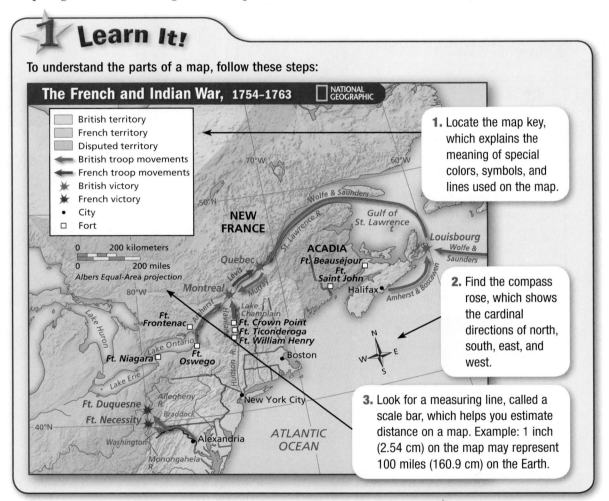

The French and Indian War, 1754–1763 · NATIONAL GEOGRAPHIC

- British territory
- French territory
- Disputed territory
- British troop movements
- French troop movements
- British victory
- French victory
- City
- Fort

0 200 kilometers
0 200 miles
Albers Equal-Area projection

1. Locate the map key, which explains the meaning of special colors, symbols, and lines used on the map.

2. Find the compass rose, which shows the cardinal directions of north, south, east, and west.

3. Look for a measuring line, called a scale bar, which helps you estimate distance on a map. Example: 1 inch (2.54 cm) on the map may represent 100 miles (160.9 cm) on the Earth.

2 Practice It!

The map above shows the territories held by Great Britain and France in North America, as well as the battles between these two countries in their quests to control the North American continent. Look at the parts of the map and then answer the following questions:

1. What color shows the disputed territory?

2. Which direction would you travel to go from Fort Oswego to Boston?

3. About how many miles was it from New York City to Fort Ticonderoga?

4. Who won the battle in Quebec?

3 Apply It!

Create a mental image of your house. Draw a map showing the location of various areas. Include a map key to explain any symbols or colors you use, as well as a scale bar to explain the size of your map compared to the real area. Finally, add a compass rose and title to your map.

Recognizing Historical Perspectives

Why Learn This Skill?

As you study historical events or read primary sources from the past, you may be surprised by the actions taking place or the beliefs being expressed. To accurately evaluate the event or statement, you must carefully consider the time period and the experiences and viewpoints of the people involved.

 Learn It!

To learn how to recognize historical perspectives, ask yourself these questions:

1. When was the statement made? To what event or time does the statement refer, and what other related events had occurred before or were occurring at the time?

2. Who is the author or speaker of the statement? What past experiences or current considerations might influence that person's viewpoint?

3. Why is it important to think critically about historical perspectives?

An 1868 treaty was supposed to bring peace, but tensions remained and erupted in more fighting. This time the conflict arose over the Black Hills of the Dakotas. The government had promised that "No white person or persons shall be permitted" to settle on the Black Hills. However, the hills were rumored to contain gold, and white prospectors swarmed into the area.

The Sioux protested against the trespassers. Instead of protecting the Sioux's rights, the government tried to buy the hills. Sitting Bull, an important leader of the Lakota Sioux, refused. "I do not want to sell any land. Not even this much," he said, holding a pinch of dust.

 Practice It!

Read the excerpt above and answer the following questions:

1. What conflict is being discussed in the excerpt above?

2. What past events and beliefs may have influenced Sitting Bull's statement? How did white and Native American beliefs about land differ at that time?

3. How does recognizing historical perspectives help you better understand the events and statements related to a historical period?

 Apply It!

Look in a current newspaper or news-magazine to find an example of a conflict between two or more groups of people. Write a short summary of how their perspectives of each other have determined their historical and current relationships.

Analyzing News Media

Why Learn This Skill?

Every citizen needs to be aware of current issues and events to make good decisions when exercising citizenship rights. To get an accurate profile of current events, you must learn to think critically about the news.

Herbert Hoover ▶

Learn It!

The following steps will help you think critically:

1. Think about the source of the news story. Reports that reveal sources are more reliable than those that do not. If you know the sources, you can evaluate them for reliability and bias.

2. Many news stories also interpret events. Such analyses may reflect a reporter's biases. Look for biases as you read or listen to news stories.

3. Ask yourself whether the news is even-handed and thorough. Is it reported on the scene or secondhand? Does it represent both sides of an issue?

AIM TO PACK COURT, DECLARES HOOVER

President Roosevelt's message to Congress asking for authority to appoint new Federal judges whenever existing ones were over 70 years old was characterized last night by Herbert Hoover, his predecessor in the White House, as a proposal for "packing" the Supreme Court to get through New Deal measures. . . .

"The Supreme Court has proved many of the New Deal proposals as unconstitutional. Instead of the ample alternatives of the Constitution by which these proposals could be submitted to the people through constitutional amendment, it is now proposed to make changes by 'packing' the Supreme Court. It has the implication of subordination of the court to the personal power of the Executive."

Practice It!

The excerpt above is from the *New York Times* newspaper of February 6, 1937. Read the passage; then answer the following questions:

1. What point is the article trying to make?

2. Is the article reporting something on the scene or secondhand?

3. Does the article reflect bias or strong opinion about the issue?

4. Is only one side of the issue presented? Explain.

Apply It!

Think of a current issue in the news that is controversial or in which public opinion is divided. Read newspaper features and editorials and watch television reports on the issue. Can you identify biases? Which reports more fairly represent the issue and the solutions? Which reports are the most reliable?

Analyzing Primary and Secondary Sources

Why Learn This Skill?

To determine what happened in the past, historians do some detective work. They comb through bits of written and illustrated evidence from the past to reconstruct events. These bits of evidence are called *primary sources.* They are records of events made by people who witnessed them. Primary sources include letters, diaries, photographs, newspaper articles, and legal documents.

This textbook, like many other history books, is a secondary source. It was written by using primary sources to explain the topics covered. The value of a secondary source depends on how well the author has used primary sources. Learning to analyze secondary sources will help you figure out whether they are presenting topics completely and accurately.

Dr. Martin Luther King, Jr. ▶

Learn It!

To analyze a **primary source**, follow these steps:

We have waited for more than 340 years for our constitutional and God-given rights . . . [W]e still creep at horse and buggy pace toward gaining a cup of coffee at a lunch counter. Perhaps it is easy for those who have never felt the stinging darts of segregation to say, 'Wait.'. . . Let us all hope that the dark clouds of racial prejudice will soon pass away.

—Dr. Martin Luther King, Jr.
Letter from Birmingham Jail, April 1963

1. Identify the author, the publication, or the document.

2. Determine when and where the document was written or illustrated.

3. Read the document or study the illustration for its content. Try to answer the five "W" questions:
   Whom is it about?
   What is it about?
   When did it happen?
   Where did it happen?
   Why did it happen?

Practice It!

The primary source above is a small part of a letter written by civil rights leader Dr. Martin Luther King, Jr., while he was in an Alabama jail.

1. When was the letter written?

2. To whom do you think the letter was written?

3. Why do you think Dr. King wrote the letter?

4. How do you know this is a primary source and not a secondary source?

Apply It!

Find a primary source and a secondary source related to a single historical topic. In several paragraphs, compare and contrast the information presented in the two sources.

Analyzing Historical Maps

Why Learn This Skill?

Historical maps show a portion of the world at a specific time in history. These maps can show physical, political, economic, climatic, or cultural information as it relates to that time period. They are useful because of the concise, visual way they present information.

1 Learn It!

To read a historical map, follow these steps:

1. Read the title to see what topic is illustrated. The specific time period is often referenced in the title.

2. Read the legend and any other text.

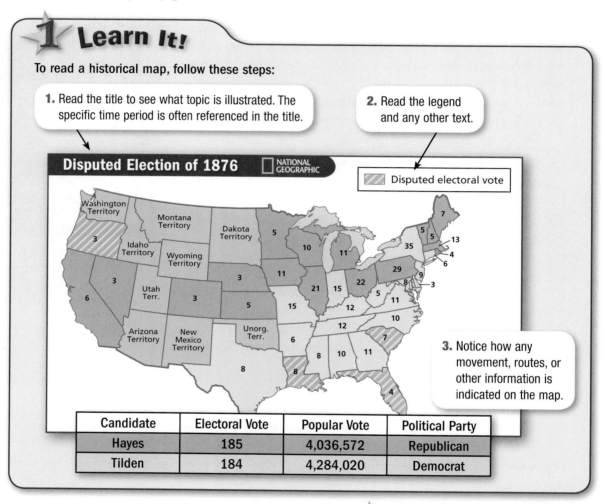

Disputed Election of 1876   NATIONAL GEOGRAPHIC

Disputed electoral vote

3. Notice how any movement, routes, or other information is indicated on the map.

Candidate	Electoral Vote	Popular Vote	Political Party
Hayes	185	4,036,572	Republican
Tilden	184	4,284,020	Democrat

2 Practice It!

Answer the following questions about the map above:

1. What event and time in history does the map cover?

2. For whom did most Northern states vote?

3. In which states were the electoral votes disputed?

4. Why are there no numbers for electoral votes in the territories?

3 Apply It!

Study the United States Territorial Growth maps on pages Ref 10–Ref 11 in the front of your textbook. Then answer these questions:

1. In which general direction did growth take place?

2. What time period is covered in the last map?

Researching on the Internet

Why Learn This Skill?

Imagine that your teacher has sent you to the Internet to research and write a report about the current makeup of the United States Congress. Knowing how to locate and choose sources that contain accurate and current information will help save you time. You will also be able to write a better and more accurate report.

Joint meeting of Congress ▶

Learn It!

Information on the Internet varies widely in its relevance and quality. Not all sources will be useful for your report on members of the Senate and House of Representatives. After choosing a search engine and typing in your topic, follow these steps to help you evaluate and select Internet resources:

1. Locate the author of the Web site and assess his/her qualifications. Is the person or organization credible and legitimate?

2. Evaluate the accuracy of the information. Are the facts on the site documented? Does the site contain a bibliography?

3. Judge whether the information is biased. Does the author present only one point of view?

4. Determine how the information is presented. Are there helpful visuals? Does the text skim the surface or offer in-depth details?

5. Review when the site was last updated. Is the information current?

6. Look for a list of links to other useful resources. Is the information on those sites appropriate and reliable?

Practice It!

Look at the following list of sources. Which would be most helpful in writing a report on the United States Congress? Explain your choices.

1. An online encyclopedia written by anyone who wants to contribute

2. www.senate.gov, the home page for the U.S. Senate

3. A student's notes on the Internet about a family trip to Washington, D.C.

4. A government site on Congressional documents drawn up between 1774 and 1785

Apply It!

Log onto the Internet to create a bibliography of six sources you might use to write your report. Explain why you would choose each source. Make sure you include information about both the House of Representatives and the Senate, including a breakdown of the membership of each.

Interpreting a Political Cartoon

Why Learn This Skill?

Political cartoons express opinions through art. The cartoons appear in newspapers, magazines, books, and on the Internet. Political cartoons usually focus on public figures, political events, or economic or social conditions. This type of art can give you a summary of an event or circumstance, along with the artist's opinion in an entertaining way.

1 Learn It!

Follow these steps to interpret a political cartoon:

1. Read the title, caption, or conversation balloons. They help you identify the subject of the cartoon.

2. Identify the characters, people, or symbols shown. Symbols are objects that stand for something else.

3. Examine the actions in the cartoon. Ask yourself: What is happening and why?

4. Identify the cartoonist's purpose; is it to persuade, criticize, or just make people think? What statement or idea is he or she trying to express?

SECESSIONISTS LEAVING THE UNION

2 Practice It!

Study the cartoon above. Then answer these questions:
1. What is the subject of the cartoon?
2. What words give clues to the meaning of the cartoon?
3. What is happening in the cartoon?
4. What message do you think the cartoonist is trying to send?

3 Apply It!

Bring a newsmagazine to class. With a partner, analyze the message in each political cartoon you find.

Writing a Case Study

Why Learn This Skill?

Have you ever wondered what can be done to help keep your community clean? A case study on environmental clean-up and recycling would help define the issue and propose various solutions to the problem.

A case study is an in-depth analysis of a particular situation or problem that could apply to a broader field. It involves thorough research and interviews to gain a better understanding of a problem and to suggest solutions. In this example, a case study might be done on the placement of recycling bins for aluminum cans to determine that action's effect on the community. This type of research tool can help both the writer and reader gain a more extensive understanding of a situation.

1 Learn It!

To learn how to write a case study, follow these steps:

1. Treat the case study like a story: introduce the problem at the very beginning of the study in a manner intended to grab the reader's attention.

2. Introduce details about the case including information on the study site, the people involved, and the central issues, in a logical manner.

3. Use short story writing techniques and plenty of dialogue to keep the narrative interesting.

4. Sum up the issue in the final paragraph. Give the reader the opportunity to come up with various positions that can be taken on the issue.

2 Practice It!

Identify a situation or event described in this book that you think could be investigated as a case study. Write a case study in which you answer the following questions:

1. Is there a problem/issue that could apply to a broader group of people?

2. What are the major issues, and who is involved?

3. What solutions have been attempted and what others could be tried?

3 Apply It!

Research to find two sources of information on the topic of banning teenagers from using cell phones while driving. Create fictional characters that might be affected by a law like this. Use your sources and your imagination to write a one-page case study on the topic.

Presidents of the United States

In this resource, you will find portraits of the individuals who served as presidents of the United States, along with their occupations, political party affiliations, and other interesting facts.

George Washington ⭐1

Presidential term: 1789–1797
Lived: 1732–1799
Born in: Virginia
Elected from: Virginia
Occupations: Soldier, Planter
Party: None
Vice President: John Adams

John Adams ⭐2

Presidential term: 1797–1801
Lived: 1735–1826
Born in: Massachusetts
Elected from: Massachusetts
Occupations: Teacher, Lawyer
Party: Federalist
Vice President: Thomas Jefferson

Thomas Jefferson ⭐3

Presidential term: 1801–1809
Lived: 1743–1826
Born in: Virginia
Elected from: Virginia
Occupations: Planter, Lawyer
Party: Republican**
Vice Presidents: Aaron Burr,
  George Clinton

James Madison ⭐4

Presidential term: 1809–1817
Lived: 1751–1836
Born in: Virginia
Elected from: Virginia
Occupation: Planter
Party: Republican**
Vice Presidents: George Clinton,
  Elbridge Gerry

James Monroe ⭐5

Presidential term: 1817–1825
Lived: 1758–1831
Born in: Virginia
Elected from: Virginia
Occupation: Lawyer
Party: Republican**
Vice President: Daniel D. Tompkins

John Quincy Adams ⭐6

Presidential term: 1825–1829
Lived: 1767–1848
Born in: Massachusetts
Elected from: Massachusetts
Occupation: Lawyer
Party: Republican**
Vice President: John C. Calhoun

Andrew Jackson ⭐7

Presidential term: 1829–1837
Lived: 1767–1845
Born in: South Carolina
Elected from: Tennessee
Occupations: Lawyer, Soldier
Party: Democratic
Vice Presidents: John C. Calhoun,
  Martin Van Buren

Martin Van Buren ⭐8

Presidential term: 1837–1841
Lived: 1782–1862
Born in: New York
Elected from: New York
Occupation: Lawyer
Party: Democratic
Vice President: Richard M.
  Johnson

William H. Harrison ⭐9

Presidential term: 1841
Lived: 1773–1841
Born in: Virginia
Elected from: Ohio
Occupations: Soldier, Planter
Party: Whig
Vice President: John Tyler

** *The Republican Party during this period developed into today's Democratic Party.
Today's Republican Party originated in 1854.*

John Tyler 10 ⭐

Presidential term: 1841–1845
Lived: 1790–1862
Born in: Virginia
Elected as V.P. from: Virginia
Succeeded Harrison
Occupation: Lawyer
Party: Whig
Vice President: None

James K. Polk 11 ⭐

Presidential term: 1845–1849
Lived: 1795–1849
Born in: North Carolina
Elected from: Tennessee
Occupation: Lawyer
Party: Democratic
Vice President: George M. Dallas

Zachary Taylor 12 ⭐

Presidential term: 1849–1850
Lived: 1784–1850
Born in: Virginia
Elected from: Louisiana
Occupation: Soldier
Party: Whig
Vice President: Millard Fillmore

Millard Fillmore 13 ⭐

Presidential term: 1850–1853
Lived: 1800–1874
Born in: New York
Elected as V.P. from: New York
Succeeded Taylor
Occupation: Lawyer
Party: Whig
Vice President: None

Franklin Pierce 14 ⭐

Presidential term: 1853–1857
Lived: 1804–1869
Born in: New Hampshire
Elected from: New Hampshire
Occupation: Lawyer
Party: Democratic
Vice President: William R. King

James Buchanan 15 ⭐

Presidential term: 1857–1861
Lived: 1791–1868
Born in: Pennsylvania
Elected from: Pennsylvania
Occupation: Lawyer
Party: Democratic
Vice President: John C. Breckinridge

Abraham Lincoln 16 ⭐

Presidential term: 1861–1865
Lived: 1809–1865
Born in: Kentucky
Elected from: Illinois
Occupation: Lawyer
Party: Republican
Vice Presidents: Hannibal Hamlin, Andrew Johnson

Andrew Johnson 17 ⭐

Presidential term: 1865–1869
Lived: 1808–1875
Born in: North Carolina
Elected as V.P. from: Tennessee
Succeeded Lincoln
Occupation: Tailor
Party: Republican
Vice President: None

Ulysses S. Grant 18 ⭐

Presidential term: 1869–1877
Lived: 1822–1885
Born in: Ohio
Elected from: Illinois
Occupations: Farmer, Soldier
Party: Republican
Vice Presidents: Schuyler Colfax, Henry Wilson

Rutherford B. Hayes 19

Presidential term: 1877–1881
Lived: 1822–1893
Born in: Ohio
Elected from: Ohio
Occupation: Lawyer
Party: Republican
Vice President: William A.
    Wheeler

James A. Garfield 20

Presidential term: 1881
Lived: 1831–1881
Born in: Ohio
Elected from: Ohio
Occupations: Laborer, Professor
Party: Republican
Vice President: Chester A.
    Arthur

Chester A. Arthur 21

Presidential term: 1881–1885
Lived: 1830–1886
Born in: Vermont
Elected as V.P. from: New York
Succeeded Garfield
Occupations: Teacher, Lawyer
Party: Republican
Vice President: None

Grover Cleveland 22

Presidential term: 1885–1889
Lived: 1837–1908
Born in: New Jersey
Elected from: New York
Occupation: Lawyer
Party: Democratic
Vice President: Thomas A.
    Hendricks

Benjamin Harrison 23

Presidential term: 1889–1893
Lived: 1833–1901
Born in: Ohio
Elected from: Indiana
Occupation: Lawyer
Party: Republican
Vice President: Levi P. Morton

Grover Cleveland 24

Presidential term: 1893–1897
Lived: 1837–1908
Born in: New Jersey
Elected from: New York
Occupation: Lawyer
Party: Democratic
Vice President: Adlai E.
    Stevenson

William McKinley 25

Presidential term: 1897–1901
Lived: 1843–1901
Born in: Ohio
Elected from: Ohio
Occupations: Teacher, Lawyer
Party: Republican
Vice Presidents: Garret Hobart,
    Theodore Roosevelt

Theodore Roosevelt 26

Presidential term: 1901–1909
Lived: 1858–1919
Born in: New York
Elected as V.P. from: New York
Succeeded McKinley
Occupations: Historian, Rancher
Party: Republican
Vice President: Charles W. Fairbanks

William H. Taft 27

Presidential term: 1909–1913
Lived: 1857–1930
Born in: Ohio
Elected from: Ohio
Occupation: Lawyer
Party: Republican
Vice President: James S.
    Sherman

Presidents of the United States

Woodrow Wilson ★ 28

Presidential term: 1913–1921
Lived: 1856–1924
Born in: Virginia
Elected from: New Jersey
Occupation: College Professor
Party: Democratic
Vice President: Thomas R. Marshall

Warren G. Harding ★ 29

Presidential term: 1921–1923
Lived: 1865–1923
Born in: Ohio
Elected from: Ohio
Occupations: Newspaper Editor, Publisher
Party: Republican
Vice President: Calvin Coolidge

Calvin Coolidge ★ 30

Presidential term: 1923–1929
Lived: 1872–1933
Born in: Vermont
Elected as V.P. from: Massachusetts; succeeded Harding
Occupation: Lawyer
Party: Republican
Vice President: Charles G. Dawes

Herbert C. Hoover ★ 31

Presidential term: 1929–1933
Lived: 1874–1964
Born in: Iowa
Elected from: California
Occupation: Engineer
Party: Republican
Vice President: Charles Curtis

Franklin D. Roosevelt ★ 32

Presidential term: 1933–1945
Lived: 1882–1945
Born in: New York
Elected from: New York
Occupation: Lawyer
Party: Democratic
Vice Presidents: John N. Garner, Henry A. Wallace, Harry S. Truman

Harry S. Truman ★ 33

Presidential term: 1945–1953
Lived: 1884–1972
Born in: Missouri
Elected as V.P. from: Missouri Succeeded Roosevelt
Occupations: Clerk, Farmer
Party: Democratic
Vice President: Alben W. Barkley

Dwight D. Eisenhower ★ 34

Presidential term: 1953–1961
Lived: 1890–1969
Born in: Texas
Elected from: New York
Occupation: Soldier
Party: Republican
Vice President: Richard M. Nixon

John F. Kennedy ★ 35

Presidential term: 1961–1963
Lived: 1917–1963
Born in: Massachusetts
Elected from: Massachusetts
Occupations: Author, Reporter
Party: Democratic
Vice President: Lyndon B. Johnson

Lyndon B. Johnson ★ 36

Presidential term: 1963–1969
Lived: 1908–1973
Born in: Texas
Elected as V.P. from: Texas Succeeded Kennedy
Occupation: Teacher
Party: Democratic
Vice President: Hubert H. Humphrey

Richard M. Nixon 37

Presidential term: 1969–1974
Lived: 1913–1994
Born in: California
Elected from: New York
Occupation: Lawyer
Party: Republican
Vice Presidents: Spiro T. Agnew, Gerald R. Ford

Gerald R. Ford 38

Presidential term: 1974–1977
Lived: 1913–2006
Born in: Nebraska
Appointed as V.P. upon Agnew's resignation; succeeded Nixon
Occupation: Lawyer
Party: Republican
Vice President: Nelson A. Rockefeller

James E. Carter, Jr. 39

Presidential term: 1977–1981
Lived: 1924–
Born in: Georgia
Elected from: Georgia
Occupations: Business, Farmer
Party: Democratic
Vice President: Walter F. Mondale

Ronald W. Reagan 40

Presidential term: 1981–1989
Lived: 1911–2004
Born in: Illinois
Elected from: California
Occupations: Actor, Lecturer
Party: Republican
Vice President: George H.W. Bush

George H.W. Bush 41

Presidential term: 1989–1993
Lived: 1924–
Born in: Massachusetts
Elected from: Texas
Occupation: Business
Party: Republican
Vice President: J. Danforth Quayle

William J. Clinton 42

Presidential term: 1993–2001
Lived: 1946–
Born in: Arkansas
Elected from: Arkansas
Occupation: Lawyer
Party: Democratic
Vice President: Albert Gore, Jr.

George W. Bush 43

Presidential term: 2001–
Lived: 1946–
Born in: Connecticut
Elected from: Texas
Occupation: Business
Party: Republican
Vice President: Richard B. Cheney

Presidents of the United States

Supreme Court Case Summaries

CONTENTS

Brown v. Board of Education
1954

In *Brown* v. *Board of Education of Topeka, Kansas*, the Supreme Court overruled *Plessy* v. *Ferguson* (1896) making the separate-but-equal doctrine in public schools unconstitutional. The Supreme Court rejected the idea that truly equal but separate schools for African American and white students would be constitutional. The Court explained that the Fourteenth Amendment's requirement that all persons be guaranteed equal protection of the law is not met simply by ensuring that African American and white schools "have been equalized . . . with respect to buildings, curricula, qualifications and salaries, and other tangible factors."

The Court then ruled that racial segregation in public schools violates the Equal Protection Clause of the Constitution because it is inherently unequal. In other words, the very fact of separation marks the separated race as inferior. The Court's decision has been extended beyond public education to virtually all public facilities and activities.

George E.C. Hayes, Thurgood Marshall, and James Nabrit, Jr., were attorneys who argued the case against segregation in *Brown* v. *Board of Education*.

Bush v. Gore
2000

The 2000 presidential election was hanging in the balance as the state of Florida recounted their disputed ballots. Candidates George W. Bush, Republican, and Al Gore, Democrat, were so close in the polls that there was a manual recount of the votes.

Bush went to the Court to stop the recount, stating that it violated the Fourteenth Amendment. The Court ruled that since the manual recount had no uniform way to judge each disputed vote equally, it did violate the Constitution and had to be stopped. As a result, Bush won Florida's electoral votes and became president.

Dred Scott v. Sandford
1857

Dred Scott was taken by slaveholder John Sanford to the free state of Illinois and to the Wisconsin Territory, which had also banned slavery. Later they returned to Missouri, a slave state. Several years later, Scott sued for his freedom under the Missouri legal principle of "once free, always free." In other words, under Missouri law enslaved people were entitled to freedom if they had lived in a free state at any time. Missouri courts ruled against Scott, but he appealed the case all the way to the United States Supreme Court.

The Supreme Court decided this case before the Fourteenth Amendment was added to the Constitution. (The Fourteenth Amendment provides that anyone born or naturalized in the United States is a citizen of the nation and of his or her state of residence.) The Court held that enslaved African Americans were property, not citizens, and thus had no rights under the Constitution. The decision also overturned the Missouri Compromise of 1820, which

Dred Scott

had outlawed slavery in territories north of 36° 30' latitude. Many people in the North were outraged by the decision, which moved the nation closer to civil war.

Furman v. Georgia
1972

This decision put a halt to the application of the death penalty under state laws then in effect. For the first time, the Supreme Court ruled that the death penalty amounted to cruel and unusual punishment, which is outlawed in the Constitution. The Court explained that existing death penalty laws did not give juries enough guidance in deciding whether or not to impose the death penalty. As a result, the death penalty in many cases was imposed arbitrarily, that is, without a reasonable basis in the facts and circumstances of the offender or the crime.

The *Furman* decision halted all executions in the 39 states that had death penalty laws at that time. Since the decision, 38 states have rewritten death penalty laws to meet the requirements established in the *Furman* case.

Gibbons v. Ogden
1824

Thomas Gibbons had a federal license to operate a steamboat along the coast, but he did not have a license from the state of New York to travel on New York waters. He wanted to run a steamboat line between Manhattan and New Jersey that would compete with Aaron Ogden's company. Ogden had a New York license. Gibbons sued for the freedom to use his federal license to compete against Ogden on New York waters.

Gibbons won the case. The Supreme Court made it clear that the authority of Congress to regulate interstate commerce (among states) includes the authority to regulate intrastate commerce (within a single state) that bears on, or relates to, interstate commerce.

Before this decision, it was thought a state could close its borders to interstate commerce. The Court affirmed, however, that a state can regulate purely internal commerce, but only Congress can regulate commerce having both intrastate and interstate dimensions.

Gideon v. Wainwright
1963

After being accused of robbery, Clarence Gideon, a poor man, could not afford to hire a lawyer. Gideon defended himself in a Florida court because the judge in the case refused to appoint a free lawyer. The jury found Gideon guilty. Eventually, Gideon appealed his conviction to the United States Supreme Court, claiming that, by failing to appoint a lawyer, the lower court had violated his rights under the Sixth and Fourteenth Amendments.

The Supreme Court agreed with Gideon. In *Gideon* v. *Wainwright* the Supreme Court held for the first time that poor defendants in criminal cases have the right to a state-paid attorney under the Sixth Amendment. The rule announced in this case has been refined to apply whenever the defendant, if convicted, can be sentenced to more than six months in jail or prison.

Hamdan v. Rumsfeld
2006

In 2004 the Bush administration began holding captured terrorist suspects at the American military base in Guantanamo Bay, Cuba. It insisted that these prisoners, as illegal enemy fighters, did not have the right of appeal to American courts. Instead, the president as commander in chief would create special military courts to hear their cases.

In 2006 the Supreme Court struck down this plan in *Hamdan* v. *Rumsfeld*. It argued that Bush's military courts, as they stood, violated both U.S. military law and international law regarding the treatment of prisoners of war. President Bush then asked Congress to pass legislation setting up military courts that met the Court's objections. Prisoners would have the right to see evidence against them, and any evidence obtained by torture would not be accepted in court. However, prisoners could be held indefinitely without trial if the military courts had determined they were being lawfully held.

In 1988 Congress officially apologized for the internment of Fred Korematsu (center) and other Japanese Americans.

Korematsu v. United States
1944

After the Japanese bombing of Pearl Harbor in 1941, thousands of Japanese Americans on the West Coast were forced to abandon their homes and businesses, and they were moved to internment camps in California, Idaho, Utah, Arizona, Wyoming, Colorado, and Arkansas. The prison-like camps offered poor food and cramped quarters.

The Supreme Court's decision in *Korematsu* v. *United States* upheld the authority of the federal government to move Japanese Americans, many of whom were citizens, from designated military areas that included almost the entire West Coast. The government defended the so-called exclusion orders as a necessary response to Japan's attack on Pearl Harbor. Only after his reelection in 1944 did President Franklin Roosevelt rescind the evacuation orders, and by the end of 1945 the camps were closed.

Marbury v. Madison
1803

During his last days in office, President John Adams commissioned William Marbury and several other men as judges. This action by Federalist president Adams angered the incoming Democratic-Republican president Thomas Jefferson. Jefferson then ordered James Madison, his secretary of state, not to deliver the commissions, thus blocking the appointments. William Marbury sued, asking the Supreme Court to order Madison to deliver the commission that would make him a judge.

The Court ruled that the Judiciary Act—the law that gave Marbury his appointment—was unconstitutional. More importantly, the *Marbury* decision established one of the significant principles of American constitutional law. The Supreme Court held that it is the Court itself that has the final say on what the Constitution means. The Court had secured for itself the power to review acts of Congress—the power of judicial review. It is also the Supreme Court that has the final say in whether or not an act of government—legislative or executive at the federal, state, or local level—violates the Constitution.

McCulloch v. Maryland
1819

Following the War of 1812, the United States experienced years of high inflation and general economic turmoil. In an attempt to stabilize the economy, the United States Congress chartered a Second Bank of the United States in 1816. Maryland and several other states, however, opposed the competition that the new national bank created and passed laws taxing its branches. In 1818 James McCulloch, head of the Baltimore branch of the Second Bank of the United States, refused to pay the tax to the state of Maryland. The case worked its way through the Maryland state courts all the way to the United States Supreme Court.

The Supreme Court declared the Maryland tax unconstitutional and void. More importantly, the decision established the foundation for expanded congressional authority. The Court held that the necessary and proper clause of the Constitution allows Congress to do more than the Constitution expressly authorizes it to do. The decision allows Congress to enact nearly any law that will help it achieve any of its duties as set forth in the Constitution. For example, Congress has the express authority to regulate interstate commerce. The necessary and proper clause permits Congress to do so in ways not actually specified in the Constitution.

Minnesota v. Mille Lacs Band of Chippewa Indians
1999

An 1855 Treaty with the United States set aside lands in present-day Minnesota and Wisconsin to several Chippewa bands as reservations at Mille Lacs but made no mention of, among other things, whether it abolished rights guaranteed by previous treaties. Minnesota was admitted to the Union in 1858. In 1990 the Mille Lacs Band and several members sued Minnesota, its Department of Natural Resources, and state officials (collectively State), seeking, among other things, a declaratory judgment that they retained their ownership rights to the land without state interference. The District Court ultimately concluded that the Chippewa retained their claim under the 1837 Treaty and resolved several resource allocation and regulation issues. The State's argument under the "equal footing doctrine," that Minnesota's entrance into the Union in 1855 extinguished any Indian treaty rights, was considered void. The Supreme Court ruled in favor of the Chippewa and the existing 1837 treaty.

In 1963 the arrest of Ernesto Miranda (left) led to a landmark decision.

Miranda v. Arizona
1966

In 1963 police in Arizona arrested Ernesto Miranda for kidnapping. The court found Miranda guilty on the basis of a signed confession. The police admitted that neither before nor during the questioning had Miranda been advised of his right to consult with an attorney before answering any questions or of his right to have an attorney present during the interrogation. Miranda appealed his conviction, claiming that police had violated his right against self-incrimination under the Fifth Amendment by not informing him of his legal rights during questioning.

Miranda won the case. The Supreme Court held that a person in police custody cannot be questioned unless told that he or she has: 1) the right to remain silent, 2) the right to an attorney (at government expense if the accused is unable to pay), and 3) that anything the person says after stating that he or she understands these rights can be used as evidence of guilt at trial. These rights have come to be called the Miranda warning. They are intended to ensure that an accused person in custody will not unknowingly give up the Fifth Amendment's protection against self-incrimination.

New York Times v. United States
1971

In June 1971, the *New York Times* published its first installment of the "Pentagon Papers," a classified document about government actions in the Vietnam War era. The secret document had been leaked to the *Times* by antiwar activist Daniel Ellsberg, who had previously worked in national security for the government. President Richard Nixon went to court to block further publication of the Pentagon Papers. The *New York Times* appealed to the Supreme Court to allow it to continue publishing without government interference.

The Supreme Court's ruling in this case upheld earlier decisions establishing the doctrine of prior restraint. This doctrine protects the press (broadly defined to include newspapers, television and radio, filmmakers and distributors, etc.) from government attempts to block publication. Except in extraordinary circumstances, the press must be allowed to publish.

Plessy v. Ferguson
1896

In the late 1800s, railroad companies in Louisiana were required by state law to provide "separate-but-equal" cars for white and African American passengers. In 1890 a group of citizens in New Orleans selected Homer Plessy to challenge that law. In 1892 Plessy boarded a whites-only car and refused to move. He was arrested. Plessy appealed to the Supreme Court, arguing that the Louisiana separate-but-equal law violated his right to equal protection under the Fourteenth Amendment.

Homer Plessy lost the case. The *Plessy* decision upheld the separate-but-equal doctrine used by Southern states to perpetuate segregation following the Civil War. The court ruled that the Fourteenth Amendment's equal protection clause required only equal public facilities for the two races, not equal access to the same facilities. This decision was overruled in 1954 by *Brown* v. *Board of Education of Topeka, Kansas* (discussed previously).

Roe v. Wade
1973

Roe v. *Wade* challenged restrictive abortion laws in both Texas and Georgia. The suit was brought in the name of Jane Roe, an alias used to protect the privacy of the plaintiff.

In this decision, the Supreme Court ruled that females have a constitutional right under various provisions of the Constitution—most notably, the due process clause—to decide whether or not to terminate a pregnancy. The Supreme Court's decision in this case was the most significant in a long line of decisions over a period of 50 years that recognized a constitutional right of privacy, even though the word "privacy" is not found in the Constitution.

Tinker v. Des Moines School District
1969

During the Vietnam War, some students in Des Moines, Iowa, wore black armbands to school to protest American involvement in the conflict. Two days earlier, school officials had adopted a policy banning the wearing of armbands to school. When the students arrived at school wearing armbands, they were suspended and sent home. The students argued that school officials violated their First Amendment right to free speech.

The Supreme Court sided with the students. In a now-famous statement, the Court said that "it can hardly be argued that either students or teachers shed their constitutional rights of freedom of speech or expression at the schoolhouse gate." The Supreme Court went on to rule that a public school could not suspend students who wore black armbands to school to symbolize their opposition to the Vietnam War. In so holding, the Court likened the students' conduct to pure speech and decided it on that basis.

United States v. Nixon
1974

In the early 1970s, President Nixon was named an unindicted co-conspirator in the criminal investigation that arose in the aftermath of a break-in at the offices of the Democratic Party in Washington, D.C. A federal judge had ordered President Nixon to turn over tapes of conversations he had with his advisers about the break-in. Nixon resisted the order, claiming that the conversations were entitled to absolute confidentiality by Article II of the Constitution.

The decision in this case made it clear that the president is not above the law. The Supreme Court held that only those presidential conversations and communications that relate to performing the duties of the office of president are confidential and protected from a judicial order of disclosure. The Court ordered Nixon to give up the tapes, which revealed evidence linking the president to the conspiracy to obstruct justice. He resigned from office shortly thereafter.

Worcester v. Georgia
1832

State officials in Georgia wanted to remove the Cherokee from land that was guaranteed to them in earlier treaties. Samuel Worcester was a congregational missionary who worked with the Cherokee people. He was arrested for failure to have a license that the state required to live in Cherokee country and for refusing to obey an order from the Georgia militia to leave Cherokee lands. Worcester then sued the state of Georgia. He claimed that Georgia had no legal authority on Cherokee land because the United States government recognized the Cherokee in Georgia as a separate nation.

The Supreme Court agreed with Worcester by a vote of 5 to 1. Chief Justice John Marshall wrote the majority opinion, which said that Native American nations were a distinct people with the right to have independent political communities and that only the federal government had authority over matters that involved the Cherokee.

President Andrew Jackson supported Georgia's efforts to remove the Cherokee to Indian Territory and refused to enforce the Court's ruling. After the ruling Jackson remarked, "John Marshall has made his decision. Now let him enforce it." As a result of Jackson's refusal to enforce the Court's order, thousands of Cherokee died on the long, forced trek to Indian Territory, known as the "Trail of Tears."

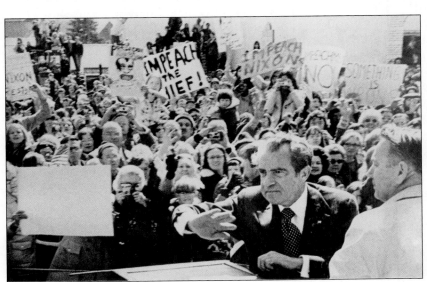

President Nixon encounters angry protesters in 1974 during the Watergate scandal.

The Magna Carta

The Magna Carta, signed by King John in 1215, marked a decisive step forward in the development of constitutional government in England. Later, it became a model for colonists who carried the Magna Carta's guarantees of legal and political rights to America.

1. . . . [T]hat the English Church shall be free, and shall have its rights entire, and its liberties unimpaired. . . . we have also granted for us and our heirs forever, all the liberties written out below, to have and to keep for them and their heirs, of us and our heirs:

39. No free man shall be seized or imprisoned, or stripped of his rights or possessions, or outlawed or exiled, or deprived of his standing in any other way, nor will we proceed with force against him, or send others to do so, except by the lawful judgment of his equals, or by the law of the land.

40. To no one will we sell, to no one deny or delay right or justice.

41. All merchants may enter or leave England unharmed and without fear, and may stay or travel within it, by land or water, for purposes of trade, free from all illegal exactions, in accordance with ancient and lawful customs. This, however, does not apply in time of war to merchants from a country that is at war with us. . . .

42. In future it shall be lawful for any man to leave and return to our kingdom unharmed and without fear, by land or water, preserving his allegiance to us, except in time of war, for some short period, for the common benefit of the realm. . . .

60. All these customs and liberties that we have granted shall be observed in our kingdom in so far as concerns our own relations with our subjects. Let all men of our kingdom, whether clergy or laymen, observe them similarly in their relations with their own men. . . .

63. . . . Both we and the barons have sworn that all this shall be observed in good faith and without deceit. Witness the abovementioned people and many others. Given by our hand in the meadow that is called Runnymede, between Windsor and Staines, on the fifteenth day of June in the seventeenth year of our reign.

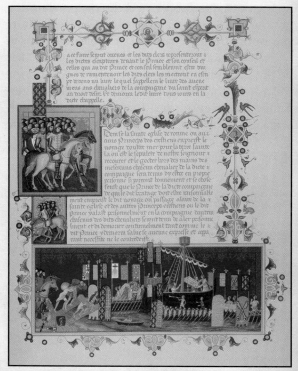

Illuminated manuscript, Middle Ages

The Mayflower Compact

*On November 21, 1620, forty-one colonists aboard the **Mayflower** drafted this agreement. The Mayflower Compact was the first plan of self-government ever put in force in the English colonies.*

In the Name of God, Amen. We, whose names are underwritten, the Loyal Subjects of our dread Sovereign Lord King James, by the Grace of God, of Great Britain, France, and Ireland, King, Defender of the Faith, etc. Having undertaken for the Glory of God, and Advancement of the Christian Faith, and the Honour of our King and Country, a Voyage to plant the first Colony in the northern Parts of Virginia; Do by these Presents, solemnly and mutually, in the Presence of God and one another, covenant and combine ourselves together into a civil Body Politick, for our better Ordering and Preservation, and Furtherance of the Ends aforesaid: And by Virtue hereof do enact, constitute, and frame, such just and equal Laws, Ordinances, Acts, Constitutions, and Officers, from time to time, as shall be thought most meet and convenient for the general Good of the Colony; unto which we promise all due Submission and Obedience. In Witness whereof we have hereunto subscribed our names at Cape-Cod the eleventh of November, in the Reign of our Sovereign Lord King James, of England, France, and Ireland, the eighteenth, and of Scotland, the fifty-fourth, Anno Domini, 1620.

The Federalist, No. 10

James Madison wrote several articles supporting ratification of the Constitution for a New York newspaper. In the excerpt below, Madison argues for the idea of a federal republic.

By a faction, I understand a number of citizens . . . who are united and actuated by some common impulse . . . adverse to the rights of other citizens. . . .

The inference to which we are brought is that the causes of faction cannot be removed and that relief is only to be sought in the means of controlling its effects. . . .

A republic, by which I mean a government in which the scheme of representation takes place . . . promises the cure for which we are seeking. . . .

The two great points of difference between a democracy and a republic are: first, the delegation of the government, in the latter, to a small number of citizens elected by the rest; secondly, the greater number of citizens, and greater sphere of country, over which the latter may be extended.

James Madison

The effect of the first difference is . . . to refine and enlarge the public views, by passing them through the medium of a chosen body of citizens, whose wisdom may best discern the true interest of their country, and whose patriotism and love of justice will be least likely to sacrifice it to temporary or partial considerations. . . .

Washington's Farewell Address

At the end of his second term as president, George Washington spoke of the dangers facing the young nation. He warned against the dangers of political parties and sectionalism, and he advised the nation against permanent alliances with other nations.

. . . Citizens by birth or choice of a common country, that country has a right to concentrate your affections. The name of American, which belongs to you in your national capacity, must always exalt the just pride of patriotism more than any appellation derived from local discriminations. With slight shades of difference, you have the same religion, manners, habits, and political principles. You have in a common cause fought and triumphed together. . . .

In contemplating the causes which may disturb our union it occurs as matter of serious concern that any ground should have been furnished for characterizing parties by geographical discriminations. . . .

George Washington

No alliances, however strict, between the parts can be an adequate substitute. They must inevitably experience the infractions and interruptions which all alliances in all times have experienced. . . .

The great rule of conduct for us in regard to foreign nations is, in extending our commercial relations to have with them as little political connection as possible. . . .

. . . I anticipate with pleasing expectation that retreat in which I promise myself to realize . . . the sweet enjoyment of partaking in the midst of my fellow citizens the benign influence of good laws under a free government—the ever-favorite object of my heart, and the happy reward, as I trust, of our mutual cares, labors, and dangers.

"The Star-Spangled Banner"

During the British bombardment of Fort McHenry during the War of 1812, a young Baltimore lawyer named Francis Scott Key was inspired to write the words to "The Star-Spangled Banner." Although it became popular immediately, it was not until 1931 that Congress officially declared "The Star-Spangled Banner" as our national anthem.

O! say can you see by the dawn's early light,

What so proudly we hailed at the twilight's last gleaming,

Whose broad stripes and bright stars through the perilous fight,

O'er the ramparts we watch'd, were so gallantly streaming?

And the Rockets' red glare, the Bombs bursting in air,

Gave proof through the night that our Flag was still there;

O! say does that star-spangled Banner yet wave,

O'er the Land of the free, and the home of the brave!

The Monroe Doctrine

In 1823 President James Monroe proclaimed the Monroe Doctrine. Designed to end European influence in the Western Hemisphere, it became a cornerstone of United States foreign policy.

. . . With the existing colonies or dependencies of any European power we have not interfered and shall not interfere. But with the Governments who have declared their independence and maintained it, and whose independence we have, on great consideration and on just principles, acknowledged, we could not view any interposition for the purpose of oppressing them, or controlling in any other manner their destiny, by any European power in any other light than as the manifestation of any unfriendly disposition toward the United States. . . .

James Monroe

Our policy in regard to Europe, which was adopted at an early stage of the wars which have so long agitated that quarter of the globe, nevertheless remains the same, which is, not to interfere in the internal concerns of any of its powers; to consider the government de facto as the legitimate government for us; to cultivate friendly relations with it, and to preserve those relations by a frank, firm, and manly policy, meeting in all instances the just claims of every power, submitting to injuries from none. . . .

Memorial of the Cherokee Nation

The Indian Removal Act of 1830 called for the relocation of Native Americans to territory west of the Mississippi River. Cherokee leaders protested the policy.

We are aware that some persons suppose it will be for our advantage to remove beyond the Mississippi. We think otherwise. Our people universally think otherwise. . . .

We wish to remain on the land of our fathers. We have a perfect and original right to remain without interruption or molestation. The treaties with us, and laws of the United States made in pursuance of treaties, guaranty our residence and our privileges, and secure us against intruders. Our only request is, that these treaties may be fulfilled, and these laws executed. . . .

. . . We have been called a poor, ignorant, and degraded people. We certainly are not rich; nor have we ever boasted of our knowledge, or our moral or intellectual elevation. But there is not a man within our limits so ignorant as not to know that he has a right to live on the land of his fathers, in the possession of his immemorial privileges, and that this right has been acknowledged by the United States; nor is there a man so degraded as not to feel a keen sense of injury, on being deprived of his right and driven into exile. . . .

The Seneca Falls Declaration

One of the first documents to express the desire for equal rights for women is the Declaration of Sentiments and Resolutions, issued in 1848 at the Seneca Falls Convention in Seneca Falls, New York. Led by Lucretia Mott and Elizabeth Cady Stanton, the delegates adopted a set of resolutions that called for woman suffrage and opportunities for women in employment and education. Excerpts from the Declaration follow.

When, in the course of human events, it becomes necessary for one portion of the family of man to assume among the people of the earth a position different from that which they have hitherto occupied, but one to which the laws of nature and of nature's God entitle them, a decent respect to the opinions of mankind requires that they should declare the causes that impel them to such a course.

We hold these truths to be self-evident: that all men and women are created equal; that they are endowed by their Creator with certain inalienable rights; that among these are life, liberty, and the pursuit of happiness; that to secure these rights governments are instituted, deriving their just powers from the consent of the governed. Whenever any form of government becomes destructive of these ends, it is the right of those who suffer from it to refuse allegiance to it, and to insist upon the institution of a new government, laying its foundation on such principles, and organizing its powers in such form as to them shall seem most likely to effect their safety and happiness. Prudence, indeed, will dictate that governments long established should not be changed for light and transient causes; . . . But when a long train of abuses and usurpations, pursuing invariably the same object, evinces a design to reduce them under absolute despotism, it is their duty to throw off such government, and to provide new guards for their future security. . . .

The history of mankind is a history of repeated injuries and usurpations on the part of man toward woman, having in direct object the establishment of an absolute tyranny over her. To prove this, let facts be submitted to a candid world. . . .

Now, in view of the entire disfranchisement of one-half the people of this country, their social and religious degradation—in view of the unjust laws above mentioned, and because women do feel themselves aggrieved, oppressed, and fraudulently deprived of their most sacred rights, we insist that they have immediate admission to all the rights and privileges which belong to them as citizens of these United States. . . .

Elizabeth Cady Stanton

The Emancipation Proclamation

On January 1, 1863, President Abraham Lincoln issued the Emancipation Proclamation, which freed all enslaved people in states under Confederate control. The Proclamation was a step toward the Thirteenth Amendment (1865), which ended slavery in all of the United States.

. . . That on the 1st day of January, in the year of our Lord 1863, all persons held as slaves within any state or designated part of a state, the people whereof shall then be in rebellion against the United States, shall be then, thenceforward, and forever free; and the Executive Government of the United States, including the military and naval authority thereof, will recognize and maintain the freedom of such persons, and will do no act or acts to repress such persons, or any of them, in any efforts they may make for their actual freedom.

That the Executive will, on the 1st day of January aforesaid, by proclamation, designate the states and parts of states, if any, in which the people thereof, respectively, shall then be in rebellion against the United States; and the fact that any state, or the people thereof, shall on that day be in good faith represented in the Congress of the United States, by members chosen thereto at elections wherein a majority of the qualified voters of such states shall have participated, shall, in the absence of strong countervailing testimony, be deemed conclusive evidence that such state, and the people thereof, are not then in rebellion against the United States. . . .

And, by virtue of the power and for the purpose aforesaid, I do order and declare that all persons held as slaves within said designated states and parts of states are, and henceforward shall be, free; and that the Executive Government of the United States, including the military and naval authorities thereof, will recognize and maintain the freedom of said persons.

And I hereby enjoin upon the people so declared to be free to abstain from all violence, unless in necessary self-defense; and I recommend to them that, all cases when allowed, they labor faithfully for reasonable wages.

And I further declare and make known that such persons, of suitable condition, will be received into the armed service of the United States. . . .

And upon this act, sincerely believed to be an act of justice, warranted by the Constitution upon military necessity, I invoke the considerate judgement of mankind and the gracious favor of Almighty God. . . .

Abraham Lincoln

The Gettysburg Address

On November 19, 1863, President Abraham Lincoln gave a short speech at the dedication of a national cemetery on the battlefield of Gettysburg. His simple yet eloquent words expressed his hopes for a nation divided by civil war.

Four score and seven years ago our fathers brought forth on this continent a new nation, conceived in liberty, and dedicated to the proposition that all men are created equal.

Now we are engaged in a great civil war, testing whether that nation, or any nation so conceived and so dedicated, can long endure. We are met on a great battlefield of that war. We have come to dedicate a portion of that field as a final resting place for those who here gave their lives that that nation might live. It is altogether fitting and proper that we should do this.

But, in a larger sense, we can not dedicate—we can not consecrate—we can not hallow—this ground. The brave men, living and dead, who struggled here, have consecrated it far above our poor power to add or detract. The world will little note nor long remember what we say here, but it can never forget what they did here. It is for us, the living, rather, to be dedicated here to the unfinished work which they who fought here have thus far so nobly advanced. It is rather for us to be here dedicated to the great task remaining before us—that from these honored dead we take increased devotion to that cause for which they gave the last full measure of devotion; that we here highly resolve that these dead shall not have died in vain; that this nation, under God, shall have a new birth of freedom; and that government of the people, by the people, for the people, shall not perish from the earth.

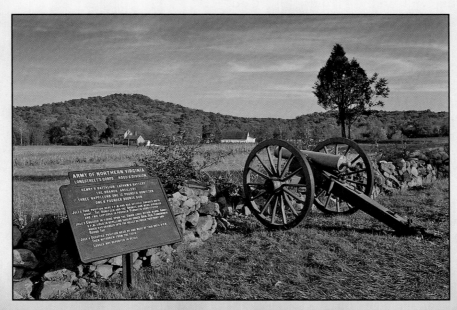

Current day photo of Gettysburg battlefield

I Will Fight No More

In 1877 the Nez Perce fought the government's attempt to move them to a smaller reservation. After a remarkable attempt to escape to Canada, Chief Joseph realized that resistance was hopeless and advised his people to surrender.

Tell General Howard I know his heart. What he told me before I have in my heart.

I am tired of fighting. . . . The old men are all dead. It is the young men who say yes or no. He who led the young men is dead. It is cold and we have no blankets. The little children are freezing to death. My people, some of them have run away to the hills, and have no blankets, no food; no one knows where they are—perhaps freezing to death. I want to have time to look for my children and see how many of them I can find. Maybe I shall find them among the dead. Hear me, my chiefs.

I am tired; my heart is sick and sad. From where the sun now stands I will fight no more forever.

Cheyenne shield

The Pledge of Allegiance

In 1892 the nation celebrated the 400th anniversary of Columbus's landing in America. In connection with this celebration, Francis Bellamy, a magazine editor, wrote and published the Pledge of Allegiance. The words "under God" were added by Congress in 1954 at the urging of President Dwight D. Eisenhower.

I pledge allegiance to the Flag of the United States of America and to the Republic for which it stands, one Nation under God, indivisible, with liberty and justice for all.

Students in a New York City school recite the Pledge of Allegiance.

The American's Creed

William Tyler Page of Friendship Heights, Maryland, wrote The American's Creed. This statement of political faith summarizes the true meaning of freedom available to all Americans. The U.S. House of Representatives adopted the creed on behalf of the American people on April 3, 1918.

I believe in the United States of America as a Government of the people, by the people, for the people; whose just powers are derived from the consent of the governed; a democracy in a republic; a sovereign Nation of many sovereign States; a perfect union, one and inseparable; established upon those principles of freedom, equality, justice, and humanity for which American patriots sacrificed their lives and fortunes.

I therefore believe it is my duty to my Country to love it, to support its Constitution, to obey its laws, to respect its flag, and to defend it against all enemies.

The Fourteen Points

On January 8, 1918, President Woodrow Wilson went before Congress to offer a statement of aims called the Fourteen Points. Wilson's plan called for freedom of the seas in peace and war, an end to secret alliances, and equal trading rights for all countries. The excerpt that follows is taken from the president's message.

. . . We entered this war because violations of right had occurred which touched us to the quick and made the life of our own people impossible unless they were corrected and the world secured once for all against their recurrence. What we demand in this war, therefore, is nothing peculiar to ourselves. It is that the world be made fit and safe to live in; and particularly that it be made safe for every peace-loving nation which, like our own, wishes to live its own life, determine its own institutions, be assured of justice and fair dealing by the other peoples of the world as against force and selfish aggression. All the peoples of the world are in effect partners in this interest, and for our own part we see very clearly that unless justice be done to others it will not be done to us. The program of the world's peace, therefore, is our program; and that program, the only possible program, as we see it, is this:

I. Open covenants of peace, openly arrived at, after which there shall be no private international understandings of any kind but diplomacy shall proceed always frankly and in the public view.

II. Absolute freedom of navigation upon the seas, outside territorial waters, alike in peace and in war, except as the seas may be closed in whole or in part by international action for the enforcement of international covenants.

XIV. A general association of nations must be formed under specific covenants for the purpose of affording mutual guarantees of political independence and territorial integrity to great and small states alike. . . .

Brown v. Board of Education

On May 17, 1954, the Supreme Court ruled in **Brown** *v.* **Board of Education of Topeka, Kansas,** *that racial segregation in public schools was unconstitutional. This decision provided the legal basis for court challenges to segregation in every aspect of American life.*

. . . The plaintiffs contend that segregated public schools are not "equal" and cannot be made "equal" and that hence they are deprived of the equal protection of the laws. Because of the obvious importance of the question presented, the Court took jurisdiction. . . .

Our decision, therefore, cannot turn on merely a comparison of these tangible factors in the Negro and white schools involved in each of the cases. We must look instead to the effect of segregation itself on public education.

In approaching this problem, we cannot turn the clock back to 1868 when the Amendment was adopted, or even to 1896 when *Plessy* v. *Ferguson* was written. We must consider public education in the light of its full development and its present place in American life throughout the Nation. Only in this way can it be determined if segregation in public schools deprives these plaintiffs of the equal protection of the laws.

Today, education is perhaps the most important function of state and local governments. Compulsory school attendance laws and the great expenditures for education both demonstrate our recognition of the importance of education to our democratic society. . . . In these days,

it is doubtful that any child may reasonably be expected to succeed in life if he is denied the opportunity of an education. Such an opportunity, where the state has undertaken to provide it, is a right which must be made available to all on equal terms.

We come then to the question presented: Does segregation of children in public schools solely on the basis of race, even though the physical facilities and other "tangible" factors may be equal, deprive the children of the minority group of equal educational opportunities? We believe that it does.

. . . We conclude that in the field of public education the doctrine of "separate but equal" has no place. Separate educational facilities are inherently unequal. Therefore, we hold that the plaintiffs and others similarly situated for whom the actions have been brought are, by reason of the segregation complained of, deprived of the equal protection of the laws guaranteed by the Fourteenth Amendment. . . .

Armed guards escort African American students.

John F. Kennedy's Inaugural Address

President Kennedy's Inaugural Address on January 20, 1961, set the tone for his administration. In his address Kennedy stirred the nation by calling for "a grand and global alliance" to fight tyranny, poverty, disease, and war.

We observe today not a victory of party but a celebration of freedom—symbolizing an end as well as a beginning—signifying renewal as well as change. For I have sworn before you and Almighty God the same solemn oath our forebears prescribed nearly a century and three-quarters ago.

The world is very different now. For man holds in his mortal hands the power to abolish all forms of human poverty and all forms of human life. And yet the same revolutionary beliefs for which our forebears fought are still at issue around the globe—the belief that the rights of man come not from the generosity of the state but from the hand of God.

We dare not forget today that we are the heirs of that first revolution. Let the word go forth from this time and place, to friend and foe alike, that the torch has been passed to a new generation of Americans—born in this century, tempered by war, disciplined by a hard and bitter peace, proud of our ancient heritage—and unwilling to witness or permit the slow undoing of those human rights to which this nation has always been committed, and to which we are committed today at home and around the world.

Let every nation know, whether it wishes us well or ill, that we shall pay any price, bear any burden, meet any hardship, support any friend, oppose any foe to assure the survival and the success of liberty.

This much we pledge—and more.

To those old allies whose cultural and spiritual origins we share, we pledge the loyalty of faithful friends. United, there is little we cannot do in a host of cooperative ventures. Divided, there is little we can do. . . .

Let us never negotiate out of fear. But let us never fear to negotiate.

Let both sides explore what problems unite us instead of belaboring those problems which divide us. . . .

Let both sides seek to invoke the wonders of science instead of its terrors. Together let us explore the stars, conquer the deserts, eradicate disease, tap the ocean depths, and encourage the arts and commerce. . . .

And so, my fellow Americans: ask not what your country can do for you—ask what you can do for your country.

My fellow citizens of the world: ask not what America will do for you, but what together we can do for the freedom of man. . . .

President Kennedy speaking at his inauguration

"I Have a Dream"

On August 28, 1963, while Congress debated wide-ranging civil rights legislation, Dr. Martin Luther King, Jr., led more than 200,000 people in a march on Washington, D.C. On the steps of the Lincoln Memorial he gave a stirring speech in which he eloquently spoke of his dreams for African Americans and for the United States. Excerpts of the speech follow.

. . . There are those who are asking the devotees of civil rights, "When will you be satisfied?"

We can never be satisfied as long as the Negro is the victim of the unspeakable horrors of police brutality. . . .

We cannot be satisfied as long as the Negro's basic mobility is from a smaller ghetto to a larger one. . . .

We can never be satisfied as long as a Negro in Mississippi cannot vote and a Negro in New York believes he has nothing for which to vote. . . .

I say to you today, my friends, that in spite of the difficulties and frustrations of the moment I still have a dream. It is a dream deeply rooted in the American dream. I have a dream that one day this nation will rise up and live out the true meaning of its creed: "We hold these truths to be self-evident, that all men are created equal."

I have a dream that one day on the red hills of Georgia the sons of former slaves and the sons of former slaveowners will be able to sit down together at the table of brotherhood.

I have a dream that one day even the state of Mississippi, a desert state sweltering with the heat of injustice and oppression, will be transformed into an oasis of freedom and justice.

I have a dream that my four little children will one day live in a nation where they will not be judged by the color of their skin but by the content of their character. . . .

. . . When we let freedom ring, when we let it ring from every village and every hamlet, from every state and every city, we will be able to speed up that day when all of God's children, black men and white men, Jews and Gentiles, Protestants and Catholics, will be able to join hands and sing in the words of the old Negro spiritual: "Free at last! Free at last! Thank God Almighty, we are free at last!"

Dr. Martin Luther King, Jr.

Glossary/Glosario

Content vocabulary are words that relate to American history content. Words that have an asterisk (*) are academic vocabulary. They help you understand your school subjects. All vocabulary words are **boldfaced and highlighted in yellow** in your textbook.

A

ENGLISH	ESPAÑOL
*abandon give up (p. 39)	*abandonar renunciar (pág. 39)
abstain to not take part in some activity, such as voting (p. 9)	abstenerse no formar parte de algunas actividades, como votar (pág. 9)
*academy a private high school; school that provides specialized training (p. 89)	*academia escuela secundaria privada; escuela que brinda capacitación especializada (pág. 89)
*achieve accomplish; gain by effort (p. 288)	*lograr conseguir; obtener con esfuerzo (pág. 288)
*accurate correct (p. 205)	*preciso exacto (pág. 205)
acid rain rain containing high amounts of chemical pollutants from the burning of fossil fuels (p. 561)	lluvia ácida lluvia que contiene grandes cantidades de sustancias químicas contaminantes provenientes de la quema de combustibles fósiles (pág. 561)
*adequate enough (p. 541)	*adecuado suficiente (pág. 541)
*adjust adapt (p. 78)	*ajustar adaptar (pág. 78)
*advocate support (p. 348)	*defender apoyar (pág. 348)
*affect to influence; have an impact on (p. 175)	*afectar influir; producir un efecto en algo o alguien (pág. 175)
affirmative action an active effort to improve educational and employment opportunities for minority groups and women (p. 508)	acción afirmativa esfuerzo activo para mejorar las oportunidades educativas y laborales de grupos minoritarios y mujeres (pág. 508)
affluence the state of having much wealth (p. 421)	afluencia estado de poseer mucha riqueza (pág. 421)
Agent Orange a chemical herbicide used to clear jungle growth in the Vietnam War (p. 472)	Agente Naranja herbicida químico usado para detener el crecimiento de la selva en la Guerra de Vietnam (pág. 472)
airlift a system of transporting food and supplies by aircraft into an area otherwise impossible to reach (p. 404)	puente aéreo sistema para transportar alimentos y provisiones con aviones en una zona imposible de alcanzar con otros medios de transporte (pág. 404)
alliance system defense agreements among nations (p. 264)	sistema de alianza acuerdos de defensa entre las naciones (pág. 264)
amend to alter; improve (p. Prologue 36)	enmendar modificar; mejorar (pág. Prologue 36)
amnesty the granting of pardon to a large number of persons; protection from prosecution for an illegal act (pp. 77, 512, 563)	amnistía otorgamiento del perdón a un gran número de personas; protección para no ser procesado por un acto ilegal (págs. 77, 512, 563)
anarchist person who believes that there should be no government (p. 303)	anarquista persona que considera que no deberían existir los gobiernos (pág. 303)
anarchy disorder and lawlessness (p. 251)	anarquía desorden y falta de normas (pág. 251)
*annual yearly (p. 249)	*anual cada año (pág. 249)

anti-Semitism hostility toward or discrimination against Jews (p. 364)

apartheid racial separation and economic and political discrimination against nonwhites, a policy formerly practiced in the Republic of South Africa (p. 518)

appeasement accepting demands in order to avoid conflict (p. 365)

arbitration settling a dispute by agreeing to accept the decision of an impartial outsider (p. 216)

armistice a temporary peace agreement to end fighting (pp. 245, 281)

arms race the competition between the United States and the Soviet Union to build more and more weapons in an effort to surpass the other's military strength (p. 420)

arsenal a storage place for weapons and ammunition (p. 19)

*****aspect** category, feature, or part (p. 453)

assembly line a system with machines and workers arranged so that each person performs an assigned task again and again as items pass before him or her (p. 151)

*****assign** appoint (p. 439)

assimilate to absorb a group into the culture of a larger population (p. 174)

*****assure** to promise (p. 416)

attitude way of thinking and acting (p. 175)

*****authority** power to decide; power to give orders and make decisions (p. 485)

autocracy government in which one person has unlimited power (p. 274)

*****aware** mindful; to have knowledge of (p. 561)

antisemitismo hostilidad o discriminación hacia los judíos (pág. 364)

apartheid separación racial y discriminación política y económica contra las personas de color, política que se practicaba anteriormente en la República de Sudáfrica (pág. 518)

pacificación aceptación de las exigencias para evitar conflictos (pág. 365)

arbitraje resolver una disputa acordando aceptar la decisión de una persona imparcial (pág. 216)

armisticio acuerdo de paz temporal para poner fin a las guerras (págs. 245, 281)

carrera armamentista competencia entre Estados Unidos y la Unión Soviética para construir cada vez más armas con el fin de superar la fortaleza militar de la otra nación (pág. 420)

arsenal lugar para el almacenaje de armas y municiones (pág. 19)

*****aspecto** categoría, característica o componente (pág. 453)

línea de ensamblaje sistema con maquinaria y trabajadores dispuestos de tal manera que cada persona realiza una tarea asignada una y otra vez a medida que pasan los artículos frente a ellos (pág. 151)

*****asignar** designar (pág. 439)

asimilar absorber a un grupo dentro de la cultura de una población más grande (pág. 174)

*****garantizar** prometer (pág. 416)

actitud forma de pensar o actuar (pág. 175)

*****autoridad** poder para decidir; poder para dar órdenes y tomar decisiones (pág. 485)

autocracia gobierno en el que todo el poder se concentra en una persona (pág. 274)

*****conciente** atento; tener conocimiento de (pág. 561)

Glossary/Glosario

B

balance of power the distribution of power among nations so that no single nation can dominate or interfere with another (pp. 264, 501)

bankruptcy the condition of being unable to pay one's debts; one's property is managed or sold to pay those to whom one owes money (p. 539)

barrio a Spanish-speaking neighborhood in a city (p. 226)

equilibrio de poderes distribución de poderes entre las naciones de tal manera que ninguna de las naciones pueda dominar a otra o interferir entre sí (págs. 264, 501)

bancarrota condición en la que una persona no puede pagar sus deudas; la propiedad de una persona se vende o administra con el fin de pagar a las personas a las que le debe dinero (pág. 539)

barrio vecindario de habla hispana en una ciudad (pág. 226) *behalf in the interest of (p. 204)

*bias prejudice; unbalanced view or consideration (p. 223)

black codes laws passed in the South just after the Civil War aimed at controlling freedmen and enabling plantation owners to exploit African American workers (p. 81)

blacklist list of persons who are disapproved of and are punished, such as by being refused jobs (p. 406)

blitzkrieg name given to the sudden, violent offensive attacks the Germans used during World War II; "lightning war" (p. 367)

blockade cut off an area by means of troops or warships to stop supplies or people from coming in or going out; to close off a country's ports (pp. 35, 466)

border ruffian Missourian who traveled in armed groups to vote in Kansas's election during the mid-1850s (p. 13)

border state state between the North and the South that was divided over whether to stay in the Union or join the Confederacy (p. 33)

bounty money given as a reward, such as to encourage enlistment in the army (p. 54)

boycott to refuse to use in order to show disapproval or force acceptance of one's terms (p. 436)

budget deficit the amount by which government spending exceeds revenue (p. 541)

*en nombre de en beneficio de (pág. 204)

*parcialidad prejuicio; punto de vista o consideración tendenciosa (pág. 223)

códigos negros leyes aprobadas en el Sur después de la Guerra Civil que apuntaban al control de los libertos y permitían que los dueños de plantaciones explotaran a los trabajadores afroamericanos (pág. 81)

lista negra lista de personas a las que se rechazaba y castigaba, por ejemplo, al negarles empleos (pág. 406)

blitzkrieg nombre que se da a los ataques repentinos, violentos y ofensivos que los alemanes realizaban durante la Segunda Guerra Mundial; "guerra relámpago" (pág. 367)

bloqueo aislamiento de un área por medio de tropas o barcos de guerra para impedir el ingreso o el egreso de suministros o personas; cierre de los puertos de un país (págs. 35, 466)

rufianes fronterizos hombres de Missouri que viajaban en grupos armados para votar en las elecciones de Kansas a mediados de la década de 1850 (pág. 13)

estado fronterizo estado ubicado entre el Norte y el Sur dividido teniendo en cuenta si formaba parte de la Unión o de la Confederación (pág. 33)

recompensa dinero otorgado como premio, por ejemplo, para incentivar el enrolamiento en el ejército (pág. 54)

boicot negarse a usar algo con el fin de demostrar desaprobación o imponer aceptación de los términos de una persona (pág. 436)

déficit presupuestario monto por el cual el gasto del gobierno excede los ingresos (pág. 541)

capitalism an economic system based on private property and free enterprise (p. 303)

carpetbagger northerner who moved to the South after the Civil War (p. 88)

cash crop farm crop raised to be sold for money (p. 97)

casualty a military person killed, wounded, or captured (p. 41)

censure to express formal disapproval of some action (p. 407)

*challenge demanding situation (p. 37)

*civil relating to citizens as individuals (p. 433)

capitalismo sistema económico basado en la propiedad privada y en la libre empresa (pág. 303)

carpetbagger norteño que se trasladó al Sur después de la Guerra Civil (pág. 88)

cultivo comercial producto agrícola que se vende por dinero (pág. 97)

víctima persona del ejército asesinada, herida o capturada (pág. 41)

censurar expresar la desaprobación formal de alguna acción (pág. 407)

*desafiar situación difícil (pág. 37)

*civil relativo a ciudadanos como individuos (pág. 433)

civil defense protective measures taken in case of attack (p. 375)

civil disobedience refusal to obey laws that are considered unjust as a nonviolent way to press for changes (p. 437)

civil war conflict between citizens of the same country (p. 13)

closed shop a workplace in which the employer by agreement hires only union members (p. 411)

coalition a group united for action (p. 537)

cold war a struggle over political differences between nations carried on by methods short of war (p. 404)

*__collapse__ break down (p. 333)

collective bargaining discussion between an employer and union representatives of workers over wages, hours, and working conditions (p. 163)

*__commission__ a group of persons directed to perform some duty (p. 94)

*__communication__ process of exchanging information (p. 234)

*__concentrate__ to focus one's effort on something (p. 379)

concentration camps prison camps used to hold people for political reasons (p. 383)

*__conclude__ decide (p. 417)

concurrent powers powers shared by the states and the federal government (p. Prologue 34)

*__conduct__ to direct the course of (p. 478)

*__conflict__ war or prolonged struggle (p. 390)

conscientious objector person who refuses military service on the basis of moral or religious beliefs (p. 478)

*__consent__ agree to (p. 281)

conservation the protection and preservation of natural resources (p. 217)

*__consist__ make up of (p. 441)

consolidation the practice of combining separate companies into one (p. 143)

*__consult__ to seek opinions or information from (p. 239)

*__consume__ to use (p. 284)

containment the policy or process of preventing the expansion of a hostile power (p. 402)

*__contrast__ large degree of difference (p. 34)

defensa civil medidas protectoras que se toman en caso de ataques (pág. 375)

desobediencia civil rehusarse a obedecer las leyes que se consideran injustas, forma no violenta de exigir cambios (pág. 437)

guerra civil conflicto entre ciudadanos de un mismo país (pág. 13)

empresa cerrada lugar de trabajo en el que el empleador contrata, por acuerdo, sólo a miembros del sindicato (pág. 411)

coalición grupo unificado para la acción (pág. 537)

guerra fría lucha por diferencias políticas entre las naciones llevada a cabo a través de métodos no bélicos (pág. 404)

*__colapsar__ derrumbar (pág. 333)

negociación colectiva discusión entre un empleador y los representantes del sindicato de los trabajadores acerca de los sueldos, las horas y las condiciones de trabajo (pág. 163)

*__comisión__ grupo de personas dirigidas para realizar tareas (pág. 94)

*__comunicación__ proceso de intercambio de información (pág. 234)

*__concentrar__ dirigir los esfuerzos a algo (pág. 379)

campos de concentración campos de prisión usados para retener a las personas por razones políticas (pág. 383)

*__llegar a una conclusión__ decidir (pág. 417)

poderes concurrentes poderes compartidos por los estados y el gobierno federal (pág. Prologue 34)

*__conducir__ dirigir el curso de (pág. 478)

*__conflicto__ guerra o lucha prolongada (pág. 390)

objetor de conciencia persona que se rehúsa al servicio militar por creencias religiosas o morales (pág. 478)

*__consentir__ aceptar (pág. 281)

conservación protección y preservación de los recursos naturales (pág. 217)

*__consistir__ estar compuesto de (pág. 441)

consolidación práctica de combinar diferentes compañías en una (pág. 143)

*__consultar__ buscar opiniones o infor mación de (pág. 239)

*__consumir__ usar (pág. 284)

contención política o proceso de prevención de la expansión de un poder hostil (pág. 402)

*__contraste__ amplio grado de diferencia (pág. 34)

*controversy arguments between opposing viewpoints (p. 512)

*convince to persuade (someone) that something is true (p. 81)

convoy a group that travels with something, such as a ship, to protect it (p. 277)

*cooperate work together (p. 402)

cooperative store where farmers bought products from each other; an enterprise owned and operated by those who use its services (p. 133)

corporation a business in which investors own shares (p. 154)

corruption dishonest or illegal actions (p. 88)

counterculture a social movement whose values go against those of established society (p. 477)

counterterrorism military or political activities intended to combat terrorism (p. 551)

*create to form; to make (p. 133)

credibility gap lack of belief; a term used to describe the lack of trust in the Johnson administration's statements about the Vietnam War (p. 479)

*credit a form of loan; ability to buy goods based on future payment (p. 88)

*currency metal coins and paper notes used as money (p. 135)

*controversia argumentos entre puntos de vista opuestos (pág. 512)

*convencer persuadir (a alguien) de que algo es verdadero (pág. 81)

convoy grupo que viaja con algo, como un barco, para protegerlo (pág. 277)

*cooperar trabajar en conjunto (pág. 402)

cooperativa tienda en la que los agricultores compraban productos entre sí; empresa que es propiedad de aquellos que utilizan sus servicios y es operada por ellos (pág. 133)

corporación empresa en la que los inversores tienen acciones (pág. 154)

corrupción acciones ilegales o deshonestas (pág. 88)

contracultura movimiento social cuyos valores van en contra de aquellos establecidos por la sociedad (pág. 477)

contraterrorismo actividades políticas o militares dirigidas a combatir el terrorismo (pág. 551)

*crear construir; confeccionar (pág. 133)

brecha de credibilidad falta de creencias; término utilizado para describir la falta de confianza en las declaraciones de la administración de Johnson acerca de la Guerra de Vietnam (pág. 479)

*crédito una forma de préstamo; capacidad de comprar bienes en función de un pago futuro (pág. 88)

*moneda monedas de metal y billetes usados como dinero (pág. 135)

D

*decade a period of ten years (p. 559)

*decline descend (p. 332)

default to fail to meet an obligation, especially a financial one (p. 333)

deferment an excuse, issued by the draft board, that lets a person be excused from military service for various reasons (p. 478)

deficit the shortage that occurs when spending is greater than income (p. 509)

deficit spending the government spending more money than it takes in (p. 541)

*definite precise or well-defined (p. 555)

demilitarized zone a region where no military forces or weapons are permitted (p. 417)

*década período de diez años (pág. 559)

*decaer declinar (pág. 332)

incumplimiento no cumplir con una obligación, especialmente del tipo financiero (pág. 333)

prórroga excusa, emitida por la junta de reclutamietno que le permite a una persona excusarse del servicio militar por diferentes motivos (pág. 478)

déficit carencia que se produce cuando el gasto es mayor que el ingreso (pág. 509)

gastos déficitarios el gobierno gasta más dinero que el que tiene (pág. 541)

*definitivo decisivo o bien definido (pág. 555)

zona desmilitarizada región donde se prohíben fuerzas o armas militares (pág. 417) *demonstration a protest march (p. 486)

*deny not allow access to (p. 222)

deport to send out of a country aliens who are considered dangerous (pp. 303, 563)

deregulation the act of cutting the restrictions and regulations that government places on business (p. 530)

desegregate to end the practice of separating or isolating people of different races (p. 413)

*detect uncover or discover the true character of (p. 310)

détente a policy which attempts to relax or ease tensions between nations (p. 501)

*device instrument or piece of equipment (p. 317)

dictator a leader who rules with total authority, often in a cruel or brutal manner (p. 363)

*dimension aspect; one element or factor among many (p. 267)

*diminish to lessen the authority, dignity, or reputation of (p. Prologue 41)

disarmament removal of weapons (p. 370)

*discriminate to treat unfairly (p. 433)

discrimination unfair treatment of a group; unequal treatment because of a person's race, religion, ethnic background, or place of birth (pp. 221, 433)

dissent disagreement with or opposition to an opinion (p. 285)

*distribute give out (p. 51)

*diverse differing from one another (p. 454)

dividend a stockholder's share of a company's profits, usually as a cash payment (p. 154)

dollar diplomacy a policy of joining the business interests of a country with its diplomatic interests abroad (p. 252)

*domestic home-based, internal (p. 410)

downsize the practice of companies laying off workers to become more efficient and to increase their earnings (p. 539)

draft the selection of persons for military service (p. 54)

dry farming a way of farming dry land in which seeds are planted deep in ground where there is some moisture (p. 123)

*dynamic active and energetic (p. 305)

*demonstración una marcha de protesta (pág. 486)

*negar no permitir el acceso a (pág. 222)

deportar sacar del país a los extranjeros que son considerados peligrosos (págs. 303, 563)

desregulación acción de reducir las restricciones y las regulaciones que el gobierno impone en el comercio (pág. 530)

abolicir de la segregación terminar de la práctica de separación o aislamiento de personas de diferentes razas (pág. 413)

*detectar revelar o descubrir el carácter real de (pág. 310)

détente política que se dirige a distender o aliviar las tensiones entre las naciones (pág. 501)

*dispositivo instrumento o pieza de un equipo (pág. 317)

dictador líder que gobierna con autoridad total, en general de forma atroz y cruel (pág. 363)

*dimensión aspecto; elemento o factor entre varios (pág. 267)

*aminorar disminuir la autoridad, la dignidad o la reputación de (pág. Prologue 41)

desarme eliminación de las armas (pág. 370)

*discriminar tratar injustamente (pág. 433)

discriminación trato injusto de un grupo; trato desigual debido a la raza, la religión, el origen étnico o el lugar de nacimiento de una persona (págs. 221, 433)

disentimiento desacuerdo con una opinión u oposición a ésta (pág. 285)

*distribuir repartir (pág. 51)

*diverso que difieren entre sí (pág. 454)

dividendo parte de las ganancias de una empresa de un accionista, en general en forma de pago en efectivo (pág. 154)

diplomacia del dólar política que une los intereses comerciales de un país con sus intereses diplomáticos en el extranjero (pág. 252)

*nacional hecho en el país, interno (pág. 410)

reducción de personal práctica de las compañías que despiden trabajadores para aumentar su eficacia y sus ganancias (pág. 539)

llamamiento a filas selección de personas para el servicio militar (pág. 54)

agricultura de secano método de cultivar la tierra seca con el que se plantan las semillas en la profundidad de la tierra, donde reciben humedad (pág. 123)

*dinámico activo y vigoroso (pág. 305)

Glossary/Glosario

E

*economy system of production, distribution, and consumption (p. 421)

*eliminate to remove; to eradicate; to end (p. 249)

embargo an order prohibiting trade with another country (p. 504)

*emerge to rise up (p. 448)

emigrate to leave one's place of residence or country to live somewhere else (p. 171)

*encounter to come upon; meet (p. 60)

*energy source of usable power (p. 510)

*enormous huge (p. 318)

*ensure make certain (p. 125)

entrenched occupying a strong defensive position (p. 57)

enumerated powers powers belonging only to the federal government (p. Prologue 34)

*environment the complex of physical, chemical, and biotic factors that surround living organisms (p. 163)

*equip furnish; provide with (p. 267)

escalate to increase or expand (p. 471)

espionage spying (p. 406)

ethnic group a minority that speaks a different language or follows different customs than the majority of people in a country (p. 172); people who share a common language and traditions (p. 263)

*eventual occurring later (p. 247)

evolution the scientific theory that humans and other living things have evolved over time (p. 321)

*exceed to be greater; to go beyond (p. 517)

*exclude shut out (p. 481)

executive order a rule issued by a chief executive that has the force of law (p. 464)

executive privilege President Nixon's belief that all White House conversations should be kept secret to protect national security (p. 511)

expansionism a policy that calls for expanding a nation's boundaries (p. 233)

expatriate a person who gives up his or her home country and chooses to live in another country (p. 319)

*expert person with advanced knowledge on a particular subject (p. 313)

*economía sistema de producción, distribución y consumo (pág. 421)

*eliminar sacar; erradicar; terminar (pág. 249)

embargo una orden que prohíbe el comercio con otro país (pág. 504)

*surgir aflorar (pág. 448)

emigrar dejar el lugar de residencia o el país para vivir en otro lugar (pág. 171)

*encuentro topar con; reunirse con (pág. 60)

*energía fuente de alimentación útil (pág. 510)

*enorme inmenso (pág. 318)

*asegurar garantizar (pág. 125)

atrincherado que ocupa una fuerte posición defensiva (pág. 57)

poderes enumerados poderes que pertenecen sólo al gobierno federal (pág. Prologue 34)

*medio ambiente complejo de factores físicos, químicos y bióticos que rodean a los organismos vivos (pág. 163)

*equipar abastecer; ofrecer (pág. 267)

escalar aumentar o expandir (pág. 471)

espionaje infiltración (pág. 406)

grupo étnico minoría que habla un idioma diferente o sigue diferentes costumbres que la mayoría de las personas en un país (pág. 172); personas con un idioma y tradiciones en común (pág. 263)

*final que ocurre después (pág. 247)

evolución teoría científica que sostiene que los seres humanos y otras formas de vida evolucionaron con el paso del tiempo (pág. 321)

*exceder sobrepasar; ir más allá (pág. 517)

*excluir negar la entrada (pág. 481)

orden ejecutiva regla establecida por un jefe ejecutivo con fuerza de ley (pág. 464)

privilegio ejecutivo creencia del Presidente Nixon acerca de que las conversaciones de la Casa Blanca debían mantenerse en secreto para proteger la seguridad nacional (pág. 511)

expansionismo política que solicita la expansión de las fronteras de una nación (pág. 233)

expatriado persona que se retira de su país de origen y decide vivir en otro país (pág. 319)

*experto persona con conocimientos avanzados sobre un tema particular (pág. 313)

Glossary/Glosario

*exploit to make use of meanly or unjustly for one's own advantage (p. 240)

export to sell goods abroad (p. 35)

*extract to remove, usually by force (p. 111)

*explotar hacer uso mezquino o injusto de las cosas para el beneficio propio (pág. 240)

exportar vender bienes en el exterior (pág. 35)

*extraer quitar, en general por la fuerza (pág. 111)

F

*factor contributing circumstance (p. 121)

fascism a political system, headed by a dictator, that calls for extreme nationalism and racism and no tolerance of opposition (p. 363)

fascist a person with extremely nationalistic views (p. 348)

federal debt the amount of money owed by the government (p. 531)

federalism the sharing of power between federal and state governments (p. Prologue 34)

feminist a person who advocates or is active in promoting women's rights (p. 453)

final last, ultimate (p. 288)

flapper a young woman of the 1920s who defied conventions in her behavior and dress (p. 317)

flexible response a plan that used special military units to fight guerrilla wars (p. 463)

free trade the absence of trade barriers so that goods flow freely among countries (p. 560)

fugitive running away or trying to run away (p. 9)

*fund source of money (p. 371)

fundamentalist a person who believes in the literal meaning of religious texts and follows strict obedience to religious laws (pp. 520, 550)

*factor circunstancia que contribuye (pág. 121)

fascismo sistema político, encabezado por un dictador, que establece nacionalismo y racismo extremos sin permitir la oposición (pág. 363)

fascista persona con puntos de vista extremadamente nacionalistas (pág. 348)

deuda federal cantidad de dinero que debe un gobierno (pág. 531)

federalismo posesión conjunta del poder entre los gobiernos centrales y estatales (pág. Prologue 34)

feminista persona que defiende los derechos de la mujer o participa en su promoción (pág. 453)

final último (pág. 288)

joven moderna mujer joven de la década de 1920 que desafiaba las convenciones en su conducta y forma de vestir (pág. 317)

respuesta flexible plan que usaba unidades militares especiales para pelear en guerras de guerrillas (pág. 463)

libre comercio ausencia de barreras comerciales de modo que los bienes circulan libremente entre los países (pág. 560)

fugitivo que se fuga o está tratando de fugarse (pág. 9)

*fondo fuente de dinero (pág. 371)

*fundamentalista persona que cree en el significado literal de los textos religiosos y obedece estrictamente las leyes religiosas (págs. 520, 550)

G

*generate create (p. 340)

genocide the deliberate destruction of a racial, political, or cultural group (p. 383)

globalism the idea that the world's economies and societies are all part of one big system (p. 559)

global warming a steady increase in average world temperatures (p. 562)

*generar crear (pág. 340)

genocidio destrucción deliberada de un grupo racial, político o cultural (pág. 383)

globalismo idea de que las economías y las sociedades de todo el mundo forman parte de un gran sistema (pág. 559)

calentamiento global aumento continuo de las temperaturas promedio en el mundo (pág. 562)

grandfather clause a clause that allowed individuals who did not pass the literacy test to vote if their fathers or grandfathers had voted before Reconstruction began; an exception to a law based on preexisting circumstances (p. 97)

grassroots movement people at the local level organizing for political action (p. 541)

greenback a piece of U.S. paper money first issued by the North during the Civil War (p. 55)

gross domestic product the value of all the goods and services produced in a nation during a one-year period (p. 543)

gross national product the total value of all goods and services produced by a nation's residents during a year, regardless of where production takes place (p. 313)

guerrilla warfare a hit-and-run technique used in fighting a war; fighting by small bands of warriors using tactics such as sudden ambushes (p. 463)

cláusula del abuelo cláusula que permitía que los individuos que no aprobaban la prueba de alfabetización pudieran votar si sus padres o abuelos habían votado antes de que se iniciara la Reconstrucción; una excepción a la ley basada en circunstancias preexistentes (pág. 97)

movimiento de las bases personas en una comunidad que se organizan para la acción política (pág. 541)

verdes billete estadounidense emitido por primera vez por el Norte durante la Guerra Civil (pág. 55)

producto interno bruto valor de todos los bienes y servicios producidos por una nación en un año (pág. 543)

producto nacional bruto valor total de bienes y servicios producidos por los residentes de una nación en un año, independientemente del lugar donde se realiza la producción (pág. 313)

guerra de guerrillas técnica de golpear y huir que se usaba para pelear una guerra; lucha de pequeños grupos de guerreros que usaban tácticas como emboscadas repentinas (pág. 463)

habeas corpus a legal order for an inquiry to determine whether a person has been lawfully imprisoned (p. 53)

Holocaust the name given to the mass slaughter of Jews and other groups by the Nazis during World War II (p. 383)

homestead to acquire a piece of U.S. public land by living on and cultivating it (p. 121)

Hull House settlement house founded by Jane Addams in Chicago in 1889 (p. 181)

human rights rights regarded as belonging to all persons, such as freedom from unlawful imprisonment, torture, and execution (p. 518)

hábeas corpus orden legal para una indagación con el fin de determinar si una persona ha sido arrestada injustamente (pág. 53)

holocausto nombre que se le dio a la masacre de judíos y otros grupos por parte de los nazis durante la Segunda Guerra Mundial (pág. 383)

cesión de tierras adquirir una porción de tierra pública de Estados Unidos al habitarla o cultivarla (pág. 121)

Hull House casa de asistencia social fundada por Jane Addams en Chicago en 1889 (pág. 181)

derechos humanos derechos que pertenecen a todas las personas, como la libertad de arresto injusto, tortura y ejecución (pág. 518)

I

*****identify** recognize (p. 162)

*****impact** effect or influence (p. 45)

impeach to formally charge a public official with misconduct in office (pp. 85, 511)

imperialism the actions used by one nation to exercise political or economic control over smaller or weaker nations (p. 234)

*****identificar** reconocer (pág. 162)

*****impacto** efecto o influencia (pág. 45)

impugnar denunciar formalmente a un funcionario público por mala conducta en el desempeño de su cargo (págs. 85, 511)

imperialismo medidas tomadas por una nación para ejercer el control político o económico sobre una nación más pequeña o más débil (pág. 234)

implied powers powers not specifically mentioned in the Constitution (p. Prologue 37)

*individual person (p. 143)

*inevitable unavoidable (p. 13)

inflation a continuous rise in the price of goods and services (pp. 55, 409)

initiative the right of citizens to place a measure or issue before the voters or the legislature for approval (p. 205)

injunction a court order to stop an action, such as a strike (p. 164)

inspect to examine carefully (p. 216)

installment buying a system of paying for goods in which customers promise to pay small, regular amounts over a period of time (p. 314)

insurgent a person who revolts against civil authority; rebel (p. 552)

integrate to end separation of different races and bring into equal membership in society (pp. 89, 434)

*integrity moral character (p. 517)

*intelligence the ability to understand and use knowledge (p. 209)

interdependent rely on one another (p. 559)

internment camp detention center where Japanese Americans were moved to and confined during World War II (p. 377)

interstate across state lines; connecting or existing between two or more states (p. 444)

*intervene to involve oneself in the affairs of another (p. 311)

*involve include (p. Prologue 39)

iron curtain the political and military barrier that isolated Soviet-controlled countries of Eastern Europe after World War II (p. 402)

ironclad armored naval vessel (p. 41)

island hopping a strategy used during World War II that called for attacking and capturing certain key islands and using these islands as bases to leapfrog to others (p. 388)

*isolate cut off or separate (p. 186)

isolationism a national policy of avoiding involvement in world affairs (pp. 233, 311)

isthmus a narrow strip of land connecting two larger land areas (p. 249)

poderes implícitos poderes no mencionados específicamente en la Constitución (pág. Prologue 37)

*individuo persona (pág. 143)

*inevitable ineludible (pág. 13)

inflación aumento continuo en el precio de los bienes y los servicios (págs. 55, 409)

iniciativa derecho de los ciudadanos de presentar una medida o un problema ante los votantes o la asamblea legislativa para su aprobación (pág. 205)

prohibición judicial orden judicial para detener una acción, como una huelga (pág. 164)

inspeccionar examinar cuidadosamente (pág. 216)

compra a plazos sistema de pago de bienes en el que los clientes prometen pagar pequeños montos en forma regular durante un período (pág. 314)

insurgente persona que inicia una rebelión contra la autoridad civil; rebelde (pág. 552)

integrar terminar la separación de diferentes razas e implantar la pertenencia igualitaria en la sociedad (págs. 89, 434)

*integridad carácter moral (pág. 517)

*inteligencia capacidad de comprender y aprovechar el conocimiento (pág. 209)

interdependientes que confían unos en otros (pág. 559)

campo de internamiento centro de detención donde los estadounidenses japoneses fueron trasladados y confinados durante la Segunda Guerra Mundial (pág. 377)

interestatal a lo largo de las líneas estatales; que conecta dos o más estados o se encuentra entre ellos (pág. 444)

*intervenir involucrarse en los asuntos de otros (pág. 311)

*implicar incluir (pág. Prologue 39)

cortina de hierro barrera política y militar que aislaba a los países controlados por la Unión Soviética de Europa Oriental después de la Segunda Guerra Mundial (pág. 402)

acorazado barco naval blindado (pág. 41)

ir de isla en isla estrategia usada durante la Segunda Guerra Mundial que consistía en el ataque y la captura de ciertas islas clave y el uso de estas islas como bases para pasar por encima a otras (pág. 388)

*aislar apartar o separar (pág. 186)

aislacionismo política nacional de evitar la participación en asuntos mundiales (págs. 233, 311)

istmo franja angosta de tierra que conecta a dos superficies más grandes (pág. 249)

Glossary/Glosario

jazz American music developed from ragtime and blues with African rhythms (p. 190)

*justify find reason to support (p. 22)

jazz música estadounidense desarrollada a partir del ragtime y el blues con ritmos africanos (pág. 190)

*justificar encontrar razones para apoyar (pág. 22)

kaiser emperor; the leader of Germany from 1871 to 1918 (p. 281)

kamikaze during World War II, a Japanese suicide pilot whose mission was to crash into his target (p. 388)

káiser emperador; líder de Alemania de 1871 a 1918 (pág. 281)

kamikaze en la Segunda Guerra Mundial, piloto suicida japonés cuya misión consistía en estrellarse contra su objetivo (pág. 388)

L

*labor to work (p. 143)

land-grant college originally, an agricultural college established as a result of the 1862 Morrill Act that gave states large amounts of federal land that could be sold to raise money for education (p. 186)

Latino American who has come to the United States from or is descended from people who came from Latin America or Spain (p. 454)

lease to hand over property in return for rent (p. 309)

levee high walls or an embankment to prevent flooding in low-lying areas (p. 555)

literacy test a method used to prevent African Americans from voting by requiring prospective voters to read and write at a specified level (p. 97)

*locate establish (p. 119)

Long Drive the herding of cattle for 1,000 miles or more to meet the railroad (p. 119)

lynching putting to death a person by the illegal action of a mob (p. 98)

*trabajar obrar (pág. 143)

universidad con dotación de tierras federales originalmente, una universidad de agricultura fundada como resultado de la Ley de Morrill de 1862 que le otorgó a los estados grandes cantidades de tierras federales que podían venderse con el fin de reunir dinero para la educación (pág. 186)

latino americano que se trasladó a los Estados Unidos y que es descendiente de personas que provienen de América Latina o España (pág. 454)

alquilar entregar una propiedad a cambio de una paga (pág. 309)

dique muros altos o terraplén para evitar inundaciones en áreas de baja altura (pág. 555)

prueba de alfabetización método usado para impedir que los afroamericanos votaran al exigirles a los votantes futuros un nivel específico de lectura y escritura (pág. 97)

*ubicar situar (pág. 119)

larga marcha pastoreo de ganado durante 1,000 millas o más hasta llegar al ferrocarril (pág. 119)

linchamiento muerte de una persona por la acción ilegal de una banda (pág. 98)

M

*major greater in size, extent, or importance (p. 179)

martial law the law applied by military forces in occupied territory or in an emergency (p. 487)

martyr a person who sacrifices his or her life for a principle or cause (p. 19)

mass media types of communication that reach large numbers of people, such as newspapers, radio, and television (p. 317)

mass production the production of large quantities of goods using machinery and often an assembly line (p. 151)

materialism attaching too much importance to physical possessions and comforts (p. 424)

*mechanism mechanical device (p. 150)

Medicaid a social program that gives the states money to help those who cannot afford to pay for their hospital bills (p. 441)

Medicare a social program that helps pay for medical care for the elderly (p. 441)

merger the combining of two or more businesses into one (p. 157)

MIAs soldiers classified as missing in action (p. 490)

migrant worker a person who moves from place to place to find work harvesting fruits and vegetables (p. 346)

*migrate relocate (p. 346)

militarism a buildup of military strength within a country (p. 264)

*minor lesser in size, extent, or importance (p. 181)

mobilization gathering resources and preparing for war (pp. 283, 373)

Model T America's first mass production car made by the Ford Motor Company (p. 151)

monopoly total control of a type of industry by one person or one company (p. 155)

muckraker a journalist who uncovers abuses and corruption in a society (p. 205)

*mutualista Mexican American self-defense group (p. 226)

*principal de mayor tamaño, grado o importancia (pág. 179)

ley marcial ley aplicada por las fuerzas militares en un territorio ocupado o en un caso de emergencia (pág. 487)

mártir persona que sacrifica su vida por un principio o una causa (pág. 19)

medios masivos de información tipos de comunicación que llegan a un gran número de personas, como los periódicos, la radio y la televisión (pág. 317)

producción en serie producción de grandes cantidades de bienes usando maquinaria y a veces una línea de montaje (pág. 151)

materialismo otorgarle mucha importancia a posesiones físicas y comodidades (pág. 424)

*mecanismo dispositivo mecánico (pág. 150)

Medicaid programa social que le otorga al estado dinero para ayudar a las personas que no pueden pagar sus gastos hospitalarios (pág. 441)

Medicare programa social que ayuda a pagar la atención médica de los ancianos (pág. 441)

fusión empresarial combinación de dos o más negocios en uno (pág. 157)

MIAs (Desaparecidos en Acción) soldados clasificados como desaparecidos en acción (pág. 490)

trabajador migratorio persona que se traslada de un lugar a otro para buscar trabajo en el cultivo de frutas y vegetales (pág. 346)

*migrar cambiar de sitio (pág. 346)

militarismo creación de fortaleza militar en un país (pág. 264)

*inferior de menor tamaño, grado o importancia (pág. 181)

movilización reunión de recursos y preparación para la guerra (págs. 283, 373)

Modelo T primer automóvil estadounidense de producción masiva fabricado por la Ford Motor Company (pág. 151)

monopolio control total de un tipo de industria por una persona o una compañía (pág. 155)

sensacionalista periodista que revela abusos y corrupción en una sociedad (pág. 205)

mutualista grupo de autodefensa Mexicano-estadounidense (pág. 226)

Glossary/Glosario

napalm an explosive material dropped from airplanes during the Vietnam War (p. 472)

National Grange the first farmers' organization in the United States (p. 133)

nationalism intense loyalty to one's nation or group and promotion of its interests above all others (p. 263)

national self-determination the right of people to decide how they should be governed (p. 287)

nativism the belief that those born in a country are superior to immigrants (p. 320)

*****network** an interconnected system of people or things (p. 11)

*****nevertheless** however (p. 59)

nomadic moving from place to place with no permanent home (p. 125)

*****normal** typical or average (p. 303)

*****nuclear** atomic (p. 420)

napalm material explosivo arrojado desde los aviones durante la Guerra de Vietnam (pág. 472)

Agricultores Nacionales primera organización de agricultores en Estados Unidos (pág. 133)

nacionalismo lealtad intensa a una nación o a un grupo y promoción de los intereses por encima de todos (pág. 263)

autodeterminación nacional derecho de las personas a decidir cómo deben ser gobernadas (pág. 287)

nativismo creencia acerca de que las personas nacidas en un país son superiores a los inmigrantes (pág. 320)

*****red** sistema interconectado de personas o cosas (pág. 11)

*****no obstante** sin embargo (pág. 59)

nómada trasladarse de un lugar a otro sin hogar fijo (pág. 125)

*****normal** típico o promedio (pág. 303)

*****nuclear** atómico (pág. 420)

*****obtain** to gain (p. 364)

*****occur** to take place (p. 465)

oligopoly market in which a few large companies control prices for an industry (p. 203)

*****outcome** result (p. 94)

override to overturn or defeat, as a bill proposed in Congress (p. 82)

*****overseas** across the ocean (p. 374)

*****obtener** lograr (pág. 364)

*****suceder** que tiene lugar (pág. 465)

oligopolio mercado en el que unas pocas compañías grandes controlan los precios para una industria (pág. 203)

*****resultado** desenlace (pág. 94)

anular revocar o derrotar, como un proyecto de ley propuesto en el Congreso (pág. 82)

*****extranjero** del otro lado del océano (pág. 374)

P

pacifist person opposed to the use of war or violence to settle disputes (p. 285)

*****partner** associate who agrees to operate a business with another (p. 155)

pension a sum paid regularly to a person, usually after retirement (p. 353)

*****perceive** to recognize; understand (p. 285)

pacifista persona que se opone al uso de guerras o violencia para solucionar conflictos (pág. 285)

*****socio** persona que acepta operar un negocio con otra (pág. 155)

pensión monto pagado a una persona de forma regular, en general después de su retiro (pág. 353)

*****percibir** reparar; entender (pág. 285)

perjury lying when one has sworn an oath to tell the truth (pp. 407, 543)

*philosophy a set of ideas and beliefs (p. 185)

poll tax a tax of a fixed amount per person that had to be paid before the person could vote (p. 97)

pool a group sharing in some activity, for example, among railroad barons who made secret agreements and set rates among themselves (p. 145)

popular sovereignty political theory that government is subject to the will of the people (p. Prologue 33); before the Civil War, the idea that people living in a territory had the right to decide by voting if slavery would be allowed there (p. 12)

*pose to present (p. 403)

poverty line a level of personal or family income below which one is classified as poor according to government standards (p. 441)

preamble the introduction to a formal document, especially the Constitution (p. Prologue 33)

*primary an election in which voters choose their party's candidates (p. 218)

*prior earlier or before (p. 551)

*proceed continue on (p. 278)

productivity how much work each worker does (p. 313)

*professional occupations requiring special knowledge or education (p. 209)

Prohibition the nationwide ban on the manufacture, sale, and transportation of liquor in the United States that went into effect when the Eighteenth Amendment was ratified in 1919 (pp. 213, 319)

*promote to help advance (p. 340)

propaganda ideas or information designed and spread to influence opinion (p. 271)

protectorate a country that is technically independent, but is actually under the control of another country (p. 246)

provisional government temporary government (p. 238)

public works projects such as highways, parks, and libraries built with public funds for public use (p. 335)

perjurio mentir cuando se juró decir la verdad (págs. 407, 543)

*filosofía conjunto de ideas y creencias (pág. 185)

impuesto de votación impuesto de una cantidad fija por persona que debía pagarse para que una persona pudiera votar (pág. 97)

conjunto grupo que comparte una actividad, por ejemplo, los barones ferroviarios que establecían acuerdos secretos y fijaban sus propias tarifas (pág. 145)

soberanía popular teoría política acerca de que el gobierno está sujeto a la voluntad de las personas (pág. Prologue 33); antes de la Guerra Civil, la idea de que las personas que vivían en un territorio tenían el derecho de decidir por votación si se permitiría la esclavitud en dicho lugar (pág. 12)

*plantear presentar (pág. 403)

línea de pobreza un nivel de ingreso personal o familiar por debajo de lo que la clasificación es pobre de acuerdo con los estándares del gobierno (pág. 441)

preámbulo introducción a un documento formal, especialmente la Constitución (pág. Prologue 33)

*primarias elección en la que los votantes eligen los candidatos de su partido (pág. 218)

*previo anterior o antes (pág. 551)

*proseguir continuar (pág. 278)

productividad cantidad de trabajo que realiza un trabajador (pág. 313)

*profesional ocupaciones que requieren conocimiento o educación especial (pág. 209)

prohibición proscripción nacional en la fabricación, venta, y transporte de licor en Estados Unidos que entró en vigencia cuando la Decimoctava Enmienda fue ratificada en 1919 (págs. 213, 319)

*promover contribuir al avance (pág. 340)

propaganda ideas o información diseñadas y difundidas para influenciar la opinión (pág. 271)

protectorado país teóricamente independiente, pero que en realidad está bajo el control de otro país (pág. 246)

gobierno provisional gobierno temporal (pág. 238)

obras públicas proyectos como autopistas, parques y bibliotecas construidos con fondos públicos para uso público (pág. 335)

Glossary/Glosario

Q

quota system an arrangement placing a limit on the number of immigrants from each country (p. 320)

sistema de cupos un acuerdo que fija un límite en el número de inmigrantes de cada país (pág. 320)

*quote to repeat the words of another (p. 531)

*citar reproducir las palabras de otra persona (pág. 531)

R

*radical extreme (p. 78)

*radical extremo (pág. 78)

ragtime a type of music with a strong rhythm and a lively melody with accented notes, which was popular in early 1900s (p. 190)

ragtime tipo de música con un ritmo intenso y una melodía animada con notas acentuadas, que era popular a principios de los años 1900 (pág. 190)

railroad barons powerful and aggressive businessmen who controlled the nation's railroads (p. 143)

barones ferroviarios empresarios poderosos y agresivos que controlaban los ferrocarriles de la nación (pág. 143)

ration to give out scarce items on a limited basis (pp. 284, 375)

ración producir artículos escasos en un período limitado (págs. 284, 375)

realism an approach to literature and the arts that shows things as they really are (p. 187)

realismo enfoque a la literatura y las artes que muestra las cosas como realmente son (pág. 187)

rebate discount or return of part of a payment (p. 145)

reembolso descuento o devolución de parte de un pago (pág. 145)

recall the right that enables voters to remove elected officials from office (p. 205)

llamar a elecciones derecho que le permite a los votantes destituir a los funcionarios electos de sus puestos (pág. 205)

recession a downward turn in business activity (p. 313)

recesión giro descendiente en la actividad comercial (pág. 313)

Reconstruction the reorganization and rebuilding of the former Confederate states after the Civil War (p. 77)

reconstrucción reorganización y reconstrucción de los antiguos estados de la Confederación después de la Guerra Civil (pág. 77)

referendum the practice of letting voters accept or reject measures proposed by the legislature (p. 205)

referéndum práctica que consiste en permitir que los votantes acepten o rechacen medidas propuestas por la asamblea legislativa (pág. 205)

*regime governing authority (p. 470)

*régimen autoridad del gobierno (pág. 470)

regionalism art or literature focused on a particular region of the country (p. 187)

regionalismo arte o literatura que se centra en una región particular de un país (pág. 187)

*register to enroll (p. 447)

*registrarse inscribirse (pág. 447)

*regulate to control (p. 8)

*regular controlar (pág. 8)

*reject refuse to accept (p. 22)

*rechazar negarse a aceptar (pág. 22)

*relax to ease (p. 501)

*relajar aliviar (pág. 501)

relief aid for the needy; welfare (p. 334)

alivio ayuda para los necesitados; bienestar (pág. 334)

reparations payment by a defeated aggressor nation for damages caused by war (p. 288)

reparaciones pago realizado por una nación agresora derrotada por los daños causados por la guerra (pág. 288)

Glossary/Glosario

republicanism favoring a republic, or representative democracy, as the best form of government (p. Prologue 33)

reservation an area of public lands set aside for Native Americans (p. 126)

reserved powers powers retained by the states (p. Prologue 34)

*****resistance** an opposing force (p. 67)

*****respond** to reply (p. 463)

*****retain** hold onto (p. 535)

revenue sharing money raised from federal taxes and given to the states for use at the state and local levels (p. 507)

*****revolution** a war to overthrow a government (p. 274)

*****rigid** firm and inflexible (p. 16)

republicanismo a favor de un república, o democracia representativa, como mejor forma de gobierno (pág. Prologue 33)

reservación área de tierras públicas reservadas para los nativoamericanos (pág. 126)

poderes reservados poderes conservados por los estados (pág. Prologue 34)

*****resistencia** fuerza opuesta (pág. 67)

*****responder** contestar (pág. 463)

*****retener** quedarse con (pág. 535)

participación en los ingresos dinero recolectado de los impuestos federales y otorgado a los estados para gastos estatales y locales (pág. 507)

*****revolución** guerra para revocar un gobierno (pág. 274)

*****rígido** firme e inflexible (pág. 16)

scalawags name given by former Confederates to Southern whites who supported Republican Reconstruction of the South (p. 87)

*****scheme** a plan (p. 353)

*****scope** range or area (p. 543)

search-and-destroy mission a strategy used in Vietnam in which American forces sought Vietcong and North Vietnamese units to destroy them (p. 472)

secede to leave or withdraw (p. 9)

secession withdrawal from the Union (p. 21)

sectionalism loyalty to a region (p. 7)

*****secure** gain control (p. 388)

segregation the separation or isolation of a race, class, or group (pp. 98, 433)

series a number of like things or events arranged in sequence (p. 65)

settlement house institution located in a poor neighborhood that provided numerous community services such as medical care, child care, libraries, and classes in English (p. 181)

sharecropping system of farming in which a farmer works land for an owner who provides equipment and seeds and receives a share of the crop (p. 89)

shareholder a person who invests in a corporation by buying stock and is a partial owner (p. 154)

*****shift** to move (p. 373)

siege military blockade (pp. 63, 380)

scalawags nombre otorgado por los primeros confederados a los blancos del Sur que apoyaban la Reconstrucción Republicana del Sur (pág. 87)

*****esquema** plan (pág. 353)

*****alcance** rango o área (pág. 543)

misión de búsqueda y destrucción estrategia usada en Vietnam en la que las fuerzas estadounidenses buscaban unidades vietnamitas y vietcong para destruirlas (pág. 472)

separarse abandonar o retirarse (pág. 9)

secesión retiro de la Unión (pág. 21)

seccionalismo lealtad a una región (pág. 7)

*****seguro** que tiene el control (pág. 388)

segregación separación o aislamiento de una raza, clase o grupo (págs. 98, 433)

serie un número de cosas o eventos similares arreglados en secuencia (pág. 65)

casa de beneficencia institución ubicada en un barrio pobre que brindaba diferentes servicios comunitarios como atención médica, atención infantil, bibliotecas, y clases de inglés (pág. 181)

aparcería sistema de agricultura en el que el agricultor trabaja la tierra para un propietario que aporta el equipo y las semillas y recibe una parte de los cultivos (pág. 89)

accionista persona que invierte en una sociedad anónima mediante la compra de acciones y es propietario parcial (pág. 154)

*****cambiar** transferir (pág. 373)

sitio bloqueo militar (págs. 63, 380)

Glossary/Glosario

*site location (p. 537)

sit-in the act of occupying seats or sitting down on the floor of an establishment as a form of organized protest (p. 443)

skyscraper a very tall building (p. 182)

slum poor, crowded, and run-down urban neighborhoods (p. 180)

socialist person who believes industries should be publicly owned and run by the government rather than by private individuals (p. 285)

sodbuster a name given to the Plains farmer (p. 123)

spectator sport sporting event that draws a crowd (p. 189)

sphere of influence section of a country where one foreign nation enjoys special rights and powers (p. 240)

square deal Theodore Roosevelt's promise of fair and equal treatment for all (p. 216)

*stable unchanging (p. 409)

stalemate a situation during a conflict when action stops because both sides are equally powerful and neither will give in (p. 416)

standard gauge the uniform width of 4 feet, 8.5 inches for railroad tracks, adopted during the 1880s (p. 144)

states' rights rights and powers independent of the federal government that are reserved for the states by the Constitution; the belief that states' rights supersede federal rights and law (p. 22)

steerage cramped quarters on a ship's lower decks for passengers paying the lowest fares (p. 172)

stock shares of ownership a company sells in its business which often carry voting power (p. 154)

stock exchange a place where shares in corporations are bought and sold through an organized system (p. 331)

*stress call particular attention to; emphasize (p. 271)

strikebreaker person hired to replace a striking worker in order to break up a strike (p. 164)

subsidy grant of money from the government to a person or a company for an action intended to benefit the public (p. 113)

*substitute replacement (p. 54)

sitio ubicación (pág. 537)

sentada acción de ocupar asientos o sentarse en el piso de un establecimiento como forma de protesta organizada (pág. 443)

rascacielos en edificiò muy alto (pág. 182)

barrio pobre barrios urbanos pobres, superpoblados y destartalados (pág. 180)

socialista persona que cree que las industrias deben ser públicas y estar dirigidas por el gobierno y no por particulares (pág. 285)

rompedor de cesped nombre otorgado al agricultor de Planicies (pág. 123)

deporte espectáculo evento deportivo que atrae a una gran multitud (pág. 189)

esfera de influencia sección de un país donde una nación extranjera goza de derechos y poderes especiales (pág. 240)

trato justo promesa de Theodore Roosevelt de un trato igualitario y justo para todos (pág. 216)

*estable que no se modifica (pág. 409)

estancamiento situación durante un conflicto en la que una acción se detiene porque ambos lados son igualmente poderosos y ninguno se rendirá (pág. 416)

medida estándar ancho uniforme de 4 pies, 8.5 pulgadas para los ferrocarriles durante la década de 1880 (pág. 144)

derechos estatales derechos y poderes independientes del gobierno federal que se reservan para los estados a través de la Constitución; creencia acerca de que los derechos de los estados superan los derechos y las leyes federales (pág. 22)

bodega espacio estrecho en la cubierta inferior de un barco para pasajeros que pagan la tarifa más baja (pág. 172)

acciones participaciones de la propiedad de una compañía que en general cuentan con poder de votación (pág. 154)

bolsa de valores lugar donde las acciones en las sociedades anónimas se compran y se venden a través de un sistema organizado (pág. 331)

*resaltar poner especial atención en; enfatizar (pág. 271)

rompehuelgas persona contratada para reemplazar a un trabajador en huelga con el fin de detener la huelga (pág. 164)

subsidio préstamo de dinero del gobierno a una persona o compañía por una acción cuya intención es beneficiar al público (pág. 113)

*sustituto reemplazo (pág. 54)

suburbs • topic

suburbs residential areas that sprang up close to or surrounding cities as a result of improvements in transportation (p. 180)

subversion an attempt to overthrow a government by persons working secretly from within (p. 406)

suffragist a man or woman who fought for a woman's right to vote (p. 210)

***sum** amount or total (p. 111)

summit a meeting of heads of government (p. 420)

supply-side economics an economic theory that proposes tax cuts as a means of stimulating the economy to produce more goods and services (p. 530)

surplus excess; amount left over after necessary expenses are paid (p. 419)

***suspend** to prevent or bar from carrying out official duties (p. 84)

sweatshop a shop or factory where workers work long hours at low wages under unhealthy conditions (pp. 161, 173)

suburbios áreas residenciales que se extienden cerca o alrededor de las ciudades como resultado de mejoras en el transporte (pág. 180)

subversión intento de derrocar a un gobierno por parte de las personas que trabajan en secreto desde adentro (pág. 406)

sufragista hombre o mujer que lucha por los derechos de las mujeres a votar (pág. 210)

***suma** monto o total (pág. 111)

cumbre reunión de los líderes gubernamentales (pág. 420)

economía del lado de la oferta teoría económica que propone recortes impositivos para estimular la economía con el fin de producir más bienes y servicios (pág. 530)

superávit exceso; cantidad que queda después de pagar los gastos necesarios (pág. 419)

***suspender** detener o prohibir la continuidad de las tareas de un funcionario (pág. 84)

fábrica donde se explota a los obreros tienda o fábrica donde los empleados trabajan muchas horas por salarios bajos y en condiciones insalubres (págs. 161, 173)

***target** an object of attack (p. 367)

***technique** skillful method (p. 313)

***technology** the use of science in commerce and industry (p. 503)

***temporary** not lasting (p. 7)

tenement a building in which several families rent rooms or apartments, often with little sanitation or safety (p. 180)

***tense** anxious or nervous (p. 381)

territory an area that is completely controlled by another country as a colonial possession (p. 246)

terrorism the use of violence by groups against civilians to achieve a political goal (p. 549)

***theme** a subject or topic of a work (p. 532)

tight money policy the practice of raising interest rates to slow personal spending (p. 508)

time zone a geographical region within which the same standard of time is used (p. 115)

***topic** subject of discussion (p. 18)

***objetivo** objeto de ataque (pág. 367)

***técnica** método especializado (pág. 313)

***tecnología** uso de ciencia en el comercio y la industria (pág. 503)

***temporal** que no dura (pág. 7)

inquilinato construcción en la que varias familias alquilan habitaciones o departamentos, en general con escaso saneamiento y seguridad (pág. 180)

***tenso** ansioso o nervioso (pág. 381)

territorio área controlada completamente por otro país como posesión colonial (pág. 246)

terrorismo uso de violencia contra los civiles por parte de grupos para lograr una meta política (pág. 549)

***tema** asunto o temática de un trabajo (pág. 532)

política monetaria restrictiva práctica de aumentar las tasas de interés para bajar el gasto personal (pág. 508)

huso horario región geográfica en la que se usa la misma hora estándar (pág. 115)

***tema** objeto de discusión (pág. 18)

Glossary/Glosario

total war war on all aspects of the enemy's life (p. 65)

totalitarian a political system in which the government suppresses all opposition and controls most aspects of people's lives (p. 364)

*trace follow back to (p. 469)

trade deficit the situation when the value of a country's foreign imports exceeds the value of its exports (pp. 517, 560)

trade union organization of workers with the same trade or skill (p. 162)

transcontinental extending across a continent (p. 113)

*transmit send from one place to another (p. 147)

*trend general direction (p. 157)

tributary a smaller river that flows into a larger river (p. 40)

*trigger to start (p. 244)

trust a combination of firms or corporations formed by a legal agreement, especially to reduce competition (p. 155)

trustbuster someone who breaks up a trust into smaller companies (p. 215)

guerra total guerra en todos los aspectos de la vida del enemigo (pág. 65)

totalitarismo sistema político en el que el gobierno reprime la oposición y controla la mayoría de los aspectos de las vidas de las personas (pág. 364)

*rastrear perseguir (pág. 469)

déficit comercial situación en la que el valor de las importaciones extranjeras de un país exceden el valor de sus exportaciones (págs. 517, 560)

gremio organización de trabajadores con el mismo oficio o destreza (pág. 162)

transcontinental que se extiende a lo largo de un continente (pág. 113)

*transmitir enviar de un lugar a otro (pág. 147)

*tendencia dirección general (pág. 157)

afluente un río más pequeño que desemboca en un río más grande (pág. 40)

*desencadenar iniciar (pág. 244)

sindicación combinación de compañías o sociedades anónimas formadas por un acuerdo legal, en especial para reducir la competencia (pág. 155)

destructor de monopolios persona que divide la empresa en compañías más pequeñas (pág. 215)

U-boat German submarine in World Wars I and II (p. 267)

unemployment insurance payments by the government for a limited period of time to people who have lost their jobs (p. 355)

*unify to join together (p. 365)

urban sprawl the spread of human settlements into natural areas (p. 561)

U-boat (submarino) submarino alemán en la Primera y Segunda Guerra Mundial (pág. 267)

seguro de desempleo pagos del gobierno durante un período limitado a las personas que perdieron sus empleos (pág. 355)

unificar poner juntos (pág. 365)

expansión urbana expansión de los asentamientos humanos en áreas naturales (pág. 561)

vaquero Hispanic ranch hand (p. 120)

vaudeville stage entertainment made up of various acts, such as dancing, singing, comedy, and magic shows (p. 189)

Vietnamization Nixon's policy that called for South Vietnam to take a more active role in fighting the war and for Americans to become less involved (p. 486)

vaquero dueño de un rancho hispano (pág. 120)

vodevil entretenimiento en un escenario que consta de varios actos, como danza, cantos, comedia y espectáculos de magia (pág. 189)

vietnamización política de Nixon que sostenía que Vietnam del Sur debía tener un papel más activo en la guerra y que Estados Unidos debía involucrarse menos (pág. 486)

Glossary/Glosario

vigilantes people who take the law into their own hands (p. 111)

*vision an imagined plan (p. 234)

vigilantes personas que toman la ley en sus propias manos (pág. 111)

*visión plan imaginado (pág. 234)

*welfare standard care; well-being (p. 355)

*widespread far-reaching (p. 127)

work relief programs that gave needy people government jobs (p. 339)

*bienestar atención estándar; saludable (pág. 355)

*generalizado trascendental (pág. 127)

alivio laboral programas en los que se repartieron empleos del gobierno a las personas necesitadas (pág. 339)

yellow journalism writing which exaggerates sensational, dramatic, and gruesome events to attract readers, named for stories that were popular during the late 1800s (p. 158); a type of sensational, biased, and often false reporting (pp. 188, 244)

periodismo amarillo escrito que exagera eventos sensacionalistas, dramáticos y atroces para atraer la atención de los lectores, su nombre proviene de las historias populares a fines de los años 1800 (pág. 158); un tipo de información sensacionalista, parcial, y, en general, falsa (págs. 188, 244)

Glossary/Glosario

Index

The following abbreviations are used in the index: m=map, c=chart, p=photograph or picture, g=graph, crt=cartoon, ptg=painting, q=quote.

A

AAA. *See* Agricultural Adjustment Act (AAA)

Abbott, E.C., *q118*

Abbott, Robert Sengstacke, 304, *p304, q304*

Abernethy, R.L., *q55*

Abilene, Kansas, 118, 119

abolitionists, Prologue 27, 10; bleeding Kansas, 13; Confederacy, opinions of, *q22*; Harper's Ferry, 18, 19; women's rights movement and, 210. *See also* anti-slavery movement

Abu Ghraib prison, 553

ACLU. *See* American Civil Liberties Union (ACLU)

Acoma, the, Prologue 2

Adams, John, Prologue 17, *pPrologue 44,* 593, *p593,* 600

Adams, John Quincy, 593, *p593*

Adams, Samuel, *qPrologue 10,* Prologue 11

Adams, Samuel Hopkins, 204, *q204*

Addams, Jane, 177, 181, *p181, q181,* 209, 211

Adventures of Huckleberry Finn **(Twain),** 187

Adventures of Tom Sawyer, The **(Twain),** 187

AEF. *See* American Expeditionary Force (AEF)

affirmative action, 508

Affluent Society, The **(Galbraith),** 424

Afghanistan, 550–51; Soviet invasion of, 519

AFL. *See* American Federation of Labor (AFL)

Africa: aid to, 464; European colonies in, 263; influence in, 234–35; World War II, 379–80

African Americans: 1948 election, 412; 1976 election, 517; Black Codes, 81–82; Christianity, 87; in the Civil War, 36, 37, 58, *g58, p58–59;* cowboys, 119, *p119;* discrimination against, Prologue 25, 97, 220, 221–25, 275, 279, 376, 433–37; draft riots, 54; educa-

tion of, 185, 186; equal rights for, 224–26; farmers, 134; Fifteenth Amendment, Prologue 58, 74, 85, *c94,* 97, 210; Freedmen's Bank, 89; Freedmen's Bureau, 78, 81–82, 89; Freedmen's schools, 78, *p78,* 81, *p81;* in government, 546; Great Depression, 346–47, 354; Great Migration, 283, 304; Harlem Renaissance, 318–19; Jim Crow Laws, 98; labor unions and, 162, 355; Lincoln assassination, 79; in military, 433; newspapers, 188; Populist Party, 136; prejudice against, 222, 347; railroad workers, 114; Reconstruction, 85, 87; rights of, 81–83, 88, 94–95, 320, 433–37; Sherman's March the Sea, 68; Spanish-American War, 245; urban migration of, *p86–87,* 179, 376, 423; voting rights of, Prologue 9, 82, 84, 86, 136, 413, 447; western settlers, 120, 122; women's clubs, 210; in World War I, *p194–95,* 275, 279, *p279;* in World War II, 375–76, *p375;* writers, 188. *See also* civil rights movement; slavery; slave trade

Agee, James, 349

Agent Orange, 472

Age of Innocence, The **(Wharton),** 187

Agnew, Spiro, 511

Agricultural Adjustment Act (AAA), 340

agriculture: dry farming, 123; during Great Depression, 340; move away from, 153; new methods of, 123; railroads and, 115; Southern, Prologue 25–Prologue 26, 96, *g97;* technology effect on, 179. *See also* farmers

Aguinaldo, Emilio, 245, 247

AIM. *See* American Indian Movement (AIM)

airplanes: Boeing jets, 483; first powered flight, 141, 148–49; Lindbergh flight, 316, 317; in World War I, 266, *p266;* in World War II, *p366–67*

Alabama, 481, 509; civil rights movement in, 443–44; readmission to Union, 84; secession, 22; statehood of, Prologue 20; steel industry in, 96

Alamogordo, New Mexico, 389

Alamo, the, Prologue 23

Alaska, *m234,* 74, 234–35, 510

Albania, 363

Alcatraz Island, 456

alcohol: temperance movement, 212, 213, 223, 319; Eighteenth Amendment, Prologue 58–Prologue 59, 212, 213, 319; Prohibition, Prologue 60; Twenty-first Amendment, Prologue 60, 320

Aldrin, Edwin "Buzz," *q149*

Alger, Horatio, 188

Algeria, 379

Algonquian groups, Prologue 1, Prologue 3

Alianza Hispano-Americo **(Hispanic-American Alliance),** 225, 226

Alien Act, 303

Alien and Sedition Acts, Prologue 17

Ali, Muhammad, *q482,* 483

Alito, Samuel Jr., 554

Allende, Salvador, 505

Allen, Frederick Lewis, 331, *q331*

Allen, Gracie, 349

Alliance for Progress, 464

Allied Powers: World War I, 265–67, 271–72, 274, 277, 279–81, 288–89; World War II, 368–71, 379–85, 390, 403. *See also* World War I; World War II

al-Qaeda, 549–51

Álvarez, Aída, 355, *p355*

Ambrose, Valerie, *q514*

Amendment(s): process of, Prologue 36, Prologue 52. *See also* Constitution of the United States (1787); specific amendments by number

America First Committee, 369

American Civil Liberties Union (ACLU), 321

American Expeditionary Force (AEF), 278–79

American Federation of Labor (AFL), 162–63, 355

American Indian Movement (AIM), 454, 456

American Party, 16

American Protective Association (APA), 221

American Railway Association, 115

American Railway Union, 164

American's Creed, The **(Page),** 612

American Socialist Party, 204

Index

D

Index

Index

Index

Index

Index

S

Index

Index

Index

neutrality policies of, 271–73, *q271*; Nobel Peace Prize of, 261; Pancho Villa, pursuit of, 253; suffrage, 211; tariff reforms, 219; Treaty of Versailles, *p286–87*, 289–90, *q289*; World War I, armistice of, 281, *q281*; World War I, beginning of, 262, 274–75, *q275*; World War I, support for, 284

Winesburg, Ohio **(Anderson),** 319

Winfrey, Oprah, 514

Winkel Tripel Projection, Ref 19, *pRef 19*

Winthrop, Elizabeth, 206–07, *p206*

Winthrop, John, Prologue 7

Wisconsin, 145, 205, 310

Wisconsin Territory, 16

Wizard of Oz, The, 349

Woman's Christian Temperance Union (WCTU), 212

women: African American, 225; Civil War (1861–1865), 50–51; education of, 209; factory workers, 161, 163, 173; first member of Congress, 273, *p273*, *q273*, 275; in government, 354, 209, 546; Harlem Renaissance, 318–19; higher education of, 186; immigrants, 174; labor unions and, 162, 163, 355; in late 1800s, 179, *p208–09*; Native American, 125; rights of, 452, 453; roles, changing of, 209–10; unequal pay, 453, *g453*; voting rights of, Prologue 9, 194, 300, 309, 317; wages of, 310; western settlers, 111, 121, 122; in workforce, 345; World War I, 282, *p282–83*, 283; World War II, *p372–73*, 373, 374, *p374*, 375

Women Appointed for Volunteer Emergency Service (WAVES), 373

Women's Army Corps (WACs), 373, 377

Women's Peace Party, *p270–71*

women's rights movement, Prologue 27

Women's Trade Union League (WTUL), 213

Wood, Grant, 349

Woods, Granville, 150

Woods, Tiger, 515

Woodstock, New York, 483

Woodward, Ellen Sullivan, 345, *q352*

Woolworth Building, 151, 182

Woolworth, F.W., 151

Worcester v. Georgia, 603

Work and Win **(Alger),** 188

Works Progress Administration (WPA), *p342*, 352, *p352–53*, *c353*, 354

World, the, 188, 243

World Trade Center, 548, *p548–49*, 549–50, *p549*

World Trade Organization (WTO), 560

World War I, 262–67, *m278*; alliance system prior to, 263, 264; American neutrality, 271–75; armies, size of, *g271*; beginning of, 265–67, *m265*; Europe after, *m288*; Germany's involvement in, *p262–63*; imperialism and, 263–64; military buildup, 264; military deaths in, *g287*; nationalism prior to, 263; reparations from, 288; sea, on the, 267; Western Front, 278, 280

World War I, U.S. involvement, 260, *p260*; events leading to, 270–75; propaganda for, 271–72, 284, *p284*; public opinion of, 285; rationing during, 284; resources for, 283; support for, 284; workers during, 283

World War II, 360–93; American neutrality, 364; beginning of, 366–69; cost of, 390; dictators, rise of prior to, 363–64; Europe after, *m402*; in Europe and Africa, 378–85, *m380*; events leading to, 362–65; military increases prior to, 367, *c367*, *g367*; in the Pacific, 386–90, *m388*; Tuskegee airmen, 317, 376, *p376*; western front, 367

World War II, U.S. involvement: events leading to, 369–71; minorities, effect on, 375–77; war economy, 373–74; wartime hardships of, 374–75; women, effect on, 375

Wounded Knee, South Dakota, 127, 129, 177, 456

WPA. *See* Works Progress Administration (WPA)

Wright, Orville, 148–49, *p148*

Wright, Richard, 349

Wright, Wilbur, 148–49, *p148, p149*

writ of habeas corpus, 53–54

WTUL. *See* Women's Trade Union League (WTUL)

WTO. *See* World Trade Organization (WTO)

Wyoming: female governor of, 301, 310; internment camps in, 600; statehood, 112; western settlers, 121; women's suffrage in, 437, 211

Yalta, 400, *p400–01*, 401, 403

Yank, Billy, *q37*

yellow journalism, 188, 243–44, 245

Yellow Kid, The **(Outcault),** 177

Yellowstone National Park, 216

Yeltsin, Boris, 536, *q536*

Yemen, 550

yeomen, Prologue 26

Yom Kippur War, 504

York, Alvin, 280

York, Duke of, Prologue 7

Yorktown, battle of, Prologue 13

Yugoslavia, 538, 544

Z

Zhou Enlai, 502

Zimmermann, Arthur, 274

Zimmermann telegram, 260, 274

Zuni, the, Prologue 2

Acknowledgments

Text Acknowledgments

Grateful acknowledgement is given authors, publishers, and agents for permission to reprint the following copyrighted material. Every effort has been made to determine copyright owners. In case of any omissions, the Publisher will be pleased to make suitable acknowledgements in future editions.

206 From *Counting on Grace* by Elizabeth Winthrop, copyright © 2006 by Elizabeth Winthrop. Used by permission of Wendy Lamb Books, an imprint of Random House Children's Books, a division of Random House, Inc.; **325** "The Negro Speaks of Rivers," from *The Collected Poems of Langston Hughes* by Langston Hughes, copyright © 1994 by The Estate of Langston Hughes. Used by permission of Alfred A. Knopf, a division of Random House, Inc.; **325** "Mother to Son," from *The Collected Poems of Langston Hughes* by Langston Hughes, copyright © 1994 by The Estate of Langston Hughes. Used by permission of Alfred A. Knopf, a division of Random House, Inc.; **450** From *The Watsons Go to Birmingham—1963* by Christopher Paul Curtis. Copyright © 1995 by Christopher Paul Curtis. Used by permission of Doubleday, a division of Random House, Inc.; **522** Excerpt from *Taking Sides*, copyright © 1991 by Gary Soto, reprinted by permission of Harcourt, Inc.

Glencoe would like to acknowledge the artists and agencies who participated in illustrating this program: SettingPace; American Artists Reps Inc.; GeoNova LLC.

Photo Credits

Cover (t)Rubberball/JupiterImages; **Cover** (b)Larry Grossman - www.retrovisions.com; **iv** (r)Military and Historical Image Bank; **iv** (l)Omikron/Photo Researchers; **v** (r)The Granger Collection - New York; **v** (l)David J. & Janice L. Frent Collection/CORBIS; **vi** (r)Flip Schulke/CORBIS; **vi** (l)Flip Schulke/CORBIS; **vii** Shannon Stapleton/Reuters/CORBIS; **viii** (tl)The Granger Collection - New York; **viii** (tr)Duomo/CORBIS; **viii** (bl)Paul J. Richards/AFP/Getty Images; **viii** (br)Motoring Picture Library/Alamy; **viii** (c)CORBIS; **ix** (b)Library of Congress - Prints & Photographs Division - LC-USZ62-17300; **ix** (t)Gene Herrick/AP Images; **x** (c)The Granger Collection - New York; **x** (t)Royalty-Free/CORBIS; **x** (b)North Wind Picture Archives; **xii** CORBIS; **xiv** (l)Bettmann/CORBIS; **xiv** (r)AP Images; **Prologue 0** Maya Barnes Johansen / The Image Works; **Prologue 0** Hudson's Bay Company Archives - Provincial Archives of Manitoba; **Prologue 1** Hudson's Bay Company Archives - Provincial Archives of Manitoba; **Prologue 2** Stock Montage - Inc./Alamy Images; **Prologue 3** Stock Montage - Inc./Alamy Images; **Prologue 3** (c)Werner Forman/Topham/The Image Works; **Prologue 3** (l)Werner Forman/Topham/The Image Works; **Prologue 3** (r)The Art Archive/Buffalo Bill Historical Center Cody Wyoming/Mireille Vautier; **Prologue 5** Private Collection - / The Bridgeman Art Library International; **Prologue 6** The Granger Collection - New York; **Prologue 7** The Granger Collection - New York; **Prologue 8** (r)Portrait of Anne Hutchinson (1591-1643) - American School - (20th century) / Schlesinger Library - Radcliffe Institute - Harvard University - / The Bridgeman Art Library; **Prologue 8** (c)SSPL/The Image Works; **Prologue 8** (l)The Art Archive/Lucien Biton Collection Paris / Dagli Orti; **Prologue 9** The Granger Collection - New York; **Prologue 9** The Granger Collection - New York; **Prologue 12** (bkgd)Bettmann/CORBIS; **Prologue 12** (inset)Massachusetts Historical Society - Boston - MA - USA/ The Bridgeman Art Library; **Prologue 14** The Granger Collection - New York; **Prologue 15** The Granger Collection - New York; **Prologue 15** REunion des MusEes Nationaux / Art Resource - NY; **Prologue 16** The Granger Collection - New York; **Prologue 17** Clark Family Collection - William Clark Papers/Missouri Historical Society - St. Louis; **Prologue 18** The Granger Collection - New York; **Prologue 19** The Granger Collection - New York; **Prologue 19** Collection of the New-York Historical Society - USA - / The Bridgeman Art Library International; **Prologue 20** Smithsonian Institution - Washington DC - USA /The Bridgeman Art Library; **Prologue 21** Smithsonian Institution - Washington DC - USA /The Bridgeman Art Library; **Prologue 21** SSPL/The Image Works; **Prologue 22** Woolaroc Museum - Bartlesville - Oklahoma - USA/SuperStock; **Prologue 23** Woolaroc Museum - Bartlesville - Oklahoma - USA/SuperStock; **Prologue 24** (c)Michael T. Sedam/CORBIS; **Prologue 24** (l)From the collection of the Old State House Museum; **Prologue 24** (r)Mormon pioneers pulling handcarts on the long journey to Salt Lake City in 1856 (colour litho) - American School - (20th century) / Private Collection - Peter Newark Western Americana / The Bridgeman Art Library; **Prologue 26** (r)The Granger Collection - New York; **Prologue 26** (r)age fotostock/Superstock; **Prologue 29** CORBIS; **Prologue 31** (t)Bettmann/CORBIS; **Prologue 31** (b)CORBIS; **Prologue 32** Steve Allen/Brand X Pictures/JupiterImages; **Prologue 32** PhotoDisc/Getty Images; **Prologue 32** Mark Wilson/Getty Images; **Prologue 33** Steve Allen/Brand X Pictures/JupiterImages; **Prologue 33** PhotoDisc/Getty Images; **Prologue 33** Mark Wilson/Getty Images; **Prologue 36** Private Collection - Peter Newark American Pictures / The Bridgeman Art Library International; **Prologue 37** Library of Congress; **Prologue 39** Matthew Cavanaugh/epa/CORBIS; **Prologue 42** (t)Bettmann/CORBIS; **Prologue 42** (c)Joe Sohm/Pan America/Jupiter Images; **Prologue 42** (b)Comstock/PunchStock; **Prologue 44** White House Historical Association; **Prologue 45** Herminio Rodriguez/AP Images; **Prologue 46** Bettmann/CORBIS; **Prologue 48** (t)Boltin Picture Library; **0** Dave King/Dorling Kindersley/DK Images; **0** Bettmann/CORBIS; **1** Bettmann/CORBIS; **4** (3)White House Historical Association; **4** (4)White House Historical Association; **4** (5)White House Historical Association; **4** (6)White House Historical Association; **4** (7)White House Historical Association; **4** (l to r - t to b)Library of Congress - Washington DC/Bridgeman Art Library; **4** (2)Lee Snider/Photo Images/CORBIS; **4** (8)SuperStock; **5** (1)White House Historical Association; **5** (2)White House Historical Association; **5** (3)White House Historical Association; **5** (l to r - t to b)SuperStock; **5** (4)Roger-Viollet / The Image Works; **7** The Granger Collection - New York; **8** The Granger Collection - New York; **11** Smithsonian American Art Museum - Washington - DC/Art Resource - NY; **11** The Granger Collection - New York; **12** Superstock; **14-15** The Granger Collection - New York; **15** Private Collection - Peter Newark American Pictures/Bridgeman Art Library; **16** (r)The Granger Collection - New York; **16** (c)CORBIS; **16** (l)David J. & Janice L. Frent Collection/CORBIS; **17** (l)CORBIS; **17** (r)Topham / The Image Works; **17** (c)Andre Jenny / The Image Works; **18** (l)Andre Jenny / The Image Works; **18** (r)Mary Evans Picture Library/The Image Works; **18** (c)CORBIS; **20-21** Mary Evans Picture Library; **21** Chicago Historical Society; **22** The Granger Collection - New York; **23** Topham / The Image Works; **25** (1)White House Historical Association; **25** (3)Library of Congress - Washington DC/Bridgeman Art Library; **25** (l to r - t to b)The Granger Collection - New York; **25** (2)CORBIS; **25** (4)Mary Evans Picture Library/The Image Works; **28** Bettmann/CORBIS; **29** David J. & Janice L. Frent Collection/CORBIS; **30** (bl)White House Historical Association; **30** (r)National Portrait Gallery - Smithsonian Institution / Art Resource; **30** (c)The Granger Collection - New York; **31** (br)White House Historical Association; **31** (c)Library of Congress; **31** (l)CORBIS; **32-33** Bettmann/CORBIS; **34** CORBIS; **35** (r)Library of Congress; **35** (l)Military and Historical Image Bank; **36** (r)MPI/Getty Images; **36** (l)Library of Congress; **38-39** Bettmann/CORBIS; **39** Bettmann/CORBIS; **41** (r)Hulton-Deutsch Collection/CORBIS; **41** (l)MPI/Getty Images; **41** (tr)CORBIS; **42-43** Omikron / Photo Researchers - Inc.; **44** (l)CORBIS; **44** (c)Royalty-Free/CORBIS; **44** (r)PhotoDisc; **46** (r)Historical Art Prints - Inc.; **46** (l)Bettmann/CORBIS; **48** (t)Courtesy Dennis M. Keesee Collection; **48-49** Medford Historical Society Collection/CORBIS; **49** (bc)Royalty-Free/CORBIS; **50** (l)CORBIS; **50** (tr)Published courtesy of the Trustees of the Boston Public Library.; **50** (br)Published courtesy of the Trustees of the Boston Public Library.; **51** The Granger Collection - New York; **52** (l)Dr. Michael Echols - American Surgical Antiques; **52** (bkgd)Library of Congress; **53** Eliot Elisofon//Time Life Pictures/Getty Images; **53** (c)Michael Macor/San Francisco Chronicle/CORBIS; **54** (b)The Granger Collection - New York; **54** (t)David A. Northcott/CORBIS; **56** (t)Bettmann/CORBIS; **56-57** MPI/Getty Images; **57** (br)Library of Congress; **57** (tr)Old Paper Studios / Alamy; **58-59** CORBIS; **59** (t)Kean Collection/Getty Images; **60** National Portrait Gallery - Smithsonian Institution / Art Resource; **61** (b)Military and Historical Image Bank; **61** (c)The Granger Collection - New York; **61** (t)David Muench/CORBIS; **64** CORBIS; **64** (t)CORBIS; **64-65** Library of Congress; **66** (l)CORBIS; **66** (r)Royalty-Free/CORBIS; **67** CORBIS; **69** Trish Gant/Getty Images; **71** (c)The Museum of the Confederacy - Richmond - Virginia/Photography by Katherine Wetzel; **71** (c)Royalty-Free/CORBIS; **71** (cr)Creatas Images/Jupiter Images; **71** (tl)Michigan Capitol Committee - photography by Peter Glendinning; **71** (b)Library of Congress; **73** CORBIS; **74** (bl)White House Historical Association; **74** (bcl)White House Historical Association; **74** (t)The Granger Collection - New York; **74** (bcl)Copyright (c) 2007 by Robert Frerck and Odyssey Productions - Inc.; **74** (c)CORBIS; **74** (bc)Chris Willson/Alamy; **74** (br)Musee Marmottan - Paris France - Giraudon/The Bridgeman Art Library; **75** (bl)White House Historical Association; **75** (bl)National Portrait Gallery - Smithsonian Institution/Art Resouce - NY; **75** (bc)The National Archives; **75** (bl)Hulton-Deutsch Collection/CORBIS; **75** (bl)White House Historical Association; **75** (bcl)White House Historical Association; **75** (bcr)White House Historical Association; **75** (bc)White House Historical Association; **75** (br)White House Historical Association; **76** (tr)Bettmann/CORBIS; **76-77** Picture History; **77** (br)CORBIS; **78** (tl)CORBIS; **78** (tr)The Granger Collection - New York; **80-81** North Wind / North Wind Picture Archives; **81** (bc)The Granger Collection - New York; **82** (tr)Bettmann/CORBIS; **82** (c)Bettmann/CORBIS; **82** (tcr)Bettmann/CORBIS; **82** (tr)REUTERS/Larry Downing/newscom; **83** Bettmann/CORBIS; **84** (tl)The Granger Collection - New York; **86** (tr)Courtesy of Special Collections - LSU Libraries - Louisiana State University; **86-87** Bettmann/CORBIS; **87** (bcl)Brooklyn Museum/CORBIS; **88** (tl)Time & Life Pictures/Timepix/Getty Images; **88** (tr)Hulton Archive/Getty Images; **90** (cl)Photo Researchers; **90** (br)North Wind Picture Archives/Alamy; **91** (tl)CORBIS; **91** (bl)Bettmann/CORBIS; **91** (br)Mary Evans Picture Library/Alamy; **92** (tr)Library of Congress - Prints & Photographs Division; **92-93** North Wind / North Wind Picture Archives; **95** Bettmann/CORBIS; **96** (bl)Bettmann/CORBIS; **96** (bcr)The Granger Collection - New York; **100** (cr)Bettmann/CORBIS; **100** (bl)Bettmann/CORBIS; **101** (tl)Library of Congress - LC-USZ62-104925; **101** (t)CORBIS; **101** (c)CORBIS; **101** (bl)CORBIS; **103** CORBIS; **104** (bl)Bettmann/CORBIS; **104-105** Museum of the City of New York - USA/Bridgeman Art Library; **108** (br)White House Historical Association; **108** (bcl)White House Historical Association; **108** (bc)White House Historical Association; **108** (br)White House Historical Association; **108** (bc)White House Historical Association; **108** (br)White House Historical Association; **108** (t)The Granger Collection - New York; **108** (c)Bettmann/CORBIS; **108** (cr)CORBIS; **108** (bc)Archivo Iconografico - SA/CORBIS; **108** (bcr)The Granger Collection - New York; **109** (bl)White House Historical Association; **109** (c)CORBIS; **109** (br)Joel Page/AP Images; **109** (bc)White House Historical Association; **109** (br)White House Historical Association; **109** (bcl)White House Historical Association; **110-111** CORBIS; **111** (br)Library of Congress - Prints & Photographs Division [LC-DIG-pga- 01999]; **112** North Wind/North Wind Picture Archives; **113** L. Berger/SuperStock; **114** (tr)The Granger Collection - New York; **114** (tcl)The Granger Collection - New York; **116** (tl)CORBIS; **116** (cr)National Archives; **118-119** SuperStock - Inc. / SuperStock; **119** (bc)Private Collection - Peter Newark American Pictures / The Bridgeman Art Library International; **120** The Granger Collection - New York; **121** (tl)Private Collection - Peter Newark Western Americana / The Bridgeman Art Library International; **121** (tr)CORBIS; **122** (bkgd)Bettmann/CORBIS; **122** (tcr)North Wind/North Wind Picture Archives; **122** (tr)The Granger Collection - New York; **122** (t)The Granger Collection - New York; **124-125** The Granger Collection - New York; **125** (bc)The Granger Collection - New York; **127** (bl)Private Collection - Peter Newark American Pictures/The Bridgeman Art Library; **127** (bc)CORBIS; **127**

(bcr)The Granger Collection - New York; **127** (cr)The Granger Collection - New York; **128** (tr)CORBIS; **128** (tl)The Granger Collection - New York; **130** (br)Washington Missourian - Karen Cernich/AP Images; **130-131** (bkgd)The Granger Collection - New York; **130-131** (b)CORBIS; **131** (cr)Bettmann/CORBIS; **131** (cl)Art Resource - NY; **132-133** CORBIS; **134** (tr)The Granger Collection - New York; **134** (tl)CORBIS; **135** The Granger Collection - New York; **137** (tr)Library of Congress - Prints & Photographs Division [LC-DIG-pga- 01999]; **137** (cr)CORBIS; **137** (bl)The Granger Collection - New York; **139** AP Images; **140** (bcl)White House Historical Association; **140** (bcr)White House Historical Association; **140** (bc)White House Historical Association; **140** (br)White House Historical Association; **140** (t)CORBIS; **140** (br)The Granger Collection - New York; **140** (b)Charles O'Rear/CORBIS; **141** (bl)White House Historical Association; **141** (bl)White House Historical Association; **141** (bl)White House Historical Association; **141** (bc)White House Historical Association; **141** (bc)White House Historical Association; **141** (br)White House Historical Association; **141** (br)The Granger Collection - New York; **141** (c)AP Images; **142-143** Private Collection - Peter Newark American Pictures / The Bridgeman Art Library International; **144** The Granger Collection - New York; **146-147** Hulton Archive/Getty Images; **147** (br)The Queens Borough Public Library - Long Island Division - Latimer Family Papers; **147** (bc)Picture Research Consultants; **148** (tl)Underwood & Underwood/CORBIS; **148** (tc)CORBIS; **148** (tr)Bettmann/CORBIS; **149** (tc)CORBIS; **149** (tl)The Granger Collection - New York; **149** (cl)The Granger Collection - New York; **149** (tc)The Granger Collection - New York; **150** (r)SSPL / The Image Works; **150** (l)Paul Almasy/CORBIS; **150** (tr)Paul Almasy/CORBIS; **152-153** Roger-Viollet / The Image Works; **153** (br)Bettmann/CORBIS; **154** A'Lelia Bundles/madamcjwalker.com/Walker Family Collection; **155** Bettmann/CORBIS; **158** (cl)Bettmann/CORBIS; **158** (l)Bettmann/CORBIS; **159** (tr)Bettmann/CORBIS; **159** (cr)CORBIS **160-161** CORBIS; **162** The Granger Collection - New York; **163** (tl)Bettmann/CORBIS; **163** (tr)Library of Congress; **165** (l to r - t to b)Private Collection - Peter Newark American Pictures / The Bridgeman Art Library International; **165** (1)AP Images **165** (3)SSPL / The Image Works; **165** (2)Paul Almasy/CORBIS; **165** (4)Bettmann/CORBIS; **165** (5)The Granger Collection - New York; **168** (bl)White House Historical Association; **168** (bcl)White House Historical Association; **168** (bl)White House Historical Association; **168** (bc)White House Historical Association; **168** (bcr)White House Historical Association; **168** (br)White House Historical Association; **168** (b)The Granger Collection - New York; **168** (b)The Granger Collection - New York; **168-169** The Granger Collection - New York; **169** (bl)White House Historical Association; **169** (bl)White House Historical Association; **169** (c)White House Historical Association; **169** (br)White House Historical Association; **169** (bl)AP Images; **169** (c)Mary Evans Picture Library / Alamy; **169** (b)Mary Evans Picture Library; **169** (b)Hulton-Deutsch Collection/CORBIS; **169** (br)The Granger Collection - New York; **170-171** Library of Congress - Prints & Photographs Division [LC-DIG-ggbain-50437]; **171** (br)CNAM - Conservatoire National des Arts et Metiers - Paris - Archives Charmet / The Bridgeman Art Library International; **172** (bl)The Granger Collection - New York; **172** (bc)Royalty-free - Getty Images; **172** (bcr)Free Agents Limited/CORBIS; **172** (br)Richard Hamilton Smith/CORBIS; **173** (bl)The Granger Collection - New York; **174** The Granger Collection - New York; **176** (t)Bettmann/CORBIS; **176** (bl)CORBIS; **177** (t) Private Collection - Peter Newark American Pictures/Bridgeman Art Library; **177** (bl)Hulton-Deutsch Collection/CORBIS; **177** (cr)Visual Arts Library (London)/Alamy; **178-179** Alvah C. Roebuck / CORBIS; **180** (tc)The Granger Collection - New York; **180** (tr)The Granger Collection - New York; **180** (tl)The Granger Collection - New York; **181** (br)The Granger Collection - New York; **181** (bl)The Granger Collection - New York; **181** (bcr)The Granger Collection - New York; **181** (bl)Wallace Kirkland//Time Life Pictures/Getty Images; **182** (tc)Mary Evans Picture Library / Alamy; **182** (tcl)The Granger Collection - New York; **182** (tr)The Granger Collection - New York; **182** (tl)The Granger Collection - New York; **184-185** Mark Rucker/Transcendental Graphics - Getty Images; **186** (bl)CORBIS; **186** (cr)Bettmann/CORBIS; **186** (br)CORBIS; **187** (tr)Bettmann/CORBIS; **187** (tr)CORBIS; **188** (t)The Granger Collection - New York; **188** (tr)The Granger Collection - New York; **189** Duomo/CORBIS; **191** (cr)Library of Congress - Prints & Photographs Division [LC-DIG-ggbain-50437]; **191** (tl)The Granger Collection - New York; **191** (c)The Granger Collection - New York; **191** (br)The Granger Collection - New York; **191** (bl)The Granger Collection - New York; **193** Bettmann/CORBIS; **194** (bcl)The Granger Collection - New York; **194-195** CORBIS; **198** (bl)White House Historical Association; **198** (bcl)White House Historical Association; **198** (bc)White House Historical Association; **198** (bcr)White House Historical Association; **198** (br)White House Historical Association; **198** (bc)White House Historical Association; **198** (t)Paul Thompson/Topical Press Agency/Getty Images; **198** (cl)Bettmann/CORBIS; **198** (cr)Bettmann/CORBIS; **198** (bc)Hulton-Deutsch Collection/CORBIS; **199** (bl)White House Historical Association; **199** (bcl)White House Historical Association; **199** (bcr)White House Historical Association; **199** (bcr)White House Historical Association; **199** (bl)Bettmann/CORBIS; **199** (bc)E.A. Kennedy III/The Image Works; **199** (c)David J. & Janice L. Frent Collection/CORBIS; **199** (br)Mike Agliolo/Photo Researchers - Inc.; **200-201** The New York Public Library / Art Resource - NY; **201** (cr)The Granger Collection - New York; **202** (tc)The Granger Collection - New York; **202** (tr)CORBIS; **202** (tl)Bettmann/CORBIS; **203** Bettmann/CORBIS; **204** (c)CORBIS; **204** (tl)The Granger Collection - New York; **204** (tr)Bettmann/CORBIS; **206** Library of Congress; **209** The Art Archive / Culver Pictures; **210** (tc)CORBIS; **210** (cl)Library of Congress; **210** (tcr)National Association of Colored Women Clubs - Inc.; **210** (tr)Bettmann/CORBIS; **211** The Granger Collection - New York; **212** (tcr)CORBIS; **212** (cl)Private Collection - Peter Newark American Pictures / The Bridgeman Art Library; **212** (r)CORBIS; **212** (tc)Kansas State Historical Society; **214-215** The Granger Collection - New York; **215** (b)The Granger Collection - New York; **216** (b)CORBIS; **216** (br)The Granger Collection - New York; **216** (bl)Private Collection/DaTo Images/The Bridgeman Art Library; **216-217** Joseph Sohm/Visions of America/CORBIS; **220-221** The Granger Collection - New York; **221** (bc)CORBIS; **222** (tr)The Granger Collection - New York; **222** (tl)The Granger Collection - New York; **223** (tr)Hulton Archive/Getty Images; **223** (tc)Bettmann/CORBIS; **224** (bl) MPI/Getty Images; **224** (br)CORBIS; **225** (br)Bettmann/CORBIS; **225** (bl)Arizona Historical Society; **227** (bl)The Art Archive / Culver Pictures; **227** (br)Bettmann/CORBIS; **227** (cl)CORBIS; **227** (tr)Private Collection/DaTo Images/The Bridgeman Art Library; **227** (br) MPI/Getty Images; **230** (bl)White House Historical Association; **230** (bc)White House Historical Association; **230** (bc)White House Historical Association; **230** (bcr)White House Historical Association; **230** (br)White House Historical Association; **230** (br)White House Historical Association; **230** (t)Private Collection/Bridgeman Art Library; **230**

(bcl)age fotostock / SuperStock ; **231** (bl)White House Historical Association; **231** (bcl)White House Historical Association; **231** (bc)White House Historical Association; **231** (bc)White House Historical Association; **231** (bcr)White House Historical Association; **231** (br)White House Historical Association; **231** (bc)The Granger Collection - New York; **231** (br)Mary Evans Picture Library / The Image Works ; **232** (tr)CORBIS; **232-233** Library of Congress - Prints & Photographs Division [LC-DIG-pga-00849]; **232-233** Library of Congress - Prints & Photographs Division [LC-DIG-pga-00849]; **234** (cl)Alaska State Archives; **234** (bcr)Holding institution; Alaska State Library - Historical Collections - PO Box 110571 - Juneau AK 99811-0571;mailto;ASL.Historical@eed.state.ak.us; **236-237** U.S. Naval Historical Center Photograph; **237** (br)The Granger Collection - New York; **238** The Granger Collection - New York; **240** (tl)Library of Congress; **240** (tl)The Granger Collection - New York; **240** (tr)Bettmann/CORBIS; **242-243** CORBIS; **243** (bcr)Lester S. Levy Collection of Sheet Music - Special Collections - The Sheridan Libraries - The Johns Hopkins University.; **243** (bc)ullstein bild / The Granger Collection - New York; **244** The Granger Collection - New York; **245** (tc)The Granger Collection - New York; **245** (tc)The Granger Collection - New York; **245** (c)David J. & Janice L. Frent Collection/CORBIS; **246** The Granger Collection - New York; **248-24** CORBIS; **249** (br)Underwood & Underwood/CORBIS; **251** (cl)CORBIS; **251** (cr)CORBIS; **251** (cr)CDC; **251** (bl)Lake County Museum/CORBIS; **252** Bettmann/CORBIS; **253** (bc)Library of Congress; **253** (cr)CORBIS; **253** (cr)CORBIS; **255** (cl)Lester S. Levy Collection of Sheet Music - Special Collections - The Sheridan Libraries - The Johns Hopkins University.; **255** (bl)CORBIS; **255** (tr)The Granger Collection - New York; **255** (l)Lake County Museum/CORBIS; **256** Columbus Memorial Library ; **257** (tr)The Granger Collection - New York; **257** (r)Bettmann/CORBIS; **259** The Granger Collection - New York; **260** (cl)White House Historical Association; **260** (b)Hulton-Deutsch Collection/CORBIS; **260** (c)The Mariners' Museum/CORBIS; **260** (cr)David Pollack/K.J. Historical/CORBIS; **260** (bl)Bettmann/CORBIS; **260** (br)Bettmann/CORBIS; **261** (cl)Bettmann/CORBIS; **261** (bcl)Bettmann/CORBIS; **261** (br)MICHAEL KOOREN/Reuters/CORBIS; **262-263** Hulton-Deutsch Collection/CORBIS; **263** (br)Austrian Archives/CORBIS; **264** The Granger Collection - New York; **265** The Granger Collection - New York; **266** (tc)The Art Archive / Dagli Orti; **266** (cr)The Art Archive / Imperial War Museum; **266** (c)CORBIS; **266** (tc)The Granger Collection - New York; **268** The Granger Collection - New York; **269** (bl)Artmedia/Heritage-Images/The Image Works ; **269** (c)Hulton-Deutsch Collection/CORBIS; **269** (br)Sally A. Morgan;Ecoscene/CORBIS; **270-271** The Granger Collection - New York; **271** (br)ullstein bild / The Granger Collection - New York; **273** Topical Press Agency/Getty Images; **274** CORBIS; **276-277** CORBIS; **277** (br)Photograph courtesy of the Pocumtuck Valley Memorial Association - Memorial Hall Museum - Deerfield - Massachusetts.; **278-279** CORBIS; **279** (br)Alamy; **280** Bettmann/CORBIS; **282-283** CORBIS; **284** (tl)The Granger Collection - New York; **284** (tcr)David Pollack/CORBIS; **284** (tcl)CORBIS; **284** (tr)Swim Ink 2 - LLC/CORBIS; **286-287** Bettmann/CORBIS; **289** Bettmann/CORBIS; **291** (br)Bettmann/CORBIS; **291** (tl)The Granger Collection - New York; **291** (cl)CORBIS; **291** (cr)The Granger Collection - New York; **291** (cr)Alamy; **292** (t)Bettmann/CORBIS; **292** (b)VSTOCK/Alamy; **293** (tc)TIME; **293** (bl)Bettmann/CORBIS; **293** (br)Bettmann/CORBIS; **295** The Granger Collection - New York; **296** (bcl)The Granger Collection - New York; **296-297** CORBIS; **300** (t)H. Armstrong Roberts/CORBIS; **300** (br)White House Historical Association; **300** (bl)Bettmann/CORBIS; **301** (cl)White House Historical Association; **301** (t)Bettmann/CORBIS; **301** (b)IOC - Olympic Museum /Allsport; **303** (r)The Granger Collection - New York; **304** (l)MPI/Getty Images; **304** (r)The Granger Collection - New York; **306** (c)CORBIS; **306** (br)Digital Image (c) The Museum of Modern Art/Licensed by SCALA/Art Resource - NY; **307** (tr)Schomburg Center/Art Resource - NY; **307** (cl)University of Illinois at Chicago - The University Library - Special Collections Department - Arthur and Graham Aldis Papers; **309** (bc)David J. & Janice L. Frent Collection/CORBIS; **309** (b)David J. & Janice L. Frent Collection/CORBIS; **310** The Granger Collection - New York; **312-313** National Motor Museum /HIP/ The Image Works ; **313** (bc)Image courtesy of The Toaster Museum Foundation - www.toaster.org; **316-317** Bettmann/CORBIS; **317** (r)Underwood & Underwood/CORBIS; **318** (c)Doug Martin; **318** (t)CORBIS; **318** (l)The Granger Collection - New York; **319** Smithsonian American Art Museum - Washington - DC/Art Resource - NY; **320** (tl)http://www.rootsweb.com/~mobarry/ schoolhouse/ schoolbook2.htm; **320-321** Albert Harlingue/Roger-Viollet/The Image Works; **323** (tl)Hulton-Deutsch Collection/CORBIS; **323** (cr)The Granger Collection - New York; **323** (tr)The Granger Collection - New York; **323** (bl)Bettmann/CORBIS; **324** (br)Smithsonian American Art Museum - Washington - DC/Art Resource - NY; **324** (tl)Miriam Berkley/AuthorPix; **327** Picture Research Consultants; **328** (l)White House Historical Association; **328** (bcr)The Library of Congress; **328** (t)Horace Bristol/CORBIS; **329** (bl)National Archives at College Park - Archives II (College Park - MD); **329** (cr)CORBIS ; **329** (bc)CORR/AFP/Getty Images; **330** (tr)American Stock/Getty Images; **330-331** Bettmann/CORBIS; **331** (b)CORBIS; **332** EFE/CORBIS; **334** Seattle Post-Intelligencer Collection;Museum of History and Industry/CORBIS; **335** Arthur Rothstein/Hulton Archive/Getty Images; **336-337** Bettmann/CORBIS; **337** (br)The Advertising Archives; **338** (t)White House Historical Association; **338** (br)Library of Congress; **338-339** Franklin D. Roosevelt Library; **340** Library of Congress - Prints & Photographs Division - LC-USZ62-17300; **342** Bettmann/CORBIS; **343** (cr)CORBIS; **344-345** Bettmann/CORBIS; **345** (br)Marion Post Wolcott /CORBIS; **346** (bl)AP Images; **346** (bc)Library of Congress; **348** (tl)The Granger Collection - New York; **348** (tl)Bettmann/CORBIS; **350** (l)Dorothea Lange/The Library of Congress; **350** (r)Underwood & Underwood/CORBIS; **351** (t)Lord Price Collection/Alamy; **351** (c)Bettmann/CORBIS; **352-353** Minnesota Historical Society/CORBIS; **354** (br)Bettmann/CORBIS; **354** (br)Reni Newsphotos - Inc./Library of Congress; **354** (b)Library of Congress; **355** (bl)NICHOLAS KAMM/AFP/Getty Images; **355** (br)White House Historical Society; **355** (bcr)Time Life Pictures/Getty Images; **355** (br)HASSAN AMMAR/AFP/Getty Images); **357** (tr)Arthur Rothstein/Hulton Archive/Getty Images; **357** (bl)Library of Congress; **357** (b)Franklin D. Roosevelt Library; **357** (tl)Horace Bristol; **359** (tr)The Granger Collection - New York; **359** AP Images; **360** (bc)White House Historical Association; **361** (bl)Jack Novak/SuperStock ; **361** (b)Bettmann/CORBIS; **361** (cl)US Air Force Museum; **361** (bcr)Owen Franken/CORBIS; **361** (cl)Bettmann/CORBIS; **362-363** Hugo Jaeger/Timepix/Time Life Pictures/Getty Images; **363** (bc)akg-images / Ernst Kutzer ; **364** Bettmann/CORBIS; **366-367** Dmitri Kessel/Time & Life Pictures/Getty Images; **368** (bl)Hulton-Deutsch Collection/CORBIS; **370** (br)Bettmann/CORBIS; **372-373** National Archives; **373** (bl)Library of Congress - Prints & Photographs Division; **374** (br)National Archives/CORBIS; **374** (bl)Bernard Hoffman/Time & Life Pictures/Getty Images; **374** (bl)Bettmann/CORBIS; **374-375** CORBIS; **376** (tc) The Mariners' Museum/CORBIS; **376** (tr)National Archives/Roger-Viollet/The Image Works; **378-379** AP Images; **379** (br)David E. Scherman//Time Life Pictures/Getty Images; **380** Hulton-Deutsch Collection/CORBIS; **381** (cr)AP Images; **381** (bl)CORBIS; **382** (br)US Signal Corps/Time Life Pictures/Getty Images; **382** (bl)Woodfin Camp & Associates; **383** (cr)Brown Brothers; **383** (cl)Bob Landry/TimePix/Getty Images; **383** (cl)Brown Brothers; **384** (tr)USHMM; **384** (c)ilian / Alamy; **384** (tc)ullstein bild/The Granger Collection - New York; **386-387** The Art Archive / Culver Pictures; **388** Bettmann/CORBIS; **389** (cr)National Archives; **389** (bl)CORBIS; **389** (cl)CORBIS; **391** (cr)Library of Congress - Prints & Photographs Division; **391** (cl)US Air Force Museum; **391** (tl)Hulton-Deutsch Collection/CORBIS; **391** (bl)Bettmann/CORBIS; **391** (tr)National Archives; **391** (br)CORBIS; **394** (cl)David J. & Janice L. Frent Collection/CORBIS; **394-395** Robert W. Kelley/Time Life Pictures/Getty Images; **398** (bcl)White House Historical Association; **398** (t)H. Armstrong Roberts / ClassicStock / The Image Works; **398** (br)Swim Ink 2 - LLC/CORBIS; **399** (bc)Bettmann/CORBIS; **399** (c)Bettmann/CORBIS; **399** (bl)White House Historical Association; **400-401** Bettmann/CORBIS; **401** (bl)Bettmann/CORBIS; **403** Reprinted from the Des Moines Registrar/Jay N. Darling - 1946; **404** (bl)Bettmann/CORBIS; **404** (cr)Hulton-Deutsch Collection/CORBIS; **406** The Granger Collection - New York;; **408-409** Ed Clark//Time Life Pictures/Getty Images; **410** (cl)Bettmann/CORBIS; **410** (br)Mark Kauffman/Time & Life Pictures/Getty Images; **411** Bettmann/CORBIS; **412** (tr)Bettmann/CORBIS; **412** (tl)Bettmann/CORBIS; **414-415** Pfc. James Cox/CORBIS; **416** (tr)Hulton-Deutsch Collection/CORBIS; **416** (tl)Library Of Congress/Getty Images; **416** (tl)CORBIS; **418** (tr)David J. & Janice L. Frent Collection/CORBIS; **418-419** Bettmann/CORBIS; **420** (b)Bettmann/CORBIS; **420** (b)Jerry Cooke/CORBIS; **420-421** Erin Patrice O'Brien/Getty Images; **421** (bc)Hugh Threlfall/Alamy; **422-423** Du Pont Company Product Information Photograph Collection. HF197234101. Courtesy of Hagley Museum and Library.; **425** (br)Swim Ink 2 - LLC/CORBIS; **425** (bc)Bettmann/CORBIS; **425** (tc)Bettmann/CORBIS; **425** (cl)Reprinted from the Des Moines Registrar/Jay N. Darling - 1946; **425** (tr)Mark Kauffman/Time & Life Pictures/Getty Images; **426** (cr)imagebroker/Alamy; **426-427** Charles E. Rotkin/CORBIS; **427** (tl)PictureNet/CORBIS; **427** (bl)Photo by Lynn Betts - USDA Natural Resources Conservation Service; **430** (bc)Bettmann/CORBIS; **430** (br)Topham/The Image Works; **430** (bl)Don Cravens/Time & Life Pictures/Getty Images; **430** (cr)Flip Schulke/CORBIS; **430** (t)Flip Schulke/CORBIS; **430** (bl)Carl Iwaski/Time & Life Pictures/Getty Images; **430** (c)White House Historical Association; **430** (bcr)OLIPHANT (c) 1971 UNIVERSAL PRESS SYNDICATE. Reprinted with permission.; **430** (br)White House Historical Association; **431** (c)Jason Laure/The Image Works; **431** (bcl)White House Historical Association; **431** (bcr)White House Historical Association; **432-433** Carl Iwaski/Time & Life Pictures/Getty Images; **435** Bettmann/CORBIS; **436** Gene Herrick/AP Images; **438-439** Bettmann/CORBIS; **440** Steve Schapiro/CORBIS; **442-443** Jack Moebes/CORBIS; **443** (br)AP Images; **445** (tr)Bettmann/CORBIS; **445** (tr)Francis Miller/Time Life Pictures/Getty Images; **445** (tr)Francis Miller/Time Life Pictures/Getty Images; **446** Hulton-Archive/Getty Images; **447** (tc)Charles Moore/Black Star; **447** (c)Paul Schutzer/Time Life Pictures/Getty Images; **448** (tl)AP Images; **448** (tr)Bettmann/CORBIS; **450** Time Life Pictures/Getty Images; **452-453** AP Images; **453** (bc)Picture Research Consultants; **454** (bc)Arthur Schatz/Time Life Pictures/Getty Images; **454** (br)Bettmann/CORBIS; **454** (cr)Collection of David J. & Janice L. Frent; **455** Bruce Kliewe/Index Stock; **457** (c)Flip Schulke/CORBIS; **457** (c)Flip Schulke/CORBIS; **457** (br)AP Images; **457** (cr)Arthur Schatz/Time Life Pictures/Getty Images; **457** (tc)Francis Miller/Time Life Pictures/Getty Images; **457** (bl)Bruce Kliewe/Index Stock; **460** (t)Sal Veder/AP Images; **460** (br) Jack Novak/SuperStock; **460** (cr)Larry Burrows/Time Life Pictures/Getty Images; **460** (bcr)White House Historical Association; **460** (bcl)White House Historical Association; **461** (c)Jack Novak /SuperStock; **461** (bcr)Collection of David J. & Janice L. Frent; **461** (bcl)White House Historical Association; **462-463** Horst Faas/AP Images; **463** (br)Bettmann/CORBIS; **464** (bl)Three Lions/Getty Images; **464** (cr)Bettmann/CORBIS; **464-465** AP Images; **468-469** Friedrich Stark / Peter Arnold - Inc.; **470** (c)Bettmann/CORBIS; **470** (br)Bettmann/CORBIS; **470** (cr)UPI/Bettmann/CORBIS; **471** Rikli/Roger-Viollet/The Image Works; **472** Vernon Merritt/Black Star; **474** (c)Bettmann/CORBIS; **475** (tl)Bettmann/CORBIS; **476** (cr)Courtesy of Robert Sharlet; **476-477** Bettmann/CORBIS; **477** (br)Hulton Archive/Getty Images; **478** (br)John Olson/Time Life Pictures/Getty Images; **480** (tl)Steve Schapiro/CORBIS; **480** (tr)Bettmann/CORBIS; **482** (tl)NASA; **482** (b)Bettmann/CORBIS; **482** (tr)George Silk/TIMEPIX/Time Life Pictures/Getty Images; **483** (tl)PhotoDisc/Getty Images; **483** (bl)Al Freni/Time Life Pictures/Getty Images; **483** (cr)Andreas Manolis/Reuters/CORBIS; **484** (cr)Wally McNamee/CORBIS; **484-485** Bettmann/CORBIS; **485** (bcl)CBS /Landov; **486** Charles Gatewood/The Image Works; **488** Steve Raymer/CORBIS; **489** Christian Simonpietri/Sygma/CORBIS; **493** a 1965 Herblock Cartoon - copyright The Herb Block Foundation; **494** (cl)AP Images; **494-495** Justin Lane/epa/CORBIS; **498** (t)White House Historical Association; **498** (bc)Lawrence Manning/CORBIS; **498** (bc)White House Historical Association; **499** (bl)Black Star; **499** (bcl)White House Historical Association; **499** (bc)White House Historical Association; **499** (bcr)White House Historical Association; **500-501** CORBIS; **501** (br)OLIPHANT (c) 1971 UNIVERSAL PRESS SYNDICATE. Reprinted with permission. All rights reserved.; **502** (tr)Bettmann/CORBIS; **502** (tcr)CORBIS; **502** (tl)Bettmann/CORBIS; **503** (tc)NASA Stennis Space Center (NASA-SSC); **504** The New Yorker Collection 1973 Alan Dunn from cartoonbank.com. All Rights Reserved.; **506-507** Gerald R. Brimacombe/Time Life Pictures/Getty Images; **508** (tl)Gary Wagner/CORBIS Sygma; **508** (tl)Bettmann/CORBIS; **508-509** Library of Congress/Getty Images; **509** Wally McNamee/CORBIS; **510** (bl)Wally McNamee/CORBIS; **510** (br)Steve Northup/Time Life Pictures/Getty Images; **510** (bcl)Dennis Brack/Black Star; **511** Alex Webb/Magnum Photos - Inc.; **512** (bc)Wally McNamee/CORBIS; **512** (cr)AP Images; **514** (t)Allstar Picture Library/Alamy; **514** (c)NASA; **514** (b)StockDisc Classic/Alamy; **515** (t)Index Stock/Alamy; **515** (bl)U.S. Mint; **515** (br)Hisham Ibrahim/Photov.com/Alamy; **516-517** Bettmann/CORBIS; **518** (cr)Robert Clay/Alamy; **518** (bcr)AUL J. RICHARDS/AFP/Getty Images; **519** Bettmann/CORBIS; **521** (br)Bettmann/CORBIS; **522** (tl)Gary Soto; **522** (br)Michael Newman/PhotoEdit; **526** (c)Jonathan Nourok / PhotoEdit; **526** (bcr)Sergei Guneyev//Time Life Pictures/Getty Images; **526** (cr)Marion Bernstein; **526** (bcl)White House Historical Association; **526** (bcr)White House Historical Association; **527** (c)Ben Sklar/AP Images; **527** (bc)Mike Greenlar / Syracuse Newspapers / The Image Works; **527** (br)Official White House Photo by Eric Draper; **527** (bl)White House Historical Association; **528-529** CORBIS; **529** (br)WARNER BROS./THE KOBAL COLLECTION; **530** (br)Wally McNamee/CORBIS; **530** (bl)Bettmann/CORBIS; **531** NASA; **532** (tcr)a 1983 Herblock Cartoon - copyright The Herb Block Foundation; **532** (tcl)Brooks Kraft/CORBIS; **534** (cl)CORBIS; **534** (b)Wally McNamee/CORBIS; **535** (br)Bettmann/CORBIS; **537** (bl)Tom Stoddart/Getty Images; **537** (br)Stuart Franklin/Magnum Photos; **538** Jacques Langevin/CORBIS SYGMA; **540** (cr)Steve Liss//Time Life Pictures/Getty Images; **540-541** Cynthia Johnson//Time Life Pictures/Getty Images; **542** (cl)CNN/AFP/Getty Images; **542** (tr)Reuters/CORBIS; **542** (cr)IM SLOAN/AFP/Getty Image; **543** (tcr)MC NAMEE WALLY/CORBIS SYGMA; **543** (tl)Library of Congress; **543** (tl)Najlah Feanny/CORBIS SABA; **543** (t)The Granger Collection - New York; **546** (tr)Reuters/CORBIS; **548-549** DOUG KANTER/AFP/Getty Images; **550-551** Mark Lennihan/AP Images; **553** Matt Cardy/Getty Images; **554** Marko Georgiev/Getty Images; **556** (cl)AP Images; **556** (l) Joseph Khakshouri/CORBIS; **558-559** Ed Kashi/CORBIS; **559** (br)White House Historical Association; **560** Motoring Picture Library/ Alamy; **562** David Young-Wolff / PhotoEdit; **563** Bob Daemmrich/Photo Edit; **565** (br)Jonathan Nourok / PhotoEdit; **565** (cr)Cynthia Johnson//Time Life Pictures/Getty Images; **565** (tl)Tom Stoddart/Getty Images; **565** (bl)DOUG KANTER/AFP/Getty Images; **566** (tr)Duane Burleson/AP Images; **566** (bl)SHANNON STAPLETON/Reuters/CORBIS; **566** (cr)Robert W. Ginn/Alamy; **567** (tl)V1/Alamy; **567** (tr)Bob Krist/CORBIS; **567** (bl)Shannon Stapleton/Reuters/CORBIS; **569** Clay Bennett / (c) 2006 The Christian Science Monitor (www.csmonitor.com). All rights reserved.; **570** (2)PhotoDisc/Getty Images; **570** (l to r - t to b)National Archives; **570** (1)Joseph Sohm/Jupiter Images; **570** (3)dynamicgraphics/Jupiter Images; **570** (6)Library of Congress; **570** (5)Brand X/Punchstock; **570** (4)PhotoDisc/Getty Images; **572** (2)Clark Family Collection - William Clark Papers/Missouri Historical Society - St. Louis; **572** (5)The Granger Collection - New York; **572** (1)PhotoDisc/Getty Images; **572** (l to r - t to b)Fototeca Storica Nazionale / Getty Images; **572** (3)Image Source/Jupiter Images; **572** (4)PhotoDisc/Getty Images; **573** Roger-Viollet / The Image Works; **574** (l)Billy Rose Theater Collection - The New York Public Library for the Performing Arts - Astor - Lenox and Tilden Foundations; **574** (r)The Granger Collection - New York; **575** (r)Bettmann/CORBIS; **575** (l)Digital Image (c) The Museum of Modern Art/Licensed by SCALA/Art Resource - NY ; **576** The Granger Collection - New York; **577** Bettmann/CORBIS; **578** AP Images; **579** Topham / The Image Works; **580** Superstock; **582** The Granger Collection - New York; **583** Library of Congress - Prints and Photographs Division [LC-USZ62-119343]; **586** White House Historical Association; **587** Bettmann/CORBIS; **589** (b)Erin Patrice O'Brien/Getty Images; **589** (t)Sandy Schaeffer/Mai/Mai/Time Life Pictures/Getty Images; **590** The Granger Collection - New York; **591** Jonathan Nourok / PhotoEdit; **592** Henryk T. Kaiser/Index Stock; **593** (tl)White House Historical Association; **593** (tc)White House Historical Association; **593** (tr)White House Historical Association; **593** (cl)White House Historical Association; **593** (c)White House Historical Association; **593** (cr)White House Historical Association; **593** (bl)White House Historical Association; **593** (bc)White House Historical Association; **593** (br)White House Historical Association; **594** (tl)White House Historical Association; **594** (tc)White House Historical Association; **594** (tr)White House Historical Association; **594** (c)White House Historical Association; **594** (cl)White House Historical Association; **594** (cr)White House Historical Association; **594** (bl)White House Historical Association; **594** (bc)White House Historical Association; **594** (br)White House Historical Association; **595** (tl)White House Historical Association; **595** (tc)White House Historical Association; **595** (tr)White House Historical Association; **595** (c)White House Historical Association; **595** (cl)White House Historical Association; **595** (cr)White House Historical Association; **595** (bc)White House Historical Association; **596** (tl)White House Historical Association; **596** (tr)White House Historical Association; **596** (tc)White House Historical Association; **596** (c)White House Historical Association; **596** (cl)White House Historical Association; **596** (cr)White House Historical Association; **596** (bl)White House Historical Association; **596** (br)White House Historical Association; **596** (bc)White House Historical Association; **597** (tl)White House Historical Association; **597** (tc)White House Historical Association; **597** (tr)White House Historical Association; **597** (cl)White House Historical Association; **597** (c)White House Historical Association; **597** (bl)Official White House Photo by Eric Draper; **597** (cr)White House Historical Association; **598** (l)C. Sherburne/PhotoLink/Getty Images; **598** (r)Bettmann/CORBIS; **599** (4)Bettmann/CORBIS; **599** (2)C. Sherburne/PhotoLink/Getty Images; **599** (3)C. Sherburne/PhotoLink/Getty Images; **599** (1)C. Sherburne/PhotoLink/Getty Images; **599** (l to r - t to b)C. Sherburne/PhotoLink/Getty Images; **600** (l to r - t to b)C. Sherburne/PhotoLink/Getty Images; **600** (2)C. Sherburne/PhotoLink/Getty Images; **600** (3)C. Sherburne/PhotoLink/Getty Images; **600** (4)C. Sherburne/PhotoLink/Getty Images; **601** (t)C. Sherburne/PhotoLink/Getty Images; **601** (tc)C. Sherburne/PhotoLink/Getty Images; **601** (b)C. Sherburne/PhotoLink/Getty Images; **601** (bc)Bettmann/CORBIS; **602** (bc)C. Sherburne/PhotoLink/Getty Images; **602** (tc)C. Sherburne/PhotoLink/Getty Images; **602** (b)C. Sherburne/PhotoLink/Getty Images; **603** (t)C. Sherburne/PhotoLink/Getty Images; **603** (c)C. Sherburne/PhotoLink/Getty Images; **603** (b)Wally McNamee/CORBIS; **604** North Wind Picture Archives; **605** Bettmann/CORBIS; **606** Bettmann/CORBIS; **607** Bettmann/CORBIS; **608** National Portrait Gallery - Smithsonian Institution/Art Resource - NY; **609** National Portrait Gallery - Smithsonian Institution/Art Resource - NY; **610** Mark Burnett; **611** (t)Shield - Unknown Southern Cheyenne - about 1880;Painted rawhide - cloth - feathers - brass bells - cowtail;Denver Art Museum Collection; Native Arts acquisition funds - 1968.330ab;(c) Denver Art Museum; **611** (b)CORBIS; **613** UPI/Bettmann/CORBIS; **614** Bettmann/Corbis; **615** Flip Schulke/CORBIS;

Election 2008

A New President

The Candidates

Because of the power and influence of the United States, the president, as our leader, has one of the most important roles in the world. Although the president is the head of just one of the three branches of government, the president—with the exception of the vice president—is the only official elected by the entire nation. As a result, the president stands as a symbol not only of the federal government, but of the entire country as well.

The Constitution lists rules about who can become president of the United States. By law, anyone who meets these qualifications is eligible.

Qualifications for U.S. President

✓ natural-born citizen

✓ at least 35 years of age

✓ a resident of the U.S. for at least 14 years

As you read about the different political candidates, what other qualities or characteristics do you think a president should have?

Notable Candidates in History

1789

George Washington runs unopposed for election as president.

1796

Presidential candidates representing two rival political parties compete for the first time: Federalist John Adams and Democratic-Republican Thomas Jefferson.

1828

Andrew Jackson and John Quincy Adams exchange personal attacks in the first true "mud-slinging" campaign.

1844

Democrat James K. Polk is the first "dark horse," or unexpected candidate, to win the presidency.

1872

Equal Rights Party nominates the first woman, Victoria Woodhull, to run for president and the first African American, Frederick Douglass, as vice president.

John McCain

Present position:
U.S. senator from Arizona

Born: August 29, 1936;
Panama Canal Zone

Lives in: Phoenix, Arizona

Education:
U.S. Naval Academy, B.S., 1958
National War College, 1974

John McCain comes from a distinguished military family. His father and grandfather were U.S. Navy admirals. McCain served as a naval pilot in the Vietnam War. His plane was shot down, and he was held prisoner by Vietnamese Communists for five years. After his release, McCain was honored as a war hero. Leaving the Navy, McCain was elected as a U.S. representative to Congress from Arizona in 1982. Four years later, he won election as a U.S. senator from Arizona. He is serving his fourth term in the Senate.

Sarah Palin

Present position:
Governor of Alaska

Born: February 11, 1964;
Sandpoint, Idaho

Lives in: Wasilla, Alaska

Education:
University of Idaho, B.S., 1987

Raised in Alaska, Sarah Palin worked as a sports reporter for local television and newspapers. In the 1990s, she served on the Wasilla, Alaska, city council and was elected the city's mayor in 1996. She later served as chairperson of the Alaska Oil and Gas Conservation Commission. In 2006 Palin was elected governor of Alaska, the first woman to hold the post. She became known for her efforts to fight corruption in Alaskan politics.

Barack Obama

Present position:
U.S. senator from Illinois

Born: August 4, 1961;
Honolulu, Hawaii

Lives in: Chicago, Illinois

Education:
Columbia University, B.A., 1983
Harvard University Law School, J.D., 1991

Of multiethnic background, Barack Obama was born in Hawaii to a white American mother from Kansas and a black father from Kenya, East Africa. After his parents divorced and his father returned to Africa, Obama stayed with his mother and was raised in Indonesia and Hawaii. Completing his higher education, Obama worked as a civil rights lawyer and taught law at the University of Chicago. In 1996 Obama was elected to the Illinois Senate and then to the U.S. Senate in 2004.

Joseph Biden

Present position:
U.S. senator from Delaware

Born: November 20, 1942;
Scranton, Pennsylvania

Lives in: Wilmington, Delaware

Education:
University of Delaware, B.A., 1965
Syracuse University, J.D., 1968

Born to a working-class family, Joseph Biden was raised in the suburbs of Wilmington, Delaware. After serving in local politics, Biden was elected to the Senate from Delaware at age 29. Through six terms in the Senate, Biden has become a skilled legislator. Having served on the Senate Judiciary and Foreign Relations Committees, Biden is known as an expert on issues related to foreign affairs, national security, drug policy, and crime.

1928
Al Smith of New York is the first Roman Catholic to gain a major party's nomination for president.

1964
Senator Margaret Chase Smith (R-Maine) becomes the first woman to seek a major party's nomination for president.

1972
Shirley Chisholm (D-New York) is the first African American woman to seek a major party's presidential nomination.

1984
Democrat Geraldine Ferraro is the first woman nominated for the vice presidency by a major party.

2000
Connecticut senator Joseph Lieberman becomes the first Jewish American to run on a national ticket.

2008
Barack Obama becomes the first African American to be elected president.

The Issues

★ ★

A host of issues–the economy, health care, and the Iraq war, for example–grabbed the attention of voters in the 2008 presidential race. When asked what issue was the most important in determining their vote for president, here is how registered voters responded one month before the election.

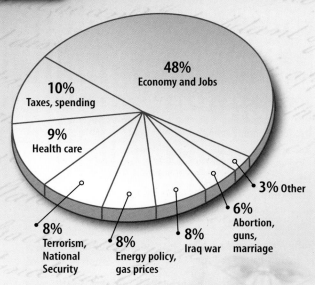

- 48% Economy and Jobs
- 10% Taxes, spending
- 9% Health care
- 8% Terrorism, National Security
- 8% Energy policy, gas prices
- 8% Iraq war
- 6% Abortion, guns, marriage
- 3% Other

VOTERS AND THE ISSUES

Source: *Newsweek* Poll conducted by Princeton Survey Research Associates International. Oct. 8-9, 2008

How the Candidates Voted

McCain's and Obama's voting records on selected issues, 2005-2008

	McCain	Obama
Trade		
Pass Central America Free Trade Agreement (2005)	Y	N
Economy and Jobs		
Increase minimum wage to $7.25 per hour (2007)	Y	Y
Pass $700 billion financial rescue package (2008)	Y	Y
Education		
Provide $52 million for community learning centers (2005)	N	Y
Shift $11 billion from corporate tax loopholes to education (2005)	N	Y
Immigration		
Allow illegal aliens to take part in Social Security (2006)	Y	Y
Begin comprehensive immigration reform (2007)	Y	Y
Declare English as the official language of the U.S. (2007)	Y	N
War on Terror		
Restrict business with foreign countries with links to terrorism (2005)	N	Y
Allow a phased withdrawal of troops from Iraq (2006)	N	Y
Reauthorize the Patriot Act (2006)	Y	Y
Preserve habeas corpus for Guantanamo detainees (2006)	N	Y
Redeploy non-essential U.S. troops out of Iraq in 9 months (2007)	N	Y

Where the Candidates Stand

REPUBLICAN

Economy and Taxes

★ Lobbyists' influence blamed for financial crisis; favors greater government oversight

★ End taxes on unemployment benefits

★ Cut capital gains tax to raise incentive to save and invest

★ Treasury Department to guarantee 100 percent of savings for 6 months

★ Lower tax rates on retirement savings plans

★ Increase tax deductions for people selling stock at a loss

Energy

★ No taxes on windfall profits

★ No drilling in the Arctic, but support for offshore drilling

★ No ethanol subsidies

★ Expand nuclear power

Health Care

★ Free-market, consumer-based

★ $5,000 refundable tax credit for health insurance to every family

Education

★ Federal government should play a limited role in public education; education primarily a state and local concern

★ Keep No Child Left Behind Act's emphasis on standards and achievement; focus on individual achievement rather than group averages

Foreign Policy

★ Iraq—early and continuing supporter of war; favors troop increase; against timetable for troop withdrawal but projects all troops home by 2013

★ Iran—use economic and diplomatic pressure, work closely with European allies

★ Trade—honor NAFTA and other agreements; international reduction of trade barriers

DEMOCRAT

Economy and Taxes

★ Federal rollback of regulations blamed for financial crisis; calls for greater government oversight

★ Tax breaks for businesses that create new jobs

★ Penalty-free withdrawals allowed from retirement savings

★ A 90-day reprieve for homeowners facing foreclosures

★ Suspend unemployment taxes and extend benefits

★ Federal lending agency to help financially-ailing cities and states

Energy

★ Tax windfall profits

★ No drilling in the Arctic and offshore

★ Provide ethanol subsidies

★ No support for nuclear power

Health Care

★ No requirements on small businesses

★ Reform of Medicare and Medicaid to reduce fraud

Education

★ Federal spending of $18 billion a year on early childhood classes, teacher recruitment, and other initiatives

★ Rewrite No Child Left Behind Act; keep emphasis on standards and accountability but offer aid to high-need schools

Foreign Policy

★ Iraq—early opponent of war; opposes troop increase; withdraw 1 or 2 brigades a month to finish within 16 months

★ Iran—use direct diplomacy; tighten economic sanctions

★ Trade—amend NAFTA to favor U.S. workers; end tax breaks for companies that outsource jobs

Historic Elections

The Election of **2008** is historic with the election of Barack Obama, the nation's first African American president. Read about other significant elections.

1800 Peaceful Transfer of Power

The election of Thomas Jefferson marked an important event in American history. At the time, the Federalists controlled the presidency and the Congress. They could have refused to step down and overthrown the Constitution. Instead, they respected the people's right to choose the president. The election of 1800 demonstrated that the power to govern could be peacefully transferred from one political party to another.

1860 Secession and War

Republican Abraham Lincoln won every Northern state and a clear victory in the Electoral College. Many Southerners did not trust a Republican president to protect their interests. For them, the only choice was to leave the Union. By March 1861, seven Southern states had seceded to form the Confederate States of America. With the Union split in two, the threat of civil war loomed on the horizon.

Election Milestones

1800 — Peaceful Transfer of Power

1824 — John Quincy Adams wins the presidency, but it requires a vote in Congress; supporters of Andrew Jackson make charges of a corrupt deal.

1840 — William Henry Harrison is the first president to die in office; Vice President John Tyler assumes the presidency, establishing a precedent that later becomes law.

1860 — Secession and War

1872 — With the passage of the Fifteenth Amendment (1870), African American males vote for the first time in a presidential election.

1876 — Reconstruction Ends

1876 Reconstruction Ends

On Election Day, Democrat Samuel Tilden had 184 electoral votes, 1 short of a majority. Republican Rutherford B. Hayes won 165 electoral votes, leaving 20 votes in dispute. When a special commission awarded all 20 disputed votes to Hayes, many people concluded that a deal had been made. The Democrats accepted Hayes as president in exchange for the removal of federal troops from the South. The era of Reconstruction was over.

1932 Government Expands

As the effects of the Great Depression worsened, Democratic candidate Franklin D. Roosevelt was elected president, promising "a new deal for the American people." Roosevelt persuaded Congress to create many new social and economic programs. When Roosevelt became president in 1933, about 600,000 people worked in the federal government. By the time he died in 1945, more than 3 million workers served in the federal government.

1960 Television Campaigns

Compared to earlier campaigns, the 1960 campaign made new use of television. Both major parties spent large amounts of money on television ads. The televised presidential debates may have been the turning point in one of the closest elections in American history. Kennedy seemed relaxed and outgoing, while Nixon struck many as formal and stiff in manner.

2000 Supreme Court Resolves Election

When the polls closed, neither Democrat Al Gore nor Republican George W. Bush had the necessary 270 electoral votes to be declared the winner. Bush held a narrow lead in Florida, but a dispute arose over ballot recounts in the state. Bush asked the Supreme Court to stop a hand recount of ballots. In *Bush* v. *Gore*, the Court ruled the election results should stand as counted. As a result, Bush won Florida and the presidency.

DEWEY DEFEATS TRUMAN

1912	1920	1932	1948	1960	2000	2008

1912 — Third party candidate Theodore Roosevelt wins 27 percent of the popular vote—the highest percentage ever for a third party.

1920 — With the passage of the Nineteenth Amendment, women vote in a presidential election for the first time.

1932 — Government Expands

1948 — Harry Truman is elected in one of the most surprising upsets in political history; early polls showed Thomas Dewey, the Republican candidate, with a big lead.

1960 — Television Campaigns

2000 — Supreme Court Resolves Election

2008 — First African American President

The Results

★ ★

Presidential Candidate	Popular Vote	% of Popular Vote	Electoral Votes
■ Obama	66,882,230	53	365
■ McCain	58,343,671	46	173

*Numbers on map show electoral votes per state.

WA 11, OR 7, ID 4, MT 3, WY 3, ND 3, SD 3, MN 10, WI 10, MI 17, NH 4, ME 4, VT 3, NY 31, MA 12, RI 4, CT 7, NJ 15, DE 3, MD 10, PA 21, OH 20, IN 11, IL 21, IA 7, NE 5, NV 5, UT 5, CO 9, KS 6, MO 11, KY 8, WV 5, VA 13, DC 3, CA 55, AZ 10, NM 5, OK 7, AR 6, TN 11, NC 15, SC 8, GA 15, MS 6, AL 9, TX 34, LA 9, FL 27, AK 3, HI 4

CONGRESSIONAL PARTY AFFILIATION*

House

Democrat 257   Republican 178

Senate

Democrat 56   Republican 41

Undecided 1
Independent 2

Source: www.senate.gov, www.house.gov

* All figures represent total number of voting members of Congress. Totals may change due to undecided races as of February 5, 2009.